NEWCOMER'S HANDBOOK

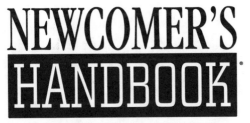

FOR MOVING TO AND LIVING IN THE

SAN FRANCISCO BAY AREA

Including San Jose, Oakland, Berkeley, and Palo Alto

4th Edition

FIRST BOOKS

503-968-6777
www.firstbooks.com

Author: Scott van Velsor (4th edition); Sabrina Crawford, Ruth Rayle, and Michael Bower (previous editions)
Editors: Linda Franklin, Linda Chaplik
Cover design and layout: Erin Johnson Design and Masha Shubin
Cover images: Erin Johnson Design, Jillian Gregg, and Nicholas Winchester
Interior design: Erin Johnson Design
Interior layout and composition: Masha Shubin
Interior photos by Scott van Velsor and Shannon Corr
Maps provided by Scott Lockheed and Jim Miller/fennana design
Transit map courtesy of Bay Area Rapid Transit

ISBN-13: 978-0-912301-74-7
ISBN-10: 0-912301-74-0

Printed in the USA on recycled paper.

Published by First Books®, 503-968-6777, www.firstbooks.com.

What readers are saying about Newcomer's Handbooks:

I recently got a copy of your Newcomer's Handbook for Chicago, and wanted to let you know how invaluable it was for my move. I must have consulted it a dozen times a day preparing for my move. It helped me find my way around town, find a place to live, and so many other things. Thanks.

– Mike L.
Chicago, Illinois

Excellent reading (Newcomer's Handbook for San Francisco and the Bay Area) ... balanced and trustworthy. One of the very best guides if you are considering moving/relocation. Way above the usual tourist crap.

– Gunnar E.
Stockholm, Sweden

I was very impressed with the latest edition of the Newcomer's Handbook for Los Angeles. It is well organized, concise and up-to-date. I would recommend this book to anyone considering a move to Los Angeles.

– Jannette L.
Attorney Recruiting Administrator for a large Los Angeles law firm

I recently moved to Atlanta from San Francisco, and LOVE the Newcomer's Handbook for Atlanta. It has been an invaluable resource—it's helped me find everything from a neighborhood in which to live to the local hardware store. I look something up in it everyday, and know I will continue to use it to find things long after I'm no longer a newcomer. And if I ever decide to move again, your book will be the first thing I buy for my next destination.

– Courtney R.
Atlanta, Georgia

In looking to move to the Boston area, a potential employer in that area gave me a copy of the Newcomer's Handbook for Boston. It's a great book that's very comprehensive, outlining good and bad points about each neighborhood in the Boston area. Very helpful in helping me decide where to move.

– no name given (online submit form)

Upon moving to Chicago from Portland, Oregon, I found myself shocked by more differences than a sales tax. Newcomer's has been amazing! I continue to use my copy years later. Newcomer's gave me contacts, confidence, and street smart tips even my native Chicago friends use. Thank you!

– Dusty W.
Chicago

TABLE OF CONTENTS

CONTENTS

CONTENTS

S AN FRANCISCO IS THE LAND OF THE '49ER GOLD RUSH, THE GREAT 1906 earthquake, and the legendary missionary expeditions of the Spanish; it is the birthplace of Levi's jeans and home of railroad empire tycoon Leland Stanford; it is host to one of greatest feats of engineering, the Golden Gate Bridge; and as a cultural epicenter, it fueled the hippie flower-power revolution, gave rise to *Rolling Stone* magazine, and played host to Beat Generation poets. Well-funded and venture capital–heavy Silicon Valley plays host to the powerhouses of modern technology like Oracle, Apple, and now Google—which occupies a large "Googleplex" off Highway 101 in Mountain View. The site teems with youthful dreamers, solitary programmers, and hundreds of millionaires thanks to Google's wildly successful public IPO in 2005. Biotechnology and software still command a sizable share of economic power in the Bay Area, but "clean tech" is emerging as the newest darling of venture capital and dominates the startup markets. While newcomers to the Bay Area may come for such employment opportunities, many come for a simpler reason—sheer love of the city itself. With thriving art, music, and literary scenes, endless opportunities to enjoy outdoor activities, and one of the country's most stunning urban landscapes, the area continues to attract young professionals, artists, and recent college graduates from all across the country, and from around the world.

Truly America's melting pot, San Francisco is home to a lively and diverse mix of cultures, including a large Chinese population, as well as substantial Vietnamese, Russian, Eastern European, Mexican, and Central and South American communities. The city is also host to a vibrant gay and lesbian community. Well known as the liberal mecca of the left coast, the Bay Area pulses with political activism—from impassioned struggles over local development issues, to heated election runoffs, to leading the charge on a host of statewide, national, and international causes: from the environment, to health care, to women's rights, to immigration reform, to gay marriage.

With stately Victorians nestled all along dramatic hilltops, the beauty and expanse of the Bay and the Pacific Ocean all around, and mountain hikes or walks in the redwoods just moments away, the city is the rarest of gems—a place that offers the culture, excitement, and opportunity of urban life with the scenic and recreational joys of the great outdoors. The Bay Area is the only place in America where you can ride a moving national landmark (cable cars) while taking in some of the world's most beautiful scenery, including the Bay, Alcatraz Island, Golden Gate Bridge, Golden Gate Park, and the city skyline itself.

Then of course, there's the weather—blissfully mild with blue skies, fog near the coast, and cooling off with light winds in the evening. Many would agree that Bay Area meteorologists have one of the easiest jobs around. The weather forecast is consistently "low clouds and fog overnight, clearing by mid-morning, giving way to afternoon sunshine," with the temperature rarely dipping below 40° or above 80° Fahrenheit. The one exception to that rule comes with the much anticipated Indian summer months of September and October, when it can get into the 80s, and on extremely rare occasions, over 100° Fahrenheit. The fall and winter rainy seasons begin with a few drizzles in October, becoming outright downpours in the rainy months of December and January, and continuing intermittently through March and sometimes into April. Communities located away from the ocean, particularly those in the South and East Bay, are, as a general rule, likely to have weather that is drier, warmer, and smoggier.

Rent-controlled San Francisco still contains some of the highest rental prices in the country, and the available rental units reflect this trend. Many are designed to be utilized by multiple roommates or shared by couples, and, in a newer twist in urban development, studio apartments in the 400-square-foot range have sprung up across the city. Newcomers looking for a city experience without the high cost of living that typically accompanies it generally look to the East Bay in cities like Oakland and Berkeley. Even cheaper are the suburbs to the south of San Francisco and to the north, east, and south of Oakland. The difference in price can be dramatic: a one-bedroom apartment in San Francisco can cost the same as an entire two-bedroom house in the outlying areas.

Real estate throughout the Bay Area is like gold, and the current downturn in the real estate market hasn't caused home sellers to lower their pricing to anywhere near affordable for the rank-and-file. Some first-time homebuyers are heading just south of the city to San Bruno and South San Francisco to take advantage of a new crop of condos; those working in Silicon Valley often opt for townhouses further south in Sunnyvale or San Jose; and families desiring single-family homes with spacious backyards are looking east to Vallejo or even Sacramento. To the north of San Francisco, in Marin County, you'll find small but burgeoning communities with dramatic landscapes, stunning vistas, and great hiking, biking and camping. East, toward Sonoma and Napa counties, are charming vineyards tucked in among rolling hills.

For those interested in purchasing a house, even with an economic recession and depressed housing prices, the median home price for the Bay Area hovers at $300,000 and for San Francisco proper, $600,000. Deals can be found—particularly with the glut of condos and townhomes on the market and the crushing foreclosure crisis—but for many in the area, realizing the American Dream of homeownership takes a backseat to economic reality. Most residents of the Bay Area have a philosophical understanding of the issue, however, and embrace the rental attitude, with the lack of responsibility for upkeep, repair, taxes, mortgage, and insurance on a piece of property valued for its simplicity of living.

This *Newcomer's Handbook®* is intended to help make your move here as seamless and enjoyable as possible. It describes San Francisco and surrounding Bay Area neighborhoods/communities in detail, and provides lists of neighborhood resources, including neighborhood web sites, police stations, post offices, libraries, hospitals, public schools, and community groups. Transportation routes are also covered. In addition to profiling area neighborhoods and communities, this guide will assist you with the biggest of Bay Area challenges: locating a new home (**Finding a Place to Live**), as well as getting your belongings here (**Moving and Storage**), setting up your bank accounts (**Money Matters**) and utilities (**Getting Settled**), where to go to buy a shower curtain, area rug, or mop and broom (**Shopping for the Home**), and places to go to kick back and relax in a welcoming patch of green (**Greenspace and Beaches**). Plus, new to this edition is **Green Living**, a chapter that addresses energy efficiency and water conservation, as well as greening your home and transportation. It's all here, and much more.

LOCAL LINGO

Like many communities, San Francisco has its own slang. If you find yourself scratching your head, here are a few phrases that may help you out:

- **The Avenues**: the numbered streets in the Sunset and Richmond neighborhoods running out toward the ocean
- **BART**: Bay Area Rapid Transit, the under- and aboveground subway-style train network that connects the East Bay and peninsula with San Francisco
- **The Boom**: the 1990s high-tech computer and internet economic explosion
- **The Bust**: the end of said dot-com explosion
- **The Chron**: *The Chronicle*, the city's major daily newspaper
- **The City (capitalized)**: the way most natives and local newspapers refer to San Francisco; wherever you are in the Bay Area, "the City" with a capital "C" always means San Francisco

- **Dogpatch**: South of the Giants' ballpark, a district just east of Hwy 280, north of Hunters Point, and bordering the Bay. Many chic industrial-style condos are built here and there is a push to develop biotech business in the area.
- **East Bay**: Alameda and Contra Costa counties, but often just refers to Oakland or Berkeley
- **Ex-dot-comers**: those who were heavily involved in the high tech explosion and have since moved on to other, often non-tech-related career pursuits
- **General**: San Francisco General Hospital
- **The Haight**: the Haight-Ashbury neighborhood, also often refers specifically to the retail shopping district along the upper section of Haight Street
- **Mavericks**: the big wave, daredevil surf competition on the West Coast, also the name of the actual surfing spot, just off the shore of Pillar Point Harbor in Half Moon Bay
- **Mitchell's**: famous locally made ice cream
- **MUNI**: Municipal Rail Network, the city's bus and light rail system
- **NoPa**: North of Panhandle. A district just north of The Haight and south of Geary Blvdoulevard
- **North Bay**: Marin and Sonoma counties
- **Oaktown**: Oakland
- **Pink Section**: special weekend arts and entertainment supplement in *The Chronicle*
- **See's**: famous locally made chocolates
- **SoMa**: area south of Market Street
- **South Bay**: Santa Clara County
- **TL**: The Tenderloin, typically refers to the rougher sections

ADDRESS LOCATOR

THE CITY

San Francisco's 43 hills prevented city planners from implementing a grand, area-wide roadway grid system, so finding any desired street address here can be a challenge. You'll want to find a good map or atlas and avoid the small tourist maps; they often distort proportions and exclude large chunks of geography that will prove important to a resident. Transit maps are useful if you're not relying on your car to get around, but they don't offer enough detailed information to serve as your primary guidance tool.

Many different types of San Francisco maps are available at stores across the Bay Area, but if you plan on being a local, get the laminated cardstock version, as you will be consulting this map often. Another smart purchase is a broad area map that lays out the major freeways surrounding and intersecting this busy slice of California. Members can also get maps free from the American Automobile Association (AAA).

With map in hand you may want to spend a few moments locating the major streets and highways listed below:

- First there's **Market Street**. It is San Francisco's main downtown street, and it starts across from the Ferry Building. As with all east-west running streets that begin at the downtown's eastern edge, address numbers begin there and increase as you head towards the ocean. Market serves as the border between the Financial District, Union Square, and Tenderloin areas to the north, and the South of Market (SoMa) district to the south. For north-south running streets, address numbering begins at Market, with the lowest numbers at Market. On streets north of Market, the numbers increase as you go north. On the other side, the street numbers increase as you travel south.

- Another main street is **Van Ness Avenue**, which runs north-south and begins one block west of 10th Street, crossing Market. It serves as part of the Highway 101 connection to the Golden Gate Bridge, along with **Lombard Street**, **Marina Boulevard**, and **Doyle Drive**. Street numbers increase as you travel north on Van Ness.

- **Geary Street** splits off from Market in the downtown area, runs east-west, and goes all the way out to the Pacific Ocean, although once it crosses into "the Avenues," its name changes to **Geary Boulevard**. Numbering begins downtown and increases as you go west.

- **"The Avenues"** is the locally accepted name for the area served by the numbered roadways in the Richmond District, **3rd Avenue** through **46th Avenue**, and it's important to know because the city also has numbered "streets," **1st Street** through **30th Street**. Don't confuse the streets and the avenues as they are entirely different neighborhoods. The avenues also extend down into the Sunset and Parkside districts. The numbered streets begin in the SoMa and run north-south until the Mission District, where they run east-west into the Potrero Hill, Bernal Heights, Castro, and Noe Valley districts after 14th Street. Thus when someone tells you that the store you want is on "24th" you'll need to clarify, "24th Street or 24th Avenue?"

- **Nineteenth Avenue** is a good roadway to become familiar with since it serves as another connector road, along with **Park Presidio Boulevard**, to the Golden Gate Bridge from **Interstate 280** and **Highway 1**. Both run into the city from San Mateo County to the south. Nineteenth Avenue splits off from 280/1 just inside the San Francisco city limits, runs right in front of San Francisco State University, out through the Sunset District, and into Golden Gate Park. Its name changes to Park Presidio Boulevard on the northern side of the park. If traffic is really bad on 19th Avenue, and it often is, **Sunset Boulevard** is just a few blocks to the west and is usually a good route through the Sunset.

- **Highway 101** also enters San Francisco from the south; however, it splits off to head for the San Francisco–Oakland Bay Bridge, where I-80 begins. Interstate 80 will take you through the northern half of the East Bay, out to Sacramento, the Sierra Nevada, and all the way to New York City.

- **Interstate 280** has a relatively new—and therefore infrequently used—extension near the Highway 101 split that drops drivers off along the Outer Mission and Dogpatch areas of the City and directly onto 6th Street at Townsend. This is a nice option to get to a Giants baseball game or simply the most direct route to the beating heart of downtown. This freeway does not reconnect to the San Francisco–Oakland Bay Bridge

- **Octavia Boulevard/Fell Street**—This connection dramatically altered the way commuters use the city streets in the area. Damage from the 1989 earthquake was finally repaired in late 2005, making this a critical east-west corridor from the bridge and Hwy 101. Follow the signs towards Golden Gate Bridge or Highway 101 North and stay towards the left. Octavia crosses Market Street in the depths of the Castro district and continues to Fell Street, which heads west towards Ocean Beach and Golden Gate Park.

- **San Francisco–Oakland Bay Bridge**, also the beginning of Interstate 80, is a double-decker hulk of steel that spans across to Treasure Island and onward to the East Bay. The bridge is under radical construction until at least 2012, however, so drivers should be aware of major rerouting and potentially crippling delays while CalTrans and union contractors build a new eastern span and tear down the old, seismically unfit section.

BEYOND SAN FRANCISCO

Two major highways, Highway 101 and Interstate 280, running north and south, connect San Francisco with the Peninsula and the South Bay while numerous highways will help you navigate the rest of the Bay Area.

- **Highway 101** is notoriously crowded and weaves through the heavily populated cities of the Peninsula and South Bay. Highway 101 goes all the way from Los Angeles up through much of the state of Washington.

- A more scenic and often less crowded drive is **I-280** (known as Junipero Serra Freeway), which starts near the Bay Bridge on the San Francisco side and goes south past Daly City, continues down the west side of the Bay, and culminates at the I-680 junction.

- Close to the San Francisco Airport, **I-380** links Highway 101 with I-280.

- **Highway 85**, also known as Stevens Creek Freeway, connects 101 with 280 from Mountain View to Cupertino.

- **Interstate 880** is another connector for 101 and 280, slicing through the city of San Jose.

- Farther north, **Highway 92** runs through the Peninsula, around San Mateo, and traverses west all the way to the coast, ending in Half Moon Bay.

- Another coastal connector and motorcyclist's dream is **Highway 84**, which links Redwood City with Woodside and then, like Highway 92, goes all the way to the coast, ending at Highway 1.
- Certainly the most scenic highway in the Bay Area, and arguably in the country, **Highway 1** twists and turns itself along the western edge of the US, going south to LA and north to Washington.

Both the San Mateo–Hayward Bridge and the Dumbarton Bridge connect the South Bay with the East Bay.

- The longest bridge in the Bay Area, the 6.8-mile **San Mateo–Hayward Bridge**, links Foster City with Hayward via Highway 92.
- The **Dumbarton Bridge** connects Fremont and Newark in the East Bay with Palo Alto and Menlo Park. The southernmost bridge crossing the Bay, the Dumbarton Bridge is part of Highway 84, which can be accessed via the Willow Road off-ramp from Highway 101.

CITY OF SAN FRANCISCO

WELCOME TO EFFERVESCENT SAN FRANCISCO, THE CHILLIEST PART of California in summertime. While the rest of the state is melting, lucky residents are swaddled in cool cotton fog that typically drops the temperature by 40 degrees. Some people will tell you to never call it "Frisco" because you'll immediately be labeled a fresh import, but that distinction has died a slow death in a veritable sea of transplants from across the country, and the world. Almost 7 million people live in the Bay Area, and about 800,000 live in San Francisco proper. The city's population almost doubles during weekdays when hundreds of thousands arrive for work, clogging the local freeways and jamming the steep and often narrow streets with steel and rubber, buses and bicycles. Traffic flowing out of San Francisco is sometimes worse than the commute into the city. In fact, some of the nation's worst morning and evening commutes are here, despite the existence of the usually efficient Bay Area Rapid Transit (BART) system. Where the BART trains don't go, more than two dozen other transit systems do, including buses, trolleys, cable cars, commuter trains, shuttles, light-rail, and ferryboats. Since the Bay Area is a commuter's cauldron, however, be prepared to add hours to your commute when using public transportation.

The shining exceptions to the sometimes challenging transportation systems of the Bay Area are the picturesque bridges. Six concrete and steel crossings span the waterways of the San Francisco Bay and provide crucial linkages between the cities by the bay. Windsurfers race alongside of the southern bridges, criss-crossing the lower portion of the bay, while sailboats, commercial shipping, Alcatraz Prison, Angel Island, and stunning industrial works are visible from the northern bridges.

Only seven by seven square miles in size, San Francisco is compact when compared to such cities as New York, Los Angeles, or Chicago. Every inch of the city teems with activity, from rollerblading, hiking, and biking in Golden Gate Park, to surfing or hang gliding at Ocean Beach, to dining or shopping in China-town or North Beach, and the list goes on.

You will quickly notice that one of the dominant features of San Francisco life is fog. The warmer central valley generates a heat pull that sucks warm air across the cold sea current running along the entire coast of North America and creates perfect conditions for mountains of dewpoint moisture. People here call it "Mother Nature's air conditioner," and it's especially prevalent—and welcome when it is 108° F—during the Indian summer months of September and October. Neighborhoods are defined by the amount of sun, or lack thereof, which shines. Some areas of the city, such as The Mission, Potrero Hill, Noe Valley, and the Castro neighborhoods, are less fog-bound than others, but you won't be able to avoid it entirely. After you've been here for a while, chances are you'll grow to love the fog, if you don't already. For those six to eight weeks of Indian summer, residents, especially in such neighborhoods as the Richmond, the Sunset District, Stonestown, and Diamond Heights, awaken in homes blan-keted by a fog so dense it almost looks solid. It usually burns away by noon, giving way to clear blue skies and temperatures into the 90s. Then, just when you can't take the heat anymore, the fog tumbles into the Bay Area from the Pacific Ocean to the west, cooling temperatures down to the 40s and 50s.

Certain smells also help to define San Francisco's neighborhoods. Fresh brewed, dark Italian and French roast coffee and baking focaccia are the scents of North Beach; steamed crab and freshly baked sourdough permeate the Northpoint/Fisherman's Wharf area; and the smell of yeasty bagels and *dim sum* waft through the air in the Richmond. A salty ocean bite spices the air along the western edge of the Sunset, and the sometimes-disturbing odor of cable car brakes hits you while descending some of the city's steepest slopes on Rus-sian Hill and Nob Hill. Visit Chinatown for the smell of exotic herbs intermingled with fresh dumplings, and throughout the city's parks you'll learn to savor the unforgettable aroma of wet eucalyptus.

Aside from its stunning physical beauty, much of San Francisco's charm and vitality stems from its ethnic diversity. The earliest non-native settlers came from Russia, Italy, Ireland, Germany, China, Japan, and the Philippines, all of them establishing their own neighborhoods at first, and then branching out. That intra-city migration continues today, most notably the Chinatown popula-tion spreading out into formerly Italian-dominated North Beach.

HISTORY AND LOCAL COLOR

Called by those who live here "the City" (with a capital C), San Francisco has a rich and vivid history. Originally the area was home to the Ohlone American

Indians; Europeans first laid eyes on the San Francisco Bay in 1579, when the English explorer Sir Francis Drake landed at Point Reyes, about 35 miles north of San Francisco. Drake, for whom that northern bay is today named, noted the sweeping vistas, thick fog, and dramatic cliffs, saying that the area reminded him of the famous White Cliffs of Dover of his homeland. But it wasn't until nearly two centuries later that colonization, led by Spanish soldiers and missionaries, began in San Francisco.

In 1776, Colonel Juan Bautista de Anza built a presidio near the Golden Gate, and later that year Franciscan priests opened Mission Dolores, which still stands in the heart of the Mission and is the city's oldest surviving building. A tiny village known as Yerba Buena ("good herb" in Spanish) sprang up between the mission and the presidio. In 1847, Yerba Buena officially became San Francisco, and in 1848 the territory was ceded to the United States at the end of the Mexican war. That same year, miners struck gold in the Sierra Nevada Mountains, and prospectors with dreams of riches packed their bags and headed west, spiraling the city's tiny population from 500 to 25,000 within a year. In 1850, the same year that California became the 31st state in the union, the City of San Francisco was officially incorporated.

From the famous '49er Gold Rush and the rowdy, lawless debauchery of the Barbary Coast days in the 19th century, to the massive devastation of the 1906 Earthquake and Fire that ushered in the 20th century, to the 1950s poetry spark that ignited the Beat Generation and electrified North Beach, to the famous 1960s "make love, not war" counterculture of Haight-Ashbury, to the political and cultural birth of the gay rights revolution and sexual liberation movement in the 1970s, San Francisco has been and continues to be the liberal heartbeat of the nation.

Culturally, the city has long been a creative mecca, drawing artists, photographers, musicians, and writers from across the country and around the world. San Francisco's illustrious past includes legions of rock and roll greats like the Grateful Dead and Jefferson Airplane, as well as notable photographers Ansel Adams, Imogen Cunningham, and Dorothea Lange. Murals painted by Diego Rivera dot the city—turning up in the most unexpected places—from the San Francisco City College campus to the stairwells of the City Club of San Francisco.

A vibrant spirit of creativity still flourishes here today, as witnessed by the Mission's rich, colorful murals, a plethora of small galleries, and a handful of world-class museums. San Francisco is also home to a thriving, tight-knit independent rock music community, a host of collective visual arts groups and spaces, and a budding local literary scene. Throughout the year, countless festivals, parades, and celebrations pay homage to the city's rich cultural heritage—from the dizzying acrobatics of the lion dancers at Chinatown's annual Chinese New Year parade, to the rhythmic beats and dancing in the streets that mark the Mission's Carnaval celebration, to the outlandish drag outfits at the yearly Gay Pride weekend extravaganza hosted in the Castro (the city is, of course, well known for its large, politically active gay and lesbian population).

Liberal bent aside, San Francisco is an economic powerhouse: Along Market Street stand the towering temples of capitalism and economic power that make up the compact downtown Financial District, home to the largest concentration of banks and financial service companies west of the Mississippi, the Pacific Stock Exchange. Also in the heart of San Francisco's downtown is Union Square, with the ultra-chic designer boutiques of Dior, Armani, and Marc Jacobs, as well as numerous upscale department stores. The square itself, an elevated open green, is perfect for resting your feet, people watching, or coffee sipping. One more thing: you won't go hungry here. There are more restaurants per capita here than in any other US city, offering every cuisine and price range imaginable. Union Square also offers free wireless access—a perk that Mayor Gavin Newsom is looking into extending to the whole city.

All of these features make San Francisco a vibrant and stimulating locale to call home. The city comprises more than two dozen neighborhoods or districts, each of which can be clearly defined, despite the fact that some are only a few blocks long and many meld into one another at the edges. The neighborhood profiles that follow this introduction focus on the general characteristics and histories of each neighborhood and provide information about housing, weather, public transit, post office locations, emergency services, hospitals, public safety agencies, and local attractions.

We start at the northeast corner of the city with the historically Italian neighborhood of North Beach, then climb up the steep slopes of upscale Nob Hill and Russian Hill, through the bustling Tenderloin, then work our way west to posh Pacific Heights, the Marina District and Cow Hollow, continuing on toward the foggy Pacific Ocean beaches of the Richmond and the breathtaking views of Seacliff. We then head south across Golden Gate Park to the crisp air and cool coastal shores of the Sunset, continuing south to Stonestown and Park Merced. Turning east we begin to work our way back toward the center of town through the colorful Victorians of Haight-Ashbury and the Western Addition, to Civic Center, and the lofts and nightclubs of SoMa. We then journey south to the murals of the Mission District, through the famous Castro, to Noe Valley, Glen Park, and Diamond Heights, before working our way up to the peaks of Potrero Hill and Bernal Heights. Then it's out to the Excelsior, Ingleside, Portola, and Visitacion Valley, before winding up at the city's southeastern-most edge, Bayview/Hunters Point, and stopping at the San Mateo County line.

HOUSING

Expect varied types of housing in San Francisco. The famous and oft-depicted Victorians are wood-framed buildings, which range from relatively simple cottages to extremely ornate gingerbread-style mansions. Styles include Italianate

Victorians, Queen Anne Victorians, and others, which you might enjoy learning to identify once you live here. Built between the 1870s and the 1910s, Victorians have interiors as distinctive as their external features. High ceilings are the norm along with elaborate ceiling fixtures and wainscoting that can range from simple wooded slats to ornate carvings. The rooms tend to be small but generally have double doors that, when opened, create one large room out of two smaller rooms, great for creating a cozy home office. Often the rooms are entered from a railway hall, which runs from the front of the house or flat to the kitchen in the back. The grander Victorians still have fireplaces and marble fixtures, and the front rooms nearly all have bay windows. Also common here are Edwardians, built in the 1900s and 1910s. Some are wooden and similar to Victorians although less ornate. They often have bay windows, but gone are the Victorian-styled railway halls and the odd little rooms. Many have double doors between bedroom and living room; some even have closets equipped with Murphy beds. Built-in oak or fir cupboards are common in the dining room. Apartment buildings, many of which were built in the 1920s, are generally of stucco and brown brick. They often sport a web of fire escapes in front and/or back, and typically are steam-heated via radiators. Often the kitchen has some built-in glass cupboards, and maybe a table and ironing board.

Many of the homes of the Richmond and Sunset districts were built during the Depression. Places built during this time are snug and comfortable, often featuring fireplaces, hardwood floors, and built-in book cabinets. Housing from the 1950s, '60s and '70s, which is scattered throughout the city, tends to be a little boxy. Rooms are smaller, walls and ceilings are plain, and bathrooms and kitchens sometimes lack windows. Once you get to South San Francisco and Daly City, you will find entire neighborhoods composed of this architectural style.

New housing borrows features from the city's past and incorporates these into modern designs. Bay windows are the norm. New condos and apartments tend to be colorful, sometimes asymmetrical, with special attention paid to natural lighting. Generally speaking, the city's newest housing is concentrated in the South of Market Area (SoMa), particularly in the Mission Bay neighborhood, which is in the midst of wide-scale redevelopment.

Throughout this book, unless otherwise noted, housing statistics are from the California Association of Realtors (CAR), www.car.org; Metro-Rent, www.metrorent.com; or DataQuick, www.dataquick.com. Visit their web sites for the latest information on local housing prices, which in today's economy, can change rapidly. The median home price according to the California Association of Realtors (CAR; www.car.org) in San Francisco proper as of March 2009 was $617,000. As of May 2009, CAR reported the median price of a Bay Area home to be $459,980, down 33% from May 2008, but median prices vary greatly from community to community within the Bay Area. For more specifics on Bay Area housing, refer to the **Finding a Place to Live** chapter.

GETTING AROUND SAN FRANCISCO

The city is notoriously tricky to navigate by car owing to an abundance of one-way streets, too many "no left turn" signs, the strangely curving main street, Market Street, which turns any semblance of grid-like order on its head, and of course, perpetual parking woes. However, San Francisco is a pedestrian- and bike-friendly city—at least for those able to navigate the steeper hills. Public transportation, made up primarily of a large army of gas and electric buses operated by San Francisco Municipal Railway (MUNI), is relatively easy to use, though getting out of town is another matter entirely. Beautifully restored antique streetcars traverse Market Street and the palm-lined bayfront of the Embarcadero, while old-time cable cars climb a few of the city's steepest hills. Bay Area Rapid Transit (known as BART) has a handful of stops in San Francisco, most of them downtown, though locals will tell you not nearly enough. But MUNI's growing light rail network, most notably the 3rd Street Light Rail expansion and talk of a future "Central Subway" metro link north of Market to Union Square and Chinatown, promises to make public transit options more efficient and pleasant to use.

CITY RESOURCES

San Francisco is a bit of an anomaly in that it is both a city and a county. Politically, the city is divided into 11 geographic districts. It is run jointly by the mayor and a Board of Supervisors—the board being elected by voters within each district.

Specific community resources and information are listed beneath each neighborhood profile, but here are a few basic citywide numbers and web sites you're likely to need, no matter which neighborhood you choose to call home.

City Web Site: www.sfgov.org
Board of Supervisors: 415-701-2311, TTY 415-701-2323
Mayor's Office: 415-554-6141
City Hall: 415-554-4933
Public Transportation: MUNI, 415-701-4500, TTY 415-701-2323, www.sfmta. com
Parks, Open Space and Gardens: For detailed information, hours, maps, and complete park listings, contact the **San Francisco Parks and Recreation Department**, 415-831-2700, www.parks.sfgov.org or the **Neighborhood Parks Council**, 415-621-3260, www.parkscan.org. For information about community gardens contact the **San Francisco Urban Gardeners League (SLUG)**, 415-285-SLUG, www.grass-roots.org/usa/slug.shtml.

NEIGHBORHOODS

NORTH BEACH, TELEGRAPH HILL

CHINATOWN

Boundaries: North: Fisherman's Wharf; **East**: The Embarcadero; **South**: Broadway; **West**: Columbus Ave (Telegraph Hill is at the east corner of North Beach, with Stockton St as the border)

Don't bring your bathing suit to **North Beach**, just an appreciation for fine Italian food and a loaded wallet. North Beach is famous for its mouth-watering aromas of olive oil, garlic, and espresso, as well as its vibrant nightlife. These perks, coupled with its close proximity to downtown, make it a favorite neighborhood for young professionals, empty-nesters, and a burgeoning Chinese-American population, many of whom are moving from nearby Chinatown.

North Beach, Telegraph Hill

Famously the one-time home of the Beat Generation, North Beach became a gathering place for poets, writers, and critical thinkers of the 1950s and '60s, coined "beatniks" by *San Francisco Chronicle* columnist Herb Caen. Adorned in black with sandals, berets, and dark glasses, beatniks opposed mainstream beliefs and spoke out against complacency. The most famous of the bunch included San Francisco's first Poet Laureate, Lawrence Ferlinghetti, who opened the City Lights Bookstore, Jack Kerouac, Allen Ginsberg, and Gary Snyder.

Historically the heart of the city's Red Light District, Broadway boasts neon signs that flicker and flash all night long, gleaming down on crowded sidewalks and a string of gentleman's clubs, host to a seemingly endless stream of bachelor parties. The late night vibe, minus the X-rated content, has spilled over onto Columbus and Grant avenues, creating a bustling nightlife with music, dancing, and late-night cafés. A smattering of blues bars line upper Grant Avenue, including the popular Grant & Green Blues Club and The Saloon, an intimate, old-time corner spot that has been serving up raucous, down-home blues since the mid 1800s, and claims to be both San Francisco's oldest bar and the world's greatest blues bar. Meanwhile the swank, art deco Bimbo's 365 Club on Columbus

North Beach

Avenue features bigger name rock bands and a velvet interior to make you feel like a 1950s movie star.

For a true San Franciscan experience head to the city's longest running musical, Beach Blanket Babylon, at Club Fugazi, 678 Beach Blanket Boulevard (Green Street). In addition to low-end blues and rock bars, upper Grant Avenue is home to trendy clothing shops and vintage jewelry stores. Because of spiraling rents, some merchants are being replaced by expensive boutiques, but no chain stores, thanks to neighborhood groups that have fought vehemently to keep North Beach's character intact.

Locals take a break from the food and frenzy of their neighborhood at Washington Square Park, one of the city's oldest public spaces. In the early morning, older Chinese-Americans congregate here, moving their limbs at glacial speed as they practice the ancient art of tai chi. At the same hour you can smell the focaccia baking across the street at Liguria Bakery, 1700 Stockton Street, in business since 1911. Throughout the day, neighbors, sunbathers, and artists gather at the park, which hosts numerous art and music festivals throughout the year. Above it all, the neo-gothic St. Peter and Paul's Catholic Church, 666 Filbert Street, towers majestically. The church, famous for its midnight Easter services, also hosts masses in both Italian and Chinese.

At dusk, Italian old timers play bocce ball at a small court near Aquatic Park, while nearby at the Joe DiMaggio Playground on Lombard and Mason streets, teens gather for pick-up basketball games and tiny tots frolic in the playground. This is where baseball hall-of-famer Joe DiMaggio swung the bat around with his kid brothers.

True to its name, there used to be a long beach along the area's northern edge, between Telegraph Hill on the east and Russian Hill on the west. Shortly after the 1906 Earthquake, the city dumped debris from the earthquake and built a series of breakwaters and piers that combined to create the tourist mecca of Fisherman's Wharf and Pier 39. At the northern end of the Embarcadero, you'll find dozens of seafood restaurants and tourist shops, including Ghirardelli Square, a former chocolate factory that still serves the dark confection in various forms.

Most North Beach residents live in three-story Edwardian apartments, flats, or condos built on the ashes of the fire from the 1906 Earthquake. North Beach still is home to many Italian families (though that number has diminished significantly over the years) as well as Chinese-Americans. Young, mostly single, professionals enjoy North Beach for its food, nightlife, and easy commute downtown. Vacancies are not always easy to come by.

If you live in North Beach and work downtown, you may decide not to own a car, as parking is difficult (sometimes downright impossible), plus buses and cable cars are frequent. If you do have a car, you'll need to get a parking permit. Remember to curb your wheels when parking on a hill. If the car is facing downhill, your front wheels must turn in towards the curb. If the car faces uphill, the front wheels should turn out from the curb. (Parking control officers will ticket you for not obeying the curbing rule.) And, set that parking brake! If your apartment doesn't come with a garage (most here don't), check www.craigslist.org and you may be able to find a garage to rent.

If you choose to make North Beach your home, undoubtedly you will find your own favorite restaurant. For breakfast, lunch, or dinner, you'll find espressos and cappuccinos available on every block. If you want to mix opera with your coffee, try Caffe Trieste at 601 Vallejo Street, one of the oldest coffeehouses in the neighborhood. If the opera's not live, it's being played on the jukebox. Neighborhood activities for hearty souls include swimming in the chilly waters at Aquatic Park, directly in front of Ghirardelli Square. The Dolphin Club and the South End Rowing Club both provide facilities and encouragement for your plunge into the cold water.

Another desirable place to live, and not as hectic as North Beach, is nearby **Telegraph Hill**. Formerly called Goat Hill, it became Telegraph Hill in 1853 because it was the site of the West Coast's first telegraph station. Here spotters scouted for ships entering San Francisco Bay through the Golden Gate. After sighting a ship, spotters used Morse code to notify port officials of the ship's impending arrival. The "Hill," as locals call the area, features breathtaking bay views, including Alcatraz Island, the former home of the notorious prison and convicts, such as Al Capone and the "Birdman of Alcatraz" (who actually never kept birds there). Here you'll

Telegraph Hill

find narrow streets lined with quaint cottages and picture-windowed condominiums, beautiful gardens, and even fewer rental vacancies than the rest of North Beach. Many residents must walk up tiny stairways and paths to their compact homes (compact due to the city's 40-foot height limit here).

Coit Tower, the most prominent feature of this area, rises 210 feet from the top of Telegraph Hill. A monument to the city's firefighters, Coit Tower was built in 1934, funded by the private contribution of Lillie Hitchcock Coit, an eccentric San Franciscan known for going against the grain (when she was 15 she served as a volunteer firefighter). The area around the tower is a romantic spot to bring a bottle of wine and watch the sunset or the boats on the Bay beneath you. If romance isn't in your cards, try climbing the 377 Filbert Street steps to Coit Tower for exercise. Listen carefully for the famous neighborhood parrots up in the trees. Though their origins are uncertain, most people believe the flock, now totaling over 100 birds, was started by a few birds that escaped from their cages. A documentary film, *The Wild Parrots of Telegraph Hill*, was recently made about these local legends and is available via www.pelicanmedia.org.

Often touted as the largest Chinatown in the USA, San Francisco's **Chinatown** is a whirlwind of culture and history. Passing through the large, ornate entry gates to the south, you wind up on the main drag, Grant Avenue. Here, you'll find a host of shops selling everything from traditional Chinese clothing, to "I heart San Francisco" T-shirts, to endless bric-a-brac. Many of the retail shops here are tourist traps—but tucked in between you can find the occasional gem—fine imported fabric stores, specialty tea shops, and vegetable stands. And of course, there are restaurants, restaurants, restaurants. Wander off the main tourist drag up Washington and Sacramento streets to find the most popular local spots. One favorite with locals and tourists alike is House of Nanking on Kearny, where you'll find long lines day and night. Stockton—which connects Chinatown to North Beach at one end and to Union Square at the other—is filled with more practical, less tourist-oriented stores. On Saturdays, this street is packed with large trucks delivering durian fruits, lychees, and Asian pears to the various markets and the sidewalk is a sea of wall-to-wall people.

The city's legacy with regard to Chinese immigrants is an ugly one.

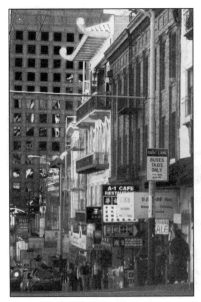
Chinatown

Chinese men began coming to California in the 1850s to help build the railroads. At first they were welcomed as a hard-working, inexpensive source of labor, but when the Gold Rush began to die out they were vilified as unwanted competitors. Demonized as the so-called yellow peril, Chinese immigrants faced severe discrimination as a series of racist laws were enacted in the 1870s and 1880s. Interracial marriages were banned, Chinese people were not allowed to own property, to vote, or to have their families join them, Chinese children attended segregated schools, and the Chinese Exclusion Act of 1882 barred further Chinese immigration.

It was amid this chaos that Chinatown was born, as restaurants, boarding houses, and opium dens sprang up around what was then the city center—Portsmouth Square—serving miners, and providing a sense of community for Chinese immigrants. Like much of the city, Chinatown was leveled in the 1906 Earthquake and Fire, and rose from the ashes with the help of a wealthy businessman into the collection of tiny storefronts, Edwardian apartments, and alleyways you see today.

Today, many elderly Chinese-Americans and recently arrived young Chinese immigrants live in Chinatown, while younger families have largely moved out to the Richmond and Sunset districts.

At night, wandering through the small alleyways you can often catch traditional Lion Dance troupes practicing, or wander into a bar for a heated game of Mahjong. And the neighborhood comes alive once a year when it hosts the Chinese New Year parade.

Web Site: www.sfgov.org

Area Code: 415

Zip Codes: 94133, 94108

Post Office: North Beach Station, 1640 Stockton St, 800-275-8777, www.usps. com

Police Station: Central Police Station, 766 Vallejo St, 415-315-2400; main non-emergency number, 415-553-0123, TTY 576-1711

Emergency Hospitals: California Pacific Medical Center, 2333 Buchanan St, 415-600-6000, www.cpmc.org; Saint Francis Memorial Hospital, 900 Hyde St, 415-353-6000, www.saintfrancismemorial.org

Library: North Beach Library, 2000 Mason St, 415-355-5626, www.sfpl.org

Public Schools: San Francisco Unified School District, 555 Franklin St, 415-241-6000, http://portal.sfusd.edu

Community Resources: Telegraph Hill Dwellers, 415-273-1004, www.thd.org; North Beach Neighbors, www.northbeachneighbors.org; Telegraph Hill Neighborhood Center, 660 Lombard St, 415-421-6443, www.tel-hi.org; North Beach Chamber of Commerce, 415-989-2220; The Dolphin Club, 502 Jefferson St, 415-441-9329; South End Rowing Club, 500 Jefferson St, 415-776-7372; Chinese Cultural Center, 750 Kearny St, 415-986-1822, www.c-c-c.org

Public Transportation: MUNI, 415-701-2311, TTY 415-701-2323, www.sfmta. com; *MUNI buses*: 15 Third, 30 Stockton, 10 Townsend, 41 Union, 39 Coit; *Cable Car:* access to Hyde St line at Ghirardelli Square area and to Mason St line at Bay and Taylor sts. MUNI bus and cable car connections to BART and Light Rail stations along Market St

RUSSIAN HILL, NOB HILL

LOWER NOB HILL

Boundaries: *Russian Hill*: **North**: Aquatic Park; **East**: Columbus Ave; **South**: Broadway; **West**: Van Ness Ave; *Nob Hill*: **North**: Broadway; **East**: Kearny St; **South**: California St; **West**: Van Ness Ave

You won't come across *samovars, piroshki,* or *borscht* on **Russian Hill**, nor will you find the graves of the Russian sailors buried here before the Gold Rush. What you will find is one of San Francisco's most charming and exclusive neighborhoods, dotted with tiny gardens and parks known only to the locals. The top of Russian Hill is crowded with high-rise condominiums and apartment buildings, serviced by brass-buttoned doormen. These buildings stand interspersed with Victorian mansions, a few converted firehouses, relatively humble Edwardian flats, and numerous dolled-up "earthquake cottages" built originally as temporary housing following the 1906 Earthquake. Tucked into the neigh-

Russian Hill

borhood, you'll find several small playgrounds for children, including the delightful Michelangelo Park on Greenwich Street and Ina Coolbrith Park off of Taylor Street. Sterling Park has public tennis courts with a stunning view of the Bay that might take an opponent's mind off the ball.

The streets are steep or winding, or both. And just when you're tired of asphalt, you'll find a surprising patch of green. Sometimes-rickety staircases ensure access to these public spaces. The architectural and green patchwork that makes up Russian Hill is embroidered together with cable car lines, invented by Andrew Hallidie back in 1873. It's said that Hallidie's pity for the horses strenuously pulling wagons up the hills is what inspired him to invent the cable cars. At its peak, the cable car system ran eight lines and more than 100 miles of track throughout the city. Today three lines remain, two of which serve both Russian Hill and Nob Hill (the Mason and Hyde lines); the third rumbles through Nob Hill and the Financial District along California Street.

Some of San Francisco's oldest homes keep watch from a lovely enclave between Taylor and Jones streets. Russian Hill boasts one of the crookedest (Lombard) and the steepest (Filbert between Hyde and Leavenworth) streets in the city. (Actually, the street with the most turns is Vermont Street in Potrero Hill, but don't tell the hordes of tourists.) The twisting Lombard Street is situated on

Russian Hill, Nob Hill

the eastern slope of Russian Hill, between Hyde and Leavenworth streets. Local residents, who pay a pretty penny for the honor of living here, are privy to the near-constant click of camera shutters and vehicle fumes, as gleeful motorists navigate the eight near-hairpin turns in just one block.

On the north side of Russian Hill is the San Francisco Art Institute, 800 Chestnut Street, with its public exhibitions and Diego Rivera murals. Although the institute educates many budding artists, most of Russian Hill is not the bohemian enclave it was in the early 1900s when poets, painters, and photographers such as Ina Coolbrith, Maynard Dixon, and Dorothea Lange populated the area. Today, bankers, suited professionals, and the so-called San Francisco elite live here.

Russian Hill's commercial area is to the west, on upper Polk and Hyde streets. You'll find excellent and pricey restaurants in Russian Hill, but for less expensive fare try one of the many hole-in-the-wall Chinese food places where owners still charge non-elite prices. Opened in 1948, Swensen's Ice Cream store, at the corner of Union and Hyde streets, is a classic San Francisco establishment. Upper Polk Street is home to small coffee shops, boutique stores selling vintage furniture and antiques, upscale consignment shops, and used bookstores. The lower half of Polk Street, once riddled by drugs and prostitution, still remains a little rough in patches bordering the Tenderloin but has been undergoing a revival in recent years, and now hosts a lively array of restaurants, bars, and cafés.

Named after the well-to-do of the post–Gold Rush era who built their enormous mansions here, **Nob Hill** is perhaps the most famous of San Francisco's hills. In 19th-century San Francisco, the newly rich were known as *nobs* or more derogatorily as *nabobs*, which was used interchangeably with the word snob. Ask around, and you'll find no one seems to mind the slightly unflattering origin of the neighborhood's name. Area residents are quite content to call Nob Hill home. Located south of Russian Hill and only minutes from downtown, Nob Hill is slightly less expensive than its northerly neighbor.

At the top of the hill are several eyesores—1960s high rises—mixed in with stately older buildings, where lucky tenants enjoy a panoramic view of the city. Some humbler apartment buildings and garden apartment bargains turn up on the market from time to time. Nob Hill's original mansions went up in smoke in the fire that followed the 1906 Earthquake, and in their stead are the city's grand hotels: the Fairmont, the Mark Hopkins, the Stanford Court, and the Clift. They all have excellent restaurants and bars, many with spectacular city and Bay views. The most famous is the Top of the Mark at the Mark Hopkins Hotel. Across the way is the Fairmont's Tonga Room, a 1960s style tiki bar replete with fabulous fruit drinks and faux rainstorms. The impressive sandstone-exterior Flood Mansion at 1000 California Street, built by James Clair Flood, who made his millions in mining stocks, is the only survivor of the grand houses of the 19th century and today houses the exclusive Pacific-Union Club.

Huntington Park, at the apex of Nob Hill, with its flowerbeds, bubbling fountains, and church bell serenades, is a lovely place to while away a Sunday afternoon (as long as you don't have to find parking). On Wednesday evenings, locals gather at the park with their dogs for a little wine and social bantering. Across the street from the park are the stunning gothic spires of the Episcopalian Grace Cathedral, home to the Cathedral Choir of Men and Boys, and host of world-renowned musicians. For interesting lectures or big performances check out Nob Hill Masonic Center at 1111 California Street (go to www.masonicauditorium.com for information about upcoming events).

Close to the city's downtown shopping, theater, and hotel district, **Lower Nob Hill** lies between California Street on the north, Powell Street to the east, Geary Boulevard to the south, and Polk Street to the west. Called Lower Nob Hill by realtors, some refer to it as "Tenderloin Heights" or "The Tendernob," due to its proximity to the Tenderloin, San Francisco's most downtrodden part of town. Lower Nob Hill is home to posh hotels, exclusive restaurants, and all of the leading private clubs. There are plenty of apartment buildings, some with art deco masterpieces like Egyptian-styled foyers or gilt-caged elevators, as well as inexpensive youth hostels. Views also run the gamut, ranging from brick walls to breathtaking urban panoramas. Many of the buildings have hidden gardens, complete with goldfish ponds and loquat trees. With some of the most plentiful and affordable studio and one-bedroom apartment options, Lower Nob Hill is a popular choice for those looking for a moderately priced, centrally located place to live. Some consider Lower Nob Hill to be the most urban of San Francisco's neighborhoods, "like Manhattan with hills," claim homesick New Yorkers. Yet oddly and fortunately, in a region of pigeons, taxi whistles, and "untrendified" diners, a definite neighborhood feel prevails here. The corner store may extend credit, the café remembers your usual, and the dry cleaner doesn't have to ask your name. Parking is impossible, although monthly rentals at commercial garages are available. The hill is traversed with bus and cable cars, but most people who live here walk to work, either to the Financial District, South of Market, or Union Square. Generally safe, centrally located, bustling, and well serviced, Lower Nob Hill is worth looking into for newcomers comfortable in such teeming surroundings.

Web Sites: www.sfgov.org, www.rhn.org; www.nobhillassociation.org
Area Code: 415
Zip Code: 94109
Post Office: Pine Street Station, 1400 Pine St, 800-275-8777
Police Station: Central Station, 756 Vallejo St, 415-315-2400; main non-emergency number, 415-553-0123, TTY 415-576-1711
Emergency Hospitals: California Pacific Medical Center, 2333 Buchanan St, 415-600-6000, www.cpmc.org; Saint Francis Memorial Hospital, 900 Hyde St, 415-353-6000, www.saintfrancismemorial.org
Library: North Beach Branch, 2000 Mason St, 415-355-5626, Main Branch, 100 Larkin St, 415-557-4400; Chinatown Branch, 1135 Powell St, 415-355-2888, www.sfpl.org
Public Schools: San Francisco Unified School District, 555 Franklin St, 415-241-6000, http://portal.sfusd.edu
Community Publication: *Nob Hill Gazette*, 5 Third St, Suite 222, 415-227-0190, www.nobhillgazette.com
Community Resources: Russian Hill Neighbors, 1819 Polk St, #221, 415-267-0575, www.rhn.org; Nob Hill Association, 1177 California St, Suite A, 415-346-8720, www.nobhillassociation.org; Cable Car Museum, 1201 Mason St, 415-474-1887, www.cablecarmuseum.org
Public Transportation: MUNI, 415-701-2311, TTY 415-701-2323, www.sfmta. com: *Russian Hill MUNI buses*: 1 California, 27 Bryant, 19 Polk, 31 Balboa, 41 Union, 45 Union-Stockton, 30 Stockton; *Cable Cars*: Hyde, Mason, and California St lines (MUNI bus and cable cars provide access to BART and MUNI Light Rail stations along Market St); *Nob Hill MUNI buses*: 1 California, 3 Jackson, 4 Sutter; *Cable Cars*: California, Mason, and Hyde lines, all Market St lines

TENDERLOIN

Boundaries: North: California St; **East**: Powell St; **South**: Market St; **West**: Van Ness Ave

Long considered San Francisco's seediest neighborhood, the Tenderloin is experiencing some improvement, with new construction and new faces. Used by many recently arrived immigrants as a kind of gateway neighborhood, you'll also find young urbanites and students living here. Located just a few blocks from Union Square, the Tenderloin is named for the days when policemen were paid more to patrol its notoriously mean streets, thereby enabling them to afford prime cuts of meat from the butcher. Others refer to it as the Theater District, with the Orpheum Theatre at 1192 Market Street; the George Coates Performance Works at 110 McAllister Street; the Golden Gate Theatre at 1 Taylor Street; and the Geary Theater at 415 Geary Street, home to A.C.T. (American Conservatory Theater), all within its boundaries. On Friday and Saturday evenings the sidewalks fill up with well-dressed theater-going crowds, and parking rates at local garages correspondingly increase.

After the devastation brought on by the 1906 Earthquake and Fire, the Tenderloin had to rebuild. In preparation for the 1915 Panama-Pacific International Exposition, small hotels with ornate architecture sprang up. In addition to these smaller hotels, many of which still remain, you'll find huge hotels, like the Hilton at 333 O'Farrell Street, and the Nikko, 222 Mason Street. During World War II, when San Francisco served as a military logistics center, many shipyard and military employees lived in the single-room hotels. Interspersed throughout the neighborhood are a number of government buildings, including the Federal and State buildings, the Main Library, City Hall, the new Asian Art Museum, and the University of California Hastings Law School.

Union Square, San Francisco's answer to New York's Fifth Avenue and Times Square, is also nearby. This shopping magnet, packed with towering upscale department stores and pricey designer fashion boutiques, recently underwent a multimillion-dollar facelift. On weekends, the square frequently hosts a variety of outdoor events and exhibits—from

Tenderloin

free jazz shows to modern technology showcases. There is also free wireless, and a fantastic outdoor café, making Union Square an increasingly popular spot to relax in the sunshine with a cup of coffee and check your e-mail. For a fantastic view, grab dessert at the

Tenderloin

Cheesecake Factory—located atop Macy's. Though it can be chilly, the outdoor balcony tables offer a bird's eye view of the hustle and bustle below.

Dozens of excellent, inexpensive Vietnamese, Chinese, and Indian restaurants dot the Tenderloin area, and on Sunday mornings and Wednesday afternoons, the Civic Center hosts a market of the old world variety, where you can buy fresh fish, fruit, and vegetables.

Tenderloin street life is busy, day and night. According to the Tenderloin Task Force, crime rates here are consistently among the city's highest. Drugs, prostitution, and burglaries are common problems and local amenities are sparse—there is no large supermarket, or even a bank, in the neighborhood. Take a drive through and you will see that the streets are full of liquor stores, saloons, X-rated movie houses, and many boarded storefronts. The recently refurbished Sgt. John Macaulay Park at O'Farrell and Larkin streets, a shining diamond in the rough, is a much welcome addition, as is the neighborhood school, Tenderloin Elementary, 627 Turk Street, in this neighborhood of 4,000-plus children. The local community resource is the Glide Memorial Church at 330 Ellis Street. Run for more than four decades by the Reverend Cecil Williams and his wife, poet Janice Mirikitani, Glide is considered a Tenderloin institution, offering a multitude of programs to help the homeless, including free meals, medical services, counseling, and job training. Many volunteers offer their services to the church throughout the year, particularly during Thanksgiving and Christmas. The church's renowned Sunday gospel services regularly draw crowds from across the city and visitors from around the world.

As you might expect, rents in the Tenderloin are much lower than in the rest of the city, and landlords may not even require the first and last month's rent when signing a lease. Affordable studios and one-bedroom apartments are also more plentiful in the Tenderloin than in any other part of town. Despite the area's rough reputation, if you search carefully, you may find a nice, clean, sunny little spot in a semi-secure art-deco building, with terrific views, an elevator, and if you are really lucky, a doorman. In addition, transportation here is top notch as many MUNI lines pass straight down Market Street, and BART stops at the Civic Center.

Web Sites: www.sfgov.org, www.tndc.org
Area Code: 415
Zip Code: 94102
Post Office: Civic Center, 101 Hyde St; Federal Building Finance Station, 450 Golden Gate Ave, 800-275-8777, www.usps.com
Police Station: Tenderloin Station, 301 Eddy St, 415-345-7300, TTY 415-474-5763; main non-emergency number, 415-553-0123
Emergency Hospitals: California Pacific Medical Center, 2333 Buchanan St, 415-600-6000, www.cpmc.org; Saint Francis Memorial Hospital, 900 Hyde St, 415-353-6000, www.saintfrancismemorial.org
Library: Main Branch, 100 Larkin St, 415-557-4400, www.sfpl.org
Public Schools: Tenderloin Elementary, 627 Turk St, 415-749-3567, http://portal.sfusd.edu
Community Resources: Bay Area Women's and Children's Center, 318 Leavenworth St, 415-474-2400; George Coates Performance Works, 110 McAllister St, 415-392-4400;Glide Memorial Church, 330 Ellis St, 415-674-6000, www.glide.org; Golden Gate Theatre, 1 Taylor St, 551-2000; Geary Street Theatre, 415 Geary St, 415-749-2228; North of Market Senior Services, 333 Turk St, 415-885-2274; Orpheum Theatre, 1192 Market St, 415-512-7770;Tenderloin Neighborhood Development Corporation, 201 Eddy St, 415-776-2151, TTY 866-427-2151, www.tndc.org
Public Transportation: MUNI, 415-701-2311, TTY 415-701-2323, www.sfmta.com; *MUNI buses*: 19 Polk, 27 Bryant, 31 Balboa, 38 Geary, 76 Marin Headlands, all Market St buses

PACIFIC HEIGHTS, MARINA DISTRICT, COW HOLLOW

PRESIDIO
PRESIDIO HEIGHTS
LAUREL HEIGHTS

Boundaries: *Pacific Heights*: **North**: Broadway; **East**: Van Ness Ave; **South**: California St; **West**: Arguello Blvd; *Marina*: **North**: Marina Blvd; **East**: Van Ness Ave; **South**: Lombard St; **West**: Lyon St; *Cow Hollow*: **North**: Greenwich St; **East**: Laguna St; **South**: Vallejo St; **West**: Divisadero St

With its sweeping Bay views, eucalyptus and cypress groves, hidden staircases, and grand mansions, many consider Pacific Heights to be one of San Francisco's most beautiful neighborhoods. Some of the mansions were rebuilt in the wake of the 1906 Earthquake and Fire that decimated much of the city while others are glorious survivors of that conflagration. This area is home to lawyers, doctors, entertainment industry moguls, corporate bigwigs, movie stars, and rock legends who enjoy the relative anonymity that San Francisco affords them. International consulates, private schools, and graceful art deco high-rises add to the aura of privilege in this elite enclave. While the houses have hidden gardens and exquisite interiors, there is no gated community feel here or any star maps for sale. Residents retain their privacy and, unlike other parts of the city, you will not see many people walking the streets—except on Halloween. With a reputation for quality treats, elaborately decorated

Pacific Heights, Marina District, Cow Hollow

mansions, and a carnival-like atmosphere, Pacific Heights is where children from all over the city beg their parents to take them for trick-or-treating.

Corner grocers are within walking distance from any point in the neighborhood. Both Sacramento and Fillmore streets have coffee shops, restaurants, and pricey boutiques. Frequently sunny and easily walkable, Fillmore Street is known for its eclectic, independently owned shops, smattering of vintage clothing stores, and luxury furniture shops. As the road crosses south into Japantown and the Fillmore District, it hosts a mix of movie theaters, live music nightclubs, and bars. Perhaps the best-kept secret here is the French bakery, Boulangerie Bay Bread, 2325 Pine Street, where the croissants and baguettes rival those made in France. Larger grocery stores are close by with Mollie Stone's, Laurel Village, and Whole Foods all along California Street.

For exercise, the Lyon Street stairs serve as an outdoor Stairmaster. Locals also use the nearby Presidio for running, hiking, biking, and golfing. Down the hill is San Francisco Bay, with its world-class sailing and windsurfing.

Buying a home on the quiet residential streets of Pacific Heights filled with majestic mansions, a multimillion-dollar proposition, is not for everyone. Traditionally one of San Francisco's most exclusive neighborhoods, renters can expect to pay a pretty penny too. But there is the occasional good deal to be found in the neighborhood's mix of Victorians, Edwardian flats, and sturdy one-bedroom apartments, which date from the 1920s and 1960s. Farther down the hill, toward Cow Hollow to the north, rents decrease slightly, and the supply

Cow Hollow

of apartments increases. Meanwhile, larger spaces and, generally speaking, lower rents can be found by heading south toward the Western Addition.

In the middle of Pacific Heights, at the corner of Jackson and Steiner streets, is Alta Plaza Park, which features stunning views of Alcatraz Island and Marin County to the north, and Mount Davidson to the south. Tennis courts and a children's playground are available. If you have a dog, visit in the morning before work and you'll be sure to meet your canine-loving neighbors. Lafayette Park on Washington Street, just across from the Spreckels Mansion, 2080 Washington Street, is another popular hangout for dogs and kids—and sunbathers when the sun comes out.

Just north of Pacific Heights, **Cow Hollow**, so-named for the herds of cattle that grazed here in the 1860s, is another pleasant place to live. One of the area's most interesting landmarks is the Octagon House at Gough and Union streets. This 19th-century oddity was built based on the belief, outlined in the book *A Home for All* by Orson Fowler, that eight-sided houses somehow made healthier residences—similar perhaps to today's Feng Shui. It is open to the public, but only a few days each month.

Once the cows were moved out of Cow Hollow, the neighborhood became exclusively residential, and it wasn't until the late 1950s that the ground-floor apartments on Union Street became storefronts and restaurants. Today, Union is crammed with trendy clothing boutiques, bars, and restaurants, the latter of which range from French (Café de Paris L'Entrecote), to Italian (Prego), to Cajun (Blue Light), to Asian (Betelnut). If you're looking for a date, check out Perry's, near the corner of Laguna Street. It's a longtime favorite pick-up place, and the food's pretty good too. Parking, especially along Union Street, between Fillmore and Van Ness, is a challenge at best, particularly on the weekends when visitors flock to the area.

Union Street is also home to a variety of popular annual festivities, including the holiday electric spectacular Fantasy of Lights, where the entire street comes aglow with twinkling white lights for the season, a June Art Festival, and San Francisco's only Spring Celebration and Easter Parade—featuring dozens of kids' activities including a bonnet contest.

After the 1906 Earthquake and Fire, San Franciscans brushed off the ash and rubble and rebuilt their city with astonishing speed. They were so proud of what they had accomplished that they leapt at the opportunity to show off to the world and hosted the 1915 Panama-Pacific International Exposition at the west end of the Marina District. Architect Bernard Maybeck designed the Palace of Fine Arts on Lyon Street, between Bay and Jefferson streets, for the expo, which today houses one of the Bay Area's most popular attractions, the Exploratorium. Much more than just a hands-on science museum, the Exploratorium is a place where you can get your whole body involved in many of the more than 600 exhibits and demonstrations. Call ahead to reserve space at the Tactile Dome (415-561-0362), a huge darkened sphere. Groups have even been known to reserve the Dome privately and explore in the buff!

Prior to the exposition, the land around the **Marina District** was created by landfill, mostly from the debris caused by the earthquake and fire. Hundreds of mostly Mediterranean-style homes were resurrected here in the 1920s and '30s. The 1989 Loma Prieta earthquake hit the Marina District hard. Along Marina Boulevard, scores of the most desirable homes and apartment buildings were destroyed by a blaze that broke out when gas lines ruptured. The homes were rebuilt to higher seismic standards, but the ground underneath remains comparatively unstable, and seismic maps show the neighborhood as a high danger area in the event of another major earthquake.

Historically, the neighborhood was a quiet area occupied by long-time residents, many of them older and of Italian descent. But in the past decade, the Marina has been transformed into the premier playground of the city's 20- and 30-something upwardly mobile set. Catching the spillover from Union Street in Cow Hollow (just a few blocks south of the Marina), Chestnut Street bustles every day of the week with trendy shops, eateries, and bars. When not shopping or eating, locals head north to the Marina Green and the Presidio for outdoor fun. The Marina Green is optimal for kite flying as well as informal soccer and football matches. Running, biking, and rollerblading are also popular along the waterfront.

The eastern end of the Marina District is home to Fort Mason, a former military facility that now houses museums, bookstores, art

Marina District

galleries, public service organizations, and a renowned vegetarian restaurant, Greens (Building A in Fort Mason), with one of the city's most spectacular waterfront views. Home to a number of nonprofit groups as well as a theater and an art gallery, the Fort Mason Center also frequently hosts exhibitions. It's a great place to take classes ranging from yoga to photography to driver's education. Stop by Fort Mason to grab a monthly newsletter and calendar or contact the center at 415-345-7500, www.fortmason.org.

At the western end of the Marina District sits the **Presidio**, the former military base, now an art, history, and cultural center, spectacular national park, and shorebird lagoon, among other things. Crissy Field, a popular spot with joggers, dog walkers, and bird watchers, offers 100 acres of open shoreline. An excellent place for an evening stroll, and a prime spot to sunbathe, pack a picnic, or view windsurfing beneath the Golden Gate Bridge on a warm day, thanks to the smooth, paved Golden Gate Promenade, Crissy Field is now also easily accessible to bicycles, wheelchairs, strollers, and rollerbladers. Substantial habitat restoration work is in progress, so just steer clear of restricted areas, which are noted by posted signs. The Crissy Field Center runs a number of environmental education programs throughout the year, with a variety of hands-on programs for children.

Unique in the national parks system, the Presidio is run jointly by the National Park Service and the Presidio Trust, an independent federal agency. The US Congress mandated that the Presidio be completely self-sufficient by the year 2013, and to that end, the Presidio Trust has had to be creative about how to stay afloat. Finding big business tenants seems to be the way the Trust has decided to go, much to the dismay of area environmentalists. *Star Wars* maverick George Lucas, headquartered at Skywalker Ranch in the North Bay, is among the first occupants. The extended San Francisco arm of Lucas Films, a new multimedia mega-complex, the Letterman Digital Arts Center, opened in the Presidio in 2005. Other large-scale future projects may include a theater built by Robert Redford's Sundance Institute. In recent years, an increasing number of nonprofit and arts organizations have set up shop here, converting former army buildings into offices.

The Presidio is also home to a small, upscale residential community with a handful of privately owned homes and large four-bedroom apartments, Navy-style. Other housing options, set aside primarily for those who work here, include a few small cottages, dormitories, and a coast-side enclave of basic, compact, affordable units known as the Baker Beach apartments, which offer stunning natural surroundings and breathtaking views at very reasonable prices.

The area called **Presidio Heights** sits between the Presidio, Presidio Avenue, Arguello Boulevard, and California Street, and differs little from Pacific Heights except for the view. Many of the homes here overlook cypress and eucalyptus groves, the golf course of the Presidio, or Julius Kahn Park. Sacramento Street, from Divisadero to Walnut, offers antique stores; chic clothing for men, women, and children; high-end consignment shops; gift shops; house-wares stores; hair and nail salons; and a smattering of restaurants with outdoor seating (bring a sweater).

Laurel Heights, which extends to Laurel Village a little farther to the south of Pacific Heights, is served by the accessible shopping area called Laurel Village. Retailers include gourmet food and wine shops, well-stocked grocery stores, including Cal-Mart and Bryan's, which has a locally famous meat market, plus several children's stores, an independent bookshop, a stationery store, a clothing boutique, a classic five-and-dime, and an old-fashioned diner. There are many ornate single-family homes, but some apartments, flats, and even brand-new condos are also available. Prices here, though perhaps a little less than Pacific Heights, are still among the city's highest.

With easy access to the Presidio, Marin County, and downtown San Francisco, many people find the Pacific Heights, Cow Hollow, and Marina neighborhoods desirable, if not always affordable. Marina and Cow Hollow attract a significant number of single professionals. For the more settled/family-oriented, Pacific, Presidio, and Laurel Heights might be your best choice.

Web Site: www.sfgov.org

Area Code: 415

Zip Codes: Pacific Heights, 94115, Marina, 94123, Presidio, 94129, Laurel and Presidio Heights, 94118

Post Offices: Marina Station, 2055 Lombard St; Presidio Station, 950 Lincoln Blvd, Building #210; 800-275-8777, www.usps.com

Police Stations: Northern Station, 1125 Fillmore St, 415-614-3400, TTY 415-558-2404, main non-emergency number, 415-553-0123

Emergency Hospitals: California Pacific Medical Center, 2333 Buchanan St, and 3700 California St, 415-600-6000, www.cpmc.org; Saint Francis Memorial Hospital, 900 Hyde St, 415-353-6000, www.saintfrancismemorial.org

Libraries: Presidio Branch, 3150 Sacramento St, 415-355-2880; Golden Gate Valley Branch, 1801 Green St, 415-355-5666; Marina Branch, 1890 Chestnut St, 415-355-2823, www.sfpl.org

Public Schools: San Francisco Unified School District, 555 Franklin St, 415-241-6000, http://portal.sfusd.edu

Community Publication: *Northside SF*, 415-931-0515, www.northsidesf.com

Community Resources: Marina Neighborhood Association, 3727 Fillmore St, #201; Cow Hollow Association, 2867 Green St, 415-749-1841; Marina Merchants Association, 2269 Chestnut St, #235, 415-567-8818; Union St Association, 1686 Union St, 415-441-7055; Presidio Homeowners' Association, 650 Presidio Ave, 415-346-4176; Pacific Heights Residents Association, 2585 Pacific St, 94115; the Exploratorium, 3601 Lyon St, 415-563-7337, TTY 353-0400, www.exploratorium.edu; Fort Mason Center, 415-345-7500, www.fortmason.org; Presidio National Park, 415-561-4323, TTY 415-561-4314, www.nps.gov/

prsf; Crissy Field Center, 415-561-3000, www.parksconservancy.org; Palace of Fine Arts, 3301 Lyon St, 415-567-6642, www.palaceoffinearts.org; Jewish Community Center, 3200 California St, 415-292-1200; Friends of the SF Pubic Library, Fort Mason, 415-771-1076

Public Transportation: MUNI, 415-701-2311, TTY 415-701-2323, www.sfmta. com; *Pacific Heights, Presidio, and Laurel Heights MUNI buses*: 1 California, 24 Divisadero, 41 Union, 45 Union-Stockton; *Marina and Cow Hollow MUNI buses*: 22 Fillmore, 28 19th Ave, 30 Stockton, 41 Union, 43 Masonic, 45 Union-Stockton

THE RICHMOND, SEACLIFF

INNER RICHMOND
OUTER RICHMOND
WEST CLAY PARK

Boundaries: *Richmond*: **North**: Lincoln Park and the Presidio; **East**: Arguello Blvd; **South**: Fulton St and Golden Gate Park; **West**: The Great Highway/Pacific Ocean; *Seacliff*: **North**: Sea Cliff Ave/Pacific Ocean; **East**: 27th Ave; **South**: California St; **West**: Lincoln Park/Legion of Honor

Although there is no definitive agreement on how this neighborhood came by its name, one popular theory credits early settler George Turner Marsh of Richmond, Australia, who, upon seeing what was then a sea of sandy dunes stretched out before him, was reminded of his distant homeland. According to urban legend, after Mark Twain visited San Francisco's Richmond District, he declared the coldest winter he ever experienced was the summer he spent in San Francisco. Located on the edge of the Pacific Ocean, this is the part of the city that is first to greet the wind and fog blowing in from the ocean, and there are many days when the rest of the city is clear and sunny while the Richmond is blanketed in fog—something to keep in mind if you are thinking about setting up house here. It's a great zone for people who like sweater weather; because of San Francisco's microclimates, it is often possible to drive just a few blocks or miles to find the sun.

In recent years, the **Inner Richmond**, composed primarily of stucco single-family homes, a smattering of lavish Edwardians, and 1920s duplexes, has increasingly attracted young professionals drawn by some of the city's most affordable rentals and the somewhat less frantic pace. It is also is home to a large Asian-American community, and is often referred to as the "New China-town," boasting some of San Francisco's best Chinese, Thai, and Vietnamese restaurants and markets. Pretty much any prepared Asian food or ingredients you can imagine are available in a host of cozy family-owned eateries and shops that are clustered along Clement Street, the main drag. Clement Street is also

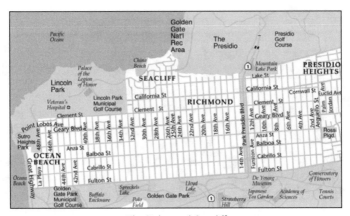

The Richmond, Seacliff

home to an array of discount shops, hardware and video stores as well as one of the city's most beloved independent bookstores, Green Apple Books, at 506 Clement Street with an annex at 520 Clement Street. Lit lovers come from all over the city to wander along the creaky hardwood floors and browse the expansive collection of new and used books, as well as videos and DVDs.

Because it's a little further inland, the Inner Richmond sometimes manages to escape the perennial fog that blankets the outer avenues—but not always. Generally, though it's not quite as cool and misty here, though outright clear and sunny days—and the accompanying warmth—are a rarity.

Though outside the main hub, with Geary Boulevard as its main artery, the neighborhood is within minutes of nearby Japantown and the Fillmore District and is still within easy, direct reach of downtown. On the flip side, heading west on Geary will lead you straight to two of the city's great natural gems, Golden Gate Park and the Pacific Ocean.

A little west, beyond the busy pulse of the Inner Richmond, lies 25th Avenue. Cutting through the central heart of the Richmond district, this road provides easy access to the Presidio, Lincoln Park, and Land's End. Featured prominently in Alfred Hitchcock's classic noir flick, *Vertigo*, Land's End is perched majestically above 32nd Avenue and El Camino Del Mar. Overlooking the Golden Gate Bridge, this segment of the Golden Gate Recreation Area offers one of the city's most breathtaking ocean vistas.

Jefferson Starship's Paul Kantner and Grace Slick used to live in the wooden house perched on the cliff at the beginning of the Land's End trail. When walking the trail, beware of flying golf balls from the not-so-talented golfers enjoying nearby Lincoln Park Golf Course. The trail winds along the coast just below the picturesque Palace of the Legion of Honor Museum, culminating at the concrete ruins of Sutro Baths. Built in 1863 but later destroyed by a fire, Sutro Baths was once the world's largest public swimming hole.

The Richmond

Formerly an army base, the nearby Presidio is now a lush national park, complete with a world-class golf course, numerous hiking and biking trails, and superb beach access. The base is prime real estate, and thanks to the fact that it is now federally protected, it won't be sold off to developers. Today, a number of non-profit organizations work in the Presidio. Private businesses are also calling the Presidio home, including George Lucas's multimedia mega-complex, the Letterman Digital Arts Center, which opened there in 2005.

When the fog lifts and the sun is shining, there is perhaps no better place to live than the **Outer Richmond**. Within walking distance of Ocean Beach and Golden Gate Park, the outer avenues are the perfect choice for lovers of the great outdoors and those looking for a little peace and quiet amid the chaos of city life. Once the city's burial ground and dismissively dubbed "the Great Sand Waste," the Outer Richmond as a neighborhood began to really take shape when waves of Russian, Irish, and European Jewish immigrants moved in following World War I. The post–World War II building boom, which went hand-in-hand with the baby boom, brought more residents, including those of Japanese and Chinese descent.

Since then the multiple generations of Asian-Americans, as well as continuing immigration waves from Russia, Eastern Europe, and Ireland, have left their indelible mark on the Outer Richmond—coming together to create one of the city's most ethnically diverse and family-oriented neighborhoods. Walking down Geary Boulevard, you can see the towering, gilded domes of Russian Orthodox Churches, grab a pint of beer at a bustling Celtic pub, or munch on *dim sum* at one of the many Chinese eateries, all while inhaling the scent of baking bread wafting from the numerous Russian bakeries.

The Outer Richmond continues to attract young families, drawn by the prospect of renting or even owning their own single-family homes with large backyards that are set along quiet streets and provide a distinctly residential feel. Once snubbed by young professionals as too removed and too dull, the neighborhood has been winning converts from the 20- and 30-something set, lured by moderate rents, plenty of on-street parking, and easy access to the Presidio. A leisurely walk through the remnants of the old Sutro Baths, breathtaking views at the historic, recently restored Cliff House, and kite flying at Ocean Beach are all just a short walk away. When it comes to beaches, the smaller, more scenic, and less crowded Baker Beach, on the edge of the Presidio, is one of the city's best-hidden gems. Here, you can enjoy the roar and crash of the thundering Pacific while taking in the fresh, salty ocean air and spectacular views of the nearby Golden Gate Bridge. A longstanding favorite with nude sunbathers, swimsuits are optional in a small section close to the bridge. China Beach, which is farther south, is a little more protected from the wind, smaller, and family friendly.

Unfortunately, those dreaming of lazy, sunshine-filled afternoons by the seashore should be forewarned—the weather here is colder than most parts of the city. Like its neighbor across the park, the Outer Sunset, which is bordered by the Pacific Ocean to its west, the Outer Richmond is typically foggy, windy, and chilly. Long pants, sweatshirts and jackets are the norm even for summer outings. Ocean temperatures hover around 56° Fahrenheit. Those who desire to brave the cold and take a plunge—and there are a few—should heed posted signs: Swim only in designated swimming areas as the undertow and rip currents are powerful and dangerous.

While the Outer Richmond is just about as far away as you can get from the hustle and bustle and still be in San Francisco, Geary Boulevard provides a direct link to the city center. The 38 Geary bus frequently traverses the busy thoroughfare—depending on traffic, downtown is roughly a 20-minute ride away.

The Outer Richmond boasts its own little gems, including the Beach Chalet Brewery, located off the Great Highway where the edge of Golden Gate Park meets the ocean, just above the Golden Gate Park Visitor's Center. The brewery, a favorite with locals and tourists alike, has spectacular 1930s murals displaying a mini history of the area, and sells large, refillable casks of locally brewed beer to go. The Java Beach Café at 1396 La Playa Boulevard is frequented by surfers, retired businessmen, and young singles who mix freely, enjoying the sound of the pounding waves across the way.

Though often socked-in with fog, the beaches, backyard barbecues, and quaint neighborhood feel make the Outer Richmond one of San Francisco's coziest places to call home. Move here and you'll get to know many on a first-name basis, including your neighbors, the butcher at the local grocery store, and quite a few restaurant proprietors.

Elite enclaves, such as West Clay Park and Seacliff, offer a peek at some of San Francisco's most spectacular mansions and stunning Golden Gate Bridge and ocean views. Sandwiched between Lincoln Park to the west and the Presidio to the east, **Seacliff** is a gorgeous neighborhood with, wouldn't you know it, sea cliffs, cypress trees, winding streets, and spectacular views of the Golden Gate Bridge. Home to San Francisco's social elite and a handful of celebrities,

Seacliff

this neighborhood boasts large houses with carefully manicured lawns and multimillion-dollar price tags.

West Clay Park, tucked in between 22nd and 24th avenues, is another unique San Francisco neighborhood, full of children and lovely houses, and perhaps best known as the home of legendary photographer Ansel Adams.

Web Sites: www.sfgov.org

Area Code: 415

Zip Codes: Inner Richmond, 94118, Outer Richmond, 94121

Post Office: Golden Gate Station, 3245 Geary Blvd; Geary Station, 5654 Geary Blvd, 800-275-8777, www.usps.com

Police Station: Richmond Station, 461 6th Ave, 415-666-8000; TTY 415-666-8059, main non-emergency number, 415-553-0123

Public Schools: San Francisco Unified School District, 555 Franklin St, 415-241-6000, http://portal.sfusd.edu

Emergency Hospitals: California Pacific Medical Center, 2333 Buchanan and 3700 California St, 415-600-6000, www.cpmc.org; UCSF Medical Center, 505 Parnassus Ave, 415-476-1000, ucsfhealth.org; St. Mary's Medical Center, 450 Stanyan St, 415-668-1000, www.stmarysmedicalcenter.org

Library: Richmond Branch, 351 9th Ave, 415-355-5600, www.sfpl.org

Community Publication: *Richmond ReView*, 415-831-0461, www.sunsetbeacon.com

Community Resources: Palace of the Legion of Honor, 34th Ave and Clement St, 415-863-3330, www.famsf.org; Lincoln Park Golf Course, 300 34th Ave, 415-221-9911, www.lincolnparkgc.com; Richmond District Neighborhood Center, 741 30th Ave, 415-751-6600, www.rdnc.org; PAR (Planning Association for the Richmond), 3145 Geary Blvd., #205, 415-974-9332, www.sfpar.org

Public Transportation: MUNI, 415-701-2311, TTY 415-701-2323, www.sfmta.com: *Inner Richmond MUNI buses*: 1 California, 2 Clement, 3 Jackson, 4 Sutter, 5 Fulton, 21 Hayes, 28L-19th Ave Limited (to Daly City BART), 29 Sunset, 31 Balboa, 33 Stanyan, 38 Geary; *Outer Richmond MUNI buses*: 1 California, 2 Clement, 3 Jackson, 4 Sutter, 5 Fulton, 18 46th Ave, 28L-19th Ave Limited (to Daly City BART), 29 Sunset, 31 Balboa, 33 Stanyan, 38 Geary; *Golden Gate Park Free Shuttle*, 415-831-2727, www.goldengateparkconcourse.org

SUNSET DISTRICT—INNER AND OUTER, PARKSIDE

GOLDEN GATE HEIGHTS
ST. FRANCIS WOOD
FOREST HILL
WEST PORTAL

Boundaries: *Sunset*: **North**: Golden Gate Park and Lincoln Way; **East**: Stanyan St; **South**: Ortega St; **West**: Great Highway/Pacific Ocean; *Parkside*: **North**: Ortega St; **East**: Dewey and Laguna Honda boulevards; **South**: Sloat Blvd; **West**: Great Highway

If you choose to make the **Sunset District** your home, be prepared with some cozy, thick sweaters, even in the summer, and know that it may be days before you actually watch a sunset here, as the neighborhood frequently is encased in fog. Rest assured, however, that the skies do clear, offering a fabulous view of the ocean and the sunset. The weather in the Sunset actually acts as a housing market deterrent, keeping values here slightly lower than in many other parts of the city. In addition, the Sunset's low crime rate, decent public schools, and manageable street parking make it an ideal family neighborhood. It is also home to students and professionals, particularly those attending classes or working at the University of California at San Francisco (UCSF) Medical Center—a premier

Sunset, Parkside

Sunset

research and teaching hospital. The neighborhood has a large Chinese-American population and many seniors as well.

Residents here are privy to one of San Francisco's greatest treasures, Golden Gate Park, right in their backyard. (See **Greenspace and Beaches** for more details.) Access to outdoor activities is easy, including endless running and bike trails, museums galore, horseback riding, rowing on Stow Lake, and soccer, polo, or lacrosse at the polo fields. You can even learn to fly fish in the park. Ocean Beach beckons from the west, where daring souls swim or surf in the cold Pacific—beware of the strong undertow. And for the more daring, Fort Funston, on the Great Highway, is a popular place to walk your dog or to hang glide. If your fear of heights dissuades you from the sport, you can still enjoy it as a spectator from the viewing area.

The Sunset comprises the **Inner Sunset** (west from UCSF Medical Center to 19th Avenue) and the **Outer Sunset** (west of 19th Avenue to the Great Highway). And, while many locals consider the entire area the Sunset, technically the homes to the south of Ortega Street and all the way to Sloat Boulevard are actually in **Parkside**; and the hilly area around Lomita and 16th avenues, known as **Golden Gate Heights**, is also considered by many as the Sunset. When the fog lifts, the views from Golden Gate Heights, perched atop a 725-foot bluff, are stunning.

Architecturally, the Inner Sunset is comprised of a number of Victorians and Edwardians, while the Outer Sunset is predominantly Mediterranean- and Spanish-style stuccos. Some of the homes along the hilly, tree-lined streets have spectacular views of the ocean and the park. Others, especially those west of 19th Avenue, are just plain unoriginal. Designed by Henry Doelger in the 1930s, they were built quickly and sold for about $5,000. While uninspiring, these "white cliffs of Doelger" usually have small gardens, and street parking is not a problem.

Two upscale neighborhoods, **St. Francis Wood** and **Forest Hill**, border the Sunset on the east; here you'll find some of the loveliest, best-tended homes in the city with prices to match. Many of the homes in St. Francis Wood, which with its large engraved entry pillars feels slightly like a gated community, were designed by renowned local architect Julia Morgan. The lots are large, giving these exquisite homes substantial space. The streets are gently winding and tree-lined.

A little farther down the hill and to the west is another of San Francisco's great hidden treasures, **West Portal**. With its 1950s charm, friendly mom-and-pop establishments, and an old-time movie house, West Portal feels like a small town you'd stumble upon somewhere in middle America. Seemingly plunked in the middle of a densely packed urban city, it is a refreshing and often overlooked family-oriented enclave, complete with quiet side streets and neatly tended single-family homes. City dwellers sometimes stumble into the heart of this quiet neighborhood quite by accident, some while riding the MUNI Metro, which runs through a tunnel here, linking it with downtown. On West Portal Avenue, an old-fashioned looking main street, independent shops and restaurants thrive and chain stores are refreshingly absent, save for a Starbucks Coffee. West Portal is just minutes from San Francisco State University via MUNI.

The main north-south artery in the Sunset is 19th Avenue, which slices through the neighborhood. (It's easy to keep track of direction here, as the streets along 19th Avenue are alphabetical from Judah Street south to Wawona Street.) Frequently crammed with vehicles, 19th Avenue links Interstate 280, coming up from San Mateo County, with Highway 1, heading north toward the Golden Gate Bridge and Marin County. (Be aware that 19th Avenue changes to Park Presidio Boulevard when it crosses Fulton Street, just north of Golden Gate Park.)

Residents of the Sunset happily boast that they can find just about everything they need within their neighborhood—from daily staples to exotic food, coin-operated laundries, electronics stores, and clothing outlets. In the Inner Sunset, the commercial areas run along Irving and Judah streets. More upscale shopping, including clothing boutiques, coffeehouses, and ethnic eateries, is centered along 9th Avenue and Irving. Go west on Irving to about 20th Avenue for the neighborhood Chinatown, which is chock full of produce markets and Asian delicacies. One block south of Irving is Judah Street, which offers easy access to the MUNI metro rail system that will take you quickly to the Financial District's Embarcadero station. A number of regular bus lines also go that way, but the rail is the most comfortable choice for those headed downtown.

At the southern end of 19th Avenue, near the Stonestown neighborhood, is San Francisco State University (SFSU). With almost 29,000 students, it is one of the largest schools in the California State University System, and thus many students call the Sunset, particularly the Outer Sunset/Parkside environs, home. The best time to find a place here is early summer, when many of the students take a year's worth of laundry home to mom and dad's house, vacating their San Francisco digs.

The Sigmund Stern Grove, located on Sloat Avenue, is a natural amphitheater surrounded by giant eucalyptus groves, redwoods, and firs. Since 1938, Stern Grove has hosted Sunday afternoon concerts for all types of music lovers. The Midsummer Music Festival features opera, operetta, symphonic, choral, jazz, rock and roll, and Broadway music...and it's all free! For the best seats, arrive early; otherwise you'll have to settle for lounging on the hillside lawn on your blanket. If you plan far enough in advance, you can call ahead and reserve a picnic table.

With its proximity to the airport and Interstate 280, many newcomers are choosing to live in the Sunset and commute to Silicon Valley. In addition, transportation to downtown San Francisco is quick, making it an optimum choice for professionals who work in the city. And, unlike most of the rest of the city, parking here is not too difficult.

Web Site: www.sfgov.org

Area Code: 415

Zip Codes: Sunset, 94122; Parkside, 94116

Post Offices: Sunset Station, 1314 22nd Ave; Parkside Station, 1800 Taraval St, 800-275-8777, www.usps.com

Police Station: Taraval Station, 2345 24th Ave, 415-759-3100, TTY 415-351-2924, main non-emergency number, 415-553-0123

Emergency Hospital: UCSF Medical Center, 505 Parnassus Ave, 415-476-1000, www.ucsfhealth.org

Libraries: Sunset Branch, 1305 18th Ave, 415-355-2808, Merced Branch, 155 Winston Dr, 415-355-2825, www.sfpl.org

Public Schools: San Francisco Unified School District, 555 Franklin St, 415-241-6000, http://portal.sfusd.edu

Community Publication: *Sunset Beacon*, 415-831-0461, www.sunsetbeacon. com

Community Resources: Sunset Neighborhood Beacon Center, 3925 Noriega St, 415-759-3690, www.snbc.org; Inner Sunset Merchants Association, 917 Irving St, 415-731-2884; Golden Gate Park, 415-831-2700, www.parks.sfgov. org; Stern Grove Festival, 415-252-6252, www.sterngrove.org

Public Transportation: MUNI, 415-701-2311, TTY 415-701-2323, www.sfmta. com; *Sunset MUNI buses*: 6 Parnassus, 17 Parkmerced, 18 46th Ave, 26 Valencia, 29 Sunset, 66 Quintara, 71 Haight-Noriega; *LRV*: N-Judah; *Parkside MUNI buses*: 17 Parkmerced, 18 46th Ave, 23 Monterey, 28 19th Ave, 29 Sunset, 35 Eureka, 48 Quintara-24th St, 52 Excelsior, 66 Quintara, 89 Laguna Honda; *LRV*: L-Taraval, K-Ingleside, M-Oceanview

STONESTOWN, PARK MERCED

LAKESHORE

Boundaries: *Stonestown*: **North**: Sloat Blvd; **East**: 19th Ave; **South**: Brotherhood Way; **West**: Lake Merced Blvd; *Lakeshore*: **North**: Sloat Blvd; **West**: Great Highway/Pacific Ocean; **East**: Lake Merced Blvd; **South**: San Francisco/San Mateo County Line; *Park Merced*: **North**: Holloway Ave.; **East**: 19th Ave; **South**: Brotherhood Way; **West**: Merced Blvd

The neighborhoods of Stonestown, Park Merced, and Lakeshore meld together and surround the compact campus of San Francisco State University (SFSU), which serves 29,000 students. Today the school is known for its education, business, and creative arts departments. In the 1960s, however, it was one of the flash points of the student protests. Well-known alumni include actress Annette Bening, pianist Vince Guaraldi (he did the music for the "You're a Good Man, Charlie Brown" cartoons), singer Johnny Mathis (rumor has it Mathis quit at SFSU after being told he'd never sing), and author Anne Rice.

The often fog-bound **Stonestown** area, simply a southern extension of the Parkside district, comes with its own mall, the Stonestown Galleria. This is a shopping destination for people from near and far that boasts major department stores, upscale boutiques, restaurants and coffee shops, a supermarket, movie theaters, medical offices, and, perhaps most important in this city, oodles of free parking. Stonestown is also the name of a pleasant collection of apartments adjacent to the Galleria. Here, you'll find scores of units, many of which are occupied by middle-aged and older residents who've lived here for years, and by students of nearby SFSU.

Just south of the campus is an even larger residential complex known as the Villas Park Merced. Metropolitan Life Insurance Company developed the

Stonestown, Park Merced

Stonestown

200-acre project in 1948 to house San Francisco's elderly. Today, it is a haven for SFSU students, especially if mom and dad are paying the rent for their garden or tower apartment that's just a five-minute walk to campus. **Park Merced**, with an array of one-, two-, and three-bedroom townhouses, is also home to many families and older residents. The multi-acre development has become a mini neighborhood in its own right, with a local grocery store, Montessori school, MUNI bus lines, lovely shaded trails, and ample greenspace. A state-of-the-art fitness center, movie theater, and conference space were recently added as part of an overall renovation effort. The shores of Lake Merced are just minutes away, as is access to I-280 and 101 south, making this a popular spot with commuters who work on the Peninsula or in the South Bay.

Across Lake Merced Boulevard, to the west of Park Merced, is Lake Merced, one of San Francisco's main reservoirs, which is surrounded by a wooded park and the 18-hole Harding Park golf course. Paddle boats and rowboats are available for rent. The western edge of Lake Merced is known as **Lakeshore**, where few San Franciscans ever visit, unless they're hang-gliders destined for the cliffs of Fort Funston or they're lucky and well off enough to have scored one of the luxury apartments or condominiums lining John Muir Drive. Rents here are steep, amenities exceptional, and the atmosphere serene, but vacancies are rare. If you can afford it and if living this far from the hustle and bustle is for you, keep checking— someone's bound to move out eventually.

Park Merced

Web Site: www.sfgov.org

Area Code: 415

Zip Codes: 94132

Post Offices: Lakeshore Plaza, 1543 Sloat Blvd, 800-275-8777, www.usps.com

Police Stations: Taraval Station, 2345 24th Ave, 415-759-3100, TTY 415-351-2924; Ingleside Station, 1 Sergeant John V. Young Lane, 415-404-4000, TTY 415-404-4009; main non-emergency number, 415-553-0123

Emergency Hospital: UCSF Medical Center, 505 Parnassus Ave, 415-476-1000, www.ucsfhealth.org

Library: Merced Branch, 155 Winston Dr, 415-355-2825, www.sfpl.org

Public Schools: San Francisco Unified School District, 555 Franklin St, 415-241-6000, http://portal.sfusd.edu

Community Resources: San Francisco Zoo, Sloat Blvd at 47th Ave, 415-753-7080, www.sfzoo.org; San Francisco State University, 1600 Holloway Ave, 415-338-1111, www.sfsu.edu; San Francisco Golf Club, Junipero Serra Blvd and Brotherhood Way, 415-469-4100; Harding Park Golf Course, Harding Dr off of Skyline Dr, 415-664-4690; Lake Merced, Lake Merced Blvd, 415-831-2700, www.lakemerced.org; Fort Funston, Fort Funston Rd and Skyline Blvd, 415-239-2366.

Public Transportation: MUNI, 415-701-2311, TTY 415-701-2323, www.sfmta.com; *Stonestown MUNI buses*: 17 Park Merced, 18 46th Ave, 23 Monterey, 26 Valencia, 28 19th Ave, 29 Sunset; *MUNI Metro*: M Oceanview; *MUNI rail*: K-Ingleside, M-Oceanview; *Lake Merced MUNI buses*: 18 46th Ave, 88 BART shuttle (to nearby Daly City BART station)

HAIGHT-ASHBURY

COLE VALLEY
BUENA VISTA PARK
PARNASSUS/ASHBURY HEIGHTS

Boundaries: *Haight-Ashbury*: **North**: Oak St; **East**: Divisadero St; **South**: Parnassus St; **West**: Stanyan St; *Buena Vista Park*: **North**: Haight St; **East**: Divisadero; **South**: Roosevelt Way; **West**: Masonic Ave; *Parnassus/Ashbury Heights:* **North**: Parnassus Ave; **East**: Buena Vista Ave and Roosevelt Way; **South**: Clarendon Ave and Tank Hill Park; **West**: UCSF Medical Center

Once dubbed "Hashbury" by legendary San Francisco columnist Herb Caen, Haight-Ashbury (or the Haight) is best known for its glory days in the sixties as the epicenter of the "make love, not war" generation. Back then the Haight was *the* place for free love, psychedelic drugs, and lazy days in the park listening to the rock bands of the time, including the Grateful Dead. But times have changed; today, the Haight has moved far beyond its counterculture and anti–Vietnam war roots to become an established and desirable neighborhood. At its core, Haight-Ashbury consists of a busy commercial zone filled with retail shops and restaurants, surrounded by restored Victorian houses, flats, and apartments. Set on tree-lined hills, the unique mansions that rock-and-roll bands once bought for a song and painted purple and orange are now tastefully restored and worth a fortune. Had you lived here in the Haight's heyday, your neighbors could have been such musical icons as Janis Joplin and members of the Grateful Dead and Jefferson Airplane, or more disturbingly, members of Charles Manson's cult.

Today, young professionals, as well as many students and employees of nearby UCSF Medical Center and the University of San Francisco, call the Haight home. Life is a tad more like it was in the 1960s the closer you get to Haight Street itself, where young people, struggling to make ends meet, often get together to share flats in large old Victorian or Edwardian houses. If you like the hubbub of a busy street, and don't mind sharing a place, such apartments are sometimes reasonably priced; some buildings feature hardwood floors, large fireplaces, views of Golden Gate Park, and cupolas.

Haight Street itself is lined with trendy boutiques selling vintage clothing, fetish shoes, used furniture, and toys for grown-ups. Not surprisingly, there are still plenty of stores that sell used records, clothes, books, comics, vintage rock-and-roll posters (even some of the "black light" variety), and new age and hippie paraphernalia, including incense, body oils, and tarot cards. Throughout the Haight vestiges of hippiedom remain, including folks with flowers in their hair wearing tie-dyes and sandals and strumming acoustic guitars. It's also commonplace to be approached on the street by folks selling all manner of illegal drugs, and there are plenty of panhandlers, some neo-hippie, some neo-punk, and some just plain annoying.

Those considering making their home here may want to "try the neighborhood out" first with a stay at the Red Victorian bed and breakfast, 1665 Haight Street, 415-864-1978, www.redvic.com. The Red Victorian Movie House, known as the Red Vic, just down the street at 1727 Haight, screens a mix of alternative, independent, and cult films. The theater is small but friendly and features bowls of yeast-flavored popcorn and old loveseats in the front rows.

Having a popular retail corridor close at hand can be both a blessing and a curse. Though Haightsters often roll their eyes at the hordes of suburban weekend warrior shoppers and tourists that crowd the sidewalks on Saturday and Sunday afternoons, living here is convenient and mostly

Haight-Ashbury

Haight-Ashbury

pleasant. All the basics are here: a good local video store, a friendly hardware shop, a mid-sized grocery store, a well-stocked bookstore, and Amoeba Music, 1855 Haight, with its mind-boggling aisles filled with new and used country, rock, blues, and everything in between—voted year after year in the *San Francisco Bay Guardian's* reader polls as the city's best music store.

Eating out is a popular pastime here, where a mix of inexpensive restaurants reflecting the city's diversity—Asian, Latin American, Italian—line the block. Spanish tapas can be had at the favorite Cha! Cha! Cha! at 1801 Haight Street. Weekends find Haight's handful of popular brunch spots serving up huge plates of eggs and waffles, with plenty of coffee and mimosas, to blurry-eyed, jam-packed crowds well into the late afternoon; arrive early if you don't want to wait in line.

Outdoor recreation, including dog walking and Frisbee playing, is an option in Golden Gate Park's "panhandle," conveniently located between Oak and Fell streets from Stanyan to Baker. The panhandle is a finger-like extension of the 1,000-plus-acre park that stretches all the way out to Ocean Beach. The park, which was once nothing but sand dunes, is laced with walking trails and has sports fields, playground equipment, an antique carousel, a science museum, an art museum, a riding stable, polo fields, an angling pond, Dutch windmills, and more.

Cole Valley, a small, friendly neighborhood located on the southern edge of Haight-Ashbury, is bounded by Carl and Cole streets. It's quieter than the Haight and home to doctors and medical students from the nearby UCSF Medical Center as well as families and young professionals. The local shopping area on Cole Street is packed with cafés, bakeries, bars, and restaurants, ranging from low-cost creperies to elegant dining. Hardware stores, flower shops, health-food stores, and dry cleaners are also available. The neighborhood pub, the Kezar Bar and Restaurant, 900 Cole, is a good place to check for any unadvertised apartment rentals. Homes here are typically a little more expensive than in the Haight. The commute to downtown is convenient; just hop on the MUNI rail N-Judah and you'll get there in less than 10 minutes.

The **Buena Vista Park** neighborhood, which surrounds the 36-acre Buena Vista Park, has curvy, hilly streets, magnificent homes, and plenty of wealthy occupants. In fact, this neighborhood has a history of well-to-do residents, including the members of the Spreckels family, who made a sweet living in the sugar refining industry. One of two Spreckels homes in the city is at the west end of the Haight, overlooking Buena Vista Park. Built in 1887 and located at 737 Buena Vista Avenue West, this mansion is exquisite, and typical of some of the other homes lining the avenue. (If you think this place is grand, take a trip over to the second Spreckels palace at 2080 Washington Street in Pacific Heights. Kind of makes one wonder if there are any openings in the sugar refinery biz.)

Visit the lookout at the top of the Buena Vista Park and you'll find a vast panorama that includes San Bruno Mountain to the south, Mount Diablo to the east, Mount Tamalpais and the Golden Gate Bridge to the north, and the Farallon islands to the west. Though right in the midst of the city, this park, with its eucalyptus groves and stately pines, makes you feel like you've left the city behind entirely. In the early morning and early evening, the park is a popular spot for local dog walkers.

For more charming neighborhoods with old, refurbished homes, check nearby **Parnassus** and **Ashbury Heights**, located south of Haight Street. These neighborhoods have plenty of ornate Victorians and Edwardians, as well as a few apartment buildings and large homes converted into apartments. Residents here claim that the wild parrots of Telegraph Hill come to visit, often in flocks of 20 or more. (To learn about these notorious birds and daily sightings, check their web page at www.pelicanmedia.org.) Rents and house prices in this area and in Buena Vista Park are higher than in the rest of the upper Haight.

Web Sites: www.sfgov.org, www.haightashbury.org
Area Code: 415
Zip Code: 94117
Post Office: Clayton St Station, 554 Clayton St, 800-275-8777, www.usps.com
Police Station: Park Station, 1899 Waller St, 415-242-3000, TTY 415-681-6487, main non-emergency number, 415-553-0123
Emergency Hospitals: St. Mary's Medical Center, 450 Stanyan St, 415-668-1000, www.stmarysmedicalcenter.org; UCSF Medical Center, 505 Parnassus Ave, 415-476-1000, www.ucsfhealth.org
Library: Park Branch (closed for one year beginning summer 2009 for renovations), 1833 Page St, 415-355-5656, www.sfpl.org
Public Schools: San Francisco Unified School District, 555 Franklin St, 415-241-6000, http://portal.sfusd.edu
Community Publication: *Haight Ashbury Voice*, found online at www.hanc-sf.org
Community Resources: The Haight-Ashbury Free Medical Clinic, 558 Clayton St, 415-746-1950, www.hafci.org; Haight Ashbury Neighborhood Council, P.O.

Box 170518, 94117, 415-753-0932, www.hanc-sf.org; Haight Ashbury Neighborhood Council Recycling Center, 780 Frederick St, 415-753-0932; Cole Valley Improvement Association, P.O. Box 170611, 94117, www.cviasf.org; Haight Ashbury Merchants, www.haightashburymerchants.com

Public Transportation: MUNI, 415-701-2311, TTY 415-701-2323, www.sfmta. com; *MUNI buses*: 5 Fulton, 6 Parnassus, 7 Haight, 33 Stanyan, 37 Corbett, 43 Masonic, 21 Hayes, 24 Divisadero, 66 Quintara, 71 Haight-Noriega: *MUNI rail*: N-Judah

WESTERN ADDITION, CIVIC CENTER

THE FILLMORE
JAPANTOWN
LOWER HAIGHT
ALAMO SQUARE
HAYES VALLEY
LOWER PACIFIC HEIGHTS
NORTH OF PANHANDLE (NOPA)

Boundaries: *Western Addition*: **North**: Pine St and Pacific Heights; **East**: Polk St and the Tenderloin; **South**: Haight St and The Lower Haight; **West**: Masonic and Richmond; *Civic Center*: **North**: Turk St; **East**: Larkin St; **South**: Market St; **West**: Gough St

Nestled between the upscale neighborhood of Pacific Heights and the colorful Haight-Ashbury, the Western Addition is one of the most ethnically and economically diverse neighborhoods in the city. Boasting rows of restored Victorians, the area's bed and breakfasts and cozy, chic restaurants are a stark contrast to auto repair shops, thrift stores, and homeless shelters scattered throughout the neighborhood. Housing choices are varied, including apartments, railway flats, colorful mansions, single-family Victorians, brand new condos, and public housing. As in most of San Francisco, living near public transit and vibrant street scenes is expensive. Despite this, affordable housing can still be found in the Western Addition because much of the area has resisted gentrification. Nearby Hayes Valley, the Fillmore, and

Western Addition, Civic Center

Japantown have all tilted in the affordable direction in recent years. The area is a mecca for the younger, "hipster" set and is steadily surviving as a place to find dive bars, legal marijuana dispensaries, nightclubs, live music, cheap eats, and thrift stores.

Until its development in the 1850s, this large land area in the center of San Francisco was a wasteland of sand dunes. Situated west of the heavily settled section of the city, the expansion into the dunes was aptly named the **Western Addition**. The neighborhood survived the 1906 Earthquake and Fire without much damage; the buildings, many of which were built on top of bedrock, did not topple, and it was beyond the downtown fire zone. After the great fire, many Japanese-Americans sought refuge here. During and after World War II, African-American G.I.'s, their families, and artists moved into the vacancies left by the interned Japanese population and cultivated a vital and energetic music scene. It was during this era that jazz flourished on Fillmore Street, with all of the musical greats of the era taking stage in one of the many nightclubs in the neighborhood, particularly the now destroyed but world famous Jimbo's Bop City at 1690 Post Street. In the decades following World War II, a city-sponsored and federally funded urban renewal plan was introduced into the area by Justin Herman, the city's 1950s redevelopment chief. Thousands of pre-1906 Victorians were bulldozed and overnight the area was reduced to a shell of its former glory in what many saw—and still see—as blatant attempts to rid the city of its African American community. For years, vacant lots scarred the once vibrant Fillmore Street and it wasn't until the real estate crunch of the 1980s and '90s that developers and real estate agents began to uncover the area's potential.

Fillmore Street, with its mix of high-end boutiques, locally owned shops, liquor stores, and cafés, is shared by both Pacific Heights and the Western Addition. Upper Fillmore, part of neighboring Pacific Heights, is lined with exclusive clothing and home design stores, trendy restaurants, an art film house, and upscale chain stores. Lower Fillmore is home to a multiplex theater, eateries, cafés, and an eclectic mix of independent neighborhood stores. Remnants of the **Fillmore District**'s 1940s jazz heyday continue today with the famous Fillmore Auditorium, John Lee Hooker's Boom Boom Room, Rasselas Jazz Club, and a new addition to that cultural heritage, Yoshi's San Francisco, which serves up high-class jazz and Japanese cuisine. Every summer, the neighborhood comes together to relive its glory days as the heart and soul of the city's jazz scene with the Fillmore Jazz Festival.

Part of the Lower Fillmore area, **Japantown** sports sushi bars, specialty stores, and cultural events. Of particular note is the Japan Center, with the Kabuki Theater Cinema Complex, the relaxing Kabuki Springs and Spa, and fun little knick-knack shops that sell products directly from Japan. Japanese necessities, from stationery and books to kimonos and cosmetics to fresh seafood and wasabi, are all available in Japantown. As you would expect, there are a number of sushi restaurants, noodle shops, and gritty karaoke bars where rooms are rented to groups of wanna-be rockstars. The Cherry Blossom Festival takes place here in April. Old Victorians, newly built public housing, and even a high-rise apartment building make up the housing options in this part of the Western Addition.

With an urban thoroughfare feel, Divisadero Street is the less gentrified artery of the Western Addition. Divisadero Street separates the **Lower Haight** from the Upper Haight or Haight-Ashbury. The Lower Haight has a distinctly different feel from its more famous sister. For the last couple of decades, students, artists, musicians, herbalists, and the like have lived in the Lower Haight's cheap and cavernous railway flats. Garages and gas stations hinder the cohesiveness of the street's commercial center, but independent and imaginative business owners maintain a stronghold in the neighborhood. A barbecue restaurant, video store, a popular record emporium, a terrific Middle Eastern deli, and many taquerias are all testament to the street's diversity. Divisadero Street is also home to several cafés, one of which has an adjoining international magazine and newspaper stand. Some of the city's cheapest gas can be found in this neighborhood at the local Arco station on Fell Street, with full-service car washing facilities available—for a fee—at the nearby and much higher priced Shell gas station.

Housing around Divisadero Street is composed mostly of Victorians split into flats and small bay-windowed apartment buildings. The sidewalks of the Lower Haight mirror the Upper Haight in many ways—packed with cafés, bars, cheap eats, secondhand retail shops, independent hair salons, and tattoo and piercing parlors. At night, the streets of the Lower Haight come alive with young hipsters out and about, touring the many neighborhood bars.

A breath of fresh air for residents and tourists alike, Alamo Square Park (between Fulton, Scott, Hayes, and Steiner streets) is four full blocks with spectacular views of the city. This steep hilltop park, whose name means "poplar tree" in Spanish, has a tennis court, windswept evergreens, weeping willows, and incredible views of the Bay and waterfront districts. Dog owners, stay-at-home mothers,

and power walkers make this park a busy, yet very safe place to enjoy the outdoors. Also here, from the peak of the Hayes Street Hill, crowds gather annually to watch thousands of costumed revelers parade past during the city's classic and burlesque Bay

Alamo Square

to Breakers race. From the northern section of the park you can see the Painted Ladies, a row of six beautifully restored Victorians that date prior to the destructive 1906 Earthquake and are featured in just about every press photograph of San Francisco. Other small parks dot the neighborhood, offering respites from the mainly urban environs.

While the Painted Ladies are iconic and represent the City around the world, they pale in comparison to many of the houses found in the Western Addition. Some of the homes, decorated in rich Victorian colors with hints of gold and silver leaf, resemble Gustav Klimt's paintings; rows of delicate pastel-painted houses look as sweet and creamy as a bag of saltwater taffies; some are painted in hippie regalia of purple, orange, and green. A few of these houses are still owned by families who bought them for a song in the mid-1940s, while others have been broken up into flats, and several serve as bed-and-breakfasts.

The **Alamo Square** neighborhood, like the rest of the Western Addition, is considerably less dangerous than it was in the 1980s. The area has received a facelift in the past two decades as large, dilapidated public housing structures have been torn down and replaced with clustered, mixed-income townhouse communities.

Within walking distance of Haight, Divisadero, and Hayes streets, life in Alamo Square offers access to the best of all worlds, as well as easy links to transportation downtown.

Hayes Valley was a little like a mole coming into the sunlight after the Central Freeway was demolished following the 1989 earthquake. Freed from the shadow

Hayes Valley

of the freeway, the area has become a hip, high-end neighborhood, with gourmet cuisine and upscale boutiques to match. Housing includes an assortment of Victorians, Edwardian flats, hidden-away cottages, new condos, and public housing townhomes. Popular, always packed cafés line Hayes, fanning out to the slightly seedier Laguna and Franklin streets. You can spend the afternoon browsing for the perfect pair of $200 high heels, gazing at contemporary art, or hunting for ultra-modern end tables. At night, foodies descend from all over the city to try out gourmet Brazilian, German, Italian, and the multiple Indian eateries, sip Belgian beer at Toronado, and sample the delights of local CAV Wine Bar. Brunch at any of the area's restaurants is a nice treat on a Sunday morning.

The biggest change here is the completion of the Octavia Grand Boulevard, which replaced the much maligned and never completed Central Freeway. The four-lane, palm-lined road

Civic Center

opened in late 2005 and is designed to carry commuters off of the freeway across Market Street and into the heart of the city. As part of the project, Patricia's Green (formerly Hayes Green), with two lawns, a playground, picnic tables and benches, now greets the arriving commuter with a small but welcome greenspace.

Lower Pacific Heights, located roughly between California Street, Presidio Avenue, Van Ness Avenue, and Geary Boulevard, was previously considered to be part of the Western Addition until realtors tagged it with the catchier name of Lower Pacific Heights. The area does differ from the bulk of the Western Addition in that it is hilly and the rents are high. Sturdy and comfortable apartments from the 1920s with brick fronts, Murphy beds, and kitchen built-ins abound in this region, sitting side by side with Victorians and mansions, as well as smaller places built in the 1960s and '70s. Neighborhood shopping can be found in Pacific Heights at the upscale Sacramento Street and Fillmore Street shopping districts.

While San Francisco's **Civic Center** does have modern condos to rent or buy and a selection of 1920s-era apartments with studios and efficiencies, with rents that are generally lower compared to some of San Francisco's more established neighborhoods, it has a much less residential feel. Centrally located and with public transportation galore, the area is busy and urban and typically the first stop that tourists take when visiting the city thanks to the BART station found there. Amenities include the ballet, the opera, the symphony, a constant string of art openings and lectures, and fine dining at elegant restaurants. The Civic Center is host to federal, state, and city buildings, including the renovated City Hall with its glowing gold trappings and marbled halls, as well as Hastings College of Law, the Asian Art Museum, and the high-tech Main Library. Some sections of the Civic Center, particularly those abutting the Tenderloin, can be a bit rough with many of the city's homeless sleeping on stoops in the area. Realtors have been known to place listings of available apartments under "Civic Center" for places that are actually in the Tenderloin—something to be aware of when you are apartment hunting. Living here may require some travel for groceries and laundry, and Civic Center's section of Market Street is still host to a number of adult entertainment spots. But, if you look hard, you may be lucky enough to find an affordable, spacious apartment with a secured entrance on a quiet street.

North of Panhandle—or NoPa, one of the City's newest named neighborhoods—stretches from Fell to Turk streets and from Divisadero to Masonic. With a sense of community and the cutting edge in modern urban renewal, this area of town features a dive-like yet wonderful music venue, the Independent; a farmer's market from July to December; fantastic dining options; and Mojo Bicycle Café, a typically unique San Francisco fusion of bike parts, repair shop, coffee bar, and pub. While not officially recognized as a neighborhood under the city's zoning codes, this area has a buzz about it that isn't going away anytime soon, due to its affordability and urban zest.

Web Site: www.sfgov.org

Area Code: 415

Zip Codes: 94115, 94117, 94102

Post Offices: Steiner St Station, 1849 Geary Blvd.; Clayton St Station, 554 Clayton St, 800-275-8777, www.usps.com

Police Stations: east of Steiner St: Northern Station, 1125 Fillmore St, 415-614-3400, TTY 415-558-2404; west of Steiner St: Park Station, 1899 Waller St, 415-242-3000, TTY 415-681-6487

Emergency Hospitals: California Pacific Medical Center, 2351 Clay St. #510, 415-392-3225, www.cpmc.org; California Pacific Medical Center, Davies Campus, Castro and Duboce streets, 415-600-6000, www.cpmc.org; Post Street Surgery Center, 2299 Post St. #108, 415-923-3770, www.poststreetsurgery.com; St. Francis Memorial Hospital, 900 Hyde St, 415-353-6000, www.saintfrancismemorial.org.

Library: Main Library, 100 Larkin St, 415-557-4400; Western Addition Branch, 1550 Scott St, 415-355-5727, www.sfpl.org

Public Schools: San Francisco Unified School District Headquarters, 555 Franklin St, 415-241-6000, *www.sfusd.edu*

Community Resources: Alliance Française de San Francisco, 1345 Bush St, 415-775-7755, www.afsf.com; Audium (a theater for audiophiles), 1616 Bush St, 415-771-1616, www.audium.org; The Fillmore, 1805 Geary Blvd, 415-346-6000, www.thefillmore.com; The Museum of Performance & Design, Veterans Building, Fourth Floor, 401 Van Ness Ave. #402, 415-255-4800, www.sfpalm. org; Ella Hill Hutch Community Center, 1050 McAllister St, 415-921-6276; War Memorial Opera House, 301 Van Ness Ave, 415-621-6600, www.sfwmpac. org/; San Francisco Ballet, 301 Van Ness Ave, 415- 861-75600, www.sfballet. org; Louise M. Davies Symphony Hall, 201 Van Ness Ave, 415-864-6000, www. sfsymphony.org; Bill Graham Civic Auditorium, 99 Grove St, www.billgrahamcivic.com; Alamo Square Neighbors Association, P.O. Box 15372, 94115, 415-248-9356, www.alamosq.org; North of Panhandle Neighborhood Association, NOPNA, P.O. Box 591504, 94159-6113, 415-267-6113, www.nopna. org; Hayes Valley Neighborhood Association, 1800 Market St, PMB #104, 94102, www.hayesvalleysf.org; Hamilton Recreation Center and Pool, 1900 Geary Boulevard, 415-292-2008

Public Transportation: MUNI, 415-701-2311, TTY 415-701-2323, www.sfmta.com: *MUNI buses*: east-west: 38 Geary, 2 Clement, 3 Jackson, 4 Sutter, 5 Fulton, 21 Hayes, 31 Balboa; north-south: 22 Fillmore, 24 Divisadero, 43 Masonic, 49 Van Ness-Mission, 47 Van Ness; inter-city: 76 Marin/Headlands; *Golden Gate Transit buses* (to and from Marin County), www.goldengatetransit.org: 10, 70, 80,93

SOUTH OF MARKET AREA (SoMa)

SOUTH PARK
SOUTH BEACH
MISSION BAY/CHINA BASIN/MISSION CREEK

Boundaries: North and **West**: Market St; **South**: 16th St; **East**: San Francisco Bay

In the 1990s, amid the dot-com boom, San Francisco's **South of Market Area** (SoMa) transformed almost overnight from a somewhat rundown commercial area to the "it" place to live and work. Old industrial warehouses were rapidly converted into Internet businesses and bustling high-end live/work lofts. But when the economic tide turned, SoMa was hit hard, as legions of small start-ups, one after another, closed up shop for good.

In the dot-com aftermath, SoMa has been forging a new identity, returning to its earlier roots as an artists' enclave, with an array of newly established art studios, galleries, and small theaters. The neighborhood also offers a smattering of fine restaurants and cafés, many of them tucked semi-secretly away.

SoMa

SoMa

Long the seat of the city's nightclub scene, SoMa provides local residents an easy walk to live music spots, busy bars, and dance clubs—something to keep in mind for those looking for a quiet neighborhood to call home. In particular, 11th, Folsom, Harrison, and Howard streets are often bustling, packed with cars, and noisy late into the night.

Housing options range from newly built condos and lofts, to small Edwardian apartments in wood-framed buildings on tiny alleyways, to residential high-rise units in the bayfront areas. Residents can walk to work in the nearby Financial District or downtown. Numerous top-name clothing and furniture outlet stores in SoMa attract shoppers citywide, including the Burlington Coat Factory, 899 Howard Street, and the ever-popular Flower Mart, 640 Brannan Street, where morning shoppers can choose from an array of fresh-cut flowers and potted plants.

You can grab a bite to eat, see a live performance, and do your laundry all in one sitting at Brainwash, 1122 Folsom Street. And Trader Joe's, Costco, Rainbow Grocery Co-op, and Whole Foods are all nearby to meet basic shopping needs.

The Moscone Convention Center (named for Mayor George Moscone, who was assassinated along with Supervisor Harvey Milk in 1978) attracts thousands of people for conventions and conferences. The Yerba Buena Center for the Performing Arts and the Museum of Modern Art solidify SoMa's flourishing art scene. A new 60,000-square-foot building for the Contemporary Jewish Museum has been installed at 736 Mission Street. The Sony Metreon, a gigantic urban techno-mall, with shops, restaurants, an IMAX theater, and a 15-screen movie theater, is situated at 101 4th Street. And just across from the Metreon is the Zeum Children's Museum, nestled in a large indoor complex that features a playground, old-fashioned merry-go-round, production studios, a bowling alley, and an ice skating rink. SoMa's heart, the sprawling expanse of lawn of the Yerba Buena Gardens, hosts a number of free outdoor events—from mini theater shows to music concerts to political fests and rallies.

Yerba Buena Lane connects Market Street to Yerba Buena Gardens, and the new Bloomingdale's shopping center dominates the fashion shopping scene in the area. Nearby 6th Street boasts a mix of hipster bars, makeshift art galleries, mini nightclubs, and inexpensive eateries. But with its smattering of boarded-up buildings,ramshackle residential hotels, and legions of homeless, this is still one of the rougher spots in town.

The **South Park** section of SoMa originated in the mid-1850s as an upscale residential area with elegant English-style townhouses. It surrounds an oval, European-style park between 2nd and 3rd and Bryant and Brannan streets, and was the first posh neighborhood in San Francisco. Today, the park remains, but the mansions do not. Wealthy San Franciscans moved to newer neighborhoods after the 1906 Earthquake and Fire ruined their homes, and in the years that followed this area became decidedly more industrial than residential. By the late 1970s photographers, graphic designers, and artists, attracted by cheap rents, moved into the neighborhood. In the 1980s a couple of restaurants tested the waters, and in the 1990s some multi-media startups rented space in warehouses that had been converted into live-work spaces, creating what was known as "Multimedia Gulch." Today, a few hardy businesses remain, but the area is now slower-paced with a decidedly residential feel. Bordering the park, you'll find excellent cafés and elegant restaurants including the South Park Café, 108 South Park Street; Ecco, 101 South Park; and the Nova Bar and Restaurant, 555 2nd Street; along with housewares and clothing shops, and architecture and design firms.

In the last decade, a massive urban renewal project has brought a number of waterfront condominium and apartment complexes to SoMa's **South Beach** area, near the west end of the Bay Bridge and along the Embarcadero, from Market Street to 3rd Street. South Beach is dominated by AT&T Park, the massive outdoor stadium that is home to San Francisco's beloved Giants baseball team. On a warm day, you can sometimes see boats floating along the marina here, hovering in hopes of catching a fly-away ball. A number of upscale bars and restaurants surround the ballpark.

Once a weedy wasteland, with crumbling, abandoned commercial buildings and pothole-filled streets, **Mission Bay**—or **China Basin** as it is referred to by old timers—is now the city's urban renewal heartland, with construction of condominiums, apartments, and office buildings, and the recently completed MUNI 3rd Street Rail project, which connects the city's southeast neighborhoods (Visitacion Valley, the Bayview, and Mission Bay) to downtown San Francisco. Long one of the city's last underdeveloped outposts, Mission Bay is undergoing a legally challenged and complex multimillion-dollar facelift—transforming more than 300 acres of abandoned rail yard to an ultramodern high-density urban hub—that will continue into the next decade.

Today, in the southwest corner of Mission Bay, the transformation is largely complete. A handful of tall condo complexes, luxury apartments, and glassy offices with ground-floor retail have sprung up in the once vacant area between 3rd and 4th streets along King Street. The swanky restaurants, winding bayfront walkways and bike paths, and well-manicured pockets of greenspace with gently swaying waterfront palms come together to create a natural extension of the revitalized Embarcadero. Folks visit to watch the boats bob in the breeze at nearby South Beach Harbor, walk along the fishing pier, and take in stunning views of the Bay Bridge or a Giants game at AT&T Park. You'll find a spacious new Safeway grocery store and a Borders bookstore on King Street. A Mission Bay branch library as well as a senior community have also recently opened in the area.

Originally part of a larger waterway—a bay, marsh, and mudflat system that connected Mission Creek to San Francisco Bay—Mission Bay was crossed by Long Bridge, a wooden causeway (where 3rd Street is now) constructed in the mid 19th century to improve links to the waterfront shipyards at Potrero Point and Hunters Point, cutting off most of Mission Creek's mouth. After the 1906 Earthquake, rubble was dumped here, filling in and further compromising Mission Bay. Then Southern Pacific Railroad settled in, using this area for its rail yards.

Long-term Redevelopment Agency plans for Mission Bay include 6,000 units of housing that mandates 28% be made available to low income citizens; 49 acres of new park space, which will include preserved wetlands; an entertainment complex; and a 43-acre UCSF Mission Bay research campus, which is already partially up and running. Many of these projects are running into local resident opposition however, and have been the subject of many lawsuits. Local activists charge that the developments are thinly disguised attempts at gentrification, long a flashpoint with the Redevelopment Agency in San Francisco.

With its distinctly modern high-density flavor, the redevelopment of Mission Bay is a good example of "new urbanism." The mixed-use matrix, being organized by one large developer, has been criticized by many for being ultramodern, too chain store friendly, and out of step with San Francisco's character, but none would disagree that this languishing area has desperately needed an overhaul. Touted by its developers as "San Francisco's newest neighborhood," Mission Bay will take a good two decades to truly come into its own, but those who enjoy an urban atmosphere and desire easy access to downtown, happening nightclubs, excellent restaurants, and the Bay should feel quite at home. Newcomers looking for a neighborhood with a more residential feel will want to head elsewhere.

Buried amid the noise of all the new construction and tucked under Interstate 280 is an old San Francisco gem, the **Mission Creek Marina**, host to a small houseboat community. Less well-to-do than Sausalito's floating home communities, the tiny, tight-knit enclave floating on Mission Creek is one of the city's hidden treasures. Established in the 1960s, this mini-oasis was once legendary for its hodgepodge of gypsies and artists—not far from a one-time traveling hobo camp near the railroad tracks—and its wild parties on the water. Today, most residents are in their 50s and 60s, have been here many years, and life is quieter, though a communal spirit is still very much alive here. Rents are very low, with only a handful of berth spaces, and turnover is almost nonexistent.

Mission Creek Park has been entirely restored and is now a haven for dog-owners living in the swank condos that line the channel. A variety of birds call this area home, giving it the feel of a tiny island of nature amid new four- and five-story towering structures.

Web Site: www.sfgov.org

Area Code: 415

Zip Codes: 94103, 94105, 94107

Post Offices: Bryant Station, 1600 Bryant St; Brannan St Station, 460 Brannan St, 800-275-8777, www.usps.com

Police Station: Southern Station, 850 Bryant St, 415-553-1373; main non-emergency number, 415-553-0123

Emergency Hospital: San Francisco General Hospital, 1001 Potrero Ave, 415-206-4478, www.sfghf.net

Library: Mission Bay, 960 4th St, 415-355-2838, www.sfpl.org

Public Schools: San Francisco Unified School District, 555 Franklin St, 415-241-6000, http://portal.sfusd.edu

Community Resources: San Francisco Museum of Modern Art, 151 3rd St, 415-357-4000, www.sfmoma.org; Yerba Buena Center for the Arts, 701 Mission St, 415-978-2787, www.ybca.org; Cartoon Art Museum, 415-227-8666, www.cartoonart.org; CounterPULSE, 1310 Mission St, 415-626-2060, www.counterpulse.org; Gene Friend Recreational Center, 6th and Folsom streets, 415-554-9532; SomArts Cultural Center, 934 Brannan St, 415-863-1414, www.somarts.org; California Historical Society, 678 Mission St, 415-357-1848; AT&T Ballpark, 24 Willie Mays Plaza, 415-972-2000, www.sfgiants.com; UCSF Mission Bay Campus, 16th and Owens streets, www.ucsf.edu/mission-bay 415-476-9000; South Beach Harbor, The Embarcadero at Pier 40, 415-495-4911, www.southbeachharbor.com; Mission Bay Park, 415-558-9063, www.missionbayparks.com; Rincon Hill Neighborhood Association, 685 Folsom St, 415-814-0143, www.rinconhillneighbors.org; SF Redevelopment Agency, 1 S Van Ness Ave, 415-749-2400

Public Transportation: MUNI, 415-701-2311, TTY 415-701-2323, www.sfmta.com: *MUNI buses*: 9 San Bruno, 12 Folsom, 14 Mission, 15 3rd St, 26 Valencia, 27 Bryant, 30 Stockton, 45; *MUNI rail*: all routes along Market St and the new T-line; *BART*: all trains along Market St; Transbay Bus Terminal for AC Transit, Sam Trans, Golden Gate Transit and Greyhound buses, on Mission St, between 1st and Fremont sts; *CalTrain Station* on 4th and King sts

MISSION DISTRICT

MISSION DOLORES

Boundaries: North and East: Highway 101; **South:** Cesar Chavez (formerly Army) St; **West:** Valencia St

Mission District

Taking its name from Mission Dolores, the whitewashed, gilded-topped monument to California's early days as the stomping ground of Spanish religious conquesting zeal, the **Mission District** is one of San Francisco's oldest neighborhoods. The traditional heart of San Francisco's Latin American community, over the years the growing intersection of emerging artists, new trendy restaurants, and young urban hipsters has turned the Mission District into one of the city's most diverse, vibrant, and distinctive neighborhoods. Amid the roving mariachi bands, you can step outside your door and grab an enormous, tasty burrito on almost every corner, enjoy a lazy, sunny afternoon in one of the city's most luscious stretches of urban greenery, Dolores Park, or get your drink on at an endless string of dive and high end bars. Just past the city's fog line, the Mission also boasts some of San Francisco's most consistent sunny, warm, and therefore most welcoming weather.

Opened in 1776, the mission, officially named Mission of St. Francis de Asis but known to all as Mission Dolores, bears the distinctive title of San Francisco's oldest building. The sixth California mission founded by Spanish missionary Father Junipero Serra, its spectacular ceiling is covered by a mural with Indian basket designs. Today, Roman Catholics from all over the city congregate for mass at Mission Dolores. The noon mass is conducted in Spanish.

From its inception as a mission, various ethnic groups have settled this area. By the 1850s, the neighborhood was filled with German and Scandinavian immigrants, with the Italians and Irish moving here en masse after the 1906 Earthquake and Fire displaced them from their North Beach and South of Market homes. In fact, the three-day fire following the 8.3 Richter earthquake leveled much of San Francisco, but stopped short at the adobe tower of Mission Dolores. So fond were locals of the Mission that, faced with the spreading flames that destroyed much of what the great earthquake missed, firefighters, hoping to preserve it, dynamited the Convent and School of Notre Dame across the way, a move later determined probably unnecessary. The anecdote remains poignant today as a testament to the neighborhood's history as well as to its inhabitants' determination and grit.

Perhaps more than any other, this neighborhood, a mix of old-timers, Mexican and Central American families, and young artists, activists, and hipsters, has a fierce sense of community unity and pride.

In the 1990s dot-com boom, tensions ran high as the Mission became a key economic and cultural battleground between preservationists and well-financed commercial opportunists. Despite the chaos and friction, when the bubble burst, an artistic and cultural vortex was left in its stead. Today, high-end restaurants sit next to independent stalwarts, such as the Roxie Theater, 3117 16th Street, an old movie house that features alternative films and documentaries; Project Artaud Theater, 450 Florida Street; and Theater Rhinoceros, 2926 16th Street. You'll also find creative paragons, such as local writer Dave Eggers' 826 Valencia, a writing center with free programs for teens, and art collaborative Cell Space, 2050 Bryant Street.

At the heart of it all is Valencia Street, the bustling epicenter for nightlife with a continuously opening string of swank "must try" eateries. Coffeehouses, restaurants, and of course bars are open late here and along 16th Street, and the proprietors won't rush you as you nurse your latte or espresso. During the day, the street is abuzz with a mix of trendy clothing stores, furniture shops, several top-notch independent bookstores, and the progressive New College, whose motto is "Education and Social Change." In recent years, the Valencia vibe has spilled over onto nearby Guerrero Street, which has seen a number of new eateries, bars, and independent boutiques open recently.

Heading south to 24th Street brings you to the heart of the Mission, where Spanish is the dominant language and Mexican taquerias and Salvadoran bakeries dot the area. The street scene is sprinkled with galleries, small shops, and amazingly colorful mural-filled alleys, especially Balmy Alley, between 24th and 25th streets and Folsom and Harrison, where every garage door and backyard fence sports a mural. The Precita Eyes Mural Arts and Visitor Center, 2981 24th Street, sponsors an art walk that features 75 murals in six blocks. And no area comes more brilliantly alive for Carnaval and the Day of the Dead.

Mission District

Filled primarily with massive, old wooden Victorians divided into two, three or more flats, the Mission is teaming with spacious three- and four-bedroom apartments—and living with multiple roommates is definitely the norm. The ability to split the rent many ways translates into some of the city's best opportunities for cheap—relatively speaking—rent. The lowest-cost rental options are shared homes where at least one person has been on the lease for a long time, and where the apartment is rent-controlled (a general rule of thumb that applies to all neighborhoods). The great rental speculation explosion of the nineties shot the prices of empty apartments way up, but in general, prices here are still lower than in much of the city. In addition to the city's first-time home buyers program, prospective homeowners may want to check out the more neighborhood-specific Mission Economic Development Association (MEDA) at 415-282-3334.

Inching west toward the Castro is **Mission Dolores**, where the vibe and the prices become increasingly more upscale. The Mission Dolores area (a rectangular neighborhood with Market Street to the north, 20th Street to the south, Church Street to the west, and Valencia Street on the east) is a quiet enclave in this often-boisterous neighborhood. It consists of classic, single-family Victorian and Edwardian houses and some contemporary apartment buildings. Rents here are higher than in the rest of the Mission, but still lower than most of the city.

Though most of San Francisco is fairly dog-friendly, the proximity of Dolores Park makes the more upscale western end of the neighborhood particularly prime for those with four-legged friends. Lined by friendly coffee shops, this stretch of rolling green, home to tennis courts, picnics, runners, and bicyclists, is the perfect place to spend Sunday in the park with George—or whomever.

On the east side of Dolores Park is Dolores Street, one of San Francisco's most attractive boulevards, which runs south from Market Street until it merges with San Jose Avenue. Unlike many of the other streets in the neighborhood, Dolores Street is a wide, divided residential boulevard with an oasis of leafy palms. Housing along Dolores Street is a mixture of traditional Mediterranean stucco houses and apartments; some of the homes are quite ornate, while others are more box-like and modern.

Transportation in the Mission is topnotch, with both MUNI buses and BART easily available.

Web Site: www.sfgov.org, www.sfmission.com
Area Code: 415
Zip Code: 94110
Post Office: Mission Station, 1198 S Van Ness Ave; Potrero Center, 1655 Bryant St, 800-275-8777, www.usps.com
Police: Mission Station, 630 Valencia St, 415-558-5400, TTY 415-431-6241, main non-emergency number, 415-553-0123

Emergency Hospital: San Francisco General Hospital, 1001 Potrero Ave, 415-206-8000, www.sfghf.net
Library: 300 Bartlett St, 415-355-2800, www.sfpl.org
Public Schools: San Francisco Unified School District, 555 Franklin St, 415-241-6000, http://portal.sfusd.edu
Community Resources: Mission Neighborhood Centers, 362 Capp St, 415-206-7752, Mission Cultural Center, 2868 Mission St, 415-643-5001 (offers classes in dance, art, and more); Women's Building, 3543 18th St #8, 415-431-1180, www.womensbuilding.org; Inner Mission Neighbors, 2922 Mission St, Suite 106, 94110; Precita Eyes Mural Arts and Visitor Center, 2981 24th St, 415-285-2287; Mission Merchants Association, P.O. Box 40280, 94110, 415-979-4171, www.missionmerchants.com; Mission Economic Development Association (MEDA), 3505 20th St, 415-282-3334, www.medasf.org; Cell Space, 2050 Bryant, 415-648-7562, www.cellspace.org; Roxie Theater, 3117 16th St, 415-863-1087, www.roxie.com; Project Artaud Theater, 450 Florida St, 415-626-4370, www.artaud.org; Theatre Rhinoceros, 2926 16th St, 415-861-5079, www.therhino.org;826 Valencia writing center, 826 Valencia St, 415-642-5905, www.826valencia.org; Dolores Park, Dolores and 19th streets, 415-831-2700
Public Transportation: MUNI, 415-701-2311, TTY 415-701-2323, www.sfmta.com: *MUNI buses*: 9 San Bruno, 12 Folsom, 14 Mission, 22 Fillmore, 26 Valencia, 27 Bryant, 33 Stanyan, 48 Quintara, 49 Mission, 53 Southern Heights, 67 Bernal Heights; *BART*: 16th St Station and 24th St Station

THE CASTRO

CORONA HEIGHTS
DUBOCE TRIANGLE

Boundaries: *Castro*: **North** and **West**: Market St; **East**: Dolores St; **South**: 22nd St

Technically known as Eureka Valley, the Castro occupies a small but vibrant area of the city that spills across Market Street into the Upper Market area. Since the 1970s, the Castro has been the center of San Francisco's dynamic and politically powerful gay community. For a number of years the Castro has hosted one of the nation's largest and most ribald Halloween celebrations. Tens of thousands of people dressed to the nines, if dressed at all, cram into the blocked-off street to stand cheek to cheek, to cheek to cheek, as a near-solid block of humanity. In recent years, the rowdy, uncontrolled vibe has been checked by better security, an army of volunteers, and more formal planning centered around large stages with live music, dancing, and cabaret-style shows. Still, every year, the highlight undoubtedly remains the dazzling array of costumed revelers informally parading up and down the street, many offering

The Castro

their own—and definitely not kid-friendly—impromptu performances.

AIDS hit this tight-knit community hard in the 1980s, transforming the freewheeling, sexual liberation spirit of the 1970s into a new kind of activism based on promoting HIV/AIDS awareness, safe sex education, scientific research, and treatment. These days, residential life in the neighborhood is quieter and increasingly family-oriented. But after dark, the heart of the neighborhood, Castro Street, with its bustling nightclubs, bars, and drag shows, still hosts a pulsing nightlife.

The Castro boasts some of the city's most beautifully maintained homes, including dozens of Victorian and Edwardian cottages, rows of two- and three-story Edwardian apartments, and a smattering of 1920s stucco flats. Streets here are often tree-lined and many of the houses have been recently renovated. Finding that perfect place in the Castro can be a challenge, as most who move into the neighborhood tend to stay for the long haul, leaving few vacancies for newcomers. Those spaces that do open tend to be in the upper middle to high end of the rental price spectrum. If you don't mind sharing, consider pooling together with two or three roommates to rent one of the neighborhood's large Victorians or, easier yet, try to find a space in an already established household. If prices seem high at first glance, don't be discouraged. A little patience and persistence can pay off.

For area shopping, Castro Street offers a variety of boutiques selling everything from jewelry, clothing, leather goods, and sexual aids to health foods, hamburgers, coffees, teas, and pastries. Castro Street is also where you'll satisfy more mundane needs, with drug, hardware, and grocery stores scattered throughout. Locals consider Cliff's Variety Store at 479 Castro Street a neighborhood fixture, offering more than just hardware.

The Castro

Taking in a show is easy at the beautiful 1930s Spanish Colonial style Castro Theatre, 429 Castro Street, with its huge Wurlitzer; arrive early to hear the resident organist pipe out live tunes. It's one of the city's cultural landmarks. If you like old movies, including musicals and art flicks, this is the place to go. It is also one of the venues for many local film festivals.

Walk across Market Street, the northern boundary of the Castro, and you'll find yourself in the **Corona Heights** area. Almost like a bedroom community for the Castro, Corona Heights has well-tended Victorian homes along steep and narrow streets. A good selection of contemporary apartments can be found in this area, many of which offer sweeping views of the southeastern section of the city and the Bay. Rentals are rare in this upscale section. Turnover is slower here than in some areas of the city, as people who put down roots here tend to stay—sometimes making rental pickings slim.

Twin Peaks shelters both Upper Market and the Castro, keeping much of the fog away, and many of these homes have sun decks in the back or on the roofs. Some even have small swimming pools. There's plenty of tight, tanned skin here, and few residents are shy about showing it off.

Children come from all over the city to visit the Randall Museum, on Museum Way in Corona Heights, which features an earthquake exhibit, live animals, art and science programs, films, lectures, concerts, and plays.

Also to the north, the three-way intersection of Market, Duboce, and Castro streets forms **Duboce Triangle**. This small, quaint, and increasingly popular neighborhood straddles the North of Market Area and the ever-extended arm of the Western Addition—both of which claim it. Yet, like so many of San Francisco's micro neighborhoods, Duboce Triangle really belongs to neither but, with its unique and individual character, truly stands on its own. Clustered around tree-lined Noe Street, this picturesque neighborhood is home to a smattering of small restaurants, cafés, and upscale shops. Bordered by Duboce Park, a small but ever-popular spot of green (especially with dog owners), Duboce Triangle boasts some of the city's most beautifully restored Victorian flats. Sandwiched between the Castro and the Lower Haight, the neighborhood is centrally located, with a large Safeway, excellent restaurants, and your choice of a popular beer joint or semi-swank martini bar, all within easy walking distance. Housing prices are on the higher end, but young professionals who can afford it are increasingly finding Duboce Triangle a good option.

Web Site: www.sfgov.org
Area Code: 415
Zip Code: 94114
Post Office: 18th St Station, 4304 18th St, 800-275-8777, www.usps.com
Police Station: Mission Station, 630 Valencia St, 415-558-5400, TTY 415-431-6241, main non-emergency number, 415-553-0123

Emergency Hospitals: San Francisco General Hospital, 1001 Potrero Ave, 415-206-8000, www.sfghf.net; California Pacific Medical Center, Davies Campus, Castro and Duboce sts, 415-600-6000, www.cpmc.org.

Library: Noe Valley Branch, 451 Jersey St, 415-355-5707, www.sfpl.org

Public Schools: San Francisco Unified School District, 555 Franklin St, 415-241-6000, http://portal.sfusd.edu

Community Resources: Metropolitan Community Church, 150 Eureka St, 415-863-4434, www.mccsf.org; Randall Museum, 199 Museum Way, 415-554-9600, www.randallmuseum.org; Eureka Valley Promotion Association, P.O. Box 14137, 94114, www.evpa.org; Castro Theatre, 429 Castro St, 415-621-6120, www.castrotheatre.com; Eureka Valley Recreation Center, 19th and Collingwood sts, 415-831-6810

Community Publications: *Castro Star*, 415-863-6397, www.sfobserver.com; *Mister SF*, www.mistersf.com

Public Transportation: MUNI, 415-701-2311, TTY 415-701-2323, www.sfmta.com: *MUNI buses*: 24 Divisadero, 33 Stanyan, 35 Eureka, 48 Quintara-24th; *MUNI rail*: F-Market, J-Church, K-Ingleside, M-Oceanview; Shuttle: S-Castro to downtown; *BART*: 24th St Station

NOE VALLEY

Boundaries: North: 22nd St; **East**: Dolores St; **South**: 30th St; **West**: Diamond Heights Blvd

Surrounded by hills, Noe Valley is geographically separate from the rest of the city, yet still easily accessible to downtown and the South Bay. In a city where you can regularly go for days or weeks without ever seeing a child under age five, Noe Valley is a bit of an anomaly as a family-friendly oasis. A mix of well-to-do young families and singles of all persuasions and from virtually every corner of the globe inhabit Noe Valley. Local comic Marga Gomez characterizes the area as ambitious and spiritual, sort of a "yuppie Tibet." Indeed, Noe has a progressive ambiance similar to Berkeley, but completely unlike its boisterous neighbor, the Castro. Residents of Noe Valley, named after Jose Noe, San Francisco's last Mexican *alcalde* (town administrator), are proud of their quiet neighborhood, their homes, and their colorful gardens.

Noe Valley

Architecturally, you'll find rows of two-story Victorian homes accompanied by a smattering of Edwardians and Tudors. And, with many homeowners busily renovating their houses, it seems there's always at least one construction project happening on every block. Some even opt to tear out an existing house and build from scratch. The array of large, single-family homes with gardens is impressive; add to this the many strollers bobbing up and down the steep hills, and you'll quickly realize you've come to a family-focused neighborhood. Children and infants are everywhere, especially at the playgrounds. Local residents designed the popular Douglass Playground, nestled underneath Twin Peaks and shaded by looming pine trees.

From Castro to Church, 24th Street is the local shopping area, and is jam-packed with coffee shops, restaurants, Irish pubs, mom-and-pop markets, one-of-a-kind clothing stores, bookshops, and vintage clothing stores as well. A quick drive east on 24th Street, and you'll end up in the heart of the Mission, where taquerias and Mexican bakeries replace the coffee shops and boutique clothing stores of Noe. Church Street, from about 24th to 30th streets, is another commercial area dotted with neighborhood stores, such as Drewes Brothers Meats at 1706 Church Street, a local favorite that has been in the neighborhood since 1889.

While it costs a bundle to live here, it hasn't a trace of chic about it. In the mornings tie-dyed t-shirt–wearing kids who attend local public schools abound, mixing in with the uniformed kids being carpooled around the city to attend private schools. There's a small town feel to this community, and overall it's a place where you'd have little to complain about. The Noe Valley Ministry, 1021 Sanchez Street, is a Presbyterian Church that also hosts community groups, classes, and concerts. Concerts vary from religious (it is a church, after all) to jazz, folk, and classical. Classes range from belly dancing to ecology. A neighborhood center for those who are expecting or are new parents is Natural Resources, 1367 Valencia Street, 415-550-2611, located one block up from 24th Street. Here, you can enroll in pregnancy, childbirth, CPR, and early parenting classes, or just peruse their library.

Noe Valley

Noe Valley offers easy access to public transit, including buses and BART. For those making the commute to the South Bay, Interstate 280 is accessible from Dolores Street/San Jose Ave, only a few minutes away. You can access Cal-Train at the 22nd Street Station.

Web Sites: www.sfgov.org, www.noevalley.com
Area Code: 415
Zip Codes: 94114, 94131
Post Office: Noe Valley Station, 4083 24th St, 800-275-8777, www.usps.com
Police Station: Mission Station, 630 Valencia St, 415-558-5400, TTY 415-431-6241, main non-emergency number, 415-553-0123
Emergency Hospitals: San Francisco General Hospital, 1001 Potrero Ave, 415-206-8000, www.sfghf.net; California Pacific Medical Center, Davies Campus, Castro and Duboce sts, 415-600-6000, www.cpmc.org
Library: Noe Valley Branch, 451 Jersey St, 415-355-5707, www.sfpl.org
Public Schools: San Francisco Unified School District, 555 Franklin St, 415-241-6000, http://portal.sfusd.edu
Community Resources: Noe Valley Ministry, 1021 Sanchez St, 415-282-2317, www.noevalleyministry.org; Friends of Noe Valley, 415-282-9918, www.friendsofnoevalley.com; Natural Resources, 816 Diamond St, 415-550-2611, www.naturalresources-sf.com
Community Publications: Noe Valley Voice, 1021 Sanchez St, 415-821-3324, www.noevalleyvoice.com
Public Transportation: MUNI, 415-701-2311, TTY 415-701-2323, www.sfmta.com: *MUNI buses*: 24 Divisadero, 33 Stanyan, 35 Eureka, 48 Quintara 24th; *MUNI rail*: J-Church, K-Ingleside, M-Oceanview; *BART*: 24th St Station

GLEN PARK, DIAMOND HEIGHTS

Boundaries: North: Clipper St; **East**: Dolores St/San Jose Ave; **South:** Bosworth St; **West**: O'Shaughnessy Blvd

Affordable property (by San Francisco standards) and a cozy neighborhood feel make **Glen Park** worth exploring. A rural community at the turn of the century, Glen Park replaced Cow Hollow, which suffered from a cholera outbreak, as the dairy capital of the area. Shortly thereafter, San Francisco bought Glen Canyon Park in 1922 and sold residential lots. Today, this hilly area located south of Noe Valley is made up of a quaint collection of single-family homes, Victorian flats, and apartments that run along narrow, curvy streets. In fact, for a moment you may wonder if you've detoured into a small, twisting mountain village. The main shopping area around Chenery and Diamond streets is nestled in the hillside surrounding the Glen Park BART Station. Close to the station you'll find a handful of cozy cafés and restaurants. For newcomers particularly concerned about temblors, this neighborhood survived last century's two great earthquakes relatively unscathed. Though slowly growing, Glen Park is still largely undiscovered, relatively quiet, and, in general, considerably less expensive than its trendy neighbor, Noe Valley. With a busy BART station at its center, transit to and from downtown San Francisco is quick and easy, as are daily commutes to the East Bay and Peninsula along the BART corridor.

Glen Park, Diamond Heights

The neighborhood is named for the lovely Glen Canyon Park, San Francisco's second largest park. Because this 70-acre park is off the beaten path, few people who live in San Francisco even know this eucalyptus-rich area exists. Many locals walk their dogs in the canyon. In addition to hiking trails, there are tennis courts, a children's playground, baseball field, and an 80-foot band of sandstone for beginner climbers. (Beware of poison oak!) The recreation center in the park has a basketball court and offers dance and art classes. (See listings below.) Another natural gem close at hand is Mount Davidson, the city's highest peak, which rises 938 feet above sea level. Here, springtime hikers can catch a glimpse of an incredible array of wildflowers.

The hilltop residential area of **Diamond Heights** was one of the last areas settled in San Francisco. Overlooking Glen Park to the north, it contains row upon row of sizable apartment complexes, a shopping center, and some superb views of the city and the San Francisco Bay below. Parking is not a problem and affordable rental housing can be found here, despite the general rule of thumb that the higher the elevation the higher the price. One drawback to living here is the fog and wind, both of which will send you scurrying for cover. Across Market Street, to the north

Diamond Heights

of Diamond Heights, sit the famous Twin Peaks. Climb up here on clear days to view the snow-capped Sierra Nevada mountain range 200 miles to the east. Nearby Sutro Tower is a strange looking structure, and many would call it an eyesore, but it's an accepted part of the San Francisco skyline. Used by television and radio stations to beam their signals to the masses below, at 981 feet, it is the tallest structure in the city.

Web Site: www.sfgov.org

Area Code: 415

Zip Code: 94131

Post Office: Diamond Heights Station, 5262 Diamond Heights Blvd, 800-275-8777, www.usps.com

Police Station: Ingleside Station, 1 Sergeant John V. Young Lane, 415-404-4000, TTY 415-404-4009; main non-emergency number, 415-553-0123

Emergency Hospitals: San Francisco General Hospital, 1001 Potrero Ave, 415-206-8000, www.sfghf.net; St. Luke's Hospital, 3555 Cesar Chavez St, 415-647-8600, www.stlukes-sf.org

Library: Glen Park Branch, 2825 Diamond St, 415-355-2858, www.sfpl.org

Public Schools: San Francisco Unified School District, 555 Franklin St, 415-241-6000, http://portal.sfusd.edu

Community Resources: Glen Park Association, P.O. Box 31292, 94131, 415-908-6728; Glen Park Recreation Center, 70 Elk St, 415-337-4705; Diamond Heights Community Association, P.O. Box 31529, 94131; Friends of Glen Canyon Park, 140 Turquoise Way, 94131, 415-648-0862; Glen Canyon Park, O'Shaughnessy Blvd and Bosworth St, 415-831-2700

Public Transportation: MUNI, 415-701-2311, TTY 415-701-2323, www.sfmta. com; *MUNI buses*: 23 Monterey, 26 Valencia, 35 Eureka, 44 O'Shaughnessy, 52 Excelsior; *MUNI rail*: J-Church line; *BART*: Glen Park Station

POTRERO HILL

DOGPATCH

Boundaries: North: 15th St; **East**: San Francisco Bay; **South**: Cesar Chavez St; **West**: Highway 101

Much like the Mission, its neighbor to the west, Potrero Hill is one of the sunniest areas of the city, as the fog seldom makes its way this far south and east. Atop Potrero Hill you'll also experience some of the best views of the Bay. Because of its proximity to Highway 101 on the west and 280 on the east, the Potrero district is easily accessible for those facing a daily freeway commute and is therefore considered a choice place to live by young professionals.

Potrero Hill

If you want to live in Potrero Hill, make sure you're ready to climb. Potrero, which means "pasture" in Spanish, was nicknamed "Billy Goat Hill" around the turn of the century when goats spent their days scrambling up the hillside. These hills also gave rise to the most crooked street in San Francisco, which is located on the slope of 20th and Vermont streets. Unlike Lombard Street, Vermont Street, with its six hairpin turns and 14.3% grade, does not play host to tourists lined up in cars waiting to experience the ride, nor is it as photogenic. In fact, you'll find many ultra-steep hills here that offer fantastic views of the city skyline below.

Housing in Potrero Hill is varied and includes many renovated Victorians, dark-shingled Edwardians, 1920s art-deco stucco apartment buildings, and not-so-attractive apartments from the 1960s and '70s, as well as more recently constructed live/work loft spaces.

Once a predominantly working class neighborhood and home to many recently arrived immigrants and artists, the neighborhood suffered the pains of rapid gentrification in the late nineties, but now has settled into a vibrant and comfortable cultural mix. Local cafés, restaurants, and groceries, primarily clustered along a few short blocks on 18th Street near Connecticut Street, are friendly neighborhood gathering spots and quiet compared to many of San Francisco's more frenetic neighborhoods. Comfortable coffeehouses, like Farley's at 1315 18th Street, dot the neighborhood, making it easy for you to grab

Dogpatch

a cup of coffee on your way out in the morning or to sit down and visit. There are also friendly corner bars, including Bloom's Saloon, 1318 18th Street, and excellent restaurants offering everything from fine French food to gourmet pizza to Thai food and tiki bar drinks. To hear rock music in an intimate setting, try the Bottom of the Hill Club on 17th Street and Missouri. Gardeners will be interested to know about the community gardens located at San Bruno Avenue and 20th Street, and Connecticut and 22nd streets. Newcomers looking to learn how to dance the tango, swing, or lindy hop should check out the Metronome Dance Center, 1830 17th Street, regularly voted by the *San Francisco Bay Guardian* readers' poll as the best place to learn to dance.

Outside of those searching for a good view or a taste of fine beer, not many venture into Potrero Hill. Consider this a bonus, particularly on those gloriously clear mornings when you can relax on your hilltop perch and pat yourself on the back for moving to the city that's spread out before you.

Heading further east to the outskirts of Potrero Hill, between Mariposa Street and Islais Creek, is a small "in between" spot, with a personality all its own, known as **Dogpatch**. A diverse neighborhood in the flats on the eastern edge of Potrero Hill, Dogpatch was recognized as a Historic District by the city of San Francisco in 2003. The area, one of the few to survive the 1906 Earthquake and Fire, includes a number of old Victorians and the city's largest collection of 19th and early 20th century workers' cottages. Today, like the rest of Potrero Hill, the area also contains a number of ultramodern live/work lofts constructed during the 1990s dot-com explosion.

Along Potrero's watery edge is a smattering of warehouses and old industrial buildings, some historically significant, some simply ghost-like shells, which speak to this area's industrial past. Known as the Central Waterfront, this spot was once home to such heavy industry giants as Tubbs Cordage Company, the Spreckels Sugar refinery, and the gasworks company that would become PG&E. At its heart is Pier 70, a long-time shipbuilding and repair hub. During World War II, under the direction of Union Iron Works/Bethlehem Steel, a flurry of ships was constructed, and in 1967, the transit tubes—57 sections, each 325 feet long and weighing 800 tons—that carry BART beneath the Bay were built here. By the 1970s manufacturing declined, and in 1982, the land was transferred to the City of San Francisco for $1. Today, the San Francisco Drydock continues with the business of ship repair, and a number of artists, drawn by low rents, have set up workspaces in this cluster of old brick buildings. Amid vacant warehouses, you'll find Agua Vista Park, with a few picnic tables and up-close views of the giant tankers and a public fishing pier (be sure to read signs about acceptable levels of fish consumption, as the Bay has high levels of mercury). Though much of Pier 70 still sits largely abandoned, with many structures in need of rehabilitation or razing, as well as environmental clean-up issues, the expansion of the nearby UCSF Mission Bay Campus and the completion of the 3rd Street Light Rail clearly demonstrate the impending redevelopment of Potrero's waterfront.

Planning sessions are afoot at the Port of San Francisco to determine the future of this massive public trust land.

Web Site: www.sfgov.org
Area Code: 415
Zip Code: 94107
Post Office: Brannan Street Station, 460 Brannan St, 800-275-8777, www.usps. com
Police Station: Bayview Station, 201 Williams St, 415-671-2300, TTY 415-671-2346, main non-emergency number, 415-553-0123
Emergency Hospital: San Francisco General Hospital, 1001 Potrero Ave, 415-206-8000, www.sfghf.net
Library: Potrero Branch, 1616 20th St, 415-355-2822, www.sfpl.org
Public Schools: San Francisco Unified School District, 555 Franklin St, 415-241-6000, http://portal.sfusd.edu
Community Publication: *The Potrero View Newspaper*, 2325 3rd St Suite 344, 415-626-8723, www.potreroview.net
Community Resources: Potrero Hill Neighborhood House, 953 DeHaro St, 415-826-8080; Potrero Hill Family Resource Center, 415-206-2121; Potrero Hill Health Center, 1050 Wisconsin St, 415-648-3022; Metronome Dance Center, 1830 17th Street, 415-252-9000
Public Transportation: MUNI, 415-701-2311, TTY 415-701-2323, www.sfmta. com: *MUNI buses*: 10 Townsend, 15 3rd St, 19 Polk, 22 Fillmore, 48 Quintara-24th St, 53 Southern Heights; *CalTrain*: 22nd St Station

BERNAL HEIGHTS

Boundaries: North: Cesar Chavez St; **East**: Highway 101; **South**: Interstate 280/Alemany Blvd; **West**: San Jose Ave

Formerly a rough, working class neighborhood, Bernal Heights, located in the southeast section of San Francisco, is now considerably safer and generally more affordable than much of the rest of the city. Indeed, because of its off-the-beaten-path location and affordable prices, many artists, musicians, writers, and young families have made Bernal Heights their home. Considered an alternative to the predominantly gay

Bernal Heights

male culture of the Castro, Bernal Heights has also become a welcoming home to a growing lesbian community. And the view from atop the brown bald hill (brown in the summer and green in the winter) offers a spectacular panorama of the city below.

Named for Don Jose Cornelio de Bernal, to whom the land was granted in 1839 by the Mexican government as part of larger parcel, Bernal Heights was originally a grazing area for cows, goats, and other livestock. By the 1860s, small plots had been sold to Irish and Italian immigrants, and farming continued, giving the area the nickname "nanny goat hill." As it was essentially unscathed after the 1906 Earthquake, Bernal Heights is where many displaced Italians from North Beach came to start anew.

Today, Bernal Heights is an intimate, progressive, and child-friendly community where neighbors know each other and come together to fight for area causes, including safer streets and improved playgrounds. Each August, residents host a hill-wide garage sale. Take a tour of this neat and tidy neighborhood and it is apparent that quite a few residents spend their free time tending their yards or planting at one of the community gardens. Many of the streets are lined with small Victorian cottages and some contemporary (1960s and '70s) box-like homes. Though the streets are narrow, parking is usually not a challenge.

Cortland Avenue hosts a number of commercial options, from a classic barbershop, coffee shops, and bookstore to produce stands and pet shops. Chain stores are almost nonexistent here and the neighborhood prides itself on supporting local, independent businesses. The recently remodeled and expanded

Bernal Heights

health food store, the Good Life Grocery at 1524 20th Street, is always bustling, as is Red Hill Books, 401 Cortland Avenue. The Liberty Café, 410 Cortland, is a local favorite for home-style cooking featuring a rotating array of fresh seasonal items. Attached, you'll find the Liberty Wine Cottage and Bakery; the smell of fresh baked goods and the cozy outdoor patio attract morning crowds, while wine buffs flock to evening tastings.

Consider heading to the Saturday morning Alemany Farmers Market at 100 Alemany Boulevard (near the 101–I-280 interchange). Many consider this, the oldest farmers market in the city, to be the most affordable. Produce and other goods come from all over the state. Bargain hunters should return on Sunday mornings when the site hosts a flea market.

Bus service in Bernal Heights is not as frequent or swift as in the neighboring Mission District. However, the neighborhood is connected to the downtown area via MUNI, and offers fast access to both 101 and I-280 for commuters.

To learn more about the neighborhood, stop by the Bernal Heights Neighborhood Center at 515 Cortland Avenue.

Web Site: www.sfgov.org
Area Code: 415
Zip Code: 94110
Post Office: Bernal Heights Finance Station, 189 Tiffany Ave, 800-275-8777, www.usps.com
Police Station: Ingleside Station, 1 Sergeant John V. Young Lane, 415-404-4000, TTY 415-404-4009; main non-emergency number, 415-553-0123
Emergency Hospitals: St. Luke's Hospital, 3555 Cesar Chavez St, 415-647-8600, www.stlukes-sf.org; San Francisco General Hospital, 1001 Potrero Ave, 415-206-8000, www.sfghf.net
Public Schools: San Francisco Unified School District, 555 Franklin St, 415-241-6000, http://portal.sfusd.edu
Community Resources: Bernal Heights Neighborhood Center, 515 Cortland Ave, 415-206-2140, www.bhnc.org; Alemany Farmers Market, 100 Alemany Blvd, 415-647-9423; The Writing Salon, for creative writing instruction, 415-609-2468, www.writingsalons.com
Public Transportation: MUNI, 415-701-2311, TTY 415-701-2323, www.sfmta.com: *MUNI buses*: 9 San Bruno, 12 Folsom, 14 Mission, 23 Monterey, 24 Divisadero, 27 Bryant, 49 Van Ness-Mission, 67 Bernal Heights

EXCELSIOR, MISSION TERRACE/OUTER MISSION, CROCKER AMAZON, INGLESIDE, VISITACION VALLEY, PORTOLA

Boundaries: *Excelsior*: **North**: Alemany Blvd; **East**: McLaren Park; **South**: Geneva Ave; **West**: Mission St; *Mission Terrace/Outer Mission*: **North** and **West**: Interstate 280; **East**: Mission St; **South**: San Mateo County Line; *Crocker Amazon*: **North** and **West**, Mission St; **North** and **East**: Geneva Ave; **South**: San Mateo County Line; *Ingleside*: **North**: Monterey Blvd; **East**: Interstate 280; **South**: San Mateo County Line; **West**: 19th Ave; *Visitacion Valley*: **North**: Mansell St; **East**: Bayshore Blvd; **South**: San Mateo County Line; **West**: McLaren Park; *Portola*: **North**: Interstate 280; **East**: Highway 101; **South**: Mansell St; **West**: Cambridge to Silver to Madison

Excelsior, Mission Terrace/Outer Mission,
Crocker Amazon, Ingleside, Visitacion Valley, Portola

Located in the foggy, windswept southern section of San Francisco, near the San Mateo County border, these neighborhoods are all primarily residential and are considered inexpensive, at least by San Francisco standards. Because of the neighborhoods' relative affordability, this is one of the rare areas in San Francisco where the dream of home ownership still remains within reach for those other than the wealthy. A true melting pot, the area is home to a variety of ethnic groups especially Asian, Latino, and African American, as well as a host of student residents, many of whom attend San Francisco City College (north of Ingleside in Sunnyside).

Visiting the **Excelsior** and **Mission Terrace/Outer Mission** neighborhoods, you'll find row upon row of single-family stucco homes, flats, apartment complexes, duplexes, and townhouses, varying from immaculate to those in need of serious renovation. Look for housing here and you may find a hidden treasure in the form of an affordable, mother-in-law rental unit tucked away in a

Excelsior

sun-baked backyard garden. Residents here have an easy commute into downtown San Francisco to the north or into the shopping mall–rich suburbia of San Mateo County to the south. Buses run frequently along Mission Street, and the two nearby BART Stations are Glen Park and Balboa Park. Geneva Avenue and Mission Street are home to inexpensive yet tasty Asian and Latin restaurants. In recent years, the Outer Mission has seen a handful of fancier, pricier eateries spring up, along with popular nightclubs and bars, which are transforming the strip of Mission Street (from Cesar Chavez south to 30th Street) into a nighttime destination spot, especially on weekends. In the summer, folks head in droves to Mitchell's Ice Cream, 688 San Jose Avenue, to sample its famous frozen confections. Family run for more than 50 years, Mitchell's was voted "best ice cream parlor" from 1996 through 2004 by the *San Francisco Bay Guardian* readers' poll.

The triangular-shaped **Crocker Amazon** lies directly south of Excelsior. These homes, and the ones in Daly City, supposedly served as the inspiration for the Malvina Reynolds song (made famous by folk singer Pete Seeger) that refers to "the little boxes, on a hilltop and they're all made out of ticky tacky." The Crocker Amazon Playground, the biggest playground in the city, is a popular family weekend outing. It's also home to San Francisco's first skateboard park. In Crocker Amazon, neighborhood lines blur with Daly City's own Crocker neighborhood boundaries. The only way to tell which town you're officially in is by the street signs—San Francisco's are white and Daly City's are blue.

Situated west of Outer Mission, the **Ingleside** district is a hodgepodge of single-family homes built in the 1920s and '30s. Ingleside was home to one of the city's first racetracks, and today's Urbano Drive traces the old racecourse. While not the safest area of San Francisco, Ingleside is far from being the most dangerous. There are a number of charming pockets along quiet winding streets where families take pride in their homes, lawns are green, traffic is sparse, and neighbors are…neighborly.

Visitacion Valley, named in 1777 by Franciscan priests, is perhaps a bit more lively than Crocker Amazon, but it's by no means exciting. What may be exciting to home seekers is that some of the least expensive homes in the city are here, both for purchase and rent. Housing includes single stuccos, wood-framed apartments, Victorian flats, townhouses, and duplexes. In an effort to improve the neighborhood, one of the city's largest and most troubled public housing projects, Geneva Towers, was demolished in 1998. The other, the 700-plus Sunnydale complex, remains and continues to struggle with difficulties arising from gang activity. Such problems still plague the neighborhood, despite residents' efforts to make the streets safer.

McLaren Park, which comes with its own golf course, makes up Visitacion Valley's western border with Excelsior. The world-famous Cow Palace sits a bit to the south of McLaren Park, along Geneva Avenue. The Beatles played at the Cow Palace, as have hundreds of other big-name acts over the years. The arena also hosts sports and boat shows, dog and cat exhibitions, consumer elec-

Vistacion Valley

tronics auctions, car auctions, motorcycle races, tractor-pulls, and, true to its cowboy roots, a popular annual rodeo.

Jutting out into the Bay, just across Highway 101, sits the large open-air stadium Candlestick Park, the current home of the National Football League's 49ers. The park is a cold and windy place, except for a few days in the summer, which was one of the reasons the Giants built their own facility in the city's South Park/China Basin/Mission Bay area. The 49ers are working on building a new stadium as well but haven't secured the necessary funding.

Just north of Visitacion Valley, and south of Bernal Heights, is **Portola**, an area similar to Bernal Heights when it comes to housing options, climate, and residential makeup. It also has a rich Italian and Jewish heritage, much of which survives to this day, especially in the thriving commercial zone along San Bruno Avenue, the district's southern border with Visitacion Valley. Local shopping options tend toward the practical, including an Italian butcher shop, mom-and-pop grocers, and flower shops. With McLaren Park nearby, there's plenty of open space for recreational activities.

Web Site: www.sfgov.org

Area Code: 415

Zip Codes: Excelsior, Outer Mission, Crocker Amazon, Ingleside, 94112; Portola, Visitacion Valley, 94134

Post Offices: Excelsior Station, 15 Onondaga Ave; Visitacion Valley, 68 Leland Ave; McLaren Station, 2755 San Bruno Ave, 800-275-8777, www.usps.com

Police Station: Ingleside Station, 1 Sergeant John V. Young Lane, 415-404-4000, TTY 415-404-4009; main non-emergency number, 415-553-0123

Emergency Hospital: San Francisco General Hospital, 1001 Potrero Ave, 415-206-8000, www.sfghf.net

Libraries: Excelsior Branch, 4400 Mission St, 415-337-4735; Visitacion Valley, 45 Leland Ave, 415-355-2848; Portola, 380 Bacon St, 415-355-5660; Ingleside Branch, 1649 Ocean Ave, 415-355-2898

Public Schools: San Francisco Unified School District, 555 Franklin St, 415-241-6000, http://portal.sfusd.edu/template/index.cfm

Community Publication: *Visitacion Valley Grapevine*, 415-467-9300, www.vivalleygrapevine.com

Community Resources: Excelsior District Improvement Association, P.O. Box 12005, 94112-0005 www.excelsiorsf.org; Visitacion Valley Children's Center, 325 Leland Ave, 415-585-9320; McLaren Park, Geneva and La Grande aves, Gleneagles International Golf Course, 2100 Sunnydale Ave, 415-587-2425, www.gleneaglesgolfsf.com

Public Transportation: MUNI, 415-701-2311, TTY 415-701-2323, www.sfmta.com: *Excelsior, MUNI buses*: 14 Mission, 29 Sunset, 43 Masonic, 49 Van Ness-Mission, 52 Excelsior, 54 Felton, *MUNI LRV*: J-Church, K-Ingleside, M-Ocean View; *Crocker Amazon, MUNI buses*: 14 Mission, 43 Masonic, 49 Van Ness-Mission, 88 BART shuttle; *Visitacion Valley, MUNI buses*: 9 San Bruno, 15 3rd St, 29 Sunset, 56 Rutland

BAYVIEW/HUNTERS POINT

Boundaries: North: Highway 280; **East** and **South**: the Bay; **West**: Bayshore Blvd

Offering some of the city's warmest weather, easy access to the Peninsula and South Bay, and majestic hilltop views of the Bay, the long neglected, troubled Bayview/Hunters Point stands today at the crossroads of change. Walking though the neighborhood, located on the sunny southeastern tip of San Francisco, you'll find evidence of this everywhere. Bright, boxy, pink, green, and yellow two-story stuccos line the rolling hillsides, while a handful of exquisite Victorians hide away amid public housing projects in various states of upkeep.

Plagued for years by economic depression, some of the city's highest violent crime rates, as well as health and environmental concerns resulting from its proximity to a large power plant, sewage treatment facility, and a former US navy shipyard, all eyes have turned to

Bayview, Hunters Point

Bayview

Bayview/Hunters Point as massive redevelopment here gets under way.

A new Saturday morning farmers market opened at Galvez Avenue and Third Street, a blessing for residents who often complained about the lack of fresh produce and other healthy food options. The historic Bayview Opera House, 4705 3rd Street, which offers music, theater and dance programs, and community classes, recently restored the theater to its original grandeur and greatly expanded its art and culture offerings.

For more than a decade, the biggest issue in Hunters Point, located in the area's southeast corner, has been the future of the 500-acre former US Naval shipyard, now a Superfund site. In 1867, Hunters Point was the first permanent dry dock on the Pacific Coast, and in 1939 the US Navy purchased the land for use as a dry dock and shipbuilding operation. During World War II, Hunters Point base, a ship repair yard, provided a large number of high-paying blue-collar jobs, and the Hunters Point/Bayview community boasted the highest percentage of home ownership in the city. But things began to slow down in the 1960s and '70s, and in 1974 the shipyards were closed. Since then the neighborhood has been plagued by high unemployment and high crime rates. Though the facility closed over three decades ago, the city and the Navy have been at odds over the environmental cleanup and transfer of land to the city. To date, the Navy has spent over $100 million to help rid the area of toxins, but residents and city officials remain concerned about higher rates of cancer and asthma among children. In 2004, a major hurdle was cleared when both sides agreed to a plan to turn the land over to city for redevelopment.

And now the first phase, a $600 million project that will include 1,600 new apartments and townhouses, with close to one-third set aside for affordable housing; 300,000 square feet of commercial space; and more than 30 acres of open space is under way. Residents and city officials are hoping new jobs created by the massive redevelopment of the shipyard will go to local residents, driving economic revitalization and social improvements in the Hunters Point and Bayview communities. Still, cleanup of the most polluted areas of the site needs to be completed, and it will likely be several decades before the face of the old shipyard is fully transformed.

With lots of undeveloped space, Hunters Point has a surprising amount of wildlife. The stunning Candlestick Point Recreation Area—home to blue herons, possums, barn owls, seals, jackrabbits, foxes, raccoons, falcons and red-tailed hawks—is popular with joggers, windsurfers, and fishermen. Though still considered rough in a many spots, this neighborhood has attracted waves of artists over the years, and continues to do so today.

Near the San Mateo County line you'll also find the home of the 49ers, Candlestick Park. There has been talk for years about rebuilding the windy outdoor stadium or finding a new spot for it altogether, but no concrete plans are under way.

Locals fear displacement as Bayview—the city's largest African American neighborhood, home to more than 4,000 families with children, and a large population of seniors—goes through growing pains. While residents are eager to improve their neighborhood, they fear being priced out of their homes by gentrification.

Web Site: www.sfgov.org
Area Code: 415
Zip Code: 94124, 94134, 94107
Emergency Hospital: San Francisco General Hospital, 1001 Potrero Ave, 415-206-8000, www.sfghf.net
Post Office: Bayview Station, 2111 Lane St; Hunters Point: San Francisco Manual Processing Facility; 180 Napoleon St, 800-275-8777, www.usps.com, www.usps.com
Police: Bayview Station, 201 Williams, 415-671-2300, TTY 415-671-2346
Library: Bayview Branch, 5075 3rd St, 415-355-5757, www.sfpl.org
Public Schools: San Francisco Unified School District, 555 Franklin St, 415-241-6000, http://portal.sfusd.edu
Community Publications: *San Francisco Bay View*, 4917 3rd St, 415-671-0789, www.sfbayview.com
Community Resources: Bayview Opera House, 4705 3rd St, 415-824-0386, www.bayviewoperahouse.org (theater, dance, African-American center, aftercare and arts programs); Burnett Child Development Center, 1520 Oakdale Ave, 415-695-5660; Shipyard Trust for the Arts, Hunters Point Shipyard, Bldg.101-1317, 415-822-0922; The Point, Hunters Point Shipyard, Building 101, 415-822-9675, www.shipyardtrust.org; Hunters Point Naval Shipyard Redevelopment, www.hunterspointcommunity.com; Southeast Community Facility, 1800 Oakdale Ave, 415-821-1534; Joseph Lee Recreation Center, 1395 Mendell St, 415-822-9040; Candlestick Point State Recreation Area, Hunters Point Expressway, 415-671-0145
Public Transportation: MUNI, 415-701-2311, TTY 415-701-2323, www.sfmta.com: *MUNI buses*: 9 San Bruno, 15 3rd, 19 Polk, 23 Monterey, 24 Divisadero, 29 Sunset, 44 O'Shaughnessey, 54 Felton

NORTH BAY

SURROUNDING AREAS

Many coming to the Bay Area choose to live outside of San Francisco proper. The reasons are varied—perhaps the city is too expensive, too congested, too foggy; some want to live in the country or suburbs; and many are looking to set up house near their office, which very often is outside of San Francisco. More than seven million people live in the nine Bay Area counties of Alameda, Contra Costa, Marin, Sonoma, San Mateo, Napa, Solano, Santa Clara, and San Francisco, and the numbers continue to increase. What follows is an overview of these counties, divided into four regions: **North Bay, East Bay, Peninsula,** and **South Bay**. The following profiles are by no means comprehensive, but are intended as a launch to your exploration of the greater Bay Area.

NORTH BAY (MARIN, SONOMA, NAPA, SOLANO COUNTIES)

MARIN COUNTY

Just north of San Francisco, across the Golden Gate Bridge, the weather is warmer and life more relaxed. Encased by the Bay on the east and the Pacific Ocean on the west, Marin County's terrain is hilly and full of oak trees, eucalyptus groves, redwoods, and other evergreens. The Coastal Miwok Indians inhabited Marin first, followed by the Spaniards, the seafarers, and eventually San Franciscans, who settled in droves after the Golden Gate Bridge opened in 1937. With easy access to San Francisco, Marin County was no longer a hidden, hard-to-reach enclave. Today with a total population just under 250,000, 84% of Marin County still consists of natural preserves, public lands, parks, open space, watershed, and agricultural lands.

Home to CEOs, CFOs, old money, and new money, Marin County has the highest average per capita income in the state, though a few less affluent artists, writers, and musicians remain. The wooded northern community once elicited hedonistic images of hot tubs and peacock feathers. The 1980 movie made from the book, *The Serial: A Year in the Life of Marin County*, parodied this milieu, and although the book was intended to poke fun at the hot-tubbing, affair-having, therapizing, divorcing stereotypes of the locals, some believe it did not stray far from the truth. These days you'll find life in Marin pretty mainstream, although vestiges of the past still can be found, particularly in the sixties-era Volkswagen mini-buses decorated with peace signs and batiked curtains, and the occasional hitchhiker waving her thumb along the roadside.

Most of the western part of Marin is dramatic, with wooded mountains and hills bordering the Pacific Ocean. California's stunning North Coast offers a visual feast, from Sausalito all the way up to the Oregon border. In the summer, sun worshippers flock to Muir Beach and Stinson Beach on the frequently glorious weekends, clogging Highway 1 and turning it into the proverbial "parking lot," one of the Bay Area's most frustrating traffic problems. Residents of Marin have one of the grandest views of the entire Bay Area, made especially photogenic when the fog hovers on the Bay or around the bridge. From Mount Tamalpais' wooded vantage point, you can often see for over 100 miles in any direction.

The southwestern end of Marin County encompasses the 1,000-acre Golden Gate National Recreation Area, which includes the Marin Headlands, Muir Woods, and the remains of wartime batteries and bunkers of Fort Cronkite. During World War II, 12-foot guns sat aimed toward the sea in the expectation of enemies invading the USA from the Pacific, invaders who, thankfully, never materialized. If you enjoy hiking or camping, you may want to make the 90-minute drive from San Francisco to the 66,000-acre Point Reyes National Seashore, north of Stinson Beach. The seashore curls gracefully around Drake's Bay, so named for the explorer Sir Francis Drake, who is credited with "discovering" San Francisco Bay in 1579.

Marin County consistently ranks among the least affordable places to live in the nation. Sausalito, Mill Valley, Tiburon, and Belvedere are the most expensive cities in the county. The towns located farther north of San Francisco, such as San Rafael, Corte Madera, and Novato, are more affordable, and the most affordable towns here are the West Marin towns of San Geronimo, Inverness, Tomales, and Marshall.

MARIN COUNTY

Web Sites: www.co.marin.ca.us, www.marin.org
Zip Codes: 94965, 94941, 94920, 94901, 94925, 94945, 94930
Area Code: 415
Sheriff: Marin County Sheriff Department, 3501 Civic Center Drive, #145, San Rafael, 415-499-7250, www.marinsheriff.org
Emergency Hospital: Marin General Hospital, 250 Bon Air Rd, Greenbrae, 415-925-7000, www.maringeneral.org
Library: Main Branch, 3501 Civic Center Drive, #414, San Rafael, 415-499-6051, www.co.marin.ca.us/depts/lb/main/
Public Schools: Marin County Office of Education, 415-472-4110, www.marin.k12.ca.us
Community Publications: *Marin Independent Journal*, 150 Alameda del Prado, Novato, 415-883-8600, www.marinij.com; *The Ark Newspaper*, 1550 Tiburon Blvd, Tiburon, 415-435-2652; *The Coastal Post*, P.O. Box 31, Bolinas, 415-868-1600, www.coastalpost.com; Marin Scope Community Newspapers (*Mill Valley Herald, Ross Valley Reporter, Twin Cities Times, San Rafael News Pointer*, and *Marin Scope*), P.O. Box 1689, Sausalito, 94966, 415-339-8510, www.marinscope.com; *Novato Advance*, P.O. Box 8, Novato, 415-898-7084; *Pacific Sun*, 835 Fourth St, San Rafael, www.pacificsun.com, 415-485-6700; *Point Reyes Light*, P.O. Box 210, Point Reyes Station, 415-663-8404, www.ptreyeslight.com

County/Community Resources: Marin Services for Women, 415-924-5995; Bay Area Discovery Museum, Fort Baker, 557 McReynolds Rd, Sausalito, 415-339-3900; Marin Civic Center, Ave of the Flags, San Rafael, 415-499-7331; City of San Rafael Community Center, 618 B St, San Rafael, 415-485-3333; Golden Gate National Recreation Area, Fort Mason, Building 201, 415-561-4700, www.nps.gov/goga; Point Reyes National Seashore, Point Reyes, 415-464-5100, www.nps.gov/pore; Muir Woods National Monument, 415-388-2595; Mount Tamalpais State Park, 801 Panoramic Hwy, Mill Valley, 415-388-2070; Marin County Parks, 3501 Civic Center Dr Rm #260, San Rafael, 415-499-6387, www.co.marin.ca.us; Corte Madera Creek Watershed, 415-456-5052, www.friendsofcortemaderacreek.org

Public Transportation: *Golden Gate Transit*, 415-455-2000; *Blue & Gold Fleet*, 415-705-8200, www.blueandgoldfleet.com; *Angel Island Ferry*, 415-435-2131, www.angelislandferry.com; *RIDES for Bay Area Commuters*, 511

SAUSALITO, MILL VALLEY, TIBURON, PETALUMA

Just across the Golden Gate Bridge, where the weather is always warmer, you'll find the upscale and highly desirable communities of Sausalito, Mill Valley, and Tiburon. **Sausalito** (population 7,374), which means "little willow" in Spanish, hosts splendid mansions with views of San Francisco and the Bay. Down on the water, the Sausalito Harbor shelters thousands of boats and houseboats,

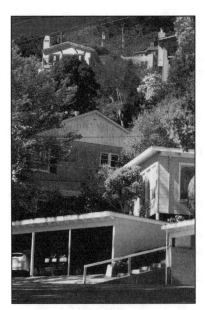

including the Taj Mahal, a replica of the Indian monument, only this one is smaller and floats. Tourists flock to Sausalito via the ferry from San Francisco, and on weekends they virtually take over Bridgeway, the main street. To avoid the crowds and overabundance of t-shirt shops and art galleries on Bridgeway, locals prefer to gather on Caledonia Street, one block east of the Bay. Away from the clicking cameras, residents of Sausalito have an active community, from the Sausalito Women's Club, which works to improve the city, to the yachties on their boats, to resident artists inspired by their surroundings. The Sausalito Arts Festival, held every Labor Day, brings people from all over the Bay Area in search of good art and live

Sausalito

Mill Valley

music. Residents celebrate the arts with the Sausalito Art Walk held the second Wednesday evening of every month from May through October on Caledonia Street.

Once a bohemian enclave, Sausalito is now joining the rank and file of the rest of the Bay Area with a wealthy population, soaring housing costs, and a number of high-tech businesses. The hills above downtown Sausalito are peppered with a broad range of abodes, from artist cabin/studios, Craftsman homes, ranch-style houses, condos, and apartments to Victorians and contemporary mansions. Many of the homes have exquisite bay views and gardens, and garage space is at a premium, especially on the hillside. Median home prices are high, but actually considerably lower than in previous years. Rental vacancies are rare and generally costly. Those commuting to San Francisco generally rely on the Sausalito Ferry or Golden Gate Transit.

Formerly a lumber town, **Mill Valley** (population 13,686) has more rentals and available property than Sausalito, and is not as touristy. Located northwest of Sausalito at the foot of Mount Tamalpais, Mill Valley has a popular downtown with charming restaurants, a coffee shop, and other stores. The famous Depot Bookstore & Café is here, located smack in the center of the town square where people play chess, hackysack, or chat with their neighbors. The square gives the city a real community feel, somewhat reminiscent of town squares in Mexico. The Mill Valley Market is another landmark, featuring a gourmet deli that's ideal for hungry bikers or hikers. Just off of Highway 101 is the Strawberry Village Shopping Center, where you'll find a large Safeway, cafés, restaurants, bookstores, and boutiques. With Mount Tamalpais as a backdrop, many Mill Valley residents spend their free time hiking, biking, or just walking the trails. Since 1905, runners have gathered to race the rigorous seven-mile Dipsea Race (www. dipsea.org), which starts in Mill Valley and ends at Stinson Beach. The Mill Valley Film Festival (www.calfilm.org), held each fall, is gaining worldwide respect.

Many of the homes here were constructed during Mill Valley's lumber days and are Craftsman types, built with exquisite redwood. You'll also find many traditional homes, some Victorians, and a number of apartments, townhouses, and condominiums. .

Located 18 miles north of San Francisco, nearby **Tiburon** (population 8,772), which means "shark" in Spanish, is even more upscale than Mill Valley and Sausalito, with homes typically priced well above Mill Valley's average. Many houses are either on the water or up in the hills. The Belvedere Peninsula sports some of the most upscale homes in Marin County. Many of these stately mansions were built more than a hundred years ago, and some have their own docks.

In downtown Tiburon you can catch the ferry to San Francisco, or better yet, to Angel Island—a delightful 750-acre state park in San Francisco Bay that is part wilderness and part former army base. In the early 1900s, many Asian immigrants came to the island first for government processing; later in the century nuclear Titan missiles were based here. Parts of the immigration station remain; you can still find graffiti, names, and even a poem etched into the walls of the buildings where the immigrants were held.

Restaurants on Tiburon's Main Street, notably Sam's Anchor Café, 27 Main Street, are popular, though pricey. The Sweden House Bistro, 35 Main Street, bakes some of the best éclairs and cookies, not to mention delicious Swedish pancakes. Views of Angel Island from the shops and restaurants on Main Street, many of which have large outdoor back patios that open out onto the Bay, are lovely. The Tiburon Playhouse movie theater, 40 Main Street, 415-435-3585, has a soundproof private viewing booth, ideal for those with infants. And a few years ago, Tiburon began hosting its own film festival, www.tiburonfilmfestival. com, which is increasingly attracting crowds from San Francisco. Boat owners can take their pick from one of three yacht clubs: San Francisco Yacht Club (in nearby Belvedere), and Corinthian and Tiburon Yacht Clubs. Bikers enjoy the

Tiburon

scenic ride on Paradise Loop or the path by Blackie's Pasture along Tiburon Boulevard.

The historic town of **Petaluma** (population 55,627) is chock-full of Victorian beauties and antique shops, country markets, and down-home restaurants. Trees and greenspaces abound and you'll find a much slower pace of life here in one of California's oldest cities. Petaluma has a burgeoning wine-making scene out among the coastal hills that frame its western reaches, but is typically home to hay fields and fruit orchards. A waterway that connects the downtown with San Pablo Bay and into San Francisco Bay proper provides the city with a vital connection for export and is also used by recreational adventure seekers for sailing, kayaking, and fishing. While commuting by car to this town can be a challenge during peak times, locals here say that it's worth the extra effort to escape the noise and frenetic energy found closer to San Francisco.

SAUSALITO
Web Site: www.ci.sausalito.ca.us
Area Code: 415
Zip Codes: 94965, 94966
Post Office: 150 Harbor Dr, 800-275-8777, www.usps.com
Police Station: 29 Caledonia, 415-289-4170
Library: 420 Litho St, 415-289-4121, www.ci.sausalito.ca.us/library
Parks, Gardens, and Open Space: Parks and Recreation Department, 420 Litho St, 415-289-4152, www.ci.sausalito.ca.us
Public Schools: Sausalito Marin City School District, 630 Nevada St, Sausalito, 415-332-3190, www.sausalitomarincityschools.org

MILL VALLEY
Web Sites: www.cityofmillvalley.org, www.millvalley.com
Area Code: 415
Zip Codes: 94941, 94942
Post Office: 751 E Blithedale Ave, 800-275-8777, www.usps.com
Police Station: One Hamilton Dr, 415-389-4100
Library: Mill Valley Public Library, 375 Throckmorton Ave, 415-389-4292,
Parks, Gardens, and Open Space: Mill Valley Parks and Recreation, 180 Camino Alto, 415-383-1370, www.cityofmillvalley.org
Public Schools: Mill Valley School District, 411 Sycamore Ave, Mill Valley, 415-389-7700, www.mvschools.org

TIBURON
Web Site: www.ci.tiburon.ca.us
Area Code: 415
Zip Code: 94920
Post Office: 6 Beach Rd, Tiburon, 800-275-8777, www.usps.com

Police Station: 1155 Tiburon Blvd, 415-789-2801
Library: 1501 Tiburon Blvd, Tiburon, 415-789-2665, www.bel-tib-lib.org
Parks, Gardens, and Open Space: Belvedere/Tiburon Recreation Department, 1505 Tiburon Blvd, Suite A, 415-435-4355, www.tiburon.org
Public Schools: Reed Union School District, 277A Karen Way, Tiburon, 415-381-1112, www.reedschools.org

PETALUMA
Web Site: www.cityofpetaluma.net
Area Code: 707
Zip Codes: 94952, 94954, 94999
Post Offices: 120 4th St, 1601 Corporate Circle, 1150 McDowell Blvd, 800-275-8777, www.usps.com
Police Station: 969 N Petaluma Blvd, 707-778-4370
Library: 100 Fairgrounds Dr, 707-763-9801, www.sonoma.lib.ca.us
Parks, Gardens, and Open Space: Petaluma Community Center, 320 N McDowell Blvd, 707-778-4380
Public Schools: Petaluma City Schools District, 200 Douglas St, 707-778-4813, www.petalumacityschools.org; McDowell Elementary, 421 S McDowell Blvd, 707-778-4745; Sonoma County Office of Education, 5340 Skylane Blvd, 707-524-2600, www.scoe.org

SAN RAFAEL

Situated north of Tiburon, **San Rafael** is the largest city in Marin County and the oldest. Founded in 1817 as a mission, San Rafael (population 57,224) is home to both blue- and white-collar populations. Compared to Sausalito and Mill Valley, rental housing here is plentiful and more affordable. Architecturally, homes range from apartments to ranch-style homes, cottages, and Mediterranean-style villas.

Nestled beneath wooded mountains, San Rafael's claim to fame is the Marin County Civic Center, a national historic landmark, designed in the early 1960s by Frank Lloyd Wright. With its salmon-colored arches and a blue-domed roof, the building's colors are intended to merge with the colors of nature. It was featured in George Lucas' first feature film, *THX-1138* (look for the golden escalator). Fourth Street, San Rafael's main drag, also found its way onto the cinematic map, as the place to cruise in your big Buick or Chevrolet in Lucas's *American Graffiti*. Throckmorton is another shopping street, home to chic clothing stores and quaint one-of-a-kind boutiques. In addition to the unique Civic Center, the Falkirk Cultural Center, 1408 Mission Ave, 415-485-3328, www.falkirkcurlturalcenter.org, is a historic Queen Anne Victorian built in 1888. The Falkirk hosts contemporary art exhibits, art classes, and poetry readings. You'll

San Rafael

also find the gorgeously restored Art Deco Christopher B. Smith Rafael Film Center here. Known to most simply as the "Rafael," the movie theater screens a selection of independent and art house films and annually plays host to the Mill Valley Film Festival (www.calfilm.org).

The San Rafael to San Francisco commute via Highway 101 can be frustrating. Many locals prefer to take the ferry or Golden Gate Transit. The ferry service is fast and scenic—board at the Larkspur Ferry Terminal. On the way out of Larkspur, the ferry passes San Quentin State Prison, still in operation, as well as Alcatraz Island, which has been closed since the mid-1960s. Drinks and snacks are served on the ride.

SAN RAFAEL
Web Site: www.cityofsanrafael.org
Area Code: 415
Zip Codes: 94901, 94902, 94903
Post Office: 40 Bellam Blvd, San Rafael, 800-275-8777, www.usps.com
Police Station: 1400 5th Ave, 415-485-3000
Library: 1100 East St, San Rafael, 415-485-3323, www.srpubliclibrary.org
Parks, Gardens, and Open Space: San Rafael Parks and Recreation Commission, 618 B St, 415-485-3333
Public Schools: San Rafael City Schools, San Rafael City Schools, 310 Nova Albion Way, San Rafael, 415-492-3200, www.srcs.org

CORTE MADERA, NOVATO, HAMILTON, FAIRFAX

Tucked between Mount Tamalpais to the west and Highway 101 to the east, the town of **Corte Madera** (population 9,378), which means "cut wood" in Spanish, is small and quaint. With slightly more affordable home prices—by Marin County standards—the town boasts a large park, historical village square and two shopping centers. Corte Madera is also home to popular independent bookstore Book Passage, 51 Tamal Vista Boulevard, whose literary events draw crowds from throughout the county. The best way to commute to the city is via the Larkspur Ferry.

Corte Madera

A little farther north, homes in **Novato** (population 50,586) are also considered affordable for this area. Novato quickly outgrew its dairy and fruit orchard days when developers built condominiums and inexpensive tract homes, but you will also find large estates hidden in the hills. Novato has the ingredients of classic suburbia, with sprawling malls, theaters, fast food eateries, and family restaurants, as well as the $100 million Buck Center for Research in Aging. Perhaps the biggest challenge about taking up residence in sunny Novato is the commute to San Francisco. It's even longer and more arduous than the San Francisco commute from San Rafael, although the Larkspur Ferry is an excellent option.

Near the edge of San Pablo Bay is old Hamilton Air Field. Opened in 1935, Hamilton Air Field was named in honor of the first American pilot to fly with the Royal Flying Corps during World War I, Lt. Lloyd Hamilton. Used at points by both the Army and the Navy, the base reached its peak of activity during World War II, when it was home to 20,000 servicemen. Decommissioned in 1975, Hamilton Air Field sat untouched for two decades while city officials, the community, and developers struggled to agree upon a plan for the site. Finally, in the 1990s, developers purchased the land from the US government for a reported $13 million and set to work on a massive redevelopment plan that included environmental cleanup, infrastructure rehabilitation, and new housing construction.

The airfield has now been transformed into a thriving planned community, sort of a small town within Novato, simply called **Hamilton.** Here, the very new—quiet culs-de-sac, new homes, outdoor trails, parks, and a large open community green—blends with the very old—restored Spanish-style buildings now converted for community uses. Clusters of modern tract homes, from spacious luxury houses to townhomes, form the heart of Hamilton. Senior apartments, as well as some affordable housing units, are also under way, though both of these are expected to have waiting lists before completion.

Other pluses include an historic outdoor amphitheater, a large park, a community swimming pool, a history museum, bat sanctuary, restored wetlands, and a city arts center home to Indian Valley Artists and a number of individual artist studios. Old hangars are in the process of being converted into office space; there are two large hotels here, and a free shuttle bus runs through the area. A few vestiges of the site's early military days linger on in the form of the US Coast Guard's Pacific Strike Team, which still maintains an installation including Coast Guard housing here.

Away from busy Highway 101, **Fairfax** is a charming small town (population 7,309) with a quaint downtown and plenty of open space for hiking, biking, horseback riding, and pondering life. Proudly defining itself as one of the most progressive and eco-conscious communities in Marin County, Fairfax has placed strict limitations on development and banned chain stores. Once a year, the community comes together for the annual Fairfax Festival, which has recently been expanded to include an EcoFest as well.

The Fairfax-Bolinas Road is not only scenic, but provides access to the coast. Fairfax's claim to fame is being home of the mountain bike, which was "invented" here in 1974. Other than the long commute to the city, the only other negative Fairfax residents must contend with is the risk of flooding from the creeks each winter.

CORTE MADERA
Web Site: www.ci.corte-madera.ca.us
Area Code: 415
Zip Codes: 94925
Post Office: Main, 7 Pixely Ave, Corte Madera, 800-275-8777, www.usps.com
Police Station: 250 Doherty Dr, Larkspur, 415-927-5150
Library: 707 Meadowsweet Dr, Corte Madera, 415-924-4844, www.co.marin.
ca.us/depts/lb/main/corte/index.cfm
Parks, Gardens, and Open Space: Corte Madera Recreation Department, 498
Tamalpais Dr, 415-927-5072, www.ci.corte-madera.ca.us
Public Schools: Larkspur School District, 230 Doherty Dr, Larkspur, 415-927-
6960, www.larkspurschools.org

NOVATO/HAMILTON
Web Site: www.ci.novato.ca.us
Area Code: 415
Zip Codes: 94945, 94948, 94949
Post Office: 1537 South Novato Blvd, 800-275-8777, www.usps.com
Police Station: 908 Sherman Ave, 415-897-4378
Library: 1720 Novato Blvd, 415-898-4623, www.co.marin.ca.us/depts/lb/main/
novato/index.cfm

Public Schools: Novato Unified School District, 1015 7th St, Novato, 415-897-4201, http://do.nusd.org

Parks, Gardens, and Open Space: Novato Community Services, 75 Rowland Way, #200, 415-899-8200, www.ci.novato.ca.us

FAIRFAX

Web Site: www.town-of-fairfax.org

Area Code: 415

Zip Codes: 94930

Post Office: 773 Center Blvd, 800-275-8777, www.usps.com

Police Station: 144 Bolinas Rd, 415-453-5330, www.fairfaxpd.org

Library: 2097 Sir Francis Drake Blvd, 415-453-8092, www.co.marin.ca.us/library/fairfax/index.cfm

Parks, Gardens, and Open Space: Fairfax Parks Department, 142 Bolinas Rd, 415-453-1584, www.town-of-fairfax.org

Public Schools: Ross Valley District, 110 Shaw Dr, San Anselmo, 415-454-2162, http://rvsd.marin.k12.ca.us/

WEST MARIN COUNTY

Though much of Marin County is super expensive, many of the homes in West Marin, which includes the coastal and sometimes tucked-away communities of **Muir Beach** (www.muirbeach.com), **Stinson Beach**, (www.stinsonbeachonline.com), **Bolinas, Nicasio, Olema, Inverness, Point Reyes Station, Tomales** (www.tomales.com), **Marshall, San Geronimo, Woodacre** and **Dillon Beach**, are slightly more affordable—though still pricey even by Bay Area standards. More information on these communities can be found at www.pointreyes.org. (To discourage the hordes of tourists that descend upon these beach

West Marin

communities, residents of Bolinas have been known to tear down the town's street sign indicating the turn-off.)

Point Reyes National Seashore is the area's crown jewel, as well as Tomales Bay, which is famous for its oysters. Filmmaker George Lucas (*Star Wars*) has his famous 4,000-acre Skywalker Ranch headquarters in Nicasio, along Lucas Valley Road. Up in Marshall, the Strauss family has been making organic milk, butter, and yogurt for years. Check your local health food store for the "skinny." In many of these towns you'll find homes, complete with redwoods and acreage, that can still be purchased for prices on the lower end of the countywide median. For lovers of the great outdoors and the quiet life, these semi-secluded small towns offer plentiful hiking, biking, and horseback riding opportunities, not to mention easy access to miles of spectacular coastline via Highway 1. In San Geronimo you'll also find a popular 18-hole golf course, and Woodacre is home to the Spirit Rock Meditation Center, 5000 Sir Francis Drake Boulevard, offering a variety of programs (www.spiritrock.org).

WEST MARIN COUNTY

Web Sites: www.co.marin.ca.us, www.marin.org, www.pointreyes.org

Zip Codes: see Marin County above

Area Code: 415

Sheriff: Marin County Sheriff Department, 3501 Civic Center Drive, #145, San Rafael, 415-499-7250

Emergency Hospital: Marin General Hospital, 250 Bon Air Rd, Greenbrae, 415-925-7000, www.maringeneral.org

Library: Main Branch, 3501 Civic Center Dr, San Rafael, 415-499-6056, www.co.marin.ca.us/depts/lb/main/

Public Schools: Marin County Office of Education, 415-472-4110, www.marin.k12.ca.us

Community Publications: *Marin Independent Journal*, 150 Alameda del Prado, Novato, 415-883-8600, www.marinij.com; *Point Reyes Light*, P.O. Box 210, Point Reyes Station, 415-663-8404, www.ptreyeslight.com; *The Coastal Post*, P.O. Box 31, Bolinas, 415-868-1600, www.coastalpost.com

County/Community Resources: West Marin Chamber of Commerce, 415-663-9232, www.pointreyes.org; San Geronimo Valley Community Center, 415-488-8888, www.sgvcc.org; Point Reyes National Seashore, Point Reyes, 415-464-5100, www.nps.gov/pore; Marin County Parks, 3501 Civic Center Drive Room #415, San Rafael, 415-499-6387, www.co.marin.ca.us; Golden Gate National Recreation Area, Fort Mason, Building 201, 415-561-4700, www.nps.gov/goga

Public Transportation: *Golden Gate Transit*, 415-455-2000

SONOMA COUNTY

North and northeast of Marin County, Sonoma County consists of rolling, green, tree- or vineyard-covered hills, dramatic coastline, seamless skies, glorious weather (most of the time), and some of the world's top chefs. Sonoma County, along with neighboring Napa County, is internationally known for the wines produced in this region. Hundreds of wineries dot the countryside, hosting visitors from around the world who come to sample and learn about the fine art of making wine. Housing options are varied, ranging from apartments and condominiums to single-family homes and stately Victorians. You'll also find farms and ranches, mobile home parks, and summer cottages.

SONOMA COUNTY

Web Site: www.sonoma-county.org

Area Code: 707

Zip Codes: 95403, 95404, 95405, 95406, 95476

Sheriff: 2796 Ventura Ave, Santa Rosa, 707-565-2650

Emergency Hospitals: Sutter Hospital, 3325 Chanate Rd, Santa Rosa, 707-576-4000; Palm Drive Hospital, 501 Petaluma Ave, Sebastopol, 707-823-8511; Santa Rosa Memorial, 1165 Montgomery Dr, Santa Rosa, 707-546-3210; Sonoma Valley Hospital, 347 Andrieux St, Sonoma, 707-935-5000

Libraries: Sonoma County Library, Petaluma Branch, 100 Fairgrounds Dr, 707-763-9801, www.sonoma.lib.ca.us

Public Schools: Sonoma County Office of Education, 5340 Skylane Blvd, Santa Rosa, 707-524-2600, www.coe.org

Community Publications: *Santa Rosa Press Democrat*, 427 Mendocino Ave, Santa Rosa, 707-546-2020, www.pressdemocrat.com; *Marin Independent Journal*, 150 Alameda Del Prado, Novato, 415-883-8600, www.marinij.com; *Sonoma Index-Tribune*, P.O. Box C, Sonoma, 95476, 707-938-2111, www.sonomanews.com

Community Resources: Sonoma Valley Chamber of Commerce, 651-A Broadway, Sonoma, 707-996-1033, www.sonomachamber.com; Sonoma Community Center, 276 E Napa St, Sonoma, 707-938-4626; Sonoma Valley Chorale, P.O. Box 816, Sonoma, 95476, 707-935-1576, www.sonomavalleychorale.org; Sonoma State University, E East Cotati Ave, Rohnert Park, 707-664-2880, www.sonoma.edu

Public Transportation: Sonoma County Transit, 800-345-7433, TTY 707-585-9817, www.sctransit.com

Parks, Gardens, and Open Space: Sonoma County Regional Parks, 2300 County Center Dr, 120A, Santa Rosa, 707-565-2041, www.sonoma-county.org/parks; Sonoma County Farm Trails, 800-207-9464, www.farmtrails.org

SANTA ROSA

Recently named one of the nation's "Most Livable Communities" by the Partners for Livable Communities, Santa Rosa prides itself on maintaining a small-town feel despite a booming population. Home to the county seat and located 50 miles north of San Francisco in central Sonoma County, the city is popular with young families, first-time homeowners, and retired seniors. Long considered one of the more affordable spots to buy a home, prices here soared in recent years. City officials here are picky about the look of new buildings and businesses, so you'll find Santa Rosa easy on the eyes. Despite the close tabs kept on development, Santa Rosa is growing (population 156,268), as is traffic congestion, especially going "cross-town" from east to west or vice versa. In addition, Highway 101, which splits the city in two going north and south, is now too narrow for the number of vehicles it must handle on a daily basis and is undergoing long-term rebuilding that further disrupts commuter traffic.

Santa Rosa

Surrounded by a handful of picturesque, lovingly restored historic neighborhoods, the downtown area comes alive every Wednesday evening from mid-May through August with the Santa Rosa Downtown Market—renowned as Sonoma County's largest farmers market. Also downtown is the Prince Memorial Greenway, a new curving terraced pedestrian and bike pathway that snakes along the banks of the Santa Rosa Creek, providing a scenic link to the city's Historic Railroad Square. In addition to scores of popular suburban ranch-style homes, Santa Rosa is also home to 14 mobile home parks, as well as two unique spots—Valley Vista I and II—where mobile home owners own the land. To encourage upkeep and maintain affordability, the city maintains a rent control program for the private parks and offers rehabilitation loans. For a taste of local history you can visit the home, greenhouse, and gardens of horticulturist Luther Burbank or take a tour of the Charles M. Schulz Museum and Research Center, named in honor of the beloved "Peanuts" creator and long-time Santa Rosa resident (www. schulzmuseum.org).

SANTA ROSA

Web Site: www.ci.santa-rosa.ca.us

Zip Codes: 95403, 95404, 95405, 95406

Area Code: 707

Post Office: 730 2nd St, 800-275-8777, www.usps.com

Police: 965 Sonoma Ave, 707-543-3600

Library: Santa Rosa Branch of the Sonoma County Library, 3rd and E sts, 707-545-0831, TTY 707-575-1206, www.sonomalibrary.org/branches/central.html

Community Resources: Downtown Market, www.srdowntownmarket.com; Sonoma County Museum, www.sonomacountymuseum.com; Wells Fargo Center for the Arts, www.wellsfargocenterarts.org, 707-546-3600

Parks, Gardens, and Open Space: Santa Rosa Parks and Recreation, www.ci.santa-rosa.ca.us/departments/recreationandparks; Hood Mountain Regional Park, 3000 Los Alamos Rd; Maddux Ranch Park, 4655 Lavelle Rd; Shiloh Regional Park, 5750 Faught Rd; Spring Lake Park, 5390 Montgomery Dr

SONOMA

Sonoma, sometimes called by locals "Slo-noma" for its tranquil, small town feel, is the commercial heart of Sonoma Valley, the so-called Valley of the Moon. Surrounded by vineyards, the entire valley is a mecca for wine lovers. On weekends, particularly in the summer, the city's population explodes as scores of tourists

Sonoma

clog Route 12 to sample world-renowned local cabernets, pinots, and merlots. A picture-postcard small community (population 9,834), rich in history, culinary treasures, and health resorts, Sonoma is also home to Sonoma State University. If you have to commute to San Francisco though, plan on at least one hour each way in the car, longer by bus.

Architecturally, single-family homes, many of them ranch style, were built between 1950 and 1970. On the outskirts, you'll find older family farms, as well as stately vineyard estates. History buffs should visit the Mission San Francisco de Solano, or Sonoma Mission, the last and northernmost of the Franciscan missions along the California Coast. Literature and nature lovers will enjoy the serene surroundings of author Jack London's former ranch and final resting place, now an 800-plus-acre state park located in nearby Glen Ellen. Heading out of the city, throughout the valley you'll find clusters of small towns and villages, many of them home to popular natural hot springs, spas, dairy farms, and of course, wineries.

SONOMA
Web Site: www.sonomacity.org
Area Code: 707
Zip Codes: 95476
Post Office: 617 Broadway, 800-275-8777, www.usps.com
Police: 175 1st St W, 707-996-3601
Library: Sonoma Branch of the Sonoma County Library, 755 Napa St, 707-996-5217, www.sonoma.lib.ca.us/branches/Sonoma.html
Parks, Gardens, and Open Space: Sonoma Parks and Public Works Department, #1 The Plaza, 707-938-3681, www.sonomacity.org; Maxwell Farms Regional Park, 100 Verano Ave

NAPA COUNTY

ST. HELENA, RUTHERFORD, YOUNTVILLE, NAPA, CALISTOGA

East of Sonoma County lies Napa Valley, a place where you can indulge your taste buds with fine wine and gourmet meals. With a mild, Mediterranean-like climate, Napa Valley produces hundreds of thousands of gallons of wine including zinfandels, merlots, cabernets, pinot noirs, and chardonnays. Premier grapes are grown on the vine, then aged in the casks, and finally bottled and corked with an end result rivaling the best in France. On weekends, thousands of wine lovers take to Highway 29, the road that runs north-south through Napa

St. Helena

County, stopping along the way at the vineyards, wineries, and picturesque small towns, such as **St. Helena**, **Rutherford**, and **Yountville**. A typical day visit might begin with one or two tastings in the cool basement of a winery, followed by a picnic lunch break in a park, then a few more wineries before dinner. If you enjoy wine and bucolic hills, it's a delightful way to spend a day. Better yet, it might be an ideal place to call home. One interesting geological note about Yountville is its recent earthquake history. In September 2000, a magnitude 5.2 earthquake struck Napa County, the epicenter of which was in Yountville, which sits about six miles northwest of Napa. It caused millions of dollars' worth of damage to buildings throughout the county, though thankfully no fatalities. Today, Yountville is known for its world-class restaurants, chief among them the French Laundry, which ranks high on the 50 Best restaurants in the World List, put together annually by World Press.

The **City of Napa** is the center of county government. If the hot air from the politicians is too much, try hot air ballooning, an ideal way to soar in Napa's

Yountville

often-sunny skies fanned by gentle breezes. Set up house here, and you can sample the wine year round. In addition to ranch-style homes, popular with families, a handful of mobile home parks—many of them designed especially for seniors—offer tranquil life for retirees.

Calistoga, at the northern end of the Napa Valley, attracts people ready to be pampered with a mud bath, herbal wrap, mineral bath, and/or a massage. (For more see the **Quick Getaways** chapter.) There's also a natural geyser, called the Old Faithful (not to be confused with Yellowstone's Old Faithful) that shoots 350° water 60 feet into the air. The owner claims Old Faithful acts erratically about 2 to 14 days before the area experiences a significant earthquake.

NAPA COUNTY
Web Site: www.co.napa.ca.us
Area Code: 707
Zip Codes: 94558, 94559, 94574, 94508
Sheriff: 1535 Airport Blvd, Napa, 707-253-4509, TTY 707-253-4344
Libraries: Napa City-County Library, 580 Coombs St, 707-253-4241, www. co.napa.ca.us/library/
Public Schools: Napa Valley Unified School District, 2425 Jefferson St, Napa, 707-253-3715, www.nvusd.k12.ca.us
Community Publications: *The Napa Valley Register*, 1615 Second St, Napa, 707-226-3711, www.napanews.com; *St. Helena Star*, 1200 Main St, C, St. Helena, 707-963-2731, www.sthelenastar.com
Community Resources: Community Resources for Children, 5 Financial Plaza #224, Napa, 707-253-0376, www.crcnapa.org; Wildlife Rescue, P.O. Box 2571, 707-224-4295; Napa County Historical Society, 1219 First St, 707-224-1739, www. napahistory.org; Napa Valley Museum, 55 Presidents Circle, Yountville, 707-944-0500, www.napavalleymuseum.org; Napa Community Resources Department, 1100 West St, 707-257-9529
Public Transportation: CalTrain, 800-660-4287; Napa Valley Transit, 800-696-6443, www.nctpa.net; Napa Valley Wine Train, 800-427-4124, www.winetrain. com
Parks, Gardens, and Open Space: Napa Valley Parks, 1195 Third St, Room 310, Napa, 707-253-4580, www.co.napa.ca.us; The Petrified Forest, 707-942-6667; Old Faithful Geyser, 707-942-6463; Bothe-Napa Valley State Park, 800-444-7275; Bothe Napa Valley State Park, 5 miles north of St. Helena and 4 miles south of Calistoga on Hwy 29/128; Bale Grist Mill State Historic Park, 3369 North Saint Helena Hwy (Hwy 29)

SOLANO COUNTY

East of Napa County, Solano County is one of the fastest growing counties in the Bay Area, with housing developments and new businesses springing up from Vallejo in the southwestern corner of the county to Vacaville and Fairfield farther inland. So-called refugees from the big city seem to be arriving en masse and are snatching up many of the new homes. Crime rates are relatively low here, and schools, in general, are better than their counterparts in San Francisco and Oakland.

SOLANO COUNTY

Web Site: www.co.solano.ca.us
Area Code: 707
Zip Codes: 94533, 94587, 95687, 95688, 94589, 94590
Sheriff: 530 Union Ave, Suite 100, Fairfield, 707-421-7000
Libraries: Solano County Library, 1150 Kentucky St, Fairfield, 866-572-7587, www.solanolibrary.com/
Public Schools: Solano County Office of Education, Superintendent's Office, 5100 Business Center Drive, Fairfield, 94534, 707-399-4400, www.solanocoe.k12.ca.us
Community Publications: *Vallejo Times Herald*, 440 Curtola Parkway, Vallejo, 707-644-1141; *Daily Republic*, 1250 Texas St, 707-425-4646; *Vacaville Reporter*, 318 Main St, Vacaville, 707-448-6401; *Benicia Herald*, P.O. Box 65, Benicia, 707-745-0733; *Dixon Tribune*, 145 East A St, Dixon, 916-678-5594; *River News Herald and Journal*, P.O. Box 786, Rio Vista, 707-374-6431
Community Resources: Six Flags Marine World, 1001 Fairgrounds Dr, Vallejo, 707-643-6722, www.sixflags.com; Solano County Fair, 707-551-2000, www.scfair.com; Solano County Family and Children Services, 421 Executive Court North, Fairfield, 707-863-3950
Public Transportation: Vallejo Baylink Ferry, 707-643-3779, www.baylinkferry.com; Vallejo Transit, 707-648-4666, www.vallejotransit.com; Vacaville City Coach, 707-449-6000, www.citycoach.com; Fairfield-Suisun Transit, 707-422-2877; RIDES, 511, www.511.org
Parks, Gardens, and Open Space: Solano County Parks, 707-784-7514, www.co.solano.ca.us

FAIRFIELD, VACAVILLE

Fairfield and **Vacaville** are typical American towns, with tract homes, apartment complexes, duplexes, townhouses, strip malls, and shopping centers. Located northeast of San Francisco along Interstate 80, they offer easy access to University of California at Davis and the state capital in Sacramento. Except for a strange blanket of fog that rolls in nightly over I-80, the weather here is dry and hot, hot, hot. On the upside, homes here are more affordable and many have

Fairfield

swimming pools. Fairfield hosts Travis Air Force Base, one of the few military installations left open in California. Vacaville's claim to fame is the local state prison that cares for mentally ill inmates. Nearby Rio Vista recently rose from the empty desert-like landscape as an oasis with the opening of Trilogy at Rio Vista, a retirement community complete with spacious homes, a state-of-the-art recreation complex, and a championship golf course.

FAIRFIELD
Web Site: www.ci.fairfield.ca.us
Area Code: 707
Zip Codes: 94533, 94587
Post Office: 600 Kentucky St, 800-275-8777, www.usps.com
Police: 1000 Webster St, 707-428-7300
Library: Fairfield Branch, 1150 Kentucky St, 866-572-7587, http://solanolibrary.com/fairfield.cfm
Parks, Gardens, and Open Space: Fairfield Park Division, 1000 Webster St, 707-428-7407, www.ci.fairfield.ca.us; Grizzly Island State Wildlife Area, Highway 12; Rockville Hills Regional Park, 2110 Rockville Rd, Rockville

VACAVILLE
Web Site: www.cityofvacaville.com
Area Code: 707
Zip Codes: 95688, 95687
Post Office: 98 Cernon St, 800-275-8777, www.usps.com
Police: 660 Merchant St, 707-449-5231
Libraries: Cultural Center Branch, 1020 Ulatis Dr, 866-572-7587, www.solanolibrary.com; Town Square Branch, 1 Town Square Pl

Parks, Gardens, and Open Space: Vacaville Community Services Department, 40 Eldridge Ave, 707-449-5655; City of Vacaville Park Facilities, 707-449-5100

VALLEJO

With home prices consistently among the lowest in the Bay Area, the City of Vallejo has become an attractive option for legions of families looking to fulfill what can seem the impossible dream here—homeownership.

San Francisco is just 32 miles away, and the high-speed Vallejo Bay Link Ferry catamaran offers one of the most pleasant commute options around. Daily, the ferry glides across the Bay, carrying 2,000 people to work in San Francisco (the stop is the Ferry Building), with the trip taking just under an hour each way. Commuting by car would take almost double the time.

Founded by General Mariano G. Vallejo in 1844, Vallejo originated as an important shipping and naval center. Around that time, a temporary capital building was built in Vallejo in 1852, but because of the area's lack of housing the legislature moved up to Sacramento. In 1853 a devastating flood then brought the legislature back to Vallejo, but they were still dissatisfied, and moved on to Benicia, and then later returned to Sacramento.

Today, Vallejo (population 121,221) is the largest city in Solano County. Best known for being home to Six Flags Marine World, a large outdoor theme and animal park, Vallejo also features an outside farmers market, a golf course, a yacht club, and the California Maritime Academy, a California State University School. Existing housing is an eclectic mix of homes, from beautifully restored Victorians to 1950s tract housing to lavish, newly built residences in the North-gate and Hiddenbrooke Golf Course neighborhoods.

In 1996, the Mare Island Shipyards closed, and the city is now in the process of converting the 5,252 acres to civilian use. Part of the conversion includes an

Vallejo

estimated $81 million environmental cleanup of lead-based paint, petroleum waste, and other toxic remnants left in the shipyard. A large commercial area is already up and running here, home to more than 70 businesses including the US Forest Service, Western Regional Headquarters. The final plans call for 1,400 new housing units ranging from apartments to single-family homes, a total of 7 million square feet of office space, new parks, and a large area of restored open space.

With the Mare Island rehabilitation under way, including plans to revitalize the downtown area and revamp the waterfront, the City of Vallejo is at a cross-roads. In the next two decades, the waterfront project will convert 110 acres into a thriving connected core of 1,090 new housing units, 562,000 square feet of commercial space, and 28 acres of parks. A new $52 million transit center to improve bus and ferry links, complete with a massive new commuter parking garage, is also in the works, as are a new performing arts center and waterfront promenade. Meanwhile, the planned $120 million downtown project will over-haul a smattering of empty lots to create 800 new housing units and 68,000 square feet of retail and office space. With so many projects in the works and a 63% rate of homeownership, it's perhaps no surprise that *Money Magazine* recently ranked Vallejo third among all medium-sized metropolitan areas in California in its report on "The Best Places to Live in America."

Web Site: www.ci.vallejo.ca.us
Area Code: 707
Zip Codes: 94589, 94590, 94591
Post Office: 485 Santa Clara St, 800-275-8777, www.usps.com
Police: 111 Amador St, 707-648-4321
Libraries: John F. Kennedy Library, 505 Santa Clara St, 866-572-7587, www.sola-nolibrary.com; Springstowne Library, 1003 Oakwood Ave
Parks, Gardens, and Open Space: Greater Vallejo Recreation District, 395 Ama-dor St, 707-648-4600, www.gvrd.org

EAST BAY

EAST BAY (ALAMEDA AND CONTRA COSTA COUNTIES)

ALAMEDA COUNTY

The East Bay is the most densely populated region of the Bay Area, from Crockett and Hercules at the northern end, through Pinole, Richmond, El Cerrito, Albany, Berkeley, Oakland, and Alameda in the center; to San Leandro, Castro Valley, Hayward, Union City, and Fremont on the southern end, and Livermore, Pleasanton, Dublin, Concord, Walnut Creek, Martinez, Pittsburg, and Antioch out east. In fact, the East Bay contains so many enclaves it's difficult to generalize about life here, except to say that it's not San Francisco. For the most part, you'll find parking the car is not as arduous a task compared to the city, rents are somewhat lower and rental property is more available, and the weather is generally clearer and warmer than in San Francisco. The biggest drawback to living in the East Bay is commuting to San Francisco by car. Fortunately, the entire area is served, and served well, by an extensive crisscrossing network of public transit systems, including buses, trains, and Bay Area Rapid Transit (BART). Another asset is the Oakland International Airport, one of the friendliest airports you're likely to find anywhere in the United States. Here, when you dial information, real human beings still answer the phone and are happy to assist you with everything from driving directions to parking suggestions, to tips for quick and easy passenger drop-off. While officials at both San Francisco International Airport and San Jose International Airport often warn passengers about overflowing parking lots, their Oakland counterpart generally can proclaim hassle-free parking.

Many fleeing San Francisco's exorbitant prices, or simply looking for more family-oriented single-family housing options, look to cities in the East Bay to call home. And the East Bay has a lot to offer. The lush parks have an array of outdoor activity options including hiking, biking, boating, picnicking, and swimming. Berkeley's Tilden Park, the crown jewel of East Bay's park system, has hiking and biking trails, a swimming hole, a carousel, a petting zoo, a steam train and much more. Another escape to the outdoors is Mount Diablo State Park, located in eastern Contra Costa County. As the highest peak in the Bay Area, Mount Diablo is a popular weekend destination for hikers, campers, and families. Oakland's 140-acre saltwater Lake Merritt, spread out beneath the downtown Oakland skyline, hosts joggers, walkers, and bikers at all times of the day. You can even hire an authentic Venetian gondola to chauffeur you on a romantic glide across the lake.

The East Bay contains several colleges and universities, most prominently the University of California, Berkeley, or "Cal" (the only school in the University of California system so called). Cal State East Bay has campuses in the Hayward hills and the Concord foothills of Mount Diablo, as well as a professional development center in Oakland. Private colleges and universities in the East Bay include Saint Mary's in the densely wooded community of Moraga, John F. Kennedy University in Orinda, and Mills College in Oakland. The northern environs of the East Bay are a stone's-throw away, if you've got a strong arm, from the University of California at Davis, Sacramento State University in Sacramento, and the University of the Pacific in Stockton.

ALAMEDA COUNTY

Web Site: www.co.alameda.ca.us

Area Code: 510

Sheriff: 1401 Lakeside Dr, 12th Floor, 510-272-6878, www.alamedacountysheriff. org

Emergency Hospitals: Alameda Hospital, 2070 Clinton Ave, 510-522-3700, www.alamedahospital.org; Fairmont Hospital, 15400 Foothill Blvd, San Leandro, 510-437-4800, www.acmedctr.org; Highland Hospital, 1411 E 31st St, Oakland, 510-437-4564, www.hghed.org; St. Rose Hospital, 27200 Calaroga Ave, Hayward, 510-264-4000, www.strosehospital.org; Kaiser Medical Center, 27400 Hesperian Blvd, Hayward, 510-784-4000, www.kaiserpermanente.org; Alta Bates Medical Center, 2450 Ashby Ave, Berkeley, 510-204-4444, www. altabates.com; Children's Hospital Oakland, 747 52nd St, Oakland, 510-428-3000, www.childrenshospitaloakland.org

Library: Alameda County Library Foundation, 2450 Stevenson Blvd, Fremont, 510-745-1500, www.aclibrary.org

Public Schools: Alameda County Office of Education, 313 West Winton Ave, Hayward, 510-887-0152, www.alameda-coe.k12.ca.us.

Community Publications: *Oakland Tribune*, 510-208-6300, www.insidebayarea. com/oaklandtribune (the Alameda Newspaper Group also owns the *Alameda Times-Star* and the *Fremont Argus*); *East Bay Express*, 510-879-3700, www. eastbayexpress.com; *Contra Costa Times* (covers Contra Costa and east Alameda County), 800-598-4637, www.ContraCostaTimes.com (also owns a handful of smaller local publications including the *Berkeley Voice*, *Alameda Journal*, the *Montclarion*, and the *Piedmonter*); *The Berkeley Daily Planet*, 510-841-5600, www.berkeleydailyplanet.com; U.C. Berkeley Publications: *The Daily Californian*, www.dailycal.org; *North Gate News On-line*, http://journalism.berkeley.edu/ngno/

County/Community Resources: Alameda One-Stop Career Center, 510-981-7564; Bananas (childcare referrals), 510-658-7353, direct referral line: 510-658-0381, www.bananasinc.org; Alameda County Social Services Agency, 510-596-0110, alamedasocialservices.org; Eden Information and Referral for Social Services, 510-537-2710, www.edenir.org; Ohlone Community College, 510-659-6000, www.ohlone.edu; Childcare Links, 510-791-9256 www. childcarelinks.org; Alameda County Art Commission, (510) 208-9646 www. co.alameda.ca.us/arts/

Public Transportation: *AC (Alameda-Contra Costa) Transit*, 510-891-4700, TTY 800-448-9790, www.actransit.org; *BART*, 510-465-2278, TTY 510-839-2278, www.bart.gov; *Alameda-Oakland Ferry*, 510-522-3300, www.eastbayferry. com; *Emery-Go-Round*, 510-451-3862, next bus hotline, 510-451-3862, www. emerygoround.com; *RIDES*, 511, www.511.org; *Amtrak*, 800-USA-RAIL, TTY 800-523-6590, www.amtrak.com; *Greyhound*, 800-231-2222, TTY 800-345-3109, www.greyhound.com

Parks, Gardens, and Open Space: East Bay Regional Park District, 2950 Peralta Oaks Court, Oakland, 94605, 888-327-2757, TTY 510-633-0460, www. ebparks.org; maintains 62 parks throughout the region, many of them with large open areas, nature trails, and shorelines

HAYWARD, FREMONT, NEWARK, UNION CITY

A sprawling, often hot, expanse of suburbia, **Hayward** (population 146,398) comes complete with a standard fare of strip malls, shopping centers, gigantic car dealerships, and fast food restaurants. This family-oriented city includes large Hispanic and Asian populations. In the eastern part of the city, California State University East Bay perches high atop a hill, offering dynamic views of the Bay Area below. Formerly called and still known locally as Cal State Hayward, the campus is in the process of expanding—adding a new Business Technology Center, revamped student union, and new housing. As is true with all of California's public colleges, though it keeps creeping up, tuition is—relatively speaking—inexpensive, and a variety of programs are geared to part-time students in the workforce looking to change careers, get new training, or simply enrich their lives.

Because of its relatively more affordable home prices, both for single-family homes and condos, Hayward continues to grow at a steady rate. Many

Hayward

new Bay Area residents opt to set down roots here and commute the 25 miles northwest to San Francisco or the 26 miles south to Silicon Valley, all for the sake of home ownership. Thanks to the San Mateo–Hayward Bridge, crossing the bay to the Peninsula is relatively easy—though commute hour traffic can be brutal despite a recent widening.

The cities of Fremont, Newark, and Union City lie to the south of Hayward, and are similar in appearance, socioeconomic components, housing options, and the like. All of these suburban communities began to absorb a mass exodus about two decades ago, as families fled San Francisco, the Peninsula and the South Bay—heading east across the bay in search of suburban family living and affordable home ownership opportunities. As a result, these towns are very family-friendly with quiet neighborhood streets, good local parks, more affordable homes, and significantly higher rates, generally speaking, of home ownership. Like Hayward, all three cities lie off of the seemingly-always-clogged I-880—which frequently resembles a parking lot during the morning and evening rush hours.

Popular with young families, **Fremont**'s largest population segment—more than 20%—is children under age 14, according to the most recent US Census. Residents here frequent Lake Elizabeth for boating, walking, and picnics. The city offers easy, direct—though not always swift—access to Silicon Valley via the Dumbarton Bridge. Two active and popular community centers—Centerville and Irvington—offer an array of community programs, classes, recreation activities and even mini branch libraries. The main route through town, Fremont Boulevard, is filled with large outdoor strip malls, and connects to the smaller neighboring town of **Newark**. For local shopping, the NewPark Mall in Newark is one of the busiest malls in the Bay Area. A little further north, **Union City** has a collection of large shopping centers right off of the freeway. The largest of these is Union Landing, on Alvarado-Niles Street. Its biggest draw on weekends is a gigantic movie theater with more than two-dozen screens.

Union City

During the Krispy Kreme craze, Union City drew hundreds of doughnut tourists—literally forming lines around the block—as it had the distinction of being among the first cities in northern California to open the popular doughnut shop. For prospective homeowners, the city's biggest enticement is its comparatively lower home prices. With relatively affordable rates, Union City boasts an owner occupancy rate of more than 70%, according to the city.

HAYWARD
Web Site: www.ci.hayward.ca.us
Area Code: 510
Zip Codes: 94540–94546, 94552, 94557
Post Offices: 822 C St; 24438 Santa Clara St; 2163 Aldengate Way, 800-275-8777, www.usps.com
Police: Hayward Police Department, 300 W Winton Ave, 510-293-7000
Library: Hayward Main Library, 835 C St, 510-293-8685; Weekes Branch, 27300 Patrick Ave, 510-782-2155, www.library.ci.hayward.ca.us.
Public Schools: Hayward Unified School District, 24411 Amador St, 510-784-2600, www.husd.k12.ca.us
Parks, Gardens, and Open Space: Hayward Area Recreation and Park District, 1099 E St, 510-881-6700, www.haywardrec.org

FREMONT
Web Site: www.ci.fremont.ca.us
Area Code: 510
Zip Codes: 94536–94539, 94555
Post Offices: Fremont: 37010 Dusterberry Way; 160 J Street; 41041 Trimboli Way; 43456 Ellsworth Street; 240 Francisco Lane, 800-275-8777, www.usps.com
Police: Fremont Police Department, 2000 Stevenson Blvd, 510-790-6800
Library: Fremont Main Library, 2400 Stevenson Blvd, 510-745-1400, TTY 888-663-0660, www.aclibrary.org
Public Schools: Fremont Unified School District, 4210 Technology Dr, 510-657-2350, www.fremont.k12.ca.us
Parks, Gardens, and Open Space: Fremont Recreation Services, 3300 Capitol Ave, Building B, 510-494-4300

NEWARK
Web Site: www.ci.newark.ca.us
Area Code: 510
Zip Code: 94560
Post Office: Newark Post Office, 6655 Clark Ave, 800-275-8777, www.usps.com
Library: Newark Library, 6300 Civic Terrace Ave, 510-795-2627
Public Schools: Newark Unified School District, 5715 Musick Ave, 510-794-2141

Parks, Gardens, and Open Space: Newark Recreation Services, Community Center, 35501 Cedar Blvd, 510-578-4437, www.ci.newark.ca.us/play/parks. html

UNION CITY

Web Site: www.ci.union-city.ca.us

Area Code: 510

Zip Code: 94587

Post Office: Main Post Office, 33170 Alvarado-Niles Road; 3861 Smith St, 800-275-8777, www.usps.com

Library: Union City Library, 34007 Alvarado-Niles Rd, 510-745-1464, TTY 510-489-1655

Parks, Gardens, and Open Space: Leisure Services Administration, 34009 Alvarado-Niles Rd, 510-675-5329, www.ci.union-city.ca.us

ALAMEDA

Located just south of Oakland, the City of Alameda (population 74,405) is almost an island, tucked alongside the East Bay. Flat as a pancake and with one long beach, Alameda connects to the mainland via a number of bridges and tunnels. In the late 1800s Alameda was a popular resort for San Franciscans and Oaklanders who sought its mild climate and comfortable sand. Seawater pools were even lighted and heated to accommodate nighttime swimmers. During World War II, the Navy built the Alameda Naval Air Station, creating a bustling naval base here until its decommissioning in 1997. Today the 800-plus acre site, now called Alameda Point, is slowly undergoing a $2-billion-plus face-lift, converting it into a mix of new residential neighborhoods, shopping areas, recreational facilities, and business parks. The terminal for the Alameda to San

Alameda

Francisco Ferry is also here. The city hasn't fully recovered from its button-down Navy days, as is evidenced by the downtown area, which still feels small and unpolished, as though from another era. Compared to the frenzy of much of the rest of the Bay Area, it seems local residents appreciate the calm, unsophisticated environment. Alameda has all your basic shopping needs, not generally in the form of chain stores.

Robert Crown Memorial Beach, equipped with picnic tables and showers, is a mile-and-a-half beach, good for beginning windsurfers and kiteboarders. Washington Park, just before the beach, has a number of tennis courts, a baseball field, and a dog park. Taking your dogs to the beach, however, could cost you a large fine. And for golfers, butting up right next to the Oakland International Airport is the Chuck Corica Golf Complex on Harbor Bay Island, One Clubhouse Memorial Road, 510-747-7800, www.golfinalameda.com

Architecturally, Alameda has some of the most beautifully restored Victorians in the Bay Area. You'll also find a few that haven't yet been renovated, and you may be lucky enough to find one at a decent price. But real estate here, once available at comparatively bargain prices, is now keeping pace with much of the Bay Area.

ALAMEDA
Web Site: www.ci.alameda.ca.us
Area Code: 510
Zip Codes: 94501, 94502
Post Offices: 2201 Shoreline Dr; 2 Eagle Rd; 1415 Webster St, 800-275-8777, www.usps.com
Police: Alameda Police Department, 1555 Oak St, 510-337-8340
Public Schools: Alameda Unified School District, 2200 Central Ave, 510-337-7000, www.alameda.k12.ca.us
Community Resources: Alameda Chamber of Commerce, 1416 Park Ave, 510-522-0414, www.alamedachamber.com; Altarena Playhouse, 1409 High St, 510-523-1553, www.altarena.org; Bill Osborne Model Airplane Field on Doolittle St, 510-747-7529; Alameda Museum and Alameda Historical Society, 2324 Alameda Ave, 510-521-1233, www.alamedamuseum.org; USS Hornet Museum, Alameda Point, Pier 3, 510-521-8448, www.uss-hornet.org; Alameda Civic Light Opera, 2200 Central Ave, 510-864-2256, www.aclo.com; Mastick Senior Center, 1155 Santa Clara Ave, 510-747-7500
Parks, Gardens, and Open Space: Recreation and Parks, 2226 Santa Clara Ave, 510-747-7529, TTY 510-522-7538, www.ci.alameda.ca.us/arpd

EMERYVILLE

Sandwiched between Oakland and Berkeley and virtually at the foot of the Bay Bridge, Emeryville was originally an industrial area, with not much else

Emeryville

happening. By the late 1980s and early 1990s, the 1.2-square-mile city set out on a path of transformation. Old industrial sites metamorphosed into huge shopping centers, warehouses became loft-style apartments and offices, and new apartments and condominiums sprang up. Today over 8,000 people call Emeryville home, while about 20,000 commute here to work at businesses such as Chiron (biotech) and Pixar (the computer animation company that created *Finding Nemo* and *WALL-E*).

To help the 20,000 employees get to work, Emeryville has a free shuttle, the Emery-Go-Round, which transports people to and from BART (MacArthur Station) and Amtrak. In addition, bike paths wind throughout the city. Another progressive attribute of Emeryville is a city-run daycare facility, known as the Child Development Center, 510-596-4343. The Center operates year-round and provides childcare services for 90 infants and toddlers whose parents are working, in training, or in school. In 1999, Ex'pression College for Digital Art, 877-833-8800, www.expression.edu, which is devoted exclusively to digital visual media and sound arts technology, opened its doors.

The city is also a regional shopping magnet, drawing people from all across the East Bay to its dense core of retail plazas. Numerous chain stores, such as Borders, Trader Joe's, and Ross Dress for Less occupy space in Emeryville. Meanwhile, IKEA's 274,000-square-foot (equivalent to five football fields), semi do-it-yourself furniture funhouse attracts people from all over the Bay Area. For food, the Emeryville Public Market, 5800 Shellmound Street, is a favorite with its inexpensive ethnic dishes, from Korean BBQ to French crepes to Japanese noodles, served cafeteria-style.

A good example of "new urbanism," most of the city's new housing takes the form of condos and townhouses situated within mixed-use plazas, such as the Bay Street development project, now nearing completion. Most Emeryville residents live in some kind of rental situation, with apartment complexes, condominiums, or loft warehouses the most common housing options. You'll find some single-family detached homes in "the triangle" area, on San Pablo Avenue, mostly

Craftsman-style houses built in the 1920s and '30s. Waterfront living is available at the 1970s-era Watergate Condominiums, which have a spectacular view of the Bay. Other Emeryville residents live in the 30-story Pacific Park Plaza, with its 650 condominium units. Although many of Emeryville's original loft residents were artists, today professionals are moving into the unique spaces created in these old industrial buildings. Emeryville's population is mostly young, single professionals and students, though a number of families are arriving.

EMERYVILLE
Web Site: www.ci.emeryville.ca.us
Area Code: 510
Zip Code: 94608, 94662
Post Office: Emeryville Branch, 1585 62nd St, 800-275-8777, www.usps.com
Police: Emeryville Police Department, 2449 Powell St, 510-596-3700
Library: Golden Gate Library, 5606 San Pablo Ave, 510-597-5023
Public Schools: Emery Unified School District, 4727 San Pablo Ave, 510-601-4000, www.emeryusd.k12.ca.us
Community Resources: Emeryville Chamber of Commerce, 5858 Horton St, Suite 130, 510-652-5223, www.emeryvillechamber.com; Emeryville Senior Center, 4321 Salem St, 510-596-3730; Emeryville Child Development Center, 1220 53rd St, 510-596-4343; Emery-Go-Round Free Shuttle, 510-451-3862 or 511, next bus hotline: 510-451-3862, www.emerygoround.com; Amtrak, 5885 Horton St, 800-USA-RAIL, www.amtrak.com; First Time Homebuyers Program, 510-596-4316.
Parks, Gardens, and Open Space: Emery Recreation Department, 4300 San Pablo Ave, 510-596-4300, www.ci.emeryville.ca.us

ALBANY

Just north of Berkeley, Albany is one of the Bay Area's best-kept secrets. Like Emeryville, it's small—just a little over one square mile, with about 17,000 residents. But here, in a city that prides itself on its small town feel, and is in no way a commuter magnet, life is decidedly family-oriented. Local public schools are considered better than average, and parents who live in other cities have been known to stretch the truth a tad in order to have their children attend Albany schools. The crime rate is among the lowest in the region, and Albany is located only 30 to 50 minutes from downtown San Francisco. Housing includes a number of single-family homes as well as apartments built in the 1940s and '50s. But people are catching on to Albany's charm, a fact reflected in rapidly increasing housing prices in the earlier years of the decade.

The commercial strip of Solano Avenue is shared with Berkeley. Once a railroad thoroughfare, Solano Avenue offers day-to-day services and shopping

Albany

options, all within walking distance from most parts of Albany. Among the selections are bookstores, boutique clothing stores, restaurants, cafés, a supermarket, and a movie theater. Locals rave about Rivoli Restaurant, 1539 Solano Avenue. Each fall the mile-long stretch of Solano Avenue is closed for the "Solano Avenue Stroll," a weekend festival of food, music, and entertainment. The west side of town, where I-80 and I-580 meet, is bounded by the Bay and home to the mudflats, which are popular with bird watchers, walkers, and joggers. An extension of the Bay Trail is under way here, as is work on Eastshore State Park. If you like to play the ponies, or just watch them run, Golden Gate Fields Racetrack, one of the largest thoroughbred tracks in the country, is also here (510-559-7300, www.goldengatefields.com).

ALBANY

Web Site: www.albanyca.org

Area Code: 510

Zip Code: 94706, 94710

Post Office: 1191 Solano Ave, 800-275-8777, www.usps.com

Police: Albany Police Department, 1000 San Pablo Ave, 510-525-7300

Library: Albany Library, 1247 Marin Ave, 510-526-3720

Public Schools: Albany Unified School District, 904 Talbot Ave, 510-558-3750, www.albany.k12.ca.us

Community Resources: Albany Chamber of Commerce, 1108 Solano Ave, 510-525-1771, www.albanychamber.org; Solano Avenue Association, 1563 Solano Ave, #101, 510-527-5358, www.solanoavenueassn.org

Parks, Gardens, and Open Space: Albany Recreation and Community Services Department, 1249 Marin Ave, 510-524-9283, www.albanyca.org

PIEDMONT

Surrounded by Oakland, but a city in itself, Piedmont is one of the wealthiest communities in the East Bay—and indeed the entire Bay Area. Incorporated in 1907, only 1.8 square miles in size, and with a population hovering around 11,000, Piedmont is a tiny enclave of large estates, mansions, tennis courts, immaculate wooded parks, and civility. This city is also known for its excellent school district. Don't go looking for an apartment here; you won't find one. As a matter of fact, rental property of any type is virtually nonexistent here. If the name Piedmont rings a bell, it may be because the local high school has for decades been the host of a national bird-calling contest, the winners of which have been invited to appear on *The Tonight Show* and *Late Night With David Letterman*.

PIEDMONT
Web Site: www.ci.piedmont.ca.us
Area Code: 510
Zip Codes: 94611, 94610, 94618, 94602, 94620
Post Office: (nearest one) 195 41st St, Oakland, 800-275-8777, www.usps.com
Police: Piedmont Police Department, 401 Highland Ave, 510-420-3000
Public Schools: Piedmont Unified School District, 760 Magnolia Ave, 510-594-2600, www.piedmont.k12.ca.us
Community Resources: City Hall, 120 Vista Ave, 510-420-3040; Piedmont Adult School, 510-594-2655, piedmontadultschool.org
Parks, Gardens, and Open Space: Piedmont Recreation Department, 358 Hillside Ave, 510-420-3070, www.ci.piedmont.ca.us

OAKLAND

DOWNTOWN OAKLAND
LAKE MERRITT
MONTCLAIR
CLAREMONT HILLS
ROCKRIDGE

For sports fans, living in Oakland means you'll have a number of professional teams to root for. Oakland is home to the NFL's Raiders, Major League Baseball's Oakland Athletics (A's), and the NBA's Golden State Warriors. The A's and the Raiders play at the Oakland Coliseum and the Warriors play at the Oracle Arena, off I-880 in southern Oakland.

As Brooklyn is to Manhattan, so Oakland has become to San Francisco. Though many commute to San Francisco for work and nightlife, Oakland,

Downtown Oakland

packed with locally owned businesses, championship sports teams, and local color and culture, including old-time movie houses, inspires civic pride and loyalty among its residents. Oakland is a happening place with all the amenities that a city of over 400,000 can offer. Home to a large and established African-American community, Oakland also boasts a growing Asian-American population. In recent years Oakland has drawn an increasing number of young artists, writers, and musicians. An excellent place to be if you play an instrument, Oakland is known locally as a kind of hipster haven. Its bustling independent music scene includes a network of nightclubs, hometown record labels, radio stations, and above all, rock bands.

The neighborhoods that make up Oakland are as different as water and oil. Generally speaking, the more upscale neighborhoods are found higher up on the hills, complete with bay views; down the hills and further west are what many would consider the rougher neighborhoods. **Downtown's** Old Oakland, adjacent to the City Center, has a collection of vintage Victorian buildings that were spared from the bulldozer. Known as Preservation Park, this area is a commercial zone, with a lovely fountain in the center. Paramount Theatre, an art deco landmark at 2025 Broadway, is another downtown highlight.

A world-class port, Oakland's waterfront teems with activity, bringing in an estimated $25 billion worth of goods each year, mostly from Asia. Situated next to the boats, Jack London Square is a destination place to dine, shop, and stroll along the waterfront, much like San Francisco's Pier 39, only not as crowded. Here, you can eat sushi and listen to jazz at the popular Yoshi's Jazz and Sushi Club, 510 Embarcadero West. Also located at the pier is Franklin Delano Roosevelt's 165-foot USS *Potomac*, which was frequented by the late president, close advisors, and congressional leaders for informal strategy sessions. Every Sunday year round, locals gather at the Pier for the farmers market, which also opens midday on Wednesdays for an extended summer season. From here you can also take the ferry into San Francisco, or just cross the street to the Amtrak station at 245 2nd Street. On Fridays, check out the Old Oakland Farmers Market, an old-fashioned open-air market filled with fruit, veggies, and seafood, held at

Lake Merritt

the revitalized Swan's Marketplace, on Ninth Street between Broadway and Clay streets, near Chinatown.

If you want the best of both worlds—city life and natural beauty—**Lake Merritt** may be your best option. Just moments from downtown, the three-mile lagoon is a scenic sanctuary amid the sometimes gritty hustle and bustle of urban life. Home to 90 species of birds, including a huge flock of Canada geese, the lake proudly bills itself as the nation's oldest wildlife refuge. During the morning, the shores are packed with joggers and dog walkers, while at night, the picturesque waters are lit up by a string of white lights, making Lake Merritt undoubtedly one of Oakland's most scenic neighborhoods.

Though not the least expensive option in town, Lake Merritt is reasonably priced. Around Lake Merritt are abundant apartments in older brick buildings from the 1920s, two- and three-bedroom homes from the 1940s and '50s, and condos from the 1960s and '70s. In the early 19th century, elite estates were built around the lake. Only one home remains today, the Camron Stanford House, 1418 Lakeside Drive. Lake Merritt residents who work in downtown Oakland enjoy a quick commute, as well as the natural beauty and outdoor recreation amenities of lakeside living. In the summer the lake comes alive with canoes, kayaks, and windsurfing, while fall ushers in breezy moonlight walks and the popular Moon Viewing Festival.

In October 1991, a massive fire struck the Oakland Hills area, destroying more than 2,500 homes and killing 25 people. Fire investigators believe an arsonist set the fire that raged for days in the hills above the city. Responding fire trucks had a difficult time trying to navigate the narrow, winding, and tree-lined roads. Though it's been well over a decade since the fires, the horrific specter of that disaster still haunts Oakland. Since the tragedy, the city implemented new fire codes and constructed roads wide enough to allow emergency vehicle accessibility to outlying areas. A mural at the Rockridge BART Station commemorates the fire victims. One of the areas hardest hit by the fires was the upscale **Montclair** district, which has been largely rebuilt. The homes immediately surrounding the main shopping area along Mountain Boulevard are wood-framed stuccos with a Mediterranean look. Others are Craftsman-style bungalows, some nearly hidden by trees and having back yards that open up to rambling redwood groves. Other homes perched on the hills are privy to views of the Bay and San Francisco. Montclair also hosts several apartment complexes for would-be renters. Many Montclair residents commute into San Francisco, which, without traffic, is only 15 to 20 minutes; with traffic it's sometimes triple that. Although Montclair is a pricey district for Oakland, purchasing a house here is considerably less costly than buying a hilltop home in San Francisco.

Montclair

The **Claremont Hills** area, just north of Montclair, also suffered from the fire of 1991. These wooded environs have large dwellings mixed in with a smattering of smaller, sometimes student-occupied homes as well as a few apartments. Access to Interstate 24 makes commuting to San Francisco or the South Bay easier. Nearby Redwood Regional Park provides for miles of secluded serenity amidst the redwoods.

Of all the areas that make up Oakland, many would argue that **Rockridge**, located south of Berkeley, offers the quintessential "neighborhood" feel. Created after the 1906 Earthquake destroyed San Francisco, this former hayfield originally was developed as a racially exclusive housing tract. Today, the area known as Lower Rockridge (between Claremont and Broadway) is an ethnically diverse and upscale area. In fact, many consider this to be one of Oakland's hippest neighborhoods. Some students and employees of UC live here, and many young professionals commuting into San Francisco or the South Bay call Rockridge home. BART's central location at College and Shafter makes the commute a breeze. Homes here are typically stucco and wood-shingled Craftsman-style bungalows with small cottage gardens. Residents can stroll along tree-lined streets to the gourmet restaurants and trendy shops clustered around the strip of College Avenue between Alcatraz and Broadway.

Upper Rockridge (above Broadway), built during the post-war housing booms of the 1920s and 1940s, extends into the hills northeast toward Lake Temescal. Many of the homes destroyed in the 1991 fire were replaced by a unique "tract" of million-dollar custom homes. As a result, housing is on the expensive end of Oakland's price scale. Apartments are scarce as the area has zoning restrictions on buildings with more than four units. Finding a rental here is easiest in the early summer when many UC students go home for the break.

Shopping and dining are the main attractions in Rockridge. Its heart is College Avenue, which boasts excellent eateries, fine antique shops, art galleries, and clothing boutiques. Rockridge Market Hall, 5655 College Avenue, touts a European-style shopping experience with specialty grocery shops located under one open-air roof. Restaurants here reflect the ethnic diversity of Oakland and include several Mexican eateries as well as Ethiopian, Italian, Japanese, Chinese, and Irish cuisine. Specialty pizza at Zachary's, 5801 College Avenue, is always standing room only. Meanwhile a mix of coffee shops and comfortable pubs with well-lit pool tables cater to locals as well as UC students that filter down from Berkeley. For those looking for a good book, Pendragon's new and used books, 5560 College Avenue, and a branch library, 5366 College Avenue, should satisfy most literary tastes.

The public schools for this district are Hillcrest Elementary and Middle School (K–8, enrollment about 275) and Chabot Elementary (K–5, enrollment about 440). Both schools traditionally rank among the top in the Oakland Unified School District.

OAKLAND

Web Sites: www.ci.oakland.ca.us or www.rockridge.org
Area Code: 510
Zip Codes: 94601–94627, 94643, 94649, 94659, 94660–94662, 94666
Post Office: Oakland Main, 1675 Seventh St, 800-275-8777, www.usps.com
Police: Oakland Police Department, 455 7th St, 510-777-3333
Libraries: Oakland Public Library, Main Branch, 125 14th St, 510-238-3134, www.oaklandlibrary.org; Asian Branch 388 9th St, Suite 190, 510-238-3400; Brookfield Branch, 9255 Edes Ave, 510-615-5725; César E. Chávez Branch, 3301 E 12th St (services in Spanish), 510-535-5620; Dimond Branch, 3565 Fruitvale Ave, 510-482-7844; Eastmont Branch, 7200 Bancroft, Suite 211 (Eastmont Town Center), 510-615-5726; Elmhurst Branch, 1427 88th Ave, 510-615-5726; Golden Gate Branch, 5606 San Pablo Ave, 510-597-5023; Lakeview Branch, 550 El Embarcadero, 510-238-7344; Martin Luther King Branch, 6833 International Blvd, 510-615-5728; Melrose Branch, 4805 Foothill Blvd, 510-535-5623; Montclair Branch, 1687 Mountain Blvd, 510-482-7810; Piedmont Avenue Branch, 160 41st St, 510-597-5011; Rockridge Branch, 5366 College Ave, 510-597-5017; Temescal Branch, 5205 Telegraph Ave, 510-597-5049; West Oakland Branch, 1801 Adeline St, 510-238-7352

Public Schools: Oakland Unified School District, 1025 Second Ave, Oakland 94606, 510-879-8200, http://webportal.ousd.k12.ca.us

Community Publications: *Oakland Tribune*, 510-208-6300, www.insidebayarea. com/oaklandtribune (also owns the *Alameda Times Star*, the *Fremont Argus* and a handful of smaller local papers); *East Bay Express*, 510-879-3700, www. eastbayexpress.com; *Contra Costa Times* (covers Contra Costa and east Alameda County), 800-598-4637, www.ContraCostaTimes.com (also owns Hills News, which puts out *Berkeley Voice*, *Alameda Journal*, the *Montclarion* and the *Piedmonter*)

Community Resources: Oakland Zoo, 9777 Golf Links Rd, 510-632-9525, www. oaklandzoo.org; McAfee Coliseum (Oakland–Alameda County Coliseum), 7000 Coliseum Way, 510-569-2121; Chabot Observatory and Science Center, 10000 Skyline Blvd, 510-336-7300, www.chabotspace.org; Oakland A's Baseball, 510-638-4900, www.oaklandathletics.com; Golden State Warriors Basketball, 510-986-2222, www.nba.com/warriors; Oakland Raiders Football, 510-864-5000, www.raiders.com; Oakland DMV, 5300 Claremont Avenue, 800-777-0133; Claremont Country Club, 5295 Broadway Terrace, 510-653-6789

Cultural Resources: Alameda County Arts Commission, P.O. Box 29004, Oakland, 94604, 510-208-9646, www.acgov.org/arts; Oakland Museum of California, 1000 Oak St, 510-238-2200, www.museumca.org; Oakland East Bay Symphony, 510-444-0801, www.oebs.org; Oakland Ballet, 510-452-9288, www.oaklandballet.org; Museum of Children's Art, 538 9th St, 510-465-8770, www.mocha.org; Pro Arts, Inc., 461 Ninth St, 510-763-4361, www.proartsgallery.org; California College of Arts & Crafts, 5212 Broadway, 510-594-3600, www.cca.edu

Parks, Gardens, and Open Space: Oakland Parks and Recreation, 250 Frank Ogawa Plaza, Suite 3330, 510-238-PARK, www.oaklandnet.com; Lake Temescal Regional Recreation Area, 6500 Broadway, 510-652-1155, www.ebparks. org/parks/temescal.htm

BERKELEY

NORTH BERKELEY
BERKELEY HILLS
SOUTH BERKELEY
CLAREMONT, ELMWOOD
DOWNTOWN/CENTRAL BERKELEY
WEST BERKELEY

Nicknamed the "The People's Republic of Berkeley" and many other more or less affectionate monikers, Berkeley conjures images of student protests, hippies, Birkenstocks, counterculture, and, above all, independent thinking. This was the first city in the nation to replace Columbus Day observances with Indigenous

Peoples Day, honoring the Native Americans who lived here before Columbus arrived. The uproar caused when the Reverend Jerry Falwell claimed that the purple Teletubby, Tinky Winky, was homosexual resulted in the Berkeley City Council passing a resolution in support of this diminutive television character. With its colorful residents and liberal leanings, Berkeley beckons the young, the politically active, and those who seek an intellectual existence. Many find it a stimulating and relaxed place to call home.

Berkeley is home to about 105,400 people from all walks of life. The city proudly proclaims that 83% of those who live here call Berkeley an "excellent" or "good" place to live. A bike-friendly, eco-conscious, and art-loving town, Berkeley boasts fantastic parks and open space for outdoor adventurers as well as excellent food from all over the world, and myriad cultural offerings. Every year locals celebrate their unique brand of civic pride with the outlandish "How Berkeley Can You Be" Parade and Festival.

The University of California at Berkeley ("Cal") and Lawrence Livermore Laboratory are the city's largest employers. Founded in 1868, Cal spreads out between the downtown area and the Berkeley Hills, and has more than 33,000 undergraduate and graduate students in attendance. The reputation of today's students is not as liberal as it was in the 1960s when Mario Savio rallied against the university's policies, sparking the free speech movement, or when Berkeley students protested the Vietnam War. Today, protests revolve around changes in admission requirements, tuition increases, and the negative impacts of state budget cuts. In addition to the many local coffeehouses, Berkeley's milieu of evening entertainment includes more than 30 movie theaters, 50 bookstores, and 400 restaurants—certainly a lot of food for thought.

North Berkeley, considered to be the calmer side of town, is home to many graduate students, professors, and young families. Strollers glide past the American Craftsman-style bungalows, rolling over to the many small parks spread throughout the area.

North Berkeley

North on Shattuck Avenue, from Rose up to Hearst, you'll find the "Gourmet Ghetto," which is equipped with restaurants and specialty shops. It was 1971 when Alice Waters pioneered serving organic food at her restaurant, Chez Panisse, 1517 Shattuck Avenue. She has since championed serving organic foods in Berkeley's public schools. Other gourmet delights in this area abound; just take a stroll down Shattuck Avenue for anything from pasta and pizza to pad thai and matzo ball soup. Intimate Walnut Square, between Walnut and Shattuck, is home to the original Peet's Coffee & Tea at 2124 Vine Street. Additional shopping is available on Hopkins Street (known as "Gourmet Ghetto West").

Following Shattuck south across University Avenue, you hit the heart of downtown. Here, you'll find a mix of shops and restaurants, and a centrally located BART station for easy access to San Francisco. There is also a cluster of movie theaters—both commercial and art house—within a short radius. Homes around the downtown area have the blessing of being both centrally located—within blocks of the action—and reasonably serene. As you move away from the main drag, streets become heavily tree-lined, shrouding stately Victorians and bungalows, roads narrow, speed limits drop, and bike lanes abound.

Up in the **Berkeley Hills**, which run from the North Campus area east to Berkeley's magnificent Tilden Park and then north to Kensington, you'll discover magnificent views and be surrounded by the lovely smell of eucalyptus. To get to the Berkeley Hills take either Euclid Avenue north all the way to Grizzly Peak, coming through Tilden Park at its northernmost entrance, or start at the football stadium and take Centennial Drive up to Grizzly Peak. Along your drive you'll see exquisite Craftsman-style homes, some with striking bay views and fabulous gardens. If you are willing to navigate the hill every day, you may be able to rent a room in one of these homes.

Along Euclid Street, the higher the ascent, the more spectacular the homes. The Berkeley Rose Garden on Euclid Street (between Eunice and Bayview Place) offers great bay views and lovely aromas. For a romantic sunset, the benches at the top of the garden are front row seats. Traveling up the hills via the Centennial route will bring you to the Botanical Gardens in Strawberry Canyon. Considered one of the world's leading gardens in terms of plant variety and quality, the gardens are home to Chinese medicinal herbs and soaring redwoods. Also on the hill is the Lawrence Hall of Science, which sports one of the best views of the city as well as a first-rate public science center with a multitude of hands-on educational programs for children and exhibits that are fun for people of all ages.

Visitors come from all over to enjoy the 2,065 acres of open meadows and forests of Tilden Park, which include 30 miles of hiking and horse trails, an 18-hole public golf course, swimming at Anza Lake, pony rides, a petting farm, carousel, and a steam train. There are no shopping options atop the hill, so you'll need to take care of all your errands before heading up.

South Berkeley

Located directly south of the campus and west of the Berkeley Hills, **South Berkeley's** population is composed predominantly of students, many of whom live in dormitories, cooperatives, and fraternity or sorority houses. This is the rowdy area of Berkeley, with activity at all times of the day and night. Some of the most architecturally interesting homes are the large mansions that house the college fraternities and sororities. The Sigmi Phi house on Durant and Piedmont is a classic Arts and Crafts style home, designed by the Greene brothers in 1909. Julia Morgan designed the outdoor Greek Theatre, and Bernard Maybeck, architect of San Francisco's Palace of Fine Arts, also made his mark on many Berkeley homes.

Much of the 1960s free speech movement and the anti-Vietnam War protests centered around Telegraph Avenue and Sproul Plaza. The plaza still hosts student protests, and when there is little to yell about, musicians, politicians, prophets, and students take center stage. Telegraph Avenue, which begins in downtown Oakland, runs into the southern side of the Cal campus. The Berkeley section of Telegraph is a bustling shopping zone catering to students with clothing, book, and music stores; coffee shops; cheap eats; and cafés. Street vendors set up daily, selling handmade jewelry and tie-dyed clothes. Locals have a choice of three well-known independent bookstores on the 2400 block: Moe's, Shakespeare & Co., and Shambhala. Every Christmas season the Telegraph Avenue Street Fair hosts an arts and crafts show. UC Berkeley has two concert sites: the outdoor Greek Theater and the indoor Zellerbach Hall, which features national and international performers. Another popular annual event is the ArtCar Fest, a motorcade showcasing some of the most creative, unique, and bizarre vehicles you'll ever see. The fest kicks off in Berkeley with a drive across the Bay Bridge to San Francisco.

The hustle and bustle of university life quiets down once you head south, away from the campus. Close to College Avenue, the **Claremont** neighborhood, bordering Oakland (east of the Elmwood District and west of the Claremont

Resort), is one of Berkeley's grandest and most expensive neighborhoods. The area is named for the huge, 22-acre resort called the Claremont Hotel Club and Spa, which is so large it can be seen from across the bay. Designed by Charles Dickey, the Claremont has tennis courts and a large outdoor swimming pool. Some of the elegant homes that make up Claremont have bay views. Two small shopping areas serve the neighborhood: the Uplands Street area and Domingo Avenue, where you'll find Berkeley's famous Peet's Coffee, across from the Claremont Resort.

Claremont

The **Elmwood District**, just down the street and west from the Claremont, is a pleasant area of two- and three-story, brown-shingle homes surrounded by tall trees. Housing here is pricey, and to supplement income, many families find tenants for their backyard cottages, basements, or attic rooms.

Downtown Berkeley's civic heart is the Martin Luther King Jr. Civic Center Park, 2151 Martin Luther King Jr. Way, a stretch of green at the foot of city hall. Berkeley's main post office and library are in the 2000 block of Allston way. Though not as chic as Fourth Street or College Avenue (see below), Shattuck Avenue offers a variety of shopping, from furniture, to clothing, to tiny boutiques, to toy stores and movie theaters. For fresh fruits and vegetables, the farmers market is a local favorite. Held twice a week on Martin Luther King Jr. Way, the market attracts people from all over seeking produce straight from the farmers. On Saturdays, the market is at Center Street and Martin Luther King (10 a.m. to 3 p.m.; on Tuesdays head for Derby Street and Martin Luther King, from 2 p.m. to 7 p.m.; on Thursdays, there is an all-organic market at Shattuck Avenue and Rose Street, open 3 p.m. to 7 p.m. (see www.ecologycenter.org/bfm for more information).

Downtown is home to Berkeley's theater scene, with the Berkeley Repertory Theatre, 2025 Addison Street, being most familiar. Though not in downtown proper, Zellerbach Auditorium on the UC Campus also sponsors live performances, from the Kirov Ballet to John Cleese.

Downtown Berkeley

Downtown's central hub for mass transit includes BART (Shattuck and Center) and AC Transit. Just down the street from the BART Station, people line up early in the morning to carpool into the city; three persons in a car constitute a carpool, plus you do not have to pay the $4 bridge toll.

Also known as the "Flatlands," **West Berkeley** is considered a transitional area with affordable fixer-upper bungalows, new lofts, and relatively inexpensive rents. This area is neither as safe nor as aesthetically pleasing as other parts of Berkeley; however, proximity to the waterfront and to the Fourth Street shopping district is an asset. South of University Avenue, along the numbered streets, you'll find a cluster of commercial warehouses and unique arts and crafts studio-shops. Nearby San Pablo Avenue is not only a major route through town, but has become a popular neighborhood gathering spot with a small stretch that's home to a smattering of restaurants, cafés, and independent boutiques. Berkeley initiatives to enhance this area are well under way including the addition of new bike routes, a revamping of the West Berkeley train station and transit plaza, and improvements to the waterfront area. The Berkeley Marina is a mecca for water sports, including sailing, kayaking, and windsurfing. On the Berkeley pier, fishing is the main pastime. Both California Adventures and the California Sailing Club offer sailing and windsurfing lessons. Also on the waterfront is Adventure Playground, a popular outdoor area for children.

Vibrant Fourth Street, which includes an inviting outdoor shopping mall, is perhaps Berkeley's most upscale shopping district, chock-full of popular restaurants, home and garden shops, boutiques, and outlet stores. Locals rave about brunch at Bette's Oceanview Diner, 1807A Fourth Street (expect a two-hour wait on Sundays). Newcomers often head to the Crate & Barrel outlet at 1785 Fourth Street to stock up on home necessities; Restoration Hardware also graces this block.

BERKELEY
Web Sites: www.ci.berkeley.ca.us

Area Codes: 510, 341

Zip Codes: 94701–94705, 94707–94709

Main Post Office: 2000 Allston Way, Berkeley, 800-275-8777, www.usps.com

Police: Berkeley Police Department, 2100 Martin Luther King Jr Way, 510-981-5900, TTY 510-981-5799

Libraries: Berkeley Public Library, Central Branch, 2090 Kittredge St, Berkeley, 510-981-6100; Claremont Branch, 2940 Benvenue Ave, 510-981-6280; South Branch, 1901 Russell St, 510-981-6260; North Branch, 1170 The Alameda, 510-981-6250; West Branch, 1125 University Ave, 510-981-6270, www.berkeleypubliclibrary.org

Public Schools: Berkeley Unified School District, 2134 Martin Luther King Jr. Way, Berkeley, 510-644-6348, www.berkeley.k12.ca.us; college: www.berkeley.edu

Community Publications: East Bay Express, 510-879-3700, www.eastbayexpress.com; *Contra Costa Times* (covers Contra Costa and east Alameda County) 800-598-4637, www.ContraCostaTimes.com (also owns Hills News, which puts out *Berkeley Voice, Alameda Journal,* the *Montclarion,* and the *Piedmonter*); *Berkeley Daily Planet*, 510-841-5600, www.berkeleydailyplanet.com; UC.Berkeley Publications: *Daily Californian*, www.dailycal.org; *North Gate News On-line* http://journalism.berkeley.edu/ngno/

Community Resources: Berkeley Chamber of Commerce, 1834 University Avenue, 510-549-7000, www.berkeleychamber.com; Tool Lending Library, 1901 Russell St, 510-981-6101; Berkeley First Source employment program, 510-981-7550; Berkeley Art Center, 1275 Walnut St, 510-644-6893, www.berkeleyartcenter.org

Cultural Resources: University of California, Berkeley Art Museum, 2626 Bancroft Way, 510-642-0808, www.bampfa.berkeley.edu; Pacific Film Archive Theater, 2575 Bancroft Way, 510-642-1124, www.bampfa.berkeley.edu; Lawrence Hall of Science, Centennial Dr below Grizzly Peak, 510-642-5132, www.lhs.berkeley.edu; Judah L. Magnes Memorial Museum, 2911 Russell St, 510-549-6950, www.magnes.org; La Pena Cultural Center, 3105 Shattuck Ave, 510-849-2568, www.lapena.org; Ames Gallery of American Folk Art, 2661 Cedar St, 510-845-4949, www.amesgallery.com; Black Repertory Group, 3201 Adeline St, 510-652-2120; Julia Morgan Center for the Arts, 2640 College Ave, 510-845-8542; Berkeley Repertory Theatre, 510-647-2949, www.berkeleyrep.org

Parks and Open Space: Berkeley Parks Recreation and Waterfront Department, 2180 Milvia St, Third Floor, 510-981-6700, TTY 510-981-6903, www.ci.berkeley.ca.us (Berkeley Community Gardening Collaborative can be reached at 510-883-9096, www.ecologycenter.org/bcgc); Marina Experience Program/Shorebird Park and Nature Center and Adventure Playground, 160 University Avenue, 510-981-6720; call the parks and recreation department for information about local climbing parks

CONTRA COSTA COUNTY

Contra Costa County, with just over one million people, is on the eastern side of the East Bay Hills, out where the weather is warm, warmer, and warmest. The population is diverse, with all economic levels represented. Housing options are also varied, ranging from old farmhouses and massive, gated apartment complexes to duplexes, condominiums, and sprawling, newly landscaped housing developments. Many apartment complexes offer swimming pools and recreation centers. Housing costs are slightly lower than most Bay Area counties.

CONTRA COSTA COUNTY

Web Site: www.co.contra-costa.ca.us

Area Codes: 510, 925

Sheriff: 651 Pine St, 7th Floor, Martinez, 925-335-1500

Libraries: Contra Costa County Library, Pleasant Hill/Central Branch, 1750 Oak Park Blvd, 925-646-6434, www.ccclib.org, branches throughout the county

Emergency Hospitals: Contra Costa Health Services: Contra Costa Regional Medical Center, 2500 Alhambra Ave, Martinez (operates community health centers in Antioch, Bay Point; Brentwood, Pittsburg, Richmond and Concord), 925-370-5000 or TTY 925-335-9959, www.cchealth.org; John Muir Medical Center, 1601 Ygnacio Valley Rd, Walnut Creek, 925-939-3000, www.johnmuirhealth.com; Mt. Diablo Medical Center, 2540 E St, Concord, 925-682-8200, www.johnmuirhealth.com; San Ramon Regional Medical Center, 6001 Norris Canyon Rd, 925-275-9200

Public Schools: West Contra Costa Unified School District, 1108 Bissell Ave, Richmond, 94801, 510-234-3825, www.wccusd.k12.ca.us; Contra Costa Office of Education, 77 Santa Barbara Rd, Pleasant Hill, 925-942-3388, www.cccoe.k12.ca.us

Community Publications: *Oakland Tribune*, 510-208-6300, www.insidebayarea.com/oaklandtribune (also owns the *Alameda Times-Star* and the *Fremont Argus*); *East Bay Express*, 510-879-3700, www.eastbayexpress.com; *Contra Costa Times* (covers Contra Costa and east Alameda County) 800-598-4637, www.ContraCostaTimes.com

Community/County Resources: Richmond Art Center, Civic Center Plaza, 2540 Barrett Ave, 510-620-6772, www.therichmondartcenter.org; Richmond Museum of History, 400 Nevin Ave, 510-235-7387; Alvarado Adobe House and Blume House (the San Pablo Historical Society), 510-215-3046; John Muir National Historic Site, 4202 Alhambra Ave, Martinez, 925-228-8860, www.nps.gov/jomu; Blake Garden, 70 Rincon Rd, Kensington, 510-524-2449; Martinez Marina, 925-313-0942; Contra Costa HIV/AIDS Program Resource Line, 925-313-6770; Recreation Services, City Hall, 525 Henrietta St, Martinez, 925-372-3510; Concord Police Community Action and Awareness Line, 925-671-3237

Public Transportation: *AC* (*Alameda-Contra Costa*) *Transit*, 510-891-4700, TTY 800-448-9790, www.actransit.org; *BART*, 510-465-2278, TTY 510-839-2278, www.bart.gov; *Benicia Transit*, 707-745-0815, *County Connection*, 925-676-7500; *RIDES*, 511, www. 511.org; *Tri-Delta Transit*, 925-754-4040, *WestCat*, 510-724-7993; *Amtrak*, 800-872-7245

Parks, Gardens, and Open Space: East Bay Regional Park District, 2950 Peralta Oaks Ct, 510-562-PARK, www.ebparks.org, maintains 62 parks throughout the region, many with large open areas, nature trails and shorelines

MARTINEZ, WALNUT CREEK, CONCORD

The City of **Martinez**, www.cityofmartinez.org, is the site of naturalist John Muir's historic home, a well-maintained hillside Victorian mansion that is open to the public. With a population of nearly 36,000, Martinez boasts average home prices a little under the county median.

Martinez

Walnut Creek, www.ci.walnut-creek.ca.us, is home to more than 64,000 people. With its fine arts programs, including the Lesher Center for the Arts and Bedford Gallery, 1601 Civic Drive, 925-295-1400, its open space projects, public gardens, equestrian center, and the Boundary Oak Golf Course, 3800 Valley Vista Road, 925-934-4775, it is considered by many to be one of the most desirable cities in Contra Costa County. Commensurate with its desirability, housing prices run higher than its neighbors.

Concord, www.ci.concord.ca.us, has the most people, with a population of about 124,000. Houses along the corridor of Highway 680 are going up rapidly because it is possible to live here and drive to Silicon Valley in under an hour. Although housing prices are increasing more rapidly than in most other areas, median home prices, according to the CAR, still tend to be on the low end for

Walnut Creek

the Bay Area. Concord is also home to an upper-division and graduate campus of Cal State East Bay.

June through September finds the homes on the east side of Highway 24's Caldecott Tunnel basking in heat. Opened in 1937, the Tunnel connects Oakland to Orinda. During the summer it's not unusual to find temperatures 60° in San Francisco and over 100° in Concord, Martinez, or Walnut Creek.

CONCORD
Web Site: www.ci.concord.ca.us
Area Code: 925
Zip Code: 94519, 94520
Post Office: 2121 Meridian Park Blvd
Library: Concord Library, 2900 Salvio St., 925-646-5455
Public Schools: Mt. Diablo Unified School District, 1936 Carlotta Dr, 925-682-8000, www.mdusd.k12.ca.us
Parks, Gardens, and Open Space: Parks Department, 2974 Salvio St, 925-671-3404

MARTINEZ
Web Site: www.cityofmartinez.org
Area Code: 925
Zip Code: 94553
Post Office: 4100 Alhambra Ave
Library: Martinez Library, 740 Court St., 925-646-2898
Public Schools: Martinez Unified School District, 921 Susana St., 925-313-0480, www.martinez.k12.ca.us; Mt. Diablo Unified School District, 1936 Carlotta Dr, 925-682-8000, www.mdusd.k12.ca.us
Parks, Gardens, and Open Space: Parks, Recreation and Community Services, 525 Henrietta St, 925-372-3580

WALNUT CREEK
Web Site: www.ci.walnut-creek.ca.us
Area Code: 925
Zip Code: 94596
Post Office: 2070 N Broadway
Library: Walnut Creek, 1395 Civic Dr, 925-646-6773
Public Schools: Walnut Creek School District, 960 Ygnacio Valley Rd, 925-944-6850,www.wcsd.k12.ca.us; Mt. Diablo Unified School District, 1936 Carlotta Dr, 925-682-8000, www.mdusd.k12.ca.us
Parks, Gardens, and Open Space: Arts, Recreation and Community Services Division, 1666 N Main St, 925-943-5858

RICHMOND

POINT RICHMOND

Richmond, the northernmost city in Contra Costa County, was established as a shipyard town with the onset of World War II. Many ships destined for the Pacific front left port from Richmond. Today, many Richmond residents are descended from individuals who arrived here for work in the mid-1930s and '40s. Richmond has since fallen upon hard times, suffering from lack of employment. Richmond has gotten a bit of a bad reputation over the years, as the city has been plagued by economic depression and high crime rates. BART quickly connects the area with nearby Oakland and Berkeley, as well as San Francisco. The city is largely African-American with a growing Latino population. Compared with the rest of the East Bay, rents and property here are much cheaper.

One lovely enclave in Richmond is **Point Richmond,** which is invitingly situated close to the bay. Here, you'll find a bayside artist/sailing community with a quaint, old-fashioned downtown with cafés and restaurants, as well as a flower shop and grocery store. The community atmosphere is cozy, with neighbors looking out for one another and shopkeepers remembering customers' names. The Richmond Yacht Club, 351 Brickyard Cove, is a popular socializing spot. Many of the homes near the yacht club have their own private docks. Public swimming is normally available in the Richmond Plunge, the Bay Area's largest heated indoor pool at 1 East Richmond Avenue, but The Plunge has been closed for extensive seismic upgrades.

RICHMOND
Web Site: www.ci.richmond.ca.us
Area Code: 510
Zip Codes: 94801–94808, 94820, 94850, 94875, 94530

Point Richmond

Post Offices: 104 Washington Ave; 1025 Nevin Ave; 2100 Chanslor Ave; 200 Broadway, 800-275-8777, www.usps.com

Police: Richmond Police Department, 1701 Regatta Blvd, 510-233-1214

Library: Richmond Main Library, 325 Civic Center Plaza, 510-620-6561

Public Schools: West Contra Costa Unified School District, 1108 Bissell Ave, 510-234-3825, www.wccusd.k12.ca.us

Community Resources: Point Richmond Online, www.pointrichmond.com; Richmond Yacht Club, 351 Brickyard Cove, 510-237-2821; Richmond Plunge, 1 East Richmond Ave, 510-620-6820; Masquers Playhouse, 105 Park Place, 510-232-4031

Parks, Gardens, and Open Space: Richmond Recreation and Parks, 3230 Macdonald Ave, 510-620-6788; East Bay Regional Park District, 2950 Peralta Oaks Court, P.O. Box 5381, Oakland, 94605, 510-562-PARK

SAN RAMON

Located about 25 miles east of Oakland, in the heart of the San Ramon Valley, is the City of **San Ramon**. What started out as a small, sleepy, well-to-do bedroom community is now a burgeoning city in its own right, with a bustling commercial center at its core and exploding job growth. Though historically known as San Ramon for more than 100 years, the city did not officially incorporate until 1983, making it a relatively new municipality. Since then, economic growth has driven a rapid population expansion along with accompanying construction, a trend that city officials expect to continue

Despite the hustle and bustle, San Ramon (population just over 50,000) retains its small town suburban charm. With its semi-secluded location, safe streets, and friendly neighborhood parks, this affluent community is the quintessential family town. More than 60% of households here are home to married couples, many with children. Spacious two-, three-, and four-bedroom single-family homes, built in the 1980s or later, dot the quiet residential roads. Many boast the well-manicured front lawns, sunny backyards, and modern amenities characteristic of newer suburban houses.

People who come to San Ramon tend to stay. Along with having one of the county's highest median incomes, San Ramon also boasts relatively high home prices. Nonetheless, the city's housing office reports that San Ramon's rate of home ownership is almost 70%. Nestled in an area of natural beauty, San Ramon is only moments away from the hiking trails of Mount Diablo, the area's highest peak at 3,849 feet. Peppered with unique rock formations and wild-flowers, Mount Diablo draws crowds from all over the Bay Area most weekends for hiking, camping, and horseback riding. From the peak on a clear day, you can see 35 of California's 58 counties.

A network of creeks dots San Ramon's landscape, which, while giving a bucolic feel, can create flooding problems during heavy rains, especially for those who live close to San Ramon, San Catanio, or South San Ramon creeks. Those looking to buy a home in these areas should consult FEMA's flood maps, www.fema.gov, and consider purchasing flood insurance.

As part of the Tri-Valley area, known for wealthy enclaves, lush golf courses, and local wineries, San Ramon shares services and amenities with a larger family of cities including Pleasanton, Livermore, and Danville. Every March, the nearby City of Dublin hosts the Bay Area's largest St. Patrick's Day celebration.

San Ramon's central commercial area, a 580-acre office park known as Bishop Ranch, is host to roughly 200 regional and corporate headquarters, including Pacific Bell, Chevron-Texaco, AT&T, Toyota, Bank of America, and United Parcel Service. Roughly 70,000 people work in San Ramon, and city officials pre-dict another 16,000 jobs will be added to the area over the next 15 years.

Like its Tri-Valley neighbors, San Ramon connects to the urban cores of Oakland, San Francisco, and San Jose via two major highways, I-680 and

San Ramon

I-580—which become severely congested during commute hours. San Ramon actively promotes the use of alternative transit and has in place several innovative programs, many of which run in partnership with local employers, the county, or neighboring cities. Incentives include $60 gas vouchers for starting a new carpool or adding a new rider, free parking and lockers at the local transit center, and the Carpool to School program, www.pooltoschool.org.

For this former village, which once boasted "San Ramon Population 100," the challenge in coming years will be to balance its historically suburban character with continuing growth.

SAN RAMON
Web Site: www.ci.san-ramon.ca.us
Area Code: 925
Zip Code: 94582, 94583,
Post Office: 12935 Alcosta Blvd, 800-275-8777, www.usps.com
Police: 2220 Camino Ramon, 925-973-2700
Library: San Ramon Library, 100 Montgomery St, 925-973-2850
Public Schools: San Ramon Valley Unified, 699 Old Orchard Dr, Danville, 925-552-5500, www.srvusd.k12.ca.us
Community Resources: San Ramon Olympic Pool and Aquatic Park, 9900 Broadmoor Dr, 925-973-3240; Senior Center, 9300 Alcosta Blvd, 925-973-3250; San Ramon Royal Vista Golf Course and San Ramon Golf Club, 9430 Fircrest Ln, 925-828-6100, www.sanramongolfclub.com; The Bridges Golf Club, 9000 South Gale Ridge Rd, 925-735-4253, www.thebridgesgolf.com; Child Day Schools and Hidden Canyon School, 18868 Bollinger Canyon Rd, 925-820-2515; San Ramon Historical Foundation, http://sanramonhistoricfoundation.org
Community Publications: *Tri-Valley Herald*, 510-208-6300, www.insidebayarea.com/trivalleyherald; *San Ramon Observer*, www.sanramonobserver.org
Public Transportation: *County Connection*, 925-676-7500, www.cccta.org; *AC (Alameda-Contra Costa) Transit*, 510-891-4700, TTY 800-448-9790, www.actransit.org; *BART*, 510-465-2278, TTY 510-839-2278, www.bart.gov; *Amtrak*, 800-USA-RAIL, TTY 800-523-6590, www.amtrak.com, *ACE (Altamont Commuter Express)*, 800-411-RAIL, www.acerail.com
Parks, Gardens, and Open Space: San Ramon Parks and Recreation and Community Center, 925-973-3200, www.ci.san-ramon.ca.us/parks; San Ramon Community Center at Central Park, 12501 Alcosta Blvd, 925-973-3350

ADDITIONAL CITY WEB SITES—CONTRA COSTA COUNTY

Antioch: www.ci.antioch.ca.us
Danville: www.ci.danville.ca.us
El Cerrito: www.el-cerrito.ca.us

Lafayette: www.ci.lafayette.ca.us
Livermore: www.ci.livermore.ca.us
Orinda: www.ci.orinda.ca.us
Pinole: www.ci.pinole.ca.us
Pittsburg: www.ci.pittsburg.ca.us
Pleasanton: www.ci.pleasanton.ca.us
San Leandro: www.ci.san-leandro.ca.us

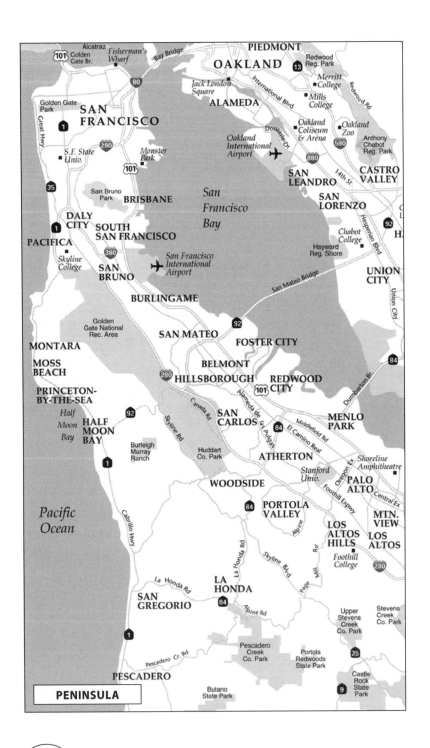

PENINSULA

THE PENINSULA (SAN MATEO COUNTY AND NORTHERN SANTA CLARA COUNTY)

SAN MATEO COUNTY

Known as "The Peninsula," San Mateo County is directly south of San Francisco, with Santa Clara County a little farther south and east. It's hard to imagine what this area was like 100 years ago when only a few small towns dotted the road between San Francisco and San Jose. Belmont, Hillsborough, Woodside, Atherton, and Palo Alto were not cities or towns, but rather garden spots with estates where wealthy San Franciscans relaxed in tranquil surroundings and glorious weather.

Today San Mateo County, which became independent of San Francisco in 1856, consists of 21 cities, many of which are booming with industry and commerce. The eastern half of San Mateo County, with easy access to Interstate 280 and Highway 101, is heavily populated and busy. Fortunately, the folks who live here have plenty of options to escape civilization since roughly the western half of the county is open space, where wooded mountains are laced with superb hiking and biking trails, campgrounds, lakes, and beaches.

Filled with single-family homes, green front lawns, and the usual array of outdoor shopping malls, San Mateo County, with its cozy suburban feel, has long attracted a more family-oriented set than its busy urban neighbor to the north. The most populous city of the county, Daly City, borders San Francisco and marks the beginning of the suburbs. Here at the northernmost edge, long-time San Francisco bedroom communities including San Bruno and South San Francisco are beginning to attract more young professionals and younger families with the development of new, more moderately priced condos and townhouses.

A little farther to the south, in the mid-county, which includes San Mateo (the city), Burlingame, and Belmont, the price of homes has been edging up, nudging past the middle-class price mark. Neatly tucked between San Francisco to the north and Silicon Valley to the south, commuter traffic here flows in both directions and can be rough during rush hours, sometimes grinding to a halt.

The Peninsula contains a number of universities and colleges, the most famous being Stanford University in Palo Alto. Other universities include Santa Clara University, San Jose State University, and Notre Dame de Namur University in Belmont. And, if you live in the center or northern portion of the Peninsula, you will not be far from San Francisco State University.

San Francisco International Airport (SFO) is located on the bayside of the Peninsula, in the South San Francisco/Millbrae/San Bruno area. The airport is a madhouse practically everyday, but especially on holidays, and is notorious for living under a perpetual cloud of fog, causing frequent flight delays. The

Peninsula is also served by the CalTrain commuter service and a number of bus lines including Sam Trans (the San Mateo County bus service), which runs into San Francisco. But by far the most exciting development in recent years here has been the expansion of BART service. Rather than terminating in Daly City, the trains have added stops further south—Colma, San Bruno, South San Francisco, Millbrae, and most exciting, SFO. The new stops offer an excellent park-and-ride option for commuters headed to San Francisco or the East Bay, though so far ridership in these areas has been a little slow to take off. BART is also working with local buses and CalTrain, which has remodeled several peninsula stations and has "baby bullet" express service between San Francisco and San Jose, to create better transit links.

People living in the East Bay commute to San Mateo County and Silicon Valley via the San Mateo–Hayward Bridge or the Dumbarton Bridge (to Fremont). During the past decade, as more and more people have moved east in search of more affordable homes, traffic has increased considerably. The San Mateo–Hayward Bridge was widened in hopes of alleviating some of the strain, but traffic along Highway 92 (the route that crosses the bridge) still frequently moves at a slow crawl during peak times. From the late afternoon into the evening, cars are frequently backed up from the ocean to the Bay (and sometimes vice versa, with coastsiders heading home from work), past jammed intersections with both of the area's major freeways—101 and 280—all along the bridge itself, and continuing well into the bottlenecks of the East Bay.

To the west, you'll find the oceanside edge of San Mateo County. This area is trimmed with Highway 1, one of the most beautiful roadways in the world, tracing the Pacific coastline from the beach city of Pacifica to the pumpkins of Half Moon Bay to the boardwalk of Santa Cruz. Be on the lookout for gray whales and dolphins. The coastline is often blanketed with fog, giving the beaches a chilly, romantic feeling.

SAN MATEO COUNTY

Web Site: www.co.sanmateo.ca.us

Area Code: 650

Sheriff: San Mateo County Sheriff's Office, 400 County Center, Redwood City, 650-365-4911

Emergency Hospitals: San Mateo Medical Center, 222 W 39th Ave, San Mateo, 650-573-2222; Sequoia Hospital, 170 Alameda de las Pulgas, Redwood City, 650-369-5811, www.sequoiahospital.org; Seton Medical Center, 1900 Sullivan Ave, Daly City, 650-992-4000, www.setonmedicalcenter.org; Stanford Medical Center, 300 Pasteur Dr, Stanford, 650-723-4000, www.stanfordhospital.org

Library: Peninsula Library System, 25 Tower Rd, San Mateo, 650-780-7018, www.plsinfo.org

Public Schools: San Mateo County Office of Education, 101 Twin Dolphin Dr, Redwood City, 650-802-5300, www.smcoe.k12.ca.us

Community Publication: *San Mateo County Times,* 650-348-4321, www.inside bayarea.com/sanmateocountytimes

Community Resources: San Mateo County Convention and Visitors Bureau, 111 Anza Blvd, Suite 410, Burlingame, 650-348-7600, www.sanmateocountycvb. com; TIES (information, advice and resources for seniors and disabled), 800-675-8437 or 650-573-3900, TTY 711

Public Transportation: *RIDES,* 511, www.511.org; *CalTrain,* 800-660-4287, TTY 415-508-6448, www.caltrain.com; *SamTrans,* 800-660-4287, TTY 650-508-6448, www.samtrans.com

Parks, Gardens, and Open Space: San Mateo County Park and Recreation Department, 455 County Center, 4th Floor, Redwood City, 650-363-4020

DALY CITY

Calling itself the "The Gateway to the Peninsula," Daly City is directly south of San Francisco, just off of Interstate 280. Immediately after the 1906 Earthquake and Fire, many San Franciscans sought refuge in the open countryside of Daly City. Today, this 7.5-square-mile city is the most populous community in the county, with over 104,000 residents.

In the Bay Area, Daly City is even more notorious for its fog than its big city neighbor to the north. It's frequently cool and gray here even when the sun is shining down on all of San Francisco. But for those who don't mind sweater weather, Daly City, which offers family-oriented living just minutes from San Francisco, may be the perfect place to call home.

Part of what gives Daly City its unique character is the fact that it is home to a large, established, and vibrant Filipino-American community. In fact, Filipino

Daly City

families who live here have nicknamed Daly City "Little Manila." Asian specialty markets are scattered throughout the city, and there is no place better in the Bay Area to grab *pancit* noodles and a tasty *lumpia* roll.

Daly City has its own BART station, located at 500 John Daly Boulevard, providing easy access to downtown San Francisco. For those driving to the station, BART provides 1,400 parking spaces; even so, these spaces fill up quickly, so arrive early or look for parking on a nearby street. San Francisco Airport is less than ten minutes away, which is a plus if you need to fly, though many locals complain about the noise. If you are commuting to Silicon Valley, it could take you anywhere from 40 minutes to 2 hours, depending on traffic.

Henry Doelger, designer of much of the bland housing that is found in parts of San Francisco's Sunset District, continued in his blah though practical style in Daly City—a one-car garage at the base that supports the common rooms, which overlook the street and are finished off with two bedrooms, one bath, and a (now) huge tree in the front yard. These "cliffs of Doelger" inspired Malvina Reynolds to write a song about Daly City homes, calling them "…the little boxes made of ticky tacky…." Indeed, though many of the homes here are painted different colors, they are very similar.

Daly City is considered one of the most affordable cities of San Mateo County. Apartments, duplexes, townhouses, condominiums, and single-family homes can be found throughout, and many of the homes on the hill have bay and ocean views.

For those who can afford it, the posh, tree-lined neighborhood of **Westlake**, bordering San Francisco, has its own shopping plaza, and is within minutes of Lake Merced. To get a feel for the neighborhood and learn all about local lore, stop in at Joe's of Westlake on the corner of John Daly Boulevard and Lake Merced Boulevard. To the west, you'll find single-family and newer luxury homes perched atop steep cliffs overlooking the pounding waves of the Pacific below. In recent years, some hillside spots have had trouble with erosion, and even landslides, so you may want to ask for a geological assessment before settling here.

In addition to the ticky tacky homes, Daly City also has one of the area's major shopping malls, the Serramonte Shopping Center. Home Depot, Nordstrom Rack, and a second Target (in case the first at Serramonte is missing that sweater you want in your size) are south on I-280 at the Metro Shopping Center in the neighboring city of Colma. Also just off the freeway, you'll find a large multiplex cinema packed every Friday and Saturday night, as well as two popular fast food pit stops—In-N-Out Burger and Krispy Kreme Doughnuts.

Locals enjoy easy access to three golf courses, including Lake Merced Country Club, which also features tennis courts. Although there is much coastline, there is little coastal access here, and so determined dog walkers have been known to frequent the path down to the city's only beach, Thornton, even though the path remains officially closed from severe storm damage due to safety concerns. You can at least enjoy looking down at the beach from the Thornton Beach Vista (west end of John Daly Boulevard, off of Skyline Boulevard /Highway 35.)

DALY CITY
Web Site: www.dalycity.org
Area Codes: 415, 650
Zip Codes: 94014, 94015
Post Office: 1100 Sullivan Ave, 800-275-8777, www.usps.com
Police Station: Daly City Police Department, 333 90th St, 650-991-8119
Emergency Hospital: Seton Hospital, 1900 Sullivan Ave, 650-992-4000, www. setonmedicalcenter.org
Library: Serramonte Main Library, 40 Wembley Dr, 650-991-8023, www. dalycitylibrary.org
Public Schools: Jefferson Elementary School District, 101 Lincoln Ave, 650-746-2400, www.jsd.k12.ca.us; Jefferson Union High School District, 699 Serramonte Blvd, #100, 650-550-7900, www.juhsd.k12.ca.us
Community Resources: Daly City-Colma Chamber of Commerce, 355 Gellert Blvd, Suite 138, 650-755-3900, www.dalycity-colmachamber.org; Doelger Senior Center, 101 Lake Merced Blvd, 650-991-8012, www.doelgercenter.com
Parks, Gardens, and Open Space: Parks and Recreation Department, 111 Lake Merced Blvd, 650-991-8015, www.ci.daly-city.ca.us/city_services/depts/park_rec/index.htm

PACIFICA

Pacifica (population 38,739), is no longer a small beach town without sidewalks. The word is out and people are moving in. Populated by middle- to upper-income families and singles who love living in fog, Pacifica (which means "peace" in Spanish) is just 15 miles south of San Francisco, and only 5 miles from the San Francisco Airport. Don't look for the town center, because it doesn't exist. What you will find instead is a string of shopping enclaves. Near the water's edge, Rockaway Beach Plaza, the Pacific Manor area, and Pedro Point, with their mix of cozy waterside cafés, seafood restaurants, pubs, antique stores, and of course surfboard shops, are alive with a quaint, quintessential beach town spirit. Others, like the Linda Mar Shopping Center east of Highway 1, have a more outdoor strip mall feel, while offering such basic necessities as a large grocery store.

People move to Pacifica for one main reason, to be close to the ocean. And you can find lovely apartments and homes, many of them overlooking the Pacific. Architecturally, the homes are mostly California ranch style, but you can also find Queen Anne Victorians and Cape Cods, a few beach shacks,

Pacifica

and a handful of new two-story luxury homes. Boxy 1970s-style two-story apartment buildings, scattered throughout the town, attract crowds of young professionals who commute via Highway 1 and Interstate 280 to San Francisco every morning. While not much to look at on the outside, many of these apartments have small balconies perfect for kicking back with a good book (and a very warm sweater) and taking in the breathtaking ocean vistas. For roughly the rent of a studio in San Francisco's Tenderloin, you can get a spacious one-bedroom with excellent views, parking, and quick and easy freeway access. Pacifica is quiet, cool, foggy, and friendly. Its traditional working-class roots have kept prices relatively affordable, but people are catching on to its charm. Pacifica offers an abundance of outdoor activities, including surfing, scuba diving, fishing, paragliding, hiking, birding, golf, tennis, and horseback riding. Surfers from all over ride the waves at Pedro Point and Rockaway Beach, and on warm days crowds cast their fishing lines off of Pacifica Pier. Most of the sandy shores here are not nearly as crowded as those in nearby Half Moon Bay; the same goes for the local parks and golf courses, except at the end of September when the city hosts thousands of visitors at the annual Pacific Coast Fog Fest. Activities include music, food, and artists' booths.

PACIFICA

Web Site: www.cityofpacifica.org
Area Code: 650
Zip Code: 94044
Post Office: 50 W Manor Dr, 800-275-8777, www.usps.com
Police Station: 2075 Coast Hwy, 650-738-7314
Libraries: Pacifica Library, 104 Hilton Way, Pacifica, 650-355-5196; Sanchez Library, 1111 Terra Nova, 650-359-3397

Public Schools: Pacifica School District, 375 Reina Del Mar, 650-738-6600, www. pacificasd.org; Jefferson Union High School District, 699 Serramonte Blvd, #100, Daly City, 650-550-7900, www.juhsd.k12.ca.us

Community Resources: Pacifica Resource Center, 1809 Palmetto Ave, 650-738-7470; Pacifica Performances, 1220A Linda Mar Blvd, 650-355-1882, www. pacificaperformances.org; Pedro Point Surf Club, http://pedropoint.typepad. com

Community Publications: *Pacifica Tribune,* 650-359-6666, www.pacificatribune. com

Beaches, Parks, Gardens, and Open Space: Parks, Beaches and Recreation Department, 1810 Francisco Blvd, 650-738-7381

HALF MOON BAY

A beachfront community about 25 miles south of San Francisco, Half Moon Bay (12,639) spans some of the most beautiful coastline in California. The smell of salt air permeates this coastal town. A little over a decade ago, the farming of flowers and specialty vegetables was one of the main occupations here. And even today you can still find excellent fresh fruits and veggies for sale at a handful of regular roadside stands. More recently the area has become a bedroom community for San Francisco and Silicon Valley, with housing prices to match.

During October, locals enjoy the annual Great Pumpkin Contest, where gourd growers from around the country bring their pumpkins and weigh-off against global competitors, hoping to enter the record books (a recent winner tipped the scales at 1229 pounds). The historic downtown area is a hodgepodge of antique shops, clothing boutiques, arts and crafts shops, tiny restaurants and cafés, and cozy bed-and-breakfasts. During the summer, the monthly flower mart is colorful and fragrant. Recreation opportunities include two golf courses,

Half Moon Bay

along with plenty of access to beaches for surfing, horseback riding, hiking, and biking. Tres Amigos, 200 Cabrillo Highway South, is a local favorite for inexpensive yet delicious Mexican food.

Nearby, you'll find a handful of smaller, semirural coastside towns including El Granada, Montara, Moss Beach, and a tiny fishing village known affectionately as Princeton-by-the-Sea. Home to Pillar Point Harbor, this little hot spot attracts surfers, sailors, and fishermen year round. Residents and visitors alike routinely venture down to the docks here to buy fresh fish and crab straight from the boats. Just off Pillar Point you'll find the world-famous Mavericks surf spot, which hosts an annual big wave contest that attracts pros from around the world. A little farther south on Highway 1 is Año Nuevo State Reserve, home to thousands of elephant seals.

Half Moon Bay is a delightful and tranquil community, which feels worlds away from the hectic pace of San Francisco or Silicon Valley. Commuting to San Francisco via Highway 1 may be delayed, especially during winter, because of mudslides around the so-called "Devil's Slide" but a new tunnel is being bored through the coastal mountain and should be completed by 2011. The old section of Highway 1 will be turned into an amazing vista trail for recreational use. Those commuting west on Route 92 marvel at the change of weather, especially in the summer, when it can be downright hot and sticky inland, but once they reach the ridge near Half Moon Bay, the fog brings instant cooling relief.

HALF MOON BAY

Web Site: www.half-moon-bay.ca.us

Area Code: 650

Zip Codes: 94018, 94019, 94038

Post Office: 500 Stone Pine Rd, 800-275-8777, www.usps.com

Police Station: 537 Kelly Ave, 650-726-8288

Library: Half Moon Bay Library, 620 Correas St, 650-726-2316, www.halfmoon baylibrary.org

Public Schools: Cabrillo Unified School District, 498 Kelly Ave, 650-712-7100, www.cabrillo.k12.ca.us

Community Resources: The Coastsider, www.coastsider.com; Coastside Children's Programs, 494 Miramontes Ave, 650-726-7413, www.coastsidechildren.org; Coastside Opportunity Center, 99 Ave Alhambra, Half Moon Bay, 650-726-9071

Community Publications: *Half Moon Bay Review*, 650-726-4424, www.hmbreview.com

Beaches, Parks, Gardens, and Open Space: Parks and Recreation Department, 535 Kelly Ave, 650-726-8297

SOUTH SAN FRANCISCO, SAN BRUNO, BRISBANE

Sometimes forgotten in the mix of suburbs extending southwards from San Francisco, **South San Francisco** ("South City") is the center of a quietly raging biotech industry. Also known as the "Industrial City," it has hundreds of companies doing research and development and, in turn, industries that support ever more esoteric industrial needs. Often resembling a sci-fi movie set, Genentech's campus sprawls over a huge portion of South City. The global company is regarded as the founder of modern bio-technology, in part because of its creation in the 1970s of a drug to combat dwarfism. South San Francisco is where your airplane actually lands when traveling to San Francisco International Airport (SFO).

South San Francisco

The neighborhoods here have the distinctly compact feel of post-WWII tract homes but many gems lie hidden amongst the gently rolling hills beneath San Bruno Mountain. Airplane noise is a given for this town and should be considered if you are sensitive to sound. In general, the western portion near Interstate 280 is more expensive than the vibrant lower southside near Highway 101.

Meanwhile next door, the city of **San Bruno** (population 41,515) has been in a home-building frenzy—adding hundreds of new condos, apartments, townhouses, and luxury homes each year. Twelve miles south of San Francisco, San Bruno, with a sleek new BART station, efforts afoot to renovate the sleepy downtown, a major mall makeover in progress, and plans to add more new housing units in the near future, is attracting crowds of young professionals. Lured by the potential to own their own condos—often a near impossibility for all but the incredibly wealthy in San Francisco—20- and 30-something singles and young families are arriving here in droves.

San Bruno the city originally took its name from San Bruno the mountain. While exploring the area in 1775, Captain Bruno Heceta spotted a large

San Bruno

mountain, which he named in honor of his patron saint, the founder of the Car-
thusian order of monks, San Bruno. In the 1820s, the land was part of a large
grant given by the Mexican government to Jose Antonio Sanchez for his military service. After the USA won the war with Mexico in 1848, Sanchez's heirs
lost their claim to the land. But their legacy lived on when in 1899 the Tanforan
Racetrack, named for Sanchez's grandson-in-law, a cowboy called Toribio Tanforan, opened. Though it burned down in 1964, the site of the old Tanforan
Racetrack still holds many fond memories—the first West Coast flight took off
from here. But the site holds many disturbing memories as well. During World
War II, the track was converted into an assembly center for Japanese Americans,
many of whom lost their homes, jobs, and businesses when they were forcibly
relocated to internment camps.

Today Tanforan is the site of a large indoor shopping center in the heart of
the city's rapidly transforming commercial/retail core. Nearby along El Camino
Real, you'll find the 24-acre outdoor shopping plaza, San Bruno Towne Center;
the new BART station; and Bayhill Drive, home to a bustling 80-acre office park
that includes the Gap's corporate headquarters.

Here too, you'll find the Crossing, a 20-acre former US Navy Administration
site that has been converted into a lively high-density, transit-oriented village.
Three hundred new apartments were recently completed here, with another 185
on the way. The site also includes 200-plus condos as well as new senior housing,
and at least 20% percent of all units are designated as affordable housing.

East San Bruno is made up of two- and three-bedroom single-family
homes from the 1950s and '60s clustered on narrow side streets off of San Bruno
Avenue, one of the city's older commercial thoroughfares, and gateway to a
twisting ribbon of freeway overpasses—Highways 101 and 380 (which heading
west connects to I-280). The area east of 101 is dominated by the airport and
businesses—long-term parking lots, rental car agencies, and hotels—that
cater to it. If you don't mind the sound of jets roaring above while you sip your

morning coffee, you can find some of the peninsula's most affordable single-family homes here.

To the west, you'll find woody, winding roads and more expensive homes, some with sweeping views of the Bay below. Skyline Boulevard (Highway 35) offers access to trails at Milagra and Sweeney Ridges, and links up with Highway 1 to carry you to nearby Pacifica's beaches in minutes. A good resource for continuing education, Skyline Community College is also here.

Downtown San Bruno, with its 1950s time warp feel, is clustered along a short stretch of San Mateo Avenue. Filled with small local eateries and retailers, and the peninsula's only casino-style card room, Artichoke Joe's, "the Avenue" has struggled to keep pace with newer shopping centers on nearby El Camino Real. But the city hasn't given up hope, and has been looking at ways to revive the languishing strip. City Park in the center of town is a local highlight, as are the light displays on the Fourth of July, when the city celebrates its designation as one of only two places on the peninsula where fireworks remain legal (the other is Pacifica).

A true natural gem, San Bruno Mountain (outside San Bruno's official city limits), is one of the largest urban open spaces in the USA, with 3,300 undeveloped acres. Home to the rare Mission Blue butterfly, the mountain is covered with hundreds of wildflowers in the spring. Curve around Guadalupe Canyon Road to the north side of the mountain and you'll find the small, tight-knit community of **Brisbane (**www.ci.brisbane.ca.us**).** With its old-fashioned downtown area, small-town vibe, and hillside homes, Brisbane is a well-kept secret—and residents want it to stay that way. But as plans inch ahead to redevelop the Baylands, an expansive former dump site alongside Highway 101, the future of the entire northern edge of San Mateo County seems destined to continue growing and changing.

SOUTH SAN FRANCISCO
Web Site: www.ssf.net
Area Codes: 415, 650
Zip Codes: 94080
Post Offices: 322 Linden Ave; 36 Chestnut Ave, 800-275-8777, www.usps.com
Police Station: SSF Police Department, 333 Arroyo Dr, Suite C, 650-877-8900
Public Schools: South San Francisco High, 400 B St, 650-877-8754; El Camino High, 1320 Mission Rd, 650-877-8806; Buri Buri Elementary, 120 El Campo Dr, 650-877-8776; Ponderosa Elementary, 295 Ponderosa Rd, 650-877-7725
Library: Main Library, 840 W Orange Ave, 650-829-3860, www.ssflibrary.net
Parks, Gardens, and Open Space: Parks and Recreation Department, 33 Arroyo Dr, 650-829-3800, www.ssf.net/depts/rcs

SAN BRUNO
Web Site: www.sanbruno.ca.gov

Police: 1177 Huntington Ave, 650-616-7100
Area Code: 650
Zip Code: 94066
Post Office: 1300 Huntington Ave, 800-275-8777, www.usps.com
Library: 701 Angus Ave West, 650-616-7078, www.ci.sanbruno.ca.us/Library
Police Station: 1177 Huntington Ave, 650-616-7100
Public Schools: San Bruno Park School District, 500 Acacia Ave, 650-624-3100, www.sbpsd.k12.ca.us; San Mateo Union High School District, 650 N Delaware St, 650-558-2299, www.smuhsd.k12.ca.us
Community Resources: Recreation Services Department, 567 El Camino Real, 650-616-7180, San Bruno Mountain Watch, 44 Visitacion Ave, Brisbane, 415-467-6631, www.mountainwatch.org; San Bruno Senior Center, 1555 Crystal Springs Rd, 650-616-7150; Skyline Community College, 3300 College Dr, 650-738-4100, www.skylinecollege.edu
Parks, Gardens, and Open Space: Parks Department, 251 City Park Way, 650-616-7180; San Bruno Mountain Park, 555 Guadalupe Canyon Pkwy

SAN MATEO, BELMONT, BURLINGAME

San Mateo, the city (94,315), has a varied population living in a variety of homes from traditional ranch styles to English Mediterranean styles, with some condominiums, modest starter homes, and huge mansions mixed in. Once the banking capital of the Peninsula, San Mateo is now a bedroom community for Silicon Valley. A mini renaissance is afoot here in the once-languishing downtown, where a wave of excellent restaurants along with a new centrally located movie theater and revamped transit center has brought new life to the area. You can browse the shops and get to know the neighbors here while sipping glasses of vino at the annual wine walk. In the heart of downtown, Central Park, with its

San Mateo

rolling grass, busy playground, rose garden, popular Japanese tea garden, and free outdoor summer concerts, draws visitors from throughout the Peninsula.

On the site of the old Bay Meadows Racetrack, the city plans to develop a massive new high-density community that would transform the town east of the railroad tracks. A recent development on the site of the old racing practice track, at the intersection of Hillsdale Boulevard and Highway 101, brought new condos, a large corporate campus for mutual fund magnate Franklin Templeton, and a new Whole Foods Market. San Mateo is feeling some growing pains as it looks to plan for the future, meet growing housing needs, and improve public transportation—yet maintain the single-family homes, greenery, and suburban charm that have been its hallmarks through the years.

Belmont

Belmont (population 25,648) has some of the highest prices in the county behind Hillsborough, Woodside, Atherton, and Burlingame. On the west side of town, most of the homes are nestled in the lush rolling hillside and it's not at all unusual to find deer trolling through your backyard in the evening. The entrance to Crystal Springs Reservoir and the San Francisco Watershed area, with winding waterside trails popular with bicyclists and joggers throughout the Peninsula, is just a few moments away off Highway 92 just west of I-280.

Belmont is primarily a residential community, with shopping largely concentrated in a few short blocks along El Camino Real, the Peninsula's main commercial thoroughfare. Residents frequently head a bit south to the cluster of upscale eateries and boutiques on Laurel Street in neighboring San Carlos. Belmont's name comes from nineteenth-century banker William Ralston, who built an 80-room mansion, which he called Belmont. Today, Ralston Avenue, named in his honor, remains the main local thoroughfare here.

Homes in **Burlingame** are a bit more upscale, with higher prices to match. For those who can afford it, this city, known for its small-town feel, elm-lined avenues, and top-notch schools, is extremely popular among young professionals planning

Burlingame

to start families. The streets here are cozy and quiet, neighborhood parks are filled with dog walkers, and the downtown sidewalks are bustling throughout the day with moms (and a few dads) pushing strollers. Filled with dozens of restaurants and upscale shops, Burlingame Avenue, the heart of this community, has a vibe similar in some ways to University Avenue in Palo Alto. Following Burlingame east across the train tracks, past the historic train station, you'll find Washington Park—a patch of green popular with stroller mommies, dog walkers, and joggers. Also in Burlingame is the Pez Museum, 214 California Drive, 650-347-2301, featuring hundreds of Pez dispensers. For those in the know, Edward Huss from Austria invented the Pez to help people quit smoking. To the north is Broadway, which, while it lives in the shadow of the more glamorous Burlingame Avenue, offers friendly, low-key local shopping and dining. In all three cities, you'll find young and old families, good schools, and tree-lined streets, a symbol of the Peninsula.

SAN MATEO
Web Site: www.cityofsanmateo.org
Area Code: 650
Zip Codes: 94401, 94402
Post Office: 1630 S Delaware St, 800-275-8777, www.usps.com
Police Station: 2000 S Delaware St, 650-522-7700
Library: San Mateo Public Library, 55 W Third Ave, 650-522-7800; Hillsdale Branch, 205 W Hillsdale Blvd, 650-522-7880; Marina Branch, 1530 Susan Ct, 650-522-7890,
Public Schools: San Mateo-Foster City School District, 51 West 41st Ave, 650-312-7777, www.smfc.k12.ca.us; San Mateo Union High School District, 650 N Delaware St, 650-558-2299, www.smuhsd.org
Community Resources: Poplar Creek Golf Course, 1700 Coyote Point Dr, 650-522-4653, www.poplarcreekgolf.com; Coyote Point Recreation Area, Coyote Point Dr, 650-573-2592; Coyote Point Museum, 1651 Coyote Point Dr, 650-342-7755, www.coyoteptmuseum.org

Parks, Gardens, and Open Space: Parks and Recreation Department, 1900 O'Farrell St, 650-522-7400, www.cityofsanmateo.org

BELMONT

Web Site: www.belmont.gov
Area Code: 650
Zip Code: 94002
Post Office: 640 Masonic Way, 800-275-8777, www.usps.com
Police Station: Belmont Police Department, One Twin Pines Ln, 650-595-7400
Library: Belmont Library, 1110 Alameda de las Pulgas, 650-591-8286
Public Schools: Belmont-Redwood Shores School District, 2960 Hallmark Dr, 650-637-4800, www.belmont.k12.ca.us; San Mateo Union High School District, 650 N Delaware St, 650-558-2299, www.smuhsd.k12.ca.us
Community Resources: 1870 Art Center, 1870 Ralston Ave, 650-595-9679, www.1870artcenter.org; Belmont Community Players, 1835 Belburn Ave, 650-599-2720, www.belmontcommunityplayers.org; Belmont Historical Society, 650-593-4213; Notre Dame de Namur University, 1500 Ralston Ave, 650-508-3500, www.ndnu.edu
Parks, Gardens, and Open Space: Parks and Recreation Department, 30 Twin Pines Ln, 650-595-7441

BURLINGAME

Web Site: www.burlingame.org
Area Code: 650
Zip Code: 94010
Post Office: 220 Park Rd, 800-275-8777, www.usps.com
Police Station: 1111 Trousdale Dr, 650-777-4100
Library: Burlingame Library, 480 Primrose Rd, 650-558-7400
Public Schools: San Mateo Union High School District, 650 N Delaware St, 650-558-2299, www.smuhsd.k12.ca.us; Burlingame School District, 1825 Trousdale Dr, 650-259-3800, www.bsd.k12.ca.us
Community Resources: Burlingame Chamber of Commerce, 650-344-1735, http://burlingamechamber.org; Burlingame Historical Society, www.burlingamehistorical.org
Parks, Gardens, and Open Space: Parks and Recreation Department, 850 Burlingame Ave, 650-558-7200

HILLSBOROUGH, ATHERTON, WOODSIDE

The Peninsula also has a handful of more upscale, exclusive, and secluded towns: Hillsborough, Atherton, Woodside, and parts of Menlo Park. If you're

Hillsborough

looking for rental property, the latter is certainly your best bet. The other three communities are heavily mansioned, with homes priced in the millions. Except for a police department and a town hall, **Hillsborough** does not have much in terms of an infrastructure and is considered to be a bedroom community. Most who live here do their shopping in Burlingame, at the upscale boutiques and chains on Burlingame Avenue.

If you dream of calling **Atherton** home, you'll need especially deep pockets. Currently home to the likes of investment mogul Charles Schwab, eBay CEO Meg Whitman, and Google pioneer Eric Schmidt, Atherton was ranked the second most expensive city in the country by a recent US Census report.

Full of lovely old estates that were once used by wealthy San Franciscans as summer residences, Atherton is a little like the West Coast's version of the Hamptons—minus the beach. Most of Atherton's homes are hard to see from the town's handful of quiet, dark residential streets, having been set back on their large lots behind thickets of foliage and large off-putting entrance gates. The

Atherton

Woodside

wealthy enclave is almost strictly residential, with no retail or commercial busi-nesses here of any kind. Residents typically stroll over to nearby Menlo Park or head a little further south to Palo Alto to meet their shopping needs. In Atherton you will also find the elite Menlo School, a prep school for grades 6–12.

Woodside, named for its wooded hillsides, has a true country feel with its steep, narrow roads, natural streams, fields of wildflowers, and towering red-woods. At its heart is a small town center that still looks a little like a trading post from California's Wild West days, complete with an old-fashioned general store. You'll frequently even see horses tied up out in front of Roberts Market, whose selection of fine delicacies belies its rugged exterior. The bulletin board out front is a kind of community clearinghouse, where you'll find everything from landscaping services, to thoroughbreds for sale, to ads looking for experienced live-in nannies. Many of Woodside's estates have substantial acreage and stables are common here, although given these homes' multimillion-dollar price tags, more CEOs than cowboys live here today. Woodside was ranked the sixth most expensive city in the country in a recent revised report by the US Census. Rich in natural beauty, the town's crowning glory is the 973-acre Huddart Park on King's Mountain Road, with its wandering wooded trails and wide open grassy meadows. A little off the beaten track, Woodside is served by sharply curving Highway 84, which connects the town with busier suburban life in Redwood City to the northeast, and with Highway 101 and I-280. Heading southwest, Highway 84 will carry you through the redwoods to the Pacific Ocean.

HILLSBOROUGH
Web Site: www.hillsborough.net
Area Code: 650
Zip Code: 94010
Post Office: 220 Park Rd, Burlingame, 800-275-8777, www.usps.com
Police Station: Police Department, 1600 Floribunda Ave, 650-375-7470

Libraries: Burlingame Library, 480 Primrose Rd, 650-558-7444; San Mateo Library, 55 W 3rd Ave, 650-522-7802

Public Schools: Hillsborough City School District, 300 El Cerrito Ave, 650-342-5193, www.hcsd.k12.ca.us; San Mateo Union High School District, 650 North Delaware St, 650-558-2299, www.smuhsd.k12.ca.us

Community Resources: *Town Newsletter*, www.hillsborough.net/depts/boards/citizens/town_newsletter.asp; also see **Burlingame** above

Parks, Gardens, and Open Space: Public Works and Parks Department, Municipal Service Center, 1320 La Honda Rd, 650-375-7444, http://www.hillsborough.net/depts/pw/parks.asp

ATHERTON

Web Site: www.ci.atherton.ca.us

Area Code: 650

Zip Code: 94027

Post Office: 3875 Bohannon Dr, Menlo Park, 800-275-8777, www.usps.com

Police Station: Atherton Police Department, 83 Ashfield Rd, 650-688-6500

Library: Atherton Public Library, 2 Dinkelspiel Station Ln, 650-328-2422

Public Schools: Menlo Park City School District, 181 Encinal Ave, Atherton, 650-321-7140, www.mpcsd.k12.ca.us; Sequoia Union High School District, 480 James Ave, Redwood City, 650-369-1411, www.seq.org

Community Resources: *The Almanac,* 650-854-2626, www.AlmanacNews.com; Holbrook-Palmer Park and Carriage House, 150 Watkins Ave, 650-752-0534

Parks, Gardens, and Open Space: Public Works, 93 Station Ln, 650-752-0535; Holbrook-Palmer Park, 150 Watkins Ave, 650-752-0534

WOODSIDE

Web Site: www.woodsidetown.org

Area Code: 650

Zip Code: 94062

Post Office: 1100 Broadway St, Redwood City, 800-275-8777, www.usps.com

Sheriff: San Mateo County Sheriff's Office, 400 County Center, Redwood City, 650-364-1811

Library: Woodside Library, 3140 Woodside Rd, Woodside, 650-851-0147, www.woodsidelibrary.org

Public Schools: Woodside Elementary School District, 3195 Woodside Rd, 650-851-1571; Sequoia Union High School District, 480 James Ave, Redwood City, 650-369-1411,www.seq.org

Community Resources: *The Almanac,* 650-854-2626, www.AlmanacNews.com; Kings Mountain Art Fair (held annually on Labor Day weekend), 650-851-2710, www.kingsmountainartfair.org; Filoli Center and Gardens, 650-364-8300, www.filoli.org; Horse Park, 650-851-2140, www.horsepark.org; The Woodside Store and history museum, 650-851-7615

Parks, Gardens, and Open Space: Huddart Park, 1100 King's Mountain Rd, 650-851-1210; Wunderlich Park, Woodside Rd, 650-851-1210

MENLO PARK

SHARON HEIGHTS

Halfway between San Francisco and San Jose, **Menlo Park**, boasting a population just over 30,000, is like old town USA where you think Kevin Arnold from "The Wonder Years" just may be cruising the street on his bicycle. A quaint, all-American city, Menlo Park's downtown Santa Cruz Avenue is lined with restaurants, coffee shops, retail stores, and ice cream shops. The quiet, tree-lined streets, public swimming pools, and tennis courts mark the 19 square miles of Menlo Park as the quintessential suburb. That's not to say nothing is going on here. Menlo Park is known for having a high number of venture capitalist companies, many of which are located along Sand Hill Road. Other noteworthy ventures include Stanford's Linear Accelerator (SLAC), which literally smashes atoms in its Menlo Park laboratory; Sun Microsystems, the largest high-tech company in the area; and the headquarters of *Sunset Magazine*.

Menlo Park received its official name in 1854 when two Irishmen, Dennis J. Oliver and D.C. McGlynn, purchased about 640 acres and built an estate, including two houses with a common entrance. On a gate, they printed the name "Menlo Park," with the date, August 1854, under it. In 1863, when the railroad came through, a railroad official looked at the gate and decided to name the station Menlo Park. The rest is history. During World War I, Menlo Park changed almost overnight from an unpopulated agricultural community into a bustling military camp housing 43,000 soldiers who trained at nearby Camp Fremont. During World War II, Menlo Park's Dibble General Hospital was built to treat thousands of soldiers injured in the South Pacific. For more about

Menlo Park

Sharon Heights

the history of Menlo Park contact the Menlo Park Historical Association and Archives, located on the lower level of the library, at 650-330-2522.

Architecturally, you'll find a range of housing options, from 1950s-style apartments to Eichler homes to ranch style homes. You can also find a number of newer apartments. The neighborhoods west of Highway 101 are more desirable. **Sharon Heights**, near the golf course, is Menlo Park's upscale neighborhood and features mountain views. With Stanford University right next door, Menlo Park is home to a number of Stanford faculty, employees, and some students. Residents also include blue- and white-collar workers, some here for generations, others recently arrived. Across San Francisquito Creek and past the stately 1,000-year-old redwood called "El Palo Alto" is the northernmost reach of Santa Clara County, and the beginning of the much-fabled Silicon Valley. Housing prices in Menlo Park are somewhat higher than you'll find in San Francisco, but here you do tend to get more house for your money. The city blocks off Santa Cruz Avenue during its annual Fine Arts Festival and its Fourth of July Parade. Both events are downright fun, attracting people from all over the area. Draeger's Supermarket, at the at 1010 University Drive, is legendary, offering only the best, from saffron to fresh brie to vine-ripe tomatoes.

Parking is easy in Menlo Park, especially since most of the homes have garages. With Interstate 280 on the west side of the city and Highway 101 near the waterfront, access to San Francisco and Silicon Valley is quick. The East Bay is accessible via the Dumbarton Bridge; CalTrain and SamTrans buses represent mass transit options.

MENLO PARK
Web Site: www.menlopark.org
Area Code: 650
Zip Code: 94025
Post Office: 3875 Bohannon Dr, 800-275-8777, www.usps.com
Police Station: 701 Laurel St, 650-330-6317
Library: 800 Alma St, 650-330-2500, www.menloparklibrary.org

Public Schools: Menlo Park City School District, 181 Encinal Ave, Atherton, 650-321-7140, www.mpcsd.k12.ca.us; Sequoia Union High School District, 480 James Ave, Redwood City, 650-369-1411, www.seq.org

Community Resources: Menlo Park Chamber of Commerce, 650-325-2818 www.menloparkchamber.com; *The Almanac*, 650-854-2626, www.Almanac News.com; Horse Park, 650-851-2140, www.horsepark.org

Parks, Gardens, and Open Space: Community Services Department, 701 Laurel St, 650-330-2200

REDWOOD CITY

Once a woody, rural, hillside community full of country cottages, open pasture, and of course redwoods, **Redwood City** is now a modern day suburbia popular with young families. The curving, tree-lined streets are filled with post–World War II Baby Boom era cozy two- and three-bedroom single-family homes with green lawns and reasonably good-sized backyards. You'll frequently find kids on bikes or skateboards cruising down the quiet residential streets here, or playing ball at one of a handful of eclectic mini parks that zigzag through the town.

Heading west into the area known as Emerald Hills, you'll find sprawling homes with spectacular views surpassing the million-dollar mark, and a few older charming country houses with stables and sizable acreage. A semi-secret swimming spot popular with kids, Emerald Lake is open in the summertime to neighborhood residents. Up in the western hills, you'll also find hiking trails and spectacular wildflowers at Edgewood Park, and Cañada College, located just off of I-280, an excellent community resource.

Downtown Redwood City is undergoing major revitalization—and the once languishing Broadway is now packed with restaurants and busy side-walk cafes. The old Fox Theatre keeps the historic vibe alive with a variety of theater and music programs, and a large new cinema complex has recently been installed. The seat of San Mateo County government is here—in a central compound that includes the courthouse, law library and county jail—and you can frequently catch D.A.'s, defense attorneys, and judges alike lunching at Bob's Courthouse Coffee Shop during the noontime hour. On the edge of the downtown area, you'll find the public library, located in a renovated historic firehouse, and Sequoia High School. Originally built as a feeder for Stanford University, this large campus with its pristine laws, shady trees, and tiled rooftops, is among the most impressive public high school campuses you'll ever see.

On the east side of town, there is a large, vibrant Latino community—and a busy commercial strip—along Middlefield Road. Homes here are a little bit cheaper, but not by much. Heading out further toward the Bay, east of Highway 101, you'll find Redwood Shores, a planned community full of newer tract homes—that has a distinct feel all its own. Similar to nearby Foster City in look and character, Red-

Redwood City

wood Shores—built on landfill—offers fantastic Bay views, lagoons, and plentiful trails. Software development powerhouse Oracle is also located here.

Redwood City's gateway proudly boasts the old-timey welcome "Climate Best By Government Test," and test or no, it's true that the weather here, as on much of the peninsula, is warm and sunny practically year-round.

REDWOOD CITY
Web Site: www.redwoodcity.org
Area Code: 650
Zip Code: 94061–5
Post Office: 855 Jefferson Ave; 1100 Broadway St; 800-275-8777, www.usps.com
Police Station: 1301 Maple St, 650-780-7100
Library: 1044 Middlefield Rd, 650-780-7018, www.rcpl.info
Public Schools: Redwood City School District, 750 Bradford St, 650-423-2200, www.rcsd.k12.ca.us; Sequoia Union High School District, 480 James Ave, Redwood City, 650-369-1412, www.seq.org
Community Resources: Redwood City San Mateo County Chamber of Commerce, 650-364-1722; www.redwoodcitychamber.com; Cañada College, 4200 Farm Hill Blvd, 650-306-3100, www.canadacollege.net
Parks, Gardens, and Open Space: Parks, Recreation, and Community Services Department, 1400 Roosevelt Ave, 650-780-7250

ADDITIONAL CITY WEB SITES—SAN MATEO COUNTY

Foster City: www.fostercity.org
Millbrae: www.ci.millbrae.ca.us
San Carlos: www.cityofsancarlos.org

NORTHERN SANTA CLARA COUNTY

A decade ago, Santa Clara County was one of the fastest growing counties in the Bay Area. Now, it's one of the fastest shrinking areas in the country. Here the feast and famine are all about one thing—jobs, job, jobs. Silicon Valley exploded with rapid growth during the 1990s high-tech boom, when it seemed just about anyone a little computer savvy could land a high-paying job, often with bonus perks and promising stock options, fresh out of college. Today, that's no longer the case. Pressures from a sagging economy, the aftermath of the dot-com crash, combined with outsourcing high-tech jobs, have made the competition for top-notch positions decidedly more fierce. Couple that with one of the most expensive housing markets in the country, and new arrivals can be in for a real challenge. Nevertheless, living here has its own rewards, and for those highly skilled programmers and engineers who can land one of the remaining premium jobs, Silicon Valley can still feel like a techie paradise.

Both Palo Alto and Mountain View are a part of Santa Clara County. They are also included as part of the amorphous Silicon Valley, a term coined by Don Hoefler, a writer for the weekly *Electronic News*. He used the name in 1971 to describe the electronic firms that were mushrooming out of Santa Clara County. However, the northern end of the county has its own distinct feel and has been able to weather the recent economic storms better than some of its southern neighbors. Palo Alto is dominated by Stanford University, while Mountain View has grown into a kind of hybrid—taking on a bit of its northern neighbor's cultural sheen, while joining the industry ranks with Sunnyvale and Santa Clara. Both cities have lovely vibrant downtown areas and the distinct advantage of being not-so-terribly-far from San Francisco as their southern counterparts.

For Santa Clara County resources, see the **South Bay** section.

PALO ALTO

OLD PALO ALTO
CRESCENT PARK
PROFESSORVILLE DISTRICT
COLLEGE TERRACE
FOREST AVENUE
BARRON PARK

While Menlo Park has street fairs, **Palo Alto** has evening balls. Indeed, Palo Alto, named after the 1,000-year-old redwood growing at the border with Menlo Park, sports a refined, cosmopolitan attitude. Located 35 miles south of San Francisco, Palo Alto is a town of cafés, bookstores, theaters, and Stanford Shopping Center, the oldest outdoor mall in the country. The city's star is the elite Stanford University, founded in 1891 by US Senator and railroad magnate

Old Palo Alto

Leland Stanford, when the local population was only 400. Living near the university offers distinct advantages, including access to an array of art exhibits, performances, cultural events, and lectures open to the public, not to mention the opportunity to enjoy walks, bike rides and picnics on the lovely, palm-lined grounds of the 8,200-acre campus.

Despite its small size relative to San Francisco and San Jose, Palo Alto boasts more than 30 parks, two community centers, seven libraries, including a children's library, an upscale shopping center, and a first-rate hospital. Along University Avenue, just a short walk from the Stanford campus, the downtown is quaint and busy, filled with cafés, bookstores, boutiques, and a wide variety of restaurants. For more of a hometown atmosphere, locals shop and dine on California Avenue. Three of the parks in Palo Alto are particularly magnificent due the natural settings and preserves within them: Arastradero Preserve, Foothills Park, and Palo Alto Baylands Nature Preserve. Today, over 62,000 folks from every corner of the globe call Palo Alto home. Thousands more commute into Palo Alto, often bringing the morning rush hour to a standstill.

In 1939, Hewlett-Packard began in a one-car garage located at 367 Addison Avenue. This garage is now a historical landmark with a plaque describing it as "the birthplace of

College Terrace

Silicon Valley." With its headquarters still in Palo Alto, today Hewlett-Packard has more than 321,000 employees in 178 countries. The 650-acre Stanford Research Park has 150 high-tech and biotech companies, including XeroxParc where GUI (Graphical User Interface), the computer mouse, and *Pong* were developed. Though the high-tech industry has struggled to get back on its feet in recent years, Palo Alto, driven by the economic engine of Stanford University, a growing crop of medical and biotech research companies, and high-tech stalwarts like HP that survived the crash, seems to have fared far better and bounced back faster than the all-tech, all-the-time cities a bit further south in Santa Clara County.

Palo Alto has more than 15 different neighborhoods, each with its own charm. Oregon Expressway divides the city, and generally speaking, the neighborhoods north of the Oregon Expressway are more established, while those south of the Expressway exemplify the expansion that took place in the late 1990s to accommodate Silicon Valley. On the north side, you'll find **Old Palo Alto** and **Crescent Park**, with their magnificent mansions, including one owned by Steve Jobs, co-founder of Apple Computer. Also on the north side is **Professorville District**, so named because it is home to many Stanford faculty members, with its wood-shingled homes (some designed by Julia Morgan and Bernard Maybeck). Another established neighborhood is **College Terrace**, nestled between Stanford University and Stanford Research Park, which is home to a mix of students, engineers, musicians, and retired people.

Slightly north of Professorville is the **Forest Avenue** neighborhood, which has newer apartments and many condominiums. This neighborhood attracts a younger crowd, many of whom frequent the nearby Whole Foods and St. Michael's Alley, a club where Joan Baez used to sing. South of Oregon Expressway, where the apricot orchards used to grow, is the largest community of Eichler homes, built from 1949 to 1970. Joseph Eichler crafted these homes, which are known for their open design (minimal interior walls in their living

Forest Avenue

Barron Park

space), shallow pitched roofs, and glass walls. Another interesting neighborhood is **Barron Park**, just west of El Camino and south of Stanford. This area has a rural feel as there are no sidewalks, plenty of grand trees, and mailboxes detached from the homes.

Finding housing in the late summer months is difficult, as you will be competing with Stanford students. Prospective homebuyers are looking cautiously at East Palo Alto, an area that has suffered higher crime rates and poverty since the early 1960s, but that seems to be turning around. A large shopping plaza near Highway 101, just off of University Avenue, includes IKEA and Home Depot. New homes are going in, and with prices significantly more moderate than those in Palo Alto, they've been selling fast.

PALO ALTO

Web Site: www.pafd.org, www.paloaltoonline.com

Area Code: 650

Zip Codes: 94301–94304, 94306, Stanford University 94309

Post Office: 380 Hamilton Ave, 800-275-8777, www.usps.com

Police Station: 275 Forrest Ave, 650-329-2413

Public Schools: Palo Alto Unified School District, 25 Churchill Ave, 650-329-3700, www.pausd.org

Libraries: Palo Alto Children's Library, 1276 Harriet St, 650-329-2436; Main Library, 1213 Newell Rd, 650-329-2436

Community Resources: Junior Museum and Zoo, 1451 Middlefield Rd, 650-329-2111; Lucie Stern Community Center, 1305 Middlefield Rd, 650-463-4900; Cubberley Community Center, 4000 Middlefield Rd, 650-329-2418; Stanford University, 650-723-2300, www.stanford.edu

Parks, Gardens, and Open Space: Parks Division, 3201 E Bayshore Rd, 650-496-6962

MOUNTAIN VIEW

Located 40 miles south of San Francisco and only 8 miles north of San Jose, Mountain View (72,000) is considered the heart of Silicon Valley. For a town that originated as a stagecoach stop in 1850, a lot has happened to this 7-square-mile city. Today it is the fourth most populated city in Silicon Valley (following San Jose, Sunnyvale, and Santa Clara, respectively), and is home to a number of high-tech companies, including AOL-Netscape Communications, Silicon Graphics, Sun Microsystems, Synopsys, and Intuit. Intel started in Mountain View before it moved to Santa Clara, and NASA's Ames Research Center is also based in Mountain View.

The population and job market exploded here during the dot-com heyday, then quickly shrank when the economy turned sour. Following the dramatic shakeup, Mountain View, like all of Silicon Valley, has been struggling to get back on even footing. Recent local economic boons include the startling success of search engine powerhouse Google, which employs more than 20,000 people, and is headquartered here.

Mountain View is predominantly home to young professionals. According to the city, more than half of the population is between 20 and 44. Locals boast that their town is well organized and clean, and the city sponsors a number of festivals, including the September Art and Wine Festival. In addition, locals also enjoy a weekly farmers market, held every Sunday on Hope Street, between Villa and Evelyn, and easy access to the popular Shoreline Park. This 660-acre park includes a golf course, bicycling and jogging trails, and a manmade lake, which is often jumping with sailors, windsurfers, paddle-boaters and shore-side picnickers. The outdoor Shoreline Amphitheatre hosts popular musicians and festivals, including Coldplay, John Mellencamp, and Ozzfest; past headliners have included Santana, Madonna, and Pearl Jam. Downtown, Castro Street,

Mountain View

with its restaurants, bars, and shops, is the pulsing center of activity during both the day and night.

Many single, high-tech professionals, young families, and students call Mountain View home. Apartments predominate the housing mix; in fact, Mountain View has more apartments than single-family homes. Homes that are here include Craftsman-style bungalows and some Eichler homes. During the high-tech boom, a number of small, single-family unit condominiums and townhouses were added to the housing pool. And the building continues today, especially in the downtown area. Neighborhoods are changing all over the city, especially around Castro Street, with the development of both residential and commercial sites. Special incentives have been given—in the form of additional floor space and higher densities—to projects located near the transit center. Recent additions to the downtown area include Park Place South Apartments, at 851 Church Street, a four-story high-density, mixed-use retail, office, and housing complex; the 44-condo Bryant Place on Bryant; and 211 apartments at Avalon Bay.

Nearby, the Mountain View Center for the Performing Arts, 500 Castro Street, 650-903-6000, is located in a newly rebuilt downtown area centered around Castro and Church streets. The former center for anti-submarine warfare on the Pacific coast, Moffett Field Naval Air Station, now decommissioned, is in Mountain View, with a large hangar for dirigibles still in existence. Some of the complex continues to be used by NASA and federal agencies. When the President flies in, he usually lands at Moffett Airfield. The city is exploring various alternatives for Moffett's future, including looking at one plan to convert 500 acres of the old airfield into a large mixed-use development for research and development companies and residential housing. Lockheed was once the major employer in the area, but after its troubles in the 1970s, high-tech firms, support industries, and more recently biotech in Mountain View, Sunnyvale, San Jose, Palo Alto, and environs are now the major employers.

MOUNTAIN VIEW
Web Site: www.ci.mtnview.ca.us
Area Code: 650
Zip Codes: 94040, 94041, 94043, 94035, 95002
Post Office: 1768 Miramonte Ave, 800-275-8777, www.usps.com
Police Station: 1000 Villa St, 650-903-6395
Library: 585 Franklin St, 650-903-6337
Public Schools: Mountain View-Whisman School District, 750-A San Pierre Way, 650-526-3500, www.mvwsd.k12.ca.us; Mountain View-Los Altos Union High School District, 1299 Bryant Ave, 650-940-4669, www.mvla.k12.ca.us
Community Resources: Mountain View Center for the Performing Arts, 500 Castro St, 650-903-6000, Mountain View Community Center, 201 S Rengstorff

Ave, 650-903-6407; Shoreline Amphitheatre, One Amphitheatre Pkwy, 650-967-3000, www.shorelineamp.com

Parks, Gardens, and Open Space: Community Services Department, Recreation Division, 201 S Rengstorff Ave, 650-903-6326

LOS ALTOS

LOS ALTOS HILLS

Set in the gentle green hills just west of Mountain View, you'll find the tranquil, upscale enclave of **Los Altos**. A well-to-do bedroom community of Silicon Valley, Los Altos is home to a number of programmers, software developers, and CEOs—many of whom cashed in their chips during the height of the dot-com frenzy. With its quiet streets and family-friendly attitude, Los Altos is a community that prides itself on its cozy village feel. Boutiques and locally owned shops line the well-manicured Main Street—which looks like a picture postcard of small town America. Here, you're likely to get to know your corner grocer, bookstore owner, and neighborhood police officer by name.

To the west, the pristine hills offer a stunning backdrop, plentiful open space, and fantastic views. And homes here have the high price tags to match. Nowhere is this truer than in the adjoining community of **Los Altos Hills**, the city's wealthier, secluded and decidedly more elite twin. Here, you'll find multi-million-dollar homes and estates hidden amid large trees, sharply twisting and ascending roads, and long, private drives. Incorporated in the 1950s to preserve the charms of rural life, homes in Los Altos Hills have a mandated minimum lot size of one acre—and several surpass that margin many times over. Mixed in with the mansions, you'll find a few stables and even a handful of family farms. A bicyclist's, walker's, and horseback rider's heaven, Los Altos Hills has 63 miles of roadside and off-road trails known as the pathway system. Open space is

Los Altos

Los Altos Hills

vast and outdoor gems abound, including the 75-plus acre Byrne Preserve, and the expansive 165-acre Rancho San Antonio Preserve. The town also owns a public horseback riding arena, the Town Riding Ring, operated jointly with the Los Altos Hills Horsemen's Association, that is free and open to all.

For activities, Hillview Community Center, near the heart of downtown Los Altos, has a variety of recreation and cultural programs, While Foothill College, spread out across a large, picturesque hillside campus in Los Altos Hills, offers not only a variety of classes, but first-rate theater performances, and a renowned radio broadcasting program, KFJC 89.7 FM. Because these neighboring communities are all about small town atmosphere and rural, upscale living, respectively, Los Altos and Los Altos Hills are short on large-scale shopping centers, big-chain grocery stores, megaplex theaters, and the like. Residents frequently head downhill to Mountain View for bulk shopping sprees and evening entertainment.

LOS ALTOS

Web Site: www.ci.los-altos.ca.us, www.losaltoshills.ca.gov

Area Code: 650

Zip Codes: 94022–94024

Post Office: 100 1st St, 800-275-8777, www.usps.com

Police Station: 1 N San Antonio Rd, 650-947-2770

Library: 13 S San Antonio Rd, 650-948-7683, www.www-lib.co.santa-clara.ca.us/losaltos

Public Schools: Los Altos School District, 650-947-1150, www.losaltos.k12.ca.us

Community Resources: Los Altos Chamber of Commerce, 321 University Ave, 650-948-1455, www.losaltoschamber.org; Los Altos Village Association, www.downtownlosaltos.org; Town Riding Ring, www.lahha.org; Foothill College, www.foothill.fhda.edu; *The Los Altos Town Crier*, www.losaltosonline.com

Parks, Gardens, and Open Space: Los Altos Recreation Department, 97 Hillview Ave, 650-947-2790, www.ci.los-altos.ca.us/recreation; Los Altos Hills Recreation Department, 26379 Fremont Rd, 650-941-7222, www.losaltoshills.ca.gov/parks-committee

SOUTH BAY (SOUTHERN SANTA CLARA COUNTY)

The heart of Silicon Valley, Santa Clara County is located on the southern tip of San Francisco Bay and extends south all the way to Gilroy (and sometimes beyond, depending on who you ask). With over 1.8 million people, the county is the center of the high-tech world, from the Internet and computing to software, communications devices, and the newest addition—due to energy and consumption concerns—clean tech (or clean technology). It is home to more than 6,000 high-tech companies including Cisco Systems, Hewlett-Packard, Apple Computer, Intel, Sun Microsystems, and many more.

Providing nearly a quarter of the jobs in the Bay Area, Santa Clara County continues to be one of the main economic engines of the area and is closely linked to the success—or failure—of Silicon Valley. Recent financial turmoil has hit the area hard, with housing prices dropping precipitously as credit markets and other pressures force a resizing of the average citizen's spending power. In the midst of this uncertainty, however, venture capital investments are funding inventors across a spectrum of fields.

Clean technology is clearly the current darling of venture-capital investment, with the region pulling down 21% of all nationwide investment—and 62% of statewide investment—in this emerging field of industry. Engineers and investors are working in earnest to create the next big thing in clean energy, from finding new ways to make solar panels to experimenting with local government energy grids. For the entrepreneurial and technological types, Santa Clara County is certainly a great place to build a career. For those that support this industry, money is infused like a saline drip from the cultural centers of power, and provides also for a rich resource of jobs in the service sector.

Housing is still quite expensive relative to the rest of the country and can top $500,000 for a middle-class house within a reasonable commute, and it goes up from there. According to a recent study by the county, only 15% of residents can actually afford a median-priced home. It thus follows that the area has a robust rental market, with everything from plush mansions to the lonely studio apartment available for those choosing to live in the area. As always in the Bay Area, craigslist.com is your ultimate resource for rental listings.

Weather-wise, you'll find Santa Clara County to be more Los Angeles than San Francisco, especially in the summertime. Away from the cooling effects of Pacific fog, the sky here is blue and the air warm at least 300 days a year. Tank tops, shorts, and flip-flops are the normal everyday wear here for about half of the year, and the area is famous locally for its hot summer nights. The Mediterranean-like climate is ideal for agriculture, which was capitalized upon by early settlers, beginning with the Ohlone Indians. The Spanish settlers came to Santa Clara County in 1777 and established El Pueblo de San Jose de Guadalupe, now known as San Jose. This community raised crops and cattle for the Spanish presidios (army bases) located in San Francisco and Monterey. In 1821, after Mexico declared its independence from Spain, San Jose became a Mexican town. Seven years later, with the signing of the Treaty of Guadalupe Hidalgo, all of California joined the United States. In 1849, during the height of the Gold Rush, San Jose was declared the first state capital. In 1851 the state capital was moved to Vallejo and then eventually to Sacramento. Through the late 1800s and into much of the 1900s, agriculture was the primary industry in the area.

It was not until the latter half of the 20th century that folks started moving to the area in earnest. With high-tech inventors like David Packard, William Hewlett, and the Varian brothers (inventors of an electron tube that helped facilitate radar and microwave technology), electronic and biotech industries began to move into areas previously occupied by farmland and orchards. According to state estimates, the city of San Jose grew from 95,000 in 1950 to over 909,000 by 1999—almost a ten-fold increase—with a population today of just over 1 million.

SANTA CLARA COUNTY

Web Site: www.sccgov.org

Area Code: 408

Zip Codes: 95109–13, 95116, 95119, 95125, 95126, 95128, 95129, 95133, 95134, 95136, 95141, 95148, 95150– 95192, and more

Sheriff: Office of the Sheriff, 55 W Younger Ave, San Jose, 800-211-2220 or 408-808-4900

Emergency Hospitals: Santa Clara Valley Medical Center, 751 S Bascom, San Jose, 408-885-5000; San Jose Regional Medical Center, 225 N Jackson Ave, San Jose, 408-259-5000; O'Conner Hospital, 2105 Forest Ave, San Jose, 408-947-2500; Good Samaritan Hospital, 2425 Samaritan Dr, San Jose, 408-559-2011; Kaiser Santa Teresa, 250 Hospital Pkwy, San Jose, 408-972-7000; Kaiser Santa Clara, 710 Lawrence Expy, Santa Clara, 408-851-1000; Community Hospital of Los Gatos, 815 Pollard Rd, Los Gatos, 408-378-6131; Saint Louise Regional Hospital, 9400 No Name Uno, Gilroy, 408-848-2000; Stanford Hospital, 300 Pasteur Dr, Stanford, 650-723-4000; El Camino Hospital, 2500 Grant Road, Mountain View, 650-940-7000

Library: Santa Clara County Library, 14600 Winchester Blvd, Los Gatos, 408-293-2326 ext 3001or 800-286-1991, www.santaclaracountylib.org (The library system includes libraries in the following cities: Campbell, Cupertino, Milpitas, Saratoga, Gilroy, Los Altos, and Morgan Hill.)

Public Schools: Santa Clara County Office of Education, 1290 Ridder Park Dr, San Jose, 408-453-6500, www.sccoe.k12.ca.us

Community Publications: *San Jose Mercury News*, 888-688-6400, www.mercurynews.com; *San Jose Post Record*, 408-287-4866; Metro, 408-298-8000, www.metroactive.com; *Silicon Valley-San Jose Business Journal*, 408-295-3800, http://sanjose.bizjournals.com/sanjose

Community Resources: Symphony Silicon Valley, 467 S First St, 408-286-2600, www.symphonysiliconvalley.org; Opera San Jose, 345 S First St, 408-437-4450, www.operasj.org; Ballet San Jose-Silicon Valley, 40 N First St, 408-288-2820; Lick Observatory, 19 miles east of San Jose on Highway 130 on top of Mount Hamilton, 408-274-5061, www.ucolick.org; Fujitsu Planetarium, 21250 Stevens Creek Blvd, DeAnza Community College Campus, Cupertino, 408-864-8814, www.planetarium.deanza.edu; Tech Museum of Innovation, 201 S Market St, 408-294-8324, www.thetech.org; American Musical Theater of San Jose, 1717 Technology Dr, 408-453-7108

Public Transportation: *Santa Clara Valley Transportation Authority (SCVTA)*, 408-321-2300, www.vta.org; *Traffic and Transit Assistance*, 511, www.511.org; *CalTrain*, 800-660-4287, www.caltrain.com

SAN JOSE

DOWNTOWN SAN JOSE
ALUM ROCK
JAPANTOWN
NAGLEE PARK
ROSE GARDEN
BURBANK/BUENA VISTA
FRUITDALE
WILLOW GLEN
EVERGREEN
EDENVALE/GREAT OAKS
SANTA TERESA
ALMADEN VALLEY

Though San Francisco gets all the attention, San Jose is actually larger in both population and physical size. With about 1 million residents, San Jose is the third largest city in California, behind Los Angeles and San Diego, and the tenth largest city in the United States. The area can be quite daunting for a new import because of its sprawling size, so learning the local freeways and main residential thoroughfares is an important step while orienting oneself to the new environment. Each of the neighborhoods has its own distinct character, but almost all of them have a less-cramped feel than most areas in the region. Traffic in this southern part of the Bay Area is quite horrendous during peak commute hours, and all roads should be avoided if at all possible during these times. San Jose International Airport (SJC) is only three miles from downtown and can be a viable option for traveling to and from the Bay Area if driving to San Francisco International (SFO) is too much of a hassle.

In the past two decades, the self-proclaimed capital of Silicon Valley has undergone a major makeover—especially in the city center. Streets and storefronts once sat neglected and empty, and local nightlife was virtually non-existent. On weekends, residents regularly hopped in their cars and headed north to San Francisco in search of entertainment and culture. Today, light rail cars glide gracefully along the streets, and the tree-lined thoroughfares of Market and First streets are packed with trendy restaurants, bars, and cafés. There is a state-of-the-art cultural arts complex—home to a performing arts center, civic auditorium, and convention center—and a handful of theaters have sprung up around its edges. Indeed, the increasingly popular southern edge of downtown has earned its own nickname, "SoFA" (South [of] First Area). The Art Walk among the many eclectic galleries makes the first Friday of each month particularly appealing. With the vibrant downtown at its heart, a thriving arts district, and an ever-growing population, San Jose is defying its reputation as a sprawling suburb and becoming a world-class city in its own right.

Downtown San Jose

Architecturally, housing runs the gamut from studio apartments to small 1950s and '60s bungalows to multimillion-dollar gated estates. Most of the housing stock is fairly new, built since 1960 to meet population demands; however, you can also find neighborhoods with historic Victorians or old ranch homes built at the turn of the century. As a general rule, the farther you get from downtown, the more suburban the neighborhood's character becomes—with larger yards, quieter streets, and mammoth outdoor strip malls.

Due to its vast size, there are dozens of neighborhoods in San Jose, some officially recognized as such by city leaders, others existing only in the hearts and minds of those residing there. Among the best-known neighborhoods are the Downtown Museum district, Rose Garden neighborhood, Naglee Park, Willow Glen, Evergreen, Santa Teresa, Almaden Valley, Japantown, Burbank, Buena Vista, Edenvale, and Great Oaks.

Today, life in San Jose, especially for the young professional set, is all about one thing—**Downtown**. Just 15 years ago many would say the city was suffering from an identity crisis. But today, the city's place as a leader in technology is clear. Since the 1980s, billions of dollars have been pumped into the downtown area, creating museums, convention centers, theaters, a light rail system, fountains, offices, restaurants, and shopping areas. For many South Bay residents, downtown San Jose is the place to be. While you'll still find older homes ranging from bungalows to mansions clustered in a handful of neighborhoods at its edges, the recent emphasis here has been on building new, ultramodern high-rise condos, apartments, and townhomes. Especially attractive to young professionals looking to be in the thick of it, Downtown housing is expected to be in continued demand.

The Plaza de Cesar Chavez, named for the legendary migrant labor leader and beloved local hero who led a series of massive, successful strikes against the grape-growing industry, is smack in the center of the museums and just across from the renovated Fairmont Hotel. The plaza has an incredible fountain with nozzles spraying water right out of the sidewalk that make it a perfect place to cool off on a hot summer day. The $140 million, 17,000-seat HP Pavilion (formerly known as the San Jose Arena), called The Tank by locals, is also here. Not only is the Arena home to the San Jose Sharks Hockey team, but it also hosts big name entertainers from around the world. The Sharks, a source of San Jose pride, continually have fans pack the pews at the venue.

A highlight of the Downtown revitalization project is the Tech Museum of Innovation, 201 South Market Street, 408-294-8324, one of the Bay Area's premier science museums. Opened in the early 1990s, the Tech quickly outgrew its original quarters, and in 1998 its new 132,000-square-foot, mango-colored facility opened at the corner of Market Street and Park Avenue. The museum boasts nearly 300 hands-on exhibits that allow visitors to do such things as design their own bicycle and ride a roller coaster. You can also get a 3-D map of your head made by a rotating laser scanner, and catch a film at the state-of-the-art IMAX Dome Theater.

On the first Friday of every month the Downtown art galleries stay open late, fostering a cultural nightlife. On Thursday evenings in the summer you can enjoy live concerts in the Plaza de Cesar Chavez. And on Friday afternoons, locals frequent the farmers market (May 1st–Dec. 12th) on San Pedro Street between Santa Clara and St. John streets.

In the heart of Downtown, from Highway 880 at the north to Highway 280 at the south, you'll find Guadalupe River Park, a three-mile ribbon of park land with many options for entertaining the family, such as the Children's Discovery Museum, a carousel, and the rapidly expanding Guadalupe Gardens along the banks of the Guadalupe River. A little farther west you'll find Overfelt Botanical and Chinese Cultural Gardens, 2145 McKee Rd, 408-251-3323, a perfect place to take an afternoon stroll through the gardens.

A popular local landmark on the west side of San Jose is the Winchester Mystery House, 525 South Winchester Boulevard, 408-247-2101, www.winchestermysteryhouse.com, where you can wander through a dizzying maze of seemingly endless hallways, trapdoors, and staircases that lead to nowhere. Designed by the eccentric heiress to the Winchester rifle fortune to ward off the spirits of those killed with rifles, the house was continually added on to until the day Sarah Winchester died. In addition to regular tours of the house and gardens, flashlight tours are given in the evenings every Friday the 13th and annually on Halloween.

Near the Winchester Mystery House, you'll find Santana Row, which directly competes with Downtown. An upscale shopping, living, and dining district, Santana Row boasts some of Bay Area's finest restaurants and designer boutiques as well as a mix of luxurious rental townhomes and flats. Hobnobbing, window shopping, and lunching here have become so popular that the area now draws people from across the Bay Area, especially on weekends.

Alum Rock

The building boom has radiated out beyond the immediate Downtown area to nearby neighborhood business districts. Thousands of apartments and condos have gone up in the areas along Alum Rock Avenue, The Alameda, West San Carlos Street, and Japantown. Nestled within Alum Rock Canyon, in the foothills of the Diablo Mountain range, is Alum Rock Park, 16240 Alum Rock Avenue. San Jose's oldest and largest park, at 720 acres, Alum Rock Park is home to the Youth Science Institute, which houses a variety of live animals and provides summer camps for kids from preschool to high school. The Mexican Heritage Plaza and Cultural Center—containing many attractions—is located in **Alum Rock**, as is the last vestige of Little Portugal.

Over 100 years old, **Japantown** bills itself as one of the last remaining authentic Japantowns in the USA. Located close to Downtown, between 1st and 7th streets and Jackson and Taylor streets, Japantown is home to single-story single-family homes as well as a handful of new condo projects. Clustered along Jackson Street between 4th and 6th streets you can find family-owned Japanese restaurants as well as handmade sweet shops. Try some homemade tofu at the San Jose Tofu Company, 175 Jackson Street. The San Jose Buddhist Church Betsuin, 640 North 5th Street, a historic temple, is frequently crowded. To learn more about the rich Japanese history in San Jose, stop by the recently expanded Japanese American Museum of San Jose, on 535 North 5th Street near Jackson. Every Sunday morning—rain or shine—locals stop by the Japantown Farmers Market on Jackson Street between 6th and 7th streets to pick up fresh vegetables, sweet treats, and fresh flowers.

The oldest neighborhood in San Jose, **Naglee Park**, is in the central core of the city just east of San Jose State University. It's bordered by Highway 280 to the south, Coyote Creek to the east, 10th Street to the west, and Santa Clara Street to the north. The neighborhood is named after General Henry Naglee, who owned a 140-acre estate and lived on 14th and East San Fernando streets. In addition to General Naglee's still-standing house, there are classic Victorian

Naglee Park

and Craftsman-style homes, and stately mansions dating from the early 1900s, some of which have been divided into apartments and duplexes. You'll also find a number of newer apartment complexes dating from the 1970s and '80s. Naglee Park locals enjoy the playground at William Street Park as well as the annual Bark in the Park Festival for dogs, hosted here each September. Then there's the Fourth of July parade, BBQs, and a playgroup for moms and tots each morning. The area has had a drastic facelift with a new City Hall, elementary school, and symphony. Newcomers looking at housing along Coyote Creek should be aware that the creek sometimes overflows in the winter months.

The **Rose Garden** neighborhood is centrally located in San Jose, west of Downtown, and bordered by the Alameda Roadway on the east, Interstate 880 on the northwest, and Naglee Avenue on the north. The area is named for the city's magnificent public rose garden located at Dana and Naglee avenues—a lovely place for an early morning stroll. Also in the neighborhood is the Rosicrucian Egyptian Museum and Planetarium, 1664 Park Avenue. With the pyramids and sphinxes, you

Rose Garden

feel like you just might be in Egypt. Housing choices in the Rose Garden neighborhood include exquisite Queen Anne Victorians, some Tudor-style homes, contemporary apartments, and many new condominiums. With San Jose State University located nearby, you'll find a lot of students here, as well as plenty of professionals and their families. Those interested in architectural preservation may want to get involved in the Rose Garden Neighborhood Preservation Association, www.rgnpa.org. The only drawback is this neighborhood's proximity to the airport and CalTrain tracks, which may present a noise problem for some.

Coming off of the freeway, you can easily miss **Burbank**, even though its main drag, West San Carlos Street, is the gateway to Downtown. The neighborhood, bounded roughly by 2nd Street, I-280, McLaughlin Avenue, and Phelan Avenue, is made up of single-family homes, apartments, and new condo developments. Within walking distance of Downtown, this neighborhood has the advantage of being a bit quieter in the evenings. West San Carlos Street, a kind of mini antique alley, is a popular shopping spot to hunt for eclectic home furnishings and vintage gems. Once a year, the community comes together for the Burbank Neighborhood Jamboree, which dates back to 1948 and hosts a variety of events including an antiques show, hot rod collections, and plenty of inflatable bounce-houses and games for the kids. Nearby, the **Buena Vista** neighborhood has a unique collection of historic bungalows with handcrafted features built between 1906 and 1930.

The **Fruitdale** area, just south of Buena Vista, is named for the fruit orchards, especially plum trees, that used to grow here. Today, middle-class homes, shopping malls, and apartments have replaced the orchards. San Jose City College, 2100 Moorpark Avenue, is also located here.

Another family-preferred area is the **Willow Glen** neighborhood, just 3 miles southwest of downtown San Jose, and easily accessible via the light rail system. Named after the willow trees that grow along the creeks and Guadalupe River, the neighborhood is composed of what used to be the town of

Burbank

Fruitdale

Willow Glen. Founded in 1927, it was annexed by San Jose just 9 years later (this is an oft-repeated story of San Jose's growth). Newcomers to Willow Glen who want to get involved in the community might consider joining the active Willow Glen Neighborhood Association, www.wgna.net, "a grassroots community organization dedicated to improving life in Willow Glen." Among other neighborhood improvement projects, this organization looks for ways to preserve the history of this area. The newly opened Los Gatos Creek trail—paved in asphalt for bicycles and strollers—is a great place for a stroll. Architecturally, you'll see the usual Victorians mixed in with Eichlers, Tudors, some ranch-style homes, and Mediterranean-style stuccos. In recent years, a number of older houses have been torn down and replaced with larger abodes, but residents have worked hard to ensure that the neighborhood maintains its old-fashioned character and charm. Walking along the quiet sidewalks here you'll find lovely lawns and well-tended gardens filled with fragrant, colorful flowers.

Young families find this neighborhood attractive because it is safe, comfortable, and more affordable than nearby Los Gatos and Saratoga. Many residents have lived here for a long time, and it seems few have plans to leave any time soon. During the winter holidays many of the houses here are adorned

Willow Glen

with twinkling lights, reindeer, and elaborate manger scenes, drawing people from all over the Bay Area for a neighborhood tour. Willow Glen's commercial area, along Lincoln Avenue, is quaint, with restaurants, coffee shops, boutiques, and antique shops. No chain stores here, as locals fight hard to keep this area a one-of-a-kind place. The neighborhood plays host to a popular farmers market every Saturday at the Garden Theater building, 1165 Lincoln Avenue.

Southeast of downtown San Jose, on the eastern side of Highway 101, is **Evergreen**, a recently developed area of the South Bay. Housing here is relatively new, much of it built beginning about 25 years ago. It's made up largely of modern apartments and large homes with three, four, and even five bedrooms. Set against the arid hills, Evergreen Community College, 3095 Yerba Buena Road, is a wonderful local resource, offering a variety of classes and a home for the local Police Academy. Students and neighbors alike enjoy the shady, tranquil green and picturesque pond on the edge of campus—a perfect spot to relax, eat lunch, and feed the ducks. Just south of the campus is the golf course, Silver Creek Valley Country Club, 5460 Country Club Parkway, and a gated community with about 1,500 Mediterranean-style homes. Evergreen feels a world away from the bustle of downtown San Jose, and residents here seem to like it that way. Newer corner malls take care of all the basics in terms of shopping, coffee, and banking needs, and the main thoroughfare, Yerba Buena Road, links the neighborhood with nearby Highway 101.

The Edenvale, Great Oaks and Santa Teresa neighborhoods are located near the end of the light rail system. In the southeast corner of the city, just north of the Blossom Hill overpass, you'll find the adjoining neighborhoods of **Edenvale** and **Great Oaks**. Built on the site of an old racetrack, many of the streets in Edenvale and Great Oaks are named after famous racehorses. Great Oaks Park forms the boundary between the two communities. Homes here tend to be ranch-style, single-family abodes and are among the more affordable in the city. Resources here are a little lacking, but there is a local shopping center and a new skate park. Both neighborhoods are part of an ongoing revitalization effort—dubbed Strong Neighborhoods Initiative by the city—to improve resources, make

Evergreen

Edenvale

neighborhoods cleaner and safer, and better connect them to one another. Information about the Initiative can be found at www.strongneighborhoods.org. To enjoy the great outdoors, head just north of Edenvale to Coyote Hellyer County Park, located along Coyote Creek and Coyote Road.

Bordered by Blossom Hill Road on the north, Santa Teresa Boulevard on the west, and Monterey Road on the east, is **Santa Teresa**. Most homes here were built in the 1960s, though new developments have been added. A lovely expanse of greenspace is located nearby at the 1,688-acre Santa Teresa County Park, along Santa Teresa's southern border. For a view of the sprawling city and surrounding mountains, climb Coyote Peak. The practical single-family tracts in these southeastern neighborhoods provide much of the housing for employees of the Almaden Research Center—a sprawling IBM Research facility that sits on a nearly 700-acre campus in the nearby valley.

Home to one of the most gorgeous landscapes in America, according to the Greenbelt Alliance, **Almaden Valley** feels like an upscale, rural suburb of San Jose.

Santa Teresa

Named for the quicksilver mines and also known as Silver Creek Valley, this large area at the southernmost edge of San Jose is roughly bordered by Almaden Expressway to the north, the Santa Teresa foothills to the east, Guadalupe Road to the west, and the city limits to the south. There is a mixture of housing here— some old, some built in the 1960s. In recent years, the area has exploded with new, multimillion-dollar mansions. Many San Jose old-timers are in shock that this neighborhood has become so high priced. Almaden Lake Park, located at the intersection of Almaden Expressway and Coleman Avenue, has a sandy beach and swim area, which comes in handy during hot summer days. Also on the lake are kayaks, paddle

Almaden Valley

boats, and windsurfers. Sitting atop Los Capitancillos Ridge, the 4,000-plus acre Quicksilver County Park is home to vast open meadows, gorgeous wildflowers, and 33 miles of hiking trails. The Almaden Expressway connects residents to state routes 85 and 87. To reduce congestion, plans are under way to widen this roadway. For more information on the neighborhood, check out the Almaden Valley Community Association, www.avca-sj.org. For a bit of history, head beyond the city limits and about 11 miles south you'll find the remnants of an historic mining town. Known as New Almaden, this little village, home to the Almaden Quicksilver Mining Museum—slated for reopening in 2010—is like a living time capsule.

SAN JOSE
Web Site: www.sanjoseca.gov
Area Codes: 408
Zip Codes: 95109–13, 95116, 95119, 95125, 95126, 95128, 95129, 95133, 95134, 95136, 95141, 95148, 95150, 95151, 95192
Post Office: 1750 Lundy Ave, San Jose, 800-275-8777, www.usps.com
Police: 201 W Mission St, 408-277-8900

Library: Dr. Martin Luther King, Jr. Library, 150 E San Fernando St, 408-808-2000, www.sjlibrary.org

Public Schools: San Jose Unified School District, 855 Lenzen Ave, 408-535-6000, www.sjusd.org

Community Publications: *San Jose Mercury News*, 408-920-5662, www.mercurynews.com; *San Jose Post Record*, 408-287-4866; Metro, 408-298-8000, www.metroactive.com; *Silicon Valley-San Jose Business Journal*, 408-295-3800, http://sanjose.bizjournals.com/sanjose

Cultural Resources: Peralta Adobe, 154 W Saint John St, 408-993-8300; History Park at Kelley Park, 1650 Senter Rd, 408-287-2290, www.historysanjose.org; Santa Clara de Asis Mission, 500 El Camino Real; Santa Clara University, 408-554-4023, www.scu.edu/mission; San Jose Museum of Quilts and Textiles, 520 S First St, 408-971-0323, www.sjquiltmuseum.org; San Jose Museum of Art, 110 S Market St, 408-271-6840, www.sjmusart.org; San Jose Institute of Contemporary Art, 560 S First St, 408-283-8157, www.sjica.org; Lick Observatory, 19 miles east of San Jose on Highway 130 on top of Mount Hamilton, 408-274-5061, www.ucolick.org; Tech Museum of Innovation, 201 S Market St, 408-294-8324, www.thetech.org; American Musical Theater of San Jose, 408-453-7100, www.amtsj.org; Opera San Jose, 345 S First St, 408-437-4450, www.operasj.org; Ballet San Jose, 40 N First, 408-288-2120, www.balletsanjose.org; San Jose Convention and Cultural Facilities (Center for the Performing Arts, Parkside Hall, Civic Auditorium, Montgomery Theater, McEnery Convention Center), 150 W San Carlos St, 408-792-4194, www.sanjose.org; Children's Discovery Museum of San Jose, 180 Woz Way, 408-298-5437, www.cdm.org

Community Resources: San Jose Silicon Valley Chamber of Commerce, 101 W Santa Clara St, 408-291-5250, www.sjchamber.com; Almaden Community Center, 6445 Camden Ave, 408-268-1133; Evergreen Community Center, 4860 San Felipe Rd, 408-270-2220; Sherman Oaks Community Center, 1800A Fruitdale Ave, 408-292-2935; Rose Garden Neighborhood Preservation Association, P.O. Box 59838, www.rgnpa.org; Willow Glen Neighborhood Association, P.O. Box 7706, 408-294-9462, www.wgna.net; Japantown Neighborhood Association, www.jtownneighbors.org

Parks, Gardens, and Open Space: Parks, Recreation and Neighborhood Services, 200 E Santa Clara St, 408-535-3570, www.sanjoseca.gov/prns; Emma Prusch Farm Park, 647 S King Rd; Alum Rock Park, 15350 Penitencia Creek Rd; Overfelt Gardens (and Chinese Cultural Gardens), 2145 Mckee Rd; Almaden Lake Park, 6099 Winfield Blvd, 408-277-5130; Kelley Park (Japanese Friendship Gardens and Happy Hollow Park and Zoo, 1300 Senter Rd, 408-277-3000, www.happyhollowparkandzoo.org are also located here); Heritage Rose Garden, 715 Spring St, 408-298-7657; Lake Cunningham Park, 2305 S White Rd, www.lakecunningham.org

SUNNYVALE

In the heart of Silicon Valley, **Sunnyvale** (pop. 130,519) remains home to many high-tech employees. Amenities include large numbers of parks and tennis courts, as well as theater groups, golf courses, a sports complex, a dance company, and much more. Home to 36,000 trees, Sunnyvale proudly calls itself a "Tree City USA." Residents here enjoy Baylands Park, 408-730-7751, located at the end of Lawrence Expressway off Highway 237, at Caribbean Drive. This 70-acre park is a bird watcher's paradise. Heritage Park, 550 East Remington Avenue, includes a pond-side plaza that is home to a community center, creative arts center, performing arts center, indoor sports complex, recreation center, and senior center.

Houses vary from multi-story condominium townhouses with the requisite pool, to red-tiled Mediterranean-style homes, to multimillion-dollar mansions. Downtown Sunnyvale has a new City Plaza, new office buildings, and a 20-screen movie theater. Historic Murphy Avenue has a number of new restaurants and shops, as well as a Saturday morning farmers market on Murphy Avenue at Washington Avenue. Recently completed projects include a new Transit Station and Plaza del Sol, 200 West Evelyn Avenue, which pays homage to the city's agricultural past with giant, colorful fruit sculptures. As part of the large-scale effort to revitalize this 184-acre central city core to create a more traditional downtown, Sunnyvale is rebuilding. There is a plan to scrap the old downtown mall, the Sunnyvale Town Center, and replace it with a large outdoor town square that will include 1 million square feet of retail space, some small office spaces, and roughly 300 new condos or townhouses.

The 23.8 square miles of Sunnyvale are said to be home to more high-tech companies than any other city in the world. Advanced Micro Devices, Network Appliance, Yahoo!, and Lockheed Martin are only a few of the hundreds of high-tech businesses that operate here. Lockheed alone employs more than 6,500 people. Back at the turn

Sunnyvale

of the century, Walter Crossman, the city's first developer, was on to something when he dubbed the scarcely populated agricultural town "the City of Destiny." If only he could see how prophetic his words were.

SUNNYVALE

Web Site: www.sunnyvale.ca.gov
Area Codes: 408
Zip Codes: 94086–94089
Post Office: 580 N Mary Ave, Sunnyvale, 800-275-8777, www.usps.com
Police: 700 All America Way, 408-730-7100
Library: Main Library, 665 W Olive Ave, Sunnyvale, 408-730-7300, http://sunnyvale.ca.gov/Departments/Library
Public Schools: Sunnyvale School District, 819 W Iowa Ave, Sunnyvale, 408-522-8200, www.sesd.org
Community Publication: *Sunnyvale Sun*, 408-200-1000, www.sunnyvalesun.com
Community Resources: Sunnyvale Chamber of Commerce, 260 S Sunnyvale Ave, 408-736-4971, www.svcoc.org; Sunnyvale Community Center Theater, 550 E Remington Dr, 408-733-6611; Sunnyvale Volunteer Resources, 408-730-7533
Parks, Gardens and Open Space: Parks and Recreation Department (and Sunnyvale Community Center), 550 E Remington Dr, 408-730-7350, http://sunnyvale.ca.gov/Departments/Parks+and+Recreation

LOS GATOS, MONTE SERENO

Considered by many to be one of the loveliest towns in the South Bay, **Los Gatos** is tucked away in the hills just east of the Santa Cruz Mountains, off of Highway 17. This community of about 29,000 is upscale, picture-perfect, woodsy, politically progressive, and prides itself on its strong sense of community. The hills are peppered with newly built mansions, especially in the Blossom Hill Manor area. More modest, early 1900s Victorians are still extant as well, but many home prices stretch into the seven figures. For an even more upscale area, visit the city of **Monte Sereno** (population 3,500), right next to Los Gatos. An old, established community, it's known for its multimillion-dollar homes sitting on expansive lots. See www.montesereno.org for more information about this quaint town.

With 15 parks and 8 playgrounds, Los Gatos offers people every opportunity to enjoy the outdoors. Year round, the Los Gatos Creek Trail, just outside the downtown on Main Street, abounds with thrill-seeking cyclists, runners, and walkers. The 5-mile path winds up into the hills and around the Lexington Reservoir, providing spectacular views guaranteed to please. For an outdoor

Los Gatos

experience more suited to the family, try the 150-acre Vasona Park, where you can picnic, rollerblade, jog, bike, or just go for a stroll. For a leisurely afternoon in the lake, rent a paddleboat. Next to Vasona Park is Oak Meadow Park, where you can ride a carousel and a miniature train, see a real Air Force jet, or just settle down for a picnic. For those with pets, the newly renovated Los Gatos Creek County Dog Park is open to dogs of all sizes.

If shopping is more your thing, you'll want to visit North Santa Cruz Avenue. This upscale shopping district is full of trendy boutiques, art galleries, restaurants, and cafés that lure people from all over the county. Warm evenings bring locals in to browse the sales, window shop, and stop for cappuccinos or a bite to eat. Singles frequent the Los Gatos Brewing Company, a brewpub at 130-G North Santa Cruz Avenue, and Steamers, 31 University Avenue. On weekends and sometimes during the week in the summer the town of Los Gatos plays host to popular free concert series at the Los Gatos Town Plaza Park and the Civic Center Lawn. In the fall, Los Gatos High School, 20 High School Court, located just a short walk from downtown,

Monte Sereno

brings in local fans to watch the Friday night football games. During the Christmas season horse-drawn carriages prance around the town. Life here is pretty good, and that's without even mentioning the weather. On average, you'll find 330 sunny days per year here. Nor is it too cold or too hot; average temperatures in January are 46° Fahrenheit, in July, 71°.

LOS GATOS

Web Site: www.town.los-gatos.ca.us
Area Code: 408
Zip Codes: 95030, 95031, 95032
Post Office: 101 S Santa Cruz Ave, 408-395-7526, www.usps.com
Police: 110 E Main St, 408-354-8600
Library: 110 E Main St, 408-354-6891, www.library.town.los-gatos.ca/us
Public Schools: Los Gatos Union School District, 17010 Roberts Rd, 408-335-2000, www.lgusd.k12.ca.us
Parks, Gardens, and Open Space: Department of Parks and Public Works, 110 E Main St, in the Los Gatos Town Hall Complex, 408-399-5781, www.losgatosca.gov/services/6a.html; Los Gatos Creek County Dog Park, 1250 Dell Ave, 408-356-2729

CAMPBELL, CUPERTINO

Other cities to consider if you are looking in the South Bay are Campbell (pop. 35,961), and Cupertino (pop. 55,981). Located in the foothills of the Santa Cruz Mountains, both communities are very suburban, with shopping malls, parks with tennis courts and play lots, and many families. In addition, major high-tech companies, including Apple, call these cities home.

Campbell borders Willow Glen and Los Gatos. The portion of Campbell between Bascom and Meridian avenues features wide, tree-lined streets with ranch-style and Eichler homes. Named after the prune yard drying days, the Pruneyard Shopping Center 1875 S Bascom Avenue offers such stores as Barnes & Noble and Trader Joe's, as well as restaurants, including the Rock Bottom Brewery, a nice place to have a burger and catch a televised sports game, and Buca di Beppo for family-style Italian food.

The old commercial heart of Campbell is along Campbell Avenue. Here you'll find Internet cafés, antique shops, dry cleaners, and a hodge-podge of ethnic restaurants and mom-and-pop stores. Nearby at 1690 S Bascom Avenue is the popular Whole Foods, a gourmet grocery store featuring health food, organic fruits and vegetables, and freshly prepared hot food. Many come here during their lunch hour or to pick up dinner on their way home from work. On Campbell Avenue at Central Avenue, a year-round farmers market held every Sunday morning—rain or shine—features farm-fresh produce and crowded stalls.

Campbell

Property prices in Campbell had increased considerably over the previous decade but are now in a sharp decline because of the housing downturn. This does not mean housing is affordable in this area of the South Bay. According to the California Association of Realtors, the median home price here was $630,000 in February 2009, down 12.5 percent from 2008. The average homes for sale are actually in the upper $800,000 range.

The 13-square-mile city of **Cupertino** grew prodigiously after World War II, first as a weekend destination for wealthy San Franciscans, and today as a thriving residential and business community. In 1950, there were only 500 homes in Cupertino; today there are more than 18,000, according to the city's consolidated housing plan, with a population of more than 55,000. Cupertino, which borders Saratoga and Sunnyvale, does not have a true downtown center, so strip malls are common. High-tech business offices include Apple Computer, which is headquartered here, and Compaq. Primarily a bedroom community, with most residents heading to San Jose for nightlife, Cupertino is popular among many families for its suburban feel and top-notch schools, which have received state and national recognition for their excellence. Travel north on Highway 9 from Saratoga, which becomes Saratoga-Sunnyvale Road, and you'll know you've arrived in Cupertino when you begin to see the many Asian restaurants and grocery stores. To the west of Saratoga-Sunnyvale Road sit the Cupertino foothills, home to million-dollar mansions with acres of open space behind them. Outdoor enthusiasts come here for mountain biking and hiking. Cupertino has a new library at 10800 Torre Avenue that even has a café next door—the popular Coffee Society—and while the Cupertino Square Mall (formerly Vallco Fashion Park Mall) seems like a sleepy place, it does have a Macy's, Victoria's Secret, and Sears. You can also find the local farmers market in the Cupertino Square parking lot every Friday morning. There is a Whole Foods in Cupertino at 20955 Stevens Creek Boulevard, and along the same street, just before Highway 85, you'll find De Anza Community College and the Flint Center, which features regular concerts by the San Francisco Symphony, Broadway plays, and other performances. Bargain hunters should check out the De Anza Flea Market, held on the first Saturday of every month at 21250 De Anza Boulevard. The swimming and picnic facilities at the 60-acre Blackberry Farm are a popular attraction; following two years of upgrading and restoration, the park reopened in July 2009. Its 9-hole golf course is also popular with locals. Those wishing for an inexpensive workout option should explore the Cupertino Sports Center, with its two racquetball courts, 17 tennis courts, and large fitness center.

Revitalization and plans for more restoration along Stevens Creek and De Anza boulevards have city planners working hard to make the area more habitable. If you are looking for a home in Cupertino, you'll find dozens of new condominiums mixed in with single-family homes and a few older homes, located along wide boulevards.

The City of Cupertino requires 15 percent of all new housing be made affordable using a Below Market Rate (BMR) qualifier. BMR rental units are made available to very low and low-income residents while a few properties for sale are made available to median and moderate-income residents. And in 2003, the City also developed a down-payment assistance program to help qualifying Cupertino teachers purchase homes in the area. (For more information, contact Neighborhood Housing Services Silicon Valley, 408-279-2600, www.nhssv.org).

CAMPBELL
Web Site: www.ci.campbell.ca.us
Area Codes: 408
Zip Code: 95008
Post Office: 500 W Hamilton Ave, 800-275-8777, www.usps.com
Police: 70 N First St, 408-866-2121
Library: Campbell Library, 77 Harrison Ave, 408-866-1991, www.santaclaracoun-
   tylib.org/campbell

Cupertino

Public Schools: Campbell Union School District, 155 N Third St, Campbell, 408-364-4200, www.campbellusd.k12.ca.us

Community Publications: *Campbell Express*, 408-374-9700, www.campbell express.com; *Campbell Times*, 408-494-7000, www.campbelltimes.com; *The Campbell Reporter*, 408-200-1000, www.mercurynews.com/campbell

Community Resources: Campbell Community Center, 1 W Campbell Ave, 408-866-2105; Campbell Chamber of Commerce, 1628 W Campbell Ave, 408-378-6252, www.campbellchamber.com

Parks, Gardens, and Open Space: Recreation and Community Services, 1 W Campbell Ave #C-31, 408-866-2105, www.ci.campbell.ca.us/recreation/parks/index.htm

CUPERTINO

Web Site: www.cupertino.org

Zip Codes: 95014, 95015

Area Codes: 408

Post Office: 21701 Stevens Creek Blvd, Cupertino, 800-275-8777, www.usps.com

Police: Santa Clara County Sheriff's Office West Valley Division, 1601 S De Anza Blvd, 408-868-6600

Library: Cupertino Library, 10800 Torre Ave, 408-446-1677, www.santaclaracountylib.org/cupertino

Public Schools: Cupertino Union School District, 10301 Vista Dr, Cupertino, 408-252-3000, http://cupertino.ca.campusgrid.net

Community Publication: *Cupertino Courier*, 408-200-1000, www.mercurynews/cupertino

Community Resources: Cupertino Chamber of Commerce, 20455 Silverado Ave, 408-252-7054, www.cupertino-chamber.org; De Anza Community College, 21250 Stevens Creek Blvd, 408-864-5678, www.deanza.edu; Quinlan Community Center and Cupertino Historical Museum, 10185 N Stelling Rd, 408-777-3120; De Anza College Flint Center for the Performing Arts, 21250 Stevens Creek Blvd, 408-864-8820;; Asian-Americans for Community Involvement, 408-975-2730; Cupertino Sports Center, 21111 Stevens Creek Blvd, 408-777-3160; Fujitsu Planetarium, De Anza Community College, 21250 Stevens Creek Blvd, 408-864-8814, www.planetarium.deanza.edu

Parks, Gardens, and Open Space: Parks and Recreation Department (and Quinlan Community Center), 10185 N Stelling Rd, 408-777-3110, www.cupertino.org//index.aspx?page=590; Blackberry Farm Golf Course, 22100 Stevens Creek Blvd, 408-253-9200

SARATOGA

Saratoga (pop. 30,216) is located 10 miles west of San Jose in the golden foot-hills of the Santa Cruz Mountains. Numerous creeks, wooded trails, and streets lined with mature oak trees fill the city's 12 square miles. The city is decidedly upscale, and like Los Gatos, the community has easy access to the outdoors. While the downtown area, on Big Basin Avenue, is where you'll find chic res-taurants and boutique shopping, the beautiful West Valley Community College lets the local farmers market take over its parking lot every Saturday morning beginning at 9 a.m.

Proximity to the Santa Cruz redwood trees put Saratoga on the map; by the mid-1800s, Saratoga had become a thriving lumber town. After lumber, agricul-ture in the form of fruit orchards—especially prunes—became the economy's mainstay. Around the turn of the 20th century, wealthy San Franciscans started building summer cottages here for weekend and summer getaways, which added tourism to the economy. Today the orchards are gone and the area is considered a bedroom community for Silicon Valley. Architecturally, you'll find many grand ranch-style estates and two-story Victorians. Famous architect Julia Morgan (best known for the Hearst Castle) designed the Saratoga Foothill Club in 1915. Of note, Steven Spielberg graduated from Saratoga High School, and actresses Olivia de Havilland and her sister Joan Fontaine began their careers in Saratoga.

One of the highlights of Saratoga is Hakone Gardens, 21000 Big Basin Way, 408-741-4994, www.hakone.com. Created in 1918 by a former Japanese imperial gardener, it is considered to be the only authentic Japanese garden in Northern California, the Japanese Tea Garden in San Francisco notwithstanding. For summer concerts, locals frequent the Mountain Winery located at 14831 Pierce Road. Another destination is the Montalvo Arts Center, 15400 Montalvo Road, a 175-acre estate with beautiful gardens, a bird sanctuary, and nature

Saratoga

trails. The center hosts concerts and plays in the outdoor amphitheater and now rents to well-heeled corporate or wedding event planners. This landmark was built in 1912 by James Duval Phelan, a three-term mayor of San Francisco and the state's first popularly elected United States Senator. He bequeathed the property—named after Garcia Ordonez de Montalvo, originator of California's name—without equivocation as a place for the "development of art, literature, music and architecture by promising students." For those lucky—or promising—enough, the center sponsors resident artists in 10 beautifully designed live/work studios.

Rock climbers come from all over the Bay Area to Castle Rock State Park at the intersection of Route 35 and Highway 9, which offers challenging belays. Overnight backpackers, day hikers, horseback riders and mountain bikers also enjoy the 32 miles of trails at the park.

SARATOGA
Web Site: www.saratoga.ca.us
Area Code: 408
Zip Code: 95070
Post Office: 14376 Saratoga Ave, 800-275-8777, www.usps.com
Sheriff: Santa Clara County Sheriff's Office West Valley Division, 408-868-6690
Library: Saratoga Library, 13650 Saratoga Ave, 408-867-6126, www.santaclaracountylib.org/saratoga
Community Publication: *Saratoga News*, 408-200-1000, www.mercurynews.com/saratoga
Community Resources: Mountain Winery, 14831 Pierce Rd, 408-741-2822, www.mountainwinery.com; Montalvo Arts Center, 15400 Montalvo Rd, 408-961-5800, www.montalvoarts.org; West Valley Community College, 12000 Fruitvale Ave, 408-867-2200, www.westvalley.edu
Public Schools: Saratoga Union School District, 20460 Forrest Hills Dr, 408-867-3424, www.saratogausd.org
Parks, Gardens and Open Space: Saratoga Parks and Recreation (also the Saratoga Community Center), 19655 Allendale Ave, 408-868-1249

SANTA CLARA

The City of Santa Clara (109,100) started out in 1777 as a Spanish mission, and later evolved into a prime agricultural region with expansive orchards as well as a lumber community. Like many of the other surrounding towns, Santa Clara reaped the immediate benefits of the old-growth redwood trees. In 1874, the Pacific Manufacturing Company set up shop, cutting down thousands of redwood trees and becoming one of the largest suppliers of wood. By 1906 Santa Clara's population had increased to a whopping 5,000. By 1950, when the semiconductor chip was developed and most of the redwoods had been cut down, many of the orchards were plowed under, making way for the industrial expansion for which Santa Clara is known today. Heavyweight companies in Santa Clara include Intel, 3COM, Applied Materials, and Yahoo!

Santa Clara is more than just high-tech industry. Founded in 1851 on mission grounds, Santa Clara University is one of the West Coast's oldest universities. Fanning out alongside Saratoga Creek is the gorgeous 52-acre Central Park, 909 Kiely Boulevard. The park is home to the famous George F. Haines International Swim Center, 2625 Patricia Drive. You'll also find a lake, lighted tennis courts, a bowling green, softball fields, basketball courts, an amphitheater, a children's play area, a 30,000-square-foot Community Recreation Center, and the Central Park Library. For a more serene sojourn in the outdoors, visit the Ulistac Natural Area, 4901 Lick Mill Boulevard, a 40-acre open space preserve featuring wooded areas, grasslands and wetlands. For more information or to get a free copy of the self-guided trail map, call 408-615-2260. Another popular family attraction is California's Great America roller coaster park, which has some of the scariest seated rides on earth. Follow the signs from Highway's 101 or 237.

Because Santa Clara developed earlier than many surrounding areas, you'll find its residential neighborhoods are older. Housing is slightly more affordable than Sunnyvale or Mountain View, and therefore more appealing to young families and those just getting started. The median sales price in this area of the South Bay is in the $495,000 range, representing a 20% decrease in 2009 over the year prior. Home to substantial Italian, Asian, and Indian immigrant populations, Santa Clara offers a wide selection of restaurants reflecting this delectable diversity.

SANTA CLARA
Web Sites: www.santaclaraca.gov, www.sccgov.org (county site)
Zip Codes: 95050, 95051
Post Office: 1200 Franklin Mall on Jackson St, 800-275-8777, www.usps.com

Santa Clara

Police: 601 El Camino Real, 408-615-4700, www.scpd.org

Library: Central Park Library, 2635 Homestead Rd, 408-615-2900

Public Schools: Santa Clara Unified School District, 1889 Lawrence Rd, 408-423-2000, www.santaclarausd.org

Community Publications: Santa Clara Visitor's Bureau, 1850 Warburton Ave, 800-272-6822, www.santaclara.org; *Santa Clara Weekly*, 408-243-2000, www.santaclaraweekly.com

Community Resources: Santa Clara Convention and Visitor's Bureau, 1850 Warburton Ave, 408-244-9202; Triton Museum of Art, 1505 Warburton Ave, 408-247-3754; Intel Museum, 2200 Mission College Blvd, 408-765-0503; Santa Clara Players Theatre, 1511 Warburton Ave, 408-248-7993; Louis B. Mayer Theatre, Santa Clara University, corner of Lafayette and Franklin Sts, 408-554-4015; California's Great America amusement park, Great America Parkway off of Hwys 101 and 237, 408-988-1776, www.cagreatamerica.com, Santa Clara University, 500 El Camino Real, 408-554-4000, www.scu.edu; Mission Community College, 3000 Mission College Blvd, 408-988-2200, www.missioncollege.org

MILPITAS

Set amid the hilly, arid backdrop of Mount Diablo to the north and Copernicus Peak to the south, the city of **Milpitas** boasts one of Santa Clara County's highest home-ownership rates. Here in this growing community of 65,000, close to 70% of households are owner-occupied. That's thanks largely to a rampant building boom, focused on what regional planners say is the key to the Bay Area's future—affordable, high density, transit-accessible housing. Working with nonprofits, developers, and federal grant agencies, Milpitas is leading the way, taking many opportunities to create new housing—including rezoning unused industrial land as high-density mixed use areas. Milpitas, as a city deep in the gut of Silicon Valley, enjoys the ebb and flow of innovative start-up companies populating the many commercial properties available. Currently, "clean tech" is driving much of the traffic.

Not surprisingly, with all the recent large-scale development, you'll find relatively modern architecture here—from older 1960s tracts of single-family ranch-style homes to a seemingly endless wave of new three- and four-story affordable apartment buildings, spacious condos, and townhomes. The good news is that housing prices have dropped rapidly and red-hot deals can still be found. According to the California Association of Realtors, median sales prices in February 2009 were $450,000, a 15% decrease from the previous year, and still quite low for the broader Santa Clara County.

Milpitas is home to a large Asian-American community. In fact, more than 50% of the city is of Asian descent, according to the most recent US census. Here, you'll find the 1.5-million-square-foot Great Mall of the Bay Area—a renovated Ford manufacturing plant—and Northern California's largest Asian market center, Milpitas Square. You'll also find a sleek, modern, and user-friendly City Hall, a recently renovated sports center, and 25 large parks (with several mini-parks scattered throughout the neighborhoods). Chief among the parks is Ed Levin County Park, with 1,539 acres of hiking trails, lawn-chair fishing, an 18-hole golf course, enormous open areas and a large off-leash dog park for dogs of all sizes. From Monument Peak you can take in sweeping views of the valley below and the southern part of San Francisco Bay. Murphy Park is popular with children, while Hidden Lake Park, as its name suggests, is a serene place to relax and watch the ducks. For a workout try the Milpitas Sports Center, 1325 East Calaveras Boulevard, where locals enjoy aerobics, yoga, swimming, water aerobics, volleyball, table tennis, and basketball in a new state-of-the-art facility.

All of this makes Milpitas an attractive and affordable option for families seeking a suburban atmosphere in which to raise their children, as well as for Silicon Valley professionals looking to own their own condo. Milpitas, whose name means "little cornfields" in Spanish, is relatively young as cities go—just barely more than 50 years old—and thus has a very modern suburban feel. A stopping point on the road between San Jose and Oakland, the area first attracted settlers in the 1850s, most of them farmers. Filled with vast orchards and sprawling sugar beet, pea, and corn fields, Milpitas remained a small agricultural community for roughly a century. During the post–World War II baby and building boom, the first of many tracts emerged in Milpitas, and in 1954, Milpitas officially became a city in its own right.

In the early 1960s Milpitas voters proved they could go it alone when they soundly defeated a ballot measure that would have made their city into an annexed arm of nearby San Jose. Milpitas leaders likened their battle for independence to the US Revolutionary War, dubbing themselves "the Milpitas Minutemen." Today, a minuteman symbol engraved on the official city seal pays

Milpitas

tribute to that legacy, and to this day, a kind of friendly local rivalry still exists with San Jose.

Milpitas has easy access to three major highways: I-680, I-880, and Highway 237, putting it within easy commuting distance of both the East Bay and Silicon Valley, though the commutes on these Bay Area roads are among the region's most brutal during peak hours. To help alleviate the strain, the city is urging commuters to consider carpooling at least once a week (visit www.511.org for more information and to sign up for the convenient online Ridematch Service).

Fortunately, the Valley Transportation Agency recently extended Santa Clara County's sleek, efficient light rail to Milpitas, greatly improving in-county commute options. Better still, extension of BART into the suburbs northwest of Milpitas is currently in the construction phase, with final completion of the $890 million project scheduled for 2014.

MILPITAS

Web site: www.ci.milpitas.ca.gov

Area Code: 408

Zip Codes: 95035, 95036

Post Office: 450 S Abel St, 800-275-8777, www.usps.com

Police: 1275 N Milpitas Blvd, 408-586-2400

Library: Milpitas Library, 40 N Milpitas Blvd, 408-262-1171, www.santaclara countylib.org/milpitas/

Public Schools: Milpitas Unified School District, 1331 E Calaveras Blvd, 408-635-2600

Community Resources: Milpitas Community Center, 457 E Calaveras Blvd, 408-586-3210; Milpitas Sports Center, 1325 E Calaveras Blvd, 408-586-3225; Milpitas Alliance for the Arts, 142 N Milpitas Blvd, Suite 330, www.milpitasarts. com; Rainbow Children's Theatre (performances at the Milpitas Community Center), 457 E Calaveras Blvd, 408-586-2777; Milpitas Chamber of Commerce, 828 N Hillview Drive, 408-262-2613, www.milpitaschamber.com

Parks, Gardens and Open Space: Recreation Service Department, 457 E Calaveras Blvd (and Milpitas Community Center), 408-586-3210

G ORGEOUS COASTS, SPECTACULAR MOUNTAINS AND HILLSIDES, parks, fantastic food, excellent weather, top-tier universities, and the diverse, vibrant, and culturally rich mecca of San Francisco combine to make the Bay Area one of the country's most desirable places to live. Not surprisingly, the region has the prices to match. This tiny slice of California ranks among the nation's most expensive places to live. Thus for many, moving here—especially to San Francisco itself—means gearing up for high rents, and often putting aside (at least for awhile) the dream of homeownership.

There are bright spots however. In an effort to meet the growing need for affordable housing, the state, local counties, and cities have banded together to create a variety of housing initiatives all designed with one goal in mind. To help meet the housing challenge, reduce congestion, and revitalize downtown areas, the regional emphasis here has been on "smart growth," with planners repeating the mantra "TOD" (Transit Oriented Development). The current trend is to focus on building mixed-use, higher density developments—creating communities that frequently have retail and office space, market rate or even luxury units, blended with below–market rate apartments, senior housing, condos, and townhouses near transportation hubs and in downtown areas. A number of municipalities and school districts have also implemented their own programs to help attract and retain high-quality police, firefighters, nurses, and teachers by putting homeownership within reach through First Time Home-buyer assistance programs.

In San Francisco, two thirds of the city's population are renters, and many live with roommates to bring costs down. Hopeful homebuyers are increasingly turning an eye to condos, townhouses, and tenancies-in-common (TIC) owner-ship. Just be aware of Homeowner Association (HOA) dues, which essentially pay for the upkeep of the building but can top $500 per month, in addition to the mortgage. If you dream of owning a home here, you may need to be a bit creative. The good news is that as a result of the housing bust, the San Francisco area is a buyer's market. For the most affordable options, many families looking for that perfect suburban dream are choosing to move into the farthest reaches of the area such as Hayward, Fremont, Livermore, Vallejo, and even sometimes as far as Hollister, which sits 45 miles south of San Jose and a full 93 miles from San Francisco.

Housing options in the Bay Area are varied. San Francisco's most distinctive dwellings are its wood-framed Victorian homes, many of which have been remodeled and turned into flats with two to four units per building. You will also find a large number of Edwardian apartment buildings, each one a castle of stone and crenellations containing dozens of units. Here in quake country, wood-framed buildings, especially if they are built on rock, are safest because they give a little when the earth moves beneath them. Virtually every large building in San Francisco has been highly reinforced against the next big earthquake. If you're especially worried about earthquakes, steer clear of homes built on landfill (like in the Marina District of San Francisco, or Foster City near San Mateo), which act like gelatin during a long duration quake. See the **Emergency Preparedness** chapter for more on this topic.

APARTMENT HUNTING

DIRECT ACTION

Many arriving in the Bay Area from other parts of the United States may be used to looking for posted rental notices on coffee shop, grocery store, and Laundromat bulletin boards, as well as on vacant apartments. However, people here rely almost entirely on one single web site: www.craigslist.org, an invention of Bay Area local Craig Newmark. Users can and do post classified advertisements without paying a dime, and the San Francisco Bay division of Craig's List is one of the most vibrant online communities in the area. Sifting through the mountains of rental advertisements can, in fact, seem like a momentous task, but with exposure and a few real-life visits it becomes easier to separate the good from the bad. Energetic souls will also call a building's manager, ask everyone they know for word-of-mouth referrals, and, when all else fails, pound the pavement and talk to people on streets or in neighborhoods where they want to live. If this seems like too much work for you, or if you haven't the time, check below under **Rental Agents, Relocation Services, Roommate Services**.

NEWSPAPER CLASSIFIED ADS

Perusing the newspaper classifieds was traditionally the most popular place to begin searching for an apartment. The listings will also give you a good sense of what you can expect to pay for rent each month. You'll see that rates vary significantly by location. Most rental ads are placed in the Sunday newspapers, which are available on Saturday at convenience stores and newsstands. Craig's List (www.craigslist.org), however, has virtually annihilated the classified markets, and only the most paltry of listings are available through printed medium. If you do not have Internet access, here is a list of local publications that have small classified sections related to rentals:

- **Contra Costa Times**, published daily, focuses on the East Bay, particularly Concord, Walnut Creek, Pleasant Hill, Martinez, Richmond, Hercules, Benicia, Antioch, Pittsburg, and Bay Point areas, 925-935-2525, www.ContraCostaTimes.com
- **The Daily Californian**, daily, UC Berkeley's student newspaper, good for rental and roommate listings, 510-548-8300, www.dailycal.org.
- **East Bay Express**, a weekly, free alternative newspaper that focuses on the East Bay. Found in newsstands and at cafés on Thursdays, 510-879-3700, www.eastbayexpress.com.
- **Marin Independent Journal**, published daily with listings for Marin, Sonoma, and Napa counties, 415-883-8600, www.marinij.com.
- **Oakland Tribune**, published daily, focuses on East Bay listings, especially Oakland, Berkeley, and Alameda areas, 510-208-6300, www.insidebayarea.com/oaklandtribune.
- **Pacific Sun**, weekly free, alternative newspaper with listings for Marin County. Good for rentals and roommate listings; found on Fridays at newsstands and cafés, 415-485-6700, www.pacificsun.com.
- **San Francisco Bay Guardian**, a free, weekly, alternative newspaper with extensive listings for San Francisco and the East Bay. Published Wednesdays, found at every café and newsstand all over the city, 415-255-3100, www.sfbg.com.
- **San Francisco Chronicle**, the most widely circulated newspaper in the area; includes listings for San Francisco, North Bay, East Bay, and Peninsula counties, and some outlying areas. The Sunday paper has the most extensive listings, 415-777-1111, www.sfgate.com.
- **San Francisco Weekly**, a free, weekly, alternative newspaper with San Francisco listings; comes out Wednesdays. Found all over the city at newsstands and cafés, 415-536-8100, www.sfweekly.com.
- **San Jose Mercury News**, published daily with the most extensive listings for the South Bay, much of the Peninsula, and areas southeast of the Bay, 408-920-5000, www.mercurynews.com.
- **San Mateo County Times**, published daily except Sunday, with listings for much of the Peninsula, 650-348-4321, www.insidebayarea.com/sanmateotimes.com.
- **Santa Rosa Press Democrat**, published daily with listings for Sonoma, Marin, and Napa counties, 707-546-2020, www.pressdemocrat.com.

OTHER RENTAL PUBLICATIONS

Many property owners pay to list their units in glossy guides that are free to prospective renters. These guides, available in racks at supermarkets, bus and BART stations, and on many street corners, are designed to make the property look like the Taj Mahal. Keep in mind that while many of them are as nice as they look in the ads, they are typically in large apartment complexes and towers.

Here are just a couple of these publications:

- **Apartment Guide**, covers San Francisco and the greater Silicon Valley, www. apartmentguide.com
- **Rental Guide**, covers San Francisco and the greater Bay Area, 415-929-7733, www. rentalguide.com

RENTAL AGENTS, RELOCATION SERVICES, ROOMMATE SERVICES

The vacancy rate is increasing across the country and the Bay Area is no exception. For the next few years many analysts predict this trend to continue. While the overall market may be flooded with newly bankrupt renters, the number of units available is increasing at a faster rate. This can make finding a comfortable home easily achievable. But for newcomers arriving in the Bay Area who want some expert help finding a place, a rental agency may be a worthwhile investment if for no other reason than to save time. When it comes to professional services, the most popular option is to sign up with a listing service, which typically charges a flat fee for access to an extensive bank of available rentals. Listings are generally accessible online and updated daily. Some agencies will also run a credit report for you and help you put together a renter's resume when you sign up. Rental agencies that offer a more tailor-made approach may do the necessary footwork to find a place for you and create customized lists, but frequently charge a percentage of the first month's rent. Sometimes a property owner will pay the fee, though this is an exception. If you have friends or coworkers in the area, ask if they can recommend a good agency. Always ask for a clear description of fees and services before entering into any binding agreements.

If you're considering a large Bay Area apartment complex, you can find passionate and free reviews by tenants at www.apartmentratings.com, a vibrant community of former and current renters. Another great source of information—also user-generated—is www.yelp.com, where dedicated people crank out reviews of everything from apartment complexes to the little Japanese restaurant down the street.

For pet owners, www.peoplewithpets.com and www.sfrent.net are great places to start when searching for tolerant landlords. The Bay Area in general is very pet-friendly (see the **Pets** section in the **Getting Settled** chapter), although pet owners typically pay a bit more for the privilege. Craig's List also has a handy search function for animal lovers under its apartments section.

Below is a partial list of Bay Area rental agencies; check the Yellow Pages under "Apartment Finding and Rental Services" for more listings:

SAN FRANCISCO

- **American Marketing Systems Inc.**, 2800 Van Ness Ave, 800-747-7784, 415-447-2000, www.amsires.com; specializes in the high-end furnished apartment market to corporate execs and vacation rentals.
- **Craig's List**, www.craigslist.com; housing is just one of the many listings found here. Check for a virtual bonanza of free apartment listings, sublets, and parking spaces. The listings are usually placed by property owners or current occupants looking to sublet their units.
- **Urban Bay Properties**, 17 Bluxome St, 415-546-3100, www.ubayp.com; specializes in lofts for sale and rent in San Francisco and the East Bay. Replete with detailed interior photos and thorough specifications. They also perform executive relocation services.
- **ApartmentRatings.com,** www.apartmentratings.com; making slumlords across the nation nervous, this web site taps into the analytical power of the people and typically rates apartment communities rather than individual rental units.
- **Move**, www.move.com; national web site includes listings for apartment rentals all around the Bay Area.
- **Roommates.com**, www.roommates.com; national roommate-finder with listings for cities across California, Basic Membership is free; Choice Membership costs are $5.99 for 3-day trial, $19.99 for 30 days, and $29.99 for 60 days.
- **Sabbatical Homes**, www.sabbaticalhomes.com; a great resource for the traveling academic. Provides global listings but has a number of home exchanges and rentals available for the Bay Area.
- **SF Real Estate Services**, 150 Lombard St, Suite 1 #1, 415-788-4488 or 415-248-8210 for rental listings, www.sfres.com; generally serving the upper-middle class renter. They also have a large database of condos and houses for sale.
- **SF Gate**, the *Chronicle*'s web site, www.sfgate.com/homes, lists rentals and homes for sale.
- **SF Rent**, 1201 Fulton St, 415-861-0777, www.sfrent.net; specializes in renting Victorian apartments that are pet friendly. Requires references and a $30 application fee.
- **SF State University Housing**, 800 Font Blvd, Mary Ward Hall, SFSU Campus, 415-338-1067, www.sfsu.edu/~housing; provides housing resources for students, faculty, and visiting scholars.
- **Saxe Real Estate**, 1999 Van Ness Ave, 415-474-2435; www.saxerealestate.com; one of the better competitors of Craig's List, this web site charges no fees but isn't as comprehensive.
- **The Rental Source**, 2013 16th St, 415-771-7685, www.therentalsource.com, charges a $20 application fee to renters.

- **Trinity Management Services**, 333 Bay St, 415-433-3333, www.trinity management.com, specializes in short-term furnished rentals for corporate clients; they do have unfurnished units for long-term lease but prices aren't listed. Upper-class listings.
- **UCSF Campus Housing Office**, 500 Parnassus Ave (for Parnassus) and 1505 4th St (for Mission Bay), 415-476-2231 and 415-514-4550 respectively, www. campuslifeservices.ucsf.edu/housing; rents university housing to students, post-docs, residents/clinical fellows and faculty.

EAST BAY/NORTH BAY

- **Apartment Guide**, www.apartmentguide.com.
- **Craig's List**, www.craigslist.com; see above for description.
- **Tenant Finders**, 3483 Golden Gate Way, Suite 217, Lafayette, 925-939-2200, www. tenantfinders.com.

PENINSULA

- **Craig's List**, www.craigslist.com; see above for description.
- **Move**, www.move.com; national web site includes listings for apartment rentals all around the Bay Area.
- **Roommate Express**, 800-487-8050, www.roommateexpress.com; national roommate-matching service with Bay Area listings; $34.00 fee
- **HIP-Homesharing**, 364 S Railroad Ave, San Mateo, 650-348-6660, www. hiphousing.org; specializes in shared housing for people with special needs, low-income family assistance, and rehabilitation of properties in San Mateo County. Call to set up an interview.

SOUTH BAY

- **Bay Area Rentals**, 900 S Winchester Blvd, Blvd #9, San Jose, 408-244-4901 or 800-706-7878 www.bayrentals.com; a friendly and exceptional service that claims a 95% success rate in placing customers. They have exclusive listings due to their contacts within the property management industry. Basic service contracts ($98) are for 90 days and include detailed listings and daily updates. Also provides listings for San Mateo, San Francisco, Contra Costa, Marin, Solano, and Alameda counties. Special services available for corporate relocation.
- **Craig's List**, www.craigslist.com; see above for description.
- **Move**, www.move.com; national web site includes listings for apartment complex rentals all around the Bay Area.
- **Roommate Express**, 800-487-8050, www.roommateexpress.com; see above for description
- **Roommates.com**, www.roommates.com; national roommate-finder with listings for cities across California, $20 for 30 days.

SUBLETS

If you're unsure how long you are going to stay in the Bay Area, or if you are having trouble finding a long-term place to lease, consider subletting an apartment or a house. A sublet allows you to rent a unit on a short-term basis while the original tenant is temporarily away. In San Francisco, subletting is quite common but buyer beware, most leases prohibit a tenant from subletting to another tenant without the landlord's approval. If it can be arranged, speak to the landlord before signing with a tenant. If you find a room, apartment, or a house to sublet for a limited time, you will usually have to vacate the premises when the original tenant returns or current contract expires. You are not considered to be the legal tenant until entering into a separate agreement with the landlord. For those choosing to stay, the landlord can require you to sign a lease at a higher rent than what you had been paying.

Subletting from a "master tenant" who is the sole lease signer, and who already lives on the premises and will continue to do so while you also live there, is common, but typically must be approved by the landlord. While it is illegal for master tenants to charge you more than the rent they pay to the landlord, they can charge you up to the full amount in rent that they are paying, an amount they must disclose in writing. The master tenant always has the right to evict you with 30 days' written notice, for any reason.

SHARING

Considering the dozens of schools and universities, the high cost of rent, and the preponderance of rambling Victorian flats—with odd-shaped little rooms and formal dining rooms that double as bedrooms—house sharing is ubiquitous in the Bay Area. For a thousand dollars a month, a studio with an efficiency kitchen may seem paltry and cramped when compared with renting a room in a house with a big kitchen, pantry, shared dining and living rooms, and a backyard, all for the same amount of rent or less. Roommate situations, however, can be challenging so careful consideration of the situation is warranted. There are households, a better term might be co-ops, comprised solely of non-smoking, cat-loving, vegetarian political activists who go to the farmers market together and share cooking duties each evening. And that's just one scenario. The options are endless.

There are two ways to enter into lease agreements with roommates. Some or all leasees can be "co-tenants," which means that whoever signs the lease with the landlord has equal rights and equal responsibilities. The worst case scenario here occurs if living together does not go as well as anticipated. Because everyone has signed the lease, everyone has the right to remain in the house and no one can force anyone else to go. The other lease option is to have a master tenant who signs the lease, pays the rent in one check, and deals with the landlord. The other roommate or roommates are then considered sub-tenants. Should you, as a sub-tenant, be unable to pay your rent, the landlord cannot go after you, but your roommate can. In fact, the master tenant can evict you with 30 days' written notice, regardless of cause. This type of situation can vary if living in San Francisco, which has strict rent control laws that protect tenants' rights. Check out the San Francisco Tenants Union, www.sftu.org, which is a great resource for legal information. Roommate situations can bring lifelong friends or a few months of living hell. While it is not legally binding, it's wise to get together with your prospective roomies to compose and sign a so-called "pre-nup," which may help to ensure promises made today won't go ignored tomorrow. For tips on what to include in your roommate agreement, check out www.ehow.com and search for "roommate agreement." You can also print out a free template at www. roommateconnection.com/2000TRC/headers/agreement.html.

If you don't mind paying a fee to find a roommate, hire a roommate service (see above under **Rental Agents, Relocation Services, Roommate Services**). The cost to match you with a roommate generally ranges from $35 to $110. If you'd rather not pay the roommate referral service fee, there are free alternatives, chief among them bulletin boards at universities, colleges, local grocery stores (generally not the chains), and coffeehouses. The Rainbow Grocery in the Mission District at Folsom and 13th Street has a large roommate board, as does the Women's Building, 3543 18th Street. In the East Bay, the bulletin board at the Whole Foods Market at Ashby and Telegraph avenues in Oakland is a popular posting place. Housing offices at universities and colleges also may be helpful.

CHECKING IT OUT

For many people, the neighborhood is just as important as the place itself, so once you've checked out a potential apartment or house, get out and walk around. Find people that live in the area and strike up a conversation. Check the city's web site. Maintain a sense of what you want and need and what you are willing to do without before you view a unit. Here are some things to consider during your search:

- Are the kitchen appliances clean and in working order? Do the stove's burners work? How about the oven? How's the kitchen sink? Is there sufficient counter and shelf space?
- Check the windows—do they open, close, and lock? Do the bedroom windows open onto a noisy or potentially dangerous area?
- How are the closets? Are they big enough to accommodate your belongings? Is there any private storage space?
- How's the water pressure? Try turning on the shower and the sink. Does the toilet flush adequately?
- Are there enough electrical outlets for your needs? Do the outlets work?
- Are there any signs of insects or other pests?

- What about laundry facilities? Are they in the building or is there a Laundromat nearby?
- Outside, do you feel comfortable? Will you feel safe at night? Is there secured parking? How many spaces? If two, are they tandem (so that one car blocks the other) or side by side? Is there an extra fee for parking? What about public transportation and shopping?
- Are you responsible for paying gas, water, or electricity? This policy varies from place to place, and paying any combination or none at all is possible.
- Watch for discrimination. The California Legislature has declared that "the opportunity to seek, obtain and hold housing without unlawful discrimination is a civil right" and it is illegal for landlords to discriminate on the basis of race, color, religion, sex, sexual orientation, marital status, national origin, ancestry, familial status, source of income or disability.

Ed Sacks' *Savvy Renter's Kit* contains a thorough renter's checklist for those interested in augmenting their own lists. The California Department of Consumer Affairs also maintains various useful documents and checklists at www.dca.ca.gov/publications/landlordbook.

STAKING A CLAIM

When you view a unit, come *prepared*. Bring your checkbook—or cold cash—so that if the place looks good, you can hold it with a deposit. Also bring a copy of your credit report for the building manager (see **Money Matters**). Landlords will often want references from your previous residences, as well as your basic employment information. Keep in mind that when you're applying for a place, landlords can require that the amount of money you earn monthly be equivalent to three times the amount of rent you are expected to pay. They can request non-smokers, they can prohibit pets other than a service dog, and they can bar you from having overnight guests for more than a certain number of nights per year. (If you think you'll have lots of visitors, watch out for a lease containing such a clause, as this may not bode well for your tenant/landlord relationship.)

LEASES/RENTAL AGREEMENTS AND SECURITY DEPOSITS

If you want a preview of what a typical Bay Area lease or rental agreement looks like, take a trip to any well-stocked office supply store. Standard lease/rental agreements are sold in tear-off pads. Of course, the numbers will not have been entered, but you'll at least get a glimpse at how most landlords handle deposits, rent due dates and grace periods, appliances, pets, and the like.

The law requires that a lease of one year or more be in writing. Every lease must also specify a termination date. If the termination date is not included, the tenant and landlord are considered to have entered into a month-to-month rental agreement. An oral agreement to rent for more than one year is considered a month-to-month rental agreement, not a lease. Also, unless it is a fixed-term lease, it will convert to a month-to-month rental agreement at the conclusion of the first tenancy period. Rarely, a landlord might ask you to sign another year-long lease.

It is customary and acceptable for California landlords to demand various combinations of upfront charges before entering into a lease or rental agreement with you. Those charges will likely include a fee for running a credit check (not refundable), the first month's rent, possibly last month's rent (which differs from a security deposit), a key deposit, sometimes a security/cleaning deposit, and, perhaps, a pet deposit. If the property manager asks for last month's rent, keep in mind it must be used for just that. That way, when you give your customary 30 days' notice of intent to vacate, you're paid up. No lease or rental agreement may include nonrefundable deposits. In California all deposits are returnable if all agreed-to conditions are met. In some cities, landlords are also required to pay interest on security deposits at the termination of the lease if the unit was held for longer than a year. If your security deposit is not returned within three weeks of your vacancy date, you can talk to a tenants' rights organization or seek recourse in small claims court. If you are a co-tenant or a sub-tenant, the landlord does not have to return your portion of the security deposit directly to you. The deposit on the unit is returned only when the entire unit is vacated, which means you will have to get your part of the deposit money from the co-tenants or master tenant.

Should you find yourself in the uncomfortable position of having to break a lease, you have a number of ways to mitigate the situation, making it less contentious, less costly to yourself, and more palatable to your landlord. If you need to move out before the lease is up, the landlord must make an effort to rent your unit and he or she may not double-dip; that is he or she may not accept rent from you (who have moved out) and a new tenant at the same time. When breaking a lease, try to do it with care and savvy. Give the landlord written notice of intent as far in advance as possible, and, if you can, try to find a new tenant for your unit, making sure the new person is financially capable of taking on the responsibility. If you know that your old unit has been rented and you are still being held responsible for the lease, take action. Speak to the new tenant, photograph a new name on your old mailbox, and seek help from a tenants' organization (see below).

RENT AND EVICTION CONTROL

Before you've secured a place of your own, be aware that San Francisco has a Rent Stabilization and Arbitration Ordinance that offers protection against some rent increases. The ordinance does not apply to post-1979 apartment units, government-regulated housing, and short-term residential hotels. For those units covered by the ordinance, landlords are allowed to raise the rent once a year, beginning on the anniversary of your move-in date, as long as a

30-day written notice is given. The amount by which the rent may be raised is determined by the San Francisco Rent Board and is announced each March. By law it will always be between 0 and 7%. In 2009 the rate stood at 2.2 %.

East Palo Alto also has rent control (see listing below). In San Jose, only mobile homes and apartments built before September 1979 are protected by rent control. An 8% rent increase is allowable yearly for these kinds of units. Berkeley is the only other rent-controlled city in the region. The rent increase allowance is variable; check with the Berkeley Rent Stabilization Program for more information (their contact information is listed below).

In the remaining parts of the Bay Area, you can expect a rent increase at the end of your lease (with 30 days' notice). Also, you can be evicted without "just cause" when your lease expires, again with 30 days' notice.

Berkeley and San Francisco have stringent eviction protection for tenants. In San Francisco there are 14 "just cause" reasons for eviction, and in Berkeley there are 12. These include failure to pay rent; failure to sign a new lease that is the same as the old lease; illegal activity on the premises; breaking the terms of the lease; willful damage to property or allowing others to damage the property (Berkeley); disturbing other tenants; refusing the landlord legal access to the premises when the landlord needs entry in order to bring the unit up to code or to make substantial repairs; an owner-move-in eviction; the landlord has received a permit to demolish the unit; a subletting tenant refuses to vacate the temporary housing offered by the landlord after the landlord has repaired the tenant's prior unit (Berkeley). In addition, a newer quirk in metropolitan areas is landlords' use of the Ellis Act, a state law permitting owners to evict tenants on the grounds that they are permanently removing the rental units from the market. Highly controversial, the law was meant to relieve the strain of management on retiring apartment owners, but has been exploited by developers in lucrative markets like San Francisco. The landlord must evict the entire building and keep it off market for five years. But a loophole in the law allows developers to convert the property into condominiums and sell the resulting units at a much higher value. Local anti-gentrification groups have fought this ordinance with varying success. The sale of property, the expiration of a rental agreement, or a change in the Federal Section 8 status of a unit does *not* constitute "good cause" for eviction.

The laws of every other locality are generally state tenancy laws. A comprehensive source of information on the legal aspects of tenancy, *California Tenants' Rights*, is published by Berkeley-based Nolo Press, 800-728-3555, www. nolo.com. Nolo also publishes the *California Landlord's Law Book*, for those on the other side of the rental property wall. Knowing the rights and responsibilities of both sides may prove valuable when it comes time to sign on the dotted line, and again when you're ready to move out, as security deposits, apartment cleaning, and repairs become potential issues of concern. Also, you can view the California Civil Code on the web, www.leginfo.ca.gov.

If you're in need of help, you can also get information on tenants' rights from a number of offices:

- **Berkeley Rent Stabilization Board**, 2125 Milvia St, 510-981-7368, www. ci.berkeley.ca.us/rent
- **California State Department of Fair Employment and Housing**, www. dfeh.ca.gov, 1515 Clay St, Suite 701, Oakland, 510-622-2973 or 800-884-1684; 2570 N First St, Suite 480, San Jose, 408-325-0344
- **East Palo Alto Rent Stabilization Program**, 650-853-3114, www.ci.east-palo-alto.ca.us
- **Eviction Defense Center**, 995 Market St #1200, San Francisco, 415-947-0797, www.evictiondefense.org
- **Housing Rights, Inc.**, 1966 San Pablo Ave, Berkeley, 510-548-8776, 800-261-2298, www.housingrights.org
- **Just Cause Oakland**, advocates for low-income tenants, 510-763-5877, www.justcauseoakland.com
- **Project Sentinel**, specializes in landlord/tenant disputes across the lower Bay Area, 888-324-7468
- **St. Peter's Housing Committee**, specializes in Latino community housing rights, 474 Valencia St, San Francisco, 415-487-9203, www.comitedevivienda. org
- **San Francisco Rent Board**, 25 Van Ness Ave, Suite 320, San Francisco, 415-252-4600, www.sfgov.org/rentboard
- **San Francisco Tenants Union**, 558 Capp St, San Francisco, 415-282-6622, www.sftu.org
- **Bay Area Legal Aid** has offices across the region, 1735 Telegraph Ave, Oakland, 510-663-4744, www.baylegal.org; call for a pre-screening.
- **Legal Aid Society Housing Counseling Program**, 408-283-1540
- **San Jose Rental Rights and Referrals**, 200 E Santa Clara St, San Jose, 408-975-4480, www.sjhousing.org

LANDLORD/TENANT RIGHTS AND RESPONSIBILITIES

In the state of California, landlords must rent premises (grounds, buildings, and units) that are free of rubbish and vermin. There must be adequate containers for garbage and recycling. The floors, hallways, and railings must be in good repair. Electrical wiring must be in good working order and up to the safety standards at the time of installation. There must be adequate and safe heating facilities. There must be hot and cold running water and a sewage disposal system. There must be plumbing, electricity, and gas, all in good working order. There must be effective waterproofing on the walls and roofs. Windows and doors must be unbroken, and locks must be in working order.

Landlords are not allowed to enter your premises without giving 24 hours' notice and receiving your permission, unless an emergency threatens damage to the unit. You must permit the landlord to enter to make repairs, and to show the apartment to prospective buyers, tenants, contractors, appraisers, and the like. The landlord is not allowed to harass you verbally or physically or make threats. A landlord can neither lock you out of the premises until you have been legally evicted nor turn off your utilities in an attempt to get you to vacate without due process. Tenants are responsible for maintaining the premises in working and sanitary condition, for paying the rent on time, and for following the rules written in the lease.

Rental situations in the Bay Area vary widely, from renting a typical apartment in a complex to renting an attic room in someone's home. To learn more about local ordinances, order the book *California Tenants: A Guide to Residential Tenants' and Landlords' Rights and Responsibilities*, available free from the Department of Consumer Affairs. Send your request to California Tenants c/o Department of Consumer Affairs, Policy & Publications Development Office, 1625 N. Market Boulevard, Suite N-112, Sacramento, CA 95834, or call (866) 320-8652 or (800) 952-5210. You can also visit www.dca.ca.gov/publications/landlordbook/catenant.pdf to download a copy

RENTER'S INSURANCE

Renter's insurance provides relatively inexpensive coverage against theft, water damage, fire, and in many cases, personal liability. In this earthquake-prone area, try to find a policy that covers earthquake damage to personal possessions. Be sure to shop around as insurance rates vary considerably. Those with several housemates may not be eligible for coverage.

Web sites can be helpful as you search for renter's insurance. A couple that may be worth investigating are www.insure.com and Quicken, www.insuremarket.com. These sites offer details about what a policy should cover and tips on making a claim. Most large insurance companies (AAA, 21st Century, etc.) also offer renter's insurance. If you own a car, a good option is to check and see if your car insurance carrier also offers renter's insurance, as you may be able to get a discount for adding a new service.

BUYING

Many people come to the Bay Area with the intention of buying a house, but the sticker price often scares them into renting and longing for life back in Kansas. Despite tough economic times, the prices of Bay Area real estate continue to command a premium.

While it's good to have a clear idea of what you want, you may need to be willing to make concessions—in terms of both price and neighborhood. To figure out what you can afford to pay for a house, the general rule of thumb is to multiply your annual salary by three or four. For example, if you make $100,000 a year, you should plan on spending no more than $400,000 on your new home. The bad news is that you will be hard pressed to find a home for $400,000 in much of the Bay Area. Another important point to remember is that you will be required to place about 20% of the purchase price as a down payment, and don't forget about closing costs, which are generally 1% to 3% of the purchase price, depending on your loan.

Before even beginning your search, most realtors suggest taking a moment to make a list of your top priorities. Think about the neighborhood, the commute, parking, schools, the number of bedrooms and bathrooms, etc. Consider your lifestyle. If you are a gourmet cook, is the kitchen spacious enough? Do you want to live in a gated community? How about a historic property? If you are looking for a fixer-upper, you'll need to consider how much time, money, and effort you will be willing to put into a place. Drafting such a list will let a real estate agent focus on what's truly important to you and your family. In addition, before meeting with a real estate agent, it's a good idea to do a little footwork on your own. Investigate the cost of properties in the neighborhood where you would like to live, and compare that to your financial situation. A good resource to check out is www.fsbo.com, an online DIY home-buying and selling web site that removes much of the overhead involved with purchasing a house. Another new resource available online through a fusion of social networking and professional real estate agents is www.trulia.com, a web site that provides comps, trends, and free advice from the hundreds of realtors that populate its forums.

ONLINE RESOURCES—HOUSE HUNTING

These days you can start your search for a home on the Internet before you even arrive in the Bay Area. While searching the web probably won't get you a house, since many are sold as quickly as they are listed, it will give you a good idea about what's on the market, where you should look once you get here, and approximately how much you can expect to pay. Not every site lists every home in the Bay Area, but every home in the Bay Area for sale is probably now listed on at least one site.

Some useful sites to help your search include:

- **www.craigslist.org**; many realtors and home owners use this web site in the Bay Area
- **www.cyberhomes.com**; lists homes for sale across the nation and lists other pertinent real estate information
- **www.realestate.msn.com**; home-buying site with information on homes for sale, finance, moving and relocating, home improvement and more
- **www.homefair.com**; realty listings, moving tips, and more
- **www.homeseekers.com**; a database system of the Multiple Listing Service
- **www.mls.com**; Multiple Listing Service—find homes for sale, realtors, and general real estate information

- **www.move.com**; lists homes for sale, apartments, roommates, and includes moving tips.
- **www.realtytimes.com**; a nice national real estate news site that provides local information
- **www.realestate.yahoo.com**; this site lists homes for sale, mortgage loans, community profiles, listings for home inspectors, real estate agents, title companies, and more
- **www.zillow.com**; lists homes for sale, real estate advice and lots of local information
- **www.ziprealty.com**; claims to be the first online real estate brokerage to host online transactions

CONDOMINIUMS, CO-OPS, TENANCIES-IN-COMMON

In the Bay Area, detached single-family homes are plentiful but usually expensive. Alternative housing options include condominiums, co-ops, and tenancies-in-common.

Condominiums or "condos" are communal associations or cooperative developments where the co-owners share interest and responsibility for the common areas (elevator, garden, laundry room, and hallways), but hold sole ownership of their unit. Condos are common in the Bay Area, and new ones are rapidly being built.

A **co-op** is a corporation; owners hold shares in the property and have voting rights. An owner has the right to sell those shares, but the board members or fellow co-op members reserve the right to refuse to sell to someone whom they consider undesirable. Co-op residences are generally in larger, older buildings.

With **tenancies-in-common**, known as TICs, co-owners usually buy an existing building of two to six units. By law, the co-owners all must live on the premises as their primary residences. The co-owners own a percentage of the entire building, but while they enjoy exclusive use of their unit, they do not own that unit outright. The finances of TIC co-owners, with regard to the building, are entwined, perhaps making it riskier to buy into than a condo. In San Francisco, TICs have become a popular option for those who want out of the San Francisco rental market but cannot afford to purchase a traditional, single-family home. San Franciscans concerned about the dwindling supply of affordable rental units in the Bay Area have opposed the recent rise in condo and TIC conversions, and now San Francisco generally restricts residential condominium conversions. The laws governing TICs shift and flow according to political currents, and you should pursue a full understanding of the current regulations regarding these complex housing contracts if contemplating this option.

FINDING A REALTOR

Certainly, buying a home is not something you do every day, and while it is possible to find a house or condo on your own, you'll probably be better off with the help of an expert. Most homes are bought through a real estate agent because of the complex funding and legal issues involved in the transaction. Even if you find a home that appeals to you, say in cyberspace, you will most likely need an agent to show you the place and complete the required paperwork.

One of the best ways to find a real estate agent is through word of mouth. Ask your friends, colleagues, or your employer's relocation administrator. Visiting open houses held in the neighborhood of your choice is another good way to meet agents. It's important to meet with and talk to a few agents before choosing one. Be sure to look for someone who will represent you as a buyer—a buyer's broker. A buyer's broker works exclusively for the prospective home-buyer, while a traditional broker works for the home seller, even though they show buyers around. A broker who works for you will bargain on your behalf, and try to get you the lowest possible price for the house, while a traditional broker's job is just the opposite—to get the seller the most money possible for the house. Make sure that whoever you choose is someone who seems trust-worthy and has a good reputation. Check a realtor's credentials, and call his or her references to find out if previous clients were satisfied.

Once you find a home you want, your realtor will help make sure that your offer is accepted, which can include pitching your "story" to the seller. When making an offer, it is also important to structure it with minimal contingencies. A real estate agent who is familiar with these and other tactics, as well as the going prices for properties, can be a great help in this market.

HOMEOWNER'S INSURANCE

For most everyone, dealing with a bank or mortgage lender is necessary when buying a new home, and getting homeowner's insurance is a required part of the process. Coverage is typically offered at 120% to 125% of the face value of your house and belongings. Factors that insurance companies consider when determining the rate of your policy include the fire resistance of your house—wood frames cost more to insure than masonry structures—and your location. Being in a high-theft neighborhood or far from a fire hydrant or fire station will add to the cost of your policy.

Earthquake insurance in the Bay Area is a good idea, although it's expensive and for a while was difficult to obtain. In 1994, as a result of the costs associated with the Northridge Earthquake, many insurance companies stopped writing new homeowner's and renter's insurance policies and some pulled out of California altogether. In response, the State of California established the **California Earthquake Authority (CEA)** in 1996, which provides basic earthquake-damage coverage. Insurance companies operating in California are required to either supply their own earthquake coverage to their policyholders or to offer the CEA's policy. For more information about the CEA call 916-325-3800 or 877-797-4300, or check out www.earthquakeauthority.com. For answers to any other insurance-related questions, contact the **California Department of Insurance** at 800-927-4357 or visit www.insurance.ca.gov.

The most common type of earthquake insurance is normally added as an endorsement on a standard homeowner's insurance policy. Typically, there is a deductible of 5% to 10%, and sometimes 15%, of the value of the home. This means that for a home currently insured at $200,000, you would have to pay $10,000 to $30,000 on damages before the insurance company would pay anything. Separate deductibles may apply to contents and structure. An important coverage is for temporary living expenses, which pays for a motel and meals if you have to move out of your home. There is usually no deductible on this coverage. The yearly cost of residential earthquake insurance is normally about $1.50 to $3 per $1,000 of coverage on the structure.

To find out more about earthquake insurance, ask your insurance agent or call the California State Department of Insurance at 800-927-4357, or visit www.insurance.ca.gov.

If you are looking at an older home, find out if it has been retrofitted. Though not required if the home hasn't had any major renovations, this is something you want to consider. Retrofitting won't guarantee your home will escape an earthquake damage-free but generally speaking, reinforced structures withstand shocks better, making them safer and reducing damage in quakes. Cost varies but can be 1% to 3% of a home's total value. For shaking maps and information on making your home safer, check out **http://quake.abag.ca.gov**. The **US Geological Survey**, www.usgs.gov, also has a wealth of information on earthquakes and earthquake safety.

ADDITIONAL RESOURCES—HOUSE HUNTING

Following are resources that may be of interest for those in the market for a new home:

- "Think Glink," **www.thinkglink.com**, a web site run by Ilyce R. Glink, a nationally syndicated columnist and best-selling writer who specializes in real estate and finance
- *How to Buy a House in California*, 12th edition (Nolo Press), by Ralph E. Warner, Ira Serkes, and George Devine
- **www.edf.org**, the web site maintained by the Environmental Defense Fund, can provide information about toxic waste issues in the geographical area for a home—a wise thing to check because the entire San Francisco Bay Area once had a heavy military presence

HAVING FOUND AND SECURED A PLACE TO LIVE, YOU NOW HAVE THE sometimes complicated task of getting your stuff here and perhaps finding storage. The how-tos follow, as well as a section detailing which agency to contact regarding consumer complaints against moving companies, information about moving with children, and specifics regarding tax-deductible moving expenses.

TRUCK RENTALS

First, determine if you are going to move it yourself or hire someone else to do it for you. If you prefer doing it all yourself, you can rent a vehicle, load it up, and hit the road. Look in the Yellow Pages under "Truck Rental" and call around and compare; also ask about any specials. Below is a list of four national truck rental companies and their toll-free numbers and web sites. For the best information, you should call a local office. Note: Most truck rental companies now offer "one-way" rentals as well as packing accessories and storage facilities. Of course, these extras are not free. If you're cost conscious you may want to scavenge boxes in advance of your move or buy some directly from a box company. (Those moving locally should check Smart and Final stores, which frequently offer empty boxes in a bin near the entrance of the store. Liquor stores are also perennial favorites for free small and mid-size boxes.)

If you're planning to move during the peak moving months (May through September), call well in advance, at least a month ahead of when you think you'll need the vehicle. Remember that Saturday is a popular moving day; you may be able to get cheaper rates if you book a different day.

Once you're on the road, keep in mind that your rental truck may be a tempting target for thieves. If you must park it overnight or for an extended period (more than a couple of hours), try to find a safe place, preferably somewhere well-lit and easily observable by you, and do your best not to leave anything of particular value in the cab. Make sure you lock the back door and, if possible, use a steering wheel lock or other easy-to-purchase safety device.

Four national self-moving companies to consider:

- **Budget**, 800-462-8343, www.budgettruck.com
- **Penske**, 888-996-5415, www.pensketruckrental.com
- **Ryder**, 800-297-9337, www.ryder.com (now a Budget company, still operating under the Ryder name)
- **U-Haul**, 800-468-4285, www.uhaul.com

COMMERCIAL FREIGHT CARRIERS AND CONTAINER-BASED MOVERS

If you don't want to drive a truck yourself, but also don't want to hire a full-service mover, there's a third option: you can hire a commercial freight carrier to deliver a trailer or container to your home. You pack and load as much of it as you need, and the carrier delivers your trailer or container to its destination. In some cases, this option can be cheaper than renting and driving your own truck, especially when you consider the cost of fuel. **ABF U-Pack Moving** (800-355-1696, www.upack.com) uses commercial 28-foot freight trailers. ABF charges by the linear foot, and you only pay for the linear feet you use (subject to a minimum charge). When you've finished loading, you install a plywood bulkhead; ABF fills the remaining space with freight, which is unloaded before the trailer is delivered to your new home.

ABF, **PODS** (866-229-4120, www.pods.com), **Door-to-Door Storage and Moving** (888-366-7222, www.doortodoor.com), and several other companies offer container-based moves. In this type of move, the carrier delivers plywood, metal, or fiberglass cubes or other containers to your home. You can take a few days—or sometimes a full month—to load the containers; when you're done loading, the company picks up the containers, transfers them to flatbed trucks, moves them to your destination city, and delivers them to your new home. You generally only pay to transport the containers you actually use, and, unlike a truck, the containers can be placed in storage at either end of the journey. However, a set of containers has a smaller storage capacity than a large truck, so this option may not work for people with large houses full of furniture. In addition, some large pieces of furniture—grandfather clocks, for example—may not fit inside the containers; if you have to move items that are very long or tall, ask the company for its containers' *interior* dimensions before you commit.

If you aren't moving an entire house and can't estimate how much truck space you will need, keep in mind this general guideline: Two to three furnished rooms equal a 15-foot truck; four to five rooms, a 20-foot truck.

MOVERS

INTERSTATE

First, the good news: Moving can be affordable and problem-free. The bad news: If you're hiring a mover, the chances of it being so are much less.

Probably the best way to find a mover is by **personal recommendation**. Absent a friend or relative who can recommend a trusted moving company, you can turn to what surveys show is the most popular method of finding a mover: the **Yellow Pages**. Then there's the **Internet**: just type in "movers" on a search engine and you'll be directed to hundreds of more or less helpful moving-related sites.

One way to check the reliability of a mover is by using **Yelp,** www.yelp.com. This user-feedback oriented web site opens thousands of businesses to the scrutiny of the masses. Also check out www.movingscam.com, another user-driven consumer review web site. And, if you are a member of Angie's List, you'll find lists of moving companies that have been rated by other members.You might ask a local realtor, who may be able to steer you towards a good mover, or at least tell you which ones to avoid. Members of the American Automobile Association have a valuable resource at hand in **AAA's Consumer Relocation Services**, which will assign the member a personal consultant to handle every detail of the move free of charge and which offers savings from discounts arranged with premier moving companies. Call 800-922-8228, www.aaa.com.

Another good resource to help you avoid problems is California-based **MoveRescue**, 800-832-1773, www.moverescue.com, which offers pre-move education and consumer assistance, all aimed at helping you avoid being scammed.

But beware! Since 1995, when the federal government eliminated the Interstate Commerce Commission, the interstate moving business has degenerated into a wild and mostly unregulated industry with thousands of unhappy, ripped-off customers annually. (There are so many reports of unscrupulous carriers that we no longer list movers in this book.) Since states do not have the authority to regulate interstate movers and the federal government has been slow to respond, you are pretty much on your own when it comes to finding an honest, hassle-free mover. That's why we can't emphasize enough the importance of carefully researching and choosing who will move you.

To aid your search for an **interstate mover**, we offer a few general recommendations:

First get the names of a half-dozen movers and check to make sure they are licensed by the **US Department of Transportation's Federal Motor Carrier Safety Administration** (**FMCSA**). With the movers' Motor Carrier (MC) numbers in hand, call 866-637-0635 or 202-385-2423 (offers the option of speaking to an agent) or go online to www.safer.fmcsa.dot.gov, to see if the carriers are licensed and insured. If the companies you're considering are federally licensed, your next step should be to check with the **Better Business Bureau**, www.bbb.org, in the state where the moving companies are licensed as well as with the states' consumer protection boards, or attorneys general (in California call the Department of Consumer Affairs, 800-952-5210, or go to www.dca.ca.gov). Also check FMCSA's **Household Goods Consumer Complaint** web site, http://nccdb.fmcsa.dot.gov, where they maintain complaints that have been filed on interstate movers. Assuming there is no negative information, you can move on to the next step: asking for references. Particularly important are references from customers who experienced moves similar to yours. If a moving company is unable or unwilling to provide references, eliminate it from your list. Unscrupulous movers have even been known to give phony references who will falsely sing the mover's praises—so talk to more than one reference and ask questions. If something feels fishy, it probably is. One way to learn more about a prospective mover: Ask them if they have a local office (they should) and then walk in and check it out.

Once you have at least three movers you feel reasonably comfortable with, it's time to ask for price quotes (always free). Best is a binding "not-to-exceed" quote, of course in writing. This will require an on-site visual inspection of what you are shipping. If you have *any* doubts about a prospective mover, drop it from your list before you invite a stranger into your home to catalog your belongings.

Regulations by FMCSA require movers to supply several documents to consumers before executing a contract. These include two booklets: *Important Information for Persons Moving Household Goods (within California)*, which must be provided at the first-person contact between the consumer and the mover, and *Your Rights and Responsibilities When You Move*; a concise and accurate written estimate of charges; a summary of the mover's arbitration program; the mover's customer complaint and inquiry handling procedure; and the mover's tariff containing rates, rules, regulations, classifications, etc. For more about FMCSA's role in handling household goods, you can go to its consumer page at www.protectyourmove.gov.

ADDITIONAL MOVING RECOMMENDATIONS

- If someone recommends a mover to you, get names (the salesperson or estimator, the drivers, the loaders). To paraphrase the NRA, moving companies don't move people, people do. Likewise, if someone tells you they had a bad moving experience, note the name of the company and try to avoid it.
- Remember that price, while important, isn't everything, especially when you're entrusting all of your worldly possessions to strangers.
- Legitimate movers charge by the hour (local moves, under 100 miles), and by weight/mileage (for long-distance moves). Be wary if the mover wants to charge by the cubic foot.

- Ask about the other end—subcontracting increases the chances that something could go wrong.
- In general, ask questions, and if you're concerned about something, ask for an explanation in writing. If you change your mind about a mover after you've signed on the dotted line, write a letter explaining that you've changed your mind and that you won't be using its services. Better safe than sorry.
- Ask about insurance; the "basic" 60 cents per pound industry standard coverage is not enough. If you have homeowner's or renter's insurance, check to see if it will cover your belongings during transit. If not, ask your insurer if you can add that coverage for your move. Otherwise, consider purchasing "full replacement" or "full value" coverage from the carrier for the estimated value of your shipment. Though it's the most expensive type of coverage offered, it's probably worth it. Trucks get into accidents, they catch fire, they get stolen—if such insurance seems pricey to you, ask about a $250 or $500 deductible. This can reduce your cost substantially while still giving you much better protection in case of a catastrophic loss.
- Whatever you do, *do not* mislead a salesperson/estimator about how much and what you are moving. And make sure you tell prospective movers about how far they'll have to transport your stuff to and from the truck as well as any stairs, driveways, obstacles or difficult vegetation, long paths or sidewalks, etc. The clearer you are with your mover, the better he or she will be able to serve you.
- Think about packing. If you plan to pack yourself, you can save some money, but if something is damaged because of your packing, you may not be able to file a claim for it. On the other hand, if you hire the mover to do the packing, they may not treat your belongings as well as you will. They will certainly do it faster, that's for sure. Depending on the size of your move and whether or not you are packing yourself, you may need a lot of boxes, tape, and packing material. Mover boxes, while not cheap, are usually sturdy and the right size. Sometimes a mover will give a customer free used boxes. It doesn't hurt to ask. Also, *don't* wait to pack until the last minute. If you're doing the packing, give yourself at least a week to do the job; two or more is better. Be sure to ask the mover about any weight or size restrictions on boxes.
- You should transport all irreplaceable items such as jewelry, photographs, or key work documents personally. Do not put them in the moving van! Consider sending less precious items that you do not want to put in the moving truck via the US Postal Service or by UPS.
- Ask your mover what is not permitted in the truck: usually anything flammable or combustible, as well as certain types of valuables.
- Although movers will put numbered labels on your possessions, you should make a numbered list of every box and item that is going in the truck. Detail box contents and photograph anything of particular value. Once the truck arrives on the other end, you can check off every piece and know for sure what

did (or did not) make it. In case of claims, this list can be invaluable. Even after the move, keep the list; it can be surprisingly useful.

- Movers are required to issue you a "bill of lading"; do not hire a mover who does not use them.
- Consider keeping a log of every expense you incur for your move, e.g., phone calls, trips to San Francisco, etc. In many instances, the IRS allows you to claim these types of expenses on your income taxes. (See **Taxes** below.)
- Be aware that during the busy season (May through September), demand can exceed supply and moving may be more difficult and more expensive than during the rest of the year. If you must relocate during the peak moving months, call and book service well in advance—a month at least—of when you plan on moving. If you can reserve service way in advance, say four to six months early, you may be able to lock in a lower winter rate for your summer move.
- Listen to what the movers say; they are professionals and can give you expert advice about packing and preparing. Also, be ready for the truck on both ends—don't make them wait. Not only will it irritate your movers, but it may cost you. Understand, too, that things can happen on the road that are beyond a carrier's control (weather, accidents, etc.) and your belongings may not get to you at the time or on the day promised.
- Treat your movers well, especially the ones loading your stuff on and off the truck. Offer to buy them lunch, and tip them if they do a good job.
- Before moving pets, attach a tag to your pet's collar with your new address and phone number in case your furry friend accidentally wanders off in the confusion of moving. Your pet should travel with you, and you should never plan on moving a pet inside a moving van. For more on moving with pets, you might want to look into *The Pet-Moving Handbook: Maximize Your Pet's Well-Being and Maintain Your Sanity*, by Carrie Straub, published by First Books (www.firstbooks.com).
- Be prepared to pay the full moving bill upon delivery. Cash or bank/cashier's check may be required. Some carriers will take VISA and MasterCard but it is a good idea to get it in writing that you will be permitted to pay with a credit card since the delivering driver may not be aware of this and may demand cash. Unless you routinely keep thousands in greenbacks on you, you could have a problem getting your stuff off the truck.

INTRASTATE AND LOCAL MOVERS

The **California Public Utilities Commission (CPUC)**, www.cpuc.ca.gov, regulates the licensing, rates, and rules of the Household Goods moving industry in California. All companies involved in the moving business must be insured and hold a license that permits them to provide moving services within or from/to California. To verify certification of your chosen mover, call the CPUC at 415-703-2782 or the **California Moving and Storage Association** (CMSA) at

800-672-1415 and have the mover's CAL T number (listed on the mover's literature) ready. The CMSA, www.thecmsa.org, is a nonprofit trade organization that offers references to legitimate movers and provides information to help consumers avoid "bandit movers" (movers that engage in unlawful practices and/or bully the customer into paying outrageous prices once the move has started). According to the CMSA, 80% of the calls to them involve complaints about bandit movers. They recommend against booking online or over the phone without investigating the company's physical address first and confirming it's licensed (with a CAL T number) with the CPUC. For moves within California, the CPUC regulations require all movers to provide each client with a written "not to exceed price" before the move commences. This price should be clearly disclosed on your Agreement for Service form. The mover will have you sign this form before the move begins.

CONSUMER COMPLAINTS—MOVERS

If a **move goes badly** and you blame the moving company, you should first file a written claim with the mover for loss or damage. If this doesn't work and it's an intrastate move, call 800-894-9444 to file a complaint with the CPUC. If the mover is a CMSA member, the CMSA will intervene on the consumer's behalf if there is a problem.

If your grievance is with an **interstate carrier**, your choices are limited. Interstate moves are regulated by the Federal Motor Carrier Safety Administration (FMCSA), 888-368-7238, www.fmcsa.dot.gov, an agency under the Department of Transportation, with whom you can file a complaint against a carrier. While its role in the regulation of interstate carriers historically has been concerned with safety issues rather than consumer issues, in response to the upsurge in unscrupulous movers and unhappy consumers, it has issued a recent set of rules "specifying how interstate household goods (HHG) carriers (movers) and brokers must assist their individual customers shipping household goods." According to its consumer page, carriers in violation of said rules can be fined, and repeat offenders may be barred from doing business. In terms of loss, however, "FMCSA does not have statutory authority to resolve loss and damage of consumer complaints, settle disputes against a mover, or obtain reimbursement for consumers seeking payment for specific charges. Consumers are responsible for resolving disputes involving these household goods matters." It is not able to represent you in an arbitration dispute to recover damages for lost or destroyed property, or to enforce a court judgment. If you have a grievance, your best bet is to file a complaint against a mover with FMCSA and with the Better Business Bureau, www.bbb.org, in the state where the moving company is licensed, as well as with that state's attorney general or consumer protection office. To seek redress, hire an attorney.

STORAGE WAREHOUSES

Storage facilities may be required when you have to ship your furniture without an apartment to receive it or if your apartment is too small for all your belongings. The CPUC regulates short-term storage (under 90 days), but not long-term or self-storage. If your mover maintains storage warehouse facilities in the city, as many do, you'll probably want to store with them. Some even offer one month's free storage. Look in the Yellow Pages under "Storage," and shop around for the best and most convenient deal. Below are a couple of major moving/ storage companies. Listing here does *not* imply endorsement by First Books.

- **Door to Door Storage**, 888-366-7222, www.doortodoor.com/storage, has warehousing for cargo containers, which it delivers to you for packing, and then its trucks transport the container back to its facilities (several throughout the Bay Area).
- **Public Storage**, 800-447-8673, www.publicstorage.com, offers locations throughout San Francisco and the Bay Area for self-service storage and truck rentals.

SELF-STORAGE

The ability to rent anything from 5' x 5' rooms to storage rooms large enough to accommodate a car is a great boon to urban dwellers. This is especially true in San Francisco, where landlords frequently rent garage space separately (for homes that have it) to monthly parkers. Collectors, people with old clothes they can't bear to give away, and those with possessions that won't fit in a sublet or shared apartment all find mini-warehouses a solution to tight living situations.

Rates for space in Bay Area self-storage facilities are competitive: Expect to pay at least $50 a month for a 5' x 5' (25 sq ft), $150+ a month for a 10' x 10' space (100 sq ft), and so on. Some offer free pick-up; otherwise you or your mover delivers the goods. If you're looking for lower rates, inquire with the storage facility for move-in specials, upper floor discounts, or other locations.

As you shop around, you may want to check the facility for cleanliness and security. Does the building have sprinklers in case of fire? Does it have carts and hand trucks for moving in and out? Does it bill monthly, or will it automatically charge the bill to your credit card? Access should be 24-hour or nearly so, and some are air conditioned, an asset if you plan to visit your locker in the summer. Is the area well lit at night and is there a security guard on-site at all times? Is the rental month to month or is there a minimum lease? Is it easily accessible from your home?

Finally, a word of warning: Unless you no longer want your stored belongings, pay your storage bill and pay it on time. Storage companies may auction the contents of delinquent customers' lockers.

Here are a few area self-storage companies. For more options, check the Yellow Pages under "Storage."

- **AAAAA Rent-A-Space**, 650-341-2964, www.5Aspace.com, offers student and senior discounts, has locations in Foster City and Moraga.
- **Central Self-Storage**, 925-930-0810, www.centralselfstorage.com, has facilities in Burlingame, Daly City, Alameda, and Corte Madera.
- **Mobile Mini, Inc.**, 866-344-4092, www.mobilemini.com, delivers storage containers from 5′ x 8′ to 40′ x 10′ that are filled then transported to your new location.
- **Public Storage**, 877-788-2028, www.publicstorage.com, has a variety of locations throughout the Bay Area, also offers pick-up and delivery services at certain locations, 866-863-4838, www.pspickup.com.

CHILDREN AND MOVING

Studies show that moving, especially frequent moving, can be hard on children. According to an American Medical Association study, children who move often are more likely to suffer from such problems as depression, low self-esteem, and aggression. Often their academic performance suffers as well. Aside from not moving more than is necessary, there are a few things you can do to help your children through this stressful time:

- Talk about the move with your kids. Be honest but positive. Listen to their concerns. To the extent possible, involve them in the process.
- Make sure children have their favorite possessions with them on the trip; don't pack "blankey" in the moving van.
- Make sure you have some social life planned on the other end. Your children may feel lonely in your new home, and such activities can ease the transition. If you move during the summer, you might find a local camp (check with the YWCA or YMCA) at which they can sign up for a couple of weeks in August to make new friends.
- Keep in touch with family and loved ones as much as possible. Photos and phone calls are important ways of maintaining links to the important people you have left behind.
- If your children are school age, take the time to involve yourself in their new school and in their academic life. Don't let them fall through the cracks.
- Try to schedule a move during the summer so they can start their new school at the beginning of the term.
- If possible, prior to the move spend some time doing fun things in the area to which you are moving, such as visiting a local playground or playing ball in a local park or checking out the neighborhood stores. With any luck your children will meet some other kids their own age.

First Books (**www.firstbooks.com**) offers two helpful resources for children. For those aged 6–11, *The Moving Book: A Kids' Survival Guide* by Gabriel Davis is a wonderful gift, and younger children will appreciate *Max's Moving Adventure: A Coloring Book for Kids on the Move* by Danelle Till. For general guidance, read *Smart Moves: Your Guide Through the Emotional Maze of Relocation* by Nadia Jensen, Audrey McCollum, and Stuart Copans.

TAXES AND MOVING

If your move is work-related, some or all of your moving expenses may be tax-deductible—so you probably want to keep those receipts. Though eligibility varies, depending, for example, on whether you have a job or are self-employed, generally, the cost of moving yourself, your family, and your belongings is tax deductible, even if you don't itemize. The criteria: In order to take the deduction your move must be employment-related, your new job must be more than 50 miles away from your current residence, and you must be at the new location for at least 39 weeks during the first 12 months after your arrival. If you take the deduction and then fail to meet the requirements, you will have to pay the IRS back, unless you were laid off through no fault of your own or transferred again by your employer. It's a good idea to consult a tax expert regarding IRS rules related to moving. However, if you're a confident soul, get a copy of IRS Form 3903 (www.irs.gov/pub/irs-pdf/f3903.pdf) and do it yourself!

ADDITIONAL RELOCATION AND MOVING INFORMATION

- **www.firstbooks.com**, relocation resources and information on moving to Atlanta, Boston, Chicago, Dallas–Ft. Worth/Houston/Austin, Los Angeles, Minneapolis–St. Paul, New York City, Portland, Seattle, Washington, D.C., as well as China and London, England. Also publisher of the *Newcomer's Handbook® for Moving to and Living in the USA*.
- *How to Survive A Move*, edited by Jamie Allen and Kazz Regelman, is a **Hundreds of Heads** guide (www.hundredsofheads.com). Divided into sections ranging from planning a move to packing tips, moving with kids, and worst moves ever, this easy-to-digest book provides the wisdom, dispensed mostly in single-paragraph bites, of hundreds of people who've lived through the experience.
- **BestPlaces**, www.bestplaces.net; compares quality-of-life and cost-of-living data of US cities.
- *How to Move Handbook* by Clyde and Shari Steiner, an excellent general guidebook
- **http://realestate.msn.com**; articles and advice.
- **The Riley Guide**, www.rileyguide.com; online moving and relocation clearinghouse. Lists moving and relocation guides and web sites, offers links to sites that cover cost of living/demographics as well as real estate links and school and health care directories.
- **American Auto Transporters, Inc**, 800-800-2580, www.shipcar.com, if you need help moving your car.
- **Worldwide ERC**, 703-842-3400, www.worldwideerc.org, a global employee relocation agency, the Employee Relocation Council, that is a professional organization offering members specialized reports on the relocation and moving industries.
- **https://moversguide.usps.com**, relocation information from the United States Postal Service.

ONE OF THE FIRST THINGS YOU'LL WANT TO DO WHEN YOU ARRIVE IN the Bay Area is set up a checking and perhaps a savings account. Opening one is usually painless. Since San Francisco is a regional financial center, there is no shortage of banks, savings and loans, and credit unions.

Most financial institutions offer a variety of account options, from no-fee checking and savings with a sizable minimum balance to inexpensive service if you do all your banking by ATM. If you have time, shop around for the best deal or if you are in a rush during the move, sign up with one of the big boys, then research other banks and change later if and when you find a better deal. Keep in mind that smaller banks may be less expensive, in terms of fees, than their colossal nationwide counterparts, while offering you a more navigable bureaucracy to deal with when you need help from your bank.

CHECKING ACCOUNTS

Setting up a checking account should be relatively quick and easy, as long as you have photo identification with your signature, an address, and some money. Some banks prefer to see that you've had an account at another financial institution, but most will not require this. Many financial institutions offer free checking account options, though most will require you to maintain a specified minimum balance in order to avoid monthly service fees. When you open your account, be sure to ask the teller for a full description of your new account, including minimum balances, available services, and fees. You may also want to ask for a map of the bank's local ATM locations in order to avoid racking up penalty charges for using another's institution's ATMs. You will typically be issued temporary checks on the spot for use until your printed ones arrive, usually within a week to 10 days. However, many merchants don't like to accept nonprinted checks. To be on the safe side, keep enough cash on hand to meet your basic needs for two weeks. Once your printed checks arrive, you should have no trouble writing checks at most places, as long as you have a driver's license or similar photo identification. Chances are you'll also get a debit/ATM card when you open your account. The card usually arrives in the mail within 7 to 10 days, ready to use. Most of your accounts can be linked to each other and to the card, making it easy to do your basic banking without ever going into a branch. Many financial institutions also offer online banking at no additional charge, which allows you to monitor your account from your personal computer.

SAVINGS ACCOUNTS

Just as easy to set up as a checking account, individual characteristics of savings accounts differ from bank to bank in fees, interest, and required minimum balances. Often your savings account can be linked to your checking account to provide overdraft protection, usually for a fee. Again, your savings account can easily be accessed with your debit/ATM card, although you may have to ask that it be set up that way.

AREA BANKS

Here's a list of some of the biggest banks in the area and their main offices. Call them for the address and phone number of neighborhood branches if you'd rather bank closer to home or work.

SAN FRANCISCO

- **Bank of America**, 345 Montgomery St, 650-622-8248, 800-622-8731, www.bankofamerica.com
- **Bank of the West**, 180 Montgomery St, 415-765-4800, 800-488-2265, www.bankofthewest.com
- **California Bank and Trust**, 465 California St, 415-875-1500, 800-355-0507, www.calbanktrust.com
- **Chase**, 401 California St, 415-788-1037, 800-788-7000, www.chase.com
- **Citibank**, 1399 Post St, 800-627-3999, 800-374-9700, www.citibank.com
- **First Republic Bank**, 111 Pine St, 800-392-1400, www.firstrepublic.com
- **Union Bank of California**, 1675 Post St, 415-202-0350, www.uboc.com
- **US Bank**, 525 Market St, 415-278-5050, 800-872-2657, www.usbank.com
- **Wells Fargo Bank**, 1266 Market St, 415-396-4424, 800-869-3557, www.wellsfargo.com

NORTH BAY

- **Bank of America**, 1000 4th St, San Rafael, 415-451-2770, 800-622-8731, www.bankofamerica.com
- **Bank of Marin**, 50 Madera Blvd, Corte Madera, 415-927-2265
- **Bank of the West**, 1313 Grant Ave, Novato, 415-897-1131, 800-488-2265, www.bankofthewest.com

- **US Bank**, 3200 Northgate Dr, San Rafael, 415-479-4804, 800-872-2657, www. usbank.com
- **Wells Fargo**, 715 Bridgeway, Sausalito, 415-332-3355, 800-869-3557, www. wellsfargo.com

EAST BAY

- **Bank of America**, 1500 Park St, Alameda, 510-273-5531; 2129 Shattuck Ave, Berkeley, 510-273-5466; 300 Lakeside Dr, Oakland, 510-273-5118; 1400 E 14th St, San Leandro, 510-649-6600; 800-622-8731, www.bankofamerica.com
- **Bank of the West**, 1969 Diamond Blvd, Concord, 925-689-4410; 11100 San Pablo Ave, El Cerrito, 510-235-2980; 2127 Broadway, Oakland, 510-444-5636; 800-488-2265, www.bankofthewest.com
- **Mechanics Bank**, Lake Merritt Plaza Building, 155 Grand Ave, Oakland, 510-251-6106; 1350 N Main, Walnut Creek, 925-210-8170
- **Union Bank**, 2333 Shattuck Ave, Berkeley, 510-843-6353; 3223 Crow Canyon Road #100, San Ramon, 925-866-0422; 1970 Franklin St, Oakland, 510-891-9505
- **US Bank**, 2424 Santa Clara Ave, Alameda, 510-747-1657, 800-872-2657, www.usbank.com
- **Wells Fargo**, 1221 Broadway, Oakland, 510-891-2011, 800-869-3557, www. wellsfargo.com

PENINSULA

- **Bank of America**, 530 Lytton Ave, Palo Alto, 650-566-8331, 800-227-5458, www.bankofamerica.com
- **Chase**, 300 Hamilton Ave, Palo Alto, 650-853-2602, 800-788-7000, www.chase. com
- **First National Bank of Northern California**, 6600 Mission St, Daly City, 650-992-8800, www.fnbnorcal.com
- **Union Bank**, 400 University, Palo Alto, 650-859-1200
- **US Bank**, 1105 El Camino Real, Menlo Park, 650-617-8330, 800-872-2657, www.usbank.com
- **Wells Fargo**, 400 Hamilton Ave, Palo Alto, 650-330-8135, 800-869-3557, www.wellsfargo.com

SOUTH BAY

- **Bank of America**, 2611 N 1st St, San Jose, 408-983-0588; 2905 Stevens Creek Blvd, Santa Clara, 408-557-6508; 921 E Arques Ave, Sunnyvale, 408-983-0588, 800-622-8731, www.bankofamerica.com
- **Bank of the West**, 2395 Winchester Blvd, Campbell, 408-379-9954; 50 W San Fernando St, San Jose, 408-947-5005; 1705 El Camino Real, Santa Clara, 408-261-1861; 800-488-2265, www.bankofthewest.com

- **Chase**, 55 W Santa Clara St, San Jose, 408-291-3331, 800-788-7000, www.chase.com
- **Union Bank**, 990 N 1st St, San Jose, 408-279-7400, www.uboc.com
- **US Bank**, 1099 Lincoln Ave, San Jose, 408-287-2710, 800-872-2657, www.usbank.com
- **Wells Fargo**, 121 Park Center Plaza, San Jose, 408-277-6535, 800-869-3557, www.wellsfargo.com

CREDIT UNIONS

Some of the best financial service deals are offered by credit unions. The goal of a credit union is to offer affordable, bank-like services, including checking and savings accounts, and low interest loans, and to do it in a way that makes fiscal sense for the organization. On the downside, credit unions usually offer fewer locations than banks and often do not have easily accessible teller machines. You'll have to pay a fee when using a non–credit union ATM. Generally, membership to a credit union is available through some kind of group affiliation, often your place of work or residence. To find out if your company sponsors one, check online at www.ccul.org for a list of dozens of Bay Area credit unions, or try:

- **Marin County Federal**, 30 N San Pedro Rd, #115, San Rafael, 415-499-9780; open to Marin County residents
- **Pacific Service Credit Union**, 245 Market St, San Francisco, 888-858-6878; open to anyone in Northern California
- **San Jose Credit Union**, 140 Asbury St, San Jose, 408-294-8800; open to anyone living, working, or going to school in San Jose

ONLINE BANKING

Today, it is rare when a bank does not offer online banking. Generally this includes balance and other account information inquiries, making transfers, paying bills, and even applying for loans. Security should be a chief concern when accessing your private financial information over the internet. While banks should encrypt your personal information and password, the user should also take standard precautions as well. Don't share your password with anyone, and change it often; don't send confidential information through e-mail or over unsecured web space; and restrict your banking interactions to private computers—not a work computer with a shared network or at an internet cafe.

Online access services and fees vary from bank to bank, so check with individual institutions for information.

CREDIT REPORTS

If you're interested in seeing a personal credit report, you can go to www.annualcreditreport.com, where you can obtain a free copy of your credit report once a year from each of the three main credit bureaus (Equifax, Experian, and

TransUnion). It's best to get a copy from each service because each company's report may be different. If you discover any inaccuracies, you should contact the service immediately and request that it be corrected. By law they must respond to your request within 30 days. Note: checking your credit report too frequently can adversely affect your credit rating.

You can also visit or call each bureau individually:

- **Equifax**, P.O. Box 740241, Atlanta, GA 30374, 800-685-1111, www.equifax. com
- **Experian**, 888-397-3742, www.experian.com
- **TransUnion**, 2 Baldwin Place, P.O. Box 2000, Chester, PA, 19022, 800-888-4213, www.transunion.com

TAXES

FEDERAL INCOME TAX

The Internal Revenue Service has offices in the Bay Area where you can pick up the forms you need to file your income tax return and get the answers to your tax questions. However, be advised that recent studies have found that the answer you get from an IRS representative often depends upon the person giving it rather than any clearly defined rule or regulation. The IRS says it is working on standardizing responses.

Many Bay Area post offices stay open until midnight on April 15th to give procrastinators extra time to fill out their return and get it in the mail with the proper postmark. To request tax forms call 800-829-3676. Tax forms are also available at most post offices and libraries during filing season (January–April), and at the Federal Building in San Francisco, 450 Golden Gate Avenue, or check online, www.irs.gov/formspubs.

IRS Taxpayer Assistance Centers can help clarify tax laws and answer specific questions about your return, your tax account, and any letters you've received from the IRS. The centers are open for walk-in assistance and no appointment is necessary. You can also get help over the phone, 800-829-1040 (individuals), or 800-829-4933 (businesses).

If you qualify for the Earned Income Tax Credit (sometimes called the "Child Tax Credit") or your income is $75,000 or less, you may qualify for free help preparing your individual return. Stop into one of the IRS Assistance Centers listed below (all open Monday–Friday, 8:30 a.m. to 4:30 p.m.) to ask for more information and to set up an appointment:

- **Oakland**: 1301 Clay St, 510-637-2487
- **San Francisco**: 450 Golden Gate Ave, 415-522-4061
- **San Jose:** 55 S Market St, 408-817-6747
- **Santa Rosa:** 777 Sonoma Ave, 707-523-0924
- **Walnut Creek**: 185 Lennon Ln, 925-935-9308

If you have ongoing unresolved issues with the IRS, contact the Taxpayer Advocate Service, 510-637-2703 or 408-817-6850.

ELECTRONIC INCOME TAX FILING

These days, many people are choosing to file their taxes electronically, by purchasing or downloading tax software, using an online tax service, or going through an accredited agency. According to the IRS, electronic filers receive their refunds in about half the time of people who file through the mail, and e-filing costs less and is more accurate than doing it the old-fashioned way.

To research the many tax filing software options, go to your search engine and type in "tax software." **Quicken Turbo Tax**, http://turbotax.intuit.com, and **H&R Block**, www.hrblock.com, are just a couple of many that are available.

For more information on electronic filing, check out **IRS E-file**, www.irs.gov/efile. This site includes features such as convenient payment options or direct deposit for those expecting a return, and offers a list of software brands and internet sites that are capable of handling both federal and state returns.

STATE INCOME TAX

California residents file state tax form 540, 540A, 540 2EZ, 540NR, or 540X. Generally much of the information for your California taxes will come directly from your completed federal return. State income tax forms and answers to your state income tax questions can be found at the State Franchise Tax Board offices:

- **San Francisco**: 121 Spear St, Suite 400, Monday–Friday, 8 a.m. to 5 p.m.
- **Oakland:** 1515 Clay St, Suite 305, Monday–Friday, 8 a.m. to 5 p.m.

For information and assistance with state taxes call 800-852-5711, www.ftb.ca.gov. State tax filing deadline is the same as for federal taxes, April 15. Tax forms are available at most post offices and libraries during tax season (January–April). You can also file online with Calfile at the Franchise Tax Board's web site, www.ftb.ca.gov/online/calfile.

SALES TAX

The local sales tax throughout the Bay Area ranges from 8.25% to 9.5%. It has risen over the years to its current level to help fund the BART transit system and to pay for earthquake damage repairs.

STARTING OR MOVING A BUSINESS

With a well-educated pool of workers, the Bay Area is a great place to start a business or move your existing business.

If your business involves sales of tangible personal property, you'll have to apply for a seller's permit from the **State of California Board of Equalization**, 800-400-7115, www.boe.ca.gov. This web site provides information about doing business in California, including employer tax forms and the *California Employer's Guide*. The Board of Equalization's information center can also answer your tax questions.

To protect your efforts and investment you should probably hire a local attorney to help you through the maze of state rules and regulations, especially if you are moving your business from another state. Resources include:

- **California State Franchise Tax Board** at 800-852-5711, www.ftb.ca.gov, the agency to check with regarding payroll, unemployment insurance, and disability insurance taxes
- **Chambers of Commerce**: Berkeley, 1834 University Ave, 510-549-7000, www.berkeleychamber.com; Oakland, 475 14th St, 510-874-4800, www.oaklandchamber.com; San Francisco, 235 Montgomery St, 12th floor, 415-392-4520, www.sfchamber.com; San Jose, 101 W Santa Clara St, 408-291-5250, www.sjchamber.com
- **Internal Revenue Service**, 800-829-1040, www.irs.gov, call them for information about an employer tax ID number
- **Referral Service of the San Mateo County Bar Association**, 650-369-4149, www.smcba.com
- **San Francisco Bar Association Lawyer Referral Service**, 415-982-1600, www.sfbar.org
- **Service Corps of Retired Executives (SCORE)**, 800-634-0245, www.score.org; call them for one-on-one counseling when starting a new business, free of charge
- **Sfbizinfo**, connects San Francisco business with services, resources and information, 888-800-8000, www.sfbizinfo.org
- **SF OEWD**, Mayor's Office of Economic and Workforce Development web site with information for businesses looking to expand or relocate in San Francisco, 415-554-6969, www.oewd.org
- **State Bar of California**, 415-538-2000, www.calbar.ca.gov
- **State of California's Department of Finance**, 916-445-3878, www.dof.ca.gov
- **US Small Business Administration (SBA)**, 800-827-5722, www.sba.gov; go online for information about starting up and financing a business, as well as learning about the SBA's services and local offices
- **Women's Initiative for Self Employment (WISE),** 415-641-3460, www.womensinitiative.org, a local nonprofit dedicated to helping low income women start and run their own businesses

C ONGRATULATIONS! YOU'VE NAVIGATED THE SEA OF LISTINGS AND secured a place to call home. Time to set up utilities and basic services and settle in. You may want to subscribe to the local paper, find a doctor, get a library card, and register to vote while you're at it. Details follow.

UTILITIES

GAS AND ELECTRICITY

To have existing service transferred to your name or to initiate gas and electric service, call **Pacific Gas & Electric Company (PG&E)**, www.pge.com. The 24-hour number is 800-743-5000, and PG&E covers San Francisco, the North Bay, East Bay, and parts of the South Bay and the Peninsula. If you're speech or hearing impaired, the TTY number is 800-652-4712, also available 24 hours. The City of Santa Clara has its own electric service, **Silicon Valley Power**, while PG&E provides gas. To find out about setting up service you can contact Silicon Valley Power between 8 a.m. and 4:55 p.m. at 408-615-2300, www.siliconvalleypower.com. The municipally owned and operated company recently added an eco-friendly option, **Santa Clara Green Power**. The program offers residents the option of choosing 100% renewable energy from wind and solar power sources. Silicon Valley Power estimates the additional monthly cost for going green at about $7.50 for the average Santa Clara household. For more information check out the web site listed above and click on the "Green Power" icon, or call 408-244-7283. The **City of Palo Alto Utilities (CPAU)**, 650-329-2161, is the only municipal utility in California that operates city-owned utility services that include electric, fiberoptic, natural gas, water, and wastewater collection.

If you have questions about utilities, contact the **Public Advisor's Office** in San Francisco toll free at 866-849-8390 or visit the **California Public Utilities Commission**'s web site, www.cpuc.ca.gov. When you first move into a new place it never hurts to verify that hot water comes out of the tap. If you don't have hot water, a little bit of household troubleshooting may be required. If the water heater is in your unit, check to see if the pilot light is on. If it's not, follow directions on the heater for lighting the flame, or, if you're nervous about doing it yourself, call your landlord or PG&E and have them do it. While you're looking at the water heater, check to see if it is strapped to the wall. Many postquake fires are started by ruptured gas lines to water heaters, and attaching the heater to the wall is an important safety precaution—and a requirement—here in earthquake country. (See **Emergency Preparedness** for more details.)

Most people pay their PG&E bills by mail or online. There are also numerous drug stores and other neighborhood businesses set up to collect money for PG&E. Customer service representatives should be able to tell you where one is in your area. You may also drop off your payments at any PG&E office. To find local payment centers visit www.pge.com, navigate to "My Account" and click "Pay in Person." A handy map function will help you find the closest location.

TELEPHONE

While there is currently only one choice in the Bay Area for "hard line" telephone connections (AT&T), some cell phone companies like Verizon, www.verizon.com, are getting into the business. With AT&T however, phone hook-up is easy; just call 800-288-2020, Monday–Friday, 8 a.m. to 7 p.m., or Saturday, 8 a.m. to 5 p.m. The TTY number is 800-397-3172, available 24 hours a day, 7 days a week. You can also visit www.att.com.

A deposit is not required, and if additional hardware doesn't need to be installed at your new residence, AT&T will waive the line connection charge. Rudimentary phone service starts at $13.50 per month and includes unlimited local calls but not long distance charges. It also doesn't include the additional maze of taxes, fees, and surcharges AT&T levies onto the bill.

Cable television provider **Comcast** is making inroads in the market with special promotions offering bundled cable, internet, and telephone services but these are subject to the vagaries of the Internet and so far, haven't replaced the old copper lines strung around the country. Prices range greatly depending on options selected. For more information visit www.comcast.com or call 800-COMCAST.

LONG-DISTANCE SERVICE

Below are a couple of the long-distance service providers available in the Bay Area. Both of these companies also offer local phone service, cellular phone service, and Internet options. For help comparing long-distance and wireless calling plans, visit the **Telecommunications Research and Action Center,** www.trac.org. The nonprofit TRAC web site also provides directory assistance via the internet.

- **AT&T**, 800-288-2020, www.att.com
- **Verizon**, 800-837-4966, www.verizon.com

CELLULAR PHONE SERVICES

These days almost everyone in California carries a cell phone and there are as many cellular carriers as there are makes and models of phones. The market is changing rapidly, so your best bet is to call around and determine for yourself which service and pricing structures best meet your needs. The web can make it easier; www.point.com, named the best web site for cell phone information by *Forbes* magazine, allows you to compare service plans in your area. San Francisco-based **TURN (The Utility Reform Network)** also operates a web site with useful consumer information on things to consider when choosing a plan, switching plans, keeping your old phone number, and deciphering cell phone charges, www.turn.org or call 415-929-8876. Following are the Bay Area's largest cellular personal communication service (PCS) providers:

- **AT&T**, 800-331-0500, www.wireless.att.com
- **MetroPCS**, 888-863-8768, www.metropcs.com
- **Sprint Nextel**, 866-866-7509, www.sprint.com
- **T-Mobile**, 1-800-866-2453, www.t-mobile.com
- **Verizon Wireless**, 800-922-0204, www.verizonwireless.com

Most businesses that sell cellular phones can also activate them for you on the spot. Many even give you the phone for free if you sign up and pay for a service contract with the company they represent. Scattered around the Bay Area are little mini-stores that carry all the latest products and services. Check the local malls or shopping strips.

AREA CODES

Here in the Bay Area, area codes are pretty straightforward and relatively easy. If you get confused, consult the Customer Guide at the front section of the White Pages. Here you'll find everything from the area code for Concord to directions on how to call Scotland. Below are the basic Bay Area codes; when calling from one to another, you'll need to dial a "1" plus the area code, then the number you are calling. Check your calling plans to see which, if any, long-distance charges may apply.

415: The master number for all of San Francisco; Marin County in the North Bay, including Marin, San Rafael, Sausalito, Novato, Mill Valley, Corte Madera, and Fairfax; and some parts of Daly City to the south

510: The East Bay: Alameda County, including Berkeley, Oakland, Alameda, Emeryville, Albany, Piedmont, Hayward, Fremont, Newark, Union City; and some parts of western Contra Costa County including Richmond

707: Further North Bay: Sonoma County, including Santa Rosa and Sonoma; Napa County including Napa, St. Helena, Yountville, and Calistoga; and Solano County, including Vacaville, Vallejo, and Fairfield

925: Outer East Bay: Contra Costa County, including Walnut Creek, Martinez, San Ramon, Dublin, and Pleasant Hill

650: The Peninsula: San Mateo County, including parts of Daly City, South San Francisco, San Bruno, Millbrae, Burlingame, San Mateo, Pacifica, Half Moon Bay, Belmont, San Carlos, Redwood City, Woodside, Atherton, Menlo Park; and some parts of northern Santa Clara County including Palo Alto and Mountain View

408: The South Bay: Santa Clara County, including San Jose, Santa Clara, Sunnyvale, Campbell, Milpitas, Cupertino, Saratoga, and Los Gatos

916: Sacramento, the state capital, and environs

WIRELESS HOTSPOTS (WI-FI)

Hundreds of businesses and libraries across the Bay Area offer free wireless Internet connectivity. If you are so equipped and need to access the Internet while waiting for your home service to be installed, a good place to start is www.wififreespot.com. In this technology-centric part of California you'd be hard-pressed to find a coffee shop or teahouse that doesn't have free wireless (unless you go to the ubiquitous Starbucks, which charges for access). Another method used by new arrivals is to park in one of the motel parking lots around any of the major airports. City-wide plans for Wi-Fi have typically ended badly in fights over providers and/or efficacy of the coverage but keep your eyes open, we may yet have a paradigm shift in public access to the world wide web.

ONLINE SERVICE PROVIDERS

Hundreds of internet service companies offer basic internet access via existing phone lines. For a complete list of Internet service providers located near you, go to www.thelist.com. You can also find a list of providers in the Yellow Pages under "Internet Access."

For high-speed Internet access, consider signing up for service on a digital subscriber line (known as DSL), or via cable modem access. Unlike a dial-up option, a DSL connection does not interrupt phone lines. DSL is limited by your residence's distance from a service "node" and as such, many of the outlying communities will not have this option. Cable Internet access is available from cable TV providers, and like DSL, the cable modem is always on and can be much cheaper if bundled with other entertainment services.

Here are a few of the companies that offer dial-up, DSL, and/or cable modem:

- **AT&T**, www.att.com, 800-288-2020
- **Comcast**, www.comcast.com, 800-COMCAST
- **Earthlink**, www.earthlink.net, 888-327-8454

- **Juno**, 800-879-5866, www.juno.com
- **Net Zero**, 888-349-0029, www.netzero.net
- **Sonic Net**, 707-522-1000, www.sonic.net
- **ZR Net**, 415-920-2226, www.zrnetservice.com

DIRECTORY ASSISTANCE

In today's web-oriented world, directory assistance does not have to cost money. Many web sites are dedicated to providing telephone listings and web sites, including the following:

- **www.411.com**
- **www.altavista.com**
- **www.anywho.com**
- **www.bigbook.com**
- **www.switchboard.com**
- **www.superpages.com**
- **www.whitepages.com**

Another great option for directory assistance is Google SMS. This service is provided by the search engine giant and is as simple as sending a text message. Key in GOOGLE (466-453) as your recipient phone number and in the message portion of the text name the city (or zip code) and business that you're trying to find. Google will almost instantly text your phone with a short list of possible matches.

CONSUMER PROTECTION—UTILITY COMPLAINTS

In the state of California, utility rates and practices relating to telephone, electric, and gas are governed by the state **Public Utilities Commission (PUC)**. The San Francisco Public Utilities Commission handles water issues. Officials at both organizations strongly suggest you take your complaints first to the utility involved. If you don't get satisfaction there, then the PUCs will listen to you.

- **California PUC**, 505 Van Ness Ave, San Francisco, Commission Docket Office in San Francisco, 415-703-2782, www.cpuc.ca.gov
- **San Francisco PUC**, 1155 Market St #4, 11th Floor, San Francisco, 415-551-3000, www.sfwater.org

Interestingly, if you have problems with the PUC, there is a public watchdog organization that keeps tabs on the effectiveness of each of the PUCs. It's called **TURN (The Utility Reform Network)**. If you don't get what you need from either PUC you may want to turn to TURN, 711 Van Ness Ave, San Francisco, 415-929-8876, www.turn.org.

With the breakup of Ma Bell and the proliferation of long-distance telephone service providers have come the inevitable scamsters. If you look at your phone bill and think you've been "slammed" (your long-distance provider or established services were changed without your approval) or "crammed" (calls you didn't make were added to your bill), and your local service provider and state attorney general's office cannot assist you, contact the **Federal Communications Commission's Consumer Center**, 888-225-5322, www.fcc.gov, or the **Federal Trade Commission**, 877-382-4357, www.ftc.gov, to file a complaint.

See the **Helpful Services** chapter for more on consumer protection.

WATER

Water in the Bay Area is provided by several water districts (see list below). Accounts and billing are handled either directly through the water district or by your city's municipal services. Bay Area renters generally are responsible for paying for water except in San Francisco apartment buildings and multi-unit flats, where usually the landlord pays.

In 1974, the United States Congress enacted a program to ensure safe drinking water for US residents. Amended in 1986, the Safe Drinking Water Act set up a comprehensive program for monitoring drinking water. Among many things, the Act banned all future use of lead pipe and lead solder in public drinking water systems, set up a monitoring system, mandated greater protection of groundwater sources of drinking water, and streamlined enforcement procedures to ensure that suppliers comply with the Safe Drinking Water provisions. In 1996, the EPA also added amendments regarding the Act that include stronger consumer protections, strengthened regulatory rules, and provided for states to access federal funds when implementing clean water actions. About 85% of San Francisco's water supply comes from Hetch Hetchy, a remote area of Yosemite National Park in the Sierra Nevada Mountains. Because of its pristine source, the quality of San Francisco's water is higher than most cities; however, it's not entirely sterile or free of all organisms. The other 15% of San Francisco's water comes from watersheds in San Mateo, Santa Clara, and Alameda counties. To preserve water quality and improve local service, the San Francisco Public Utilities Commission has embarked on a $4.3 billion program to repair and upgrade its regional water system.

Outside of San Francisco, about two thirds of the state, or 22 million people, obtains water from the San Francisco Bay and the Sacramento Delta (located northeast of Contra Costa County) through a series of pumps and canals. In the South Bay, concern remains over water contamination caused by the gasoline additive methyl tertiary butyl ether (MTBE), mixed with gasoline to make it burn cleaner. When scientists discovered that MTBE can contaminate groundwater, and is not as readily removable as other contaminates, then-Governor Gray Davis ordered a statewide phase-out of the additive. MTBE is now officially banned, and massive clean-up efforts have taken place across the state to ensure the safety of drinking water. Nevertheless, areas that were impacted, like the Santa Clara Valley Water District, are still keeping a watchful eye on water supplies to determine whether further action is necessary. The likelihood of having MTBE in the groundwater may depend on how close you live to a gas station. If you are within 1,000 feet, check with the station to find out if they have ever had any leaks or spills. If you are moving to the South Bay, contact the Santa Clara Valley Water District, 408-265-2600, www.valleywater.org, for more information about the MTBE issue. Another good source of information is the State Water Resources Control Board, 916-341-5455, www.swrcb.ca.gov.

If you are living in the city and are concerned about the quality of your tap water, contact the **San Francisco PUC** at 415-551-3000. Those outside of San Francisco can contact the **Water Quality Control Board, San Francisco Bay Region**, 1515 Clay St, Suite 1400, Oakland, 510-622-2300, www.waterboards. ca.gov/sanfranciscobay, and ask them to send you a copy of their annual report on water quality. If you feel the need to take extra precaution, contact a private laboratory to perform water quality tests. Check the Yellow Pages under "Laboratories-Analytical" or get a referral from your county health department.

For further questions on tap water quality, contact the **California Department of Public Health**, 916-558-1784, www.cdph.ca.gov; the **US Environmental Protection Agency Safe Drinking Water Hotline**, 800-426-4791; or the **Water Quality Association**, 630-505-0160, www.wqa.org. Information regarding home water filtration systems is covered in an Environmental Protection Agency pamphlet, "Home Water Treatment Units: Filtering Fact from Fiction," www.epa.gov/ogwdw.

To **set up water service** you will need to contact one of the following water districts or municipal services. Most of the web sites included here provide detailed information about setting up your account, as well as the county's annual water quality report:

- **Alameda County Water District**, 43885 S Grimmer Blvd, Fremont, 510-668-4200, www.acwd.org
- **Contra Costa Water District**, 1331 Concord Ave, Concord, 925-688-8000, www.ccwater.com
- **East Bay Municipal Utility District**, 375 11th St, 866-403-2683, www.ebmud. com
- **Marin Municipal Water District**, 220 Nellon Ave, Corte Madera, 415-945-1455, www.marinwater.org
- **North Marin Water District**, 999 Rush Creek Pl, Novato, 415-897-4133, www. nmwd.com, serves Novato and parts of West Marin
- **City of Palo Alto Utilities (CPAU)**, 250 Hamilton Ave, Palo Alto, 650-329-2161, www.cpau.com
- **San Francisco Water Department**, 1155 Market St, San Francisco, 415-551-3000, www.sfwater.org
- **Santa Clara Valley Water District**, 5750 Almaden Expy, San Jose, 408-265-2600, www.valleywater.org; to set up service contact one of the following:

- **California Water Service Co**, 650-917-0152, www.calwater.com, serves San Carlos, San Mateo, South San Francisco, Woodside, Los Altos and some areas of Cupertino, Menlo Park, Mountain View, and Sunnyvale
- **San Jose Municipal**, 3025 Tuers Rd, San Jose, 408-535-3500, www. sjmuniwater.com, and Great Oaks Water, 15 Great Oaks Blvd, Suite 100, 408-227-9540, www.greatoakswater.com, serve San Jose
- **San Jose Water Co.**, 110 W Taylor St, San Jose, 408-279-7900, www.sjwater. com, serves Campbell, Los Gatos, and Saratoga, and parts of the cities of San Jose and Cupertino
- **Sonoma County Water Agency**, 404 Aviation Blvd, Santa Rosa, 707-526-5370, www.scwa.ca.gov to set up service in Sonoma County contact one of the following:
  - **Santa Rosa Water District**, 707-543-4200, serves Santa Rosa
  - **City of Sonoma Public Works**, #1 The Plaza, Sonoma, 707-938-3332, serves Sonoma

GARBAGE/RECYCLING

In San Francisco landlords pay for garbage collection for apartments, and for some duplexes and single-family homes. Homeowners must order and pay for disposal service; the collection fee is based on how many trashcans you fill up each week. One company, **Allied Waste**, provides the vast majority of garbage service in the Bay Area. All cities now provide a bulk pickup option—typically twice a year—that allows the homeowner or renter to relieve themselves of bulky garbage. The best way to determine your local garbage service provider is to contact your city's public works department or contact one of the following companies:

- **Allied Waste**, serving Daly City, Colma, Broadmoor, 650-756-1130, www. alliedwastedalycity.com
- **Allied Waste of San Mateo County**, serving Atherton, Belmont, Burlingame, East Palo Alto, Foster City, Half Moon Bay, Hillsborough, Ladera, Menlo Park, North Fair Oaks, Redwood City, San Carlos, and San Mateo, 650-592-2411; www.alliedwastesanmateocounty.com
- **Allied Waste Services**, serves most of Contra Costa County, 925-685-4711, www.alliedwasteservicesofcontracostacounty.com
- **Marin Sanitary Services**, Marin County, 415-456-2601, www.marinsanitary.com
- **Norcal Waste Systems of San Jose**, 408-576-0057, provides service in San Jose
- **Norcal Waste Systems: Sunset Scavenger**, 415-330-1300, and **Golden Gate Disposal & Recycling Co**, 415-626-4000, provide service to San Francisco
- **South San Francisco Scavenger**, northern San Mateo County (South San Francisco, Brisbane, Millbrae), 650-589-4020, www.ssfscavenger.com
- **StopWaste.org (Waste Management, Alameda County [north])**, 510-891-6500, www.stopwaste.org

Curbside recycling collection is available throughout the Bay Area and is included in the cost of your other garbage pickup. In San Francisco, residents of apartment buildings with fewer than five units are responsible for picking up the approved plastic containers themselves. Landlords are responsible for setting up recycling programs if the building has five or more units. Landfill space is scarce in the Bay Area, making recycling all the more important. To find out more about recycling in the Bay Area contact:

- **Acterra**, 650-962-9876, www.acterra.org
- **Marin Recycling Center**, 415-453-1404
- **Palo Alto Zero Waste Program,** 650-496-5910
- **RecycleWorks,** San Mateo County, 888-442-2666, www.recycleworks.org
- **Santa Clara County Recycling Hotline**, 408-924-5453 or 800-533-8414, www.recyclestuff.org
- **SF Recycling & Disposal**, 415-330-1400
- **SF Environment,** 415-355-3700, www.sfenvironment.org
- **StopWaste.org (Waste Management, Alameda County [north])**, recycling hotline 877-786-7927, www.stopwaste.org

Earth 911 offers a wealth of information on recycling including what items can and cannot be recycled, how to find local recycling centers, and instructions for dealing with hazardous waste, 800-253-2687, www.earth911.com. For information specifically dealing with beverage container collection centers, call the **California Department of Conservation** at 800-732-9253.

If you've got a green thumb and you'd like to compost, contact the **San Francisco League of Urban Gardeners (SLUG)** at 415-285-7584. They call it the ROT-line, as opposed to a HOT-line. In the East Bay the ROT-line is run by **StopWaste.org (Alameda County Waste Management Authority)**, 510-444-7645.

AUTOMOBILES

DRIVER'S LICENSES

If you've moved here from out-of-state and you want to drive in California, you have 10 days from your arrival to apply for a new driver's license from the Department of Motor Vehicles (DMV). While there is no penalty for filing late and no method for law enforcement to determine your residency status, if you are pulled over for a traffic violation after the 10-day grace period, the officer can give you an additional citation if you admit to living in California for more than 10 days. You will need to bring your current driver's license and a birth certificate or passport for proof of age to your appointment. If the name that you use is different than the one on this document, you will also need to provide a marriage certificate or dissolution of marriage, adoption, or name change document that shows your current name.

Once there, you will be asked to fill out a formal application, provide your Social Security Number, and pass a vision test. You will also be required to pass a written test on traffic laws and road signs. You have three chances to pass this test, which has 36 questions. To give yourself a quick refresher course, you can take a sample test on the DMV's web site: www.dmv.ca.gov/pubs/interactive/tdrive/exam.htm. Once you pass, you'll have your thumbprint scanned and your picture taken. Your new license will be mailed to you. In the meantime, the DMV will issue an interim license good for 60 days. When driving with an interim license, always keep a valid photo ID handy (out-of-state driver's license or passport).

A note to international newcomers: If your license is from another country, you will also be required to take a driving skills test.

A driver's license costs $28 and it is good for up to four years, expiring on your birth date. If you are moving to the Bay Area from within California, you have 10 days to notify the DMV of your address change; call or visit www.dmv.ca.gov.

The DMV also handles the issuance of **state identification cards**. In order to get one you'll need to bring a birth certificate or passport and provide your Social Security number. The fee is $24 and the card is valid for six years. Seniors can get ID cards free that are good for 10 years.

AUTOMOBILE REGISTRATION & INSURANCE

If you bring a car into the state of California, be prepared to jump through bureaucratic hoops. In general, it isn't a huge issue to bring your car or truck in from out-of-state, but the Golden State sets the national—and arguably global—standard for exhaust emissions on vehicles and has strict laws to regulate these gases. New cars that are 49-state legal cannot be imported into California unless they have more than 7,500 miles on them. The car must be inspected by the DMV or a law enforcement officer and typically smog-checked. The DMV requires that emission control devices on your car operate correctly; any non-diesel vehicle that is four years old or older must pass an emissions test. Most service stations will do the test for less than $50. When you've received emission certification, bring it, along with your current automobile registration and checkbook, to the nearest DMV. Registration is good for one year and can vary in cost, sometimes in the hundreds of dollars for newer cars. Note that the DMV will not accept payment via credit cards.

Newcomers from out-of-state will sometimes be surprised to learn that vehicles operating on the streets and highways of California are required to have both rear and **front license plates**. Driving without a front plate is technically illegal here and while enforcement is spotty, the ticket can be expensive because in addition to a fine, a violation requires a working hours field trip to a local police station for verification of compliance.

All California drivers are required by law to carry liability insurance on their vehicles and to show proof of coverage when registering an automobile at the DMV. Insurers have estimated that 30% to 40% of the drivers on California roads are not properly covered, although avoiding this mandate has become increasingly difficult because DMV is rapidly digitizing and communicating with insurers.

DMV OFFICES

The DMV in San Francisco is notorious for its long lines. If you can, spare yourself this frustration and instead go to the DMV in Marin County or San Mateo County. Wherever you go, you should make an appointment, which could be the difference between a half-hour wait and a two-hour wait. The DMV has a 24-hour hotline that handles all appointments. The automated 24-hour number is 800-921-1117; TTY 800-368-4327. Appointments can also be made online—highly recommended—at www.dmv.ca.gov. When heading to your appointment, make sure to show up early—not late—they won't wait for you! A note about hours: In general, DMV offices are open 8 a.m. to 5 p.m. on Mondays, Tuesdays, Thursdays and Fridays. Due to budget cuts, offices now open one hour later on Wednesdays—at 9 a.m. More information about operating hours, driver's license requirements, and vehicle registration can be found online at www.dmv.ca.gov.

SAN FRANCISCO/NORTH BAY
- Corte Madera, 75 Tamal Vista Blvd
- San Francisco, 1377 Fell St

EAST BAY
- Concord, 2070 Diamond Blvd
- El Cerrito, 6400 Manila Ave
- Fremont, 4287 Central Ave
- Hayward, 150 Jackson St
- Oakland, 501 85th Ave; 5300 Claremont Ave
- Walnut Creek, 1910 N Broadway

PENINSULA/SOUTH BAY
- Daly City, 1500 Sullivan Ave
- Redwood City, 300 Brewster Ave
- San Jose, 111 W Alma Ave
- San Mateo, 425 N Amphlett Blvd
- Santa Clara, 3665 Flora Vista Ave

PARKING

SAN FRANCISCO

In the City of San Francisco, vacant parking spaces are some of the most sought-after real estate. Many residential areas require parking permits, which allow neighborhood residents or temporary guests to park without time limits in the neighborhood. Those without a permit are required to move their cars frequently, usually after two hours. If you're not sure if your neighborhood or the neighborhood you are visiting requires a residential parking permit, check for signs posted along the street. Also check to see when the street sweeper is coming—illegally parked vehicles on street-sweeping days will be slapped with a $65 ticket.

Newcomers to the steep streets of San Francisco may not be familiar with "curbing" their front wheels on an incline. In this mountainous city it is the law and will merit a $50 ticket if not done properly. Runaway vehicles are a real danger here. When parking downhill with over 3% grade, it is required that the front wheels touch the curb and that the tires are turned toward the sidewalk. When parking uphill, the tires must be turned outward from the curb and brought back to rest against the sidewalk.

The city is also experimenting with parking meter cards that can be purchased using an online portal, http://services.sfgov.org/mtacards, or bought separately at local retail businesses. These are for use in the new single-meter or multiple-space parking meters, over 23,000 of which have been installed to replace the old coin-only style. The new meters still accept coins and an hour parked next to one of these ubiquitous street fixtures will set you back three dollars. That's a large handful of quarters so if you plan on parking in the metered areas often, a parking card is recommended.

Residential Parking Permits are available at the Customer Service Center, 11 South Van Ness Ave, 415-701-3000. In order to get your permit you'll need to bring valid car registration that shows your new address, which means you'll first need to visit the nearby DMV. Also bring another proof of address: your lease, a utility bill with your address on it, a bank statement, or a personalized check. Your driver's license is not an acceptable proof of residency. The full-fledged parking permit is good for a year and will set you back $74. For more information on the program, call 415-554-5000.

When it comes to parking in San Francisco's downtown core, your choices are limited to streetside meters or parking garages. There are more than 10,000 garage spaces in the downtown area, and they are certainly the most costly option. Fees vary somewhat; in general, depositing your car in one of these spots will cost $20 to $30 a day. Some outdoor lots in the South of Market area will sell you a monthly spot for as little as $100, but more often than not those lots are sold out. For general information on parking in San Francisco, call

SFMTA at 415-701-4500 or check online at www.sfmta.com. Here are just a few of San Francisco's downtown parking garages:

- **Ellis-O'Farrell Garage**: 123 O'Farrell St, 415-986-4800, 925 spaces
- **Fifth and Mission Yerba Buena Garage**: 5th and Mission St, 415-982-8522, www.fifthandmission.com, 2500+ spaces
- **Portsmouth Square Garage**: 733 Kearny St, 415-982-6353, www.sfpsg.com, 500+ spaces
- **St. Mary's Square Garage**: 433 Kearny St, 415-956-8106, 600+ spaces
- **Sutter-Stockton Garage**: 444 Stockton St, 415-982-8370, 1800+ spaces
- **Union Square Garage**: 333 Post St, 415-397-0631, 900+ spaces

There are many more lots in the city, so if the one you want to patronize is full or closed you'll only need to drive a couple of blocks and you'll probably find one with space. While driving around watch for the metered parking spaces, but make certain you read and understand all the postings. The only people faster at their jobs than the meter readers are the tow truck operators they call out. **To pay a parking citation** by phone, have your VISA or MasterCard ready and dial 415-255-3999, or you can pay online at http://services.sfgov.org//dptpark.

COLORED CURBS

You'll need to know the meaning of painted curbs:

- **Red:** Fire Zone—don't even think of parking here
- **Yellow:** Commercial loading zone only, for times posted
- **White:** Passenger pick-up or drop-off and valet only
- **Green:** Temporary (usually 20–30 minutes) parking only—as posted
- **Blue:** Handicapped parking only, special placard required

PARKING FINES

The city of San Francisco Department of Parking and Traffic issues 7,000 tickets every month. Meter readers troll the streets throughout the day, and enforcement of parking rules here is aggressive. If you get a ticket, pay it right away. Delaying payment can significantly increase your fine—doubling and in some cases even tripling what you owe. Below is a list of current fees for common violations.

Failure to block wheels (curbing your tires)	$45
Meter violation	$50
Meter violation downtown	$60
Parking in a red zone	$85
Parking in a white zone	$85
Parking in a yellow zone	$70
Parking in a green zone	$60
Parking on a sidewalk	$100
Failure to move car for street sweeper	$50
Residential permit zone violation	$60
Blocking a bike lane	$100

Blocking a driveway . . . . $85 (If a resident calls
to complain, you can
also be towed)
Double parking. $75
Abandoned vehicle. $210
Parking in a bus zone $250
Blocking wheelchair access ramp $250
Illegally parking in a blue (handicapped) zone $300

SURROUNDING AREAS

Fortunately parking is easier in outlying areas and there is plenty of street parking in most cities; in fact there have been cases of people moving out of San Francisco just for the parking. Some cities require a residential permit allowing you to park in your neighborhood for an extended period of time. To obtain a residential parking sticker in Sausalito, call the **Sausalito Parking Services**, 415-289-4149. Most of the other cities in Marin do not require parking stickers. For information on parking tickets, towing, and other unpleasantness in the North Bay, contact the **Marin County Traffic Authority**, 800-281-7275.

In the East Bay, Oakland residents should call the **Oakland Parking Bureau**, 510-238-3099, or the **Traffic Division of the Superior Court**, 510-627-4701, located in Oakland. In Berkeley, contact the Berkeley **Residential Preferential Parking (RPP) Program**, Finance Customer Service Center, 510-981-7200. For UC Berkeley call the **UC Berkeley Parking and Transportation Office**, 510-643-7701.

In the South Bay/Peninsula, call **Palo Alto Parking Permits**, 650-329-2317; **San Mateo Parking Permits, Residential & City Parking Facilities**, 650-522-7300; and in San Jose, contact the **Residential Parking Permits** at 408-535-3850.

GETTING YOUR TOWED CAR BACK

If your car is towed in San Francisco, your first step should be to call the **DPT Tow Line** 415-865-8200 to find out why it was towed and what you need to do (read: how much you'll need to pay) to get it back. Once you've figured out how much you owe, you'll need to settle your fees with **AutoReturn**, 450 7th Street, 415-865-8200 (7 days / 24 hours). To obtain your vehicle's release you must appear in person with photo identification and be prepared to pay not only the towing cost and ticket but also any outstanding parking tickets written against the vehicle, and storage costs. Ouch!

In surrounding Bay Area counties, if your car is missing, call the local police station first and they will provide you with the name of the towing company contracted out by that city. Police department numbers are listed at the end of the neighborhood profiles.

OFFICIAL DOCUMENTS

VOTER REGISTRATION

Registering to vote in the Bay Area is easy. Frequent voter registration drives literally bring the process to you, along downtown sidewalks, in malls, and in public transit facilities. You can also register by visiting the **Registrar of Voters** or **Elections Department** in the county where you live, or by going to the California Secretary of State's **voter registration web site**, www.sos. ca.gov/elections/elections_vr.htm. The deadline to register is 15 days before an election.

You can register with any political party in California, sign up as an independent, or decline to state a party affiliation. Voters may cast their ballots in person or vote via absentee ballot. If you want to vote absentee, you must call your local registrar's office and request the forms. Be sure to allow ample time, usually about a month, for them to receive your forms in the mail. Your registrar's office will be able to tell you what the cut-off date is for sending in an absentee ballot.

Here are the locations and phone numbers for voter registration officials in each of the nine Bay Area counties:

- **San Francisco**, City Hall, Room 48, San Francisco, 415-554-4375
- **Alameda**, 1225 Fallon St, Oakland, 510-272-6933
- **Contra Costa**, 555 Escobar St, Martinez, 925-335-7800
- **Marin**, 3501 Civic Center Dr, San Rafael, 415-499-6456
- **Napa**, 900 Coombs St, Room 256, Napa, 707-253-4321
- **San Mateo**, 40 Tower Rd, San Mateo, 650-312-5222
- **Santa Clara**, 1555 Berger Dr, Building 2, San Jose, 408-299-8683
- **Solano**, 675 Texas St, Fairfield, 707-784-6675
- **Sonoma**, 435 Fiscal Dr, Santa Rosa, 707-565-6800

LIBRARY CARDS

San Francisco is home to one of the finest city libraries in the world. Opened in early 1996, **The Main Library**, 415-557-4400, www.sfpl.org, across the Civic Center plaza from City Hall, holds more than one million books, magazines, and research tomes. It also provides Internet access and multimedia presentations via dozens of computers. The entire library system's card catalog is accessible at terminals on every floor. Library cards are free, and you don't have to be a San Francisco resident to get one. Just bring proper ID, such as a driver's license, and something else with your current address on it, such as a utility bill. The card is valid at all San Francisco library branches; addresses and phone numbers are listed in the Neighborhoods section of this book. The Main Library, at 100 Larkin Street, is easy to get to; it's just a short walk through the United Nations Plaza from the Civic Center BART/MUNI station. For more information on local branch libraries, see neighborhood listings, and for more on specialty libraries, see the **Cultural Life** chapter.

PASSPORTS

You need to apply in person for new passports. A number of post offices and local city halls are set up to provide this service; check http://iafdb.travel.state.gov for the office closest to you. You'll need to bring two identical 2" x 2" photographs, proof of US citizenship (birth certificate, social security card, old passport), and a valid photo identification (driver's license, state ID card, military ID), and you'll have to fill out the application available at the passport office. The fee for a new passport is $75. For general information contact the **National Passport Information Center,** 877-487-2778, TTY 888-874-7793, or visit www.travel.state.gov.

If you just need to renew your passport, you can do it by mail. Simply fill out the renewal application (DS-82)—available online at www.travel.state.gov—and send it, along with your old passport, two identical 2" x 2" photos, and a check for $75 made out to the US Department of State, to National Passport Processing Center, P.O. Box 90155, Philadelphia, PA, 19190-0155. When renewing or ordering a new passport in person, add another $25.

Passports generally take about six weeks to arrive by mail, but can take longer, so it's a good idea to take care of your passport well in advance. If you need it sooner, you can pay $60 to expedite the process—plus overnight charges there and back. Expedited passports should arrive within 2 weeks. If you've been called out of the country on an emergency, it is possible to get a passport sooner—in some cases even on the same day, but it will cost extra for speedy service. If this is the case, your first step should be to call the **National Passport Information Center** (see number above). You can also contact the **San Francisco Passport Agency** directly at 877-487-2778 for assistance in making an appointment. The services at this office are reserved for those in need of expedited service. The San Francisco Passport Agency, located at 95 Hawthorne Street, 5th Floor, is open Monday–Friday from 9 a.m. to 4 p.m for appointments only. If you are outside San Francisco, check with your local city hall. In San Jose, the **Santa Clara County Recorders Office** at the County Government Center, East Wing, 70 West Hedding Street, 408-299-5669, can process your passport application within 10 to 14 days. Passports are good for 10 years (for adults).

BROADCAST AND PRINT MEDIA

TELEVISION STATIONS

Broadcast television reception in the Bay Area is fairly good, unless you live in a particularly hilly area, in which case hooking up to the cable is the way to go. If you're not interested in cable, a standard roof antenna will probably suffice to pull in most of the stations listed below. Apartment dwellers may want to consider getting a pair of "rabbit ears," a small indoor antenna that sits on top of the television set. Be aware of the recent changes related to the federal government's mandated shift from analog signals to all digital. If you are using antennas to connect to the airwaves, a digital converter box is necessary. The feds have set up a clearinghouse for this transition at www.dtv2009.gov that provides guidance and coupons for the purchase of a converter at any local electronics store.

Channel	Call Letters	Network	Location
2	KTVU	Fox	Oakland
4	KRON	Independent	San Francisco
5	KPIX	CBS	San Francisco
7	KGO	ABC	San Francisco
9	KQED	PBS	San Francisco
11	KNTV	NBC	San Jose
14	KDTV	Univision (Spanish)	San Francisco
20	KOFY	KOFY-TV	San Francisco
26	KTSF	Independent	San Francisco
32	KMTP	Minority Television Project	San Francisco
36	KTEH	PBS	San Jose
44	KBHK	UPN	San Francisco
66	KFSF	Univision	Vallejo

CABLE AND SATELLITE TELEVISION

If broadcast television (those listed above) doesn't provide you with adequate entertainment options, you'll probably need to get cable or a satellite dish. Cable and satellite television are available throughout the nine Bay Area counties, with service levels governed by agreements reached with municipalities. Availability of satellite is limited if there are large objects—like the apartment complex—in the path of a signal. Each provider offers various packages based on how many channels you wish to receive. Naturally, the more channels you receive, the more you pay.

Here are some of the largest local providers:

- **AT&T**, 800-331-0500, TTY 866-241-6567, www.att.com
- **Comcast**, 800-266-2278, www.comcast.com
- **Direct TV**, 800-531-5000, TTY 800-779-4388, www.directv.com
- **Dish Network**, 888-825-2557, www.dishnetwork.com

RADIO STATIONS

There are 80 radio stations located within the nine-county Bay Area, 30 AM and 50 FM. AM reception is fairly consistent throughout the area, with no special equipment needed. FM reception can be spotty, especially if you live in a hilly area of San Francisco (which is most of the city), the East Bay, or North Bay. You may need an FM antenna in those areas. Here are some of the most listened-to stations in the Bay Area and their formats.

AM

SAN FRANCISCO

KQKE 960	Liberal Talk Radio
KCBS 740	News
KNTS 1220	News, Talk and Sports
KEAR 610	Religious
KGO 810	News, Talk, Sports
KIQI 1010	Hispanic
KNBR 680	Talk, Sports
KYCY 1550	Talk, Sports
KSFO 560	Conservative Talk
KSRO 1350	News, Talk, Sports
KSFB 1260	Religious

NORTH BAY

KDYA 1190	Gospel
KRRS 1460	Hispanic
KPIG 1510	AAA Americana
KDIA 1640	Talk, Christian
KSRO 1350	News, Talk, Sports

SOUTH BAY/PENINSULA

KTCT 1050	Sports
KSJX 1500	Vietnamese
KLIV 1590	News
KAZA 1290	Hispanic
KZSF 1370	Spanish
KNTS 1220	News, Talk, Sports
KTCT 1050	Talk, Sports
KLOK 1170	Spanish

EAST BAY

KDYA 1190	Gospel
KMKY 1310	Children, Disney
KNEW 910	Talk
KQKE 960	Liberal Talk Radio
KVTO 1400	Asian

FM

SAN FRANCISCO

KALW 91.7	News and Information (NPR, BBC, CBC)
KBRG 100.3	Romantic, Hispanic
KISQ 98.1	Classic Soul
KBLX 102.9	Adult Contemporary
KCSM 91.1	Jazz
KDFC 102.1	Classical
KFOG 104.5	Adult Alt. Rock
KFRC 99.7	Adult Contemporary
K101 101.3	Adult Contemporary
KSFB 100.7	Contemporary Christian
KITS 105.3	Live 105, Modern Rock
KKSF 103.7	Smooth Jazz
KMEL 106.1	Hip Hop
KOIT 96.5	Light Rock
KUFX 98.5	Modern Rock
KPFA 94.1	News, Information, Variety
KPOO 89.5	Music, Talk, Variety, Listener Sponsored
KQED 88.5	Public Radio News, Information (NPR)
ALICE 97.3	Modern Adult Contemporary
KUIC 95.3	Adult Contemporary
KYLD 94.9	Urban Top 40
KSJO 92.3	Spanish
KUSF 90.3	College, Alternative Rock, Multicultural
KRZZ 93.3	Spanish
KIFR 106.9	Talk
KFOG 104.5	Adult alternative
KBWF 95.7	Modern Country
KSAN 107.7	Classic Rock

EAST BAY

KALX 90.7	College, Alternative Rock
KKDV 92.1	Adult Contemporary
KPFA 94.1	Public Radio Liberal News, Culture

NORTH BAY

KJZY 93.7	Jazz
KVRV 97.7	Classic Rock
KSXY 98.7	Popular Top 40

SOUTH BAY/PENINSULA

KBAY 94.5   Soft Rock
KVRV 97.7   Classic Rock
KEZR 106.5   Adult Contemporary
KFJC 89.7   Alternative Rock
KZSU 90.1   Eclectic Music

NEWSPAPERS AND MAGAZINES

- **Asian Week**, 809 Sacramento St, San Francisco, 415-397-0220, www.asianweek. com
- **Bay Area Business Woman**, classified listings of local businesses, seminars, classes, events, 707-938-0700, P.O Box 320, Sonoma, www.babwnews.com
- **Bay Area Consumers' Checkbook**, evaluates quality and prices of local service firms and stores; 800-213-7283, www.checkbook.org
- **Contra Costa Times**, published daily with East Bay listings, focusing on Concord, Walnut Creek, Pleasant Hill, Martinez, Richmond, Hercules, Benicia, Antioch, Pittsburg, and Bay Point areas, 925-943-8235, www.ContraCostaTimes.com (also owns Hills Newspapers, a handful of smaller local publications including the Berkeley Voice, Alameda Journal, the Montclarion, and the Piedmonter)
- **East Bay Express**, 510-879-3700, www.eastbayexpress.com, a free weekly alternative paper; focuses on the East Bay. Great resource for Arts & Culture listings; found in newsstands and at cafés.
- **East Bay Monthly**, distributed free throughout the East Bay, 1301 59th St, Emeryville, 510-658-9811, www.themonthly.com
- **Marin Independent Journal**, published daily with listings for Marin, Sonoma, and Napa counties, 415-883-8600, www.marinij.com
- **Metro**, 408-298-8000, www.metroactive.com/metro, the South Bay's alternative weekly
- **Oakland Tribune**, published daily with a focus on the East Bay, especially Oakland, Berkeley, and Alameda, 510-208-6300, www.insidebayarea.com/ oaklandtribune (the Alameda Newspaper Group also owns the Alameda Times-Star, the Fremont Argus, and a handful of smaller local papers)
- **Pacific Sun**, a free, weekly alternative; listings for Marin County. Found in newsstands and cafés. Good for rentals and roommate listings, 415-485-6700, www.pacificsun.com.
- **San Francisco Bay Guardian**, weekly free alternative paper with extensive listings for San Francisco and the East Bay. Published Wednesdays. Found at every café, corner store, and newsstands all over city. Good for Arts & Culture listings, 415-255-3100, www.sfbg.com.
- **San Francisco Business Times**, 275 Battery St, San Francisco, 415-989-2522

- **San Francisco Chronicle**, the most-read newspaper in the area; includes listings for San Francisco, North Bay, East Bay, Peninsula counties, and some outlying areas, 415-777-1111, www.sfgate.com
- **San Francisco Examiner**, daily free tabloid that publishes local news, 866-733-7323, www.examiner.com/san_francisco.
- **San Francisco Magazine**, 243 Vallejo St, San Francisco, 415-398-2800, www.sanfranmag.com, glossy, upscale San Francisco lifestyle magazine
- **SF Weekly**, a free weekly alternative paper with San Francisco listings. Great for Arts & Culture listings; published Wednesdays; found all over city at newsstands and cafés, 415-536-8100, www.sfweekly.com.
- **San Jose Mercury News**, published daily; most extensive listings for the South Bay as well as much of the Peninsula and southern East Bay, 408-920-5000, www.mercurynews.com
- **San Mateo County Times**, published daily except Sunday with listings for much of the Peninsula, 650-348-4321, www.insidebayarea.com/sanmateocountytimes
- **Santa Rosa Press Democrat**, published daily; listings for Sonoma, Marin and Napa counties, 707-546-2020, www.pressdemocrat.com
- **7 x 7 Magazine**, San Francisco lifestyle, fashion, food, design, celebrity magazine, 888-260-4269, www.7x7.com

FINDING A PHYSICIAN

Much like finding a place to live in the Bay Area, finding a physician is never easy. You must first consider your needs—are you looking for a pediatrician, family physician, OB/Gyn, or all of the above? Do you want someone who staffs the hospital nearest you? Are you interested in an MD or an osteopath? And perhaps most importantly, does your health plan limit whom you can see? Here in the Bay Area you will find cutting-edge, top-notch care at the **University of California San Francisco Medical Center** located at 505 Parnassus Avenue, 888-689-8273, famous for its pioneering work in areas such as pediatrics, high-risk obstetrics, organ transplantation, cancer care, cardiac care, neurosurgery, and orthopedics. However, because it is an educational facility, you may have students observing you. Probably the most popular way to find a good doctor is through word of mouth, talking to friends, neighbors, colleagues, or other doctors. To assist in your research, consider ordering the book *Top Doctors* from the *Bay Area Consumers' Checkbook*, which lists the Bay Area's outstanding physician specialists. Go to www.checkbook.org, or call 510-763-7979 and ask for the latest version of *Top Doctors*; there is a charge for the service. See the **Helpful Services** chapter for more information about *Consumers' Checkbook*. To determine if a physician you are considering is board certified, check with the American Board of Medical Specialties Board Certification Verification at 847-491-9091, or go online to www.abms.org.

If you are strapped for cash while in transition, the **Haight Ashbury Free Medical Clinic**, 558 Clayton Street, 415-746-1967, www.hafci.org, offers free primary health care and specialty care, including podiatry, chiropractic care, pediatrics, HIV testing, comprehensive HIV treatment services, and community information and referral services. The Medical Clinic welcomes everyone who walks through the door. However, the clinic is unable to treat emergency medical problems, such as broken bones, severe bleeding, trauma, abdominal pains, etc. For emergency medical problems, go immediately to the nearest hospital emergency room.

If you've only recently arrived in the Bay Area and find yourself in sudden need of a physician, the **Traveler's Medical Group**, 490 Post Street, Suite #225, 415-981-1102, can send a doctor who speaks your language, 24 hours a day, 7 days a week.

Hopefully you'll never need the following: The **Medical Board of California**, 2005 Evergreen Street, Suite 1200, Sacramento, CA 95815, 800-633-2322, TTY 263-0935, www.medbd.ca.gov, and the **Osteopathic Medical Board of California**, 1300 Natinoal Drive, Suite 150, Sacramento, CA 95834, 916-928-8390, www.ombc.ca.gov, are the two state organizations that handle complaints against medical professionals in California. Write or call for more information.

PETS

PET LAWS & SERVICES

If you're bringing Fido, Fluffy, or Spot with you to the Bay Area, you're no doubt wondering which local ordinances may apply to your dog or cat. Area agencies can answer your specific questions about leash laws, immunizations, and the like, or at least refer you to the right organization. **SF DOG** (San Francisco Dog Owners Group), 415-339-7461, www.sfdog.org, has a comprehensive web site that lists dog-friendly areas, events, and important contact numbers. Your courthouse should be able to provide details about licensing your pets and local leash laws. Additional pet services found in the Bay Area include pet sitters and boarding and grooming establishments. Look in the Yellow Pages under "Pet Services."

You and Fido can take MUNI together, but your dog must pay her own way and wear a muzzle; non-service animals cannot ride during peak hours, 5–9 a.m. and 3–7 p.m. Guide dogs can ride all public transit at no charge and do not need to be muzzled. Call 415-701-4500, TTY 415-701-2323, for more information. Also noteworthy is **PAWS**, which stands for "Pets are Wonderful Support," an organization dedicated to preserving the relationship of people with AIDS and their pets; call 415-979-9550 to volunteer or visit www.pawssf.org for more information. The *Dog Lover's Companion to the Bay Area* by Maria Goodavage provides valuable information for the best places to explore, sleep, and eat with your dog in the nine Bay Area counties. There is even a glossy quarterly magazine devoted to dogs called *Bark*, www.thebark.com, 2810 8th Street, Berkeley, 510-704-0827.

What follows is a list of animal shelters, adoption services, and rescue and resource groups:

SAN FRANCISCO
- **Animal Care & Control**, 1200 15th St, 415-554-6364, TTY 415-701-2323, www.sfgov.org/acc
- **PAWS (Pets Are Wonderful Suppor)**, 415-979-9550, www.pawssf.org
- **Pets Unlimited Adoption Center**, 2343 Fillmore St, 415-568-3058, www.petsunlimited.org
- **Rocket Dog Rescue**, 415-642-4786, www.rocketdogrescue.org
- **SF DOG (Dog Owners Group)**, 415-339-7461, www.sfdog.org
- **SF Society for the Prevention of Cruelty to Animals (SPCA)**, 2500 16th St, 415-554-3000, www.sfspca.org

EAST BAY
- **Benicia-Vallejo Humane Society**, 1121 Sonoma Blvd, Vallejo, 707-645-7905, www.bvhumane.org
- **Berkeley-East Bay Humane Society**, 2700 9th St, Berkeley, 510-845-7735, www.berkeleyhumane.org
- **East Bay SPCA**, 8323 Baldwin St, Oakland, 510-569-0702, www.eastbayspca.org
- **Home at Last Animal Rescue**, 510-237-1625, www.homeatlastrescue.org
- **Milo Foundation Berkeley**, Pet Food Express adoption site, Berkeley, 415-454-6456, www.milofoundation.org
- **Tri-Valley SPCA Maddie's Adoption Center**, 4651 Gleason Dr, Dublin, 925-479-9670 www.eastbayspca.org

SOUTH BAY/PENINSULA
- **Homeless Cat Network**, 650-286-9013, www.homelesscatnetwork.org
- **Humane Society Silicon Valley**, 2530 Lafayette St, Santa Clara, 408-727-3383, www.hssv.org
- **Peninsula Cat Works**, 650-329-9570, www.peninsulacatworks.org/index.php
- **Peninsula Humane Society**, 12 Airport Blvd, San Mateo, 650-340-8200, www.peninsulahumanesociety.org
- **A Safe Haven For Cats**, 270 Redwood Shores Pkwy, Redwood City, 650-802-9686, www.safehavenforcats.com

NORTH BAY

- **Humane Society of Sonoma County**, 5345 Highway 12 West, Santa Rosa, 707-542-0882 www.sonomahumane.org
- **Marin County Humane Society**, 171 Bel Marin Keys Rd, Novato, 415-883-4621, www.marinhumanesociety.org
- **Napa County Humane Society**, 3265 California Blvd, 707-255-8118, www.napahumane.org
- **Second Chance Rescue**, 415-506-0161, www.hopalong.orgcom

FINDING A VETERINARIAN/EMERGENCY HOSPITALS

To alleviate the high cost of veterinarian bills, you may want to consider obtaining health coverage for your pet. Contact the national organization **Veterinary Pet Insurance**, 888-899-4874, www.petinsurance.com, or the pet HMO **Pet Assure**, 888-789-7387, www.petassure.com, for more details.

Most neighborhoods have at least one vet. To limit your travel time, try a vet in your area first. The best way to get the inside scoop on vets is to frequent the dog park and talk to neighborhood owners, but www.yelp.com is another great option. In addition to adoption services, the **San Francisco SPCA**, 2500 16th Street, 415-554-3000, also runs a full-service animal hospital and operates a spay-neuter clinic.

Or try the **California Veterinary Medical Association's** site at 916-649-0599 or www.cvma.org. You choose the city in which you are interested, and they will give you in-depth details about selected vets there. The CVMA's parent organization at www.avma.org will also give you information on your critter questions.

If your pet has ingested anything poisonous, contact **ASPCA National Animal Poison Control Center**, 24-hour emergency information service, 888-426-4435; there is a $60 charge. You can also go straight to an emergency pet hospital at the following locations:

SAN FRANCISCO

- **All Animals Emergency Hospital**, 1333 9th Ave, 415-566-0531, open weekday evenings from 6 p.m. to 8 a.m., weekends from noon on Saturday to 8 a.m. on Monday
- **Balboa Pet Hospital**, 3329 Balboa St, 415-752-3300
- **Pets Unlimited Veterinary Hospital**, 2343 Fillmore St, 415-563-6700, open 7 days a week, 24 hours for emergencies
- **San Francisco Veterinary Specialists**, 600 Alabama St, 415-401-9200, www.sfvs.net, 24-hour emergency services

NORTH BAY

- **Calistoga Pet Clinic**, 2960 Foothill Blvd, Calistoga, 707-942-0404, one vet on call for emergencies

- **Madera Pet Hospital**, 5796 Paradise Dr, Corte Madera, 415-924-1271
- **Novato Veterinary Hospital**, 7454 Redwood Blvd, Novato, 415-897-2173; evening calls will be directed to call emergency number
- **Pet Emergency Center**, 901 E Francisco Blvd, #C, San Rafael, 415-456-7372, www.petemergencycenter.com, 24-hour emergency services
- **San Francisco Veterinary Specialists**, 901 East Francisco Blvd, 415-455-8317, www.sfvs.net, 24-hour emergency services

EAST BAY
- **All Bay Animal Hospital**, 1739 Willow Pass Rd, Concord, 925-687-7346
- **Berkeley Dog and Cat Hospital**, 2126 Haste St, Berkeley, 510-848-5041, www.berkeleydogandcat.com
- **Pet Emergency Treatment Service of Berkeley**, 1048 University Ave, after-hours emergency services, 510-548-6684

SOUTH BAY/PENINSULA
- **Adobe Animal Hospital**, 396 First St, Los Altos, 650-948-9661, www.adobe-animal.com, 24 hour emergency care
- **Mayfair Veterinary Hospital**, 2810 Alum Rock Ave, San Jose, 408-258-2735
- **Skyline Pet Hospital**, 170 Skyline Plaza, Daly City, 650-756-4877
- **Stanford Pet Clinic**, 4111 El Camino Real, Palo Alto, 650-493-4233

OFF-LEASH AREAS

San Francisco is a dog lover's paradise. Berkeley is the birthplace of *Bark* magazine, and the greater Bay Area has been adding off-leash dog runs at a record clip.

In San Francisco, one in four families includes a dog, according to local dog owners' group **SF Dog**. Four-legged furry friends are more than welcome at a multitude of neighborhood parks, beaches, and even some cafés. While most of these spots have posted signs requiring pups to stay on their leashes, there are a number of designated off-leash runs and play areas where your pet can frolic freely—and legally. See the list below for dog park locations.

That said, by far and away the most popular off-leash spots in San Francisco, all located within the Golden Gate National Recreation Area (GGNRA), became strictly on-leash four years ago. But the story doesn't end there.

Every morning, evening, and weekend, these hot spots—the sandy shores of Fort Funston, Ocean Beach, and Crissy Field—are packed with wall-to-wall Golden Retrievers, Labs, and German Shepherds jogging alongside their owners. Some dogs are on leash, as the new rules require, while many others, in open defiance of the rules, are not.

Created in 1979, GGNRA's original pet policy allowed dogs to run off-leash in these areas, as well as North Baker Beach, Fort Miley, and Lands End. But in 2001, amid loud protests, the National Park Service—citing concerns about sensitive habitats, bird life, and eco-restoration areas, abruptly revoked this privilege. In response, many dog owners have refused to comply.

Luckily, there are a host of neighborhood parks, open greenspaces, and fenced runs available. Below is a list of designated spots where your doggy can run free, hassle-free.

A note about off-leash etiquette: Off-leash does not mean out of control. Dogs must always be under your direct supervision, and under strict voice control. This is especially important in unfenced off-leash areas. You should always carry a leash, ask fellow dog owners if your pup can play with their pets before releasing him into the pack, and always, always, always carry waste baggies and pick up after your pet!

SAN FRANCISCO DESIGNATED OFF-LEASH AREAS

- **Alamo Square Park**, western half of the park, along Scott Street between Hayes and Fulton sts
- **Alta Plaza Park**, second park terrace, Clay Street between Scott and Steiner sts
- **Bernal Heights**, dogs roam free beside their owners all along the trails that wind along the top of the hill, Bernal Heights Blvd
- **Buena Vista Park**, this green spot with great city views has trails and open hilly green grass popular with pooches and their owners, Buena Vista West at Central Ave
- **Corona Heights**, upper field with fenced area near the base of the hill, adjacent to Randall Museum, Roosevelt Way, and Museum Way
- **Dolores Park**, south of tennis courts, north of soccer field, 16th St between Church and Dolores sts
- **Douglass Park**, 26th and Douglass sts
- **Eureka Valley Park**, fenced area, 19th St and Collingwood, east of baseball diamond (on a trial basis)
- **Golden Gate Park**, four off-leash areas: southeast section bounded by Lincoln Way, King Dr, 2nd and 7th aves; northeast section at Stanyan and Grove sts; south central area bounded by King Dr, Middle Dr, 34th and 38th aves; fenced training area in the north central area near 38th Ave and Fulton
- **Lafayette Park**, near Sacramento St between Octavia and Gough sts
- **Lake Merced**, north side of lake area provides lots of space for free roaming with your dog, Lake Merced Blvd and Middlefield Dr
- **McKinley Square**, western slope, San Bruno Ave and 20th St
- **McLaren Park**, two off-leash areas: top of hill at Shelly Dr and Mansell St; south section via 1600 block of Geneva or 1600 block of Sunnydale—dogs must remain outside of sensitive habitat area
- **Mountain Lake Park**, east end of park, north of Lake St at 8th Ave
- **Potrero Hill Mini-Park**, 22nd St between Arkansas and Connecticut sts
- **St. Mary's Park**, lower park terrace, fenced area, Murray Ave and Justin Dr

- **Stern Grove**, north side, Wawona St between 21st and 23rd aves
- **Upper Noe Park**, fenced area adjacent to ball field, Day and Sanchez sts (on a trial basis)

UNOFFICIAL OFF-LEASH AREAS

As mentioned above there is quite a bit of controversy over some of San Francisco's most popular puppy sites, Fort Funston, Crissy Field, and Ocean Beach. Duboce Park, Duboce and Steiner streets, has been an "unofficial" dog park for years. However, it has never been legally designated for off-leash use.

For additional details on city off-leash sites listed here, or for more information on citywide dog run areas, contact the Parks and Recreation Department at 415-831-2700 or the SF DOG, 415-339-7461, www.sfdog.org.

BAY AREA OFF-LEASH AREAS

Outside of San Francisco check out Palo Alto People for Unleashed Pet Space (PUPS), 650-562-1777, www.canineworld.com/pups, and South Bay Pet Talk, www.southbaypettalk.com/pet_friendly.php; www.dogpark.com and www.thedogpark.com are also good resources.

EAST BAY

- **Cesar Chavez Park**, 11 Spinnaker Way, Berkeley
- **Crown Memorial Beach**, Alameda
- **Del Mar Dog Park**, Del Mar Dr at Pine Valley Rd, San Ramon
- **Dracena Park**, 130 Dracena, Piedmont
- **Drigon Dog Park**, fake fire hydrants, dog bone–shaped walkway, jumps, tunnels, separate small dog and large dog areas, Mission Blvd and 7th St, Union City
- **East Bay Regional Parks**: The majority of parks in the district allow dogs to be off-leash in most open space and trail areas (with a list of exceptions) as long as they are under control at all times, and the owner is carrying a leash. The park system includes a number of gems for pet lovers including a dog-swimmable shoreline at Lake Del Valle, and the puppy paradise Point Isabel—which has its own set of guidelines (see below). For detailed dog rules, off-leash areas, park listings, and trail maps visit www.ebparks.org.
- **Hardy Dog Park**, fenced, off-leash, 2.16 acres, 491 Hardy St, Oakland
- **Lake Elizabeth Dog Park**, at Central Park and Lake Elizabeth, fenced area near softball camp side of the lake, off of Stevenson Blvd, 40000 Paseo Padre Pkwy, Fremont
- **Leona Heights Park**, Campus and Canyon Oaks Dr
- **Livermore Canine Park**, Murdell Lane, Livermore
- **Lower Washington Park**, recently expanded to a half acre, 8th and Westline, Alameda

- **Marina Park**, Marina and Fairway, San Leandro
- **Memorial Park—Dog Run**, 1.3-acre fenced dog run within Memorial Park, Bollinger Canyon Rd at San Ramon Valley Blvd, San Ramon
- **Newhall Dog Park**, areas for big and small dogs, Ayers and Turtle Creek, Concord
- **Ohlone Dog Park** (Martha Scott Benedict Memorial Park), dogs allowed off-leash in entire park, membership group publishes monthly newsletter, SCOOPs, and hosts potluck meetings, Grant St and Hearst Ave, Berkeley, www.ohlonedogpark.org
- **Paso Nogal Park**, Paso Nogal Rd and Morello Ave, Pleasant Hill
- **Piedmont Park**, 711 Highland Avenue, Piedmont
- **Point Isabel Regional Shoreline**, 21 acres of run-free shoreline; official off-leash area is along the south side of the canal; Central Ave, exit off I-80 East or I-580 West, Richmond, www.pido.org. Point Isabel Dog Owners and Friends, a dog owner membership group, provides biodegradable doggy waste bags, publishes a newsletter, and sponsors monthly clean-ups. At the end of the day, you can stop by the popular Mudpuppy's Tub & Scrub and Sit & Stay café, www.mudpuppys.com, in the park to sign your pup up for a doggie bath, pick up treats and toys, and grab some coffee and snacks for yourself.
- **San Lorenzo Community Park**, half-acre site on the west side of the 30-acre park, 1970 Via Buena Vista, San Lorenzo

NORTH BAY

- **Bayfront Park**, popular 2-acre dog park, Camino Alto and Sycamore Ave, Mill Valley
- **Camino Alto Open Space Preserve**, end of Escalon Dr, West of Camino Alto, Mill Valley
- **DeTurk Roundbarn Park**, 819 Donahue St, Santa Rosa
- **Doyle Park Dog Park**, fenced dog park is behind the stadium, 700 Hoen Ave, Santa Rosa
- **Field of Dogs**, San Rafael, 3540 Civic Center Dr, fenced two thirds of the area behind Marin Civic Center, www.fieldofdogs.org
- **Galvin Dog Park**, in Don Galvin Park, next to Golf Course, 3330 Yulupa Ave, Santa Rosa
- **Larkspur—Piper Park**, 250 Doherty Dr (behind police station)
- **Marin Headlands Trails**, there are several entrances, one is at the Coastal Trail off Bunker Rd, near Rodeo Beach, Marin
- **Mc Dog**, within John F. McInnis County Park, Highway 101 to Smith Ranch Rd, San Rafael
- **Northwest Community Dog Park**, Marlow off of Gurneville Rd, Santa Rosa
- **O'Hair Park**, Novato, located on Novato Blvd, just west of Sutro in San Marin

- **Remington Dog Park** (also known as the Sausalito Dog Park), fenced area within the Martin Luther King Park, on Bridgeway and Ebbtide Ave, Sausalito, http://dogpark-sausalito.com
- **Rincon Valley Dog Park**, in Rincon Valley Community Park, fenced pond area for dogs, separate fenced large and small dog areas, 5108 Badger Rd, Santa Rosa
- **Rodeo Beach and Lagoon**, from the Marin Headlands Visitor Center, follow the sign west, Sausalito
- **San Pedro Mountain Open Space Preserve**, North Point San Pedro Rd, to Woodoaks Dr to the end, San Rafael
- **Terra Linda–Sleepy Hollow Divide Open Space Preserve**, end of Ridgewood Dr, San Rafael

PENINSULA

- **Boothbay Park**, Boothbay Ave and Edgewater Lane, Half Moon Bay
- **Burlingame Dog Park**, fenced area in Washington Park, Burlingame Ave east of train tracks, Burlingame
- **Cipriani Park Dog Exercise Area**, 2525 Buena Vista Ave, Belmont
- **Coastside Dog Park**, Wavecrest Rd near the Smith Field ball fields, off of Highway 1, Half Moon Bay, http://coastdogs.org
- **Foster City Dog Exercise Area**, 600 Foster City Blvd, Foster City
- **Foster City Dog Run**, fenced run, Foster City Blvd and Bounty, Foster City
- **Greer Park**, West Bayshore Rd and Amarillo St, Palo Alto
- **Heather Park**, Portofino and Melendy drs, San Carlos
- **Hoover Park**, Cowper Street between Loma Verde and Colorado aves, Palo Alto
- **Mitchell Park**, 3800 Middlefield Rd, Palo Alto
- **San Bruno Dog Park**, fenced area, Maywood and Evergreen, San Bruno
- **Shoreline Dog Park**, Shoreline Recreation Area, east end of Shoreline Blvd, Mountain View

SOUTH BAY

A good resource for area dog parks is http://www.wagntrain.com/dog_parks.htm. In addition, the City of San Jose plans to build a dog park in each of its 10 districts; for a current listing, go to http://www.sjparks.org/dogparks.asp.

- **Hellyer Park**, 1-acre enclosed area near Shadowbluff picnic area, 101 to Hellyer Ave, San Jose
- **Las Palmas Park**, Russet and Danforth drs, Sunnyvale
- **Lincoln Park**, fenced area, Wabash and West San Carlos, San Jose
- **Miyuki Dog Park**, small dirt enclosed area, Miyuki Dr and Autotech Ln, off of Santa Theresa Blvd, San Jose
- **Percolation Ponds**, off-leash running and swimming, Noble Ave north of Piedmont, San Jose

- **Santa Clara Dog Park**, 3450 Brookdale Dr, Santa Clara
- **Watson Dog Park**, San Jose's first official dog park, has a separate fenced small dog area, benches, picnic tables and grass, East Jackson and 22nd, San Jose

A WORD ABOUT SAFETY

San Francisco, and indeed the Bay Area, suffers from the same problems with crime as does most every other large metropolitan area. What's unusual here is that San Francisco suffers from an inordinate number of pedestrian fatalities. More pedestrians than occupants of motor vehicles were killed in car accidents in San Francisco during the previous 10 years, according to a recent study by the San Francisco Injury Center of UCSF. Pedestrian injuries were heavily concentrated in the downtown area of San Francisco and along heavily trafficked corridors. Be careful when you walk, bike, or drive.

Because police can't be everywhere all the time, you need to be aware of your own safety. Fortunately, common sense can reduce your chances of being victimized. Below are a few simple urban safety tips:

- Walk with determination, and remain aware of your surroundings at all times.
- If you're carrying a handbag or backpack, do so with the strap across your chest. However, if someone demands what you are carrying, give it up! Your life is much more valuable than anything you're carrying.
- On the street, you do not owe a response to anyone who asks for one. This may seem callous but it is better to err on the side of bad manners than bad judgment.
- At all costs, avoid getting into a car with a stranger.
- On the bus, ride in the front next to the driver.
- Keep clear of abandoned/deserted areas; if you must go into an area that you feel may be unsafe, do it in the daytime and, if possible, with someone else.
- Lock your house, both when you leave and when you are at home.
- If you like to jog, try to find a running partner, particularly if you run at night.
- Know where the local police and fire stations are located.
- If something does happen to you or if you witness a crime, notify the police immediately.

Neighborhood Watch programs are on the increase throughout the Bay Area, but they're not in every community yet. These programs encourage neighbors to get to know each other and watch out for each other, and to notify authorities of anything suspicious. Check with the police department in your neighborhood to find out if a watch program is up and running, and if not, you may want to take the lead and set one up yourself. You can also visit the neighborhood watch web site at www.ncpc.org, which gives you general safety information and instructs you on how to set up a neighborhood watch in your neighborhood. In addition, the District Attorney's office set up a community DA program where district attorneys in San Francisco volunteer in their own neighborhood and share their expertise.

The San Francisco Police Department is always looking for volunteers to assist in crime prevention, neighborhood policing, and other areas. For more information, contact the Reserve Coordinator, 850 Bryant Street, Room 535, San Francisco, 415-553-1643, or fill out a request for information online at the police department's web site, www.sfgov.org/police.

In San Francisco and many other neighborhoods in the Bay Area, crime statistics are available online and can help pinpoint areas with high crime rates.

Finally, if you are a victim of a crime, contact the police immediately, by dialing 911. For family violence, the crisis hotline is 800-799-7233 (non-emergency) or 911 for emergencies. For more listings, see **Crisis Lines** in the **Useful Phone Numbers and Web Sites** chapter.

If you have a complaint against a police officer in San Francisco contact the Office of Citizen Complaints, 415-241-7711 or TTY 415-241-7770. In Oakland contact the Citizens' Police Review Board, 510-238-3159. In San Jose, contact the Office of the Independent Police Auditor, 408-794-6226. You can also contact the police department in question directly.

N OW THAT YOU'VE FOUND A PLACE TO HANG YOUR HAT, AND YOU'VE taken care of some of the basics like turning on electricity and making sure your stove works, it's time to make your place feel like home. This chapter covers appliance rentals, domestic services, finding an automobile repair shop, receiving and sending packages, as well as services for people with disabilities, information for international newcomers, a resource section for gays and lesbians, and more.

RENTAL SERVICES

Most Bay Area rental apartments come fully equipped with all of the basic essentials you'll need—refrigerator, stove, etc.—with one exception. Your odds of getting a washer and dryer in San Francisco are only about 50/50, especially if you opt, as many do, for an older Victorian or Edwardian flat, in which case your odds are even worse. If you'd rather not shlep to the local Laundromat with all your neighbors, you might consider renting a washer and dryer. However, always be sure to check with your landlord first about logistics—where to hook it up and who will pay the increased water (the owner if you're lucky) and electricity (almost always you) bills. Who knows, in the process you may even be able to convince them to purchase one instead. It's worth a try.

If you're buying a house or condo and wind up missing a key appliance, or want to replace an old one with a newer one, or find yourself in the rare but odd studio rental with a "partial kitchen," you may want to check into appliance rental options. Generally speaking, you'll probably save money by opting to buy instead of renting—even buying on credit is financially better. But you just may need to rent something temporarily to get you started.

MAJOR APPLIANCE RENTAL

SAN FRANCISCO/NORTH BAY
- **Rent-A-Center**, 2853 Mission St, 415-282-2522, or 800-422-8186, www. rentacenter.com
- **Rent-A-Center**, 1375 Fillmore St, 415-567-3313, or 800-422-8186, www. rentacenter.com
- **Rent-A-Center**, 3475 Sonoma Blvd, Vallejo, 707-643-1733, or 800-422-8186, www.rentacenter.com
- **Rent-A-Center**, 711 Stony Point Rd #6, Santa Rosa, 707-542-6522, or 800-422-8186, www.rentacenter.com

EAST BAY
- **Rent-A-Center**, 3400 International Blvd, Oakland, 510-532-0210, or 800-422-8186, www.rentacenter.com

PENINSULA/SOUTH BAY
- **Mike's Appliance Rental**, 1224 Lynhurst Way, San Jose, 408-266-5640
- **Rent-A-Center**, 1789 E Capitol Expy, San Jose, 408-532-0274
- **Rent-A-Center**, 1605 W San Carlos St, San Jose, 408-287-2183, or 800-422-8186, www.rentacenter.com

DOMESTIC SERVICES

HOUSEKEEPING

Depending on how many long hours you spend at work, you may find there just isn't enough time to keep up with domestic details, particularly house cleaning. Rest assured, the Bay Area has plenty of people who'd be more than happy to clean your abode, for a fee. Many housekeepers advertise on coffeehouse, grocery store, university/college bulletin boards, and Craig's List (www.craigslist. org), as well as in newspaper classifieds. In San Francisco, **Parent's Place**, 1710 Scott St, 415-359-2454, has a bulletin board full of ads posted by people looking for housecleaning and childcare jobs. **Professional housecleaning services** are listed in the Yellow Pages under "House Cleaning." Here are a few numbers to get you started.

SAN FRANCISCO
- **City Maids**, 415-665-6633, www.sfcitymaids.com
- **Maid Green**, 415-839-6105, www.maidgreensf.com; this service uses non-toxic supplies, and specializes in working with families and children
- **Marvel Maids**, 877-627-8358, www.marvelmaids.com
- **Merry Maids**, 415-221-6243 or 800-637-7962, www.merrymaids.com
- **New Dimensions**, 415-731-4900, www.ndclean.com/agency.html

- **Self-Help for the Elderly**, 415-677-7600, www.selfhelpelderly.org; free temporary at-home assistance for qualified seniors and the disabled, particularly in Chinatown but also across the Bay Area

NORTH BAY
- **A Maid to Shine**, 415-379-9400, www.amaidtoshine.com
- **Merry Maids**, 415-455-9191 or 800-637-7962, www.merrymaids.com,

EAST BAY
- **Dana's Housekeeping**, 510-654-6880, www.danashousekeeping.com
- **Marvel Maids**, 877-627-8358, www.marvelmaids.com
- **Merry Maids**, 510-521-5878, 510-614-6243, or 800-637-7962, www.merrymaids.com

PENINSULA
- **Bay Area Maintenance**, 650-368-3906, www.bayareamaintenance.net
- **City Maids**, 415-665-6633, www.sfcitymaids.com
- **Marvel Maids**, 877-627-8358, www.marvelmaids.com
- **Merry Maids**, 650-572-8200 or 800-637-7962, www.merrymaids.com,

SOUTH BAY
- **Complete Cleaning**, 408-248-4162
- **Marvel Maids**, 877-627-8358, www.marvelmaids.com
- **Merry Maids**, 408-978-6273 or 800-637-7962, www.merrymaids.com

PEST CONTROL

As with the rest of the USA, the Bay Area has some cockroaches, ants, and termites, but in general there are far fewer pests here than in many parts of the country. Some older buildings, especially those with restaurants on the premises, are prone to cockroaches. In winter months ants can be a problem. Fleas may bug you in the late fall, particularly if you live near the beach, at ground level, or have pets. Pigeons can become bothersome if they decide to roost on the ledges of your building, especially near the entryway – protect your head! In warmer, damper regions, mosquitoes can be a nuisance. Alameda, San Mateo, Santa Clara, Marin, Sonoma, Napa, Solano, and Contra Costa counties have mosquito abatement programs. Some homes also suffer from termites; if you are in the market to buy a house, consider having it inspected for termites. In more rural areas ticks, raccoons, opossums, and skunks can be a problem.

If you are renting your place, it is the landlord's responsibility to keep your premises free from vermin, although keeping your home or apartment clean always helps. Nontoxic and humane means of controlling pests are available. Check the Yellow Pages or Internet under "Pest Control Services" for listings.

MAIL SERVICES

If you're in between addresses but still need a place to get your mail, there are dozens of businesses that will rent you a mailbox. You can also rent a mailbox at your local post office, though many have a waiting list. The following mail service companies are located in San Francisco. Check your Yellow Pages or the Internet under "Mailing Receiving and Forwarding Services" for a location near you.

- **Aim Mail Center**, 221 King St, 415-495-6776, www.aimmailcenters.com
- **Jet Mail**, 2130 Fillmore St, 415-922-9402
- **Mail Access**, 2261 Market St, 415-626-2575, www.mail-access.us
- **Mail Boxes Etc. (MBE)** and **UPS Stores**: 268 Bush St, 415-765-1515; 3701 Sacramento St, 415-221-9882; 4104 24th St, 415-824-1070; 601 Van Ness Ave, 415-775-6644; 2370 Market St, 415-431-0121, 2443 Fillmore St, 415-922-6245; 1032 Irving St, 415-566-2660; multiple other San Francisco and Bay Area locations; to find the store nearest you, visit www.theupsstore.com or www.mbe.com
- **Postal Annex**, 100 1st St, 415-882-1515; 350 Bay St #100, 415-772-9022

For mailing services, packaging help, faxing, and copying try

- **FedEx**, 1967 Market St, 415-252-0864; 1155 Harrison St, 415-552-4628; 1800 Van Ness Ave, 415-292-2500; 100 California St, 415-834-0240; 369 Pine St, 415-834-1053, www.fedex.com

MAIN POST OFFICES

Neighborhood post offices are listed at the end of each neighborhood profile. Check there for the one nearest you. For postal rates, post office locations, zip codes, and more, you can also contact the post office at 800-275-8777, www.usps.com, or try any of the post offices listed below.

SAN FRANCISCO/NORTH BAY
- **Napa**, 1625 Trancas St (Monday–Friday, 9 a.m. to 5 p.m.; closed Saturday)
- **San Francisco**, 1300 Evans Ave (Monday–Friday, 7 a.m. to 8:30 p.m.; Saturday, 8 a.m. to 2 p.m.)
- **San Rafael**, 40 Bellam Boulevard (Monday–Friday, 8:30 a.m. to 5 p.m.; Saturday, 10 a.m. to 1 p.m.)
- **Santa Rosa**, 730 2nd St (Monday–Friday, 8 a.m. to 6 p.m.; Saturday, 10 a.m. to 2 p.m.)

EAST BAY
- **Berkeley**, 2000 Allston Way (Monday–Friday, 9 a.m. to 5 p.m.; Saturday, 9 a.m. to 3 p.m.)
- **Concord**, 2121 Meridian Park Blvd (Monday–Friday, 9 a.m. to 6 p.m.; Saturday, 9 a.m. to 2 p.m.)

- **Emeryville**, 1585 62nd St (Monday–Friday, 8:30 to 5 p.m.; Saturday, 8 a.m. to 2 p.m.)
- **Walnut Creek**, 2070 N Broadway (Monday–Friday, 8:30 a.m. to 5 p.m.; closed Saturday)

PENINSULA/SOUTH BAY
- **Palo Alto**, 2085 E Bayshore Rd (Monday–Friday, 8:30 a.m. to 5 p.m.; closed Saturday)
- **San Mateo**, 1630 S Delaware St (Monday–Friday, 8:30 a.m. to 5 p.m.; Saturday, 9 a.m. to 12:30 p.m.)
- **San Jose**, 1750 Lundy Ave (Monday–Friday, 8:30 a.m. to 8 p.m.; closed Saturday)

JUNK MAIL

Everyone gets it, and most hate it—junk mail. There are a number of strategies for curtailing the onslaught. Try writing a note, including your name and address, asking to be purged from the **Direct Marketing Association's list** (Direct Marketing Association's Mail Preference Service, P.O. Box 9008, Farmingdale, NY 11735). This may work, although some catalog companies need to be contacted directly with a purge request. Another option is to call the **"Opt-out" line** at 888-567-8688 and request that the main credit bureaus not release your name and address to interested marketing companies pushing "pre-approved" credit and insurance offers. To keep telemarketers at bay, you can also register your home and cell phone numbers with the **National Do Not Call Registry**, 888-382-1222, TTY 866-290-4236, www.donotcall.gov.

SHIPPING SERVICES

- **DHL Worldwide Express**, 800-225-5345, www.dhl.com
- **FedEx**, 800-463-3339, www.fedex.com
- **United Parcel Service (UPS)**, 800-742-5877, www.ups.com
- **US Postal Service Express Mail**, 800-275-8777, www.usps.com

AUTOMOBILE REPAIR

Everything in your world is going great: you have a place to live, a good job, the sun is shining…and then your car breaks down. If this happens on the freeway, hopefully you already have some kind of service plan that will get your car towed to a service station. The American Automobile Association, known as AAA, is a popular plan (see below). Insurance companies that offer auto insurance, as well as some fuel companies, have auto emergency plans similar to AAA. Your next dilemma—how do you find a reputable auto repair place? This is not an easy process, no matter where you live. Probably the most popular way to find a repair place is to ask around—friends, co-workers, neighbors, etc—but www.yelp.com is rapidly gaining a reputation as the go-to place for service reviews. Going to your auto dealer, while generally a reliable option, can be expensive. **Value Star**, a leading rating organization of local service businesses and professionals, is headquartered in Oakland. To use their rating service, go to www.valuestar.com or call 888-298-8100. Remember, it's always a good idea to check with the **Better Business Bureau** (see below under **Consumer Protection**) to find out if any complaints have been filed against a service station you are considering using. And finally, on the lighter side, try calling *Car Talk* on National Public Radio, 888-CAR-TALK, or just tune in to KQED 88.5 FM, at 10 a.m. on Saturday or Sunday as Click and Clack, the Tappet brothers, discuss, in a most humorous fashion, cars and the problems of their owners. You can also pick up handy auto tips on their web site: www.cartalk.com.

AAA (AMERICAN AUTOMOBILE ASSOCIATION)

Founded at the turn of the century by Jim Wilkins, proprietor of the Cliff House, the American Automobile Association (AAA) began as an automobile club when there were only a dozen self-propelled vehicles navigating the hills of San Francisco. Today, more than 3.8 million people belong to AAA. Basic membership costs $54 a year plus a one-time $17 enrollment fee. As a member, you receive 24-hour emergency road service, free maps, travel services, discounts at numerous hotels, DMV services, and more. If you are caught out of gas, have a flat tire, or worse yet, a blown transmission, AAA can come rescue you. Just call their **Emergency Road Service Number** at 800-AAA-HELP (800-222-4357). You can also call 800-922-8228 to find an office near you or visit the web site for California AAA, www.csaa.com.

CONSUMER PROTECTION

The *Bay Area Consumers' Checkbook* is a pro-consumer guide published by the Center for the Study of Services. It is a nonprofit magazine, free of advertising, created "to provide consumers information to help them get high quality services and products at the best possible prices." The quality of information is excellent. Articles can be ordered online at www.checkbook.org or through the mail, call 510-763-7979, Monday-Friday, 8:30 a.m. to 2:30 p.m. There is a fee for ordering articles. A subscription to the magazine is $34 for two years; call the same number used for ordering articles.

For consumer protection information regarding utilities see **Consumer Protection—Utility Complaints** in the **Getting Settled** chapter.

Got a beef with a merchant or a company? Several agencies monitor consumer-related businesses and will take action when necessary. It goes without saying that the best defense against fraud and consumer victimization is to avoid it—read contracts before you sign them, save all receipts and canceled checks, get the name of telephone sales and service people, and check a contractor's license number with the Department of Consumer Affairs for complaints. But sometimes you still get stung. A dry cleaner returns your blue suit, but now it's purple and he shrugs. A shop refuses to refund as promised on the expensive gift, which didn't suit your mother. Your landlord fails to return your security deposit when you move. After $898 in repairs to your automobile's engine, the car now vibrates wildly, and the mechanic claims innocence. Negotiations, documents in hand, fail. You're angry, and embarrassed because you've been had. There is something you can do.

- **Better Business Bureau: San Francisco**, Alameda, Contra Costa, San Mateo, and Marin counties, 510-844-2000; Santa Clara and Santa Cruz counties, 408-278-7400; maintains consumer complaint files about businesses. You can also research businesses on their web site at www.goldengate.bbb.org.
- **California Attorney General**, 800-952-5225, or TTY 800-735-2929, www.ag.ca.gov, maintains a public inquiry unit that reviews consumer complaints.
- **California State Directory Information Service**, 800-807-6755 or TTY 916-464-1580
- **California Department of Consumer Affairs**, 800-952-5210 or TTY 800-326-2297, www.dca.ca.gov, is a state agency that investigates consumer complaints.
- **Contractors State License Board**, 800-321-2752, www.cslb.ca.gov
- **SF District Attorney**, 415-553-1751, www.sfdistrictattorney.org, maintains a consumer protection unit that investigates and mediates consumer/business disputes.

MEDIA-SPONSORED CALL FOR ACTION PROGRAMS

The following are consumer advocacy programs operated by Bay Area television/radio stations:

- **KGO Seven On Your Side**, 900 Front St, San Francisco, CA 94111, 415-954-8151
- **KRON-TV Contact 4**, 1001 Van Ness Ave, San Francisco, CA 94109, 415-441-4444
- *San Jose Mercury News* **Action Line**, 750 Riddler Park Dr, San Jose, CA 95190, 888-688-6400

LEGAL MEDIATION/REFERRAL PROGRAMS

- **The Bar Association of San Francisco**, 310 Battery St, San Francisco, 415-982-1600, www.sfbar.org, runs early mediation program jointly with San Francisco Superior Court
- **California Community Dispute Service**, 502 7th St, San Francisco, 415-865-2520, www.cacds.org
- **East Bay Community Mediation**, 1968 San Pablo Ave, Berkeley, 510-548-2377, www.seedscrc.org

LEGAL ASSISTANCE FOR THE ELDERLY

- **Legal Assistance for Seniors**, 464 7th St, Oakland, 510-832-3040
- **Legal Assistance to the Elderly**, 995 Market St, San Francisco, 415-538-3333

SMALL CLAIMS COURTS

The maximum amount of money you may sue for in small claims court is $7,500, and in accordance with state law, one individual may file up to two cases per year.

The **California Department of Consumer Affairs** maintains a helpful web site, www.dca.ca.gov/smallclaims, with information on small claims court in general, including a useful booklet, "How to Use Small Claims Court," that you can download. The site also has information and individual contacts for each county. Here are a few local county web sites to get you started.

- **Alameda County**, www.alameda.courts.ca.gov
- **Contra Costa County**, www.cc-courts.org
- **Marin County**, www.marincourt.org
- **San Mateo County**, www.sanmateocourt.org
- **Santa Clara County**, www.sccsuperiorcourt.org
- **Solano County**, www.solanocourts.com
- **Sonoma County**, www.sonomasuperiorcourt.com

SERVICES FOR PEOPLE WITH DISABILITIES

Long before there was an Americans with Disabilities Act, the Bay Area's sensitivity to the needs of the disabled was raised by a group of handicapped college applicants who fought for admission to the Berkeley campus of the University of California. Their efforts, in the early 1970s, not only achieved the group's goal but also spawned the **Independent Living Center**, which now boasts offices across the country. Its representatives work hard to protect the rights of the disabled, and the centers offer training and rehabilitation services to those with disabilities, as well as referrals to support groups and organizations.

Rose Resnick's Lighthouse for the Blind and Visually Disabled provides assistance, equipment, support, and referrals to the visually impaired. Fully trained guide dogs are available through **Guide Dogs for the Blind**, which is based in Marin County. **The Hearing and Speech Center of Northern California** provides testing, education, support, and referrals to the hearing impaired.

A great resource for accessible sports and recreation in the Bay Area can be found at the **Bay Area Outreach & Recreation Program**, a Berkeley nonprofit. They feature year-round activities for youth and adults and have an adaptive cycling program.

Here's how to get in touch with several helpful organizations:

- **The ARC of San Francisco (Association of Retarded Citizens)**, 1500 Howard St, 415-255-7200, www.thearcsanfrancisco.org
- **Bay Area Outreach & Recreation Program,** 600 Bancroft Wy, Berkeley, 510-849-4616, www.borp.org
- **Center for Independent Living**, 2539 Telegraph Ave, Berkeley, 510-841-4776, TTY 510-848-3101, www.cilberkeley.org
- **Deaf and Disabled Telecommunications Program**, provides free service to the hearing disabled, 877-546-7414, TTY 800-867-4323, www.ddtp.org
- **Deaf Services of Palo Alto**, P.O. Box 60651, Palo Alto, 650-856-9262, interpreters@dspa.org
- **Guide Dogs for the Blind**, 350 Los Ranchitos Rd, San Rafael, 415-499-4000
- **Hearing and Speech Center**, 1234 Divisadero St, San Francisco, 415-921-7658, TTY 415-921-8990
- **Independent Living Resource Center**, 649 Mission, 3rd Floor, San Francisco, 415-543-6222, TTY 415-543-6698, www.ilrcsf.org
- **The Janet Pomeroy Center (Recreation Center for the Handicapped)**, 207 Skyline Blvd, 415-665-4100www.janetpomeroy.org
- **Rose Resnick Lighthouse for the Blind**, 214 Van Ness Ave, 415-431-1481; TTY 415-431-4572
- **Support for Families of Children with Disabilities**, 2601 Mission St, 415-920-5040, www.supportforfamilies.org

GETTING AROUND

All BART stations are wheelchair accessible with elevators at every station, and discount tickets are available. Most public transit buses throughout the Bay Area are also equipped to handle wheelchairs by use of ramps and lifts. Fares are significantly lower for the disabled. For more information on public transit options for the disabled call the appropriate transit agency (BART, MUNI, AC Transit, SamTrans, and CalTrain are listed in the **Transportation** chapter). Wheelchair rentals are available at a number of medical equipment and supply businesses. You can also purchase new and used wheelchairs at various stores. Check under "Wheelchairs" in the Yellow Pages or online.

Applications for handicapped parking permits are available at any local **Department of Motor Vehicles** and online at www.dmv.ca.gov, or you can request to have an application mailed to you by calling 800-777-0133. Once you complete the application, it must be signed by your doctor and brought to any local DMV office, or returned by mail to the address listed on the application. There is no fee for disabled placards.

COMMUNICATION

The **California Telephone Access Program** offers free assistance devices for the deaf, as well as the hearing-, speech-, mobility-, and visually impaired—from amplified phones, to voice enhancers, to large-button phones, to TTYs. **TTY** is a small telecommunications device with a keyboard for typing and a screen for reading conversations. TTY is sometimes also referred to as **TDD (Telecommunications Device for the Deaf)**. Experts will come to your home to install the equipment and help train you to use it. To get started contact TTY 800-806-4474 or Voice: 800-806-1191; for services in Spanish TTY 800-896-7670, or Voice: 800-949-5650; for service in Hmong: 866-880-3394; or Cantonese: 866-324-8754; or Mandarin: 866-324-8747. You can also drop by the walk-in center, CTAP Oakland Service Center, 1970 Broadway, Suite 650, Oakland, open Monday through Friday, 9 a.m. to 6 p.m.

California also has a telephone relay service, which provides a communication system for the hearing- and speech-impaired. This system allows people who are deaf or hard of hearing to phone people who do not have a TTY. The operator will contact your party and relay your conversation. **Speech to Speech Relay Service (STS)** assists those who can hear but have a speech disability, and use a voice synthesizer or voice enhancer. A specially trained operator re-voices what is being said by the STS user. The STS user hears the other party's voice directly. No special telephone equipment is required. This service is free except for any toll charges. Also now available is an Internet-based relay service. Text-users who are deaf, hard of hearing, or speech-disabled can make a relay call by connecting with an Internet Relay Operator who, in turn, dials the phone number of the other party and manages the conversation between the two.

- **TTY**: 800-735-2922 or 711
- **STS**: 800-854-7784 or 711
- **Internet** : www.ip-relay.com; www.myrelay.com; www.sprint-crs.com
- **Voice**: 877-546-7414, or 711

If you need help with sign language, contact the following organizations. They usually require one week's notice. **Bay Area Communication Access**, 415-356-0405, TTY 415-356-0376, www.bacainterp.com; **Hands On Bay Area**, 415-541-9616.

HOUSING

Some of the organizations listed above can help you with finding accessible housing, including the **Independent Living Center** in San Francisco at 415-543-6222 and the **Center for Independent Living** in Berkeley, 510-841-4776.

INTERNATIONAL NEWCOMERS

Immigration rules and regulations have become increasingly strict and bureaucratic in the USA since 9/11. If you are planning to relocate from abroad, your first step should be to visit the US consulate in your home country and find out what you need to do to prepare; that way you can have all of your paperwork in order ahead of time, and hopefully avoid any problems or delays when you arrive. The consulate should be able to provide you with information specific to your situation—applications for permanent residency, guest worker programs, and student visas, etc., as well as information on green cards, naturalization, seeking asylum, and becoming a US citizen.

A variety of helpful information can be found online at the **US Citizen and Immigration Services** web site: www.uscis.gov. If you have specific questions, you can also contact the USCIS national customer service center: 800-375-5283 or TTY 800-767-1833.

For further assistance, you can also schedule an appointment with **USCIS**. Below are the addresses of local USCIS district and satellite offices:

- **San Francisco District Office**: 444 Washington St, San Francisco
- **Asylum Office**: 75 Hawthorne St, #303S, San Francisco, 415-293-1234
- **Oakland Application Support Center**: 2040 Telegraph Ave, Oakland
- **South Bay Office**: 1887 Monterey Rd, San Jose

Once you've settled in, you may want to get in touch with the consulate from your home country. The consulate can often be a useful starting point when you're getting settled—providing information on local community groups and organizations that may be of interest, as well as assisting with questions you may have about your move to the USA. For US citizens planning to travel abroad—especially for work, school, or an extended stay—the consulate is also the place to go to find out about rules and regulations, visas, etc. Below is a list of the major offices in San Francisco:

INTERNATIONAL CONSULATES IN SAN FRANCISCO

- **The Consulate General of Australia**, 1800 18th St, 415-362-6160
- **The Consulate General of Austria**, 580 California St, 415-951-8911
- **The Consulate General of Egypt**, 276 Mallorca Wy, 415-346-9700, www. egy2000.com
- **The Consulate General of Brazil**, 300 Montgomery St, Suite 900, 415-981-8170, www.brazilsf.org
- **The British Consulate General**, 1 Sansome St, Suite 850, 415-617-1300, www.ukinusa.fco.gov.uk
- **The Consulate General of Canada**, 580 California St, 415-834-3180
- **The Consulate General of Chile**, 870 Market St, 415-982-7662, www.chileanconsulatesfo.org
- **The Consulate General of China**, 1450 Laguna St, 415-674-2900, www. chinaconsulatesf.org
- **The Consulate General of Ecuador**, 235 Montgomery St, Suite 944, 415-982-1819, www.consuladoecuadoraf.org
- **The Consulate General of El Salvador**, 507 Polk St, Suite 280, 415-771-8524, www.elsalvadorsf.org

- **The Consulate General of France**, 540 Bush St, 415-397-4330, www.consulfrance-sanfrancisco.org
- **The Consulate General of Germany**, 1960 Jackson St, 415-775-1061
- **The Consulate General of Greece**, 2441 Gough St, 415-775-2102
- **The Consulate General of Guatemala**, 785 Market St, 415-896-9181
- **The Consulate General of Honduras**, 870 Market St, Suite 449, 415-392-0076
- **The Consulate General of India**, 540 Arguello Blvd, 415-668-0662, www.cgisf.org
- **The Consulate General of Indonesia**, 1111 Columbus Ave, 415-474-9571, www.kjrisfo.net
- **The Consulate General of Ireland**, 100 Pine St, 33rd Floor, 415-392-4214, www.israeliconsulate.org
- **The Consulate General of Israel**, 456 Montgomery St, Suite 2100, 415-844-7500
- **The Consulate General of Italy**, 2590 Webster St, 415-931-4924, www.italcons-sf.org
- **The Consulate General of Japan**, 50 Fremont St, Suite 2300, 415-777-3533, www.sf.us.emb-japan.go.jp
- **The Consulate General of the Republic of Korea**, 3500 Clay St, 415-921-2251
- **The Consulate General of Luxembourg**, One Sansome St, Suite 830, 415-788-0816, http://sanfrancisco.mae.lu
- **The Consulate General of Mexico**, 532 Folsom St, 415-354-1700, www.sre.gob.mx/sanfrancisco
- **The Royal Norwegian Consulate General**, 20 California St, 6th floor, 415-986-0766
- **The Consulate General of Peru**, 870 Market St, Suite 1067, 415-362-5185
- **The Consulate General of The Philippines**, 447 Sutter St, Philippine Center Building, 415-433-6666
- **The Consulate General of Portugal**, 3298 Washington St, 415-346-3400
- **The Consulate General of the Russian Federation**, 2790 Green St, 415-928-6878, www.consulrussia.org
- **The Consulate General of The Republic of Singapore**, 595 Market St, Suite 2450, 415-543-4775, www.mfa.gov.sg/sanfrancisco
- **The Consulate General of Spain**, 1405 Sutter St, 415-922-2995, www.maec.es/consulados/sanfrancisco
- **The Consulate General of Sweden**, 120 Montgomery St, Suite 2175, 415-788-2631
- **The Consulate General of Switzerland**, 456 Montgomery St, 415-788-2272, www.eda.admin.ch/sf
- **The Consulate General of Ukraine**, 530 Bush St, Suite 402, 415-398-0240, www.ukrainesf.com
- **The Consulate General of Vietnam**, 1700 California St, Suite 430, 415-922-1707, www.vietnamconsulate-sf.org

IMMIGRATION RESOURCES

- **Bureau of Immigration and Customs Enforcement**, www.ice.gov
- **Customs & Border Protection**, www.cbp.gov
- **Department of Homeland Security**, www.dhs.gov
- **General Government Questions**, 800-333-4636, www.usa.gov
- **Social Security Administration**, 800-772-1213, www.ssa.gov
- **US Bureau of Consular Affairs**, www.travel.state.gov
- **US Department of State, Visa Services**, www.state.gov
- **US Bureau of Citizenship and Immigration Services—Green Cards, Visas, Government Forms,** www.uscis.gov

IMMIGRATION PUBLICATIONS

You can download a useful guide, "**Welcome to the United States: A Guide for New Immigrants**" free at www.uscis.gov/newimmigrants. The booklet includes information on your rights and responsibilities as well as the steps to take to become a US citizen. Another publication you may find helpful is the **_Newcomer's Handbook for Moving to and Living in the USA_**, by Mike Livingston (First Books).

MOVING PETS TO THE USA

- **_The Pet-Moving Handbook_** (First Books) covers domestic and international moves, via car, airplane, ferry, etc. Primary focus is on cats and dogs.
- **Cosmopolitan Canine Carriers,** based in Connecticut, 800-243-9105, www.caninecarriers.com, has been shipping dogs and cats all over the world for over 25 years. Contact them with questions or concerns regarding air transportation arrangements, vaccinations, and quarantine times.

GAY AND LESBIAN LIFE

After years of grassroots fundraising, the **Lesbian, Gay, Bisexual and Transgender Center of San Francisco**, known simply as "The Center," opened its doors in 2002 at the corner of Market Street and Laguna. Today, the bright, primary-colored, multimillion-dollar, spacious, 40,000-square-foot facility proudly flying the rainbow flag provides a variety of programs for the LGBT community, their families and friends, including parenting classes, HIV support groups, 12-step programs, and a wide range of arts activities and presentations. The Center also has a drop-in youth center, a large auditorium for special events, a senior space, a reading room, an art gallery, a bulletin board with dozens of resources, child care, offices for a handful of nonprofit groups, a computer room, a café, and a fantastic roof terrace. To find out more, drop by 1800 Market Street, call 415-865-5555, or check out www.sfcenter.org.

For gay and lesbian nightlife, dance clubs, comedy, and theater, the Castro and the Mission districts are the places to go. For the leather-loving set, a handful of clubs in SoMa are hopping every night. SoMa is also home to the Stud, one of the oldest gay club/bars around, which frequently draws a mixed crowd to its popular dance nights.

The biggest gay celebration in town is the annual **Gay Pride Parade** in June. Festivities are held all over the city, especially in SoMa and The Castro. See **A Bay Area Year** for more detail. Also in June, check out **The International Lesbian & Gay Film Festival**, put on annually by Frameline, 415-703-8650, www.frameline.org. For a mini tour through the evolution of queer politics, culture, and identity in San Francisco check out www.shapingsf.org/ezine/gay, part of the excellent history project **Shaping San Francisco**. For LGBT-friendly worship, check out the **Gay and Lesbian** section of **Places of Worship** in the **Getting Involved** chapter.

PUBLICATIONS

- **Bay Area Reporter**, 395 9th St, San Francisco, 415-861-5019, www.ebar.com, has been around for almost 30 years and offers entertainment listings, hard news, sports, classifieds, personals, and more. It is distributed citywide every Tuesday; free.
- **San Francisco Bay Times: The Gay, Lesbian, Bi, Trans Newspaper**, 3410 19th St, San Francisco, 415-626-0260, offers news, reviews, employment listings, therapy and support groups, etc. Distributed citywide every other Thursday; free.
- **Curve**, a glossy magazine with lesbian-related news, politics, style, travel, social issues and entertainment content; www.curvemag.com.

BOOKSTORES

- **A Different Light Bookstore**, 489 Castro St, 415-431-0891, www.adlbooks. com, is arguably the premier gay and lesbian bookstore.
- **Modern Times**, 888 Valencia St, 415-282-9246, www.mtbs.com, is a progressive bookstore with a good selection of lesbian, bi, and gay literature.

W HEN MOVING TO A NEW AREA, ONE OF THE MOST CHALLENGING and overwhelming prospects parents face is finding good childcare and schools. While the process is not an easy one, with time and effort it is possible to find what you are looking for, be it in-home or onsite daycare, an after-school program, or a good public or private school, and even colleges and universities. The keys, of course, are research and persistence. Often the best advice comes from those with the most first-hand experience, namely, other parents.

PARENTING PUBLICATIONS

If you have childcare concerns upon arriving here, it's a good idea to pick up a copy of **Bay Area Parent**, a free monthly magazine that includes a calendar of events and articles on parenting resources in San Francisco and the Bay Area. The same company also publishes several related publications including **B.a.b.y. (The Best Advice for Baby & You)** and **Parenting Bay Area Teens**. To subscribe, call their office at 650-655-7600, or visit them online at http://bayareaparent.parenthood.com. **Parents' Press**, 1454 Sixth Street, Berkeley, CA 94710, 510-524-1602, offers online magazines for parents: www.parentspress.com and www.parent-teen.com (for families with teens).

DAYCARE

Probably the best way to find a good daycare provider is by referral from someone you know and trust. That said, being new to the Bay Area might limit such an option for you. The **California Childcare Resource & Referral Network**, 111 New Montgomery Street, 7th floor, San Francisco, CA 94105, 415-882-0234, www.rrnetwork.org, an information service that provides referrals to childcare agencies throughout California, should be able to assist you with your search. **The National Association for the Education of Young Children (NAEYC)** may be helpful as well. Call or write for a list of daycare centers in your area, accredited by them: 202-232-8777, NAEYC, 1313 L St NW, Suite 500, Washington, DC 20005, or search their childcare provider database at www.naeyc.org. You can also use this service to find accredited nursery schools.

Those affiliated with a major university in the Bay Area may have access to a university-operated referral agency or a university-run childcare center. Inquire at the student services desk of your university. Sometimes university graduate student divisions provide such referrals and services.

For a childcare referral agency in your area check with the following:

SAN FRANCISCO/NORTH BAY

- In San Francisco, contact **Children's Council of San Francisco**, 445 Church St, San Francisco, 94114, 415-276-2900, Child Care Resource and Referral Line: 415-343-3300, www.childrenscouncil.org.
- **Wu-Yee**, 888 Clay St, Lower Level, Joy Lok Family Resource Center, San Francisco, 94108, 415-391-4956, www.wuyee.org, an agency devoted to servicing the needs of San Francisco's large Cantonese-speaking community, operates six childcare centers in the Tenderloin, Chinatown, and Visitacion Valley. Both agencies provide a variety of services in English, Spanish, and Cantonese, including training for childcare providers, health and safety training, needs assessment and food programs, resource library, parent support information about employing in-home workers, referral service for licensed childcare, and listings of nanny services.
- In Marin County, contact **Marin Child Care Council**, 555 Northgate Dr, San Rafael, Suite 105, 94903, 415-472-1092, Childcare Referral Line: 415-479-2273, www.mc3.org.

EAST BAY

- For childcare referrals in Alameda County contact **Bananas**, 5232 Claremont Ave, Oakland, 94618, 510-658-7353, direct referral line: 510-658-0381, www.bananasinc.org; or **Child Care Links,** 1020 Serpentine Ln, Suite 102, Pleasanton, 94566, 925-417-8733, www.childcarelinks.org.
- For referrals in Hayward, San Leandro, and the Tri-Cities Area, call **4Cs of Alameda County**, 22351 City Center Dr, Suite 200, Hayward, 94541, 510-582-2182, www.4c-alameda.org, childcare referral lines: 510-582-2182 (Hayward, San Leandro, San Lorenzo, and Castro Valley) and 510-713-2557 (Fremont, Newark, and Union City).
- In Contra Costa County, call **Contra Costa Child Care Council**, 2280 Diamond Blvd, Suite 500, Concord, 94520, 925-676-5437, www.cocokids.org.

PENINSULA/SOUTH BAY

- For the San Mateo area, consult with **Child Care Coordinating Council of San Mateo County (4Cs)**, 2121 El Camino Real, Suite A-100, San Mateo, 94403, 650-655-6770, www.thecouncil.net.

- The **Community Child Care Council of Santa Clara County**, 2515 N First St, San Jose, 95131, 408-487-0747, childcare referrals: 408-487-0749, www.4c.org, provides information and referrals in Santa Clara County.

WHAT TO LOOK FOR IN DAYCARE

When searching for the best place for your child, be sure to visit prospective daycare providers—preferably unannounced. In general, look for safety, cleanliness, and caring attitudes on the part of the daycare workers. Check that the kitchen, toys, and furniture are clean and safe. Observe the other kids at the center. Do they seem happy? Are they well behaved? Ask for the telephone numbers of other parents who use the service and talk to them before committing. It's a good idea to request a daily schedule—look for both active and quiet time, and age-appropriate activities. Since the weather in California allows for year-round outdoor activities, such as sports, games, and field trips, make sure the childcare curriculum includes such things.

Keep in mind that being licensed does not necessarily guarantee service of the quality you may be seeking. If you think a provider might be acceptable, check to see if they're licensed and not in trouble for anything. To find out if a daycare is licensed, check the online registry of the **California Community Care Licensing Division**, www.ccld.ca.gov or contact the **California Child Care Resource & Referral Network**, 111 New Montgomery Street, 7th floor, San Francisco, CA 94105, 415-882-0234, www.rrnetwork.org, or any of the county referral agencies listed above.

For drop-in childcare while you go shopping or to a movie, try a **KidsPark Center**. They have two locations close to the major shopping malls in Silicon Valley (Oakridge and Valley Fair) and accept children aged 2–11 years. Call 408-213-0973 or visit www.kidspark.com for more information.

In 2009 rates were $7.50 per hour for one child with discounted rates for siblings. They limit the number of hours that you can use their service (5 hours per day and up to 15 hours per week) to ensure that the center provides drop-in rather than regular childcare. There is also a one-time $25 registration fee per family. While reservations are not necessary, it's a good idea to call first to be sure they have room on a particular day.

NANNIES

If you are looking for a nanny, in San Francisco or Silicon Valley you can expect to pay $1,400 to $2,000 per month for a live-in nanny, and $13 to $25 per hour for a part-time nanny, depending on the nanny's experience, education, the number of kids in your family, and whether housekeeping and driving are expected. Many agencies can assist you in finding a qualified nanny. Online, try the local **Nanny Network** at www.nannynet.net or call them at 925-256-8575. This organization provides reliable nanny referral services within Alameda and Contra

Costa counties. In San Francisco and Marin counties, **In-House Staffing @ Aunt Ann's,** 415-749-3650, www.in-housestaffing.com, matches families with baby nurses, nannies, and babysitters. **A Special Nanny**, 408-358-1065, www.specialnanny.com, provides nanny care and aides for children with special needs throughout the greater Bay Area. Another useful place to look is **Town and Country Resources**, www.tandcr.com, 415-567-0956 (San Francisco), 650-326-8570 (Palo Alto). They place childcare and household professionals in homes, including nannies, baby nurses, personal assistants, housekeepers, and cooks.

Be sure to check all references prior to hiring someone. Many parents choose to run background checks on prospective nannies. **Trustline**, 800-822-8490, www.trustline.org, a nonprofit state-affiliated background checking agency and registry, conducts fingerprint searches through both FBI and California Department of Justice records, and name searches for child abuse reports. This service is available to all prospective childcare employers, but keep in mind that searches usually take three to four weeks to complete.

If you decide to hire a nanny without using an agency, you will need to take care of taxes, disability, unemployment insurance, and social security. For information, call 800-NANITAX or check www.4nannytaxes.com.

AU PAIRS

The US Information Agency oversees and approves the organizations that offer this service where young adults between the ages of 18 and 26 provide a year of in-home childcare and light housekeeping in exchange for airfare, room and board, and a small stipend per week. The program offers a valuable cultural exchange between the host family and the (usually European) au pair, as well as a flexible childcare schedule for parents. Unfortunately, the program only lasts one year and the au pairs don't have the life or work experience of a career nanny. Nevertheless, in California au pairs are a popular way to satisfy families' childcare needs. In the Bay Area, most au pairs come from Poland, Germany, France, and Scandinavia. The agencies that bring over the au pairs run background checks before making placements, and orientation and training sessions once the placements have been made. Here are some of the agencies you can contact if you'd like to find an au pair:

- **Au Pair Care**, 800-428-7247, www.aupaircare.com
- **Au Pair in America**, 800-928-7247, www.aupairinamerica.com
- **Cultural Care Au Pair**, 800-333-6056, www.culturalcare.com
- **Interexchange, Au Pair USA**, 800-479-0907 or 800-287-2477, www.aupairusa.org

SCHOOLS

Choosing the right school for your child was probably a difficult task in your old community; factor in moving to a new city, and, for many, it becomes a stressful proposition. Add to that the reputation of California's public schools—overcrowded, staffed by underpaid and inexperienced teachers, etc.—and the search for the right school can be downright intimidating. Many parents who are new to the area rush to the conclusion that the only way to offer their child a good education here is to shell out a lot of money for an expensive private school. In fact, the Bay Area offers a great multitude of schooling possibilities, including an excellent public charter program, public and private year-round schooling programs, and myriad private options.

CHOOSING A SCHOOL

Quantitative measures such as graduation rates and test scores are important, but just as important are the subjective impressions and feelings you and your child will gain from visiting a prospective school. That's why the crucial ingredients for finding the right school are visit, visit, visit, and talk, talk, talk.

When visiting a school, your gut reactions will tell you a lot. Ask yourself these questions:

- Am I comfortable here? Will my child be comfortable here?
- Does the school feel safe? Are the bathrooms clean and free of graffiti?
- Does this school meet her/his learning style? Are elementary-age students moving around naturally, but staying on task?
- What are the halls like in junior high and high schools when classes change—how are students interacting with one another and with their teachers as their class changes?
- Are students actively engaged in discussions or projects? Is student work displayed?
- Ask elementary teachers about reading and math groups and if children move up as they build skills.
- Find out if there are any special programs offered to assist new students with their transition to their new school.
- Check for after-school or enrichment activities that your child will enjoy.
- Ask if parents are encouraged to volunteer in the classroom.
- Look at the faculty and curriculum as well as facilities and equipment. Are adults a presence in all parts of the building and grounds? Are the computer labs up-to-date with enough computers? Are instructional materials plentiful and new? Do textbooks cover areas you think are important? Does the school have a clearly articulated mission statement? Do the teachers that you observe seem to teach with that mission in mind? Can teachers speak articulately about the mission of the school and the educational philosophy? Do you see opportunities for your child to do things he/she likes to do—art, music, science, etc.?
- Finally, if the school that you are visiting is located near one of the Bay Area's many colleges and universities, ask whether there are programs that bring

college students to schools for presentations and talks. Inquire about field trips to the Bay Area's museums and other attractions.

Although satisfying answers to all these questions might be a somewhat unrealistic and time-consuming dream, with research and visits, you will be able to find a good match for your child's needs and interests. The time put in at the front end of the decision-making process is definitely worth the effort.

To find out about California Public Schools' statewide accountability programs, funding, and reform efforts, as well as district and school-by-school breakdowns of recent test scores and campus rankings, visit the **California Department of Education's** web site, www.cde.ca.gov.

Another excellent site for gathering specific information about Bay Area schools is called **Great Schools**, www.greatschools.net. This nonprofit organization is dedicated to providing clear and objective information about local schools. Visit their web site to learn about schools' test scores, programs, facilities, student body size, and teacher qualifications.

To orient yourself to the public schools in the Bay Area, you might want to consult some of the many helpful publications available in your local bookstore or online. **School Wise Press** has a number of useful resources and links on their web site, www.schoolwisepress.com. They also publish a handful of resource books, and have two online "ask an expert" columns that offer parents advice on everything from understanding test scores to applying for school transfers. For more information, call 415-337-7971. For straightforward explanations of California's complex education policies and reform efforts, check out the non-profit **EdSource**, www.edsource.org. If your head isn't already swimming, you can find additional facts and figures at **Ed-Data**, www.ed-data.k12.ca.us, a joint effort between the state and EdSource to provide accessible data to parents.

To become better acquainted with schools in your district, consider contacting the for-profit organization **SchoolMatch Inc.**, 800-992-5323, www.schoolmatch.com, which maintains a database including information on student-teacher ratios, test scores, and per-pupil spending for public and private schools. The cost for a comprehensive district "report card" is $34. Prices are higher if not ordered online. SchoolMatch's "full search service" will give you a statistical analysis of up to ten school systems in your requested area.

PRESCHOOLS

Preschools, typically for children ages 3 to 5, offer youngsters a chance to start off on the right foot, at a critical period in their early development. Multiple studies have shown that good early childhood education lays a foundation that leads to higher levels of achievement and academic aptitude throughout the school years, and beyond. Currently, there are far fewer top-notch programs than there are families with young children. Thus, the most popular preschools all have waiting lists. As a newcomer, it's a good idea to thoroughly research schools and once you find one you like, sign up as far in advance as possible. There are a wide range of programs available, from co-ops that offer parent participation and education, to Montessori. To find accredited programs, contact the **National Association for the Education of Young Children (NAEYC)**, 202-232-8777, 1313 L St NW, Suite 500, Washington, DC 20005, www.naeyc.org. The national **Head Start** program, www.nhsa.org, 703-739-0875, helps low-income families and children ages 0–5.

Proposition 10, the California Children and Families Act of 1998, also helps fund early childhood development services to children from prenatal to 5 years of age. For more information about programs contact **California Children & Families Commission**, First 5, 2389 Gateway Oaks Drive, Suite 260, Sacramento, CA 95814, 916-263-1050, www.ccfc.ca.gov.

BAY AREA PUBLIC SCHOOLS

California's schools are in turmoil. Thirty-plus years ago California spent more money on public schools than most other US states. However, due to property tax cuts implemented in 1978 by Proposition 13, California's spending on schools dropped dramatically—from one of the highest per pupil spending levels to near the bottom of that list today. And its overall performance went with it. California student achievement on national standardized tests ranks in the bottom third of states. Despite efforts that began in 1996 to reduce class size, focusing first on the early grades of K–3, and for high school freshmen, California still has one of the highest ratios of students per teacher in the nation.

In the late eighties, concerned California voters passed Proposition 98 to guarantee that minimum levels of school funding must be met. However, the "guarantee" has proven to be less than solid as the state continues to struggle in the throes of a fiscal crisis. In 2004, Governor Arnold Schwarzenegger diverted $2 billion from the education fund—cited as a loan to cover the state's bottom line—but much to the dismay of many teachers and parents, the "loan" has yet to be repaid. On top of that, districts are contending with spiraling healthcare and retirement benefit costs. With public schools receiving fewer and fewer state dollars, a number of districts routinely issue pink slips to teachers, unsure of whether the funds to pay their salaries will return from the state in the coming year. To save funds, districts have cut back on support staff—school librarians, secretaries, and janitors, cut extracurricular and enrichment programs, and a number of districts with declining enrollments have closed down campuses entirely. In 2005, the San Francisco School Board, citing financial troubles and an ongoing annual decrease in its student rolls of about 800 children, voted to close four local schools. There have been feisty board meetings, mass protests, and demonstrations, including a 70-mile march to Sacramento by parents and teachers pleading for more money for the West Contra Costa school district, which was forced to make severe cutbacks in 2004.

Meanwhile the national education reform effort, **No Child Left Behind (NCLB)**, has become a prickly bone of contention among educators. Bogged down by federal requirements to cut class sizes and meet performance testing standards, without the funds attached to implement the changes, NCLB has left many schools reeling. To further complicate matters, not all school districts here are funded in the same way.

On the brighter side, a number of counties and cities have come together and taken it upon themselves to pass bond initiatives to help upgrade and retrofit ailing buildings, provide new equipment, science centers, and recreation facilities for their local schools. Parent groups and concerned residents have also chipped in to keep art and music programs—which have often landed on the chopping block—alive. In San Francisco initiatives were approved to restore public school arts, physical education, and other extras cut by state funding, and to add funds for after-school activities, childcare subsidies, and additional programs. Innovative efforts are under way to help educate the state's large ESL (English as a Second Language) population. Meanwhile in an effort to attract and retain good teachers, several districts have started offering to assist educators with the high costs of housing through **First Time Homebuyer Programs**.

California has a dizzying array of assessment tests and performance evaluations that even confuse many education experts. How a school measures up, according to these, in general can been seen in the annual **Academic Performance Index (API)** report—which measures various tests results on an overall scorecard. Looking at the API, you can find district and school-by-school test scores, as well as overall rankings on a scale of 1 through 10, 10 being the highest. To see how your neighborhood schools stack up, visit http://api.cde. ca.gov/reports.asp.

In 1994 Bay Area public schools adopted an **open enrollment** policy, which offers a student the option to enroll in any public school in his/her district, space permitting, if parents believe that the school within a student's immediate vicinity is not right for their child. Often with top schools, particularly high schools, there are waiting lists, and open spots are granted by lottery. If your transfer request is declined, you can appeal to the governing district school board.

Throughout the Bay Area, the length of the academic year is becoming more flexible. Now you can decide whether a **traditional ten-month** or the newly adopted and increasingly popular **yearlong academic program** is the best for your child. For instance, educators at Allendale Elementary in Oakland, one of the largest year-round elementary schools in the Bay Area, believe that year-round education offers advantages to children who, during long summer breaks, would otherwise not be exposed to educational activities. San Francisco is trying a new approach on a few campuses dubbed "Dream Schools." By keeping kids in school longer, offering more rigorous academics, enhanced extracurricular activities—and requiring uniforms—the program seeks to provide challenges and opportunities for local kids, particularly in poorer neighborhoods.

In the past decade, California public education has seen the growth of the **charter school** movement. Unlike most public schools, charter schools, which are bound by their own charter agreements, are free from some of the traditional school regulations. A charter school is a public program created by a group of individuals, usually teachers, parents, and community leaders, that must have approval of the local school district governing board. First and foremost, the purpose of a charter school is to improve student learning. To do this, many charter schools promote the use of innovative teaching methods, expand the learning base outside the class-room, and encourage parent/community involvement in the school. Charter school enrollment is voluntary and not determined by geographic location, which means parents can select any school, as long as space allows. While most charter schools do not focus on specific subjects (as do magnet schools, which often specialize in lan-guage arts or the sciences), their charters propose certain programmatic guidelines for the general educational process. For example, Aurora High School in Redwood City guarantees its students personalized learning plans, which are created to help students realize their full potential. Several charter schools in San Francisco, including Gateway and Leadership high schools, have been quite successful.

Because charter schools are designed with more academic freedom and flex-ibility, they are not bound by most of the regulations in the state Education Code. In some cases, charter schools have been a wonderful success. In other cases, concerns have arisen that standards aren't high enough. In California, stu-dents in charter schools are required to take part in the Standardized Testing and Reporting Program. If students in a given charter school do not perform at a certain level or meet certain goals listed in their charter agreement with the local school district governing board, the school may be closed.

In the current fiscal climate, charter schools have become more controversial, as districts worry about adding new campuses, and spreading scant resources too thin. As a result, getting charter schools approved has become increasingly difficult. For more information about charter programs and charter school policies in the Bay Area, visit www.uscharterschools.org.

Although individual class years in many public schools tend to be fairly large, there is always an opportunity for your child to get individualized attention. Inquire about programs for children with special needs, including those with learning dis-abilities or programs for gifted and talented children (GATE). Again, the importance of visiting schools and asking lots of questions before enrolling your child cannot be underestimated.

BAY AREA SCHOOL DISTRICTS

First, you might want to check out the school district information at the end of each neighborhood listing earlier in this book. In addition, the following school organizations will provide you with information concerning schools in your area, as well as details about referrals, enrollment, testing, and any available special programs.

- For official information on public schools in **San Francisco**, contact the **San Francisco Unified School District**, 555 Franklin St, 415-241-6000, www. sfusd.edu. This district oversees 59,000 students in over 100 schools as well as many specialized educational programs in the city.
- If you plan to reside in the **North Bay**, consult the **Marin County Office of Education**, 1111 Las Gallinas Ave, San Rafael, 94903, 415-472-4110, www. marin.k12.ca.us
- For information on the **East Bay**, go to the **Alameda County Office of Education**, 313 W Winton Ave, Hayward, 510-887-0152, www.acoe.org/acoe
  - **Fremont Unified School District**, with a total enrollment of around 31,000. Contact them at 4210 Technology Dr, Fremont, 94538, 510-657-2350, www.fremont.k12.ca.us.
  - **Hayward Unified School District** enrolls 24,000 students, 24411 Amador St, Hayward, 94540, 510-784-2600, www.husd.k12.ca.us.
  - **Oakland Unified School District**, with enrollments of around 50,000 students in its more than 100 schools, can be contacted at 1025 Second Ave, Oakland, 94606, 510-879-8200, www.ousd.k12.ca.us
- For information on **Contra Costa County**, visit the **Contra Costa County Office of Education**, 77 Santa Barbara Rd, Pleasant Hill, 94523, 925-942-3388, www.cccoe.k12.ca.us.
- Those on the **Peninsula** should contact the **San Mateo County Office of Education**, 101 Twin Dolphin Dr, Redwood City, 94065, 650-802-5300, www. smcoe.k12.ca.
- For information on **Silicon Valley** and **South Bay** schools, visit the **Santa Clara County Office of Education**, 1290 Ridder Park Dr, San Jose, 95131, 408-453-6500, www.sccoe.k12.ca.us, which incorporates 33 elementary, high, and unified school districts.

PRIVATE AND PAROCHIAL SCHOOLS

In San Francisco, an estimated 25% to 30% of children attend private and parochial schools. If you are ready to finance your child's studies, there are many different private programs in the Bay Area. You'll find private schools, which offer educational programs based on particular learning philosophies, including Montessori and Waldorf programs, as well as parochial schools, which often provide more traditional settings and curriculum. The diverse educational offerings of private schools and their smaller classroom sizes often better accommodate children's individual talents and interests. To find a private school that suits your needs, visit **www.baprivateschools.com,** which offers a guide to private schools in the Bay Area and includes information, locations, and links to private and parochial schools. Other helpful publications on finding a good private school include *Peterson's Private Secondary Schools*, www.petersons.com; *The Handbook of Private Schools*, www.privateschoolsearch.com; *Private High Schools of the San Francisco Bay Area* by Betsy Little and Paula Molligan; and *Private Schools of San Francisco & Marin Counties (K-8): A Parents' Resource Guide* by Susan Vogel.

PRIVATE SCHOOLS

- For information on area Montessori schools, contact **Montessori Schools of California**, 16492 Foothill Blvd, San Leandro, 94578, 510-278-1115, www.montessorica.com.
- For **Waldorf schools** check the following:
  - San Francisco Waldorf School, K–8, 2938 Washington St, San Francisco, 94115, 415-931-2750; High school, 470 West Portal Ave, San Francisco, 415-431-2736 www.sfwaldorf.org
  - Marin County, 755 Idylberry Rd, San Rafael, 94903, 415-479-8190, www.marinwaldorf.org
  - East Bay, 3800 Clark Rd, El Sobrante, 94803, 510-223-3570, www.eastbay-waldorf.org
  - Silicon Valley, Waldorf School of the Peninsula K-8, 11311 Mora Dr, Los Altos, 94024, 650-948-8433, www.waldorfpeninsula.org
- **Challenger Schools** are famous for their engaging approach to elementary and middle school education. Their mission: "to prepare children to become self-reliant, productive individuals; to teach them to think, speak, and write with clarity, precision, and independence; and to inspire them to embrace, challenge, and find joy and self-worth through achievement." Call 888-748-1135, 408-377-2300, or 408-245-7170, or visit www.challengerschool.com for more information.

PAROCHIAL SCHOOLS

- Information regarding Catholic schools in San Francisco, San Mateo, and Marin counties is provided by the **Archdiocese of San Francisco Department of Catholic Schools**, One Peter Yorke Way, San Francisco, 94109, 415-614-5660, www.sfcatholicschools.org.
- The **Archdiocese of Oakland, Department of Catholic Schools**, 2121 Harrison St, Oakland, CA 94612, 510-628-2154, www.csdo.org, can give you information for Alameda and Contra Costa counties.
- In the South Bay, contact the **Archdiocese of San Jose, Office of Education**, 1150 North 1st St, San Jose, 95112, 408-983-0185, www.dsj.org.
- For information on **Jewish education** in the Bay Area, go to www.sfjcf.org/resource, where you'll find *The Resource: A Guide to Jewish Life in the Bay Area*, which provides listings and brief information on all the Jewish schools in the Bay Area.

Since admission to private schools can be competitive, the sooner you call a school to find out about admission deadlines and open houses the better. The registration process begins as early as October of the year prior to the desired academic start date. Be sure to visit schools to learn about their unique philosophies and teaching methodologies. As private schools are not required to follow state standards (though most do), a visit can be an extremely important aspect of the admissions process. Many parents and children have a visceral reaction when walking into a school, and can often sense whether a school is "right" for them. Since private schooling is expensive and signing up for a private program is an often-arduous task, finding a good match between child and school is important.

HOMESCHOOLING

Homeschooling is becoming increasingly popular in the state of California at large, and in the Bay Area specifically. Many parents believe that they, with their in-depth knowledge of their child's psychological and intellectual needs, are better suited to design an educational program that will engage and challenge their youngsters to the utmost. If you have the time and energy to plan and execute a comprehensive study program for your children, you'll find many organizations to assist you. For information and support for your homeschooling project, visit the **HomeSchool Association of California** at www.hsc.org. The mission of this organization is to provide information, monitor legislation, and cultivate connections among homeschoolers and the society at large. Another organization that might be helpful is **California Homeschool Network**, www.californiahomeschool.net; it too provides information on homeschooling and works to protect the rights of the family to educate children at home.

ADDITIONAL PARENTING RESOURCES

- **Parents Place**, www.parentsplaceonline.org: In **San Francisco,** it offers a drop-in playgroup for children 5 and under every Tuesday, where kids can play and parents can meet, 1710 Scott St, Koret Family Resource Center, San Francisco, 415-359-2454. A variety of programs are also available in **Palo Alto**, 650-688-3040, **San Rafael**, 415-491-7958, and **Sonoma**, 707-571-8131.
- **Support for Families of Children with Disabilities**, 415-282-7494, 2601 Mission St, Suite 606, www.supportforfamilies.org: Support groups for children, siblings, and parents—some in Spanish or Cantonese—as well as a parent mentor program, workshops, a drop-in center and resource library, a help line, short-term counseling, and a newsletter.
- **La Leche League,** www.llli.org: provides a wealth of information on breastfeeding and also runs support groups at locations throughout the Bay Area.

- **Petit Appetit**, 415-601-4916, www.petitappetit.com: San Francisco–based resource for preparing all-natural food for babies and toddlers, offers private and group classes, cookbook, and food services.

EAST BAY
- **The Nurture Center**, 3399 Mt. Diablo Blvd, Lafayette, 925-283-1346, www. nurturecenter.com: Provides childbirth information, support groups for new parents.

SOUTH BAY/PENINSULA
- **Las Madres Neighborhood Playgrounds**, 877-527-6237, www.lasmadres.org: South Bay group that hosts regular mommy and baby park days in local parks, field trips, parties, educational speaker nights, classes, discounts, Mom's Night Out, Couple's Night Out, baby sitting co-ops, sit 'n play groups, and more.
- **Community Arts & History Support Family Institute**, 408-251-1776, www. cahsworld.org/cahs_family.html: Runs family support groups in San Jose, Milpitas, and Santa Clara.
- **Parents Helping Parents**, 1400 Parkmoor Ave, San Jose, 408 727-5775, www. php.com: Family resource center serving parents of special-needs kids. Extensive network of education, referrals, support groups, community events, and online tools.
- **Special Parents Information Network (SPIN)**, www.spinsc.org: Though based in Santa Cruz, this group has a wealth of online information with links to support and information services throughout California for parents of children with special needs and disabilities.

HIGHER EDUCATION

California, the Bay Area in particular, is world renowned for its quality institutions of higher learning. Whether you are looking to enroll in a Bachelor's, Master's, continuing education, or night degree program, or interested in attending a lecture series or evening theatrical performance, the list of possibilities is endless. A few notable colleges and universities are included in the following list.

SAN FRANCISCO
- **Golden Gate University,** 536 Mission St, 800-448-4968, www.ggu.edu, is a private, nonprofit, and accredited program, located in the downtown area. It offers a wide variety of graduate and undergraduate programs in business, law, and public administration.
- **San Francisco State University**, 1600 Holloway Ave, 415-338-1111, www. sfsu.edu; part of the California State University system, SFSU offers a wide range of undergraduate and graduate degrees. Serving more than 30,000 students a year, SFSU is one of the largest schools in the CSU system.

- **University of San Francisco**, Parker and Fulton Sts, 415-422-5555, www. usfca.edu; founded in 1855 by Jesuit fathers, USF was San Francisco's first institution of higher learning. It is fully accredited and beautifully situated on a 50-acre hilltop. USF offers undergraduate and graduate degrees in nursing, business, education, law, and many other disciplines.

NORTH BAY

- **Dominican University of California**, 50 Acacia Ave, San Rafael, 415-457-4440, www.dominican.edu; affiliated with the Catholic Church, Dominican is known for its counseling psychology, education, and music programs; offers Bachelor's and Master's degrees.
- **Sonoma State University**, 1801 East Cotati Ave, Rohnert Park, 707-664-2880, www.sonoma.edu, was founded in 1960 and is one of the youngest universities in the California State University system. Located 50 miles north of San Francisco, the 220-acre campus east of Rohnert Park reminds many of a park. Degrees and certificates offered in a wide variety of disciplines.

EAST BAY

- **California State University, East Bay**, formerly California State University, Hayward, has two main campuses. One is situated on a hilltop overlooking the city of **Hayward** to the west, and the other is in the **Concord** foothills of Mt. Diablo. CSUEB also has a new professional development center in downtown Oakland. Located at 25800 Carlos Bee Blvd, Hayward, 510-885-3000, and 4700 Ygnacio Valley Rd, Concord, 925-602-4700; www.csuhayward.edu.
- **John F. Kennedy University**, locations in Berkeley, Pleasant Hill and Campbell, www.jfku.edu; founded in 1964, JFKU offers courses geared toward the adult student looking for a BA and/or MA degree, in fields such as counseling, library or museum arts, management, law, and liberal arts.
- **Mills College**, 5000 MacArthur Blvd, Oakland, 510-430-2255, www.mills.edu; founded in 1852, Mills is the oldest women's college in the western United States. Mills has a long history of excellence in the fields of liberal arts and science. The college offers women undergraduate and graduate degrees, and admits men to some graduate programs.
- **Saint Mary's College**, 1928 St Mary's Rd, Moraga, 925-631-4000, www.stmarys-ca.edu, founded in 1863 by the Christian Brothers, is located in the hilly, wooded, secluded community of Moraga. Classes are small and instruction excellent. Offers undergraduate and graduate degrees.
- **University of California, Berkeley**, 510-642-6000, www.berkeley.edu, is considered by many to be the finest school in the UC system. Founded in 1868 and located on a 1,500-acre wooded urban campus, UC Berkeley has top-notch facilities, faculty, and course offerings in hundreds of disciplines, undergraduate and graduate. Entrance competition is stiff, to say the least.

PENINSULA/SOUTH BAY

- **San Jose State University,** One Washington Square, San Jose, 408-924-2000, www.sjsu.edu, is located in the heart of Silicon Valley in downtown San Jose. SJSU offers some unique opportunities including the use of the nation's only undergraduate nuclear science lab, its own deep-sea research ship, and centers for the study of Beethoven and John Steinbeck. Graduate programs also offered.
- **Santa Clara University** is considered by many to be one of the finest universities in the country. Santa Clara was founded in 1851 by the Jesuits and is recognized as California's oldest institution of higher learning. Today it is known for its law, business, and engineering schools. Located at 500 El Camino Real, Santa Clara, 408-554-4000, www.scu.edu.
- **Stanford University,** 650-723-2300, www.stanford.edu, is certainly one of the nation's premier universities. Stanford is located in comfortable Palo Alto, at the northern end of Silicon Valley. Established in 1885 by former California Governor and Senator Leland Stanford and his wife Jane, Stanford is known for its excellence in the arts and sciences, and its highly regarded faculty and facilities, including its medical center.

SURROUNDING AREAS

- **University of California, Davis,** Mrack Hall, Davis, 530-752-1011, www.ucdavis.edu, is located about 70 miles northeast of San Francisco and 15 miles west of Sacramento. UCD is a top-notch research university offering undergraduate and graduate degrees in a wide range of fields. A beautiful college town, the city of Davis is known for being one of the most bicycle-friendly communities in the nation.

W ITHOUT EXAGGERATION, IT IS FAIR TO SAY THAT THE BAY AREA IS a shopper's paradise. Whether you like to shop in familiar chain stores or enjoy finding unique boutiques, they're all here. If you don't want to spend a lot, used clothing, furniture, and appliances are available at secondhand stores, such as the Salvation Army or Goodwill, which run their own department stores. Numerous flea markets abound, and because of the mild climate, garage and yard sales occur year round. Discount shopping is also available from one end of the Bay Area to the other. If money is of no concern, you can be sure you'll have plenty of opportunities to hand it over to a delighted sales associate at an upscale emporium.

MALLS/SHOPPING CENTERS

No matter what you're looking for or how much or how little you're willing to spend, you can probably find it at one of the following Bay Area shopping destinations. Check their web sites for mall specials, directions, and store directories.

SAN FRANCISCO
- **The Cannery/Del Monte Square**, 2801 Leavenworth St, 415-771-3112, www. thecannery.com
- **Crocker Galleria**, One Montgomery St, 415-393-1505, www.shopatgalleria. com
- **Embarcadero Center**, One Embarcadero Center, 415-772-0700, www.embarcaderocenter.com
- **Ghirardelli Square**, 900 N Point St, 415-775-5500, www.ghirardellisq.com
- **Japan Center**, Post St between Webster and Laguna, www.sfjapantown.org
- **Metreon**, A Sony Entertainment Center, 101 4th St, 415-369-6000, http:// westfield.com/metreon

- **Stonestown Galleria**, 3251 20th Ave, 415-759-2626, www.stonestowngalleria.com
- **Westfield San Francisco Centre**, 865 Market St, 415-512-6776, http://westfield.com/sanfrancisco

NORTH BAY

- **Larkspur Landing Shopping Center**, Larkspur Landing Circle, Larkspur
- **Northgate Mall**, Los Ranchitos Rd and Las Gallinas Ave, San Rafael, 415-479-5955, www.shopatnorthgate.com
- **Strawberry Village**, Redwood Highway Frontage Rd, Mill Valley, www.strawberryvillage.com
- **Town & Country**, Corte Madera, 415-924-2961
- **The Village**, Hwy 101 and Paradise Dr, Corte Madera, 415-924-8557, www.villageatcortemadera.com

EAST BAY

- **Alameda Towne Centre**, 523 S Shore West, Alameda, 510-521-1515, www.alamedatownecentre.com
- **Bayfair Mall**, 15555 14th St, San Leandro, 510-357-6000, http://bayfair.mallfinder.com
- **Hilltop Mall**, 2200 Hilltop Mall Rd, Richmond, 510-223-1933
- **Jack London Square**, 866-295-9853, www.jacklondonsquare.com
- **NewPark Mall**, 2086 Newpark Mall, Newark, 510-794-5523, www.newparkmall.com
- **Sun Valley**, 1 Sunvalley Mall, Concord, 925-825-0400, www.shopsunvalley.com
- **The Willows**, 1975 Diamond Blvd, Concord, 925-825-4001, www.willowsshoppingcenter.com

PENINSULA

- **Hillsdale Mall**, San Mateo, 650-345-8222, www.hillsdale.com
- **Serramonte Center**, Daly City, 650-301-3360, www.serramontecenter.com
- **The Shops at Tanforan**, San Bruno, 650-873-2000, www.theshopsattanforan.com
- **Stanford Shopping Center**, Palo Alto, 650-617-8200, www.stanfordshop.com
- **Town & Country Village**, El Camino Real and Embarcadero Rd, Palo Alto, 650-325-3266, www.tandcvillage.com
- **Westlake Shopping Center**, Daly City, 650-301-3000, www.shopwestlakecenter.com

SOUTH BAY

- **Great Mall of the Bay Area**, Milpitas, 408-956-2033

- **Oakridge Mall**, San Jose, 408-578-2912, http://westfield.com/oakridge
- **The Pruneyard**, Campbell, 877-367-0006, www.thepruneyard.com
- **Santana Row**, San Jose, 408-551-4611, www.santanarow.com
- **Westfield Valley Fair Mall**, Santa Clara, 408-248-4451, http://westfield.com/valleyfair

OUTLET MALLS

Whether these places actually offer more affordable merchandise than elsewhere is debatable but what is certain is their nationwide popularity and rapid growth. Check the web at www.outletsonline.com for more information. In the South Bay, the city of Gilroy is famous for its outlets—packed together along Highway 101. Bay Area residents frequently take special weekend trips just for shopping. Below are a few of the outlet malls located in the Bay Area:

- **Gilroy Premium Outlets**, 681 Leavesley Rd, Highway 101 at Leavesley exit, Gilroy, 408-842-3729, www.premiumoutlets.com/gilroy
- **Great Mall of the Bay Area**, 447 Great Mall Drive, Milpitas, www.simon.com/mall/default.aspx?ID=1250
- **Marina Square**, 1201 Marina Blvd, San Leandro,.www.marinasquarecenter.com
- **Vacaville Commons**, 321 Nut Tree Rd, Vacaville, 707-447-5755, www.premiumoutlets.com/vacaville

DEPARTMENT STORES

- **Gumps**: The upscale grand dame of San Francisco department stores, Gumps stocks furniture and other home accessories with special attention paid to *objets d'art*, impeccably displayed. The service is top-notch; 135 Post St, 800-882-8055, www.gumps.com
- **JC Penney**: This national department store chain sells just about everything you'd need for your home, including major appliances, televisions, stereos, VCRs, linens, bedding and furniture as well as clothing, shoes, jewelry, and cosmetics. Numerous Bay Area locations, but none in San Francisco, including Tanforan, San Bruno, 650-873-4100; Southland Mall, Hayward, 510-783-0300; Richmond Hilltop Mall, Richmond, 510-222-4411, www.jcpenney.com
- **Macy's**: The Union Square store is reportedly the largest in the nation, outside of the flagship store in Manhattan. You could fully stock your closets and furnish your entire home here if you were so inclined, as Macy's carries clothing, shoes, linens, bedding, appliances, cookware, gourmet items, luggage, and more. Service, once notoriously bad, has improved of late. Bay Area locations include **San Francisco**: Union Square, Stockton & O'Farrell sts, 415-397-3333; **Peninsula**: 1 Serramonte Center, Daly City, 650-994-3333; **East Bay**: Bayfair Mall, San Leandro, 510-357-3333; **North Bay**: Northgate Mall, San Rafael, 415-499-5200, www.macys.com

- **Neiman-Marcus**: The opulent Texan retailer carries expensive non-necessities, has nice restaurants, a fairly good gourmet department, and is known for the Christmas tree in the rotunda. Geary at Stockton, San Francisco, 415-362-3900; 400 Stanford Shopping Center, Palo Alto, 650-329-3300, www.neimanmarcus.com.
- **Nordstrom**: Employees at this Seattle-based retailer have a reputation for being helpful, courteous, and knowledgeable about the products they sell. Merchandise ranges from shoes and clothing for the entire family to jewelry and cosmetics, though no home furnishings. Perhaps most popular here are the women's shoe sales. Their online service is top-notch, http://shop.nordstrom.com. Bay Area locations include: **San Francisco**: Westfield Shopping Centre, 865 Market St, 415-243-8500; Stonestown Galleria, 285 Winston Dr, 415-753-1344; **Peninsula**: Hillsdale Mall, San Mateo, 650-570-5111; **North Bay:** The Village at Corte Madera, 1870 Redwood Hwy, Corte Madera, 415-927-1690; **East Bay**: 1200 Broadway Plaza, Walnut Creek, 925-930-7959.
- **Saks Fifth Avenue**: This upscale retailer features clothing, jewelry, cosmetics, objets d'art. Located in San Francisco at 384 Post St on Union Square, 415-986-4300, www.saksfifthavenue.com
- **Wilkes Bashford**: Strictly speaking, Wilkes Bashford isn't a department store since it sells only clothing and decorative items, but most department stores don't sell much else these days either. What you'll find here is high-end, high-style gear in a low-key, service-oriented environment, without the cookie cutter feel of many chain stores. Three locations: 375 Sutter St, San Francisco, 415-986-4380; 450 Stanford Shopping Center, Palo Alto, 650-322-7080; 57 Throckmorton Ave, Mill Valley, 415-381-5183, www.wilkesbashford.com.

DISCOUNT DEPARTMENT STORES AND OUTLETS

Discount chains such as **Target**, **Kmart**, and **Wal-Mart** all do business throughout the Bay Area. Check the Yellow Pages or the Internet for the nearest location. Below are a few of the discount outlet stores in the area.

- **Georgiou Outlet**, 512 7th St, San Francisco, 415-554-0150
- **Loehmann's**, 222 Sutter St, 415-982-3215, is a local favorite for discount designer clothes and shoes for both men and women
- **Nordstrom Rack**, 555 9th St, San Francisco, 415-934-1211; Metro Shopping Center, 81 Colma Blvd, Colma, 650-755-1444; the discount rack for all the Nordstrom stores
- **North Face Outlet**, 1238 Fifth St, Berkeley, 510-526-3530
- **Rochester Big & Tall**, for men, 700 Mission St, San Francisco, 415-982-6455; 319 S Winchester Blvd, San Jose, 408-244-8255; 1337 N Main St, Walnut Creek, 925-407-1000, www.rochesterclothing.com

COMPUTERS/ELECTRONICS/APPLIANCES

The Bay Area offers plenty of options when it comes to buying anything computer-related. This is, after all, the headquarters of the global digital revolution. Locations are in San Francisco unless otherwise noted. In addition, dozens of individually owned and operated electronics and appliance stores as well as all the familiar national chains can be found throughout the Bay Area. The list below includes some well-known computer and electronics retailers, and you can check the Yellow Pages or Internet for additional options.

- **Apple Store**, for the latest in everything Mac, One Stockton St, San Francisco, 415-392-0202; 3251 20th Ave, Stonestown Shopping Center, San Francisco, 415-242-7890; 1301 Burlingame Ave, Burlingame, 650-340-1167; 1516 Redwood Hwy, Corte Madera, 415-927-5820; 5656 Bay St, Emeryville, 510-350-2400; 451 University Ave, Palo Alto, 650-617-9000; 925 Blossom Hill Rd, Oakridge Shopping Center, San Jose; 408-362-4930; 1129 S Main St, Walnut Creek, 925-210-2020; 2855 Stevens Creek Blvd, Santa Clara, Valley Fair Shopping Center, 408-551-2150, www.apple.com/retail
- **We Fix Macs**, 1245 Laurelwood Rd, Santa Clara, 408-850-3300; 3159 El Camino Real, Palo Alto, 650-813-6161; www.allmac.com
- **Best Buy**, 1717 Harrison St, San Francisco, 415-626-9682; 2675 Geary Blvd, San Francisco, 415-409-4960; 200 Colma Blvd, Colma, 650-756-8711; 1250 El Camino Real, San Bruno, 650-244-5139; 180 Donahue St, Marin City, 415-332-6529; 3700 Mandela Pkwy, Emeryville, 510-420-0323; 1127 Industrial Rd, San Carlos, 650-622-0050; 3090 Stevens Creek Blvd, San Jose, 408-241-6040; for more Bay Area locations visit www.bestbuy.com
- **Fry's**, 340 Portage Ave, Palo Alto, 650-496-6000; 600 E Hamilton Ave, Campbell, 408-364-3700; 1077 East Arques Ave, Sunnyvale, 408-617-1300; 550 E Brokaw Rd, San Jose, 408-487-1000, www.frys.com

BEDS, BEDDING, & BATH

Some area department stores sell bedding as well as beds. For their names, locations, and phone numbers see the previous entries under **Department Stores**. Here's a list of just some of the San Francisco stores that deal exclusively in these items.

- **Bed Bath and Beyond**, 555 9th St, 415-252-0490; call 800-462-3966 or check www.bedbathandbeyond.com to find numerous other Bay Area locations
- **Duxiana**, 1803 Fillmore St, 415-673-7134
- **Earthsake**, 1772 4th St, Berkeley, 510-559-8440, www.earthsake.com
- **Mancini's Sleepworld**, 2950 Geary Blvd, San Francisco, 415-750-0500; 3806 El Camino Real, San Mateo, 650-212-0200; www.sleepworld.com
- **Mattress Discounters**, multiple locations, 800-289-2233, www.mattressdiscounters.com,

- **McRoskey Airflex Mattresses**, 1687 Market St, San Francisco, 415-861-4532; 220 Hamilton Ave, Palo Alto, 650-327-1966; www.mcroskey.com
- **Oysterbeds**, 1400 Tennesse St, 415-643-0818, www.oysterbed.com
- **Scheuer Linens**, 340 Sutter St, 415-392-2813
- **Warm Things**, 3063 Fillmore St, San Francisco, 415-931-1660; 6011 College Ave, Oakland, 510-428-9329; www.warmthingsonline.com

CARPETS & RUGS

- **Carpet Connection**, Hudson Ave, San Francisco, 415-550-7125
- **Claremont Rug Company**, 6087 Claremont Ave, Oakland, 510-654-0816, fine antique carpets
- **Conklin Brothers**, 1801 S Grant St, San Mateo, 650-432-6063
- **Cost Plus World Market**, 2552 Taylor St, San Francisco, 415-928-6200; 890 Jefferson Ave, Redwood City, 650-701-1820; 101 Clay St, Oakland, 510-834-4440, www.worldmarket.com
- **The Floor Store**, 5327 Jacuzzi St, Suite 2A, Richmond, 510-527-3203
- **Omid Carpets**, 590-10th St, San Francisco, 415-626-3466, a full range of Oriental carpets
- **Pier One Imports**, 3535 Geary Blvd, San Francisco, 415-387-6642; 2501 El Camino Real, Redwood City, 650-364-6608; 20610 Stevens Creek Blvd, Cupertino 408-253-4512; 1009 Blossom Hill Rd, San Jose, 408-978-9555, www.pier1.com

FURNITURE

There are too many furniture stores in the Bay Area to list them all, but here are a few well-known names to get you started in your search for perfect and affordable home furnishings.

- **Cort Furniture Clearance Center**, 2925 Meade Ave, Santa Clara, 408-727-1470; 426 El Camino Real, San Bruno, 650-615-0406; 1240 Willow Pass Rd, Concord, 925-609-9127; www.cort.com/furniture
- **Crate & Barrel**, 55 Stockton St, San Francisco, 415-982-5200; Stanford Shopping Center, Palo Alto, 650-321-7800,; Hillsdale Shopping Center, San Mateo, 650-341-900; 301 Santana Row, San Jose, 408-247-0600; Crate & Barrel Outlet Store, 1785 4th St, Berkeley, 510-528-5500; for more Bay Area stores check out www.crateandbarrel.com
- **Flegel's**, 1654 2nd St, San Rafael, 415-454-0502; 870 Santa Cruz Ave, Menlo Park, 650-326-9661; www.flegels.com
- **Fumiki Wholesale**, 888 Brannan St, San Francisco, 415-255-4625, www.fumikiwholesale.com
- **Hoot Judkins**, offers a wide selection of finished and unfinished furniture at reasonable prices; 1269 Veterans Blvd, Redwood City, 650-367-8181; 1400 El Camino Real, Millbrae, 650-952-5600; www.hootjudkins.com

- **IKEA**, 4400 Shellmound St, Emeryville, 510-420-4532; 1700 E Bayshore Road, East Palo Alto, 650-323-4532, www.ikea.com
- **Limn**, high-end cutting-edge design furniture and housewares; 290 Townsend St, San Francisco, 415-543-5466, www.limn.com
- **Macy's**, Union Square, San Francisco, 415-397-3333
- **Nest**, San Francisco: 2300 Fillmore St, 415-292-6199; 2340 Polk St, 415-292-6198; East meets West eclectic; www.nestsf.com
- **Noriega Furniture**, 1455 Taraval St, San Francisco, 415-564-4110; www.noriegafurniture.com
- **Scandinavian Designs**, 317-South B St, San Mateo, 650-340-0555; 2101 Shattuck Ave, Berkeley, 510-848-8250; 1212 4th St, San Rafael, 415-457-5500; www.scandinaviandesigns.com
- **Slater/Marinoff**, 1823 4th St, Berkeley, 510-548-2001
- **The Wooden Duck**, 2919 7th St, Berkeley, 510-848-3575; 1848 Fourth St, San Rafael, 415-453-0345; www.thewoodenduck.com
- **Z Gallerie**, 2154 Union St, San Francisco, 415-567-4890; 1731 4th St, Berkeley, 510-525-7591; 215 Corte Madera Town Center, 415-924-3088; 378 Santana Row, San Jose, 408-615-9863, www.zgallerie.com
- **Zonal**, distressed and "found" furniture, San Francisco: 568 Hayes St, 415-255-9307; www.zonalhome.com

HOUSEWARES

Most department stores carry dishes, glassware, and other items needed for the home, so if you have a favorite you can start there. There are also numerous specialty outlets from which to choose, including the following:

- **Bed Bath and Beyond**, 555 9th St, 415-252-0490; call 800-462-3966 or check www.bedbathandbeyond.com to find numerous other Bay Area locations
- **Cost Plus World Market**, 2552 Taylor St, 415-928-6200, www.worldmarket.com
- **Crate & Barrel**, 55 Stockton St, San Francisco, 415-982-5200; Stanford Shopping Center, Palo Alto, 650-321-7800; Hillsdale Shopping Center, San Mateo, 650-341-900; 301 Santana Row, San Jose, 408-247-0600; Crate & Barrel Outlet Store, 1785 4th St, Berkeley, 510-528-5500, for more Bay Area stores check out www.crateandbarrel.com
- **IKEA**, 4400 Shellmound St, Emeryville, 510-420-4532; 1700 E Bayshore Rd, East Palo Alto, 650-323-4532; www.ikea.com
- **Pier One Imports**, Pier One Imports, 3535 Geary Blvd, San Francisco, 415-387-6642; 2501 El Camino Real, Redwood City, 650-364-6608; 20610 Stevens Creek Blvd, Cupertino 408-253-4512; 1009 Blossom Hill Rd, San Jose, 408-978-9555, www.pier1.com
- **Pottery Barn**, 2390 Market St, San Francisco, 415-861-0800; 2100 Chestnut St, 415-441-1787; for other Bay Area locations check www.potterybarn.com

- **Sur La Table,** 77 Maiden Ln, San Francisco, 415-732-7900; Ferry Building Marketplace, 415-262-9970; 1806 Fourth St, Berkeley, 510-849-2252; 23 University Ave, Los Gatos, 408-395-6946; cookware, kitchenware, linens, small appliances, and tableware; www.surlatable.com
- **Viking Home Chef,** 6422 Mission St, Daly City, 650-756-3931; 633 Laurel St, San Carlos, 650-654-3100; www.vikingappliance.com
- **Williams Sonoma,** 340 Post St, San Francisco, 415-362-9450; 2 Embarcadero Center, San Francisco, 415-421-2033; Stonestown Galleria, San Francisco, 415-242-1473; Hillsdale Mall, San Mateo, 650-574-2818; 180 El Camino Real, Palo Alto, 650-321-3486; The Village, Corte Madera, 415-924-6799

HARDWARE/PAINTS/WALLPAPER/GARDEN CENTERS

Nearly everything you might need to fix up your new place is readily available at a local hardware store, but if the local store doesn't have that special color of paint you want for the sun porch you can head for one of many cavernous home improvement centers (see below). Unless otherwise indicated, the following hardware stores and garden centers are in San Francisco.

- **Bauerware Cabinet Hardware,** 3886 17th St, 415-864-3886, www.bauerware.com; offers offbeat and eclectic knobs, pulls, and handles
- **Restoration Hardware,** 1733 4th St, Berkeley, 510-526-6424; Hillsdale Mall, San Mateo, 650-577-9807; 281 University Ave, Palo Alto, 650-328-4004
- **Victoriana SF Moulding,** 2070 Newcomb Ave, San Francisco, 415-648-0313; specializes in Victorian moldings, wallpapers, draperies, tiles, fabrics, carpets, and more

ACE HARDWARE STORES

- **Cliff's Variety,** 479 Castro St, 415-431-5365
- **Cole Hardware,** 956 Cole St, 415-753-2653
- **Discount Builders,** 1695 Mission St, 415-621-8511
- **Fredericksen's Hardware,** 3029 Fillmore St, 415-292-2950
- **Standard 5 & 10,** 3545 California St, 415-751-5767

TRUE VALUE HARDWARE STORES

- **Creative Paint,** 5435 Geary Blvd, 415-666-3380
- **Sunset Hardware,** 3126 Noriega St, 415-661-0607
- **True Value Hardware,** 2244 Irving St, 415-753-6862

GARDENING STORES

- **Broadway Terrace Nursery,** 4340 Clarewood Dr, Oakland, 510-658-3729
- **Native Here Nursery,** focuses on California native plants; 101 Golf Course Dr, Berkeley, 510-549-0211

- **Plant'It Earth**, 661 Divisadero St, 415-626-5082
- **Smith and Hawken**, 800 Redwood Hwy, Mill Valley, 415-381-1800; 1330 10th St, Berkeley, 510-527-1076; 26 Santa Cruz Ave, Los Gatos, 408-354-6500; 705 Stanford Shopping Center, Palo Alto, 650-321-0403
- **Sloat Garden Centers**, A full range of garden supplies, plants and trees, classes, and friendly and helpful advice; 3rd Ave between Geary and Clement, San Francisco, 415-752-1614; 2700 Sloat Blvd, San Francisco, 415-566-4415; 2000 Novato Blvd, Novato, 415-897-2169; 1580 Lincoln Ave, San Rafael, 415-453-3977; www.sloatgardens.com
- **Summer Winds Garden Center**, 4606 Almaden Expy, San Jose, 408-266-4400; 725 San Antonio Rd, Palo Alto, 650-493-5136

HOME IMPROVEMENT CENTERS

The big do-it-yourself centers are located outside of San Francisco, but the ones listed below are all within a 15- to 30-minute drive of the city.
- **Orchard Supply Hardware (OSH)**, 2245 Gellert Blvd, South San Francisco, 650-878-3322; 900 El Camino Real, Millbrae, 415-873-5536; 1151 Anderson Dr, San Rafael, 415-453-7288; 1025 Ashby Ave, Berkeley, 510-540-6638
- **Home Depot**, 2 Colma Blvd, Colma, 650-755-9600; 2001 Chess Dr, San Mateo, 650-525-9343; 1125 Old County Rd, San Carlos, 650-592-9200; 1781 E Bayshore, East Palo Alto, 650-462-6800; 1933 Davis St, San Leandro, 510-636-9600; 11939 San Pablo Ave, El Cerrito, 510-235-0800; www.homedepot.com

SECONDHAND SHOPPING

The Advertiser is a weekly newspaper that lists items sold by individuals or at flea markets. The publication is free and can be found at most supermarkets and many newsstands. Call 415-863-3151 to sell or buy anything from cars to computers, from bedroom sets to budgies. Using the Internet for this type of shopping has become a San Francisco tradition, and locally founded Craig's List (www.craigslist.org) is your one-stop-shop for all of the aforementioned items, and then some.

Your mother might call it secondhand but today that pair of 1970 elephant bottoms in the bottom of a box in the basement may be high fashion "vintage" to an aficionado. In San Francisco, dressing in stylish cast-offs has been all the rage for decades and there are scores of stores at which to try your luck. There are also plenty of shops that sell secondhand items that don't quite qualify as vintage. Vintage is consistently more expensive than secondhand and usually in excellent condition. Shopping for secondhand furnishings can be just as much fun as shopping for new. The chance of finding a lost heirloom adds to the excitement of saving a bit of cash. Here are a few places to begin your bargain-hunting adventure. Locations are San Francisco unless otherwise noted.
- **The Apartment**, 3469 18th St, vintage furniture, 415-255-1100

- **Attic Shop**, 1317 Pine St, 415-474-3498, secondhand
- **Berkeley Outlet**, 711 Heinz Ave, Berkeley 510-549-2896
- **Community Thrift Store**, 623 Valencia St, 415-861-4910
- **Cottrell's Moving and Storage**, 150 Valencia St, 415-431-1000
- **Goodwill**, 86 11th St, 415-575-2197, has multiple other San Francisco and Bay Area locations, www.sfgoodwill.org
- **Home Consignment Center**, 863 E Francisco Blvd, San Rafael, 415-456-2765, www.thehomeconsignmentcenter.com, many other locations in the Bay Area
- **Hospice by the Bay Thrift Shop**, 910 Lincoln Ave, San Rafael, 415-459-4686; 910 Grant St, Novato, 415-893-9036, www.hospicebythebay.org
- **Mickey's Monkey**, 218 Pierce St, vintage furniture, 415-864-0693
- **Out of the Closet**, 100 Church St, 415-252-1101, many other locations across the Bay Area with cheap vintage and used clothing; www.outofthecloset.org
- **People's Bazaar**, 3258 Adeline St, Berkeley, 510-655-8008; www.peoples-bazaar.com
- **Repeat Performance**, 2436 Fillmore St, 415-563-3123, vintage
- **St. Vincent de Paul Society**, 6256 Mission St, Daly City, 650-992-9271, secondhand, has multiple other Bay Area locations; www.svdpusa.org
- **Salvation Army**, 1500 Valencia St, 415-401-0698, secondhand, has multiple Bay Area locations; www.salvationarmyusa.org
- **Thrift Center**, 1060 El Camino Real, San Carlos, secondhand, 650-593-1082
- **Thrift Town**, 2101 Mission St, 415-861-1132, secondhand, second floor features furniture and housewares, www.thrifttown.com
- **Town School Closet**, 1850 Polk St, 415-929-8019, vintage

FLEA MARKETS

- **Alemany Flea Market**, 100 Alemany Blvd, specializes in antiques, every Sunday
- **Berkeley Flea Market**, 1937 Ashby Ave, Berkeley, 510-644-0744, Saturdays and Sundays, 7am-7pm, a nonprofit, community flea market.
- **Coliseum Public Market**, 5401 Coliseum Way, Oakland, 510-534-0325, Tuesday-Sunday
- **Midgley's Country Flea Market**, 2200 Gravenstein Hwy South, Sebastopol, 707-823-7874, weekends
- **Mission Village Flea Market**, 2050 Bryant St, eclectic goods, including occasional music equipment, collectibles; you can even get help fixing your bike at the popular bike kitchen, 415-648-7562, Sundays; www.cellspace.org
- **Norcal Swap Meet**, Laney College, Oakland, 510-769-7266, Sundays daily 5am-5pm
- **San Jose Flea Market**, 1590 Berryessa Road, San Jose, 408-453-1110 x246 or 800-BIG FLEA, open Wednesday through Sunday from dawn til dusk; this is a

huge flea market with everything old for sale, plus live music, fresh produce, dozens of food stands, two playgrounds, and more; www.sjfm.com

ANTIQUES

There are pages of antique dealers listed in the San Francisco Yellow Pages; check there first for stores in your neighborhood. The 400 block of Jackson Street, in San Francisco's Financial District, is known for its high concentration of antique stores. Most of the Jackson Street dealers are members of the Antique Dealers Association of California, and if they don't have what you're looking for they can steer you in the right direction. Market Street at Franklin has several lower priced antique shops. Sacramento Street in Presidio Heights has an array of fine antique shops. In Marin County, San Anselmo has a small antique row along Sir Francis Drake Boulevard.

FOOD

The Bay Area is blessed with a wide selection of supermarket chains that range from inexpensive to downright exorbitant. The budget grocery stores offer bulk quantities of your regular fare while the more expensive stores emphasize fresh produce, organics, and imported goods. The big grocery chains fall in between those two extremes. For budget shopping head for **Foods Co.**, **Food 4 Less**, **Grocery Outlet**, **Smart and Final**, or **Pak-N-Save**. **Safeway**, **Lucky**, and **SaveMart** are the next rung up the ladder. **Trader Joe's** offers an array of high-quality foods, as well as beers and wines, for reasonable prices. **Andronico's** reigns supreme at the high end. **Whole Foods** is the big chain health food store, and **Mollie Stone's** is a more local natural foods chain.

SPECIALTY GROCERS

SAN FRANCISCO
- **Bombay Bazar**, 548 Valencia St, 415-621-1717, has a variety of Indian spices, food, and clothing, not to mention the fantastic Bombay Ice Creamery next-door—featuring flavors like rose, cardamom, and clove
- **Chinese** food markets—featuring some of the best priced produce in town—are sprinkled throughout Chinatown, Irving St in the Sunset, and Clement St in the Richmond District
- **Cost Plus World Market**, 2552 Taylor St, 415-928-6200, www.worldmarket.com; a discount clearing house for nonperishable imports with a variety of wines, beers, teas, and chocolates as well as housewares
- **Ferry Building Marketplace**, the Embarcadero at Market St, 415-983-8000, www.ferrybuildingmarketplace.com; features a number of specialty shops including the North Bay's Cowgirl Creamery Cheese Shop, Acme Bread Com-

pany, and the San Francisco Fish Company. The outdoor plaza also hosts one of the Bay Area's most popular farmers markets (see details below).

- **Good Life Grocery**, 448 Cortland Ave, 415-648-3221; friendly Bernal Heights shop with a good selection of produce, fine cheeses and wines
- **Mollie Stone's**, 2435 California St, 415-567-4902; 635 Portola Dr, 415-664-1600, www.molliestones.com; a large, upscale natural foods shop with a wide selection, and several additional locations throughout the area
- **Rainbow Grocery and General Store**, 1745 Folsom St, 415-863-0620, www.rainbowgrocery.org; this popular eco-friendly, worker-owned co-op has a vast selection of bulk products from grains to pastas to teas, organic produce, a huge vitamin and mineral selection, and an amazing olive bar. You'll have to go elsewhere for your meat though.
- **Whole Foods**, 1765 California St, 415-674-0500; 399 4th St, 415-618-0066, www.wholefoodsmarket.com; the natural food giant offers a wide array of bulk products, a large prepared foods area, a decent house brand, popular salad bar, and everything to meet your basic grocery needs. Many other stores are sprinkled around the Bay Area.

NORTH BAY

- **Mill Valley Market**, 12 Corte Madera, Mill Valley, 415-388-3222
- **Mollie Stone's**, 100 Harbor Dr, Sausalito, 415-331-6900; Bon Air Shopping Center, Greenbrae, 415-461-1164; www.molliestones.com
- **Whole Foods**, 414 Miller Ave, Mill Valley, 415-381-1200; 340 3rd St, San Rafael, 415-451-6333; www.wholefoodsmarket.com

EAST BAY

- **Berkeley Bowl**, 2020 Oregon St, Berkeley, 510-843-6929; a beloved local favorite that draws shoppers from throughout the Bay Area, offers bulk foods, organic produce, seafood, and a wide variety of goods and great prices
- **Cheese Board Collective**, 1504 Shattuck Ave, 510-549-3183, http://cheeseboardcollective.coop; this popular Berkeley co-op has a rotating variety of freshly baked breads, a wide selection of cheeses and a tasty pizza place a few doors down at 1512 Shattuck Ave
- **Cost Plus World Market**, 101 Clay St, Oakland, 510-834-4440, www.worldmarket.com
- **G.B. Ratto and Co**, 821 Washington St, Oakland, 510-832-6503; ethnic import sausages, great fun
- **Market Hall**, 5655 College Ave, Oakland, 510-250-6000; specialty stores for wine, coffee, tea, pasta, produce, poultry, meat, and fish
- **Monterey Market**, 1550 Hopkins, Berkeley, 510-526-6042; incredible produce
- **Monterey Fish Market**, 1582 Hopkins St, Berkeley, 510-525-5600
- **Pacific East Mall**, 3288 Pierce St, Richmond, 510-527-3000

- **Whole Foods**, 3000 Telegraph Ave, Berkeley, 510-649-1333, www.whole foodsmarket.com

PENINSULA/SOUTH BAY
- **Cosentino's** vegetable haven, South Bascom and Union aves, San Jose, 408-377-6661; vegetables, bulk items, ethnic condiments
- **Cost Plus World Market**, 423 Serramonte Blvd, Daly City, 415-994-7090
- **Draegers**, 1010 University Ave, Menlo Park, 650-324-7700; imported cheeses, deli, produce and wine
- **Mollie Stone's**, 164 South California Ave, Palo Alto, 650-323-8361; 1477 Chapin Ave, 650-558-9992, Burlingame; 22 Bayhill Shopping Center, San Bruno, 650-873-8075; 49 W 42nd Ave, San Mateo, 650-372-2828, www.molliestones.com
- **Takahashi**, 221 S Claremont St, San Mateo, 650-343-0394; Southeast Asian, Hawaiian, and more
- **Whole Foods**, 774 Emerson St, Palo Alto, 650-326-8676; 1250 Jefferson Ave, Redwood City, 650-367-1400; 1010 Park Place, San Mateo, 650-358-6900; www.wholefoodsmarket.com

MAKE-AND-TAKE MEAL ASSEMBLY

An option for those who are too busy to rustle up a home-cooked and healthy meal for themselves or their family is the popular "Make-and-Take" stores in the area. This service typically provides a food preparation space, ingredients, and dish cleanup with a resident chef to help would-be cooks assemble fancy restaurant-style meals. Most of them also have the option for users to simply drop in and pick up the meals fully prepped for your kitchen, and many do everything but set the table for you by delivering right to your door. Here are a few options available in the Bay Area.
- **Dream Dinners** has many locations throughout the Bay Area, including: 2307 Blanding Ave, Suite F, Alameda, 510-337-1105; 390 El Camino Real, Suite R, Belmont, 650-595-4545; 5685 Cottle Rd, San Jose, 408-363-3968; www.dreamdinners.com
- **Chef Dane's**, 1725 De La Cruz Blvd, Santa Clara, 408-538-1380; 2879 Ygnacio Valley Rd, Walnut Creek, 925-939-2433; www.chefdanes.com
- **Dinners Galore**, 51 Wright Brothers Ave, Livermore, 925-456-3257; www.dinnersgalore.com
- **Sous Kitchen**, in-house assembly and delivery options for the entire Bay Area; 975 Industrial Rd, Suite D, San Carlos, 650-508-0800; www.souskitchen.com
- **Deeelish**, has pick-up onsite or delivery options across the Bay Area via FedEx, 700 El Camino Real, Suite 170, Menlo Park, 650-325-6325; www.deeelishmeals.com

WAREHOUSE SHOPPING

Costco, www.costco.com, a giant in the club-shopping business, features cavernous warehouse-type facilities stacked from floor to ceiling with restaurant-trade items, such as gallon jars of olives, mayonnaise, six-packs of everything from chopped tomatoes to pet food, tires, cleaning supplies, clothing, and pharmaceuticals. Basic membership costs $50 a year, and there are over 20 locations around the Bay Area.

FARMERS MARKETS

San Francisco is surrounded by some of the most productive farmland in the world (the San Joaquin Valley, and the counties of Sonoma, Salinas, and Monterey), and many of the men and women who run these farms take at least one day a week to hawk their fruits and vegetables at **Farmers Markets** all around the Bay Area. Organic produce is also available and most sellers will offer you a taste before you buy. Below is a list of some of the markets held in or close to San Francisco. You can also get organic, locally grown, fresh and tasty fruits and veggies delivered weekly from Planet Organics, www.planetorganics.com, 800-956-5855. Users can set up many different varieties of "surprise" vegetable and fruit deliveries or customize a weekly delivery with everything from seafood to tinfoil.

SAN FRANCISCO CITY & COUNTY
- **100 Alemany Blvd**, Saturday, dawn to dusk, year round
- **Ferry Plaza on the Embarcadero**, Tuesday, 10 a.m. to 2 p.m.; Saturday, 8 a.m. to 2 p.m.
- **Fillmore Farmers' Market**, O'Farrell and Fillmore sts at the Fillmore Center Plaza, Saturday 9 a.m. to 1 p.m., year round
- **United Nations Plaza**, Market St (between 7th and 8th sts), Sunday and Wednesday 7 a.m. to 5 p.m., year round

MARIN COUNTY
- **Corte Madera**: Village Shopping Center, Wednesday, noon to 5 p.m., year round
- **Novato**: Downtown (Grant Ave between Reichert and Machin aves), Tuesday, 4 p.m. to 8 p.m., April–September
- **San Rafael**: Civic Center parking lot, Sunday and Thursday, 8 a.m. to 1 p.m., year round
- **Sausalito**: Bridgeway and Tracy, Friday, 4 p.m. to 8 p.m., May–October

SAN MATEO COUNTY
- **Daly City**: Serramonte Center, Thursday, 9 a.m. to 1 p.m., and Saturday, 10 a.m. to 2 p.m., year round
- **Menlo Park**: Crane and Chestbut, Sunday, 9 a.m. to 1 p.m., year round

- **Millbrae**: 200 Broadway, Saturday, 8 a.m. to 1 p.m., year round

ALAMEDA COUNTY

- **Berkeley**: Center St at MLK (Martin Luther King) Way, Saturday, 10 a.m. to 3 p.m., year round
- **El Cerrito**: El Cerrito Plaza, Tuesday and Saturday, 9 a.m. to 1 p.m., year round
- **Oakland**: Jack London Square, Sunday, 10 a.m. to 2 p.m., year round

SANTA CLARA COUNTY

- **Cupertino**: Cupertino Square parking lot, Wolfe Rd at I-280, Friday, 9 a.m. to 1 p.m., year round
- **Palo Alto**: Hamilton and Gilman, Saturday, 8 a.m. to noon, May–December
- **San Jose downtown**: Jackson between Sixth and Seventh, Sunday, 8 a.m. to noon, year round

To find a farmers market in another locale call 800-949-FARM or check www.cafarmersmarkets.com.

COMMUNITY GARDENS

Why shop for fruit and veggies when you can grow your own? San Francisco, Berkeley, and Oakland are home to a variety of community gardens ranging from dense urban forests tucked in larger city parks to tiny backyard fields at local churches, schools, and community centers. Most of the time, you'll be assigned a plot of your own to care for and sometimes there is a waiting list. But urban gardening is a great way to get outdoors, enjoy the fresh air, and meet your neighbors. For information about community gardens in San Francisco, contact the **San Francisco League of Urban Gardeners (SLUG)**, 2088 Oakdale Ave, 415-285-SLUG, www.grass-roots.org/usa/slug.shtml.

SAN FRANCISCO

- **25th and De Haro Garden**, 25th and De Haro sts
- **3rd St Community Garden**, 6698 3rd St
- **Adam Rogers Garden**, 1220 Oakdale Ave
- **Alice St Community Gardens**, Bonifacio and Lapu Lapu sts
- **Alioto Park Community Garden**, Capp and 20th sts
- **Argonne Community Garden**, between 15th and 16th aves and Fulton and Cabrillo sts
- **Arkansas Friendship Garden**, 22nd St between Arkansas and Connecticut sts
- **Arlington Community Garden**, Arlington St and Highland Ave
- **Bayshore Gardens and Roses**, Bayshore Blvd near 3rd St and LeConte
- **Bernal Heights Garden**, Bernal Heights Blvd between Gates and Banks sts
- **Brooks Park**, Ramsell and Shields sts
- **Candlestick Point Garden**, 1105 Carroll Ave

- **Central YMCA Rooftop Garden**, 220 Golden Gate Ave
- **Clipper Community Garden**, Clipper St near Grandview Ave
- **Connecticut St Garden**, 22nd and Connecticut sts
- **Corona Heights Garden**, Corona Heights Park, 16th and Flint sts
- **Crags Court Garden**, end of Crags St off of Berkeley Way
- **Daniel E. Koshland Community Learning Garden and Page St Community Garden**, Page and Buchanan sts
- **Dearborn Community Garden**, between 17th and 18th sts and Valencia and Guerrero sts
- **Fort Mason Garden**, north of Building 201, Fort Mason
- **Golden Gate Senior Center Garden**, 6101 Fulton St
- **Good Prospect Garden**, Prospect St and Cortland Ave
- **Hooker Alley Garden**, Mason St between Bush and Pine sts
- **Howard Langton (SoMa) Garden**, Langton Alley and Howard St
- **Howard St Garden**, Howard St near 12th St
- **Juri Commons Community Garden**, between Guerrero and San Jose sts and 25th and 26th sts
- **La Grande Community Garden**, end of Dublin St near Russia St
- **McLaren Park Garden**, Leland Ave and Hahn St
- **Michelangelo Community Garden**, Greenwich St between Jones and Leavenworth sts
- **Miller Memorial Garden**, Brewster and Rutledge
- **Mission Creek Gardens**, 300 Channel St
- **New Liberation Community Garden**, Divisidero and Eddy sts
- **Noe Beaver Garden**, Noe and Beaver sts
- **Noe Valley Library Garden**, 451 Jersey St
- **Ogden Terraces Community Garden**, Ogden St between Prentiss and Nevada sts
- **Park St Community Garden**, end of Park St, west of Mission St;
- **Potrero Del Sol**, Potrero Ave and Cesar Chavez St
- **Potrero Hill Community Garden**, San Bruno Ave and 20th St
- **Rolph Playground Garden**, Potrero Ave between 25th and Cesar Chavez sts
- **Rose/Page Garden**, Page St between Laguna and Octavia sts
- **Sunset Community Garden**, 37th Ave and Pacheco St
- **Telegraph Hill Neighborhood Center Garden**, 660 Lombard St
- **Visitacion Valley Garde**n, Arleta St, between Alpha and Rutland sts
- **White Crane Springs Garden**, 7th Ave, near Lawton St
- **Wolfe Lane Community Garden**, Rutledge and Mullen

BEYOND SAN FRANCISCO

For information on Community Gardens in **Oakland**, contact the city's **Community Gardening Coordinator**, 250 Frank Ogawa Plaza, Suite 3330, Oakland, 94612, 510-238-2197.

- **Arroyo Viejo**, 79th Ave and Arthur St, Oakland
- **Bushrod**, 584 59th St, Oakland
- **Golden Gate**, 1068 62nd St, Oakland
- **Lakeside Horticultural Center Kitchen Garden**, 666 Bellevue Ave, Oakland
- **Marston Campbell**, between 16th and 18th sts and Market and West sts, Oakland
- **Temescal**, 876 47th St; Verdese Carter, 96th and Bancroft aves, Oakland

Berkeley is very community garden-friendly and many schools have educational gardens; to find out more contact **Berkeley Community Gardening Collaborative**, P.O. Box 2801, Berkeley, CA 94702, 510-883-9096, www.ecologycenter.org/bcgc.
- **BYA Community Garden**, Allston Way between Bonar and West sts, Berkeley
- **Karl Linn Community Garden**, Peralta Ave and Hopkins St, Berkeley
- **Northside Community Gardens**, Northside Ave and Hopkins St, Berkeley
- **Ohlone Community Garden**, Hearst and McGee aves, Berkeley
- **People's Park Gardens**, Bowditch St between Dwight Way and Haste St, Berkeley
- **Peralta Community Art Garden**, Peralta Ave near Hopkins St, Berkeley
- **South Berkeley Community Garden**, Martin Luther King Jr. Way and Russell St, Berkeley
- **UC College of Natural Resources Garden**, Walnut and Virginia sts, Berkeley
- **West Berkeley Senior Center**, Senior Gardening, 1900 6th St, Berkeley

For **San Jose**, check the web site, www.sjcommunitygardens.org. In other cities, contact the local park and recreation department for information on community gardening programs.

ETHNIC FOOD DISTRICTS

San Francisco reportedly has so many restaurants that everyone who lives here could sit down to dinner at the same time, and there would still be table space left over for visitors. It's a city that, simply put, loves to eat, and to eat well. Thanks to a wealth of diverse cultural influences, San Francisco boasts not only some of the finest ethnic eateries in the USA, but some of the best markets as well. Whether you want a hard-to-find hot chili pepper from Mexico, handmade Japanese soba noodles, or freshly baked Russian rye bread, you can find it here.

The Mission: The heart of San Francisco's vibrant Latin American community, 24th Street between Potrero Avenue and Valencia Street, and Valencia and Mission streets between 16th and Cesar Chavez, the Mission boasts a wide variety of traditional Mexican bakeries; mom 'n pop groceries stocked with fresh produce, homemade tortillas, and imported specialties; and makeshift corner stands with everything from flowers to mangoes to oranges sold from the back of pick-up trucks. If you're looking for food on the go, you can frequently find the famous Tamale Lady selling her cheap and tasty specialties late into the night at local bars.

Chinatown: Chinese moon pies, steamed pork buns, roasted duck, rice candy, Asian pears, and starfruit are all available here in a dense collection of markets, bakeries and the ever-popular produce stands. The markets are always packed during the day and on Sundays, trucks with the latest imported fruits and vegetables often don't even bother to unload, opting instead to sell their goods directly to the gathering crowds. Grant Street between Market Street and Broadway is the main thoroughfare, but you'll find shops all along Washington, Stockton, Kearny, and smaller surrounding streets as well. Goodies from China, Thailand, Vietnam, and all across Asia can be found in the Inner Richmond on Clement Street between 4th and 9th avenues, referred to by many as "new Chinatown." Shops and restaurants also spill over onto nearby Geary Boulevard and California Street.

North Beach: While most of this old world district is populated with fancy sit-down restaurants today, you can still find a few gems—bakeries with fresh foccacia, delis offering fine imported cheeses, olive oil, and sweets, markets that sell freshly made pastas to go, and of course cafés that will pack their premium coffee and espresso for you to take home. Broadway and Columbus are the main streets here, but Grant, Union, and Vallejo streets, especially near Washington Square Park, are also filled with shops.

Japantown: "town" is kind of a misnomer here—Japan mall might be more appropriate, as the Japanese markets are almost all clustered under one roof here at the Kintetsu Mall, better known as Japan Center, on Geary Boulevard and Fillmore Street. A handful of smaller shops are also clustered alongside the mall on Post Street. In Japantown, you can find a remarkable array of Japanese delicacies from udon noodles, to seaweed wraps for sushi, to the latest in anime art. And yes, there are karaoke bars here as well. If you feel like taking a break from shopping, the fantastic Kabuki Day Spa is quietly hidden away here at the foot of Japan Center, near the Kabuki multiplex cinema, which annually plays host to the Asian American Film Festival. Even though Japantown is small, you can't miss it—just look for the large pagoda in the central outdoor plaza.

The Richmond: While the Inner Richmond is known for its Asian markets along Clement Street, the Outer Richmond is all about Russia and Eastern Europe. Here, you'll find locals lining up every morning to nab loaves of exquisite, freshly baked breads, as well as markets that carry imports from Russia, Hungary, Romania, and the Czech Republic.

RESTAURANTS

Depending on your interest in food, dining out here can be a convenience, a diversion, a hobby, a sport, a religion, or a vocation. Offering every cuisine imaginable, the San Francisco Bay Area is one of the food capitals of the world, with more restaurants per person than any other area in the USA. In fact, many new arrivals to the Bay Area are part of the food industry, serving as wait staff, suppliers, growers, chefs, managers, investors, etc. If you are interested in learning more about dining out in the Bay Area, check out the weekly reviews features and columns in the *San Francisco Weekly* and the *San Francisco Bay Guardian* newspapers. You can also check out the food lover's trusty old companion, *Zagat Survey, San Francisco Bay Area Restaurants*, www.zagat.com.

WINES

- **Beltramos**, 1540 El Camino Real, Menlo Park, 650-325-2806, wines and beers
- **BevMo!**, for Bay Area locations of this adult beverage superstore, check www. bevmo.com
- **Cost Plus World Market**, 2552 Taylor St, San Francisco, 415-928-6200; Westlake Center, Daly City, 415-994-7090; 101 Clay St, Oakland, 510-834-4440, www.worldmarket.com
- **The Jug Shop**, 1590 Pacific Ave, San Francisco, 415-885-2922, 800-404-9548, www.jugshop.com
- **K&L Wine Merchants**, 3005 El Camino Real, Redwood City, 877-559-4637; 638 4th St, San Francisco, 415-896-1734, www.klwines.com, wine-of-the-month clubs, free newsletter, huge selection
- **The Wine Stop**, 1300 Burlingame Ave, Burlingame, 650-342-5858

And don't forget to visit the hundreds of wineries in Napa and Sonoma.

WITH ALL THE DIVERSE AND HIGHLY ACCLAIMED CULTURAL EVENTS in the Bay Area, you may have trouble deciding what to do first. San Francisco boasts a world-class symphony and chorus, opera, ballet, and a vibrant live theater scene, with everything from the experimental and off-beat to big, brash Broadway musicals. And the surrounding Bay Area presents rich and varied cultural offerings as well. It's a rare evening here when one of the current stars of the pop music scene is not appearing locally. South of Market, the official nightlife district, is the nightclub hub.

Art lovers indulge themselves at major museums in San Francisco's down-town area and in Golden Gate Park as well as in smaller galleries throughout the City. Oakland, Berkeley, and the South Bay have myriad museums and galleries as well. Science museums, aquariums, planetariums, and top-notch zoos also abound. The South Bay, not surprisingly, has a number of technology-oriented museums.

All of the Bay Area's newspapers print entertainment schedules on a reg-ular basis, so you'll have no trouble finding out what's happening. The most comprehensive listing can be found in the *San Francisco Chronicle's* Sunday "Datebook." The *Chronicle* also publishes a daily "Datebook" section in the morning newspaper. San Francisco's *Bay Guardian* weekly and the *SF Weekly* also have extensive listings and movie reviews, and they're free. Look for them in street-side racks and cafés. A brief listing of special events/celebrations/fes-tivals can also be found in the chapter, later in this volume, entitled **A Bay Area Year**.

Tickets for most events and performances may be purchased at the venue box offices or by calling **Ticketmaster** at 800-745-3000, TTY 800-943-4327, or you can order online at www.ticketmaster.com. It's always a good idea to get your tickets as far in advance as possible since many shows, concerts, exhibits, and events sell out in advance. When calling ahead, have your credit card ready and be prepared to pay service fees (if your sense of thrift won't allow you to pay the often-steep service fees, buy your tickets in person at the box office). For discount, same-day tickets to San Francisco theater productions and full-price tickets to other selected local events, check out the **TIX Bay Area** ticket booth on the east side of Union Square. This is where last-minute open seats are sold for half-price; although your choices are usually limited, you can score great bargains. Call TIX at 415-433-7827. Also check out Brown Paper Tickets, www.brownpapertickets, which bills itself as the first and only fair-trade ticketing company. Other ticket agencies are listed in the Yellow Pages or on the web under "Tickets" or "Event Ticket Sales."

MUSIC—SYMPHONIC, OPERA, CHORAL

SAN FRANCISCO/NORTH BAY

- The **San Francisco Symphony** is one of the country's premier orchestras. The symphony and its **Chorus** have both won Grammy awards and toured much of the world, performing to packed houses and critical acclaim. World-renowned conductor Michael Tilson Thomas, known as MTT, runs the show and is famous for his innovative approach. Along with showcasing Beethoven and Mozart as well as classics of American music, the symphony has paired with such unusual partners as SF heavy metal legend Metallica for a special sold-out show. When at home, the San Francisco Symphony and Chorus perform separately and in tandem at their glittering glass, brass, and concrete home, the $33 million Louise M. Davies Symphony Hall. Opened in 1980, the structure underwent an acoustic upgrade in 1992. The concert hall and box office are located in the Civic Center area, at 201 Van Ness Ave. Call the ticket office at 415-864-6000 or purchase tickets and view the full concert calendar online at www.sfsymphony.org. Ticket prices start around $10 and go up from there. Each new concert season kicks off in early September with a swank black tie and ball gown gala, and runs through June.
- The **San Francisco Opera** performs at the War Memorial Opera House, right across Van Ness Avenue from City Hall, north of Davies Symphony Hall. This company attracts many of the opera world's biggest stars and is known for its often-lavish productions. Tickets can be on the expensive side, with decent seats starting around $85. However, so-called "rush tickets" can be purchased the day of the show, after 11 a.m. until one hour before curtain, at the Opera box office, 301 Van Ness Ave. Call the day before to check for ticket availability. The curtain comes up on the opera season with a gala event in September and continues into the summer. For more information or to order tickets, call 415-864-3330. The opera also presents free performances in Stern Grove, Golden Gate Park, and Yerba Buena Gardens during the summer. Visit www. sfopera.com for more details and schedules.

- The highly acclaimed vocal ensemble **Chanticleer** calls San Francisco home. This a cappella group of 12 men works year round, traveling all over the world, performing live and making new recordings. The ensemble specializes in "early music," but is also adept at classical choral works, jazz, pop, and spirituals. Catch them when they're in town—you'll be amazed by what you hear. To find out more, contact Chanticleer at 415-252-8589, www.chanticleer.org.
- San Francisco's own **Kronos Quartet** specializes in modern, experimental music, and they, too, travel the globe, playing to sold-out audiences. Check newspaper entertainment guides for the few times Kronos is in the Bay Area to play for its adoring local followers. If you like modern chamber music, you're sure to become one of Kronos's many fans. For a schedule of upcoming performances, check out www.kronosquartet.org.
- If you'd like to hear some of the professional musicians of the future, the place to go locally is the **San Francisco Conservatory of Music**. The Conservatory has recently moved to a beautiful new venue at 50 Oak St. Frequent concerts are staged here, featuring classical and contemporary solo and ensemble performers. For more information on upcoming events at the conservatory, call 415-864-7326 or visit www.sfcm.edu.
- At **San Francisco Community Music Center**, 544 Capp St, 415-647-6015, www.sfcmc.org, you can take a class or view inexpensive, sometimes free performances by students, instructors, and professionals of worldwide acclaim.
- At the striking Frank Lloyd Wright–designed Civic Center in San Rafael you can hear the **Marin Symphony**. Call 415-479-8100 or visit www.marinsymphony.org for more details.

The areas surrounding San Francisco and the North Bay host an abundance of classical musical offerings. Not all musical groups have permanent homes; instead, some play at a variety of locations, which means that people have an opportunity to hear live classical music pretty close to home no matter where they live.

EAST BAY

In Contra Costa County the **Lesher Center for the Arts** houses a number of performance companies such as the **Contra Costa Chamber Orchestra**, the **Diablo Light Opera Company**, and the **Center REPertory Company**, 1601 Civic Drive, Walnut Creek, 925-943-7469, www.lesherartscenter.org.

The East Bay also offers:

- **Berkeley Opera**, 2640 College Ave, Julia Morgan Center for the Arts, Berkeley, 925-798-1300, www.berkeleyopera.org
- **Berkeley Symphony Orchestra**, various locations, 510-841-2800, www.berkeleysymphony.org
- **Oakland East Bay Symphony**, 2025 Broadway, the Paramount Theatre, Oakland, 510-444-0801 or order tickets through www.ticketmaster.com, www.oebs.org

PENINSULA

In the groves of academe at Stanford University you can hear the **Stanford Symphony Orchestra**, the **Symphonic Chorus**, and the **Chamber Chorale**. Visit http://events.stanford.edu for a full events listing, or contact 650-723-2300.

- **Palo Alto Chamber Orchestra**, various locations, Palo Alto, 650-856-3848, www.pacomusic.org
- **Palo Alto Philharmonic**, various locations, www.paphil.org
- **West Bay Opera**, Lucie Stern Theatre, Palo Alto, 650-424-9999, www.wbopera.org

SOUTH BAY

- **Cupertino Symphonic Band**, various locations, 408-262-0471, www.netview.com/csb
- **Opera San Jose**, the California Theatre, 345 S First St, San Jose, 408-437-4450, www.operasj.org
- **San Jose Wind Symphony**, various locations, 408-927-7597, www.sjws.org
- **Symphony Silicon Valley**, performances at the California Theatre, 345 S First St, 408-286-2600, www.symphonysiliconvalley.org

CONTEMPORARY MUSIC

San Francisco draws star entertainers as well as up-and-comers from all over the world. The city also has its own incredibly vibrant local music scene. If you're into hip hop, dance music, rowdy pick-up bars, and late-night clubbing, check out SoMa. About a decade ago, this area became the target of "clean-up" efforts instituted by then-head of the Southern Police Station, Capt. Dennis Martel. Frequent vice squad raids by the SFPD and the Federal Bureau of Alcohol led to tighter restrictions on club operating hours and ultimately shut down many of the city's most popular clubs. To this day, it's extremely difficult to get an after-hours license in San Francisco, so you'll be hard pressed to find anything (legally) open after 2 a.m. The best-known exception is **Ten 15**—a massive multi-tier dance club with different DJs spinning in every room. Long lines form every Friday and Saturday when the club is open all night long, 1015 Folsom Street, www.1015.com.

Rock and roll hipsters spend their nights following beloved local bands and DJs who spin at a seemingly ever-rotating pool of tiny bars and intimate nightclubs scattered throughout the city. Currently, 6th Street—where rents are cheap, space is freely available, and neighbors don't complain—is home to a crop of new nighttime hot spots. In recent years, a number of new bands, small clubs, and art/music spaces have also sprung up in Oakland—enticing die-hard San Francisco music lovers across the bridge on Friday and Saturday nights.

For the latest on local bands, shows, and venues, check out the alternative weeklies: the *San Francisco Bay Guardian*, *SF Weekly*, and the *East Bay*

Express. There are also a host of free monthly magazines devoted entirely to local music—for example, *West Coast Performer* and *Mesh*. You can pick these up at local music stores and at many coffee shops. In the wired world, there are also a number of popular online music sites. Try www.foopee.com/punk/the-list, the internet version of **"The List"**—Steve Koepke's tried and true old-school photocopied punk and indie rock listing—for a weekly lowdown on Bay Area shows, good for lovers of more underground/less mainstream music. You can also sign up for the **Squid List**, http://laughingsquid.com/squidlist/events, a daily e-mail list of noncommercial/underground music, art, culture, and performance events. You can check their online event calendar at the same web address. Many events are posted on the bulletin boards of the popular social site **MySpace**, www.myspace.com. MySpace has an area specifically devoted to music. **Yahoo** (www.yahoo.com) also hosts a variety of subscriber bulletin board and discussion groups, including the popular **SF Indie List**. You have to register to use these sites and online community services, but membership is free. **Noise Pop**, the all-about indie rock festival held every February, is the place to check out local emerging rock stars and hot out-of-town acts, www.noisepop.com.

If big arena rock is your cup of tea, no doubt the name Bill Graham will be familiar to you. Graham, the prolific Bay Area concert promoter, died in 1991 returning from a Huey Lewis and the News concert on a windy night when his helicopter hit a transmission tower in the North Bay. Today Graham is best remembered for his early years in the 1960s and 1970s promoting San Francisco psychedelic rockers the Grateful Dead and Jefferson Airplane, first at local art spaces and later at the Fillmore. These days, the company he founded, **Bill Graham Presents (BGP)**, presses on, bringing big-time rock and roll acts to the Fillmore and the Warfield, as well as the large, centrally located Civic Center, now officially renamed the Bill Graham Civic Auditorium.

In the East Bay, the **Oakland Coliseum** (currently officially named, but called by no one, Oracle Coliseum) is one of the Bay Area's premier outdoor concert sites for big-name pop stars; it also has an indoor stage. A number of other outdoor facilities are used for concerts, chief among them the **Shoreline Amphitheatre** in Mountain View and the **Sleep Train Pavilion** in Concord. Both have covered seating up front, close to the stage, and loads of uncovered lawn behind the seats. Bring a blanket, stretch out, and listen to the music. Though it's not outdoors, Madonna and Bette Midler both performed at the **HP Pavilion** in San Jose, skipping San Francisco—which lacks a space large enough to host them—entirely.

Jazz and blues are the hallmarks of North Beach, especially along upper Grant Avenue. While it's no longer the Beat Generation mecca—and you'll be hard pressed to find a smoky bar with young intellectuals hanging on the words of a solo performer waxing poetic to a bongo backbeat—you will find a mix of late night jazz clubs and down home country and blues dive bars. Spots like

Grant & Green Blues Club and **The Saloon** are longtime favorites. Late into the night, jazz lovers congregate for cappuccino nightcaps and lively chats at the neighborhood's late night coffee houses.

Wherever you go be forewarned, there is no smoking indoors in public places in San Francisco—or in any of California for that matter. Smoking is officially banned in restaurants, bars, and clubs throughout the state. Of course, a handful of places have figured out a way around the law by providing suction fans or indoor/outdoor combination rooms.

For the latest on who's playing where and when, you can consult the weeklies listed earlier in this section, the *San Francisco Chronicle's* weekend "Datebook," or the paper's web site, www.sfgate.com.

BAY AREA CONCERT FACILITIES

- **Sleep Train at Concord**, 2000 Kirker Pass Rd, Concord, 925-363-5701,
- **Cow Palace**, Geneva Ave and Santos St, Daly City, 415-404-4111, www.cow-palace.com
- **Fillmore**, 1805 Geary Blvd, San Francisco, 415-346-6000
- **Great American Music Hall**, 859 O'Farrell St, San Francisco, 415-885-0750, www.gamh.com
- **Greek Theater**, UC Berkeley (near football stadium), Berkeley, 510-642-9988
- **HP Pavilion**, 525 W. Santa Clara St, San Jose, 409-287-6655
- **Oakland Coliseum & Arena**, Hegenberger Rd and I-880, Oakland, 510-569-2121, www.coliseum.com
- **Shoreline Amphitheatre**, One Amphitheatre Pkwy, Mountain View, 650-967-3000, www.livenation.com
- **Warfield Theatre**, 982 Market St, San Francisco, www.ticketmaster.com

NIGHTCLUBS

We offer a list of places to get you started, though this list is by no means comprehensive. Call ahead: here today, gone tomorrow is often the case in this fast-paced scene.

SAN FRANCISCO

- **Biscuits & Blues**, 401 Mason St, 415-292-2583, www.biscuitsandblues.com; blues, hosts a weekly Mardi Gras party Tuesday nights at 8:45 p.m. with the Fat Tuesday Band; there's a full-service restaurant upstairs that serves up home-style Cajun cuisine including jambalaya and fried chicken—and there's a raw oyster bar.
- **Bottom of the Hill**, 1233 17th St, 415-621-4455, www.bottomofthehill.com; this long-reigning king of the indie rock music scene hosts up-and-coming local bands and touring favorites; the outdoor patio is the place to mix and

mingle, and to escape the noise, as well as a haven for smokers; when the weather is nice, the Sunday BBQs are a great way to while away the day.

- **Café du Nord**, 2170 Market St, 415-861-5016, www.cafedunord.com; the stairwell that leads you down to this swanky little dark club reveals du Nord's former days as a bootleggers' paradise during Prohibition; you can catch up-and-coming local rock bands and in-house jazz regulars with a pint of speakeasy ale in your hand; arrive early to grab a bite to eat and a cozy table.
- **Edinburgh Castle**, 950 Geary St, 415-885-4074, www.castlenews.com; the stage here is tiny, but the friendly pub atmosphere, excellent beer, and support of emerging bands make it a great place to check out new local rock acts; the Castle also hosts a handful of intimate but popular dance nights, including the beloved Brit pop night, and drinkers square off for a test of wits at the Castle Quiz trivia night every Tuesday at 8:30 p.m.
- **Fillmore**, 1805 Geary Blvd, 415-346-6000; this old-fashioned, ornate, and stalwart hall was closed for several years after being ravaged by the 1989 Loma Prieta Earthquake. But today, you can once again wander through and admire the walls lined with posters and photos from its glory days in the 1960s and '70s while you listen to today's rock and roll greats; a new upstairs lounge hosts DJs and smaller acts that play between sets on the main stage as well as a snack bar to soothe your late night munchies. Arrive extra early to snag one of the premier balcony tables and leave quickly afterward to garner one of the venue's free concert posters.
- **Hotel Utah**, 500 4th St, 415-546-6300, www.thehotelutahsaloon.com; a dive in the best sense of the word, with bar-style rock and blues bands, Monday night open mike.
- **Noe Valley Ministry**, 1021 Sanchez St, 415-454-5238, www.noevalleyministry.com; hosts the Noe Valley Music Series in a 110-year-old Victorian church, with a mix of world, jazz, folk, and classical performances.
- **Pearl's**, 256 Columbus Ave, 415-291-8255, www.jazzatpearls.com; this famous jazz and blues 1930s-style supper club with French and Spanish food in the heart of North Beach offers two live music shows every Monday–Saturday at an 8 p.m. dinner show and a 10:30 p.m. cocktail show.
- **Plough & Stars**, 116 Clement St, 415-751-1122; voted "Best Irish Pub" by the *SF Weekly*, the club offers a variety of imported pints and live Irish music Tuesday through Sunday, free most nights with a cover charge on Friday and Saturday.
- **Slim's**, 333 11th St, 415-522-0333, www.slims-sf.com; opened in 1988 by legendary R&B artist Boz Scaggs, this mid-size club in the heart of SoMa hosts rock, hip hop, and blues touring and local acts.
- **330 Ritch**, 330 Ritch St, 415-902-3125; DJ dance nights, world, hip hop, hosts long-running popular Brit pop dance night, Pop Scene, every Thursday night.

NORTH BAY

- **19 Broadway**, 19 Broadway, Fairfax, 415-459-1091, www.19broadway.com; open seven nights a week, with two shows nightly, rock to raga, Monday nights open jam sessions.

EAST BAY

- **Ashkenaz**, 1317 San Pablo Ave, Berkeley, 510-525-5054, www.ashkenaz.com; all ages, rock, hip hop, funk, blues, world, country.
- **Freight & Salvage**, 1111 Addison St, Berkeley, 510-548-1761, www.freight andsalvage.org; coffee house with coffee, tea and desserts, acoustic, rock, blues, world, country; youth 16 and under half price, $1 off for seniors.
- **Kimball's Carnival**, 215 Washington St, Oakland, 510-444-6136, www.kim-ballscarnival.com; music, dining, and billiards.
- **La Pena Cultural Center**, 3105 Shattuck, Berkeley, 510-849-2568; hip hop, soul, world.
- **Starry Plough**, 3101 Shattuck Ave, Berkeley, 510-841-2082; small, friendly pub atmosphere with local rock, country and world music acts, shows are frequently $5.
- **Yoshi's**, 510 Embarcadero West, Oakland, 510-238-9200, www.yoshis.com; this club in the heart of Jack London Square is where the giants of jazz play when they come to town; tickets are pricey, but shows are top-notch and you can enjoy sushi and classic Japanese fare at the adjoining restaurant. Shows are Monday–Saturday at 8 p.m. and 10 p.m., Sunday at 2 p.m. and 8 p.m.

PENINSULA

- **Los Altos Bar and Grill**, 233 3rd St, Los Altos, 650-948-3524; rock, jazz
- **Pioneer Saloon**, 2925 Woodside Rd, Woodside, 650-851-8487; country, rock

SOUTH BAY

- **The Blank Club**, 44 S Almaden Ave, San Jose, 408-292-5265, www.theblank club.com; rock
- **Boswell's**, Pruneyard Shopping Center, 1875 S Bascom, Campbell, 408-371-4404; rock
- **J.J.'s Blues**, 3439 Stevens Creek Blvd, San Jose, 408-243-6441; blues, rock, hip-hop

SWING

Swing is the "in" thing here and has been for the last several years. What was an underground youth movement has caught the imagination of old timers, former hippies, young people, and everyone in between. There are numerous swing bands, swing street fairs, and swing clubs, and now the old swank night spots like Bimbos and Top of the Mark hire young swing bands to keep their patrons hopping. Vintage clothing stores have run out of original 1940s swing attire, so smart young designers are making their own replicas of everything from zoot suits for men to flattering floral print rayons for the gals. Almost every venue hosts pre-event dance classes for the beginner, so there's no excuse not to lindy. Check out the Lindy List, www.lindylist.com, for Bay Area–wide classes and happenings.

BALLET & DANCE

At any given time dance lovers in the Bay Area can enjoy watching Celtic step dancing, Native American dancing, Russian or Balkan dancers, and modern dance companies. Look in the newspaper or any of the local weeklies for listings.

SAN FRANCISCO/NORTH BAY

- **Dance Mission Theater**, run by Dance Brigade, hosts a variety of shows, from performances by the resident six-woman contemporary company to Afro-Cuban festivals; it's also a popular spot to take classes in everything from hip hop to salsa, to modern dance, to Afro-Brazilian, 3316 24th St (at Mission) 415-826-4441, www.dancemission.com.
- **Fat Chance Belly Dance**, a San Francisco institution, performs tribal-style belly dancing at a variety of festivals and events, as well as offering drop-in dance classes, for women only, at the studio, 670 S Van Ness Ave, 415-431-4322, www.fcbd.com.
- **Marin Ballet**, various locations, 415-453-6705, www.marinballet.org, performs the Nutcracker every Christmas at the Marin Veterans Memorial Auditorium, 3501 Civic Center Dr.
- Michael Smuin, formerly a choreographer with the San Francisco Ballet, started his own company, **Michael Smuin Ballet**. They perform modern and classical pieces often reworked by Smuin at various locations, including the Yerba Buena Center for the Arts, 701 Mission St, and the Mountain View Center for the Performing Arts, 500 Castro St. Call 415-495-2234 or visit www.smuinballet.org for information.
- **ODC Theater** (Oberlin Dance Collective, with its roots at Oberlin College) performs modern dance at ODC Dance Commons, 351 Shotwell St, 415-863-6606, www.odcdance.org, and elsewhere. They also put on the popular "Velveteen Rabbit" for children each December at Yerba Buena Center for the Arts.
- The **San Francisco Ballet** is a small company with a big reputation. The ballet season follows the opera season, starting with the perennially popular "Nutcracker" in November and proceeding throughout the late winter and spring. Performances are at the War Memorial Opera House at Van Ness and Grove. For performance and ticket information call 415-865-2000, or visit www.sfballet.org.

- **Theatre Flamenco of San Francisco**, 1144 Rhode Island, 415-826-2477, enlivens the Spanish dancing scene.
- Other modern dance troupes include **Deborah Slater Dance Theatre**, 415-267-7687, **Margaret Jenkins Dance Company**, 415-861-3940, and **Footloose Dance Company and Shotwell Studios**, 415-289-2000, www. ftloose.org. This is only a partial list. New companies form, combine, and move in all the time.

EAST BAY

- **Axis Dance Company** is a contemporary ensemble that integrates dancers with disabilities who create and perform their own original works; various locations, 510-625-0110, www.axisdance.org.
- **Cal Performances** presents dancers of world renown who perform through UC Berkeley at the Greek Theater, Hertz Hall, or Zellerbach Auditorium, 510-642-9988; www.calperfs.berkeley.edu.
- **Julia Morgan Center for the Arts,** 2640 College Ave, Berkeley, 510-845-8542, www.juliamorgan.org, offers a wide variety of arts programs. The Center also houses the **Berkeley Ballet Theater**, which boasts the inclusive motto, "where all can dance," features both adult and youth companies, and teaches ballet lessons, 510-843-4687, www.berkeleyballet.org.

PENINSULA/SOUTH BAY

- **Ballet San Jose Silicon Valley**, 40 N First St, San Jose, 408-288-2800, www. balletsanjose.org, showcases classic and contemporary works from *Romeo and Juliet* to *The Little Mermaid*; the ballet school's educational outreach program is dedicated to serving young audiences.
- **Peninsula Ballet Theatre**, various locations, 650-342-3262, presents a variety of classical ballet performances at affordable prices, including an annual rendition of the *Nutcracker* popular with families, www.peninsulaballet.org.
- **San Jose Dance Theatre**, 408-286-9905, www.sjdt.org, hosts classics and children's favorites including *Alice in Wonderland*, *Sleeping Beauty*, *Beauty and the Beast*, and of course the *Nutcracker*.

THEATER

The San Francisco theater scene is an active one offering works that range from experimental to mainstream. The theater district, located two blocks west of Union Square on Geary Street, is where you'll find the Curran and Geary theaters. The Curran stages musicals as well as shows being prepared for the trip to New York's Great White Way. The Geary Theater plays host to what many would consider more serious productions, such as works by Shakespeare, Chekhov, and Sam Shepard. It is also is home to one of the country's most respected companies, the American Conservatory Theatre. The Golden Gate Theater, in the nearby Tenderloin district, stages big, splashy musicals. The surrounding streets are on the seedy side, which puts many people off when it comes to attending shows here. However, there is safety in numbers, so if possible, stick with the crowd when traveling through this area.

Once you leave the theater district, productions take on a less commercial, more experimental feel, and there are many to choose from. Of course, local high schools, colleges, and universities also mount shows, as do many local theater groups. Look for listings for all of the above in newspaper entertainment guides, or call the theaters. Here are just a few **San Francisco theaters**:

- **American Conservatory Theater (ACT)**, San Francisco's major professional theater company, based at the Geary Theater, 415 Geary St, 415-749-2228, www.act-sf.org
- **Brava**, 2781 24th St, 415-641-7657, social and political issues
- **Club Fugazi**, 678 Beach Blanket Blvd (Green St) 415-421-4222, home of the immensely popular *Beach Blanket Babylon*. www.beachblanketbabylon.com
- **Curran**, 445 Geary Street, 415-551-2000, www.shnsf.com, Broadway shows
- **Eureka Theatre**, 215 Jackson St, 415-788-7469, music, plays, classes
- **Exit Theatres**, 156 Eddy St, 415-673-3847, www.theexit.org
- **Fort Mason Box Office** (Cal Theater, Young Performers Theater, etc.), Fort Mason, 415-345-7575, new and old plays, comedy and drama
- **Golden Gate**, 1 Taylor St, 415-551-2000, www.shnsf.com, musicals
- **Intersection for the Arts**, 446 Valencia St, 800-838-3006, www.theintersection.org, plays, readings, musicals, music, and dance
- **Lorraine Hansberry**, 533 Sutter St, known for top-notch African-American drama; www.lhtsf.org
- **Magic Theatre**, Fort Mason, Building D, 415-441-8822, www.magictheatre.org, experimental
- **Marines Memorial**, 609 Sutter Street, 415-771-6900, varied, www.marinesmemorialtheater.com
- **New Conservatory Theatre Center**, 25 Van Ness Ave, 415-861-8972, traditional, new, musical, gay and lesbian themes; www.nctcsf.org
- **Orpheum**, 1192 Market St, 415-551-2000, www.shnsf.com, opera, musicals, serious drama
- **Post Street Theatre**, 450 Post St, 2nd Floor, 415-771-6900, www.unionsquaretheatres.com, drama, new works, classics
- **Theatre Rhinoceros**, 2926 16th St, 415-861-5079, www.therhino.org, gay and lesbian themes

NORTH BAY

- **Marin Community Playhouse**, 27 Kensington Rd, San Anselmo, 415-456-8555, films, lectures, dance, drama, music
- **Marin Shakespeare Company**, 415-499-4488, www.marinshakespeare.org, various locations

- **Marin Theatre Company**, 397 Miller Ave, Mill Valley, 415-388-5208, www. marintheatre.org, new plays and classes
- **Mountain Play Association**, Mt Tamalpais State Park, 415-383-1100, www. mountainplay.org, yearly outdoor summer musicals in a fantastic Greek Theatre–style venue

EAST BAY

- **Actors Ensemble of Berkeley**, 1301 Shattuck Ave, 510-841-5580; www.aeofberkeley.org
- **Aurora Theatre Co.**, 2081 Addiston St, Berkeley, 510-843-4822, old standards and new plays; www.aurotheatre.org
- **Berkeley Repertory Theatre**, 2025 Addison St, Berkeley, 510-647-2900, www.berkeleyrep.org, nationally known, new, and reworked plays
- **Black Repertory Group**, 3201 Adeline St, Berkeley, 510-652-2120; www. blackrepertorygroup.org
- **Contra Costa Civic Theatre**, 951 Pomona Ave, El Cerrito, 510-524-9132; www.ccct.org
- **Lesher Center for the Arts**, 1601 Civic Dr, Walnut Creek, 925-943-7469, www. lesherartscenter.org
- **Diablo Light Opera**, Lesher Center for the Arts, 1601 Civic Center Dr, Walnut Creek, 925-943-7469, www.dloc.org
- **East Bay Center for the Performing Arts**, 339 11th St, Richmond, 510-234-5624, www.eastbaycenter.org

PENINSULA

- **Broadway by the Bay**, San Mateo Performing Arts Center, 600 North Delaware St, San Mateo, 650-579-5565, www.broadwaybythebay.org
- **Palo Alto Players**, 1305 Middlefield Rd, Palo Alto, 650-329-0891, www. paplayers.org, full season of shows at reasonable prices
- **TheatreWorks**, Mountain View Center for the Performing Arts, 500 Castro St, and Lucie Stern Theater, 1305 Middlefield Rd, Palo Alto, 650-463-1960, www. theatreworks.org

SOUTH BAY

- **City Lights Theater Company**, 529 S Second St, San Jose, 408-295-4200, www.cltc.org, eclectic new plays
- **Louis B. Mayer Theatre**, Santa Clara University, Santa Clara, 408-245-2978
- **San Jose Repertory Theatre**, 101 Paseo de San Antonio, 408-367-7255, www.sjrep.com, classics and originals
- **San Jose Stage Company**, 490 S First St, San Jose, 408-283-7142, www. sanjose-stage.com, off-Broadway shows
- **Santa Clara Players**, Santa Clara Community Center, Santa Clara, 408-248-7993, www.scplayers.org

- **Shady Shakespeare**, Sanborn Skyline County Park, 6055 Sanborn Rd, Saratoga, 408-264-3479, www.shadyshakes.org/, outdoor theater, season runs August–September

MOVIES—ART, REVIVAL, INTERNATIONAL

Mainstream theaters, some of which still offer bargain matinees in the afternoon, show the latest Hollywood blockbusters and are located throughout the Bay Area. Below is a list of harder-to-find "art houses" that specialize in foreign and alternative films.

SAN FRANCISCO
- **Artists' Television Access**, 992 Valencia St, 415-824-3890
- **Bridge**, 3010 Geary Blvd, 415-267-4893
- **Balboa**, 3630 Balboa St, 415-221-8184, www.balboamovies.com
- **Castro**, 429 Castro St, 415- 621-6120, www.castrotheatre.com
- **Clay**, Fillmore at Clay St, 415-267-4893
- **Embarcadero**, 1 Embarcadero Center, 415-267-4893
- **Four Star**, Clement St and 23rd Ave, 415-666-3488, www.hkinsf.com/4star
- **Lumiere**, California St at Polk St, 415-267-4893
- **Opera Plaza**, Van Ness Ave at Golden Gate Ave, 415-267-4893
- **Red Vic**, 1727 Haight St, 415-668-3994
- **Roxie**, 3117 16th St, 415-863-1087
- **Vogue**, Sacramento St and Presidio Blvd, 415-346-2288

SURROUNDING BAY AREA
- **Stanford Theater**, 221 University Ave, Palo Alto, 650-324-3700
- **Camera 12 Cinemas**, 201 S Second St, San Jose, 408-998-3300, www.cameracinemas.com
- **Los Gatos Cinemas**, 41 N Santa Cruz Ave, Los Gatos, 408-395-0203, www.cameracinemas.com
- **Christopher B. Smith Rafael Film Center**, 1118 Fourth St, San Rafael, 415-454-1222, www.cafilm.org
- **New Pacific Film Archive Theater**, 2725 Bancroft Ave, Berkeley, 510-642-0808, www.bampfa.berkeley.edu

FILM FESTIVALS

The Bay Area hosts several annual film festivals. If you're a film buff, you'll want to mark your calendar.
- **Festival Cine Latino** (Fall), 415-513-5308
- **International Lesbian & Gay Film Festival** (June), 415-703-8650, www.frameline.org
- **Jewish Film Festival** (July), 415-621-0556, www.sfjff.org

- **Mill Valley Film Festival** (October), 415-383-5256, www.cafilm.com
- **San Francisco International Asian American Film Festival** (March), 415-863-0814, www.naatanet.org
- **San Francisco International Film Festival** (April), 415-561-5000, www.sffs.org

COMEDY

There's a lot to laugh about in life, and San Francisco provides ample opportunity to do so at a number of comedy clubs. Some headline the big names in modern comedy, including San Francisco natives Margaret Cho and Marga Gomez, and touring stand-ups Jamie Kennedy and Bill Maher.

Others offer open-mike opportunities for up-and-coming jokesters. If your funny bone needs tickling, here are a few of the places you may want to visit for comic relief:

- **Cobb's**, 915 Columbus Ave, San Francisco, 415-928-4320, www.cobbscomedyclub.com
- **Comedy on the Square**, various locations, comedy, 415-646-0776, www.comedyonthesquare.com
- **Punch Line**, 444 Battery St, San Francisco, 415-397-7573, www.punchlinecomedyclub.com
- **Rooster T. Feathers**, 157 W El Camino Real, Sunnyvale, 408-736-0921, www.roostertfeathers.com

MUSEUMS

San Francisco is blessed with excellent art museums, most notably the M.H. de Young Memorial Museum (undergoing renovations) in Golden Gate Park, the Asian Art Museum, the San Francisco Museum of Modern Art at Yerba Buena Gardens, and the California Palace of the Legion of Honor in Lincoln Park. Those are the big ones. Throughout the Bay Area are also many smaller art museums and galleries, as well as museums related to history, culture, and science, and interesting one-of-a-kind centers. Here's a sampling:

ART MUSEUMS

SAN FRANCISCO/NORTH BAY
- **Museum of the African Diaspora,** 685 Mission St, 415-358-7200; www.moadsf.org; celebrates and explores the art, culture and history of the African Diaspora, and features an interactive theater and immersive exhibitions. Kids 12 and younger are free.
- **Asian Art Museum**, 200 Larkin St, 415-581-3500, www.asianart.org; featuring artwork, ceramics, architectural displays, jade and textiles from China, Korea, India, Tibet, Japan and Southeast Asia. This is the largest museum of its type

on the West Coast and is indicative of the Bay Area's large Asian population. On Thursdays, the museum is free after 5 p.m. and stays open until 9 p.m. Kids 11 and younger free.

- **California Palace of the Legion of Honor**, 415-750-3600; a beautiful building perched atop a hill in Lincoln Park, it was given to the city in 1924 by the Spreckels family as a monument to the state's war dead. The art collection features European art from the medieval to the 20th century including a cast of Rodin's *The Thinker*, which sits outside the main entrance. Free on Tuesday, under age 12 free; www.famsf.org/legion.
- **Headlands Center for the Arts**, 944 Fort Barry, Sausalito, 415-331-2787, www.headlands.org.
- **M.H. de Young Museum**, named for Michael de Young, a former publisher of the *San Francisco Chronicle*, this museum has been located in Golden Gate Park since construction of the park began in 1917. The dramatically trans-formed new museum (reopened in fall 2005) features a stunning observatory tower as well as American works from Colonial to Modern, and African, British, Egyptian, Greek, Roman, and Asian items. The museum is also the site of many lectures and gala events. Call 415-750-3600 for more information. www.famsf.org/deyoung.
- **Museo Italo Americano**, Fort Mason, Building C, 415-673-2200, free for chil-dren 11 and under.
- **Performing Arts Library and Museum**, 401 Van Ness Ave, fourth floor, 415-255-4800, www.sfpalm.org, free.
- **SF Craft and Folk Art Museum**, 51 Yerba Buena Ln, 415-227-4888, youth 18 and under free; free the first Wednesday of the month, when the museum stays open until 7 p.m., and free every Saturday from 10 a.m. to noon; www.mocfa.org.
- **San Francisco Museum of Modern Art (SFMOMA)** at Yerba Buena Gardens, one of the most exciting buildings in the city. Swiss architect Mario Botta de-signed the building, and its massive cylindrical skylight is a sight to behold. Exhibits include works by Henri Matisse, Pablo Picasso, and Jackson Pollock, to name just three. SFMOMA was the West Coast's first museum dedicated solely to 20th century art. Located at 151 3rd St, 415-357-4000, www.sfmoma.org. On Thursdays the MOMA is open until 9 p.m. and is half price after 6 p.m. Children 12 and under free. Free on the first Tuesday of the month.
- **Yerba Buena Center for the Arts**, 701 Mission Street, 415-978-2700, www.ybca.org; under age 12 free. Free the first Tuesday of the month.

EAST BAY
- **Judah L. Magnes Memorial Museum**, 2911 Russell St, Berkeley, 510-549-6950, www.magnes.org; Jewish art and objects, under 12, free.

- **Oakland Museum**, 1000 Oak St, 510-238-2200; www.museumca.org; California art and history, open late the first Friday of the month, under age 12 free.
- **University Art Museum**, 2626 Bancroft Way, Berkeley, 510-642-0808, http://www.bampfa.berkeley.edu/; free the first Thursday of the month.

PENINSULA/SOUTH BAY

- **Cantor Arts Center,** 328 Lomita Dr, Palo Alto, 650-723-4177, www.stanford.edu; features modern art, sculpture, photography, and international exhibits; the highlight here is the outdoor Rodin Sculpture Garden, with 20 bronze statues by Auguste Rodin, including "The Gates of Hell"; admission is free.
- **San Jose Museum of Quilts and Textiles**, 520 S First St, 408-971-0323, www.sjquiltmuseum.org; features contemporary and traditional quilt making and textile design.
- **De Saisset Museum**, Santa Clara University, 500 El Camino Real, 408-554-4528; www.scu.edu/desaisset; large print collection, art and history, free admission.
- **Palo Alto Cultural Center**, 1313 Newell Rd, 650-329-2366, www.cityofpaloalto.org/depts/csd/activities_and_recreation/attractions/art_center/; features contemporary local artwork.
- **San Jose Museum of Art**, 110 S Market St, San Jose, 408-271-6840, www.sjmusart.org; features 20th century traveling exhibits.
- **San Jose Institute of Contemporary Art**, 560 S First St, San Jose, 408-283-8155, www.sjica.org.
- **Triton Museum of Art**, 1505 Warburton Ave, Santa Clara, 408-247-3754, www.tritonmuseum.org; features modern art.

HISTORY AND CULTURAL MUSEUMS AND CENTERS

- **Cable Car Museum**, 1201 Mason St, 415-474-1887, www.cablecarmuseum.org; get a close look at the history and inner workings of the nation's only moving landmark, San Francisco's world famous cable cars.
- **California History Center**, 21250 Stevens Creek Blvd, DeAnza College Campus, Cupertino, 408-864-8987, http://www.deanza.edu/califhistory.
- **Cartoon Art Museum**, 655 Mission St, San Francisco, 415-227-8666, www.cartoonart.org.
- **Chinese Culture Center**, Holiday Inn, Third Floor, 750 Kearny St, San Francisco, 415-986-1822, www.c-c-c.org.
- **Chinese Historical Society of America**, 965 Clay St, San Francisco, 415-391-1188, www.chsa.org; San Francisco's Chinatown has long been one of the largest Chinese communities in the country, and this small museum is dedicated to the Chinese-American story.

- **Contemporary Jewish Museum**, 736 Mission St, San Francisco, 415-655-7800, www.thecjm.org; this modest historical museum doubles as an art museum featuring works by Jewish artists.
- **Cupertino Historical Museum**, 10185 N Stelling Rd, Quinlan Community Center, Cupertino, 408-973-1495.Falkirk Cultural Center, 1408 Mission Ave, San Rafael, 415-485-3328, www.falkirkculturalcenter.org.
- **Jack London Square and Village**, Embarcadero between Alice and Broadway in Oakland, here you'll find shops and restaurants as well as a museum of African Antiquities. The Jack London Museum is at 30 Jack London Square.
- **Living Museum of Printing**, 1802 Hayes St, The Presidio, San Francisco, 415-668-2542, www.arionpress.com; comprising Arion Press, M&H Type, and the Grabhorn Institute, this living, breathing museum of book arts was designated an "irreplaceable cultural treasure" by the National Trust for Historic Preservation.
- **Marin History Museum**, 1125 B St, San Rafael, 415-454-8538, http://www.marinhistory.org.
- **Maritime Museum**, Hyde St Pier, San Francisco, 415-561-6662; www.maritime.org.
- **Mission San Rafael**, 1104 5th Ave, San Rafael, 415-454-8141; www.saintraphael.com.
- **Museum of American Heritage**, 351 Homer Ave, Palo Alto, 650-321-1004, http://www.moah.org; historical tableaux of day-to-day life.
- **National Japanese American Historical Society**, 1684 Post St, San Francisco, 415-921-5007, http://www.njahs.org/.
- **Paramount Theatre**, 2025 Broadway, Oakland, 510-465-6400, www.paramounttheatre.com.
- **Peralta Adobe**, 154 W St. John St, San Jose, 408-918-1055, www.historysanjose.org; tours by appointment.
- **San Francisco Museum and Historical Society**, free exhibits at City Hall and Pier 45, 415-537-1105, http://www.sfhistory.org.
- **San Jose History Park** at Kelley Park, 1650 Senter Rd, 408-287-2290, www.historysanjose.org.
- **Santa Clara de Asis Mission**, 500 El Camino Real, San Jose, 408-554-4023, http://www.missionart.com/hSC/p-sc.html.
- **Saratoga Historical Museum**, 20450 Saratoga-Los Gatos Rd, Saratoga, 408-867-4311, http://www.saratogahistory.com.

SCIENCE MUSEUMS & ZOOS

The Bay Area is a world scientific research center, home to the Lawrence Livermore and Lawrence Berkeley laboratories, medical research facilities at UCSF, and Stanford University Medical Center. In Silicon Valley, and elsewhere in the Bay Area, the next generation of computer, communications, and medical technologies is being developed. That said, you don't have to be a tech guru or rocket scientist to enjoy the abundant science museums in the Bay Area. Below is a partial list:

SAN FRANCISCO

- **Aquarium of the Bay**, which opened in 1996 at the tourist magnet of Pier 39, takes visitors literally into the aquarium through a long viewing tunnel. All around you the aquarium's residents glide by in an environment that can make you feel as though it is people, rather than fish, that are on display, 415-623-5300.
- **California Academy of Sciences** has been completely rebuilt and upgraded for the 21st century and now features some of the most innovative displays of tropical rainforests, aquariums and reptile tanks. Founded in 1853, the Academy of Sciences was and is the oldest scientific institution in the western United States but was closed for over 10 years for the overhaul. The facility includes the **Morrison Planetarium** and the **Steinhart Aquarium**. One of the aquarium's most popular attractions is the Fish Roundabout, which allows you to watch as all manner of water creatures, including shark, bat rays, and eel, glide around you in a 100,000-gallon tank. There are astounding displays of reptiles and amphibians, as well as a varied display of underwater plant life. Call 415-379-8000 or visit www.calacademy.org for information on the academy and the aquarium. Free the first Wednesday of the month.
- **Exploratorium**, located in the Palace of Fine Arts in the Marina district, is a true "hands on" scientific experience for everyone. There are nearly 700 exhibits, many of them interactive, and all highly educational. One of the most popular attractions is the Tactile Dome. Reservations are required for the opportunity to tumble around inside this darkened dome, where you rely on nothing but touch and sound. Located at 3601 Lyon St, 415-397-5673, www.exploratorium.edu.
- **San Francisco Zoo**, this 65-acre facility is perhaps best known for its koalas and Gorilla World. The koalas are a real treat to see as they cling, fast asleep, to their habitat's eucalyptus branches. The gorilla display is reportedly one of the world's largest. There's also a Children's Zoo, which allows kids to pet some of the animals, and an Insect Zoo. Located on Sloat Blvd at 47th Ave, 415-753-7080, www.sfzoo.org.

NORTH BAY

- **Bay Area Discovery Museum**, Fort Baker, 557 McReynolds Rd, Sausalito, 415-339-3900, www.baykidsmuseum.org; hands-on exhibits for kids.
- **San Francisco Bay Model Visitor Center**, 2100 Bridgeway, Sausalito, 415-332-3871, no charge.

EAST BAY

- **Holt Planetarium–Lawrence Hall of Science**, Centennial Dr, Berkeley, 510-642-5132, www.lawrencehallofscience.org
- **Oakland Zoo**, Oakland Zoo, 9777 Golf Links Rd, 510-632-9525, www.oaklandzoo.org
- **UC Berkeley Botanical Gardens**, 200 Centennial Dr, 510-643-2755, http://botanicalgarden.berkeley.edu; offers plants and hiking trails.

PENINSULA AND SOUTH BAY

- **Children's Discovery Museum of San Jose**, 180 Woz Way, 408-298-5437, www.cdm.org.
- **Hiller Aviation Museum**, 601 Skyway Rd, San Carlos Airport, San Carlos, 650-654-0200.
- **Intel Museum**, 2200 Mission College Blvd, Santa Clara, 408-765-0503.
- **Lick Observatory**, 19 miles east of San Jose on Highway 130 near Mount Hamilton, 408-274-5061, www.ucolick.org.
- **Art Museum of Los Gatos**, 4 Tait Ave, Los Gatos, 408-354-2646, /www.museumsoflosgatos.org/.
- **Fujitsu Planetarium**, 21250 Stevens Creek Blvd, DeAnza College Campus, Cupertino, 408-864-8814, www.planetarium.deanza.edu.
- **NASA Ames Research Center**, Moffett Field, Mountain View, 650-604-6274, www.nasa.gov/centers/ames/events/index.html.
- **Stanford Linear Accelerator**, 2275 Sand Hill Rd, Menlo Park, 650-926-2204, www.slac.stanford.edu, offers tours six times per month.
- **The Tech Museum of Innovation**, 201 S Market St, San Jose, 408-294-8324, www.thetech.org.

CULTURE FOR KIDS

There is so much for kids to do culturally in the Bay Area that they'll grow up before they can try it all. Besides numerous technical, history, science, nature, ethnic, and art museums, there are dozens of dance, theater, poetry, and musical performances aimed at or composed of children. Now that schools are less inclined to offer an array of language classes, kids can learn another language at some of the local cultural institutes as well. During the holidays, the **San Francisco Ballet** performs its version of *The Nutcracker* and the **ODC** performs a modern version of the *Velveteen Rabbit*. This smattering of listings for events and places that children might enjoy represents only a little of what the Bay Area has to offer.

SAN FRANCISCO

- **Exploratorium**, the **San Francisco Zoo**, and the **Aquarium of the Bay** are made for kids. See descriptions above under **Science Museums & Zoos**.

- **Randall Junior Museum**, 199 Museum Way, 415-554-9600, www.randallmuseum. org; a perennial favorite among children, this museum features an earthquake exhibit, live animals, art and science programs, films, lectures, concerts, and plays.
- **Yerba Buena Gardens**, 4th and Mission sts, www.yerbabuenagardens.com, offers gardens, paths, waterfalls and fountains full of birds. At one end, you'll find the high-tech museum **Zeum**, an ice-skating rink, a kid-sized bowling alley, a playground, and a merry-go-round; at the other, the **Sony Metreon**, 415-369-6000, www.metreon.com, is home to 15 movie screens, an IMAX theater, restaurants, hot dog stands, shops, arcades, and a Where the Wild Things Are interactive exhibit.
- **Zeum**, 221 4th St, 415-820-3320, www.zeum.com, part of the large arts complex at Yerba Buena Gardens, includes hands-on science and technology exhibits for children, an outdoor playground, and an old-fashioned merry-go-round.

SURROUNDING BAY AREA
- **Berkeley Youth Orchestra**, 2322 Shattuck Ave, Berkeley, 510-663-3296, www.berkeley-youth-orchestra.org.
- **Billy Jones Wildcat Railroad**, Oak Meadow Park, Los Gatos, 408-395-7433, www.bjwrr.org.
- **Children's Discovery Museum of San Jose**, 180 Woz Way, 408-298-5437, www.cdm.org.
- **Coyote Point Museum for Environmental Education**, 1651 Coyote Point Dr, San Mateo, 650-342-7755, www.coyotepointmuseum.org; nature museum and animal center, hands-on children's exhibits.
- **Emma Prusch Farm Park**, 647 S King Rd, San Jose, 408-926-5555.
- **Happy Hollow Park and Zoo**, 1300 Senter Rd, San Jose, 408-277-3000, www. happyhollowparkandzoo.org.
- **Marin Dance Theatre**, 1 St. Vincent's Dr, San Rafael, 415-499-8891, www.mdt. org, children and adult classical ballet classes and performances.
- **Oakland Youth Orchestra**, 1428 Alice St, Oakland, 510-832-7710, www.oyo. org.
- **Palo Alto Junior Museum and Zoo**, 1451 Middlefield Rd, Palo Alto, 650-329-2111, http://friendsjmz.org.
- **Winchester Mystery House**, 525 S Winchester Blvd, San Jose, 408-247-2101, www.winchestermysteryhouse.com.
- **Young People's Symphony Orchestra**, Berkeley, 510-849-9776, www.ypso-music.net.

LITERARY LIFE

New York may be home to the major publishing houses, but San Francisco has a literary legacy and pulsing life all its own. The city's illustrious roster of once-wrote-heres includes beloved humorist Mark Twain, detective noir master Dashiell Hammett, and legendary newspaper columnist Herb Caen. And across the bay, Oakland proudly claims classic literary legend Jack London, for whom its waterfront square is named, as one of its own.

In the 1950s and '60s, San Francisco was a favorite stomping ground of Beat greats Allen Ginsberg and Jack Kerouac, while in the 1970s Armistead Maupin began a local soap-opera-esque newspaper serial that shined a light on San Francisco life, and eventually became the famed novel *Tales of the City*.

But those who think San Francisco's glory days as a writers' haven are long gone should take a closer look. Beneath the surface, a young, feisty new community of novelists, essayists, poets, and publishers is rising—forging an active local literary community and commanding national attention. Independent bookstores, community spaces like Dave Eggers' **826 Valencia**, which offers free writing workshops for teens, and the Grotto, a writers' collective that offers a variety of seminars, are coming to the fore. And while the big city loves the limelight, the East Bay—Berkeley and Oakland in particular—is home to some of the best spoken word and hip hop poetry groups around.

Below you'll find a list of some of the Bay Area's best-loved independent bookstores, many of which host regular readings; cafés and clubs that host storytelling and open mike nights; writers' groups; local literary publications; and annual events. Local libraries, which offer a variety of programs—not to mention endless books to choose from, all for free—are an excellent place to start.

BOOKSTORES

The Bay Area has a large number of good independent, specialized, and used bookstores, many of which host author readings and other literary programs. Check their bulletin boards or get on their mailing or e-mail lists to be notified of upcoming events. Below is a list of just some of these, though once you move here, you'll probably discover many more. The university towns of Palo Alto and Berkeley have many good new and used bookstores encircling their campuses. Here are some of the familiar standards as well as a few interesting local independents worth visiting. Unless otherwise noted, the following establishments are in San Francisco.

- **Adobe Book Shop**, 3166 16th St, 415-864-3936; the store employees arranged all of the books here in color order, a la the rainbow. But not to worry, the art exhibit was only temporary and things are now back to "normal." Adobe hosts popular reading nights and occasional music and art events.
- **Alexander Book Co.**, 50 2nd St, 415-495-2992, www.alexanderbook.com; this three-level store in the heart of the Financial District specializes in African American literature and children's books, also maintains a large poetry collection.

- **Black Oak Books,** www.blackoakbooks.com, hosts author events at the main store, 1491 Shattuck Ave, Berkeley, 510-486-0698
- **Book Passage**, 51 Tamal Vista Blvd, Corte Madera, 415-927-0960 and 1 Ferry Plaza, #46, San Francisco, 415-835-1020, or 800-999-7909, www.bookpassage.com; known for its great support of local authors, frequent readings, and writing workshops.
- **Booksmith**, 1644 Haight St, 415-863-8688, www.booksmith.com, offers a wide collection of new and used books, as well as a substantial magazine section. Recent author events have showcased everyone from local Green Party activist Medea Benjamin to baseball superstar Jose Canseco to ex-Monty Python member and current travel writer Michael Palin
- **Bound Together Book Collective**, 1369 Haight St, 415-431-8355, specializes in anarchist and progressive books.
- **Builders Booksource**, 1817 Fourth St, Berkeley, 510-845-6874, www.buildersbooksource.com; offers architectural, design, and construction books for the amateur and professional.
- **Citylights Bookstore**, 261 Columbus Ave, 415-362-8193, www.citylights.com; the legendary Beat Generation bookshop founded by San Francisco's first poet laureate, Lawrence Ferlinghetti, was the first paperback bookstore in the country. Its creaky wooden floors and endless shelves are probably the best place to browse late in the evening. The store has an excellent collection of fiction, a poetry room upstairs, and a nook dedicated to zines; the store showcases local authors, operates its own publishing house, and hosts frequent poetry and fiction events.
- **Dog Eared Books**, 900 Valencia St, 415-282-1901, offers a great collection of used fiction—from the classics to recent works.
- **Get Lost Books**, 1825 Market St, 415-437-0529, www.getlostbooks.com, offers travel-related books, maps, and gear.
- **Green Apple Books and Music**, 506 Clement St, and annex at 520 Clement St, 415-387-2272, www.greenapplebooks.com, offers a huge selection of used books, a wide fiction selection including small presses, a large magazine collection, and used CDs, DVDs, and videos.
- **Kepler's Books**, 1010 El Camino Real, Menlo Park, 650-324-4321, www.keplers.com; boasts an expansive collection of fiction and nonfiction, special children's section, and frequent author events, highly knowledgeable staff; stays open late and is next door to an outdoor café.
- **Marcus Books**, 1712 Fillmore St, 415-346-4222, and 900 Martin Luther King Jr Way, Oakland, 510-652-2344, specializes in African American, African, and Caribbean literature.
- **Moe's Books**, 2476 Telegraph Ave, Berkeley, 510-849-2087, www.moesbooks.com, an East Bay favorite, Moe's features an excellent, huge collection of used fiction and nonfiction.

- **Modern Times**, 888 Valencia St, 415-282-9246, www.mtbs.com, hosts frequent author events and a large leftist politics section, occasionally has music events too.
- **Nolo Press Outlet Bookstore**, 950 Parker St, Berkeley, 510-549-1976, www.nolo.com, publishes a variety of easy-to-read legal guides.
- **San Francisco Mystery Book Store**, 4175 24th St, 415-282-7444, offers mystery and detective books as well as out-of-print pulp fiction.
- **William Stout**, 804 Montgomery St, 415-391-6757, stoutbooks.com, specializes in books on architecture and design.

BOOKSTORE CHAINS

These days there are pretty much two main players that dominate the big league bookstore game all across the country, Borders and Barnes & Noble. A few discount-style bookshop chains remain in local shopping malls. The Bay Area is also home to a handful of West Coast chains.

- **Barnes & Noble**, 2550 Taylor St, San Francisco, 415-292-6762; 11 W Hillsdale Blvd, San Mateo, 650-341-5560; 3600 Stevens Creek Blvd, San Jose, 408-984-3495; www.barnesandnoble.com
- **Books Inc.**, Stanford Shopping Center, Palo Alto, 650-321-0600; 3515 California St, San Francisco, 415-221-3666, various other locations throughout the area, www.booksinc.net, specializes in discounted books. They have a good cookbook section. They also have a spot at SFO if you need to pick up something to read on the airplane.
- **Borders Books Music Movies & Café**, 15 Ranch Dr, Milpitas, 408-934-1180; 400 Post St, San Francisco, 415-399-1633; 5903 Shellmound, Emeryville, 510-654-1633; 588 W Francisco Blvd, San Rafael, 415-454-1400, www.bordersstores.com; have their own coffee shops inside where you can read, flip through magazines, or study.

RESOURCES

In addition to libraries and bookstores, San Francisco has a collection of active literary groups, creative collectives, nonprofits, and publications that host regular events. A great source of information is the *Literary Supplement*, a special pull-out section published quarterly in the *San Francisco Bay Guardian*.

- **826 Valencia**, 826 Valencia St, 415-642-5905, www.826valencia.org; Dave Eggers' strange pirate booty shop in the front/writing center in the back offers free youth writing classes and occasional adult workshops and events, and is also home to *McSweeney's*, an excellent literary quarterly.
- **The Alternative Press Expo (APE)**, www.comic-con.org/ape, held every spring at the Concourse Exhibition Center in San Francisco, showcases independent authors, publishers, and comic artists from all over.

- **Berkeley Poetry Slam**, 510-841-2082, www.daniland.com/slam; this popular open mike night showcases up-and-coming poets and spoken word artists and regularly draws crowds from throughout the Bay Area. Held every Wednesday at the Starry Plough, 3101 Shattuck Ave, Berkeley. Sign-up to read at 7:30 p.m.; show starts at 8:30 p.m.
- **City Arts and Lectures**, 415-392-4400, www.cityarts.net, brings big-wig talents and off-beat cult favorites to town for packed lectures, usually at the Herbst Theater.
- **The Commonwealth Club**, 595 Market St, 415-597-6700, www.commonwealthclub.org, hosts a range of impressive guests from political heavyweights to cultural icons to literary giants; membership and single-ticket options available.
- **Friends of the San Francisco Public Library**, offers a way to get involved with your local library and operates two book bays with excellent deals: 391 Grove St, San Francisco, 415-626-7500; www.friendssfpl.org.
- **The Grotto**, www.sfgrotto.org, writers' collective space whose members frequently offer workshops and seminars at various locations, including a multimedia series in conjunction with the SF Public Library.
- Every year, **Litquake**, www.litquake.org, a week-long extravaganza of fiction and nonfiction, celebrates local literary life with readings by some of the Bay Area's best-known authors.
- **Porchlight**, 415-571-0998, www.porchlightsf.com, a storytelling series hosted by local authors Beth Lisick and Arline Klatte, presents stories on specific themes at 7 p.m. on every third Monday of the month at Café Du Nord, 2170 Market St. Recent themes have included *Pants on Fire: A Show about Lies* and *More, More, More: Stories of Obsession*.
- **Selected Shorts**, public radio broadcast of actors reading short stories by notable authors, Saturdays at 8 p.m., KQED 88.5 FM.
- **Writers with Drinks**, 415-647-2888, www.writerswithdrinks.com, is a "spoken word variety show" hosted at 7:30 p.m. on the second Saturday of every month by *Other Magazine* at the Make Out Room, 3225 22nd St.

SPECIALTY LIBRARIES

The **Main Library** in San Francisco, 100 Larkin Street, puts on a variety of excellent programs throughout the year from author readings, to poetry workshops for teens, to noontime film screenings—and they're all free. Call them at 415-557-4400 or visit www.sfpl.org to find out about current events. Local branch libraries are also a great resource; check the neighborhoods sections for more details and contact information. Home to two top-tier universities, Stanford and the University of California at Berkeley, and a cutting-edge scientific research facility at UCSF, the Bay Area offers a wide array of specialty libraries and research centers. Below are just a few. All libraries are located in San Francisco unless otherwise noted.

- **Alliance Française**, 1345 Bush St, 415-775-7755, www.afsf.com, maintains a large library of French books, videos, CDs, and magazines, as well as works in French with accompanying English translations. Alliance also offers a variety of French language classes and programs. Library open to all, but borrowing privileges are reserved for members and students enrolled in classes.
- **Bureau of Jewish Education**, 639 14th Ave, 415-751-6983; www.bjesf.org
- **The Foundation Center and Library,** 312 Sutter St, in the World Affairs Council Building, Ste 606, 415-397-0902, http://foundationcenter.org/sanfrancisco; for nonprofits, artists, students, and scholars, this is the place to go for information about grants and special funding opportunities. Anyone can use the library—which is full of stacks and stacks of helpful resource materials—and the staff is extremely knowledgeable. The online database is available on a first-come, first-served basis, and there are also frequent specialized workshops.
- **Holocaust Center of Northern California**, 121 Steuart St, Suite 10, 415-777-9060; www.hcnc.org
- **Hoover Institution Library and Archives**, Hoover Tower at Stanford University in Palo Alto, 650-723-1754, www.hoover.org, offers a mind-boggling collection of first-hand historical accounts recording major political, social, and economic transformations, with more than 1.6 million volumes, 60 million archive documents, and 100,000 original political posters. The institute is free and open to the public, but borrowing privileges are reserved for Stanford students, faculty, and research affiliates. The reading tower is worth a trip in itself for the spectacular views of the Peninsula.
- **Japanese American National Library**, 1619 Sutter St, 415-567-5006, *www.janlibrary.org*
- **The Law Library** houses a wealth of legal documents and information on various aspects of federal and state law. Access is free to the public, but borrowing privileges are reserved for members of the state bar in good standing and practicing law in the City and County of San Francisco; judges of courts within the City and County of San Francisco; and municipal, state, and federal officers. If you meet these requirements, you may qualify for a library card. There are three locations:
  - **Veterans War Memorial Building**, 401 Van Ness Ave, Room 400, 415-554-6821, www.sfgov.org/site/sfll_index.asp (main location)
  - **Monadnock Building**, 685 Market St, Se 420, 415-882-9310 (special emphasis on business law)
  - **Courthouse Reference Room**, Courthouse, 400 McAllister St, Room 512, 415-551-3647 (quick answers to last-minute court preparations)
- **Performing Arts Library and Museum**, 401 Van Ness Ave, fourth floor, 415-255-4800, www.sfpalm.org, houses books, artwork, photographs, newspaper

clippings, audio recordings, sheet music, video tapes, design plates, and artifacts that chronicle the history of dance, music, theater, and theater design in the San Francisco Bay Area. The museum is home to the archives of many local performing arts organizations. Check the web site for special programs, presentations, and events.

THE BAY AREA IS ONE OF THE BEST URBAN PLAYGROUNDS IN THE WORLD. With its ocean beaches, wide-open greenspaces, nearby mountain ranges, and all the activities that accompany such environs, it may be difficult to decide what to do with your free time. Surfing (with a wet suit) at Ocean Beach is one option, as well as kayaking, windsurfing, or rowing—though probably not in the ocean. Biking, hiking, and running in Golden Gate Park, the Presidio, or Mount Tamalpais are popular choices; bird watching at the Palo Alto Baylands is fabulous; and these are only a few of the opportunities available. However, if all you really want to do on your day off is kick back and be a spectator, you are in luck. The Bay Area has plenty of professional and college teams to cheer on.

PROFESSIONAL

Bay Area sports fans are blessed (although some might say cursed) with professional teams in all of the major leagues: baseball, basketball, football, hockey, and soccer. For the latest, consult the sports section of the *San Francisco Chronicle*, *Oakland Tribune*, *Marin Independent Journal*, or the *San Jose Mercury News*, or visit your team's web site.

BASEBALL

One of the Bay Area's most intense sports rivalries exists between the National League **San Francisco Giants** and the American League **Oakland Athletics** (the A's), and passions run high on both sides. Among the most popular matches are the inter-league games where the Giants and the A's face off against each other. The last time the A's and Giants met in the World Series was in 1989, a series disrupted by the October 17th Loma Prieta earthquake that rattled Candlestick

Park. (The game was canceled, and the A's went on to win the series four games to three.)

- **San Francisco Giants** (National League), AT&T Park, 24 Willie Mays Plaza, San Francisco, CA 94107, 415-972-2000, www.sfgiants.com; the big news for the Giants is their gorgeous stadium, a 40,800-seat ballpark in China Basin that was completed in March 2000. For those wanting to attend a game, there are a number of ways to purchase tickets: online at http://sanfrancisco.giants.mlb.com; at the stadium's Double Play Ticket Window; from www.tickets.com, 877-473-4849; or from any Giants Dugout Store—check the Giants' web site for more details. Individual ticket prices for the 2009 season ranged from $14 for bleacher seats all the way up to $110. Season tickets are readily available. For those on a more last-minute schedule, 500 day-of-the-game tickets are available at the stadium two hours before each scheduled home game.
- **Oakland Athletics** (American League), Oakland (Oracle) Coliseum, I-880 and Hegenberger Rd, Oakland, 510-638-4900, http://oakland.athletics.mlp.com. A's fans have a reputation for throwing a good party, and the bleachers—where you can catch the game live for a mere $9—can get rowdy at times, especially during heated night games. If this sounds like a fun night out, you can track down tickets several ways: purchase online at the A's web site (web address above); purchase through www.tickets.com, 877-493-2255; or go to the Oakland Coliseum ticket window. Ticket prices for the 2009 season ranged from $9 for bleacher seats to $55 for a MVP Box seat.

BASKETBALL

The NBA's **Golden State Warriors** play their home games in Oakland's Oracle Arena, just off I-880 in Southern Oakland, from November through June. Tickets can be purchased at the Warrior Ticket Office, 888-479-4667, or at the Oracle Arena on the day of the game. For more information check the Warriors' web site, www.nba.com/warriors.

FOOTBALL

Similar to the baseball rivalry between the A's and the Giants, competition between the **Oakland Raiders** and the **San Francisco 49ers** is fierce. These teams, two of the most successful franchises in the National Football League, rarely play each other because they are in different conferences, but when they do, the air is thick with anticipation and the cheers are passionate and loud.

- The **Raiders** play at Oakland (Oracle) Coliseum, I-880 and Hegenberger Rd, Oakland, 510-864-5000, www.raiders.com. For tickets, call 800-RAIDERS or purchase them at www.ticketmaster.com.
- The **San Francisco 49ers**, www.sf49ers.com, play at Candlestick Park, which is notoriously cold and windy. For tickets call the 49ers' ticket office, 415-

464-9377, or purchase tickets through Ticketmaster on the web at www.ticketmaster.com.

HOCKEY

The **San Jose Sharks** of the National Hockey League are the ice hockey team for the Bay Area. Pre-season starts in September; the season runs until April. They play in the HP Pavilion (aka San Jose Arena), affectionately known as the "Shark Tank." Tickets for the Sharks are available at the arena ticket office, 408-998-8497, or through Ticketmaster at www.ticketmaster.com. Consult the Sharks' web site, http://sharks.nhl.com, for more information.

HORSE RACING

Pack your mint juleps and don your Kentucky Derby hat—horse racing is not far from San Francisco. Just across the bay you can attend **Golden Gate Fields**, located at 1100 Eastshore Highway, in the City of Albany. Entrance fees range from $4 to $15, depending on the location of your viewing stand. Winter/Spring season runs from December through June. For more information call 510-559-7300 or visit www.goldengatefields.com.

SOCCER

The year 1996 brought professional soccer to the Bay Area for the first time in years, in the form of Major League Soccer's San Jose Clash. At the inaugural match against DC United, the Clash won, 1-0. Today, the renamed **San Jose Earthquakes**, www.sjearthquakes.mlsnet.com, play at Santa Clara University's Buck Shaw stadium. The season runs from April through September. For ticket information call the San Jose Earthquakes' ticket sales office at 408-556-7700. You can also purchase tickets through Ticketmaster on the web at www.ticketmaster.com.

COLLEGE SPORTS

If you'd like to watch the sports stars of tomorrow, check out one of the Bay Area college or university teams. Probably the most closely followed collegiate sports contest in the Bay Area is football's annual Big Game that pits the **University of California Golden Bears** against the **Stanford Cardinal**. It's usually a spirited event, and a consistent sellout, so get your tickets early.

Another popular attraction is the Stanford women's basketball team. Under Coach Tara VanDerveer, the Stanford women have been one of the best teams in the country, and Cardinal fans are hoping that trend continues. **Stanford University** plays basketball at Maples Pavilion and football at Stanford Stadium, both located on the university campus in Palo Alto. For information call 650-723-4591 or check www.gostanford.com. The **University of California**

at Berkeley plays basketball in the Harmon Arena and football at Memorial Stadium, both on the Berkeley campus. For more information call 800-462-3277, or check www.calbears.com.

The following schools also stage sporting events:

- **Cal State East Bay**, 510-885-3000, www20.csueastbay.edu
- **San Francisco State University**, 415-338-2218, www.sfstategators.com
- **San Jose State University**, 877-757-8849, www.sjsuspartans.com
- **St. Mary's College**, 925-631-4392, www.stmarys-ca.edu/athletics
- **Santa Clara University**, 408-554-4063, www.santaclarabroncos.com

PARTICIPANT SPORTS & ACTIVITIES

The Bay Area is a haven for sports enthusiasts. Popular activities include walking, running, biking, hiking, camping, sailing, tennis, baseball, football, soccer, swimming, lifting weights, and aerobics. Crissy Field in the Golden Gate National Recreation Area is home to some of the world's best windsurfing, and Mount Tamalpais and the Marin Headlands have excellent hiking and biking trails. Area **Parks and Recreation Departments** can assist those interested in specific programs:

- **California Department of Parks and Recreation**, P.O. Box 942896, Sacramento, 94296, 916-653-6995, 800-777-0369, www.parks.ca.gov
- **East Bay Regional Park District**, 2950 Peralta Oaks Court, P.O. Box 5381, Oakland, 94605, 888-327-2757, TTY 510-633-0460, www.ebparks.org
- **Marin County Parks**, 3501 Civic Center Dr, Room #260, San Rafael, 94903, 415-499-6387
- **Mid-Peninsula Regional Open Space District**, 330 Distel Circle, Los Altos, 94022, 650-691-1200, www.openspace.org
- **Napa Valley Parks**, 1195 Third St, Room 310, Napa, 94559, 707-259-5933, www.napaoutdoors.org
- **San Francisco Recreation and Parks Department**, 501 Stanyan St, San Francisco, 94117, 415-831-2700, www.parks.sfgov.org
- **San Mateo County Park and Recreation Department**, 455 County Center, 4th Floor, Redwood City, 650-363-4020, www.eparks.net
- **Santa Clara County Park and Recreation**, 298 Garden Hill Dr, Los Gatos, CA 95032, 408-355-2200, www.parkhere.org
- **Solano County Parks**, 707-784-7514, www.co.solano.ca.us
- **Sonoma County Regional Parks**, 2300 County Center Dr, 120A, Santa Rosa, 707-565-2041, www.sonoma-county.org/parks

Parks and recreation departments for specific cities are listed below:

- **Alameda Recreation and Parks**, 1327 Oak St, 510-747-7529, TTY 510-522-7538, www.ci.alameda.ca.us/arpd

- **Berkeley Parks Recreation and Waterfront Department**, 2180 Milvia St, Third Floor, 510-981-6700, TTY 510-981-6903
- **Cupertino Parks and Recreation Department (and Quinlan Community Center)**, 10185 N Stelling Rd, 408-777-3120
- **Daly City Parks and Recreation Department**, 111 Lake Merced Blvd, 650-991-8001
- **Emeryville Recreation Department**, 4300 San Pablo Ave, 510-596-4395
- **Foster City Parks**, 650 Shell Blvd, Foster City, 650-286-3380
- **Fremont Recreation Services**, 3300 Capitol Ave, Building B, 510-494-4300
- **Hayward Area Recreation and Park District**, 1099 E St, 510-881-6700, www. haywardrec.org
- **Menlo Park Community Services Department**, 701 Laurel St, 650-330-2200
- **Mill Valley Parks and Recreation Commission**, 26 Corte Madera Ave, 415-383-1370
- **Milpitas Recreation Service Department**, 457 E Calaveras Blvd, 408-586-3210
- **Mountain View Community Services Department**, Recreation Division, 201 South Rengstorff Ave, 650-903-6331
- **Newark Recreation and Community Services**, 37101 Newark Blvd, 510-578-4000
- **Novato Community Services**, 75 Rowland Way, #200, 415-899-8200, www. cityofnovato.org
- **Oakland Parks and Recreation**, 250 Frank Ogawa Plaza, Suite 3330, 510-238-PARK, TTY 510-615-5883
- **Pacifica Parks**, Beaches and Recreation Department, 650-738-7381
- **Palo Alto Parks and Golf Division**, 3201 East Bayshore Rd, 650-496-6962
- **Piedmont Recreation Department**, 358 Hillside Ave, 510-420-3070
- **Redwood City Recreation**, 1400 Roosevelt Ave, Redwood City, 650-780-7250
- **Richmond Recreation & Parks Department**, 3230 Macdonald Ave, 510-620-6793
- **San Bruno Recreation Services Department**, 251 City Park Way, 650-616-7180
- **San Jose Parks Recreation and Neighborhood Services**, 200 E Santa Clara St, 408-535-3570, www.sanjoseca.gov/prns
- **San Rafael Parks and Recreation Commission**, 618 B St, 415-485-3333, www.cityofsanrafael.org/parkandrecreation
- **San Ramon Parks and Recreation and Community Center**, 925-973-3200 or visit www.ci.san-ramon.ca.us/parks/
- **Santa Rosa Parks and Recreation**, Steele Lane Community Center, 415 Steele Lane, 707-543-3282
- **Sausalito Parks and Recreation Department**, 420 Litho St, 415-289-4152
- **Sunnyvale Parks and Recreation Department,** 550 E Remington Dr, 408-730-7350
- **Greater Vallejo Recreation District**, 395 Amador St, 707-648-4600, www. gvrd.org

BASEBALL/SOFTBALL

Play ball! There are a number of softball and baseball leagues around the Bay Area. The **Northern California Amateur Softball Association** sponsors slow and fast pitch adult and junior leagues. For more information, visit their web site at www.norcalasa.org. For **Little League** contact www.littleleague.org, and for **Pony Baseball/Softball** contact www.pony.org.

City parks and recreation departments are another good place to look for baseball and softball games. (See above and also see **Neighborhood** listings.)

BASKETBALL

San Francisco has a **professional/amateur basketball league**, one for men and one for women. Teams play at Kezar Pavilion on Stanyan and Waller streets. Check www.sanfranciscoproam.com for information about dates and times. For something a little less competitive, check with your local parks and recreation department (see above) or try your community gymnasium or health club, which may have its own league. **Dream League,** www.dreamleague.org, runs programs for at-risk teens. **San Francisco Gay Men's Basketball**, www. sfgba.com runs the **Castro Basketball League** at the Upper Noe Recreation Center and open court games at the 6th Street Gym. The **YMCA**, 415-777-9622, www.ymcasf.org, offers organized youth programs and pick-up games for all ages. **Dolores Park**, at 19th Street and Dolores, also almost always has a pick-up game going.

BICYCLING

Numerous biking trails and bike lanes throughout the Bay Area offer a wide variety of terrain and views. One of the most exciting developments in recent years was the installation of a biking/walking trail ringing the entire bay. While only portions of the Bay Trail have been built to date, supporters insist it will eventually be completed, and will be a definite boon to cyclists.

According to California law, bike riders younger than 18 must wear a bike helmet. Violators are subject to fines.

If pro-bicycle activism interests you, consider joining the local Critical Mass campaign. Since 1992, this bicyclists' movement (they adamantly call themselves a "movement" and not a "group") has taken to the streets on the last Friday of every month. Literally hundreds (sometimes thousands) gather at Justin Herman Plaza and then bicycle, en masse, through the city streets. Their goal is to make their presence known, in the hope that drivers will be more courteous and city leaders will be inspired to make the streets safer for cyclists. This monthly "movement" usually has a police escort to protect them from irate drivers who resent being held up by the group.

Some of the best biking in **San Francisco** is in Golden Gate Park, along the Embarcadero and the Golden Gate Promenade beneath the south end of the Golden Gate Bridge. The stretch runs from the Marina all the way to Fort Point. For more information about trails in San Francisco, bicycle groups, and resources, contact the **San Francisco Bicycle Coalition**, 995 Market Street, Suite 1150, 94103, 415-431-BIKE, www.sfbike.org.

The South Bay and the Peninsula have more than 440 miles of biking trails. On the **Peninsula**, the Long Ridge Open Space Preserve provides lovely views, great oaks, grassy knolls, and some of the best single track riding in the area. The trail parallels Skyline Blvd between Page Mill Road and Highway 9. Another great ride is along Montebello Road just off Stevens Canyon Road in **Cupertino**. Here, you'll find creeks, steep hills, and the Ridge Winery. Upper Stevens Creek County Park is another spectacular ride with steep canyons amidst hardwood forests. For more information about biking in the mid-Peninsula, contact the **Silicon Valley Bicycle Coalition** at 408-806-8582, http://bikesiliconvalley.org. Another good resource for maps and hooking up with other bikers is through the **Trail Center**, www.trailcenter.org.

Taking your bike across to the biking trails in the **East Bay** and **Marin County** is a fairly easy task as the BART system accommodates bicycles in the last train car, during non-commute hours. Some bus systems also accommodate bikes, as do the many ferryboats that crisscross the bay. Marin Headlands and Mount Tamalpais are fantastic areas to ride. For more information call the **Bicycle Trails Council of Marin**, www.btcmarin.org. In the East Bay check with **The Bicycle Trail Council for the East Bay**, 510-466-5123, www.btceb.org. For some exceptional trails try Tilden Park (see under **Hiking**), Redwood Regional Park, Wildcat Canyon, and Briones Park.

There are many bicycle shops in the Bay Area; consult your Yellow Pages for local listings.

BOWLING

Some might argue that it's not quite a sport, but few would argue that it's a lot of fun. Since the much-bemoaned closure of the famous Japantown Bowl, the city has been left with just two bowling spots. But, you can find more opportunities in the rest of the Bay Area:

- **The Rooftop at Yerba Buena Center Gardens Ice Skating and Bowling Center**, 750 Folsom St, San Francisco, Skating Center, 415-820-3541; www.skatebowl.com
- **Presidio National Park Bowl**, Building #93 (between the Presidio's Moraga and Montgomery streets), San Francisco, 415-561-2695, www.presidiobowl.com
- **Albany Bowl**, 540 San Pablo Ave, Albany, 510-526-8818, www.albanybowl.biz
- **Southshore Lanes**, 300 Park St, Alameda, 510-523-6767

- **Bel Mateo Bowl**, 4332 Olympic Ave, San Mateo, 650-341-2616
- **Fourth St Bowl**, 1441 N Fourth St, San Jose, 408-453-5555
- **Redwood Lanes**, 2580 El Camino Real, Redwood City, 650-369-5584
- **Moonlite Lanes**, 2780 El Camino Real, Santa Clara, 408-296-7200
- **Palo Alto Bowl**, 4329 El Camino Real, Palo Alto, 650-948-1031
- **Serra Bowl**, 3301 Junipero Serra Blvd, Daly City, 650-992-3444
- **Sea Bowl**, 4625 Coast Highway, Pacifica, 650-738-8190, www.seabowl.com

CHESS

Throughout the day you can see groups eagerly gathering around a small line of checkered tables on **Market Street** near the corner of 5th Street. If you're looking for a good pick-up match, this is the place; all levels are welcome. Tables are usually set up by 2 p.m. and taken down at dusk. It generally costs 50 cents to join a game, and often players agree to bet $1 per match. Another outdoor spot with more atmosphere hasn't quite caught on yet, but if you don't mind bringing your own pieces and your own opponent, you can play at one of the stone tables with built-in game boards at **Yerba Buena Gardens**. The tables are located on the southwest side of the gardens, near the pedestrian bridge to the Zeum, and there's no place better to be on a sunny afternoon.

In the North Bay, the **Depot in Mill Valley** has permanent chess tables set up throughout the square. Donated by famed local music promoter Bill Graham, these tables are busy with pick-up games of both casual and speed chess from afternoon until evening; occasionally a pro even stops by.

A good first stop for chess-loving newcomers is **The Northern California Chess Association**, P.O. Box 136, Berkeley, CA 94701, www.calchess.org. Cal Chess maintains lists of active local clubs, events, and tournaments. Below are a few club contacts to get you started. For more information also try the **US Chess Federation**, www.uschess.org.

- **Fremont Chess Club**, meets Fridays at 8 p.m. at 3375 Country Dr, Fremont, www.fremontchessclub.org
- **Kolty Chess Club**, meets Thursday evenings at the Campbell Community Center, Campbell, 408-866-6686, www.fofv.org
- **The Mechanics' Institute Chess Club**, 57 Post St, San Francisco, 415-421-2258, www.chessclub.org; daily drop-in games, Tuesday night marathons, programs for children
- **San Mateo-Burlingame Chess Club**, meets Thursdays at 7 p.m. at the Burlingame Lions Club, 990 Burlingame Ave, Burlingame, new players welcome, 650-591-8857, www.BurlingameChessClub.com

If you're interested in chess lessons try one of the following or look under "Chess Instruction" in the Yellow Pages:

- **Academic Chess**, 888-442-4377, www.academicchess.com; classroom and after-school programs

- **The Berkeley Chess School**, P.O. Box 10073, Berkeley, 94707, 510-843-0150, www.berkeleychessschool.org; teaches chess in Bay Area schools, runs summer chess camps, and offers Friday night chess games
- **Know Chess**, 4019 Rector Common, Fremont, 510-770-1300, www.knowchess. com; programs throughout Bay Area schools for children

FENCING

Those interested in the fine art of the foil may want to contact the **Northern California Division of the United States Fencing Association**, www.norcalfence.org, which keeps a list of local fencing teachers, as well as information on competitions. **The Bay Cup**, www.thebaycup.org, sponsors Bay Area fencing competitions for youth and adults at various skill levels, and maintains a list of active clubs in the area and information on fencing summer camps. Another good source of information is www. fencing.net, a national web site that offers information on technique, tournaments, and equipment, and also hosts discussion forums. Below are a few local clubs and instruction centers; many colleges and universities have competitive fencing teams, and a few park and recreation departments also offer classes. Contact your local park and recreation department to find out about offerings in your neighborhood.

SAN FRANCISCO
- **Golden Gate Fencing Center**, 2417 Harrison St, 415-626-7910, www. gofencing.com
- **Halberstadt Fencers' Club**, 621 S Van Ness Ave, 415-863-3838, www.halberstadtfc.com
- **Massialas Foundation at Halberstadt**, www.fencingUSA.com
- **Coastside Fencing Club**, 3201 Balboa St, 415-518-8869, www.coastsidefencers. com

PENINSULA AND SOUTH BAY
- **Accademia di Scherma Classica**, 14 Bancroft Rd, Burlingame, 650-401-3838, www.scherma.org
- **California Fencing Academy**, 5289F Prospect Rd, San Jose, 408-865-1950, www.calfencingacademy.com
- **Cardinal Fencing** (Stanford Fencing Club), 341 Galvez St, Stanford, 650-925-3601, www.cardinalfencingclub.com
- **Elite Musketeers Fencers Club**, 160-B Constitution Dr, Menlo Park, 650-353-0717, www.emfc.net
- **The Fencing Center**, 110 Stockton Ave, San Jose, 408-298-8230, www. fencing.com
- **First Place Fencing Club**, 835-B E San Carlos Rd, San Carlos, 650-592-1619, www.firstplacefencing.com

EAST BAY

- **East Bay Fencers' Gym**, 1429 Martin Luther King Jr Way, Oakland, 510-451-2291, www.eastbayfencers.com
- **Fremont Fencers**, 3355 Country Dr, Fremont, and Centerville Community Center, Fremont, 510-791-4324, www.fremontfencers.com
- **Las Positas Fencing Center**, Physical Education Complex at Las Positas College, Livermore, contact Coach Stephen at murraylpfc@yahoo.com for more information, www.laspositasfencingcenter.com
- **Pacific Fencing Club**, 2329 Santa Clara Ave, Alameda, 510-814-1800, www.pacificfencingclub.com
- **Sport Fencing Center**, 5221 Central Ave #9, Richmond, 510-528-5110, www.sportfencingcenter.com
- **Sword Play Fencing Academy**, 1061 Shary Circle, Suite A-1, Concord, 925-687-9883, www.swordplayfencing.net

NORTH BAY

- **La Spada Nimica**, 309 Todd Way, Mill Valley, 415-388-8939, www.fencing.franklurz.com
- **Marin Fencing Academy**, P.O. Box 518, San Anselmo, CA 94979, 415-458-4271, www.marinfencing.com
- **Sonoma Fencing Academy**, 239 Water St, Petaluma, 707-763-8290, www.sonomafencing.com

FISHING

You'll find a large number of fishing spots across the Bay Area (the following only details a smattering of the fishing opportunities). Check with your local outfitter for more ideas. In San Francisco, people fish for bass, perch, shark, and even crab right off the pier near Crissy Field in the Presidio. The piers near Fisherman's Wharf are also popular fishing spots.

Lake Merced is stocked with trout and catfish, but water quality can vary depending on the time of year. Check the Lake Merced Task Force web site at www.lmtf.org for up-to-date information on the conditions. Lake Anza, north of Berkeley in Tilden Park, is open for fishing throughout the year. Oakland's Lake Temescal, located next to the junction of highways 24 and 13, is stocked periodically with rainbow trout. Other fish in Lake Temescal include largemouth bass, red-eared sunfish, bluegill, and catfish. The pier in Pacifica is also a popular spot as well as a great place to watch the sunset.

For those more interested in fishing on the open ocean, check www.sfsportfishing.com, where the San Francisco Bay Area commercial fishing fleets have pooled charter information onto one page. This web site lists the fleet of boats leaving from the Fisherman's Wharf, Emeryville Marina, Berkeley Marina, Half Moon Bay, Point San Pablo, Sausalito, and San Rafael. The California Department of Fish and Game, 1416 Ninth Street, Sacramento, requires you to obtain a permit/license to fish, but be advised that because of the virtual collapse of the salmon runs along the Pacific Northwest, fishing for these delectable finned friends has been banned for the foreseeable future. Local fisherman, however, are retooling to focus on other species of fish. You can find more information about this, and all things fish and wildlife, at 916-445-0411, www.dfg.ca.gov. Or visit your local bait and tackle store.

If you're planning to take your catch of the day home for dinner, you should be aware that because of higher mercury levels, PCBs, and other chemicals found in the San Francisco Bay, public health officials advise adults to eat a maximum of two servings per month of fish caught in Bay waters. Striped bass over 35 inches long—as well as croakers, surfperches, bullheads, gobies, and shellfish from the Richmond Harbor Channel—should not be eaten at all. Pregnant women, nursing mothers, and children should not eat more than one serving of SF Bay fish per month. They should avoid entirely striped bass over 27 inches and shark. These advisory guidelines do not apply to salmon, anchovies, herring, and smelt from the Bay; other fish caught in the delta or ocean; or commercial fish. For more information check out www.dfg.ca.gov.

ULTIMATE FRISBEE AND DISC GOLF

Contact the local **Ultimate Players Association**, 800-872-4384, www.upa.org, for more information.

For disc golfers, San Francisco has a new 18-hole course in **Golden Gate Park**, at Marx Meadow between 25th and 30th avenues on the north side of the park off of Fulton Street. For more information check out the **San Francisco Disc Golf Club**, www.sfdiscgolf.org, which also lists courses throughout the Bay Area.

GOLFING

The Bay Area is home to a fantastic array of golf courses. San Francisco offers a Resident Golf Card, good for booking advance tee times and local course discounts. The card costs $45 and is valid for one year. Contact Parks and Recreation for more information, 415-831-2700.

SAN FRANCISCO

- **Gleneagles**, 2100 Sunnydale Ave, 415-587-2425, 9-hole course in McLaren Park.
- **Golden Gate Park Golf Course**, 47th Ave and Fulton St, Golden Gate Park, 415-751-8987; 9-hole course, a good spot for beginning golfers.
- **Harding Park**, 1 Harding Rd, 415-664-4690, www.harding-park.com; undoubtedly the most popular public course in San Francisco, and host to

a variety of competitions; situated near the beach at Lake Merced, 18-hole tournament course and 9-hole practice course.

- **Lincoln Park Golf Course**, 34th Ave and Clement St, 415-221-9911, www.lincolnparkgc.com; a local favorite, this 18-hole course offers sweeping scenic views of the Golden Gate Bridge; make a day of it, walk the nearby Lands End trail after your game, and stop to take in the latest exhibit at the Palace of the Legion of Honor Museum.
- **Presidio Golf Club**, 300 Finley Rd (in the Presidio), 415-561-4661, www.presidiogolf.com; not just for high-ranking military officers anymore, this 18-hole course set in the lush Presidio National Park is now open to the public.

NORTH BAY
- **Indian Valley Golf Club**, 3035 Novato Blvd, Novato, 415-897-1118, www.ivgc.com, 18 holes, instruction, bar and grill.
- **Mare Island Golf Course**, 1800 Club Dr, Vallejo, 707-562-4653, www.mareislandgolfclub.com, recently expanded into a full 18-hole facility.
- **McInnis Park Golf Center**, 350 Smith Range Rd, San Rafael, 415-492-1800, www.mcinnisparkgolfcenter.com, 9 holes, golf academy, driving range, miniature golf course, batting cages, restaurant.
- **Mill Valley Golf Course**, 280 Buena Vista Ave, Mill Valley, 415-388-9982, 9 holes.
- **Napa Municipal Golf Course at Kennedy Park**, 2295 Streblow Dr, Napa, 707-255-4333, www.playnapa.com, 18 holes.
- **Peacock Gap Golf & Country Club**, 333 Biscayne Dr, San Rafael, 415-453-4940, www.peacockgapgolf.com, 18 holes, two putting greens, driving range, instruction, restaurant and bar.
- **San Geronimo Golf Course**, 5800 Sir Francis Drake Blvd, San Geronimo, 415-488-4030, 18 holes.
- **Stone Tree**, 9 StoneTree Lane, Novato, 415-209-6090, www.stonetreegolf.com, new 18-hole championship course.

EAST BAY
- **Chuck Corica Golf Course**, 1 Clubhouse Memorial Rd, Alameda, 510-747-7800, two 18-hole courses, par 3 executive course, putting greens, restaurant, lighted driving range.
- **Lake Chabot Golf Course**, 11450 Golf Links Rd, Oakland, 510-351-5812, 27 holes, panoramic views.
- **Metropolitan Golf Links**, 10051 Doolittle Dr, Oakland, 510-569-5555; practice your swing at this local driving range.
- **Montclair Golf Course**, 2477 Monterey Blvd, 510-482-0422, 9-hole course.
- **Tilden Park Golf Course**, Grizzly Peak Blvd and Shasta Rd, Berkeley, 510-848-7373, 18 holes.

PENINSULA/SOUTH BAY

- **Blackberry Farm**, 22100 Stevens Creek Blvd, Cupertino, 408-253-9200, www. blackberryfarm.org, 9-hole course.
- **Cinnabar Hills**, 23600 McKean Rd, San Jose, 408-323-7815, www.cinnabarhills.com, 27 holes.
- **Coyote Creek,** 1 Coyote Creek Golf Dr, San Jose, 408-463-1400, www.coyote creekgolf.com, two 18-hole courses.
- **Crystal Springs**, 6650 Golf Course Dr, Burlingame, 650-342-4188, www.play crystalsprings.com, 18-hole championship course, tournaments, restaurant and bar.
- **Deep Cliff Golf Course**, 10700 Clubhouse Lane, Cupertino, 408-253-5357, 18-hole course.
- **Half Moon Bay Golf Links**, 2 Miramontes Point Rd, Half Moon Bay, 650-726-4438, www.halfmoonbaygolf.com, two 18-hole championship courses, ocean views, lessons, restaurant.
- **Mariner's Point**, end of Mariner's Island Blvd, Foster City, 650-573-7888, www.marinerspoint.com, 9 holes, bayside course.
- **Palo Alto Municipal Golf Course**, 1875 Embarcadero, Palo Alto, 650-856-0881 www.paloaltogolfcourse.com, recently renovated 18-hole championship course, lighted driving range, restaurant and bar, putting green area.
- **Poplar Creek**, 1700 Coyote Point Dr, San Mateo, 650-522-4653, www.poplar creekgolf.com, 18 holes, restaurant, junior golfer program.
- **San Jose Municipal Golf Course**, 1560 Oakland Rd, San Jose, 408-441-4653, 18 holes.
- **Santa Clara Golf and Tennis Club**, 5155 Stars & Stripes Dr, Santa Clara, 408-980-9515, 18 holes, restaurant, Santa Clara residents get preferential rates and tee time sign-ups at this municipal course.
- **Sharp Park Golf Course**, foot of Sharp Park Rd off Interstate 280, Pacifica, 650-355-8546 or 650-359-3380, 18 holes.
- **Shoreline Golf Links**, 2600 North Shoreline Blvd, Mountain View, 650-903-4653, 18 holes.

HANG GLIDING/PARAGLIDING

Originated by French mountain climbers eager to descend the mountain before sundown, paragliding is a popular sport in the Bay Area. Venture down to Fort Funston to watch the paragliders and hang gliders soar through the air. Suspended in a harness, hang gliders are attached to large kite-like gliders that help them sail through the air. Increasingly popular is the art of tandem gliding, where two people ride the same glider together. If you've never been before, check out a program or club that can offer you lessons in the basics—launching, turning, and landing. For more information check out the **US Hang Gliding Association's** web site, www.ushpa.aero and www.all-about-hang-gliding.com.

Local clubs include **The Fellow Feathers Fort Funston**, www.flyfunston.org; the **Marin County Hang Gliding Association**, www.mchga.org; and the **Bay Area Paragliding Association**, www.sfbapa.org. There are a number of options for lessons, including the **San Francisco Hang Gliding Center**, 510-528-2300, www.sfhanggliding.com, which offers gliding lessons at Mt. Tamalpais in Marin.

HIKING

If taking off for a hike away from the urban bustle is something that strikes your fancy, you'll have many opportunities to indulge without straying too far from home. San Francisco offers plenty of hikes, including the famous **Golden Gate Bridge walk** (the Bridge is about a mile and a half long). Contact the folks at the Golden Gate Bridge Plaza, San Francisco, 415-921-5858, for more details. Longer hikes can be found at **Presidio National Park** in San Francisco. Along the water, Crissy Field is a popular place for walking and running. A wide paved pathway along the waterfront makes this area accessible to wheelchairs and baby strollers as well. **Marin Headlands**, just beyond the northern end of the Golden Gate Bridge, is nice. An enjoyable option for a long afternoon is to take the ferry to Angel Island to hike the island. **Mount Tamalpais** in Marin County and **Tilden Park** in the Oakland/Berkeley hills are great places to explore. Drive a little further north (about 90 minutes) to the popular **Point Reyes National Seashore** for exceptional hiking and views. See also **Trails** in the **Running** section, later in this chapter.

If you want to escape for more than a day, consider **Yosemite National Park**, located about a four-hour's drive to the east, in the Sierra Nevada Mountains. Yosemite is a popular vacation destination for Bay Area residents, many of whom visit in the fall or early spring to avoid the summer tourist season. Despite what you may have heard about the crowds in the park, though, the only consistently crowded part is Yosemite Valley; if you set out on foot for the high country, you can leave the motor homes behind. For more park information contact **Yosemite National Park**, Wilderness Permits, P.O. Box 577, Yosemite, CA 95389, 209-372-0200. **Lake Tahoe** and the **Sierras**, which offer prime hiking and camping, are also about four hours away. Consult with the **Forest Service** for the best hikes: US Forest Service, 1323 Club Dr, Vallejo, 94592, 707-562-8737, TTY 707-562-9240, www.fs.fed.us/r5

HORSEBACK RIDING

Public trails and riding areas abound on the coast in and around Half Moon Bay, as well as in the wooded hills of Woodside, Portola Valley, and in Marin County. The East Bay regional parks (see details below) offer a variety of boarding and trail options, and on the peninsula **Huddart Park** in Woodside is a popular riding spot. And whether you're an expert or beginner, you can saddle up at one of the popular stables in Half Moon Bay that offer guided rides along the water's edge. In the North Bay, the **National Golden Gate Recreation Area** offers a range of spectacular horse-friendly coastal trails, and **Miwok Stables** in Tennessee Valley, 415-383-8048, runs guided rides in the park.

In the East Bay, you can rent a horse for a trail ride at **Las Trampas Stables**, **Little Hills Regional Recreation Area**, **Las Trampas Regional Wilderness**, in Danville, 925-838-7546, and trails are available for horses at **Tilden Regional Park**, Berkeley. There are also stables in a handful of East Bay regional parks including the **Chabot Stables and Skyline Equestrian Center**, in Anthony Chabot Regional Park, Skyline Boulevard and Keller Avenue; call East Bay Parks at 888-327-2757 for more information. For further information on places to take guided rides, rent horses for the day, or take lessons, see "Horse Rentals" and "Horse Stables" in your local Yellow Pages or online.

KAYAKING

Sea kayaking is another way to enjoy the Bay. It's best to kayak early in the morning when the water is more likely to be calm. The semi-secluded, relatively calm waters of Tomales Bay, in Marin County, are protected from the pounding waves of the Pacific and the winds of nearby Inverness, making this one of the most popular spots in the Bay Area for this sport. Contact **Tomales Bay State Park**, 415-669-1140.

- **Blue Waters Kayaking**, Point Reyes National Seashore, Inverness, 415-669-2600, www.bwkayak.com
- **California Adventures**, 2301 Bancroft Way, Berkeley, 510-642-4000
- **California Canoe & Kayak**, 409 Water St, Oakland, 510-893-7833, www.calkayak.com
- **Environmental Traveling Companions**, Fort Mason Center, Building C, 415-474-7662, www.etctrips.org
- **Sea Trek Ocean Kayaking Center**, Schoonmaker Point Marina, Sausalito, 415-488-1000, www.seatrek.com

RUNNING

Running clubs are a great way to get in shape, enjoy the outdoors, and make new friends in a new city. Many Bay Area clubs welcome walkers as well as those training for marathons, and several sponsor their own events and races. Most have some sort of annual membership fee, in the $20–$30 range, which helps support the club.

- **Golden Gate Running Club**, www.goldengaterunningclub.org; Sunday runs in the park at 10 a.m., followed by brunch, open to all ability levels, track workout Wednesday night at Kezar Stadium, meeting at the southeast corner of the track at 7 p.m.

- **Hoy's Excelsior Running Club**, www.runexcelsior.org; regular Tuesday and Thursday 6 p.m. track runs at Kezar Stadium, Sunday morning long Golden Gate Park and Bay Area trail runs, competitive teams.
- **Lake Merritt Joggers and Striders**, 510-644-4224, www.lmjs.org; club hosts runs at Lake Merritt in Oakland every fourth Sunday at 9 a.m: 5K, 10K, 15K, and a 5K walk. On the morning of San Francisco's Bay-to-Breakers, the club sponsors an alternative race in the Berkeley Hills—the Tilden Tough Ten, the first race in the renowned Triple Crown Trail Championship.
- **Palo Alto Run Club**, www.parunclub.com; 5- to 7.5-mile runs on the first Sunday of the month, at 8:30 a.m., followed by a pot-luck tailgate brunch; Wednesday runs 6:15 p.m. leave from the Lucie Stern Community Center, 1305 Middlefield Rd, in Palo Alto.
- **Pamakid Runners Club**, 415-333-4780, www.pamakids.org; weekly fun runs, racing teams practice at Kezar Stadium on Thursdays at 6:30 p.m.
- **San Francisco Dolphin South End Runners**, 415-978-0837, www.dserunners.com; open to all levels and encourages women runners, older runners, beginners, and kids. Walkers welcome. The DSE holds runs throughout San Francisco almost every Sunday at 9 a.m. and sponsors special challenge events throughout the year.
- **San Francisco FrontRunners**, men's contact, 415-821-7988, women's contact, 415-587-6256, www.sffrontrunners.com; club for the LGBT community and friends, regular Tuesday evening run starting at the Ferry Building and along the Embarcadero and then dinner, and Saturday morning run and then brunch—beginning at Stow Lake in Golden Gate Park, open to walkers.
- **San Francisco Road Runners Club**, 415-273-5731, www.sfrrc.org; Saturday 7:45 a.m. runs at Marina Green divided into pace groups, training programs for beginners and marathon and half-marathon runners, Tuesday and Thursday track runs at Kezar Stadium at 6:30 p.m., distance runs throughout San Francisco and Marin County.
- **Stevens Creek Striders**, www.stevenscreekstriders.org; runs every Saturday at 8:30 a.m. in Stevens Creek County Park, followed by breakfast. From April through late October a group also runs at Rancho San Antonio County Park & Open Space Preserve in Cupertino on Tuesdays and Thursdays at 6 p.m.
- **Tamalpa Runners' Association**, www.tamalparunners.org; holds regular runs on Mt. Tamalpais; racing teams for road, cross country, and distance trips; coaching and youth activities; Saturday 9 a.m. 7- to 10-mile fun run on Mt. Tam, Tuesday morning training sessions, Wednesday night 7-mile runs at Blackie's Pasture in Tiburon.

RACES

- **Bay to Breakers**, 415-359-2800, www.baytobreakers.com; San Francisco's moveable Mardi Gras includes as many (or more) costumed revelers as serious racers and begins with a massive hail of tortilla throwing, from the Embarcadero up the Hayes Street Hill through Golden Gate Park, 12K, May

- **Bridge to Bridge**, 12K (shorter 7K route) run from the Bay Bridge to the Golden Gate, October
- **Escape from Alcatraz**, www.tricalifornia.com; Triathlon—world-class 1.5-mile swim from Alcatraz Island in the San Francisco Bay, 18-mile bike ride out the Great Highway, through the Golden Gate Park, concluding with an 8-mile run through the Golden Gate National Recreation Area, finishing at the Marina Green, June
- **San Francisco Marathon**, 888-958-6668, www.runsfm.com; also shorter half-marathon and 5K run/walk option, July

TRAILS

With its fantastic weather and stunning landscape, the Bay Area has a host of amazing trails, including those listed below:

SAN FRANCISCO
- **The Coastal Trail**: Runs from the Golden Gate Bridge just over 9 miles south through China Beach, Land's End, and the Cliff House, Lake Merced, and Fort Funston.
- **The Embarcadero**: This long concrete, palm-lined promenade stretches along the Bay from the Ferry Building to Fisherman's Wharf for about 2 miles.
- **Golden Gate Park**: The city's main park has a number of trails of varying length, both paved and dirt. A 7.4-mile perimeter loop goes around the entire park; a 2-mile loop circles around Stow Lake and goes up Strawberry Hill.
- **Golden Gate Promenade**: This 3.5-mile multi-use path at Crissy Field is extremely popular with joggers, walkers, bicyclists, and dog walkers; the paved path starts a little past the Yacht Harbor and ends near the Fort Point Coast Guard Station. This run offers fantastic views of the Bay and the Golden Gate Bridge. If you're feeling really ambitious, you can even run across the bridge—but be warned, it's usually quite windy!
- **Lake Merced**: Check out the 4.5-mile paved and dirt loop alongside the water at Lake Merced Boulevard and Skyline.
- **Ocean Beach**: You can run on the sand or along the esplanade. The run alongside the beach is pretty flat and you can make it a few blocks or a few miles—depending on your endurance; head up toward the Cliff House for great views and a steeper workout.

For more information on San Francisco trails, contact **The Golden Gate National Recreation Area**, 415-561-4700, www.nps.gov/goga, or the **San Francisco Recreation and Park Department,** 415-831-2700, www.parks.sfgov.org

PENINSULA AND SOUTH BAY

- **Edgewood Park**: This park has a handful of dirt hillside trails trekking up and downhill amid the dense forested areas and the open grasslands. In the spring, the fields here are blanketed with colorful wildflowers. The trails are also excellent for hikers; see bulletin boards in the park for information on free guided nature walks. Main park entrance is at Edgewood Rd off of I-280 in Redwood City.
- **Huddart Park**: Set in the high hills amid lush redwoods, the park offers a number of trails of varying length and difficulty; park entrance is at the top of Kings Mountain Road in Woodside.
- **Rancho San Antonio Open Space Preserve**: A popular site with runners and hikers, the reserve offers more than 20 miles of scenic, hilly trails; Cristo Rey Dr off of Foothill Expy in Mountain View.
- **San Bruno Mountain**: Twelve miles of trails snaking up and downhill. Summit Trail heads 1,314 feet to the top and boasts the best views; wildflowers and butterflies abound in the spring. Main park entrance is at Guadalupe Canyon Pkwy in Brisbane, $3 fee for cars.
- **Sawyer Camp Trail**: This 12-mile waterside loop is the most popular trail on the peninsula. The path is paved with some dirt areas, and mostly flat. You'll meet lots of fellow runners here, as well as bicyclists, walkers, parents pushing strollers, and rollerbladers. The scenic trail winds around the blue waters of Crystal Springs Reservoir, and mile markers are posted along the way to help you keep track. The main entrance is at Skyline Blvd and Highway 92 in San Mateo.
- **Stanford University**: Lots of paved trails weave through the Palo Alto palm tree–lined campus; routes are popular with bikers and walkers too. For a map check www.stanford.edu.
- **Sweeney Ridge**: Steep and rolling coastal hills with ridges overlooking the peninsula and the Pacific Ocean. There are three trails with about 10 miles of space; the Sweeney Ridge Trail is the easiest. Take Sneath Lane west to Sweeney Ridge or you can access the main trail from Skyline College, just off of parking area 2, San Bruno.

For more information on Peninsula trails, contact the **San Mateo County Park and Recreation Department**, 650-363-4020, www.eparks.net; for more on South Bay trails, contact Santa Clara County Park and Recreation, 408-355-2200, www.parkhere.org.

EAST BAY

- **Coyote Hills Regional Park**: Offering vistas of the Bay, marshlands, hills, and multiple trails, the Alameda Creek Trail is a popular, long, paved, flat 12-mile trail along the south side of the creek from the mouth of Niles Canyon west to the Bay; there's an additional 3.5-mile loop trail making the run west from

Niles Canyon along the trail, through Coyote Hills, and back again a full marathon length. There are markers along the way at quarter-mile intervals; 8000 Patterson Ranch Rd, Fremont.
- **Nimitz Way**: One of the most popular multi-use pathways in the East Bay, this paved 8-mile trail starting at Inspiration Point has terrific views; Wildcat Canyon Rd, Tilden Park, Berkeley.

For more information on East Bay trails, contact the **East Bay Regional Park District,** 510-562-PARK, www.ebparks.org.

NORTH BAY
- **The Dipsea Trail**: This 7.1-mile trail from Mill Valley to Stinson Beach is probably the best known trail in the North Bay. Twisting dirt trails wander amid shady trees, bringing you through Mt. Tamalpais State Park, Muir Woods National Monument, and the Golden Gate Recreational Area. There are a few steep steps to climb at one point along the way—676 to be exact!
- **The Marin Headlands**: There are a number of trails here, including several near Point Bonita Lighthouse and Hawk Hill with spectacular views of San Francisco and the Golden Gate Bridge.
- **Tennessee Valley**: Follow the main trail from to the beach and back, about 4 miles total. Take the Highway 1 exit off of 101, and follow the signs.
- **Wolf Ridge Loop**: This 5.5-mile path starts at Rodeo Beach and climbs almost 900 feet upward before dropping back down to sea level again. Rodeo Beach has strong currents and undertows; swimming here is not recommended.

For more information on Marin County trails, contact the **Golden Gate National Recreation Area**, 415-561-4700, www.nps.gov/goga, or Marin County Parks, 415-499-6387.

ROCK CLIMBING

To keep your finger muscles in shape, the Bay Area has a number of climbing gyms including:
- **Berkeley Ironworks**, 800 Potter St, Berkeley, 510-981-9900
- **Mission Cliffs**, 2295 Harrison St, San Francisco, 415-550-0515, www.touchstoneclimbing.com
- **Planet Granite Rock Climbing**, 924 mission St, San Francisco, 415-692-3434; 100 El Camino Real, Belmont, 650-591-3030; 815 Stewart Dr, Sunnyvale, 408-991-9090; www.planetgranite.com
- **Twisters Gym**, 2639 Terminal Blvd, Mountain View, 650-967-5581
- **Vertex Climbing Center**, 3358a Coffey Lane, Santa Rosa, 707-573-1608, www.climbvertex.com

A number of local parks in Berkeley also have excellent outdoor climbing areas:

- **Contra Costa Rock Park**, 869-A Contra Costa Ave
- **Cragmont Rock Park**, 960 Regal Rd
- **Glendale La Loma Park**, 1339 La Loma Ave
- **Great Stoneface Park**, 1930 Thousand Oaks Blvd
- **Grotto Rock Park**, 879 Santa Barbara Rd
- **Indian Rock Park**, 1950 Indian Rock Ave
- **Mortar Rock Park**, 901 Indian Rock Ave
- **Remillard Park**, 80 Poppy Lane

For more information contact the **Berkeley Parks, Recreation and Waterfront Department**, 2180 Milvia St, Third Floor, 510-981-6700.

SAILING

According to aficionados, the sailing and windsurfing in San Francisco Bay is top-notch. The annual opening day on the Bay brings out hundreds of sailors and spectators each May. Although sailing is possible here year round, this event serves as the ceremonial, if not official, kickoff of the summer sailing season. Throughout the year the Bay is the place for various sailing regattas, from the casual Friday night beer can race to the competitive world championship.

Many of the local yacht clubs have summer sailing programs for children and classes for adults wanting to learn how to sail. For information on sailing schools, check out the nonprofits and clubs below or look in the Yellow Pages under "Sailing Instruction."

SAN FRANCISCO

- **Cal Sailing Club**, nonprofit membership sailing club that offers lessons at the Berkeley Marina, membership is $69 for 3 months or $200 per year, all activities are free to members—lessons, cruises, and use of the club's sailboats and sailboards; visit www.cal-sailing.org to become a member or find out more.
- **Lake Merced, Learn-to-Sail** program for at-risk youth on Lake Merced, offered by America True with the San Francisco Parks and Recreation Department and San Francisco State University; contact America True, Pier 40, San Francisco, 415-974-1018, www.americatrue.org.
- **The Lake Merritt Boating Center** offers beginning, intermediate, and advanced sailing classes, youth programs and summer camp at Lake Merritt. Advanced classes also take to the waters of the San Francisco Bay from the Oakland Estuary. Windsurfing, kayaking, canoeing, and rowing programs are also available at the lake, 568 Bellevue Ave, Oakland, 510-238-2196.
- **Robert W. Crown Memorial Beach**; during summer weekends you can rent sailboards and take lessons at this shoreline gem, located at 8th St and Otis Dr in Alameda; contact the East Bay Regional Park District for more information, 510-562-PARK.

- **Sailing Education Adventures**; this nonprofit offers adult beginning and advanced classes, and youth summer sailing camps; boats are located at the Clipper Yacht Harbor in Sausalito, Building E, Room 235, Fort Mason Center, San Francisco, 415-775-8779, www.sailsea.org.
- **Shoreline Aquatic Center**, 3160 North Shoreline Blvd, Shoreline Park, Mountain View, offers sailing, windsurfing, and kayaking lessons and youth summer sailing camps on a 50-acre manmade salt lake 650-965-7474, www. shorelinelake.com.

SCUBA AND FREE DIVING

Northern California's waters are not warm, so be sure you have a thick wetsuit when you scuba dive in Monterey Bay. If you have strong lungs, try free diving (diving without a tank) for abalone off the northern coast of California by Mendocino. Make sure to get a fishing license if you are catching abalone or any fish. Also familiarize yourself with the rules regarding size and limits. Contact the **Department of Fish and Game** at 916-227-2245, www.dfg.ca.gov, for more information.

- **Any Water Sports**, 1130 Saratoga, San Jose, 408-244-4433, www.anywater. com
- **Cal School of Diving**, 1750 6th St, Berkeley, 510-524-3248, www.caldive.net
- **Diver Dan's**, 2245 El Camino Real, Santa Clara, 408-984-5819
- **Mistix State Park Reservation System**, Point Lobos, Bluefish Cove, Whalers Cove, and Monastery Beach (the latter is for experienced divers only), 800-444-7275, www.reserveamerica.com
- **Monterey Bay Harbormaster**, 831-646-3950
- **Monterey Bay Dive Center**, 225 Cannery Row, Monterey, 831-656-0454, www.mbdcscuba.com

SKATING—ROLLER/IN-LINE/ICE

Every Friday night in-line skaters, sometimes more than 500 at a time, meet at San Francisco's Ferry Building to tour the city on wheels.

Roller-skating, in-line skating (rollerblading), and skateboarding (see below) are all popular activities in San Francisco, especially on weekends in Golden Gate Park. If you don't own your own skates, head for Fulton Street along the northern end of the park in the morning and look for the brightly colored rent-a-skate vans parked there. Alternatively, there are plenty of skate shops that will be more than happy to outfit you in the latest gear.

If you'd rather skate at an ice rink, you're in luck. After years without a regular indoor ice skating rink, San Francisco now offers an NHL-sized (200' by 85') hockey rink at the Yerba Buena Gardens downtown.

SAN FRANCISCO
- **DLX SF Skateboards**, 1831 Market St, 415-626-5588
- **FTC Skate Shop**, 1632 Haight St, 415-626-0663, www.ftcsf.com
- **Golden Gate Park Skate & Bike**, 3038 Fulton St, 415-668-1117
- **Skates on Haight**, 1818 Haight St, 415-752-8375
- **Yerba Buena Center Gardens Ice Skating and Bowling Center**, 750 Folsom St, 415-820-3532

NORTH BAY
- **Adrenaline Zone Sports**, 124 Calistoga Rd, Santa Rosa, 707-538-7538
- **Brotherhood Board Shop**, 1240 Mendocino Ave, Santa Rosa, 707-546-0660
- **Redwood Empire Ice Arena**, 1667 West Steele Lane, Santa Rosa, 707-546-7147, www.snoopyshomeice.com

EAST BAY
- **Golden Skate**, 2701 Hooper Dr, San Ramon, 925-820-2525, www.thegoldenskate.com, roller-skating rink
- **Oakland Ice Center**, 519 18th St, Oakland, 510-268-9000

PENINSULA/SOUTH BAY
- **Belmont Iceland**, 815 Country Rd, Belmont, 650-592-0532
- **Sharks Ice at San Jose (formerly Ice Center of San Jose)**, 1500 S Tenth St, San Jose, 408-279-6000
- **Ice Center of San Mateo**, 2202 Bridgepoint Pkwy, San Mateo 650-574-1616
- **Ice Oasis**, 3140 Bay Rd, Redwood City, 650-364-8090
- **Redwood Roller Rink**, 1303 Main St, Redwood City, 650-369-5558
- **The Winter Lodge**, 3009 Middlefield Rd, Palo Alto, 650-493-4566, www.winterlodge.com

SKATEBOARDING

When the X Games came to San Francisco in 1999, kids of all ages and adults packed the bayside bleachers for a chance to see legends like Tony Hawk take on seemingly impossible vertical feats. These days, that daredevil waterside legacy lives on in the summertime at Pier 7, which, while not a sanctioned spot, is a popular gathering place for skaters. Years after shouting the mantra "skateboarding is not a crime," and tangling with frustrated office building owners over oh-so-sleek and inviting staircases, planters, and benches, skateboarding is finally getting its due, and its own public space. Skateparks are popping up all over the peninsula, offering kids and adults alike a place to flip kick and ollie freely—and legally. Below are a just a few local favorite spots; check with your local park and recreation department to find the spot closest to you, visit www. caliskatz.com or www.sk8parklist.com, or check out *Thrasher*, www.thrasher-magazine.com or *Transworld* magazine, www.skateboarding.com.

Most parks operated by parks require safety gear—helmets, knee and elbow pads; many allow roller blades and a handful also allow BMX bikes, but call ahead to find out. San Francisco has only one official skate park, but the greater Bay Area has stepped up to offer skaters quite a bit more.

SAN FRANCISCO

- **Crocker Amazon Skate Park**, Crocker Amazon Playground, Geneva Ave and Moscow St, 415-831-2700; bowl, ramps, rails, and ledges

EAST BAY

- **Alameda Skatepark**, 1177 W Redline Ave, Alameda Point, Alameda, 510-747-7529; recently revamped with design input from local skateboarders, this 15,000-square-foot park has a bowl, banks, a pyramid, ledges, and excellent views
- **Antioch Skatepark**, 4701 Lone Tree Way, at Prewett Family Park, Antioch, 925-779-7070, www.ci.antioch.ca.us
- **Berkeley Skatepark**, Harrison and Fifth sts, Berkeley, 510-981-6700; 18,000 square feet, double bowl, ramps
- **510 Skateboarding**, 2500 Telegraph Ave, Berkeley, 510-843-1863
- **Kennelly Skatepark**, Moraga Ave off of Pleasant Valley Rd, Piedmont, 510-420-3070; bowl, concrete features
- **Livermore Skatepark**, east end of Pacific Ave, in Sunken Gardens Park, Livermore, 925-373-5700, 11,000 square feet, bowls, fun box, pyramid, rails
- **Pleasanton Skateboard Track**, Sports and Recreation Park, Parkside Dr and Hopyard Rd, Pleasanton, 925-931-5340;10,000-square-feet Skatetrack is located at the front of a 105-acre Sports Park

SOUTH BAY AND PENINSULA

- **Campbell Skatepark**, 1 West Campbell Ave, Campbell, 408-866-2105, www.ci.campbell.ca.us; pyramid, quarter pipe, fun box, rails, half pipe
- **Derby Skatepark**, 508 Woodland Way, Santa Cruz, 831-420-5270; Derby is a classic, one of the first public skateparks in this area with a long concrete snakerun and bowls
- **Greer Skateboard Park**, 1098 Amarillo Ave, in Greer Park, Palo Alto, 650-329-2390; popular three-bowl complex
- **Millbrae YMCA Skatepark**, 451 Millbrae Ave, YMCA, Millbrae, 650-697-6852; $5 entrance fee, at the Peninsula Family YMCA
- **Mountain View Skatepark**, 201 S Rengstorff Ave at Crisanto Ave, northwest corner of Rengstorff Park, Mountain View, 650-903-6331; Sundays the park is reserved exclusively for skaters age 12 and under from 9:30 to 11:30 a.m; ramp, quarter pipe, mini half pipe, fun box, rails

- **Phil Shao Memorial Skatepark**, St. Francis St off of Jefferson St, in Red Morton Park, Redwood City, 650-780-7250; 13,000 square feet, bowl, concrete features
- **Sunnyvale Skatepark**, 540 Fair Oaks Ave, in Fair Oaks Park, Sunnyvale, 408-730-7350; 18,500 square feet, big bowl, vertical and street course elements, local favorite

NORTH BAY
- **Mill Valley Skatepark**, Sycamore Ave, east end of the middle school parking lot, Mill Valley, 415-383-1370
- **Novato Skatepark**, 1200 Hamilton Parkway, at Sport Court Island, Novato, 415-893-1100; 15,000-square-foot park, bowls, walls, curbs, stairs, rails, and ramps
- **Santa Rosa Skatepark**, 1725 Fulton Rd, at Youth Community Park, Santa Rosa, 707-543-3292; pool-style features, concrete half acre, three bowls connected by runs, fun box, curb

SKIING

Sierra Nevada ski resorts are about a four-hour drive east of the Bay Area, along Interstate 80 and Highway 50. If you don't own skiing equipment, several local businesses will rent everything you need to hit the slopes or cross-country ski trails in style, including the national chain **REI** (Recreational Equipment Incorporated), 1338 San Pablo Avenue, Berkeley, 510-527-4140, www.rei.com. Also check **Lombardi Sports**, 1500 Jackson Street, San Francisco, 415-771-0600. For additional outfitters, try the Yellow Pages under "Ski Equipment-Retail" or www.yelp.com.

SKYDIVING

Call one of the listings below for information about lessons, equipment, and getting connected with an instructor for this exhilarating sport:
- **Bay Area Skydiving,** Byron, 925-634-7575, www.bayareaskydiving.com
- **Skydive Monterey Bay**, 888-229-5867, www.skydivemontereybay.com

SOCCER

Soccer is a popular sport in the Bay Area. If you are interested in organized games, contact your local parks and recreation department (see above). The **Palo Alto Adult Soccer League (PAASL)**, for men and women ages 25 and over, has an informative web site about local and international soccer, www.paasl.org. PAASL games generally take place at Jane Lathrop Stanford Middle School (next to Mitchell Park) in Palo Alto. Also included on the PAASL web site is a list of pick-up games in the Bay Area. Many such pick-up games are now so crowded that participation may be limited to the first 20 players to arrive.

Bring both a white and a colored t-shirt. For youth, the **American Youth Soccer Organization (AYSO)** is the main organization with teams throughout the Bay Area, offering boys and girls a chance to play outdoors, 800-872-2976, www. soccer.org.

SWIMMING

For those few days when it actually gets hot enough to swim outdoors in San Francisco, you might want to check out a public pool; visit www.parks.sfgov.org for more information. Hours vary, so the best bet is to call ahead. Below is a list of public pools in San Francisco, unless otherwise noted:

- **Alameda Swim Center**, 2256 Alameda Ave, Alameda, 510-522-8107
- **Angelo Rossi**, Arguello Blvd and Anza St, 415-666-7014
- **Balboa Park**, Ocean and San Jose aves, 415-337-4701
- **Coffman Swimming Pool**, Visitacion and Hahn, 415-337-4702
- **Garfield Pool**, 26th and Harrison sts, 415-695-5001
- **Hamilton Recreation Center**, Geary Blvd and Steiner St, 415-292-2001
- **King Swimming Pool**, Keith and Carroll sts, 415-822-2807
- **Sava Swimming Pool**, 19th Ave and Wawona St, 415-753-7000

Some private clubs have pools, including the **Golden Gateway Tennis and Swim Club (GGTSC)**, 370 Drumm St, 415-616-8800, the **Bay Club** at 1 Lombard St, 415-433-2550, and the **Presidio YMCA** at the Presidio, 415-447-9680.

Outdoors, **Lake Anza**, north of Berkeley, in Tilden Park has a sandy beach that is sheltered from the wind. Lifeguards are posted here during the swim season, April 15 to October 15. Picnic grounds are located nearby. There is an entrance fee to the swim area, which has changing rooms and a refreshment stand. The lake is open for fishing throughout the year.

Originally constructed as a storage lake for drinking water, **Lake Temescal**, next to the junction of highways 24 and 13 in Oakland, was opened to the public in 1936. Temescal is a popular urban oasis, with many coming for swimming, fishing, sunbathing, and picnicking. The swim area is open spring through fall. Lifeguards are on duty during posted periods. A snack stand is nearby, and many facilities are accessible to the disabled. There are picnic areas at both ends of the lake (several of them can be reserved for groups), and eight acres of lawn. For more information about Temescal, call 510-562-PARK.

People actually swim in San Francisco Bay, and some more than once. Many such intrepid souls belong to **The Dolphin Club**, 502 Jefferson St, 415-441-9329 or the **South End Rowing Club**, 500 Jefferson St, 415-776-7372. After a cold dip, you can enjoy the clubs' sauna and shower facilities.

TENNIS AND RACQUET SPORTS

San Francisco alone boasts 140 public tennis courts, most of which operate on a first-come, first-served basis. At the east end of **Golden Gate Park** are 21 courts that may be reserved by calling 415-753-7100. There are also quite a few private clubs in and around San Francisco, including the **Golden Gateway Tennis and Swim Club**, 370 Drumm, 415-616-8800; **The Bay Club**, 1 Lombard St, 415-433-2550; **San Francisco Tennis Club**, 645 5th St, 415-777-9000; and the **California Tennis Club**, 1770 Scott St, 415-346-3611. In addition, the **Presidio YMCA** has access to the numerous courts spread throughout the Presidio. Call 415-447-9622 for details. For more information about public tennis and lessons in San Francisco, call 415-751-5639. For courts outside San Francisco check with your local parks and recreation department (see above).

VIDEO ARCADES

Does Ms. Pac-Man make your heart sing? Are you a sucker for Dance Dance Revolution? Whichever it is, you can get your game on at Bay Area arcades, mini golf lands, and family fun centers. If you're feeling hungry too, pizzerias—most notably the massive kids' party land **Chuck E. Cheese**—are usually a good bet to get your gaming fix.

SAN FRANCISCO
- **Metreon**, a Sony Entertainment Center, 101 4th St, San Francisco, 415-369-6000,http://westfield.com/metreon
- **Pier 39**, San Francisco, www.pier39.com

NORTH BAY
- **Pinky's Pizza Parlor**, 345 3rd St, San Rafael, 415-453-3582
- **Starbase Arcade**, 1545 4th St, San Rafael, 415-459-7655, www.starbasearcade.com

SOUTH BAY AND PENINSULA
- **Capitol Flea Market**, 3630 Hillcap Ave, San Jose, 408-225-5800
- **Great Mall**, 447 Great Mall Dr, Milpitas, 408-956-2033
- **Malibu Castle**, 320 Blomquist St, Redwood City, 650-367-1906, www.malibugrandprix.com
- **Milpitas Golfland**, 1199 Jacklin Rd, 408-263-6855, www.golfland.com/milpitas
- **Nickel City**, 1711 Branham Lane, San Jose, 408-448-3323
- **Santa Cruz Boardwalk**, 400 Beach St, Santa Cruz, 831-423-5590, www.beachboardwalk.com.
- **Town and Country Billiards**, Mission and San Pedro, Daly City, 650-992-7900

EAST BAY
- **Escapade Family Entertainment Center**, in the Public Market, Emeryville, 510-653-3323

VOLLEYBALL

Whether you are a pro looking to join an indoor tournament team or a parent looking to sign your kids up for some outdoor summer fun, the Bay Area offers a variety of options for volleyball lovers. Many local park and recreation departments offer lessons, leagues, and special summer camps. If you're new in town, and looking to join a league, a good place to start is the **Northern California Volleyball Association (NCVA)**, 72 Dorman Ave, San Francisco, 415-550-7582, www.ncva.com. Another good resource is www.volleyball.org/bay_area.
- **City Beach Volleyball**, 4020 Technology Pl, Fremont, 510-651-2500, and 2911 Mead Ave, Santa Clara, 408-654-9330, www.citybeach.com/sports/, sponsors tournaments and runs two game facilities that offer indoor and outdoor volleyball classes.
- **Industrial Volleyball League, Inc.**, 947 Emerald Hill Rd, Redwood City, 650-365-2666, www.ivlinc.com., organizes indoor volleyball competition on the Peninsula and in the South Bay, and runs an open play night for individuals and teams on Fridays from 7 p.m. to 10 p.m. in the large gym at Wilcox High School, 3250 Monroe St, Santa Clara; the fee is $6.
- **Stanford University** runs a popular volleyball clinic for adults in the summer; the cost is $100 per session; for more information or to sign up visit www.gostanford.com/marketplace/events/volleyball-adult-form.html or call 800-782-6367.

WINDSURFING

San Francisco Bay hosts some of the world's best windsurfing. The inexperienced should take instruction before heading out on the Bay, as understanding the ocean's tides and currents is key to staying safe. Check www.iwindsurf.com for updates on wind speed and direction on the Bay. (True windsurfing addicts can even get a pager called "call of the wind," that beeps in with updates on the Bay's wind and tide conditions.) Favorite local spots to ride the wind include **Crissy Field/Golden Gate Bridge**, 415-561-4700, and **Candlestick Point Recreation Area**, 415-671-0145, in San Francisco; **Crown Beach** in Alameda, 510-562-7275; and **Brannan Island State Park** in the Sacramento Delta, 916-777-6671, home of Windy Cove.

Area windsurfing clubs and outfitters include:

SAN FRANCISCO
- **San Francisco Board Sailing Association**, www.sfba.org

- **WOW: Women on Water**, 415-385-1224, www.uswindsurfing.org/WOW/ WOWhome.htm; women's windsurfing club offers lessons at Crown Beach in Alameda

EAST BAY
- **California Adventures**, Berkeley Marina, 510-642-4000
- **California Sailing Club**, Berkeley Marina, www.cal-sailing.org (see **Sailing** for more information)

SOUTH BAY
- **Helm Ski and Windsurf**, 333 N Amphlett Blvd, San Mateo, 877-975-4332
- **Shoreline Aquatic Center**, 3160 N Shoreline Blvd, Mountain View, 650-965-7474, www.shorelinelake.com

THE SACRAMENTO DELTA
- **Delta Windsurf Co.**, 3729 W Sherman Island Rd, Isleton, 916-777-2299

YOGA

Yoga is popular in the Bay Area, and many health clubs offer yoga classes. In addition, several studios are devoted solely to the fine art of bending, stretching, and breathing. Here are a few:

SAN FRANCISCO
- **Funky Door Yoga**, 1336 Polk St at Pine, 415-673-8659 (Bikram); for other San Francisco locations check out www.funkydooryoga.com
- **Integral Yoga**, 770 Dolores, 415-821-1117, www.integralyogasf.org
- **Iyengar Yoga Institute of San Francisco**, 2404 27th Ave, 415-753-0909, www.iyisf.org
- **Mindful Body**, 2876 California St, 415-931-2639, www.themindfulbody.com
- **Yoga Society of San Francisco**, 2872 Folsom St, 415-285-5537, www.yssf.com
- **Yoga Tree**, multiple locations, 415-626-9707, www.yogatreesf.com

NORTH BAY
- **Bikram Yoga San Rafael**, 1295 2nd St, San Rafael, 415-453-9642, www.sanrafaelyoga.com
- **Yoga Center of Marin**, 142 Redwood Ave, Corte Madera, 415-927-1850, www.yogacenterofmarin.com

EAST BAY
- **4th Street Yoga**, 1809C 4th St, Berkeley, 510-845-9642, www.4thstreetyoga.com
- **Funky Door Yoga**, 2567 Shattuck Ave, Berkeley, 510-204-9642 (Bikram), www.funkydooryoga.com
- **Piedmont Yoga Studio**, 3966 Piedmont Ave, Piedmont, 510-652-3336, www.piedmontyoga.com

PENINSULA/SOUTH BAY
- **Willow Glen Yoga**, 1188 Lincoln Ave, San Jose, 408-289-9642, www.willowglenyoga.com
- **Yoga Source**, 158 Hamilton Ave, Palo Alto, 650-328-9642

HEALTH CLUBS, GYMS, YMCAs

The Bay Area has no shortage of health clubs, so whether you're seeking the latest, most up-to-date exercise machine with a pulse-pumping soundtrack or the quietest, most peaceful yoga center, you can find it here.

SAN FRANCISCO
- **Bay Club**, 150 Greenwich St, 415-433-2200, www.sfbayclub.com
- **Club One**, 1 Sansome St, 415-399-1010; 450 Golden Gate Ave, 415-876-1010; 1755 O'Farrell St, 415-749-1010; 535 Mason St, 415-337-1010
- **Crunch**, five locations in San Francisco, 888-227-8624, www.crunch.com
- **Curves**, 2529 Van Ness Ave, 415-771-0445, women only; for other locations in San Francisco and throughout the Bay Area, visit www.curves.com
- **Gold's Gym**, 2301 Market St, 415-626-4488; 1001 Brannan St, 415-552-4653, www.goldsgym.com.
- **Golden Gateway Tennis and Swim Club**, 370 Drumm St, 415-616-8800, www.ggtsc.com
- **24 Hour Fitness**, numerous locations, 800-204-2400
- **Valencia Street Muscle and Fitness Center**, 333 Valencia St, 415-431-9700, www.valenciastmuscle.com
- **YMCA**, 169 Steuart St (Embarcadero), 415-957-9622; Presidio, 415-447-9622; Stonestown, 333 Eucalyptus Dr, 415-242-7100; Chinatown (men only), 855 Sacramento St, 415-576-9622; Central, 220 Golden Gate Ave, 415-885-0460
- **YWCA**, 1830 Sutter St, 415-775-6502

NORTH BAY
- **Gold's Gym**, 10 Fifer Ave, Corte Madera, 415-924-4653, www.goldsgym.com
- **Mill Valley Health Club**, Mill Valley, 415-380-8787
- **Nautilus of Marin**, 3020 Bridgeway, Sausalito, 415-331-3020
- **24 Hour Fitness**, 1001 Larkspur Landing Cir, Larkspur, 415-925-0333

EAST BAY
- **Curves**, 7282 San Ramon Rd, 925-875-1193; 1129 Catalina Dr, 925-960-9199; 1991 Santa Rita Rd, Suite I, Pleasanton, 925-600-9612; women only; www.eastbaycurves.com
- **In Forma**, 23 Orinda Way, #A, Orinda, 925-254-6877, www.informaorinda.com
- **World Dance Center**, 1901 San Pablo, Berkeley, 510-528-1958
- **YMCA**, 2330 Broadway, Oakland, 510-451-8039, www.ymcaeastbay.org

PENINSULA/SOUTH BAY

- **Curves**, 839 Emerson St, Palo Alto, 650-566-1515; women only; for more locations visit www.curves.com
- **Optimum Results,** 2624 Fayette Dr, Mountain View, 650-941-9148
- **Prime Physique Fitness Specialists**, 3635 Union Ave, San Jose, 888-348-8663
- **Right Stuff Health Club-Women**, 1147 S De Anza Blvd, San Jose, 408-973-1088
- **YMCA**, 4151 Middlefield Rd, #211, Palo Alto, 650-856-3955

SPORT AND SOCIAL CLUBS

Sport and social clubs offer organized athletic activities specifically geared towards singles. One part athletic outing, one part date night, they offer an alternative way for singles to meet through shared activities. Ski clubs and hiking groups hosting short getaways are the most popular here. And often good old-fashioned coed leagues offered through your local parks department serve the same purpose. Whether your love is diving, rock climbing, or bowling, the best way to find a club is to look in the Yellow Pages or online under the specific sport. Below are a few to get you started:

- **Bay Area Ski Connection**, www.jaws.com/baski/home.html; a clearinghouse of information on local clubs, here you'll find links to various Bay Area singles ski and snowboard clubs, information on group travel, and the singles racing league.
- **Golden Gate Sport & Social Club**, 415-921-1161, www.ggsportandsocialclub. com; based in San Francisco, offers adult recreational sports leagues including softball, soccer, basketball, and night bike riding, coed activities, parties and social nights, membership is free.
- **Single Sailors Association of Alameda**, www.singlesailors.org; for beginning and experienced sailors alike, the group organizes lunch and dinner sails to Tiburon, Sausalito, and San Francisco as well as multi-day cruises to the Delta, Drakes Bay, Monterey, and other spots. Membership is $87 ($55 renewal). Meetings are the second Thursday of every month, 6:30 p.m. social hour, 7:30 p.m. at Ballena Bay Yacht Club, 1150 Ballena Blvd, Alameda.
- **The Diving Singles Club**, www.divingsingles.com; Silicon Valley singles club based around a shared love of scuba diving. The group organizes several diving trips every month to Monterey for beginner to advanced divers, and also hosts get-togethers occasionally for dinner, hiking, and wine tasting. Membership is free.

PARKS

Everyone knows about San Francisco's Golden Gate Park, and many have heard about the Presidio and Marin Headlands, but most newcomers are probably unaware of the profusion of gem-like parks scattered throughout the Bay Area. These little havens, some of them perched atop hillsides, are perfect for romping with the kids, taking in the views, and breathing in the misty morning air. In fact, in San Francisco alone there are 230 parks and recreation facilities; among them, you'll find 6 scenic golf courses and 52 playgrounds—not bad for a city of 48 square miles. And then there are the beaches…

If you're interested in National Parks beyond the Presidio, discussed below, refer to **National Parks** in the **Quick Getaways** chapter.

SAN FRANCISCO

GOLDEN GATE PARK

The idea to create a large park in San Francisco first surfaced in the mid-1860s as city leaders strategized about how to wrest control of a large, sandy area occupied by squatters. Today this area spreads out about three miles from its eastern border of Stanyan Street to the Pacific Ocean, is about a half mile wide, and separates the Richmond district to the north from the Sunset to the south.

Visit Golden Gate Park and you will find that the rolling sand dunes of the 1800s have been transformed into rolling fields of green and wooded groves. The method for turning the land into the greenspace it is today was reportedly hit upon by accident. It seems William Hammond Hall, the park's designer and its first Superintendent (1871–1876), noticed a horse's barley nosebag fall to the sand and then sometime later, the barley that spilled sprouted. Hall took note of this and decided to plant barley, grass, and other plants throughout the sandy areas needing transformation, and the rest is history. Hall is also credited with keeping traffic moving slowly through the park by insisting on the design of park roads that twisted and turned.

Hall appointed John McLaren as Assistant Superintendent, and by 1890, McLaren, a native of Edinburgh, Scotland, became Superintendent. He went on to make a name for himself by continuing the transformation process. Word has it that with the advice of horticulturists from around the world as to what kinds of plants and trees might thrive in this region, he alone planted more than one million trees in the park. Following his death in 1943, "Uncle John," as he was lovingly known, was honored by City leaders who named the park's headquarters (his former home) after him, the McLaren Lodge.

Today Golden Gate Park is the City's 1,017-acre playground, seven days a week. It's huge—New York's Central Park comes in at a mere 840 acres. No matter what the weather, you'll find walkers, joggers, roller skaters, and bike riders out using the trails. The meadows and groves are popular picnic sites. (The grills require reservations on weekends; see below.) The park also boasts numerous lakes and streams, baseball diamonds, soccer fields, tennis courts, playgrounds, an antique carousel, two art museums, a science museum and an aquarium, a Japanese tea garden, and much more. You can get your groove on with free swing dancing lessons every Sunday at Lindy in the Park from 11 a.m. to 2 p.m, weather permitting, beginner's lesson at noon. This activity is located just behind the new De Young Museum. For more information visit www.lindyinthepark.com. Despite all the activity, Golden Gate Park also offers quiet places for those seeking a bit of solitude.

For further information or reservations visit www.parks.sfgov.org or call:

- **Beach Chalet Visitor Center**, 415-751-2766
- **Boating** (Stow Lake), 415-752-0347
- **Fly casting** (Angler's Lodge), 415- 386-2630
- **Golf** (9-hole course), 415-751-8987
- **Guided walks**, 415-263-0991
- **Japanese Tea Garden**, 415-668-0909
- **Lawn bowling**, 415-487-8787
- **M. H. de Young Art Museum**, 415-750-3600
- **Park Senior Center**, 415-666-7015
- **Permits & Reservations**, 415-831-5500
- **Sharon Arts Studio**, 415-753-7004
- **Strybing Arboretum**, 415-661-1316
- **Tennis** (21 courts), 415-831-6302

PRESIDIO NATIONAL PARK

Located at the northern tip of the San Francisco peninsula, the 1,480-acre Presidio is one of the City's biggest treasures. Only recently made part of the

National Park system, it was originally settled by the Spanish in 1776, and functioned as a military post. In 1847, under US rule, its military functions continued, serving as a training base for Union troops in the Civil War and, in the aftermath of the 1906 Earthquake that destroyed much of San Francisco, as a refuge for displaced residents. During World War II, the Presidio functioned as command center for the Sixth Army Command. It wasn't until October 1, 1994, when the National Park Service assumed control, that the US Sixth Army packed up and moved out. It is now part of the Golden Gate National Recreation Area and boasts some of the City's prime real estate, with more than 100 miles of roads and wooded trails, ocean vistas, and a world-class golf course. Bikers and hikers enjoy the trails that meander through the eucalyptus groves; windsurfers and kite surfers head for Crissy Field. Fishermen look for crab, bass, perch, shark, or whatever else will bite at the pier near Fort Point.

Unique in the National Park System, the Presidio is run by the Presidio Trust, an independent federal agency, in combination with the National Park Service. The US Congress has mandated that the Presidio be completely self-sufficient by the year 2013, and to that end, the Presidio Trust has had to be creative about how to accomplish self-sufficiency. Finding big business tenants seems to be the way the Trust has decided to go. The San Francisco arm of Lucas Films, LucasFilms Ltd, runs the Letterman Digital Arts Center, a multi-media mega-complex here. Area organizations and businesses have offices here, including nonprofits and some dot-coms, and the Presidio is also a residential area with houses and apartments—available primarily to those who work here. Regardless of the politics surrounding how best to manage the area, the Presidio is a valued San Francisco icon, offering art, history, and cultural centers, a shorebird lagoon, and recreation space. For more information on what the park has to offer, call the **Visitor's Center** at 415-561-4323. Military history buffs may want to visit the **Presidio Army Museum**, at Funston Avenue and Lincoln Boulevard, 415-561-4331. Golfers interested in teeing off at the **Golf Course** call 415-561-4661. Keglers can try out the park's 12-lane **Bowling Alley** in Building #93 (between Moraga and Montgomery streets); call 415-561-2695 for more information. Visit the Presidio's web site at www.nps.gov/prsf, and check the **Sports and Recreation** chapter for more details about these and other sports.

ADDITIONAL SAN FRANCISCO PARKS

- **Sigmund Stern Memorial Grove**, 19th Ave and Sloat Blvd, 415-252-6252
- **Harding Park**, popular public golf course, Harding Dr off Skyline Dr, 415-664-4690
- **McLaren Park**, University and Woolsey sts
- **Dolores Park**, Dolores and 19th sts
- **Balboa Park**, Ocean Ave and San Jose St
- **Glen Canyon Park**, Bosworth St and O'Shaughnessy
- **Crocker Amazon**, Moscow and Italy sts

Most San Francisco neighborhoods have parks with playgrounds, tennis courts, various flora and fauna, views, and secluded sunbathing groves. **Washington Square Park** in North Beach, **Alamo Square Park** at Fulton and Scott streets, **Lafayette Park** and **Alta Plaza** in Pacific Heights, and **Buena Vista Park** in the Haight are just a few. For more information about parks and recreational opportunities in your area, call the **San Francisco Parks & Recreation Department**, 415-831-2700, or visit their web site at www.parks.sfgov.org.

BEYOND SAN FRANCISCO—BAY AREA PARKS

The park system throughout the rest of the Bay Area is vast and varied. Included here are city, county, and national parks. There are too many parks to list completely but the following will give you an idea of what to expect.

For information about additional parks in the western United States, call the **National Park Services' Pacific West Information line** at 415-561-4700.

NORTH BAY

Part of the Golden Gate National Recreation Area, **Marin Headlands** is located on the Marin side of the Golden Gate Bridge, and offers spectacular views of the city, the bridge, and the ocean. Hiking, camping, and mountain biking are available, and it's only moments away from the city. Near Rodeo Beach you'll find the Marine Mammal Center, 415-289-SEAL(7325), which provides shelter and medical assistance to elephant seals and sea lions. For more information about the Marin Headlands, contact the Visitors' Center in Sausalito at Bunker Road, 415-331-1540, or visit the Golden Gate National Recreation Area's web site at www.nps.gov/goga or call 415-561-4700.

Located in the center of San Francisco Bay is **Angel Island State Park**. People come here mostly by ferry, though a few arrive via sailboats. Ferries leave from Tiburon, San Francisco (at Pier 41, Fisherman's Wharf), and Vallejo. Once on the island, you can hike, bike, picnic, camp, enjoy a softball game, or even climb the 750-foot Mount Livermore. For more information about Angel Island, call 415-435-1915 or visit www.angelisland.org. For the San Francisco and Vallejo ferries, call the Blue and Gold Fleet at 415-705-8200. For information about the Tiburon Ferry, call 415-435-2131.

Mount Tamalpais (elevation 2,586 feet), in Mount Tamalpais State Park, features 50 miles of hiking and biking trails. On clear days, the views of San Francisco Bay and the city are stunning, especially by Trojan Point and Pantoll. You can even see the Farallon Islands, some 25 miles out to sea. In the spring the outdoor Mountain Theater presents plays. For information about Mount Tamalpais, call 415-388-2070. On your way to Mount Tamalpais, you'll pass **Muir Woods**, an eerily beautiful grove of ancient redwoods. Visit in the winter when there are fewer tourists, lots of greenery, and creeks that are running full blast.

For more information call 415-388-2595 or visit the Golden Gate National Park Recreation web site at www.nps.gov/goga.

Samuel P. Taylor State Park, 15 miles west of San Rafael on Sir Francis Drake Boulevard, offers over 2700 acres of hilly forested countryside, complete with hiking trails, fire roads, and a paved bike trail. The groves of redwoods and Papermill Creek make the area a popular camping spot. For more information, call 415-488-9897. To reserve a campsite (61 sites), contact Reserve America at 800-444-7275, www.reserveamerica.com

Located between the towns of Bolinas and Tomales, **Point Reyes National Seashore** includes 80 miles of coastline and 70,000 acres of pristine wilderness. Amidst its rugged bluffs, wooded canyons, dense forests, and open meadows, you'll find spectacular hiking, biking, camping, bird watching, and whale watching. Mountain lions live here, so if visiting with children, be sure to keep them nearby at all times. In 1995, a fire destroyed some 13,000 acres of the park, and though you can still see the effects of the fire, most of the area has recovered. For information about camping at Point Reyes, contact the Visitors' Center at 415-464-5100, ext. 2. Make sure to reserve camping sites ahead of time.

To learn more about city parks in Marin County, contact the **Marin County Department of Parks and Recreation** at 415-499-6387, www.co.marin.ca.us/depts/PK/Main/pos/parks.cfm.

EAST BAY

The East Bay has some spectacular parks, especially up in the Berkeley and Oakland hills. Call the **East Bay Regional Park District** at 888-327-2757 or TTY 510-633-0460 for information or visit their web site at www.ebparks.org.

In Berkeley, the Aquatic Park, at Seventh and Heinz streets, is alive with the sounds of sculling teams and migrating birds. You can join a kite-flying contest at Berkeley Marina off University Avenue in Berkeley, 510-981-6740. Many would argue that the crown jewel here is **Tilden Park**. Located in North Berkeley, it has hiking trails and Anza Lake for swimming (see **Sports and Recreation** for swimming details), a merry-go-round, miniature trains, golf course, a steam train, and a petting zoo. For more information, call 510-843-2137.

Tucked away in Oakland are a number of lovely green havens. **Lake Temescal Recreation Area**, 510-652-1155, has a reservoir for swimming and trout or bass fishing. Only a few miles from downtown Oakland, **Redwood Regional Park** offers stately redwoods, horseback riding, a swimming pool, and picnic areas. At **Anthony Chabot Regional Park** you can row along the 315-acre lake—no swimming allowed though. To reserve one of the 75 campsites (fees run $20–$28), call 888-327-2757. Another Oakland Park is the 425-acre **Joaquin Miller Park**, off Highway 13 on Joaquin Miller Road, where you'll find plenty of hiking trails. If you drive up Skyline Boulevard check out the **Chabot Obser-**

vatory and Science Center, 510-336-7300, with its high-powered telescopes, planetarium, and Dome IMAX theater.

In Richmond, **Wildcat Canyon** offers hiking trails that are less crowded than many other Bay Area trails.

In Alameda you can walk lazily along **Crown Memorial Beach**, Shoreline Drive, 510-521-7090, or if you are energetic, try windsurfing or kitesurfing. The **Crab Cove Visitor Center**, which offers marine education as well as tide pooling, is another favorite recreation spot. Call 510-521-6887 for more details.

In Contra Costa County check out the 19,000-acre **Mount Diablo State Park**, 925-837-2525, for hiking, camping, mountain biking, and incredible city views.

Located between Martinez and Lafayette is the hilly **Briones Regional Park**, 888-EBPARKS (888-327-2757). Its 6,117 acres offer 45 miles of trails through meadows and wooded areas among lakes and waterfalls.

PENINSULA

In San Mateo County, along Highway 1 from Pacifica to Santa Cruz, you'll find stunning coastline, big waves, and lovely beachcombing. Because of the large volume of readily available food, the largest shark in the world patrols this area. Attacks are rare, however, and surfers by the thousands ride the waves along this stretch of coast. Located about 55 miles south of San Francisco is the **Año Nuevo State Reserve**, which hosts the world's largest breeding colony of northern elephant seals. Every year, the elephant seals mate and give birth to their 75-pound pups along the sand dunes. This is truly a remarkable area and if you are lucky, you may witness a female giving birth. Breeding season is from December to late March. For more information, call 650-879-0227.

On the San Francisco Bay, the **Coyote Point County Recreational Area**, Coyote Point Drive, 650-573-2592, has a well-visited Nature Museum along with swimming, boating, windsurfing, and some kite-boarding. Windsurfing is also popular near **Candlestick Park State Recreation Area**, a few miles south of Coyote Point and near the San Francisco Airport. **Crystal Springs Reservoir**, located 13 miles south of San Francisco on Interstate 280, is another refuge as well as a source of water for San Francisco and the surrounding areas. Trails here are used for hiking, biking, and horseback riding. The reservoir itself holds 22.6 billion gallons of Hetch Hetchy water for delivery to San Francisco and northern peninsula towns.

At **Huddart County Park** in Woodside, you'll find groves of second growth redwoods. To reserve a picnic area, call (650) 363-4021 or use their online system, http://reservations.eparks.net/index.asp?park_idno=7. The park also features a playground designed specifically for the physically challenged. Additional San Mateo County Parks are **Memorial Park**, where you can fish for trout, plunge into a swimming hole, hike, bike, ride, or visit a nature museum; the 7,500-acre

Pescadero Creek County Park with ridgetop ocean views and hiking and biking; and the **Sam MacDonald County Park** with 42 miles of hiking trails. Call 650-879-0238 for camping information at the above parks.

For more information on **San Mateo's County Parks** call the **Parks and Recreation Department** at 650-363-4020.

There are also many preserves and open spaces such as **Pulgas Ridge Open Space Preserve** in San Carlos and the **Thornewood Open Space Preserve** in Woodside. Call the **Mid-Peninsula Regional Open Space District Office** at 650-691-1200 or go to www.openspace.org to learn more.

SOUTH BAY

There are 28 parks in Santa Clara County; contact the **Santa Clara Department of Parks and Recreation** at 408-355-2200 or visit www.parkhere.org. Below is just a sampling.

The 3,600-acre **Sanborn Skyline County Park**, nestled in the Santa Cruz Mountains between the city of Saratoga and Skyline Boulevard, is a steep and wooded area. It offers camping, an outdoor theater, and a youth hostel; call 408-867-9959 for more information. Here, you'll also find Silicon Valley's only outdoor Shakespearean company, Shady Shakespeare, http://www.shadyshakes. org. **Stevens Creek County Park**, in Cupertino, 408-867-3654, is great for riding or bicycling around its reservoir. Within the City of San Jose is **Alum Rock Park**, 408-259-5477, which has trickling mineral springs, as well as hiking, biking, and horseback riding trails.

Bird lovers from all over the country flock to **Palo Alto's Baylands Preserve**. Here, among the 2,000 acres of bird-beckoning salt marsh, you'll find more than 100 species of birds, including white egrets, California clappers, and thousands of tiny shorebirds. In the fall and winter the tiny black rail makes its appearance. For more details call 650-329-2506 or check www.cityofpaloalto. org. Remember to bring your binoculars.

With more than 87,000 acres, **Henry Coe State Park** is the largest state park in northern California. People come to hike, mountain bike, backpack, camp, fish, and ride horses. Located in Morgan Hill (south of San Jose), the park has blue oaks, ponderosa pines, wild pigs, deer, birds, and much more. There is a $5 per vehicle parking fee. For more information, call the visitor center at 408-779-2728 or visit their web site at www.coepark.org.

BEACHES

If you think all of California's beaches are like the ones seen on "Baywatch," erase that image from your mind. Those are southern California beaches. Northern California beaches are much different than the miles-long oceanfront playgrounds seen on TV. Weather here is frequently foggy and cold, and the undertow can be extremely dangerous. Although Bay Area beaches do host hardy surfers and sunbathers, you won't be out of place if you consider the beaches here more akin to the North Sea—places to walk with a stick and a dog and warm clothing.

Often socked-in by morning fog, temperatures along the shore rarely top the 70s, even by mid-afternoon. Nevertheless, **San Francisco** boasts a number of popular beaches. In addition to the beaches listed below, dog walkers love the beach at **Fort Funston**, south of **Ocean Beach**, and nudists throw caution to the wind at **Land's End** (located on the northern edge of Lincoln Park). **China Beach**, a few steps away from popular **Baker Beach**, is a small, secluded stretch of sand adjacent to the upscale Sea Cliff neighborhood. Daring swimmers willing to endure the cold Bay water take the plunge at the beach in **Aquatic Park** near Fisherman's Wharf.

In **Marin County**, **Stinson Beach** is perhaps the Bay Area's most popular beach (see listing below for more details). As a matter of fact, it is so popular that on summer weekends you should beware of the thousands of vehicles, and inevitable traffic jams, on Highway 1 along the coast north of San Francisco as city dwellers rev up their engines in search of peace and quiet. Keep in mind that the car trip there includes a winding road, which can make even the sturdiest stomach queasy. For clothing-optional beaches in Marin try **Muir Beach**, just before Stinson. Just past Stinson is the town of Bolinas, which has a small beach, popular for surfing.

The **San Mateo County** coastline offers much quieter beaches, so if you'd like to avoid the crowds, head south from San Francisco down Highway 1, through **Pacifica** and **Half Moon Bay** and keep your eyes peeled for a beach that fits the bill. Remember, though, that the water is cold, and the currents are strong. For more details on the state beaches listed below and others throughout the Bay Area, check out www.parks.ca.gov.

To find out more about area parks and to make camping reservations, call 800-444-7275 or log onto the **National Recreation Reservation Service** at www.recreation.gov. The **National Park Service** is located in Fort Mason, Building 201, San Francisco, 415-561-4700, www.nps.gov.

SAN FRANCISCO AND NORTH BAY BEACHES

- **Ocean Beach**: San Francisco's main beach is a long, flat, sandy shoreline stretching out along the city's western edge, just a few steps from the foot of Golden Gate Park. Packed with sun worshipers on those rarest of days when the weather is warm, Ocean Beach is popular year-round with surfers, hang-gliders, paragliders, kite fliers, city strollers, joggers, and dog walkers (officially on-leash). The weather here is typically foggy and brisk, with high wind gusts that kick sand into your food and your face; waters here are icy and the waves are rough so swimming is hazardous; on summer evenings, the beach lights up (on the northern end only) with campfire gatherings. Highway 1, easily accessible from the MUNI: N Judah and L Taraval.

- **Baker Beach**: Smaller than Ocean Beach, but also more picturesque, Baker Beach is nestled at the bottom of the deeply wooded Point Lobos, just beneath the Golden Gate Bridge—offering great views of the bridge and the Marin Headlands; North Baker is a popular nude beach. On a nice day, sunbathing is the main activity here.
- **Point Reyes**, 415-464-5100, www.nps.gov/pore/visit.htm, is one of the Bay Area's greatest gems with 100 square miles of beaches, forests, marshes, and trails snaking along the northern coastline—a great place to camp and spend the weekend hiking, kayaking, biking, bird watching, picnicking, or just relaxing. The rough Pacific currents make swimming in the ocean dangerous, but many intrepid water-lovers take the cold plunge at Bass Lake, dubbed by the park service as the best unofficial place to take a dip. The hike to Bass Lake via the Coastal Trail can be challenging in spots.
- **Tomales Bay State Park**, 415-669-1140: Right next to Point Reyes, this 2,000-acre park is home to four protected, gentle, and surf-free beaches, making it a prime spot for swimming, boating, and kayaking; four miles north of Inverness on Pierce Point Road.
- **Stinson**, www.stinsonbeachonline.com: This well-loved long sandy beach and adjoining 51-acre park are packed with wall-to-wall families in the summertime; swimming is permitted here and there are lifeguards on duty from May through October. There are also lots of picnic tables and a snack bar open during peak season, plus restrooms and showers are available. If you want to avoid the crowds, try visiting on a weekday. Take Highway 1 to the Stinson Beach exit.
- **Red Rock Beach**: This popular "clothing optional" beach is about half a mile south of Stinson Beach, at Milepost 11 on Highway 1. There's a turnout for parking, but no signs. It's about a 15-minute hike down a steep trail to the water. There are no facilities at Red Rock Beach, and poison oak is reportedly rampant here so wear shoes on the trail and use caution.

For more information on San Francisco and Marin County beaches, contact the **Golden Gate National Recreation Area**, San Francisco, 415-561-4700, www.nps.gov/goga.

PENINSULA, SOUTH BAY, AND EAST BAY BEACHES

- **Half Moon State Beach**, a half-mile west of Highway 1 on Kelly Avenue, is actually three beaches under one title: Dunes, Francis, and Venice combine to make up four miles of broad, sandy beaches along Highway 1. For those interested in an overnight experience, Francis Beach has a campground for tents and RVs. Reservations are recommended. **Francis Beach**, end of Kelly Avenue in Half Moon Bay; **Venice Beach**, end of Venice Boulevard off Highway 1;

Dunes Beach, end of Young Avenue off Highway 1. Contact Half Moon Bay Beaches, 650-726-8819, for more information. Campsite reservations must be made through Reserve America by calling 800-444-PARK (7275) or through their web site at www.reserveamerica.com.

- **San Gregorio State Beach**: A perennial favorite with families and school field trips, San Gregorio's clay cliffs and caves, hiking trails, and picnic facilities make it a perfect children's adventure land. There is also an estuary here, home to many birds. The beach is located 10.5 miles south of Half Moon Bay on Highway 1. Call 650-879-2170 for more information.
- **Año Nuevo State Reserve**: Fifty-five miles south of San Francisco a rocky point juts out into the ocean—home to the largest mainland breeding colony in the world for the northern elephant seal. During the breeding season, December through March, access to the reserve is available by guided walks only. This 4,000-acre reserve is truly something special, well worth a day trip. For more information call 650-879-0227.
- **Montara State Beach**: The tide pools and fishing are great here. Point Montara also has one of the best youth hostels in the country—offering visitors the chance to spend the night at the lighthouse 20 miles south of San Francisco, on Highway 1. There are two beach access points from the bluff area. One access is across from Second Street. The second access is located about a half-mile north on the ocean side of Highway 1. The paths down to the beach are steep. Dogs are allowed on leash. For information on staying overnight contact American Youth Hostels, 650-728-7177.
- **Pacifica**, 650-738-7381, www.cityofpacifica.org: Pacifica has a handful of spectacular beaches; Linda Mar (also known as Pacifica State Beach) runs along a wide curving mouth, and is popular with families. Kids love what locals call the world's most beautiful Taco Bell, while the wave-pounded shores here and at nearby Rockaway are favorites with surfers. All of Pacifica's beaches are accessible from Highway 1 in Pacifica.
- **Pescadero State Beach**, 650-879-2170: The sandy shores, rocky cliffs, and picnic tables make this a popular family spot in the summer; get here early to check out the tide pools. Across the highway Pescadero Marsh Natural Preserve is an excellent spot for bird watching. The beach is located about 15 miles south of Half Moon Bay on Highway 1.
- **Robert W. Crown Memorial State Beach**: The City of Alameda's 2.5-mile sandy playground is a popular spot for family picnics, BBQs, and windsurfing; swimming is permitted year-round. The beach is also home to the Elsie Roemer Bird Sanctuary and Crab Cove marine reserve. Rental sailboards and lessons are available on summer weekends. Visit www.ebparks.org for more information, or call 510-521-7090 or 888-EBPARKS (888-327-2757).

LIVING ON THE WEST COAST IS TRULY A BLESSING FOR MANY, THOUGH it is not without risk. While bad weather events are not as much of an issue as they can be in the arctic upper Midwest, the hurricane-prone coastal South, or the tornado-torn heartland, the concern here is with earthquakes. While only chance dictates who will be in the wrong place at the wrong time during a quake, there are precautions you can take to aid your survival, including establishing a family emergency plan and creating a stock of emergency supplies (see the end of the chapter). The following sources of general information and assistance may also be helpful:

- **American Red Cross Bay Area Chapter,** 415-427-8000 (disaster preparedness information), www.bayarea-redcross.org; for a 24-hour disaster hotline dial 866-272-2237
- **California Office of Emergency Services**, 916-845-8510, www.oes.ca.gov
- **Federal Emergency Management Agency (FEMA)**, 800-621-FEMA or TTY 800-462-7585, www.fema.gov

EARTHQUAKES

One of the biggest fears about living in California is earthquakes. While most natives aren't too frightened by the swaying or bumps of small temblors, no one relishes the thought of the proverbial "big one." San Francisco has been victimized by major earthquakes twice in nearly 100 years: 1906 and 1989. In 1906 the 8.3 magnitude quake toppled buildings and sparked fires that destroyed much of the city, and killed 700 people. The 1989, 7.1 magnitude Loma Prieta temblor killed 67, brought down a section of a major East Bay freeway, dislodged part of the San Francisco–Oakland Bay Bridge, sparked fires in the Marina district, and brought the World Series to an abrupt, albeit temporary, halt. And without a doubt, the San Francisco Bay area will be hit with more earthquakes. In fact, earthquake experts say there is a 62% chance that the Bay Area will be hit by the "Big One," an ominous shaker of 6.7 or greater, by 2032. While no one can control the whims of Mother Nature, if you choose to settle down in earthquake country, there are many preventative steps you can take to help keep you, your loved ones, and your home safe.

HOME PREPARATION AND INSURANCE

Simple steps you can take prior to an earthquake that will make your home a bit safer include fastening computers, televisions, and other big pieces of equipment to desks and counters so that they won't fall off during the quake. Large furniture items, such as bookcases, should be bolted to the wall. Small items, such as fragile collectibles, should be taped or glued to their shelves or stuck with clay or museum wax. Strap the water heater and other large appliances to the wall. The folks in the earthquake supply stores will be more than happy to sell you what you need to do this or go to a hardware/home supply store and get the equivalent. Chances are it will be less expensive at the latter. For information about retrofitting your home contact the **California Earthquake Authority**, 916-325-3800, www.earthquakeauthority.com. They'll tell you what needs to be done to your home to make it safer and will give you information on contractors and financing. Additional information on seismic safety can be found at http://quake.abag.ca.gov. *Peace of Mind in Earthquake Country* by Peter Yanev might also be useful.

Bolted wood frame buildings (such as Victorians) are considered quite safe, and steel-reinforced concrete buildings (such as downtown skyscrapers) are reasonably safe. The most dangerous building to be in during a quake is one made of non-reinforced masonry. For this reason, brick buildings can no longer be constructed in San Francisco, but a handful of older ones remain. Many such buildings have warning plaques in their entryways. Dozens of San Francisco buildings are still being retrofitted following the 1989 earthquake. You might want to find out whether the building you live or work in has been retrofitted or bolted.

If you're buying a home in California the seller is required by law to tell you if the property is in the vicinity of an earthquake fault line. Before buying you may want to engage the services of a civil engineer to give your prospective home the once-over, just to make sure it's as safe as it can be. Rental property owners are not required to disclose information about nearby faults to prospective tenants.

Property owners are strongly advised to buy a homeowner's insurance policy that covers quake damage. The California Insurance Commissioner requires that companies that sell homeowners and renters policies in California must also offer earthquake insurance. The most common type of earthquake insurance is normally added as an endorsement on a standard homeowner's insurance policy. Typically, there is a deductible of 5 to 10%, and sometimes

15%, of the value of the home. An important coverage is temporary living expense, which pays for motel and meals if you have to move out of your home. There is usually no deductible on this coverage. The yearly cost of residential earthquake insurance is normally about $1.50 to $3 per $1,000 of coverage on the structure. To find out more about earthquake insurance, ask your insurance agent or contact the **California State Department of Insurance** at 800-927-HELP (4357), http://www.insurance.ca.gov.

WHAT TO DO DURING AN EARTHQUAKE

- If you're inside when the earth shifts, remember the three potentially life-saving words that all California school children know by heart—duck, cover, and hold. Get under a strong table or desk. Cover your head and face to protect them from broken glass and falling debris. Hold onto the table or desk and be prepared to move with it. Stay there until the shaking stops. Do not run outside. Stay away from windows and avoid elevators and stairwells. Keep an eye out for falling objects.
- If you're driving when the earthquake strikes, pull over to the shoulder of the road. Stay away from bridges, overpasses, power lines, and large buildings. Remain in your car and wait for the shaking to stop.
- If you're outside, go into an open area away from trees, power lines and buildings.
- If you're in a crowded public area, stay calm, do not jam the exit, and avoid elevators and stairwells. Look for a safe place to duck and cover until passage is safe and clear.

AFTER THE SHOCK

- One of the first things you should do following a quake is check to see if your natural gas line is leaking. If you detect a leak, and only if you detect a leak, turn the shutoff valve. Quake-prepared residents leave the appropriate tool for shutting off the gas valve right next to it at all times. Remember, don't turn the gas off if you don't think it's leaking. The gas company will no doubt be very busy fixing numerous emergency problems following the earthquake so it may be days before someone can get to those who shut things off unnecessarily. If your water supply is working fill the tub and sinks with water. Although the pipes are running now they may not later and you can use this water for washing. Outside, check for downed utility lines, and turn on the radio for instructions and news reports.
- Stay calm, help others, make sure all household members and pets are safe and accounted for. Turn the radio on for emergency announcements, and follow emergency workers' instructions. To leave roads clear for emergency vehicles, avoid driving. Check gas, water, electrical, and sewer lines, and turn

off anything that appears to be leaking or broken at the source. Report any problems immediately to your utility company.

- Check your home for damages—paying attention to the roof, foundation, and chimneys, as well as cracked walls, etc.
- Check for downed power lines; steer clear and warn others to stay away.
- Be prepared for aftershocks.
- If you must leave your home, leave a note telling others where you are.
- If you have to leave your residence and haven't found your pets or they have run off or hidden, remember to leave food and water. Leave the toilet seat up, fill the bathtub, open cans of food and tear open entire bags of dry food. It might be several days before you are allowed to return.

BASIC EARTHQUAKE FACTS: BAY AREA FAULTS

The mother of all Bay Area faults, and the source of much geological anxiety, is the San Andreas. Named in 1895 by geologist A.C. Lawson for the San Andreas Lake, a pond roughly 20 miles south of San Francisco, this master fault spans almost the entire length of California. A fault system made of up of various segments, the San Andreas is more than 800 miles long, and at its greatest depth, dips 10 miles beneath the surface. Here, two of the continent's great tectonic plates, the Pacific and the North American, meet, creating what geologists call a strike slip fault—for the way the plates crash, then dip, one beneath the other. Earthquakes in the San Francisco Bay Area result from the pressure buildup and strain across the region as these plates push against one another. From the San Andreas, a web of smaller faults splinter off, weaving in and out from inland areas all along the coast. These smaller Bay Area faults include the Rodgers Creek, Concord–Green Valley, Greenville, Hayward, San Gregorio, and Calaveras faults.

For more interesting facts about the science of earthquakes, as well as up-to-the-minute information on quakes happening all over the world, visit the US Geological Survey's informative web site at www.usgs.gov.

Other **earthquake information sources**:

- **American Red Cross Bay Area Chapter**, 415-427-8000, www.bayarea-redcross.org, offers disaster preparedness information; for a 24-hour disaster hotline dial 866-272-2237
- **California Earthquake Authority**, 916-325-3800, www.earthquakeauthority.com, for seismic safety and earthquake insurance information
- **California Office of Emergency Services**, 916-845-8510, www.oes.ca.gov
- **California Seismic Safety Commission**, 1755 Creekside Oaks Dr, Suite 100, Sacramento, 95833, 916-263-5506, www.seismic.ca.gov, publishes "The Homeowner's Guide to Earthquake Safety" as well as other materials on quake preparedness
- **Federal Emergency Management Agency (FEMA)**, 800-621-FEMA or TTY 800-462-7585, www.fema.gov

- **Northern California Earthquake Data Center at UC Berkeley Seismology Laboratory**, http://quake.geo.berkeley.edu
- **US Geological Survey**, 345 Middlefield Rd, Menlo Park, 94025, 888-275-8747, www.usgs.gov; this office helps to determine the size of the quakes and offers a treasure trove of information on all things seismic

DISASTER KITS AND SAFETY PLANS

Aside from luck, the secret to surviving a local disaster is found in the time-proven Boy Scout adage "be prepared." There are dozens of good books on the market about how to get ready for a seismic onslaught or terrorist strike, and plenty of free information available from local, state, and federal agencies. They all tell you that you need to be ready to be on your own for three to seven days, because it may take that long for emergency crews to restore power, water, and telephone service to affected areas. You should also have at least a basic disaster kit prepared. Remember to store your supplies away from areas likely to be damaged in a big earthquake. The kit should include the following:

- Water (at least one gallon per person, per day)
- Food for each family member and your pets (canned goods such as stews, beans, soups, evaporated milk, cereals, granola bars and nuts, dried fruit, cookies)
- Non-electric can opener
- Flashlights and extra batteries
- Portable radio and extra batteries
- Blankets/sleeping bags/pillows
- Camping stove or your barbecue with plenty of appropriate fuel
- Swiss Army knife or similar tool
- Cooking and eating utensils, paper plates and cups
- Proper sized tent
- Water purification tablets
- Small bottle of chlorine bleach
- Toiletries, including toilet paper, feminine hygiene products, and contact lens supplies, diapers
- Waterproof matches
- Plastic garbage bags and ties
- Toys, games, cards, crosswords, paper and pencils, books
- Red lipstick to scrawl a message on the front of the building door (or ruins) if you must leave
- Sturdy shoes
- Rain gear
- Sunglasses and sunscreen
- Dust masks
- Cold weather clothing, gloves, scarves, hats
- Fire extinguisher

- Whistle
- Pet carrier and photos of your pets to identify them if they take off
- A basic tool kit with hammer, pliers, wrenches, etc., for minor repairs
- Cash (bank ATMs may not work after a big temblor and merchants may not be accepting credit cards!)
- First aid kit, including the following:
  - plastic adhesive strips
  - ACE bandages
  - gauze pads and tape
  - scissors
  - tweezers
  - safety pins
  - chemical ice packs
  - cotton balls or swabs
  - aspirin or the equivalent
  - antibiotic ointments
  - hydrogen peroxide
  - rubbing alcohol
  - insect repellent
  - thermometer
  - over-the-counter medications for diarrhea and upset stomach
  - first aid manual
  - prescription medications that are not past their expiration dates

Once you've gathered everything together, put it all in a container, such as a big plastic garbage can with a lid, and stash it in a place that's not likely to be buried in a quake. If you're living in a house, the backyard may be best. If you're living in an apartment building you'll have to be creative when it comes to protecting your kit.

Several Bay Area stores sell earthquake/disaster preparedness equipment and information. They also sell earthquake kits as well as individual components. These can be pricey, but when you consider that your life, following a major quake, may depend on how well prepared you are, it is probably worth the expense. Here are just a few of the stores specializing in quake supplies:

- **Earthquake Supply Center**, 3095 Kerner Blvd, San Rafael, 415-459-5500, 800-728-8531, www.earthquakesupplycenter.com
- **Earth Shakes**, 1004 Oak Grove, Burlingame, 650-548-9065, www.earth-shakes.com
- **REI—Recreational Equipment Inc.**, 840 Brannan St, San Francisco, 415-934-1938, 1338 San Pablo Ave, Berkeley, 510-527-4140; 1119 Industrial Rd, San Carlos, 650-508-2330; other locations, www.rei.com

As you put your disaster kit together you should also come up with a **family emergency plan**, in case disaster strikes when you're not all in the same place. You can do the same thing with your apartment building neighbors. Emergency preparedness experts say you should:

- Agree on someone out of the area you can all call to check in, for example, Aunt Mildred in Omaha. She'll want to know how you are as well, so let her be the clearinghouse for family information. Make sure each family member knows the number. The only chink in this armor is that telephone lines and satellite service may not be working for a few days—keep trying; eventually they will be restored.
- Should your home suffer severe damage, create a planned meeting place, such as the local high school football field or a department store parking lot, someplace that is not likely to come tumbling down during an initial quake or any aftershocks.

NOW THAT YOU'VE FOUND A PLACE TO LIVE, UNPACKED, AND GOTTEN settled into your new home, it's time to get involved in the community. This chapter lists a variety of options for participation, from volunteering in the area to joining a place of worship.

VOLUNTEERING

Giving back to the community is a rewarding experience. Whether you are skilled at building houses, caring for the elderly, tutoring underprivileged children, or canvassing neighborhoods (having bilingual skills in any of these areas can be particularly useful), you can find a volunteer project that suits your talents and beliefs. Helping out in your new community is also a great way to meet people and can make the transition to an unfamiliar place less stressful.

HOW YOU CAN HELP

THE HUNGRY AND THE HOMELESS

Scores of volunteers concern themselves with shelters for the city's homeless. Jobs include monitoring and organizing the shelters; providing legal help; ministering to psychiatric, medical, and social needs; raising money; manning phones; and caring for children in the shelters. Many people solicit, organize, cook, and serve food to the destitute at sites throughout the city. Still others deliver meals to the homeless and the homebound.

CHILDREN

If involvement with children is especially appealing, you can tutor in and out of schools, be a big brother or sister, teach music and sports in shelters or at local community centers, run activities in the parks, entertain children in hospitals, and accompany kids on weekend outings. Schools, libraries, community associations, hospitals, and other facilities providing activities and guidance for children are all worth exploring.

HOSPITALS

The need for volunteers in both city-run and private hospitals is manifold: From interpreters to laboratory personnel to admitting and nursing aides, many volunteers are required. Assistants in crisis medical areas—emergency rooms, intensive care units, and the like—are wanted if you have the skills, as are volunteers to work with victims of sexual abuse. If you just want to be helpful, you might assist in food delivery or work in the gift shop.

THE DISABLED AND THE ELDERLY

You can read to the blind, help teach the deaf, work to prevent birth defects, and help the developmentally delayed and disabled, among others. You can also make regular visits to the homebound elderly, bring hot meals to their homes, and teach everything from nutrition to arts and crafts in senior centers and nursing homes.

EXTREME CARE SITUATIONS

Helping with suicide prevention, Alzheimer's and AIDS patients, rape victims, and abused children is a special category demanding a high level of commitment—not to mention emotional reserves and, in many cases, special skills.

THE CULTURE SCENE

Area museums are constantly in need of volunteers to lead tours or lend a hand in any number of ways. Libraries, theater groups, and ballet companies have plenty of tasks that need to be done. Fundraising efforts also require many volunteers to stuff envelopes and make phone calls. The Public Broadcasting Service (PBS) is a good example. Its large volunteer staff raises money for its stations through extensive on-air fundraising campaigns that include collecting pledges.

THE COMMUNITY

Work in your neighborhood. You can help out at the local school, community garden, neighborhood block association, nursing home, settlement house, or animal shelter.

VOLUNTEER REFERRAL SERVICES

If you know the specific entity for which you'd like to volunteer, the best idea is to contact them and inquire about volunteer opportunities. Otherwise, the agencies listed below can put you in touch with the many service organizations in the Bay Area in need of your assistance.

- **Center for Volunteer and Nonprofit Leadership of Marin**, 415-479-5710, www.centerforleadershipmarin.org
- **HandsOn Bay Area**, 135 Bluxome St, San Francisco, 415-541-9616, www.handsonbayarea.org
- **Hayward Area Volunteer Services**, 510-881-6710
- **SmartVolunteer**, www.smartvolunteers.com, this national organization matches professionals with volunteer opportunities within nonprofit organizations
- **Volunteer Center of San Francisco** (also serving San Mateo County) 415-982-8999, San Mateo County, 650-235-3550, www.thevolunteercenter.net
- **Volunteer Center of the East Bay** (serving Contra Costa and Alameda counties), 925-472-5760, 925-778-0165, 510-232-0163, www.helpnow.org

PLACES OF WORSHIP

San Francisco's diversity is most evident in the multitude of churches, temples, ashrams, mosques, and other houses of worship to be found throughout the Bay Area. Below is a list describing just a few of the many religious organizations here. For more information about worship in the Bay Area, talk to leaders or fellow congregants at your current place of worship. You'd be surprised by how many people across the USA have ties to the San Francisco area. To find a place of worship close to your new home, check the Yellow Pages under "Churches," "Synagogues," "Mosques," etc., or go online and do a key word search. You can also check out www.yelp.com/c/sf/churches.

CHURCHES

BAPTIST

- **Ebenezer Baptist Church**, 275 Divisadero St, San Francisco, 415-431-0200
- **First Chinese Baptist Church of San Francisco**, 1-15 Waverly Pl, San Francisco, 415-362-4139; www.fcbc-sf.org; serving San Francisco since its inception in 1880, the Waverly location is newly renovated and seismically retrofitted. The congregation is multi-generational, bilingual, and bicultural.
- **Third Baptist Church, Inc.**, 1399 McAllister St, San Francisco, 415-346-4426, www.thirdbaptist.org, headed by pastor Amos Brown, former member of the San Francisco Board of Supervisors; youth activities, broadcasts regular radio program.

EASTERN ORTHODOX

- **Greek Orthodox Cathedral of the Annunciation**, 245 Valencia St, San Francisco, 415-864-8000, www.annunciation.org, hosts fantastic, packed events with Greek music, food, and dancing; its whitewashed façade evokes the beauty of the Greek islands.
- **Greek Orthodox Cathedral of the Ascension**, 4700 Lincoln Ave, Oakland, 510-531-3400, www.groca.org; this cathedral is known for its lovely stained glass. Overlooking the Bay Area from atop the Oakland hills, the church offers youth and senior programs and a choir.
- **Greek Orthodox Diocese of San Francisco**, 372 Santa Clara Ave, San Francisco, 415-753-3075, www.sf.goarch.org
- **Holy Virgin Cathedral**, 6210 Geary Blvd, 415-221-3255, located in the Outer Richmond, in the heart of San Francisco's vibrant Russian community, towers majestically above the fog. This dazzling Russian Orthodox cathedral—with its five ornate golden domes and stunning frescoes—is a true San Francisco landmark. The church offers services in Russian and is also home to a Russian high school. It's definitely worth seeing, regardless of your faith. While in the neighborhood, be sure to check out the wonderful Russian bakeries nearby.
- **Russian Orthodox Church of Our Lady of Kazan**, 5725 California St, 415-752-2502, www.kazanchurch.org, is located in the Richmond District. The church's glistening, onion-domed cathedral with mosaics, icons, and frankincense is an exquisite place to visit, even if you aren't a member. The singing is spectacular. Several Russian bakeries and restaurants nearby offer mouthwatering breakfasts and lunches after services.

EPISCOPAL

- **Grace Cathedral**, and the **Episcopal Diocese of California**, 1055 Taylor St, San Francisco, 415-749-6300, www.gracecathedral.org; perched atop Nob Hill, this is a lovely cathedral, complete with stained glass windows, murals, and lofty ceilings. Episcopalians come from all over the city to worship here. In particular, midnight mass on Christmas Eve, the Easter service that includes an egg roll at nearby Huntington Park, and the Evensong on Sundays are attended by members and non-members alike. The church also hosts concerts and indoor/outdoor art exhibits, and offers an associated boys' school, a cafe, and a shop of religious items including music and Christmas cards. Just walking inside or strolling through the outdoor labyrinth offers a peaceful and meditative experience. There are a number of other Episcopal churches throughout the city and the Bay Area.

JEHOVAH'S WITNESSES

Jehovah's Witnesses in San Francisco can contact the **Excelsior Congregation**, 11 Bright St, San Francisco, 415-586-9194, or to find your local Kingdom Hall, visit www.watchtower.org.

LATTER DAY SAINTS/MORMON

Whether or not you are a member of the Church of Jesus Christ of Latter Day Saints, the **Mormon Temple**, 4770 Lincoln Avenue off of Highway 13 in Oakland, is well worth a visit. Built in the 1960s and nested high in the Oakland hills overlooking the Bay, this impressive temple and its five spires dominate the skyline and can be seen from miles away. The church boasts a large, active membership from throughout the Bay Area, including a large Asian-American community. The temple itself is reserved for religious services, but the exquisitely kept grounds and visitors' center are open to the public. For more information call 510-531-3200. For more information on finding a ward near you visit www.lds.org.

LUTHERAN

- **St. Mark's Lutheran Church**, 1111 O'Farrell St, San Francisco, 415-928-7770, www.stmarks-sf.org, is known for its music programs and social outreach activities; childcare provided all Sunday morning.
- **St. Matthews Lutheran Church**, 3281 16th St, San Francisco, 415-863-6371, www.stmatthews-sf.org, offers services in German as well as English.
- **West Portal Lutheran Church**, 200 Sloat Blvd, San Francisco, 415-661-0242, www.westportallutheran.org, multicultural community.
- **Zion Lutheran Church and School**, 495 9th Ave, San Francisco, 415-221-7500, www.zionsf.org, traditional and contemporary services.

METHODIST

There are a large number of Methodist churches throughout San Francisco and the Bay Area. To find one near you, go to www.umc.org.
- **Glide Memorial Methodist Church**, 330 Ellis St, San Francisco, 415-674-6000, www.glide.org; the charismatic Reverend Cecil Williams, a prominent San Francisco figure, and his poet wife, Janice Mirikitani, have instituted 52 programs at Glide including food giveaways, recovery meetings, classes, and housing programs. But what draws parishioners, the down and out, tourists, the movers and shakers of San Francisco society, and many others, at least once, is the lively music and singing at the services.

PRESBYTERIAN

- **Calvary Presbyterian Church**, 2515 Fillmore St, San Francisco, 415-346-3832, www.calvarypresbyterian.org, located at the top of the hill in Pacific Heights, offers concerts, a preschool, and singles and elder groups.
- **Menlo Park Presbyterian Church**, 950 Santa Cruz Ave, Menlo Park, 650-323-8600, www.mppc.org, is a popular church with loads of groups for singles and single parents, group activities, and outreach programs.
- **Noe Valley Ministry**, 1021 Sanchez St, San Francisco, 415-282-2317, www.noevalleyministry.org, holds popular concerts, including jazz, folk, classical, and religious music. The church also offers community classes that range from belly dancing to ecology.
- **The Old First Presbyterian Church**, 1751 Sacramento St, San Francisco, 415-776-5552, www.oldfirst.org, claims to be the oldest Presbyterian church in the city. The church also frequently hosts popular chamber music concerts. For more information visit www.oldfirstconcerts.org.

QUAKER

Known worldwide for promoting peace and justice, as well as fellowship and spirituality, the Quakers, also known as the Religious Society of Friends, have an active meeting house in San Francisco, at 65 Ninth Street, a library that includes multimedia offerings on Quaker history and peace studies as well as children's books, and a school, http://sffriendsschool.org. The San Francisco Friends hold an open-to-all silent peace vigil in front of the Federal Building at Golden Gate and Larkin streets every Thursday at noon. The San Francisco meeting house holds regular worship services every Sunday at 11 a.m; newcomers are encouraged to attend the Orientation to Meeting held beforehand at 10:40 a.m. To find out more, contact **San Francisco Friends Meeting**, www.sfquakers.org. Outside of San Francisco, to find the meeting house nearest you visit www.quakerfinder.org.

ROMAN CATHOLIC

There are 48 different Catholic parishes in San Francisco. For a comprehensive list, contact the San Francisco Archdiocese at 415-614-5500, or check their web site, www.sfarchdiocese.org. The office of the Archdiocese of San Jose, 900 Lafayette Street, Suite 301, 408-983-0100, www.dsj.org, can tell you about churches in the South Bay. Numerous churches in the Bay Area offer services in Italian, Chinese, Tagalog, French, Spanish, Latin, Vietnamese, Korean, and more. Check the web sites listed above to find one that may be of interest to you.

- **The Cathedral of St. Mary of the Assumption,** 1111 Gough St, San Francisco, 415-567-2020, www.stmarycathedralsf.org, is the main church of the diocese in San Francisco. Referred to as St. Mary's Cathedral, it is a bright and airy modern structure, completed in 1971 after the original cathedral burned down.

- **Mission Dolores**, 3321 16th St, San Francisco, 415-621-8203, www.missiondolores.org, the oldest building in the city (dating from 1776), is rich in history and tucked on the edge of Dolores Park. Sunday services are at 8 a.m. and 10 a.m. for English speakers; there is a noon mass in Spanish.
- **St. Dominic's**, 2390 Bush St in San Francisco, 415-567-7824, www.stdominics.org, has a school for children, K–8, a special shrine to St. Jude, and holds weekday and evening masses, morning prayer sessions, and services in Spanish at 1:30 p.m. every Sunday.
- **St. Ignatius**, Fulton and Parker sts, San Francisco, 415-422-2188, www.stignatiussf.org, you can see the gorgeous, towering spires of this Jesuit parish, located on the University of San Francisco campus, from many of the city's hilltops—watching the sun set over this magnificent work of architecture is simply stunning.
- **St. Vincent de Paul Church**, 2320 Green St, San Francisco, 415-922-1010, www.svdpsf.org, has one of the largest and most active young adult groups, meets every second and fourth Monday of the month (not every other Monday), from 7:30 p.m. to 9 p.m.

SEVENTH-DAY ADVENTISTS

Known for their worship music programs, Seventh-day Adventist churches are located throughout the city—including churches specifically dedicated to Chinese, Japanese, Latin American, Russian, and gay and lesbian communities. For newcomers, a good place to start is the **San Francisco Central Seventh-day Adventist Church**, 2889 California St., 415-921-9016, www.sfcentral.org. The church offers a variety of services, including Saturday services, and Sabbath school for children. To find a church or school near you visit www.adventistdirectory.org.

UNITARIAN UNIVERSALIST

Known for their progressive views, social activism, and embrace of people from varied religious backgrounds, Unitarian Universalist churches are active throughout the Bay Area. For a list of local churches go to www.uua.org.

- **First Unitarian Universalist Church and Center**, 1187 Franklin St, San Francisco, 415-776-4580, www.uusf.org, welcomes people of all faiths, operates the King's Gallery art space, and offers a variety of programs including a Social Justice Committee, UUs for Peace, the Faithful Fools Street Ministry (addressing poverty through art and activism), a Wednesday night bridge club, and a choir.

JEWISH CONGREGATIONS

The **Jewish Community Center** at 3200 California St, San Francisco, 415-292-1200, www.jccsf.org, offers Jewish education classes and workshops, social and singles events, programs for interfaith couples and families, preschools, after-school programs, a teen center, summer and day camps, youth sports classes and leagues, dance, music, ceramics and art classes, and older adult programs. In Palo Alto, the **Oshman Family Jewish Community Center**, 650-852-3500, www.paloaltojcc.org, also offers classes and community events.

For a wealth of information log onto the Jewish Community Federation's web site, www.sfjcf.org, where you can find out about volunteer opportunities, trips to Israel for young people, and a great deal more. *Resource: A Guide to Jewish Life in the Bay Area*, www.sfjcf.org/resources/guide/, is an excellent guide to Jewish life in the Bay Area and maintains a thorough list of local congregations, organizations, and social events.

For more on Jewish congregations and organizations in the Bay area, go to www.jweekly.com, where you can bring up information about cooking, personal ads, classifieds, entertainment, a calendar of events, and more.

There are at least 20 different Jewish congregations in the City. Below are just a few.

CONSERVATIVE

* **Beth Sholom**, 301 14th Ave, San Francisco, 415-221-8736, www.bethsholomsf. org, is a traditional conservative congregation with more than 500 member households.

ORTHODOX

* **Chabad of Noe Valley**, 94 29th St, San Francisco, 415-821-7046, www. chabadnoevalley.org, offers Shabbat and holiday services, Torah study, and a variety of other programs.

PROGRESSIVE REFORM

* **Sha'ar Zahav**, 290 Dolores St, San Francisco, 415-861-6932, www.ShaarZahav. org, is a progressive reform synagogue for people of all sexual identities.

RECONSTRUCTIONIST

* **Keddem Congregation**, 650-494-6400, www.keddem.org, a community-led congregation based in Palo Alto.

REFORM

- **Beth Israel Judea**, 625 Brotherhood Way, San Francisco, 415-586-8833, www.bij.org; a center for progressive, egalitarian Judaism; offers services on Fridays at 7:30 p.m., and Saturdays at 10 a.m.
- **Congregation Emanu-El**, 2 Lake St, San Francisco, 415-751-2535, www.emanuelsf.org, housed in a beautiful temple, it's one of the centers of reform Jewish life in San Francisco. Also on-site you'll find the Elizabeth S. and Alvin I. Fine Museum.
- **Temple Sherith Israel**, 2266 California St, San Francisco, 415-346-1720, www.sherithisrael.org; services Fridays at 6 p.m. and Saturdays at 10:30 a.m.

ISLAMIC CENTERS

There are dozens of mosques, Islamic community centers, libraries, schools, and political and social groups in the Bay Area. For starters, in San Francisco contact the **Islamic Society of San Francisco** at www.islamsf.com; in the South Bay, contact the **Muslim Community Association of the San Francisco Bay Area**, 408.727.7277, www.mcabayarea.org. You can reach the **South Bay Islamic Association** at www.sbia.net, which offers details about Bay Area mosque locations, schools, elder groups, restaurant listings, charities, and more.

FAR EASTERN SPIRITUAL CENTERS

HINDU

To find out more about the practice of Hinduism and its related yogic meditations, visit the **Sivananda Yoga Vedanta Center**, 1200 Arguello Boulevard, 415-681-2731, www.sfsivananda.org. A number of yoga centers are sprinkled throughout the city; however, the **Mindful Body**, 2876 California Street, 415-931-2639, was voted one of the best places to practice yoga by the *San Francisco Bay Guardian*.

- **Hindu Temple and Cultural Center**, 3676 Delaware Dr, Fremont, 510-659-0655, www.fremonttemple.org.
- **The Vedanta Society of Northern California** at 2323 Vallejo St, 415-922-2323, www.sfvedanta.org, while not a religious organization, offers lectures, scripture classes, a bookshop, and library.

BUDDHISM

The **San Francisco Buddhist Center**, at 37 Bartlett St, 415-282-2018, www.sfbuddhistcenter.org, is a good resource for newcomers wanting to contact other Buddhist centers in the Bay Area.

Bay Area Zen Buddhist centers offer peaceful and sheltered environments for ceremonies, meals, meditations, chanting, and more, to members and non-members alike. The old brick **Zen Center** at 300 Page Street, in San Francisco, 415-863-3136, and Marin County's **Green Gulch Farm Zen Center** in Muir Beach, 415-383-3134, are just two of the many centers in the Bay Area. (Vegetables grown at Green Gulch are used at Green's Restaurant in Fort Mason.) For more information and links to local centers, visit www.sfzc.com.

GAY AND LESBIAN

- **A Common Bond**, the support network for current and former gay, lesbian, bisexual, and transgender Jehovah's Witnesses, began in San Francisco and has expanded nationally. The group meets in the various homes of its members. For more information check out www.gayxjw.org.
- **Congregation Sha'ar Zahav**, 290 Dolores St, San Francisco, 415-861-6932, www.shaarzahav.org, is a reform synagogue for people of all sexual identities.
- **Dignity San Francisco**, San Francisco, 415-681-2491, www.dignitysanfrancisco.org, is for Catholic gay, lesbian, bisexual, and transgender people and their friends. Services are held at the Seventh Avenue Presbyterian Church, 3129 7th Ave.
- **Metropolitan Community Church**, 150 Eureka St, San Francisco, 415-863-4434, www.mccsf.org, offers social activities, recovery groups, counseling. The parishioners also serve meals to and provide showers for the homeless, and tutor children at the Harvey Milk Civil Rights Academy.
- **Most Holy Redeemer Church** (Catholic), 100 Diamond St, San Francisco, 415-863-6259, www.mhr.org, offers services, reconciliation and confession, and AIDS support groups.
- **Saint Francis Lutheran**, 152 Church St, San Francisco, 415-621-2635, www.st-francis-lutheran.org; this entire church was expelled from the mainstream Lutheran Church in 1996. They offer over 30 self-help groups, senior meetings, and bingo.

RELIGIOUS STUDIES

- **The Graduate Theological Union**, 1798 Scenic Ave, Berkeley, 510-849-8272, www.gtu.edu, nicknamed Holy Hill, is on the north side of the University of California at Berkeley. It includes the Pacific School of Religion, the Bade Museum (of religious items), the Flora Lamson Hewlitt Library, at 2400 Ridge Rd, 510-649-2500, as well as six schools of theology and six religious centers. Combined, these schools and centers offer seminars on every imaginable subject about any known religion. For more about lectures, presentations, and public prayer services, call 510-649-2400.

THE MISSIONS

For California history buffs, Roman Catholics, or anyone who wants to get a sense of old California, a tour of some of Northern California's missions is a must. Spanish missionaries settled California during the 1700s and several mission sites are still in existence today. Some are active, consecrated churches, others exist only as crumbling remnants.

- **Mission Dolores**, 3321 16th St, 415-621-8203, www.missiondolores.org, in the heart of San Francisco, is the area's most well known and still operating mission.
- Little of **Santa Clara's** original mission remains, but a replica has been placed on the University of Santa Clara campus, 500 El Camino Real, Santa Clara, 408-554-4000.
- **Mission San Jose**, 43300 Mission Boulevard in Fremont has been reconstructed and re-consecrated.
- **Mission San Rafael**, 1104 5th Avenue, 415-456-3016, once a sanitarium for the California natives who were sickened by exposure to European diseases, is today a consecrated church.

If you want to head out of town to see the historic sites, check out **Mission Soledad**, 36641 Fort Romie Road, Soledad; **Sonoma Mission**, 114 East Spain Street, Sonoma, 707-938-1519; or **Carmel Mission**, 3080 Rio Road in Carmel. To find out more, visit www.californiamissons.com.

C ALIFORNIA HAS TYPICALLY BEEN ON THE FOREFRONT OF ENVIRON-
mental stewardship since passage of the California Environmental
Quality Act (CEQA) in 1970. This powerful law required developers to
analyze and report on the potential environmental impact of their project,
and in many cases, required them to mitigate damages to the environment.
Most states in the country follow a different—and less stringent—set of federal
guidelines. This set the stage for an existential battle between California and
the federal government with regard to environmental standards, which continues to this day. Interestingly, however, the new federal guidelines on vehicle
fuel-efficiency standards, recently adopted by the Obama administration, are a
carbon copy of California's tough regulations. As a result of these efforts, residents of California generally enjoy clean air, massive sections of undeveloped
waterways, and tax incentives to "green" their lives.

GREENING YOUR HOME

The simplest method of going green is to reduce the size of your home. Units
that are clumped together—like high-rise complexes or mixed-use buildings—
take advantage of shared utilities and more importantly, minimize exposure
to the outside world and its variable temperatures. Many "eco-homes" have
sprung up in the Bay Area recently, like **Arterra Condominiums** and the **Mission Bay Homes**, both managed by Urban Bay Properties, 415-546-3100, www.
ubayp.com. If you're in the market for a dwelling that utilizes limited resources
efficiently, be sure to take a look at them or other green buildings. Another
option is to purchase a home and revitalize it with an eye on the environment
and saving energy. The following are listings that will help the DIY'er achieve
this goal.

GREEN REMODELING

A good place to start is with an organization funded by the City of San Francisco, "SF Environment," which can be found at www.sfenvironment.org. In addition to listing approved green businesses and suppliers, this web site provides information on many aspects of green living. Many homes in the Bay Area are in dire need of the very basic improvements that will save you money on energy costs. Insulation and fans in the attic, dual-pane windows, high-efficiency toilets, modern water heaters, central heating/cooling units, and EnergyStar-rated appliances were all typically left out of pre-1970s construction. Upgrading to modern systems can really pay off in the long run and is considered the cheapest method of improving energy consumption because older technologies are, quite simply, obsolete and expensive to operate.

For basic building supplies, lumber, and such innovations as "wheatcore" doors, which contain pressed wheat straw under a veneer of hardwood, check out these suppliers (as well as Big Box retail home-improvement chains):

- **Ashby Lumber (ACE)**, 824 Ashby Ave, Berkeley, 510-843-4832, www.ashbylumber. com
- **Ecohome Improvement**, 2617 San Pablo Ave, Berkeley, 510-644-3500, www. ecohomeimprovement.com
- **Golden State Lumber**, 1100 Anderson Dr, San Rafael, 415-454-2532, www. goldenstatelumber.com
- **SilverWalker**, 117 S 2nd St, Richmond, 888.633.4533, www.silverwalker.com
- **Sunnyvale Lumber**, 44580 Old Warm Springs Rd, Fremont, 510-651-8730, www.sunnyvalelumber.com

For recycled building materials:

- **Habitat for Humanity**, 2619 Broadway, Oakland, 510-251-6304, www.habitateb.org
- **Reusable Lumber Company**, Woodside, 650-529-9122, www.reusablelumber.com
- **The ReUse People**, 9235 San Leandro Blvd, Oakland, 510-383-1983, http:// thereusepeople.org
- **Urban Ore**, 900 Murray St, Berkeley, 510-841-7283
- **Whole House Building Supply & Salvage**, 1955 Pulgas Rd, East Palo Alto, 650-328-8731, www.driftwoodsalvage.com

Or try a full service option by contacting an eco-friendly design shop:

- **Zwanette Design**, 1777 Yosemite Ave, Suite 115, San Francisco, 415-595-3000, www.zwanettedesign.com

LANDSCAPING

Landscaping using plants that are indigenous to the area and don't require large amounts of water or fertilizers is a smart method of going green, right in your front yard. San Francisco–based Bay Natives (www.baynatives.com) is a great resource about this type of gardening, and for the South Bay, try Yerba Buena Nursery in Woodside (www.yerbabuenanursery.com). Both are excellent repositories of plant species that thrive in the Bay Area climate and soils. Also, take a look at the free *Bay-Friendly Gardening Guide* at www.stopwaste.org/docs/gardeningguide.pdf.

You can also try a full service option by contacting these or other contractors in the area:

- **A Scape Artist**, 1195 Pine Ave, San Jose, 650-759-2455, www.ascapeartistonline.com
- **Ploughshares Nursery**, 2701 Main St, Alameda, 510-898-7811, www.ploughsharesnursery.com
- **St. John Landscapes**, Patricia St. John, 1635 Le Roy Ave, Berkeley, 510-848-5673, www.stjohnlandscapes.com

ENERGY EFFICIENCY

As mentioned previously, any home that hasn't had the benefit of modern upgrades to its systems can be quite wasteful. Governmental web sites like California's www.energy.ca.gov, or www.coolcalifornia.org, are treasure-troves of useful information on improving both energy usage and the environment. Cash incentives are provided by the government—often in the form of tax breaks—for homeowners and businesses that adopt these improvements. Flex Your Power, www.fypower.org, is a great resource for these programs, and also provides tips for saving money in the hot summer months. For federal standards regarding appliances, check www.energystar.gov for a wealth of information and shopping advice.

RENEWABLE ENERGY

Most of the area's utility companies provide a method of purchasing green power and, as a by-product of your choice, supporting the effort to increase the amount of renewable energy the utilities use. Check the **Getting Settled** chapter for contact information for your local electrical provider. California also has innovative and fully funded programs for people who choose to mount solar panels on their roofs. The California Solar Initiative has an informative web site that contains everything you'll need to know about joining the solar "grid," 415-355-5586, www.gosolarcalifornia.ca.gov.

WATER CONSERVATION

Allocation of water resources in the Bay Area—and California at large—is a big deal, and constantly on the minds of regulators and politicians charged with overseeing the usage of this precious commodity. Contracts signed between states and cities over the past 100 years have divided the water "ownership" into fractional and fiercely competing parties. Cities like Oakland run advertising campaigns begging consumers to turn off the tap while brushing their teeth, while farm cooperatives post billboards along major highways reminding citizens of the importance of locally grown food (which of course requires locally available water). Since California is such a huge producer and exporter of nuts, fruits, vegetables, and rice, the politics of the water-rights issue veer quickly to global trade policy, individual property rights, and the protection of endangered species (like the Delta smelt, which in 2009 caused the shutdown of 90% of farmers' surface water in the San Joaquin Valley; studies had demonstrated the drastic decline in population of this fish, which many scientists believe to be a key indicator of the health of the ecosystem).

Many water agencies across the state are enacting mandatory water rationing each summer because the supply of water is precariously tight. Much higher charges will occur if your household exceeds this threshold. More information can be found about water issues at the State Water Resources Control Board's web site, 916-341-5300, www.swrcb.ca.gov. Useful tips about conservation can be found at Save Our Water, 916-669-2762, www.saveourh2o.org.

GREEN PRODUCTS AND SERVICES

Many companies have jumped on board the green "revolution" and purport to be the latest innovation in environmental excellence. These claims have led to the creation of competing standards—such as ASTM, LEED, Green Globes, and other rating systems—with regard to environmental impact and friendliness of the product or service to the ecosystem as a whole. At the moment, there isn't a single universally agreed-upon standard for measuring the "green-ness" of these things, so due diligence is required from the consumer. Check out www.buildinggreen.com and search for "Behind the Logos" to access a 2008 article detailing the latest standards on the market.

GREENER TRANSPORTATION

Since the Bay Area has relatively efficient public transportation systems, many residents can choose to forgo a car entirely and ride the rails, buses, or boats that crisscross the area. Check the **Transportation** section for information about car sharing and other transportation options.

The freeways are always packed with traffic, particularly during peak commute times, so carpooling becomes a viable option if HOV (High-Occupancy

Vehicle) lanes are available. Generally, you can use this lane if three or more people are in the car. Motorcycles can use this lane with a single rider. Also, hybrid vehicles that qualify (super ultra-low emission vehicles, SULEV) sometimes have a special CleanAir sticker to allow the owners to drive alone in the HOV lane. This is a trial program—you can't get a sticker anymore—due to expire in 2011, but it proved so popular that it probably will be expanded and extended once the state has a chance to evaluate transportation data. Check the Department of Motor Vehicles, http://dmv.ca.gov/vr/decal.htm, and the Air Resources Board, www.arb.ca.gov, for more information.

For service to your hybrid vehicle, check out the innovative Luscious Garage, www.lusciousgarage.com, a woman-owned business, housed in a converted building in San Francisco, that specializes in the upkeep of these fuel-efficient vehicles.

ALTERNATIVE FUELS

California has many alternative fueling stations but care should be taken when traveling across the state to ensure options are available. A handy web site, www.cleancarmaps.com, 800-861-7759, solves this problem, listing everything from electrical charging outlets to biodiesel gas stations across California, Nevada and Arizona. Purchasing cars or trucks that use these fuels encourages the manufacturers and government to continue production of alternative options and will, in time, reduce the cost associated with them.

BY CAR

California is widely known for its "car culture." However, if you are planning to live and work in San Francisco, having a car—with the endless hassles of parking, the merciless traffic, and the staggering price of gas—can often seem more a hindrance than a help. Living car-free in San Francisco is common, thanks to an excellent public transportation system that makes getting around town easy and inexpensive. However, living car-free outside San Francisco is quite a different story. Despite the best efforts of alternative transportation advocates, a long history of poor regional planning, abysmal connections, and sparse suburban options have left those who live and/or work outside the city little choice but to get into their cars and go. Thus Bay Area freeways clog every weekday morning, afternoon, and evening, often to the point of gridlock. Millions of residents here commute to work using their vehicles, and a majority are driving alone. Newcomers should note the slow rebuilding of the eastern span of the Bay Bridge and planned rerouting of bridge traffic onto a temporary section of S-track while CalTrans (California Department of Transportation) tears down and connects traffic to the new earthquake-safe single-deck span on the Oakland side of the Bay. The project is slated to be completed by 2013, but numerous road closures and the temporary rerouting take a heavy toll on commuters. If you plan on living in the more affordable East Bay and working in San Francisco or the Peninsula, these delays should be considered carefully.

Bay Area transportation planners have been doing their best to deal with the rapidly expanding population of cars on the freeways, as well as neighborhood activists who do not want a freeway in their backyards, and the planners seem to be making an impact, albeit slowly. The number of solo drivers has been slowly decreasing, as the stress- and money-saving option of carpooling becomes more popular. And with the recent opening of its much anticipated airport extension—which includes several new stops along the peninsula including SFO—BART has also become a way of life for many of those who work along its corridor. Plans are in the works to extend BART farther still, to provide better links between Santa Clara and Alameda counties. And with plans inching forward throughout the region to create so-called transit corridors—improving links among BART, CalTrain, light rail, ferries, buses, and shuttles as well as expanding bike and pedestrian pathways—commuters may soon have more reliable, easy-to-use, eco-friendly options.

For details on Bay Area transit options including fares, routes, and schedules as well as traffic updates, ridesharing, bicycling, and trip planning options, check out 511, a phone and web information service provided by the Metropolitan Transportation Commission (MTC). Simply dial 511 from anywhere in the nine Bay Area counties, 24 hours a day, 7 days a week, or visit www.511.org.

TRAFFIC

It cannot be said enough. The Bay Area has some of the worst traffic in the country, particularly if you must travel with the hordes in a high-volume direction, such as from the South Bay to San Francisco in the morning or vice versa in the evening. Particular routes remain stubborn problems—most notoriously the dreaded Bay Bridge commute, which brings throngs of East Bay residents to work in San Francisco and back, backing up not only Interstate 80 but the connecting highways as well as several city blocks starting in the late afternoon. In fact, the MTC named the Bay Bridge morning commute the area's most congested strip of highway. Replacing the South Bay as the new heart of the Bay Area's traffic woes, the East Bay now boasts three of the Bay Area's worst commutes along Interstate 580 in eastern Alameda County. If taking BART or some other form of mass transit is not feasible, the travel information line, 511 (no area code needed), will give you up-to-the-minute highway condition reports for the entire Bay Area. Or tune into KALW-FM at 91.7, KGO-AM at 810, and KCBS-AM at 740, during morning and afternoon commute hours. Real-time traffic incidents are available at http://cad.chp.ca.gov and now http://maps.google.com has real-time traffic information overlaid on their maps.

CARPOOLING

Rides for Bay Area Commuters Inc. is a free carpool and vanpool matching service. To be matched with a fellow commuter who is on a similar work schedule and lives and works close to you, call the service at 511 or check www.511.org. In the Bay Area you'll find carpool lanes, also called diamond or HOV (high-occupancy vehicle) lanes on the major freeways. The number of passengers required to qualify as a carpool and the hours during which the lane may be used exclusively by buses, vanpools, and carpools varies. Call 511 for more details, or check your route for posted information. During commute hours, 5 a.m. to 10 a.m., and 3 p.m. to 7 p.m., the Bay bridges offer free tolls for those driving with three or more people in a vehicle. Commute hours for the Golden Gate Bridge are 5 a.m. to 9 a.m. and 4 p.m. to 6 p.m. There are also 150 Park & Ride lots throughout the area where you can leave your car and meet up with a van- or carpool. Use 511.org's Rideshare to join—there's no need to drive down that lonesome highway all alone!

CAR SHARING

If you prefer to live car-free but need your own set of wheels every once in awhile for errands, moving, etc., car sharing programs let you reserve cars by the hour. In San Francisco and the East Bay, **City CarShare** maintains a fleet of cars, from hybrids to minivans, that can be picked up and dropped off at a variety of locations. They have a choice of plans, including special rates for some universities and organizations. For more information call 415-995-8588 or visit www.citycarshare.org. Another popular car sharing service is **Zipcar**, www.zipcar.com, 415-495-7478. Zipcar offers a variety of plans to choose from. Gas and insurance are included with both of these services.

CAR RENTALS

All the big rental outfits are represented in the Bay Area, most with numerous locations. Here are a few numbers to get you started:
- **Alamo**, 877-222-9075, TTY 800-522-9292, www.alamo.com
- **Avis**, 800-230-4898, www.avis.com
- **Budget**, 800-527-0700, www.budget.com
- **Dollar**, 800-800-3665, TTY 800-232-3301, www.dollar.com
- **Enterprise**, 800-261-7331, TTY 866-534-9270, www.enterprise.com
- **Hertz**, 800-654-3131, TTY 800-654-2280, www.hertz.com
- **National**, 877-222-9058, TTY 800-328-6323, www.nationalcar.com
- **Thrifty**, 800-847-4389, www.thrifty.com

TAXIS

The Bay Area is served by a number of cab companies, but they are not always easy to find and it almost always seems that once you sight a cab it's already full. Particularly on a rainy day, holidays (especially Halloween and New Year's), and during rush hour, it is best to call ahead. If you are already out and about and need a cab, you might have better luck hailing one in front of a hotel, a department store, or a hospital.

SAN FRANCISCO
- **De Soto Cab**, 925-277-9999
- **Luxor Cab**, 415-282-4141
- **SuperShuttle**, 415-558-8500, TTY 866-472-4497

- **Veteran's Cab**, 415-552-1300

NORTH BAY
- **Marin Cab**, 415-455-4555
- **Marin Door-to-Door,** 415-457-2717
- **North Bay Cooperative Taxi**, 415-332-2200
- **Yellow Cab of Marin County**, 415-453-6030

EAST BAY
- **Berkeley Yellow**, 510-528-9999
- **Contra Costa Cab**, 925-235-3000
- **Veteran's Cab**, 510-533-1900
- **Yellow Cab**, 510-317-2200

PENINSULA
- **Burlingame Rainbow Cab**, 650-344-6718
- **Hillsborough Yellow Cab**, 650-340-0330
- **Merit Taxi**, 650-571-0606
- **Peninsula Cab Co.**, 650-344-2627
- **Yellow Cab,** 650-321-1234

SOUTH BAY
- **American Cab**, 408-988-3300
- **Santa Clara Cab**, 408-773-1900
- **United Cab**, 408-971-1111
- **Yellow Cab**, 408-293-1234

BY BIKE

Many Bay Area residents commute to work by bicycle. To find out everything you need to know about using your bike as transportation in the Bay Area call 511 (no area code needed) and ask for the "**RIDES Bicycle Resource Guide**" or check www.511.org. At this site you can find out about bike racks at your place of work, track down a bike buddy, learn about bicycle routes and lanes, and find a bicycle club. If you choose this manner of commuting, make sure to purchase a bike light for the winter months, and wear a helmet! Bicycles are allowed on BART with the following restrictions: Bikes are allowed on at the Embarcadero Station during morning commute hours (7:05 a.m. to 8:50 a.m.) only for trips to the East Bay. For the evening commute (4:25 p.m. to 6:45 p.m.), bicycles coming from the East Bay must exit at the Embarcadero Station. During morning and evening commute hours, bikes are not allowed in the 12th and 19th Street Oakland Stations. During non-commute times, bicyclists are allowed in any car except for the first car. There is no extra cost for bringing your bike. Most ferries and buses (not all) also accommodate bikes. But be forewarned, most city bus racks can only hold one bicycle at a time! And note that bikes are not allowed on cable cars or historic streetcars.

For the latest about proposed bike routes, bicycle commuting initiatives, safety information, and bike laws, visit **California's Department of Transportation** web site, www.dot.ca.gov/hq/tpp/offices/bike Another resource is the **San Francisco Bicycle Coalition** at 415-431-BIKE (2453), www.sfbike.org. To learn more about recreational bicycling in the Bay Area, consult the **Sports and Recreation** chapter.

A note of interest: on the last Friday of every month, **Critical Mass**, a large group of bike riders, gathers at the Ferry building in downtown San Francisco to ride together throughout the city. Their intent is to be noticed, particularly by city leaders and drivers, in the hope that more attention will be paid to biking as an alternative form of transportation.

PUBLIC TRANSPORTATION

BAY AREA RAPID TRANSIT (BART)

The king of local transportation systems is Bay Area Rapid Transit, a high-speed, above- and below-ground train system that whisks travelers between San Francisco, the East Bay, and San Mateo County, through one of the world's longest underwater tunnels. BART transports about 350,000 people daily, and has a reputation for being clean, quiet, and on time.

Currently BART runs five lines on more than 100 miles of track between 43 stations. When the extension to the San Francisco International Airport opened, it brought with it three additional stations en route—South San Francisco, San Bruno, and Millbrae. Trains currently run weekdays from 4 a.m. to midnight, Saturdays, 6 a.m. to midnight, and Sundays, 8 a.m. to midnight. Fares are based on distance traveled, starting at $1.75 one way. Discount tickets (75% off) for senior citizens, children 5–12 years old, persons with disabilities who have proper identification, and students on a chaperoned field trip are sold at participating banks, retailers, social service agencies, and other community-based organizations. These tickets are not sold at any of the BART stations.

BART stations are also connection points for local bus services, making it fairly easy to get just about anywhere in the Bay Area on public transit. You can pick up free transfers from BART stations in San Francisco and Daly City for discounts on connections with MUNI. All BART stations are wheelchair accessible. Bicycles are allowed on BART; see **By Bike** above for details. For schedule and fare information drop by the Customer Service window at the Lake Merritt BART station in Oakland, or at the Embarcadero or Montgomery Stations in San Francisco during normal business hours, or call 510-465-2278 (Oakland, Berkeley, San Leandro), 415-989-2278 (San Francisco, Daly City) or 650-992-2278 (South

San Francisco/San Bruno/San Mateo); TTY 510-839-2220. Other numbers are listed at their informative web site, www.bart.gov.

SAN FRANCISCO MUNICIPAL TRANSPORTATION AUTHORITY (MUNI)

San Francisco's public transportation system employs a variety of vehicles including diesel and electric buses, electric trolleys (some of them vintage), MUNI Metro light-rail vehicles, and the world-renowned cable cars. In total, MUNI operates 80 lines, 17 of them express, as well as special service to Candlestick Park for 49ers games and other events. In general, service is available 24 hours, although not on all lines. The current adult fare is $2 one way. Cable car rides cost $5. Exact change is required on all MUNI vehicles, except for the cable cars. Transfers are available on all MUNI lines, as are discounts for seniors, youths and the disabled. A monthly pass costs $15.00 for seniors, youths, and disabled people, and $55.00 for everyone else. The monthly pass is also valid on specific BART, CalTrain, and SamTrans routes within the city (routes 24B and 34 and only within San Francisco), as well as cable cars. If you are taking BART and then MUNI, you can get a 25-cent discount on your bus ride. Just stop off before you exit the BART gates near the addfare machine to pick up a transfer discount coupon.

You can also always request a transfer to ride on another MUNI bus for free from the MUNI bus driver. Bus transfers are valid for 90 minutes and can be used for any direction. The popular light rail service has been gradually expanding over the years, and the 3rd Street extension "T" Line—linking southeast San Francisco with downtown—opened in late 2006.

For more information on MUNI service call 311 inside San Francisco, 415-701-2311; TTY 415-701-2323 or visit their web site at www.sfmta.com. Call 415-701-4485 or TTY 415-701-4730 for information about services for passengers with disabilities.

ALAMEDA–CONTRA COSTA TRANSIT (AC)

AC Transit, 510-891-4700, TTY 800-448-9790, www.actransit.org, the bus system connecting the East Bay to San Francisco, serves Alameda and Contra Costa counties. Widely used are the commute-hour Transbay Express Routes from San Francisco to cities in the East Bay such as Oakland, Berkeley, Alameda, Emeryville, Richmond, and more. AC Transit also connects with all East Bay BART stations. Ticket prices vary depending on distance traveled; they range from $2–4 (adult fare) to $1–2 for seniors, the disabled, and those under 17. You can purchase transfers for 25¢. Transfers from BART are $1.75.

SAN MATEO COUNTY TRANSIT (SAMTRANS)

SamTrans, 800-660-4287, TTY 650-508-6448, www.samtrans.com, provides Peninsula residents with local bus service and offers routes to downtown San Francisco. It also offers direct service from SFO to downtown San Francisco, making it possible for airline passengers to get to and from the airport entirely on public transit. The cost varies depending on distance traveled. Adult fares start at $1.75, Seniors/Disabled at 75¢, and aged 17 and under at $1.00.

GOLDEN GATE TRANSIT (GGT)

Golden Gate Transit, 511, 415-455-2000; TTY 711, www.goldengatetransit.org, provides **local bus service** for Marin County communities, as well as **commuter bus and ferry service** between Marin and Sonoma counties and downtown San Francisco (see below).

ADDITIONAL BUS SERVICES

- **Contra Costa County Connection** provides local bus service in Contra Costa County, call 925-676-7500, www.cccta.org.
- **Santa Clara Valley Transit Authority** (VTA) offers bus and light rail service to the South Bay, call 800-894-9908, 408-321-2300; TTY 408-321-2330, www.vta.org.

FERRIES

ALAMEDA/OAKLAND

Providing an aquatic link to downtown San Francisco for East Bay residents, the **Alameda/Oakland Ferry**, 510-705-8204, www.eastbayferry.com, is similar to the Golden Gate ferry service outlined below. Those who use the boat regularly often develop friendships that continue on land, and you can be sure plenty of professional networking takes place on board. The boats leave seven days a week from Oakland's Jack London Square, at the foot of Broadway, and from Alameda's Main Street terminal. They dock at San Francisco's Ferry Building and at Fisherman's Wharf. Food and beverage service is available. One-way fares range from $1.50 for a Short Hop between Alameda and Oakland to $6.25 for Adult Fare; and ticket books are also available.

VALLEJO

Baylink, 707-643-3779 or 877-643-3779, www.baylinkferry.com, operates a daily commuter ferry service from San Francisco to Vallejo. One-way fares are $6.50 to $13, and various passes are also available.

HARBOR BAY

The **Harbor Bay Ferry**, 510-769-5172, www.alamedaharborbayferry.com, operates from the San Francisco Ferry Building to Bay Farm Island (part of the City of Alameda) in the East Bay. Travel time is approximately 30 minutes. One-way fares are $6.50 for adults, with various passes available. The ferry runs Monday through Friday only, and does not operate on most major holidays.

GOLDEN GATE

The **Golden Gate Ferry Service**, 415-455-2000, www.goldengateferry.org, is the premier north county water link, with daily service connecting San Francisco with Larkspur and Sausalito. The ferries depart for San Francisco from the Larkspur Ferry Terminal and a Sausalito dock located just off Bridgeway, the city's main street. There is plenty of free parking at the Larkspur facility and metered parking close to the Sausalito launch point. There is no more civilized or more relaxing way to commute than on the ferry, and more and more people are choosing to take the boat these days. Drinks and snacks are served. The trip across the bay takes about 30 minutes. The cost varies depending upon distance traveled, with one-way fares ranging from $3.70 to $7.45.

ADDITIONAL FERRY SERVICE

- **Angel Island–Tiburon Ferry**, 415-435-2131, www.angelislandferry.com
- **Blue and Gold Fleet**, 415-705-8200, www.blueandgoldfleet.com

COMMUTER TRAINS

CALTRAIN

For Peninsula and South Bay residents, the commuter rail option is CalTrain, 800-660-4287, TTY 415-508-6448, www.caltrain.com. This service runs between Gilroy in the South Bay and San Francisco's Fourth Street Station. Once you get to San Francisco you'll need to take a bus, light-rail, cab, or walk to the Financial District. Fares on CalTrain are based on distance traveled within "zones," range from $2.50 to $11.25, and can be purchased at any CalTrain station. From San Jose, trains run Monday–Friday, 4:30 a.m. to 10:30 p.m., and from San Francisco, 4:55 a.m. to 12:01 a.m. Bikes are allowed in the northernmost car, which is the designated bicycle car. Some trains also have an added, second bicycle car.

AMTRAK

Amtrak trains don't board in San Francisco; instead you take the Amtrak bus at the Ferry Building, Pier 39 (near Fisherman's Wharf), or at Powell and

Market, which will then drive you over the Bay Bridge to the Amtrak station in Emeryville. Or you can take BART, disembark at the Richmond station, and catch an Amtrak train upstairs at the same station. Oakland has a new train station just two blocks off Jack London Square at Embarcadero and Alice Street. Amtrak provides connecting bus service to San Francisco, or you can head off on your own and catch the ferry. In San Francisco, Amtrak is located at 65 Cahill just south of the Alameda. Here you can connect up with local commuter trains and buses.

For more information call the central line at 800-USA-RAIL (872-7245), TTY 800-523-6590, or check www.amtrak.com. When visiting online, look for "Hot Deals," where you'll find discounts of up to 60% on long-distance coach train tickets. Regional Amtrak information can be found at Amtrak California, www.amtrakcalifornia.com, which lists local specials and promotions.

ALTAMONT COMMUTER EXPRESS (ACE)

Altamont Commuter Express is a commuter train service for those traveling between Stockton and San Jose, with additional stops in Lathrop/Manteca, Tracy, Livermore, Pleasanton, Fremont, and Santa Clara. Currently, there are two morning and two afternoon trains. Fares depend on the distance traveled. Weekly and monthly passes are available. For more information, contact 800-411-RAIL (7245) or visit the ACE web site at www.acerail.com.

GREYHOUND

Greyhound has numerous stations throughout the Bay Area. For more information, call 800-231-2222, TTY 800-345-3109, or visit their web site at www.greyhound.com.

AIRPORTS & AIRLINES

SAN FRANCISCO INTERNATIONAL AIRPORT (SFO)

Located 15 miles south of downtown San Francisco, SFO sits just off Highway 101 near the Peninsula cities of Millbrae and San Bruno. The granddaddy of Bay Area airports, it has undergone a massive reconstruction that befits the transportation hub that it is. One warning: fog can be a problem, causing delays, especially during the summer.

There is no shortage of transportation options between the airport and San Francisco. One of the best is BART, which runs directly to SFO, where it connects with a new air tram that will shuttle you straight to your terminal. Be sure to check the schedule ahead of time though, as service is less frequent outside rush hours and on weekends. A taxi or a limo will set you back about $40. One of the many shuttle vans, such as SuperShuttle, 415-558-8500, TTY 866-472-4497, www.supershuttle.com, will cost about $17 (additional passengers in your party are $10 each) but you may have to sit through a number of stops before you get to your destination (they claim no more than three stops per trip). If you've got time to kill and want to conserve cash, catch a SamTrans bus at one of several stops right outside the terminals for a ride directly into downtown San Francisco. (For more on SamTrans see above.)

For more information on SFO call 800-435-9736, or visit their web site at www.flysfo.com. Airlines serving SFO include:

- **Air Canada**, 888-247-2262, www.aircanada.ca
- **Air China**, 800-882-8122, www.airchina.com.cn/
- **Air France**, 800-237-2747, www.airfrance.com/us
- **AirTran**, 800-247-8726, www.airtran.com
- **Alaska**, 800-252-7522, www.alaskaair.com
- **American**, 800-433-7300, www.aa.com
- **British Airways**, 800-247-9297, www.britishairways.com
- **Continental**, 800-523-3273, www.continental.com
- **Delta**, 800-221-1212, www.delta.com
- **Hawaiian Airlines**, 800-367-5320, www.hawaiianair.com
- **Japan Airlines**, 800-525-3663, www.ar.jal.com/en
- **JetBlue**, 800-538-2583, www.jetblue.com
- **Lufthansa**, 800-645-3880, www.lufthansa.com
- **Mexicana**, 800-531-7921, www.mexicana.com
- **Northwest-KLM**, 800-225-2525, www.nwa.com
- **Qantas**, 800-227-4500, www.qantas.com
- **Southwest Airlines**, 800-435-9792, www.southwest.com
- **US Airways**, 800-428-4322, www.usairways.com
- **United**, 800-864-8331, www.united.com
- **Virgin America**, 877-359-8474, www.virginamerica.com
- **Virgin Atlantic**, 800-821-5438, www.virgin-atlantic.com

OAKLAND INTERNATIONAL AIRPORT

This East Bay airport is easier to use than San Francisco International for one simple reason: It is much smaller than its trans-bay Goliath. While SFO is serviced by many major US and international carriers, Oakland Airport focuses on commuter and low-cost airlines, the most popular being Southwest and the United Shuttle. Oakland Airport is fairly easy to get in and out of by car, but be aware that taking BART there will require switching to a shuttle bus at the Coliseum stop ($2.00 extra fee). Parking is usually available at Oakland Airport, even during peak holiday travel periods. The airport is located at the west end of Hegenberger Road, a clearly marked exit from Highway I-880.

Airlines serving Oakland Airport include:

- **Alaska**, 800-426-0333, www.alaskaair.com
- **Allegiant Air**, 702-505-8888, www.allegiantair.com

- **Delta**, 800-221-1212, www.delta.com
- **Hawaiian Airlines**, 800-367-5320, www.hawaiianair.com
- **Jet Blue**, 800-538-2583, www.jetblue.com
- **Mexicana**, 800-531-7921, www.mexicana.com
- **Southwest Airlines**, 800-435-9792, www.southwest.com
- **United Express**, 800-241-6522, www.united.com
- **US Airways**, 800-428-4322, www.usairways.com

For general information on Oakland Airport call 510-563-3300, www.flyoakland.com. For the latest on airport parking call 510-563-3200.

SAN JOSE INTERNATIONAL AIRPORT

Located just north of downtown, San Jose International Airport, like Oakland Airport, is relatively easy to navigate and to find parking. Large and small air carriers fly to San Jose International. For general information call 408-501-0979 or look at their web site at www.sjc.org.

Some of the airlines serving San Jose include:
- **Alaska**, 800-252-7522, www.alaskaair.com
- **American**, 800-433-7300, www.aa.com
- **Continental**, 800-525-0280, www.flycontinental.com
- **Delta**, 800-221-1212, www.delta.com
- **Mexicana**, 800-531-7921, www.mexicana.com
- **Northwest-KLM**, 800-225-2525, www.nwa.com
- **Southwest**, 800-435-9792, www.southwest.com
- **United**, 800-241-6522, www.united.com

ONLINE RESOURCES—AIR TRAVEL

A number of travel-related web sites all tout great deals including Travelocity.com, Expedia.com, Orbitz.com, and Cheaptickets.com—take your pick. If cost far outweighs convenience, check Priceline, www.priceline.com, where you may be able to pin down a cheap fare at an inconvenient hour (often in the middle of the night). Some airlines post last-minute seats at a reduced rate, usually online on web sites like www.airfarewatchdog.com. Northwest, www.nwa.com, posts last-minute cybersavers on Wednesdays at 12:01 a.m. Check with other airlines' web sites for similar deals.

To register a complaint against an airline, contact the Department of Transportation: 202-366-4000, TTY 800-877-8339, Office of Aviation Enforcement and Proceedings, 1200 New Jersey Ave, SE, Washington, DC 20590.

Information about flight delays can be checked online at www.fly.faa.gov.

U NTIL YOU FIND YOUR FIRST BAY AREA HOME OR APARTMENT, YOU'LL need an interim place to hang your hat. Besides hundreds of hotels, motels, and bed & breakfasts aimed at San Francisco's considerable tourist trade, there are old-fashioned, homey residential clubs in better neighborhoods that may be more economical. Also, although most of the hotels in the city are downtown or at Fisherman's Wharf, there are neighborhood hotels where you can get a sense of what it might be like to live in a particular area of San Francisco. If you are an adventurous and/or budget-minded newcomer, you may want to consider one of the single-room occupancy hotels, called SROs, that dot much of downtown. Keep in mind that these establishments typically offer just a small room with little more than a bed, dresser, chair, and a desk. They are popular because they are cheap and because they rent by the day, week, or month. Be wary, though, because these low-rent buildings are often located in the seedier parts of town—6th and Mission streets south of Market, and the Tenderloin, which is just north of Market.

Reservations for bigger, more mainstream and chain hotels can be had by calling a hotel directly or through a reservation service such as, among others, **Central Reservation Service**, www.crshotels.com, 800-555-7555, **Quikbook**, www.quikbook.com, 800-789-9887, or **San Francisco Reservations**, www. hotelres.com, 800-737-2060. Always ask about the cancellation policy when booking through discount sites, as charges may apply. Some companies ask for full payment upon making the reservation.

Low rates quoted below are for one person per night, and for the most part, high rates quoted are for two persons per night. Of course, prices are subject to change depending on the season. If you are a real bargain hunter, try negotiating a lower price.

Unless otherwise noted, all listed establishments are in San Francisco.

RESIDENCE CLUBS

Residence clubs offer secure housing, maid service, some meals, community rooms for television, videos, reading, games, message service, and the opportunity to meet dozens of people in the same situation as yourself. They are not the cheapest form of housing, but the pampering you receive while you search for something permanent may be worth the added expense. Prices per week typically range from $210 for a shared room for students to $375 and up.

- **Gaylord Suites**, 620 Jones St, 415-673-8445, www.gaylordsuites.com, a pretty, California Mission–style hotel
- **Kenmore Residence Club**, 1570 Sutter St, 415-776-5815, www.kenmorehotelsf.com
- **Monroe Residence Club**, 1870 Sacramento St, 415-474-6200, www.monroeresidenceclub.com
- **Vantaggio Suites**, 3 locations in San Francisco: Turk St, 415-922-0111, O'Farrell St, 415-885-0111, Post St, 415-614-2400, www.vantaggiosuites.com

INEXPENSIVE HOTELS

San Francisco has a range of basic, inexpensive motels and hotels located downtown and along outer Lombard Street in the Marina. Prices range from as little as $50 to $165 per night. The greater Bay Area has a variety of options too, many of them located just off of major highways.

- **Capri Motel**, 2015 Greenwich St, 800-975-2905, 415-346-4667, www.motelcaprisfo.com; located in a residential neighborhood in the Marina district
- **Comfort Inn**, 2775 Van Ness Ave, 415-928-5000, 825 Polk St, 415-673-0411, and 1370 Monument Blvd, Concord, 925-827-8998
- **Days Inn**, many locations throughout the Bay Area, suites with kitchenettes available; call 800-329-7466, www.daysinn.com
- **Hotel Beresford**, 635 Sutter St, 800-533-6533, 415-673-9900, www.beresford.com/beresford, close to Union Square
- **The Phoenix Hotel**, 601 Eddy St, 800-738-7477, www.jdvhotels.com, a San Francisco legend, this arty hotel is built around an enclosed courtyard pool, with popular adjoining bar; a frequently used pit stop for touring rock bands; good for young, energetic, music-loving set
- **Royal Pacific Motor Inn**, 661 Broadway, 800-545-5574, 415-781-6661, www.royalpacificmotorinn.com; free parking included (a San Francisco rarity!); close to Chinatown and North Beach
- **San Remo**, 2227 Mason St, 800-352-7366, www.sanremohotel.com, a charming old hotel (it has chain toilets) with odd-shaped rooms, shared bathrooms, a Victorian ambiance, a wine bar, and lots of European guests; located in North Beach

- **Seal Rock Inn**, 545 Point Lobos Ave, 888-732-5762, 415-752-8000, www. sealrockinn.com, located on the ocean, in the fog belt of the Richmond district; a good place to stay if you want to get a taste of the Richmond or Sunset districts

MEDIUM-PRICED HOTELS

The next step up, mid-range hotels run a bit more; room rates vary from about $125 to $250 per night; many of these hotels offer online special rates. Locations are San Francisco unless otherwise noted.

- **Berkeley City Club**, 2315 Durant Ave, Berkeley, 510-848-7800, www.berkeleycityclub.com
- **Berkeley Travelodge**, 1820 University, Berkeley, 800-578-7878, 510-843-4262, www.travelodge.com
- **Chancellor Hotel**, 433 Powell St, 800-428-4748, 415-362-2004, www.chancellorhotel.com, Union Square location, meeting facilities available
- **Claremont Hotel Club and Spa**, 41 Tunnel Rd, Berkeley, 800-551-7266, 510-843-3000, www.claremontresort.com, a rambling Victorian spa
- **Courtyard by Marriott**, 299 2nd St, 800-321-2211, 415-947-0700, www.marriott.com/courtyard
- **Cupertino Inn**, 10889 North De Anza Blvd, Cupertino, 800-222-4828, 408-996-7700, event services and business amenities
- **Holiday Inn Express Hotel and Suites**, 93 W El Camino Real, Mountain View, 800-445-7774, 650-967-6957, www.hitowncenter.com, geared for business travelers, offers a variety of extended stay options
- **Hotel Boheme**, 444 Columbus Ave in North Beach, 415-433-9111, www.hotelboheme.com; an ode to the beatniks
- **Hotel California (Best Western)**, 580 Geary St, 800-227-4223, www.hotelca.com/sanfrancisco; 5 other Best Western hotels located in San Francisco
- **Hotel Rex**, 562 Sutter St, 800-433-4434, 415-433-4434, www.thehotelrex.com, cozy boutique hotel in the heart of the theater district with tasty restaurant downstairs
- **Hotel Sierra Suites**, 3915 Rivermark Plaza, Santa Clara, 408-486-0800; geared for extended stay
- **Hotel Vertigo**, 940 Sutter St, 415-885-6800, www.hotelvertigosf.com, located in lower Nob Hill; the site of the Empire Hotel, made famous in Hitchock's classic *Vertigo*
- **King George Hotel**, 334 Mason St, 800-288-6005, 415-781-5050, www.kinggeorge.com, downtown, an interesting, skinny, green building with a popular tea room
- **Oakland Marriott**, 1001 Broadway, Oakland, 510-451-4000, www.marriott.com, downtown with great views of Lake Merritt and the Bay

- **San Ramon Marriott**, 2600 Bishop Dr, San Ramon, 925-867-9200, www.marriott.com

LUXURY HOTELS

The finest the Bay Area has to offer; if you can afford to splurge, you'll be well taken care of here:

- **The Clift**, 495 Geary St, 800-697-1791, 415-775-4700, www.clifthotel.com/#/home; located downtown, considered to be one of the best in the city; lobby designed by Philippe Starck, houses the elegant Redwood Room, an ever-popular piano bar
- **The Fairmont**, 950 Mason St, 866-540-4491, 415-772-5000, www.fairmont.com, at the top of Nob Hill, one of the city's opulent, old-world hotels
- **The Fairmont**, 170 South Market St, San Jose, 866-540-4493, 408-998-1900, www.fairmont.com/sanjose, in the heart of downtown
- **Garden Court Hotel**, 520 Cowper St, Palo Alto, 800-824-9028, 650-322-9000, *www*.gardencourt.com, downtown location, central to Silicon Valley, Stanford University
- **The Grand Hotel**, 865 W El Camino Real, Sunnyvale, 800-786-0827, 408-720-8500, www.svgrandhotel.com
- **The Grand Hyatt**, 345 Stockton St, 415-398-1234, www. grandsanfrancisco.hyatt.com, downtown
- **Hotel Drisco**, 2901 Pacific Ave, 800-634-7277, 415.346.2880; in Pacific Heights, an old gem with great views
- **Hotel Los Gatos**, 210 E Main Street, Los Gatos, 866.335.1700, 408.335.1700, www.jdvhotels.com/hotels/los_gatos; central to Silicon Valley
- **Hotel Sausalito**, 16 El Portal, Sausalito, 888-442-0700, www.hotelsausalito.com
- **The Mark Hopkins**, One Nob Hill Circle, 415-392-3434, www.markhopkins.net, old-fashioned luxury atop Nob Hill, what a view!
- **Ritz-Carlton**, 600 Stockton St, 415-296-7465, www.ritzcarlton.com/en/Properties/SanFrancisco, in Nob Hill, luxurious
- **Stanford Park Hotel**, 100 El Camino Real, Menlo Park, 866-241-2431, 650-322-1234, www. stanfordparkhotel.com/hotel, adjacent to Stanford University, Palo Alto, the Peninsula and South Bay
- **Westin St. Francis**, 335 Powell St, 800-937-8461, 415-397-7000, www.westinstfrancis.com, luxurious grand hotel in the heart of Union Square

EXTENDED-STAY ESTABLISHMENTS

Generally, extended-stay residences cater to corporations rather than individuals. However, many will rent directly to people who are moving to a new city. And if you are getting assistance from your employer as part of a job relocation, this can be a great way to start out. In general, short-term rentals are less costly than extended hotel stays and give you a comfortable, homey place to rest your head when you arrive, while leaving you time to house hunt in person. Most offer month-to-month or week-to-week fully furnished accommodations—typically in studios or one-bedroom apartments with kitchens—and the majority require a 30-day minimum stay. Higher end spots can also come loaded with hotel-style amenities including laundry service, restaurants, and fitness centers. You can check out the following, or any of the standards such as Residence Inns or Courtyards at Marriott.

- **BridgeStreet Worldwide**, 800-278-7338, www.bridgestreet.com, has several corporate housing sites in San Francisco, including Avalon at Mission Bay, as well as apartments in the East Bay, Peninsula, and South Bay; weekly, monthly and year-long rentals available. Fully furnished units, fitness facilities, parking, families welcome.
- **Suite America** (short-term rentals nationwide), 800-784-8341, 510-429-9700, www.suiteamerica.com
- **ExecuStay**, 888-340-2565, www.execustay.com, a nationwide Marriott Hotel–affiliated service that offers fully furnished apartments, kitchens, and in-unit washers and dryers; some apartments can also accommodate pets and children.
- **Key Housing Connections**, 800-989-0410, www.keyhousing.net, offers furnished accommodation Bay Area–wide for a minimum of 30 days, depending on availability.
- **Oakwood Corporate Apartments**, 877-902-0832, www.oakwood.com; this company has properties all over the Bay Area, and beyond. Fully furnished apartments are customized to suit your needs. The minimum stay is generally 30 days, some locations allow shorter stays. Prices vary depending on location.
- **Trinity Management Services**, San Francisco, 415-433-3333, www.trinitymanagement.com; studios and one-bedrooms, furnished or unfurnished, leases available from one month to one year. Trinity Properties offer numerous short-term rentals around San Francisco. Pets not allowed.

SUBLETS

Many people opt to stay in one of the many vacant apartments left behind by San Francisco's globetrotting denizens. Really great deals can be found, and furnished apartments are the norm. Check www.craigslist.org under "sublets/temporary" for more information. You can also post a free "want" advertisement if you plan ahead.

BED & BREAKFASTS

There are hundreds of B&Bs in the Bay Area, ranging in price from as low as $65 per night for a simple room in a private home to as much as $200 per night for an opulent unit in an historic Victorian or a self-contained carriage house or private cottage. **Bed and Breakfast International** has been providing information and reservations about local B&Bs since 1978 and boasts connections to more than 300 B&Bs and similar lodgings. Check out Bed and Breakfast International on the web at www.ibbp.com.

HOSTELS/YMCAs

In addition to the facilities listed below, you can find out more information on local youth hostels at www.hostelweb.com or www.hiusa.org

SAN FRANCISCO/NORTH BAY

- **Adelaide Hostel**, 5 Isadora Duncan Ln, 877-359-1915, www.adelaidehostel. com, basic, funky, private rooms and dorm style options, full of budget-minded Europeans; located in downtown San Francisco
- **AYH City Center**, 685 Ellis St, 415-474-5721, www.sfhostels.com/city-center
- **AYH Hostel Union Square**, 312 Mason St, 415-788-5604, www.sfhostels. com/downtown
- **AYH Hostel Fisherman's Wharf**, Fort Mason, Bldg #240, 415-771-7277, www. sfhostels.com/fishermans-wharf
- **Globetrotters Inn**, 494 Broadway, 415-346-5786, www.globetrottersinn.com
- **HI Marin Headlands**, 941 Fort Berry, Sausalito, 415-331-2777, www.norcal-hostels.org/marin, dorms and private rooms
- **YMCA**, 631 Howard St, Suite 500, 415-777-9622, www.ymcasf.org. From this main web site, check for locations throughout the City

SOUTH BAY

- **Hidden Villa Hostel**, 26870 Moody Rd, Los Altos Hills, 650-949-8650, www. hiddenvilla.org/hostel.php
- **Sanborn Park Hostel**, 15808 Sanborn Rd, Saratoga, 408-741-0166, 408-741-9555, www.sanbornparkhostel.org

ACCESSIBLE LODGING FOR THE DISABLED

The Bay Area is very sensitive to the needs to the disabled and offers numerous options for those with disabilities. Check with your hotel before booking to ensure their accessibility features.

A couple of helpful web sites are:

- **www.onlyinsanfrancisco.com/plan_your_trip/access_guide.asp**; from here, print out a thorough access guide to the Bay Area that includes hotels as well as major city attractions
- **www.accessnca.com**, a web site with links to accessibility options for travel throughout Northern California

AS WONDERFUL AND DIVERSE AS THE BAY AREA IS, EVERYONE LIKES to get away from city living now and again. Whether it's skiing, water sports, scenery, gambling, historical tours, wining and dining, or just rest and relaxation, there are dozens of nearby destinations to suit most anyone. Interesting possibilities abound outside the immediate Bay Area; in fact, you can go skiing on Saturday and sailing on Sunday, and be back to work by Monday. Following are just a few of the many quick getaways Northern California has to offer.

NORTH OF SAN FRANCISCO

If you don't want to drive far and you want to keep an eye on San Francisco, **Angel Island** may be the ticket. Located in the middle of San Francisco Bay, Angel Island is a short jaunt, either by ferry or sailboat, and a good place to picnic, barbecue, join a softball game, bike, kayak, hike the scenic trails, and camp. Call 415-435-1915 or visit www.angelisland.org for more information. For the San Francisco and Vallejo ferries, contact the Blue and Gold Fleet at 415-705-8200; the Tiburon Ferry information is at 415-435-2131.

In Marin County, a stay in a cedar lodge with meals included is available at **Green Gulch Farm Zen Center**, 1601 Shoreline Highway, Sausalito, 415-383-3134, www.sfzc.org/ggf. Here you can witness a Japanese tea ceremony, join in classes and meditation, and even learn about organic gardening. Most of the fruits and vegetables grown at Green Gulch end up as a vegetarian meal at Greens Restaurant in Fort Mason. If this kind of getaway appeals to you, get a copy of *Sanctuaries, the Complete United States: A Guide to Lodging in Monasteries, Abbeys, and Retreats* by Jack and Marcia Kelly.

On a hot summer day, you may want to drive windy Highway 1, past the Green Gulch Farm Zen Center, and venture to **Stinson Beach** for sunbathing, body surfing, swimming, or just exploring the shore. Be aware that you may not be the only one with this plan; traffic can be horrible. Another great beach getaway is **Point Reyes National Seashore**, which includes 30 miles of coastline and 70,000 acres of pristine wilderness. Amidst its rugged bluffs, wooded canyons, dense forests, and open meadows, you'll find spectacular hiking, biking, camping, bird watching, and whale watching. For information about camping at Point Reyes contact the Visitors' Center at 415-464-5100, www.nps.gov/pore. Make sure to reserve camping sites ahead of time.

One of the most popular Bay Area getaways is a journey to **Napa** and **Sonoma counties** for fine wines and steaming mud. If you're a gourmand, these areas offer dozens of world-renowned **vineyards** and **wineries**, most with tours, tastings, and some with fine restaurants. Connoisseurs recommend Auberge du Soleil, 180 Rutherford Hill Road, Rutherford, www.aubergedusoleil.com; Tra Vigne, 1050 Charter Oak Ave, Saint Helena, www.travignerestaurant.com; and The French Laundry, 6640 Washington Street, Yountville, www.frenchlaundry. com. You can even take a wine train to eat, drink, and view the gentle landscape all the way from St. Helena to Napa, without having to designate a driver. For information about the train call 800-427-4124 or check out the Wine Train web site, http://winetrain.com.

Napa and Sonoma counties also host numerous **spa-type resorts**. Facilities range from the funky to the glamorous. Most of the spas are in the town of Calistoga. Below is a list of some of the spas, many of which have indoor and outdoor pools, mineral baths, steam rooms, dirty but oh so cleansing mud baths, salt scrubs, massage, and more. This list is far from comprehensive:

- **Calistoga Spa Hot Springs**, 1006 Washington St, Calistoga, 866-822-5772, 707-942-6269, www.calistogaspa.com.
- **Dr. Wilkinson's Hot Springs**, 1507 Lincoln Ave, Calistoga, 707-942-4102, www.drwilkinson.com
- **Fairmont Sonoma Mission Inn**, 100 Boyes Blvd, 866-540-4499, 707-938-9000, www.fairmont.com/sonoma
- **Indian Springs**, 1712 Lincoln Ave, Calistoga, 707-942-4913, www.indianspringscalistoga.com
- **Lavender Hill Spa**, 1015 Foothill Blvd, Calistoga, 800-528-4772, 707-942-4495, www.lavenderhillspa.com

If all this isn't enough, you can ride a hot air balloon, take a tram up a mountainside, sail through the air on a glider, hike, bike, horseback ride, picnic, or shop at posh designer outlets. For further information about the entire region, go to www.co.napa.ca.us or www.sonoma.com.

Another North Bay getaway is a visit to the old logging region of **Russian River**. In the 1920s and '30s, the area was a working-class summer resort. During and after the Depression it suffered from neglect and overuse, and was quite deteriorated by the 1970s when entrepreneurs arrived and began restoring the old buildings. Today Russian River is again a resort destination with lodging, fine restaurants, wineries, camping, hiking, horseback riding, and more. The natural environs of the Russian River, with its sandy beaches, redwood groves, and placid river, make it a pleasant place to spend a day or even a weekend. Canoeing down the river is a popular way to explore the area. Begin in Forestville and the local canoe company will meet you and your canoe 10 miles downriver in Guerneville. After canoeing, take a trip down the Russian River Wine Road (www.wineroad. com) to sample fine wine. For more information about the many things to do here, contact the Russian River Visitors Center, www.russianriver.com at 877-644-9001, 707-869-9000 or visit www.russianriver.com

Heading toward the coastline around **Mendocino**, located about three and half hours north of San Francisco, you'll encounter breathtaking scenery. The town of Mendocino reminds some of fishing villages on the East Coast. You can watch for whales, wade in the tide pools, hike in Mendocino Headlands State Park, 707-937-5804, or camp among redwoods at Van Damme State Park, 707-937-5804. At the **Jug Handle State Reserve** you can view tectonic uplifts and pygmy forests. If riding horses along the beach appeals to you, take a trail ride at Ricochet Ridge Ranch, **888-873-5777**, 707-964-7669. Many opt to explore the area by train, allowing the engineer of the Skunk Train to do the driving through 40 miles of redwoods and gulches, 866-457-5865, www.skunk-train.com.

The community of **Sea Ranch**, located 100 miles north of San Francisco on Highway 1, offers house rentals with ocean views and nearby trails. Abalone diving, kayaking, horseback riding, and swimming are only some of the activities, not to mention the golf course. For more details go to www.searanch-getaway.com or call 800-643-8899.

Fort Bragg, about four hours north of San Francisco on Highway 1, was built to protect the peace-loving Pomo Indians from less peaceful settlers, though the actual fort hasn't been here since the 1860s. These days Fort Bragg is a lumber town, and during the annual Paul Bunyan Days you can watch lumberjacks test their skill in a number of competitions. Contact the Mendocino Coast Fort Bragg Chamber of Commerce at 707-961-6300 or visit www.mendocinocoast.com for more information.

PENINSULA/SOUTH BAY

The coastline from San Francisco all the way south to Santa Cruz offers a scenic getaway with bluffs, beaches, and great surfing spots. In Half Moon Bay, you can pick pumpkins at any of the numerous pumpkin patches along the highway; in October, check out the Art and Pumpkin Festival. Sixty miles south of San Francisco brings you to **Año Nuevo State Reserve**, home to large numbers of northern elephant seals. The reserve offers memorable tours during breeding season from December to March. Call 650-879-0227 for more information.

Monterey/Carmel is also known as John Steinbeck country, as he based many of his novels here, including *Cannery Row*, *Of Mice and Men*, and *The Grapes of Wrath*. Now the canneries are closed, and resorts and tourist sites stand in their stead. At the Monterey Bay Aquarium you can come eye to eye with strange-shaped sunfish or marvel at the elegant jellyfish. For more information on the region, go to www.monterey.com.

These days, Carmel is tourist oriented—full of restaurants, art galleries, gift shops, inns, and hotels—and is an easy place for children and elderly folks to get around. The scenery is spectacular, with sea lions and coves, rocky beaches, wind-whipped cypress trees, and well-maintained indigenous gardens. Nor can we forget the famous Pebble Beach Golf Course, where Tiger Woods etched his name into the golfing record books, winning the 100th US Men's Open by 15 shots. The Carmel Mission on Rio Road and Lasuen Drive, 831-624-1271, dates from 1797. The missionaries assigned here must have counted their blessings to be in such a scenic place and gentle climate. In the early 1900s, Carmel-by-the-Sea became a mecca for artists and writers. Robert Louis Stevenson, Ansel Adams, Sinclair Lewis, Edward Weston, Upton Sinclair, and Mary Austin settled at one time in Carmel. Poet Robinson Jeffers' home has been made into a museum; contact Tor House, www.torhouse.org, 831-624-1813 for details. The Henry Miller Library, with memorabilia from that famous author, is located nearby in Big Sur. Call 831-667-2574, or check www.henrymiller.org for more details. Residents and tourists alike gather to watch the sunset at Nepenthe Restaurant along the cliffs of Big Sur, 48510 Highway One, 831-667-2345.

Those looking for a more spiritual outing may want to drive to **Big Sur** to visit the famous Esalen Institute/Hot Springs, 831-667-3000, www.esalen.org. The institute, designed to foster personal and social transformation, offers seminars, lodging, dining, hot springs, a pool, massages, and awesome views of the California coastline.

On the northern part of Monterey Bay sits **Santa Cruz**, a striking contrast to the more conservative town of Carmel. The bohemian-hippie enclave of Santa Cruz is as lovely as any beach town, with wind-swept trees, rolling hills, and ocean vistas, though most outsiders come here for the Santa Cruz Beach Boardwalk, 400 Beach Street, 831-423-5590, www.beachboardwalk.com. Here you can ride the wooden roller coaster or the merry-go-round and experience an old-style amusement park. The University of California at Santa Cruz, with its laid-back student body, adds to the beachy feel of this friendly town—despite its many resident panhandlers. Visit the Santa Cruz Municipal Wharf for the Santa Cruz Surfing Museum on West Cliff Drive, 831-420-6289. Come in the summer and sit on the beach to listen to Summertime Summer Nights Concerts, or attend an opera at the Capitola Theatre, 120 Monterey Avenue, Capitola, 831-462-3131. If thrift shopping is your thing, junk-stores on Capitola

Avenue are quite popular; they even offer a guide and map for your convenience. For a perfect place to watch the sunset or build a fire on the beach after dusk, try New Brighton, Seacliff, Rio del Mar, or Manresa state beaches. There are fire rings for barbecues and roasting marshmallows. For more information, check www.scccvc.org/things/beachlist.cfm or www.ci.santa-cruz.ca.us.

Amateur and professional geologists alike flock to the epicenter of the 1989 Loma Prieta quake at what's known as the **Earthquake Trail** in **Nisene Marks State Park**. Located 80 miles south of San Francisco, just a few miles outside of Santa Cruz, the area is lovely, sheltered by pines and oaks with gentle streams running through. There are 10,000 acres of forest here, so plenty of non-geology folk visit as well. Visit www.santacruzstateparks.org/parks/nisene for more information. Call the Aptos Chamber of Commerce at 831-688-1467 or visit their web site, www.aptoschamber.com, for further sightseeing and hotel ideas.

SIERRAS AND GOLD COUNTRY

Twenty-five miles north of Auburn in the **Sierra Nevada foothills** is **Gold Country**. View what the '49ers experienced when they flocked here from around the world in search of their fortunes. In this old mining territory you can pan for gold, swim, or sun on a rock while being sprayed by the cooling foam of the Yuba River. Bird watching is popular, or if you're a homesick Northeasterner, come in the autumn to take in the brilliantly colored maple and aspen leaves. In summer and fall you can fish for trout or bass. Hiking is possible at Buttermilk Bend and Independence Trail, or if you're up to it, try the steep Humbug Trail. Call 800-655-6569, or check out www.nevadacitychamber.com for information. Some of the best whitewater rafting and kayaking can be had along the American, Stanislaus, Tuolumne, and Merced rivers, all weaving through the Sierra foothills.

In winter, many head north on I-80 to ski in the Sierras. There are dozens of choices in **Lake Tahoe** for downhill or cross-country skiers. You can also ice-skate, snowboard, or sled. Lake Tahoe is loads of fun in the summer, too. That's when folks go water-skiing in the icy waters of Lake Tahoe. You can also kayak, river raft, or even try inner tubing the chilly Truckee River. Camping, rock climbing, and hiking in the Sierras are first rate. If you want to reserve a roof over you head, contact Lake Tahoe Central Reservations at 888-434-1262 or at www.gotahoenorth.com.

Nearby, **Reno**, which proudly sports the moniker "The Biggest Little City in the World," in big flashing lights, offers a mini Las Vegas–style quick getaway. Roulette wheels, card tables, cocktails, and slot machines are the name of the game here. Along with 24-hour casino entertainment, you'll find hearty buffets, big name country and pop music performers, late night lounge acts, and a host of golf courses including PGA Tour host Montreux Golf and Country Club. For more information contact 775-337-3030 or www.reno-sparkschamber.org. For hotel and resort reservations check out www.reno.com

NATIONAL PARKS

To learn about the camping and tour reservation system for the National Park system, visit www.nps.gov. For reservations, visit www.recreation.gov or call 877-444-6777, TTY 877-833-6777. The National Park Service Office for the Bay Area is located at Fort Mason, Building 201, 415-561-4700.

YOSEMITE NATIONAL PARK

Beloved by Californians and out-of-state tourists alike, Yosemite is a popular destination for many, though most Bay Area visitors come in the fall, after the summer crowds have gone. President Theodore Roosevelt called Yosemite "the most beautiful place on earth," and it seems photographer Ansel Adams and naturalist John Muir were equally awestruck, having spent years here documenting the incredible natural beauty, including Half Dome, El Capitan, and Nevada Falls. Yosemite has gotten much more popular and crowded since Muir and Adams made their way around the valley. The valley floor is often packed with tourists, and many try to avoid it, preferring to head to the backcountry hiking trails. Intrepid folks hike 17 steep miles to the top of Half Dome, while rock climbers finesse their way up El Capitan. There's a hut system for luxury backcountry camping, but the permits for these are issued by lottery and therefore can be difficult to obtain. Wilderness permits are required for any overnight travel into the park's backcountry; call 209-372-0740 for more details about hut and wilderness permits. For more details about Yosemite, contact Yosemite National Park, P.O. Box 577, Yosemite, CA 95389, 209-372-0200 or check www.nps.gov/yose or www.yosemitepark.com.

NATIONAL FOREST SERVICE

If you are planning a camping trip, call the National Forest Service's toll-free reservation line at 877-444-6777, TDD, 877-833-6777. You can also make your reservation online at www.recreation.gov.

A LMOST EVERY DAY OF THE YEAR THERE IS SOMETHING SPECIAL TO DO or see in this culturally rich region. Many local events take place on an annual basis so you can look forward to them year after year. Here are just a few of the celebrations and events you may want to experience for yourself. Specific dates are not provided as they may change depending on the particular year. Locations are provided when possible, although they too sometimes change from year to year. If none is given, then assume San Francisco and call for details.

JANUARY

- **Chinese New Year Celebrations** begin toward the end of the month and go into February in Chinatown, San Francisco, 415-986-1370, www.chineseparade.com
- **Golden Gate Kennel Club Dog Show**, Cow Palace, Daly City, 415-819-5773, www.goldengatekc.com
- **Martin Luther King, Jr., Birthday Celebration**: San Francisco Annual Freedom March from CalTrain station to Civic Center, SF Martin Luther King Civic Committee, 415-643-5121, www.sfmlk.org; for information about events happening throughout the Bay Area, contact the Northern California Martin Luther King, Jr., Birthday Observance Committee, 510-562-3372, www.norcalmlk.org
- **Peninsula Orchid Society Show & Sale**, Fair Oaks Community Center, 1400 Roosevelt Ave, Redwood City, 650-780-7500 http://penorchidsoc.org
- **San Jose International Auto Show**, McEnery Convention Center, San Jose, 408-792-4194, www.motortrendautoshows.com/sanjose
- **Tall Ships Exposition**, Jack London Square, Oakland, 800-200-5239, www. jacklondonsquare.com

- **Tet Festival**, Vietnamese New Year (sometimes in February), in San Francisco at the Civic Center and Tenderloin District, 415-351-1038; huge celebration in the South Bay, Santa Clara County Fairgrounds, San Jose, 408-494-3247
- **Whale Watching** (through March), Point Reyes National Seashore, 415-669-1534, www.pointreyes.net

FEBRUARY

- **Arts of Pacific Asia Show**, Fort Mason, 310-455-2886, www.caskeylees.com
- **Black History Month Celebrations**, Oakland Museum of California, Oakland, 510-238-2200, www.museumca.org; Oakland Public Libraries, Oakland, 510-238-3136 or www.oaklandlibrary.org; Westlake Park, Daly City, 650-991-8001; MLK Jr. Community Center, San Mateo, 650-522-7470
- **Chinatown Community Street Fair**, Chinatown, www.sanfranciscochinatown.com
- **Chinese New Year Celebration,** Bay Area Discovery Museum, Sausalito, 415-339-3900, www.badm.org/home
- **Chinese New Year Parade**, Chinatown, 415-391-9680, www.chineseparade.com, long-running nighttime parade
- **The Marin Show: Art of the Americas**, Marin Center, San Rafael, 310-822-9145, www.marinshow.com, known as the "Superbowl of Native American art collecting"
- **Pacific Orchid Exposition**, Fort Mason, 650-548-6700, www.orchidsanfrancisco.org
- **Russian Festival**, Sutter and Divisadero sts, 415-921-7631, www.russiancentersf.com

MARCH

- **International Women's Day Celebration**, call San Francisco location, 415-422-5662
- **Russian River Wine Barrel Tasting**, local wineries strut their stuff; call for locations in Sonoma County, 800-723-6336, www.wineroad.com
- **Saint Patrick's Day Parade**, Market St, San Francisco, 415-586-4826
- **San Francisco International Asian American Film Festival**, 415-863-0814
- **Sonoma County Home and Garden Show**, Sonoma County Fairgrounds, Santa Rosa, 707-545-4200, www.sonomacountyfair.com
- **White Elephant Sale**, benefits Oakland Museum of California, call for location, Oakland, 510-536-6800, www.whiteelephantsale.org

APRIL

- **Bodega Bay Fisherman's Festival**, benefit for Bodega Bay community services; Westside Park, Bodega Bay, 707-875-3866, www.bbfishfest.com

- **Cal Day**, open house at UC Berkeley for the community, www.berkeley.edu/calday/
- **Cherry Blossom Festival**, Japantown, 415-563-2313, www.nccbf.org
- **Earth Day Events**, Civic Center Park, Berkeley, 510-548-2220, multiple events and locations in Oakland, 510-238-7611; College of Marin, Marin, 415-457-8811
- **Grand National Rodeo**, for the cowpoke inside us all, Cow Palace, Daly City, 415-404-4111, www.grandnationalrodeo.com
- **Opening Day on the Bay**, kicks off the local yachting season on the San Francisco Bay, 415-331-0702, www.picya.org
- **San Francisco International Film Festival**, 415-561-5000, www.sffs.org
- **Spring Garden Festival**, Marin Art & Garden Center, Ross, 415-455-5260, www.magc.org
- **Youth Arts Festival**, Berkeley Arts Center, Berkeley, 510-644-6893, www.berkeleyartcenter.org

MAY

- **American Pacific Heritage Festival**, Bay Area Discovery Museum, Sausalito, 415-339-3900, www.badm.org/home
- **Arboretum Plant Sale**, San Francisco Botanical Garden Nursery, www.sfbotanicalgarden.org
- **Bay to Breakers**, a seven-mile, cross-city, run/walk, with incredible sights and costumes, in San Francisco, 415-359-2800, www.baytobreakers.com
- **Carnaval**, Latin street party in San Francisco, 24th and Mission sts, 415-621-2255, www.carnavalsf.com
- **Cinco de Mayo Celebration**, Stanford University, Palo Alto, 650-723-2089; downtown San Jose, 408-277-4000
- **Cinco de Mayo Parade**, in San Francisco, 24th and Mission sts, 415-647-1533, www.sfcincodemayo.com
- **Hometown Days**, local arts & crafts, Burton Park, San Carlos, 650-574-2700, www.sancarloshometowndays.com
- **Marin Greek Festival**, Zorba would feel welcome, Nativity of Christ Church, Ignacio, 415-883-1998, www.nativityofchrist.org
- **New Living Expo**, a must for New Age aficionados, Concourse in San Francisco, 415-382-8300, www.newlivingexpo.com
- **Nikkei Matsuri Japanese Festival**, Japantown, San Jose, www.nikkeimatsuri.org
- **Oakland Greek Festival**, Greek Orthodox Cathedral, Oakland, 510-531-3400, www.oaklandgreekfestival.com
- **Santa Clara Valley's WWII Experience**, Pacific Hotel Gallery, San Jose, 408-287-2290

- **Stanford PowWow**, massive gathering of Native Americans, Stanford University, Palo Alto, http://powwow.stanford.edu
- **Tiburon Wine Festival**, Point Tiburon Plaza, Tiburon, 415-435-5633, http://tiburonwinefestival.homestead.com/

JUNE

- **Black & White Ball**, open to the public, this glamour symphony fundraiser is held every other year in San Francisco, call for locations, 415-864-6000.
- **Chamarita Pentecostal Festival**, Portuguese extravaganza, IDES Hall, Half Moon Bay, 650-726-2729, www.coastsidelive.com
- **Haight Ashbury Street Fair**, fun and frolic at the free love flash point, Haight and Ashbury sts, San Francisco, www.haightashburystreetfair.org
- **Juneteenth Celebration**, marking Lincoln's Emancipation Proclamation: San Francisco parade and celebration, Fillmore St, 415-931-2729, www.sfjuneteenth.org
- **Lesbian Gay Bisexual Transgender Celebration & Parade**, also known as the Gay Pride Parade, numerous San Francisco locations, 415-864-0831
- **Mill Valley Wine & Gourmet Food-Tasting**, Downtown Plaza, Mili Valley, 415-388-9700, www.millvalley.org/main
- **Milpitas Summer Concert Series**, through August, call for locations, Milpitas, 408-586-33210
- **North Beach Festival**, an Italian blowout, Washington Square Park in North Beach, San Francisco, www.sfnorthbeach.org/NBFestival
- **Novato Art, Wine & Music Festival**, Old Town, Novato 415-897-1164, www.novatochamber.com
- **San Anselmo Art & Wine Festival**, San Anselmo Ave, San Anselmo, 707-829-5064
- **San Francisco Jazz Festival** summer sessions, call for locations, June–October, 866-920-5299, www.sfjazz.org
- **San Jose Gay Pride Festival & Silicon Valley Pride Parade**, Discovery Meadow, San Jose, www.sanjosepride.com
- **Sonoma-Marin Fair**, Petaluma Fairgrounds, Petaluma, 707-283-3247, www.sonoma-marinfair.org
- **Stern Grove Midsummer Music Festival**, in San Francisco, Stern Grove, June–August, 415-252-6252, www.sterngrove.org
- **Sunnyvale Art & Wine Festival**, downtown Sunnyvale, 408-736-4971, www.artsopolis.com/event/detail/44177
- **Trips for Kids Bike Swap**, huge bicycle event serving at-risk youth, San Rafael, www.tripsforkids.org
- **Twilight Concerts in the Park**, Tuesday nights through July, various parks, Palo Alto, 650-463-4940, www.cityofpaloalto.org

- **Union Street Festival**, Cow Hollow event with music, art, and gourmet food, Union and Fillmore sts, San Francisco, 800-310-6563, www.unionstreetfestival.com

JULY

- **Alameda County Fair**, Alameda County Fairgrounds, Pleasanton, 925-426-7610, www.alamedacountyfair.com
- **Berkeley Kite Festival** and **West Coast Kite Flying Championships**, Cesar Chavez Park, Berkeley, 510-235-5483, www.highlinekites.com
- **Big Time Festival at Kule Loklo**, Native American Trade Festival, Bear Valley Visitor Center, Point Reyes National Seashore, south of Olema; 415-464-5140, www.nps.gov/pore/planyourvisit/events_bigtime.htm
- **Chinese Summer Festival**, Kelly Park, San Jose, 408-842-1625, www.chcp.org
- **Festa Italia**, plenty of pasta and pesto, San Mateo, 650-349-9879, www.festa-foundation.org
- **Fillmore Jazz Festival**, Fillmore and California sts, 800-310-6563, www.fillmorestreetjazzfest.com
- **Fourth of July Celebrations**, call for details: San Francisco, fireworks at Pier 39, 415-705-5500, www.pier39.com; Alameda, 510 747-7400; Berkeley, 510-981-CITY; Redwood City, 650-365-1825, www.parade.org; San Jose, 408-277-4000; Oakland, 866-295-9853, www.jacklondonsquare.com
- **Gilroy Garlic Festival**, a pungent party, Christmas Hill Park, Gilroy, 408-842-1625, www.gilroygarlicfestival.com
- **Jewish Film Festival**, various venues within the city, 415-621-0556, *www.sfjff.org*
- **Los Altos Art & Wine Festival**, downtown Los Altos, 650-949-5282, www.downtownlosaltos.org
- **Marin County Fair**, Marin County Fairgrounds, San Rafael, 415-499-6800, www.marinfair.org
- **Marin Shakespeare Festival**, Dominican College, San Rafael, 415-499-4488, July–September, www.marinshakespeare.org
- **Midsummer Mozart Festival**, call for locations, 415-627-9141, www.midsummermozart.org
- **Obon Festival**, Buddhist Church, San Jose, 408-293-9292, www.sjbetsuin.com
- **Puerto Rican Cultural Festival "Dia de San Juan,"** History Park, San Jose, 888-200-1488, www.wrprc.org
- **San Francisco Jazz Festival** summer sessions, call for locations, June–October, 866-920-5299, www.sfjazz.org
- **San Jose America Festival**, Discovery Meadow, San Jose, 408-841-8411, www.americafestival.com
- **San Jose International Mariachi Festival, Guadalupe River Park, San Jose,** 408-928-5564, www.sanjosemariachifestival.com

- **Scottish Highland Games**, Dunsmuir House, Oakland, 510-562-0328, www. dunsmuir.org
- **Shakespeare in the Park,** free performances, Pleasanton, Cupertino, and San Francisco, 415-558-0888, www.sfshakes.org
- **Stern Grove Midsummer Music Festival**, in San Francisco, Stern Grove, June–August, 415-252-6252, www.sterngrove.org
- **Summer Festival & Chili Cook-off**, Mitchell Park, Palo Alto, 650-463-4921, www. cityofpaloalto.org
- **Youth Arts Festival**, Yerba Buena Arts Center and Zeum, 415-285-2287, www.precitaeyes.org

AUGUST

- **Concours d'Elegance**, fine wine and vintage cars along a beautiful stretch of coastline, Pebble Beach, 831-622-1700, www.pebblebeachconcours.net
- **Good Guys Rod and Custom Classic Car Show**, Alameda County Fairgrounds, Pleasanton, 925-838-9876, www.good-guys.com
- **Nihonmachi Street Fair**, a celebration of Japanese culture, Japantown, www.nihonmachistreetfair.org
- **Palo Alto Festival of the Arts**, University Ave, Palo Alto, 831-438-4751, www.mla-productions.com
- **Park Street Art & Wine Faire**, Park St, Alameda, 510-523-1392, www.shop-parkstreet.com
- **San Francisco Aloha Festival**, Pacific Islander cultural celebration, San Francisco Presidio Main Parade Grounds, 415-281-0221, www.pica-org.org/AlohaFest
- **San Francisco Jazz Festival**, summer series continues, call for locations, June–October, 866-920-5299, www.sfjazz.org
- **San Jose Jazz Festival**, Plaza de Cesar Chavez, San Jose, 408-288-7557, www. sanjosejazz.org
- **San Mateo County Fair**, San Mateo County Expo Center, San Mateo, 650-574-3247, www.sanmateocountyfair.com
- **Santa Clara County Fair**, Santa Clara County Fairgrounds, San Jose, 408-494-3247, www.thefair.org
- **Stern Grove Midsummer Music Festival**, in San Francisco, Stern Grove, June–August, 415-252-6252, www.sterngrove.org
- **West Marin Music Festival**, call for locations, 415-663-9650

SEPTEMBER

- **Black Diamond Blues Festival**, Diamond and 5th sts, Pittsburg, 510-836-2227, www.bayareabluessociety.net
- **California Small Brewers Festival**, microbrew beer bash, Discovery Park, Sacramento, www.calbrewfest.org

- **Chocolate Festival**, Ghiradelli Square, 415.775.5500, www.ghirardellisq. com/ghirardellisq/events.php?id=2
- **Fall Arts Festival**, Old Mill Park, Mill Valley, 415-381-8090, www.mvfaf.org
- **How Berkeley Can You Be? Festival**, 510-644-2204, www.howberkeleycany-oube.com
- **Mountain View Art & Wine Festival**, Castro St, Mountain View, 408-968-8378, www.chambermv.org
- **Opera in the Park**, free arias, Sharon Meadows, Golden Gate Park, 415-861-4008, http://sfopera.com
- **Pacific Coast Fog Fest**, clearly a good time in the fog, Palmetto & Salada Aves, Pacifica, 650-355-8200, www.pacificcoastfogfest.com
- **Renaissance Pleasure Faire**, journey back to Elizabethan England, Hollister, September–October, 408-847-3247, www.norcalrenfaire.org
- **San Francisco Blues Festival**, Great Meadow, Fort Mason, 415-979-5588, www.sfblues.com
- **San Francisco Fringe Festival**, a celebration of the offbeat, call for locations, 415-931-1094, www.sffringe.org
- **San Francisco Heart Walk**, Justin Herman Plaza, 1 Market St, 415-228-8420, www.sfheartwalk.org
- **San Francisco Jazz Festival** summer sessions, call for locations, June-October, 866-920-5299, www.sfjazz.org
- **Sausalito Art Festival**, Bay Model Visitors Center and Marinship Park, Sausalito, 415-331-3757, www.sausalitoartfestival.org
- **Santa Clara Art & Wine Festival**, Central Park, Santa Clara, www.santaclaraartandwinefestival.com
- **Sir Francis Drake Kennel Club Dog Show**, Marin Center, San Rafael, 415-472-3500, www.sfdkc.og
- **Solano Stroll**, massive street fair, Solano Ave, Albany and Berkeley, 510-527-5358, www.solanoavenueassn.org/strol.htm

OCTOBER

- **Castro Street Fair**, Castro St, 415-841-1824, www.castrostreetfair.org
- **Day of the Dead Community Festival**, Oakland Museum of California, Oakland, 510-238-2200, www.museumca.org
- **Fleet Week**, celebrating San Francisco's long relationship with the US Navy, Marina wharf, 415-599-5057
- **Half Moon Bay Pumpkin Festival**, Main St, Half Moon Bay, 650-726-3491, www.miramarevents.com/pumpkinfest
- **Halloween Celebration**, Jack London Square, Oakland, www.oaklandcvb.com

- **Halloween at the Winchester Mystery House**, a sprawling, 160-year-old Victorian mansion, San Jose, 408-247-2101, www.winchestermysteryhouse. com
- **Harvest Festival**, various locations across the Bay Area, 415-447-3205, www. harvestfestival.com
- **Italian Heritage Day**, honoring, among others, Christopher Columbus, North Beach, 415-703-9888, www.sfcolumbusday.org
- **Mill Valley Film Festival**, call for locations, Mill Valley, 415-383-5256, www. cafilm.org/mvff/index.html
- **Open Studios**, a citywide, month-long tour of artists' studios, 415-861-9838, www.artspan.org
- **Pacific Fine Arts Festival**, Santa Cruz Ave, Menlo Park, www.pacificfinearts.com
- **Sandcastle Classic**, architects vs. amateurs in sandcastle building, Ocean Beach, www.leap4kids.org
- **San Francisco Jazz Festival**, call for locations, June–October, 866-920-5299, www.sfjazz.org
- **Sequoia Auto Show**, Sequoia High School, Redwood City, 650-368-8212
- **Sonoma County Harvest Fair**, Santa Rosa, 707-545-4200, www.sonomacounty-fair.com

NOVEMBER

- **American Indian Film Festival**, Palace of Fine Arts, 415-554-0525, www. aifisf.com
- **Arts & Crafts Faire**, Mill Valley Community Center, Mill Valley, 415-383-1370, www.cityofmillvalley.org
- **Celebration of Craftswomen**, Fort Mason, 415-731-5539 www.celebra-tionofcraftswomen.org
- **Christmas Tree Lighting**: Ghirardelli Square, 415-775-5500, http://www.ghi-rardellisq.com/ghirardellisq/events.php?id=16
- **Dias de los Muertos (Day of the Dead)**, Mexican celebration of spirits, parade, altars in the park, great costumes and food, 24th and Bryant sts to Garfield Park, the Mission District, 415-722-8911, www.dayofthedeadsf.org
- **Festival of Lights Parade**, downtown, Los Altos, 650-949-5282, www.down-townlosaltos.org
- **Great Dickens Christmas Faire**, travel back in time to 19th Century London, Cow Palace, Daly City (runs through early December), www.dickensfair.com
- **Harvest Festival**, various locations across the Bay Area, 415-447-3205, www. harvestfestival.com
- **Jack London Square Tree Lighting**, Jack London Square, Oakland, www.jacklon-donsquare.com
- **San Francisco International Auto Show**, Moscone Center, 415-331-4406, www. sfautoshow.com

- **Thanksgiving Farmers Market**, Civic Center, San Rafael, 415-472-6100, www.marinfarmersmarkets.org
- **Union Square Tree Lighting**, Christmas window displays, Union Square, San Francisco, 415-781-7880
- **Union Street Fantasy of Lights**, Union St between Franklin and Steiner sts, San Francisco, 800-310-6563
- **Veterans Day Parade**, Market St, 415-554-6036; downtown San Jose, 408-993-0729
- **Victorian Christmas**, Open House, Angel Island, 435–3972, www.angelisland.org
- **Winter Wonderland & Parade of Lights**, downtown San Rafael, 415-720-5591

DECEMBER

- **Berkeley Artisans Holiday Open Studios**, check their web site for locations and hours, berkeleyartisans.com
- **Christmas in the Park**, Plaza de Cesar Chavez, San Jose, 408-995-6635, www.christmasinthepark.com
- **Christmas Revels**, Scottish Rite Temple, Oakland, 510-452-9334, http://californiarevels.org
- **Christmas at Sea**, holiday fair with a nautical bent, Hyde St Pier, 415-561-7170
- **Hanukkah Family Celebration**, Osher Marin Jewish Community Center, San Rafael, 415-444-8000; locate other Hanukkah events via the Jewish Community Federation web site, www.sfjcf.org
- **Heritage Holiday**, San Jose Historical Museum, San Jose, 408-287-2290
- **Kwanzaa Celebration**, Bay Area Discovery Museum, Sausalito, 415-339-3900, www.badm.org/home
- **Kwanzaa Gift Show**, Oakland Marriott Convention Center, Oakland, 510-534-1594 www.kwanzaagiftshow.com
- **Lighted Yacht Parade**, Jack London Square & Waterfront, Oakland, 866-295-9853, www.lightedyachtparade.com
- **Lighted Yacht Parade**, Sausalito, 415-331-7262
- **Messiah Sing**, Point Reyes Station, 415-663-9232
- **Marin County Holiday Antique & Collector's Fair**, Marin Center, San Rafael, 415- 383-2252
- **San Jose Holiday Parade**, downtown, San Jose, 408-794-6200, www.holidayparade.com
- **Sing-a-long Messiah**, Santa Rosa High School Auditorium, Santa Rosa, 707-579-4094, www.sing-along-messiah.org
- **Sing-it-yourself Messiah**, Davies Symphony Hall, 415-401-9229, www.sfsinfonietta.org
- **Trains for Tots**, South Bay, Peninsula, and San Francisco stops with Santa along the CalTrain corridor, 800-660-4287, www.caltrain.com

THERE ARE HUNDREDS, IF NOT THOUSANDS, OF BOOKS ABOUT SAN Francisco and the Bay Area. Below is a small selection of guides, works of fiction, and historical books that will help you get acquainted with your new home.

ART

- *Art in the San Francisco Bay Area: 1945-1980: An Illustrated History* by Thomas Albright
- *Artful Players: Artistic Life in Early San Francisco* by Brigitta Hjalmarson
- *Bay Area Wild: A Celebration of the Natural Heritage of the San Francisco Bay Area* by Galen Rowell; captures the natural beauty of the Bay Area with the author's photographs and insightful text

FICTION AND LITERATURE

- *The Best of Adair Lara* by Adair Lara
- *Bombardiers* by Po Bronson
- *China Boy* by Gus Lee
- *City Lights Pocket Poets Anthology*, Lawrence Ferlinghetti, Editor
- *Daughter of Fortune* by Isabel Allende
- *Everyone Into the Pool: True Tales* by Beth Lisick
- *Eyes of a Child* by Richard North Patterson
- *Flower Drum Song* by C.Y. Lee
- *A Heartbreaking Work of Staggering Genius* by Dave Eggers
- *The Joy Luck Club* by Amy Tan
- *Letters from the Earth* by Mark Twain
- *Lonesome Traveler* by Jack Kerouac
- *The Maltese Falcon* by Dashiell Hammett
- *McTeague* by Frank Norris

- *Our Lady of Darkness* by Fritz Leiber
- *San Francisco Stories: Great Writers on the City* edited by John Miller
- *The Subterraneans* by Jack Kerouac
- *San Francisco Poems* by Lawrence Ferlinghetti
- *Tales of the City* by Armistead Maupin
- *Jack London Stories of Adventure* by Jack London
- *Valencia* by Michelle Tea
- *West from Home: Letters of Laura Ingalls Wilder, San Francisco, 1915* by Laura Ingalls Wilder
- *The Woman Warrior* by Maxine Hong Kingston

LOCAL LIT JOURNALS
- *McSweeney's*
- *Instant City: A Literary Exploration of San Francisco*

FOOD

- *Bread and Chocolate: My Food Life in San Francisco* by Fran Gage
- *The Cheese Board: Collective Works: Bread, Pastry, Cheese, Pizza* by Alice Waters and the Cheese Board Collective
- *Chez Panisse Cooking: New Tastes and Techniques* by Paul Bertolli with Alice Waters
- *The Chowhound's Guide to the San Francisco Bay Area*
- *Eat This San Francisco* by Dan Leone
- *The Eclectic Gourmet Guide to San Francisco* by Richard Sterling
- *Farm City: The Education of an Urban Farmer* by Novella Carpenter
- *Patricia Unterman's San Francisco Food Lover's Guide* by Patricia Unterman
- *San Francisco in a Teacup* by Ulrica Hume; where to find tea, accoutrements, and afternoon teas
- *The San Francisco Chronicle Cookbook Volume II* by Michael Bauer
- *San Francisco a la Carte* by the Junior League of San Francisco
- *Zagat Survey, San Francisco Bay Area Restaurants*

HISTORY

- *Baghdad by the Bay* by Herb Caen
- *The Barbary Coast* by Herbert Asbury
- *Historic San Francisco* by Rand Richards
- *The Mayor of Castro Street: The Life and Times of Harvey Milk* by Randy Shilts
- *Reclaiming San Francisco History, Politics, Culture; a City Lights Anthology* edited by James Brook, Chris Carlsson, and Nancy J. Peters
- *San Francisco: A Cultural and Literary History* by Mick Sinclair
- *San Francisco Then & Now* by William Yenne

- *Tales of San Francisco* by Samuel Dickson
- *The World of Herb Caen* by Herb Caen
- *The Wild Parrots of Telegraph Hill* by Mark Bittner

KIDS

- *Best Hikes with Children: San Francisco's North Bay* by Bill McMillon with Kevin McMillon
- *The Cable Car and the Dragon* by Herb Caen
- *The City by the Bay: A Magical Journey Around San Francisco* by Tricia Brown
- *Fun Places to go with Children in Northern California* by Elizabeth Pomada
- *Humphrey, the Lost Whale: A True Story* by Wendy Tokuda and Richard Hall
- *San Francisco* by Deborah Kent
- *San Francisco: A Mini-History* by Phyllis Zauner

LIVING HERE

- *Connecting in San Francisco* by Diane de Castro; once you've found your job and your home, this'll help you find friends
- *How to Get a Job in the San Francisco Bay Area* by Robert Sanborn and Will Flowers

OUTDOORS

- *Adventuring in the San Francisco Bay Area* by Peggy Wayburn; information about camping, hiking, fishing, area wildlife and weather
- *Backcountry Adventures: Northern California* by Peter Massey and Jeanne Wilson
- *Bay Area Backroads* by Doug McConnell
- *Cruising Guide to San Francisco Bay* by Carolyn Mehaffy and Bob Mehaffy
- *Bay Area Bike Rides* by Ray Hosler
- *East Bay Trails: Outdoor Adventures in Alameda and Contra Costa Counties* by David Weintraub
- *Foghorn Outdoors: 101 Great Hikes of the San Francisco Bay Area* by Ann Marie Brown
- *Foghorn Outdoors Bay Area Biking: 60 Of the Best Road and Trail Rides* by Ann Marie Brown
- *Golden Gate Trailblazer: Where to Hike, Walk and Bike in San Francisco and Marin* by Jerry Sprout and Janine Sprout
- *Inside/Out Northern California: Best Places Guide to the Outdoors* by Dennis J. Oliver
- *The New San Francisco at Your Feet: Best Walks in a Walkers' City* by Margot Patterson Doss; offers a selection of walking tours rated for their difficulty
- *Roaming the Backroads of Northern California* by Peter Browning

- **Sailing the Bay** by Kimball Livingston; about sailing on San Francisco Bay
- **San Francisco Running Guide: The 45 Best Routes in the Bay Area** by Bob Cooper
- **Short Bike Rides in and Around San Francisco** by Henry Kingman

SAN FRANCISCO GUIDES

These off-beat and theme-oriented guides to San Francisco will get you out and exploring, but away from the hordes of tourists.

- **Broke-Ass Stuart's Guide to Living Cheaply in San Francisco** by Stuart Schuffman; this cult-ish guide has many of the area's cheapest bargains and is written in plain, hilarious English
- **The Dog Lover's Companion to the Bay Area** by Maria Goodavage; the name says it all—amongst the concrete walls of the City, there are places for your dog
- **Get Lost! The Cool Guide to San Francisco** by Claudia Lehan; a hip guide to the Bay Area
- **Romantic Days and Nights in San Francisco: Intimate Escapes in the City by the Bay** by Donna Peck; with this book, you can truly leave your heart in San Francisco
- **Footsteps in the Fog, Alfred Hitchcock's San Francisco** by Jeff Kraft; the master of cinematic suspense shot a number of his famous films in and around San Francisco
- **Ghost Hunter's Guide to the Bay Area** by Jeff Dwyer; full of local legends and lore
- **Jazz on the Barbary Coast** by Tom Stoddard
- **San Francisco As You Like It: 20 Tailor-Made Tours for Culture Vultures, Shopaholics, Non-Bohemians, Fitness Freaks, Savvy Natives, and Everyone Else** by Bonnie Wach; there's an old hippie tour, a tour for gourmet lovers, kids tours, and others
- **San Francisco Bizarro** by Jack Boulware; proving the old adage that truth is definitely sometimes stranger than fiction
- **San Francisco Noir** by Nathaniel Rich; a look at the city's rich past as a the stunning backdrop for a host of Hollywood whodunits
- **San Francisco Secrets** by John Snyder; full of little-known information about the city for lovers of trivia and history
- **Underground Guide to San Francisco** by Jennifer Joseph; if you need a new tattoo or an unusual museum to show a visiting friend, here's the guide for you

SHOPPING

- **Bargain Hunting in the Bay Area** by Sally Socolich
- **Mr. Cheap's San Francisco** by Mark Waldstein

ONCE YOU ORDER PHONE SERVICE OR MOVE INTO YOUR NEW address, Valley Yellow Pages will deliver the White and Yellow Pages to your door. To get them faster, call 800-350-8887 and have them deliver the books to you by UPS—this will take three to five days. To obtain a phone book from outside your county you will have to order by mail or go to the local Chambers of Commerce for your area. You can access the Yellow Pages online at www.valleyyellowpages.com Although not as extensive as the print Yellow Pages, the list below should be of some assistance:

AMBULANCE, all areas, 911

ANIMALS

- **Animal Bites**, 911
- **Animal Control**, 415-554-6364
- **Homeless Cat Network**, 650-286-9013, www.homelesscatnetwork.org
- **Hopalong & Second Chance Rescue**, 415-267-1915, www.hopalong.org
- **Humane Society of Contra Costa County**, 925-279-2247, www.cchumane.org
- **Humane Society of East Bay**, 510-569-0702, www.eastbayspca.org
- **Humane Society of Marin County**, 415-883-4621, www.marinhumanesociety.org
- **Humane Society of Peninsula**, 650-340-8200, www.peninsulahumanesociety.org
- **Humane Society Silicon Valley**, 408-262-2133, www.hssv.org
- **Humane Society of Sonoma County**, 707-542-0882, www.sonomahumane.org
- **Pets Unlimited**, 415-563-6700, www.petsunlimited.org

- **San Francisco Lost Pet Services**, 415-567-8738, www.sfgov.org/acc
- **Silicon Valley Friends of Ferals**, www.svff.org
- **SPCA (Society for the Prevention of Cruelty to Animals)**, 415-554-3000, www.sfspca.org

AUTOMOBILES

- **American Automobile Association (AAA)**, 800-AAA-HELP, 800-922-8228, www.csaa.com
- **BBB Auto Line**, 703-276-0100, www.bbb.org
- **California Department of Motor Vehicles**, 800-777-0133, TTY 800-368-4327, www.dmv.ca.gov

SAN FRANCISCO

- **AutoReturn**, if you suspect your vehicle has been towed, 415-865-8200, www.autoreturn.com
- **City Tow**, 415-621-8605
- **DMV,** 800-777-0133 to speak with an agent

PARKING AND TRAFFIC
SAN FRANCISCO

- **San Francisco Municipal Transportation Agency**, www.sfmta.com
- **Information**, 415-701-2311
- **Citation Division**, 415-701-3000; Pay Traffic/Parking Citations with Credit Card, 415-701-3099, 800-531-7357, or online at www.sfmta.com/parking
- **Parking Permits**, 415-701-3000
- **Towed Vehicles**, 415-865-8200

NORTH BAY

- **DMV**, 800-777-0133, TTY 800-368-4327, www.dmv.ca.gov
- **Marin Parking Authority**, 800-281-7275; in San Rafael 415-458-5333; in Sausalito 415-289-4149

EAST BAY

- **DMV**, 800-777-0133, TTY 800-368-4327, www.dmv.ca.gov
- **Oakland Parking Bureau**, 800-500-6484
- **Traffic Division of the Superior Court, Oakland,** 510-627-4701

PENINSULA/SOUTH BAY

- **DMV**, 800-777-0133, TTY 800-368-4327, www.dmv.ca.gov
- **San Mateo, Parking Permits, Residential & City Parking Facilities,** 650-522-7326

BIRTH/DEATH CERTIFICATES

- **Alameda County**, 510 272-6362, www.acgov.org/auditor/clerk
- **Marin County**, 415-499-7215
- **San Francisco County Health Department**, 415-554-2700, www.sfdph.org
- **San Mateo County**, 650-363-4500, www.smcare.org
- **Santa Clara County**, 408-299-2481, www.sccgov.org

CITY/COUNTY GOVERNMENT

SAN FRANCISCO
- **Assessor-Recorder's Office**, 415-554-5596
- **Board of Supervisors**, 415-554-5184
- **California Governor**, 916-445-2841, http://gov.ca.gov
- **California Public Utilities Commission**, Public Advisor's Office in San Francisco, 866-849-8390, www.cpuc.ca.gov
- **California Registrar of Voters**, 916-657-2166, TTY 800-833-8683
- **City Attorney**, 415-554-4700
- **City Hall**, 415-554-4000
- **County Clerk**, 415-554-4950
- **District Attorney**, 415-553-1752
- **Health Department**, 415-554-2500
- **Marriage Licenses**, 415-554-4950
- **Mayor's Office**, 415-554-6141
- **Parks and Recreation**, 415-831-2750, www.parks.sfgov.org
- **Recycling Program**, 415-255-3700, www.sfenvironment.org
- **Rent Stabilization Board**, 415-252-4600, www.sfgov.org/rentboard
- **Residential Parking Permits**, 415-701-3000
- **San Francisco Public Utilities Commission**, 415-554-3155, www.sfwater.org
- **San Francisco Unified School District**, 415-241-6000, http://portal.sfusd.edu/template/index.cfm

NORTH BAY—ONLINE
- **Corte Madera**, www.ci.corte-madera.ca.us
- **Fairfax**, www.town-of-fairfax.org
- **Marin County**, www.co.marin.ca.us, www.marin.org
- **Mill Valley**, www.cityofmillvalley.org
- **Napa County**, www.co.napa.ca.us
- **Novato**, www.ci.novato.ca.us
- **San Rafael**, www.cityofsanrafael.org
- **Sausalito**, www.ci.sausalito.ca.us
- **Santa Rosa**, www.ci.santa-rosa.ca.us
- **Sonoma County**, www.sonoma-county.org
- **Tiburon**, www.ci.tiburon.ca.us

EAST BAY—ONLINE

- **Alameda City**, www.ci.alameda.ca.us
- **Alameda County**, www.co.alameda.ca.us
- **Albany**, www.albanyca.org
- **Antioch**, www.ci.antioch.ca.us
- **Berkeley**, www.ci.berkeley.ca.us
- **Concord**, www.ci.concord.ca.us
- **Contra Costa County**, www.co.contra-costa.ca.us
- **Danville**, www.ci.danville.ca.us
- **Fremont**, www.ci.fremont.ca.us
- **El Cerrito**, www.el-cerrito.org
- **Emeryville**, www.ci.emeryville.ca.us
- **Hayward**, www.ci.hayward.ca.us
- **Livermore**, www.ci.livermore.ca.us
- **Martinez**, www.cityofmartinez.org
- **Newark**, www.ci.newark.ca.us
- **Oakland**, www.ci.oakland.ca.us, www.oaklandnet.com
- **Piedmont**, www.ci.piedmont.ca.us
- **Pinole**, www.ci.pinole.ca.us
- **Pittsburg**, www.ci.pittsburg.ca.us
- **Pleasanton**, www.ci.pleasanton.ca.us
- **Richmond**, www.ci.richmond.ca.us
- **San Leandro**, www.ci.san-leandro.ca.us
- **San Ramon**, www.ci.san-ramon.ca.us
- **Union City**, www.ci.union-city.ca.us
- **Walnut Creek**, www.walnut-creek.org

PENINSULA/SOUTH BAY—ONLINE

- **Atherton**, www.ci.atherton.ca.us
- **Belmont**, www.ci.belmont.ca.us
- **Brisbane**, www.ci.brisbane.ca.us
- **Burlingame**, www.burlingame.org
- **Campbell**, www.ci.campbell.ca.us
- **Cupertino**, www.cupertino.org
- **Daly City**, www.ci.daly-city.ca.us
- **Foster City**, www.fostercity.org
- **Half Moon Bay**, www.half-moon-bay.ca.us
- **Hillsborough**, www.hillsborough.net
- **Los Gatos**, www.town.los-gatos.ca.us
- **Menlo Park**, www.ci.menlo-park.ca.us
- **Millbrae**, www.ci.millbrae.ca.us
- **Mountain View**, www.ci.mtnview.ca.us
- **Pacifica**, www.cityofpacifica.org

- **Palo Alto**, www.cityofpaloalto.org
- **Redwood City**, www.ci.redwood-city.ca.us
- **San Bruno**, www.sanbruno.ca.gov
- **San Carlos**, www.cityofsancarlos.org
- **San Jose**, www.sanjose.org
- **San Mateo City**, www.ci.sanmateo.ca.us
- **San Mateo County**, www.co.sanmateo.ca.us
- **Santa Clara City**, http://santaclaraca.gov
- **Santa Clara County**, www.sccgov.org
- **Saratoga**, www.saratoga.ca.us
- **South San Francisco**, www.ci.ssf.ca.us
- **Sunnyvale**, http://sunnyvale.ca.us
- **Woodside**, www.woodsidetown.org

COMMUNITY EVENTS AND RESOURCES ONLINE

- *Bay City Guide,* www.baycityguide.com
- **City of San Francisco**, www.sfgov.org
- **KTVU Channel 2**, www.ktvu.com
- *San Francisco Bay Guardian,* www.sfbg.com
- *San Francisco Chronicle,* www.sfgate.com
- **San Francisco Citysearch**, http://sanfrancisco.citysearch.com
- **San Francisco.com**, www.sanfrancisco.com
- *San Francisco Magazine,* www.sanfranmag.com
- *San Jose Mercury News,* www.mercurynews.com
- *SF Weekly,* www.sfweekly.com

CONSUMER AGENCIES

- **Alameda County Bar Association**, 510-302-2222
- **Better Business Bureau, Oakland Branch,** 510-844-2000, http://bbb.gold-engate.org
- **California Attorney General**, 800-952-5225, TTY 800-735-2929, http://caag.state.ca.us
- **California Department of Consumer Affairs**, 800-952-5210, www.dca.ca.gov
- **California Public Utilities Commission**, 415-703-2782
- **California State Directory Information Service**, 800-807-6755, TTY 916-464-1580, www.cold.ca.gov
- **Department of Consumer Complaints**, 800-952-5210
- **Federal Communications Commission**, 888-225-5322, TTY 888-835-5322, www.fcc.gov
- **Federal Citizen Information Center** (and Consumer Action Handbook), 888-878-3256, www.pueblo.gsa.gov, www.consumeraction.gov

- Federal Trade Commission, 877-382-4357, www.ftc.gov
- Financial Consumer Information, www.mymoney.gov
- San Francisco Bar Association Lawyer Referral Service, 415-989-1616
- San Francisco District Attorney, 415-553-1752
- San Francisco Public Utilities Commission, 415-554-3155, www.sfwater.org
- San Mateo County Bar Association, 650-298-4030
- Santa Clara County Bar Association, 408-287-2557
- State Bar of California, 800-843-9053, www.calbar.ca.gov
- Telecommunications Research and Action Center (TRAC), www.trac.org
- The Utility Reform Network (TURN), 415-929-8876, www.turn.org

CRISIS LINES

- Gay Youth Talk Line, 415-863-3636
- Suicide Prevention, 415-781-0500
- Suicide Prevention, Marin, 415-499-1100
- Westside Crisis Services, 415-355-0311

ALCOHOL AND DRUG DEPENDENCY
- Alcoholics Anonymous, 415-674-1821, www.aasf.org
- Behavioral Health Services Community Access, 888-246-3333
- Cocaine Anonymous, 415-821-6155
- Contra Costa County AA, 925-939-4155
- East Bay AA, 510-839-8900
- Marin County Alcoholics Anonymous, 415-499-0400
- Napa County AA, 707-255-4900
- Narcotics Anonymous, 415-621-8600, www.sfna.org,
- San Mateo County AA, 650-577-1310
- Santa Clara County AA, 408-374-8511
- Smoker's Hotline, 800-662-8887

CHILD ABUSE/PROTECTION
- Alameda County Child Protective Services, 510-259-1800
- Child Abuse Council of Santa Clara County, 408-299-2071
- Marin Child Abuse Prevention Council, 415-507-9016
- Marin Child Protective Services, 415-473-7153
- Domestic Violence Hotline, 800-799-7233; for emergencies dial 911
- San Francisco Child Abuse Prevention Center, 415-668-0494
- San Francisco TALK 24hr Family Support Center, 415-441-5437

RAPE/DOMESTIC VIOLENCE
- Bay Area Women Against Rape (Crisis Line), 415-647-7273

- **Casa de Las Madres**, 877-503-1850, www.lacasadelasmadres.org (offers shelter and advocacy to battered women and children)
- **Marin Rape Crisis Center**, 800-670-7273
- **National Domestic Violence Hotline**, 800-799-7233
- **San Francisco General Hospital 24-hour Rape Treatment Center**, 415-437-3000
- **Women Against Rape**, 415-647-7273, www.sfwar.org
- **YWCA Rape Crisis Center** (Crisis Hot-Lines), 408-287-3000, 650-493-7273

ENTERTAINMENT

- **San Francisco Events**, 415-391-2001
- **www.sgbg.com**
- **www.sfgate.com**
- **www.sfstation.com**
- **www.sfweekly.com**
- **Theatre Bay Area (discount tickets)**, 415-430-1140
- **Ticketmaster at 415-512-7770**, www.ticketmaster.com
- **777-FILM**, www.moviefone.com

EARTHQUAKE INFORMATION

- **American Red Cross, Bay Area Chapter,** 415-427-8000, www.bayarea-red-cross.org
- **Bay Area Quake Information**, http://quake.abag.ca.gov.
- **California Earthquake Authority**, 916-325-3800, www.earthquakeauthority.com
- **California Seismic Safety Commission**, 916-263-5506, www.seismic.ca.gov
- **Federal Emergency Management Agency (FEMA)**, 800-621-3362, TTY 800-462-7585, www.fema.gov
- **US Geological Survey**, 888-275-8747, 650-853-8300, www.usgs.gov

ELECTED OFFICIALS

SAN FRANCISCO CITY AND COUNTY
- **Mayor's Office**, 415-554-6141, TTY 415-701-2323
- **Board of Supervisors**, 415-554-5184, TTY 415-554-5227
- **City Hall**, 415-554-4000
- **County Clerk**, 415-554-4950
- **District Attorney**, 415-553-1752
- **Assessor-Recorder**, 415-554-5596

STATE OF CALIFORNIA
- **Governor's Office**, 916-445-2841, www.gov.ca.gov

- **State Assembly**, 916-319-2856, www.assembly.ca.gov
- **State Senate**, 916-319-2856, www.sen.ca.gov

UNITED STATES

- **US Senate**, 202-224-3121, www.senate.gov
- **US House of Representatives**, 202-224-3121, TTY 202-225-1904, www.house.gov
- **White House**, 202-456-1111, TTY 202-456-6213, www.whitehouse.gov

EMERGENCY NUMBERS

- **24-Hour SF Rape Treatment Center**, 415-437-3000
- **FEMA Disaster Assistance Information**, 800-621-3362, TTY 800-462-7585, www.fema.gov
- **Fire**, Police, Medical Emergency, 911
- **Office of Emergency Services**, 415-558-2700
- **Poison Control Hotline**, 800-222-1222, www.poison.org
- **San Francisco Fire Department**, non-emergency, 415-558-3200
- **San Francisco General Hospital**, 415-206-8000, 24-hour Emergency Services, 415-206-8111
- **San Francisco Police Department** non-emergency, 415-553-0123

HEALTH AND MEDICAL CARE

- **American Board of Medical Specialties—Board Certification Verification**, 866-275-2267
- **Berkeley Drop-in Center**, 510-653-3808
- **Berkeley Free Clinic**, 800-625-4642, www.berkeleyfreeclinic.org
- **Cancer Care**, 800-813-4673, www.cancercare.org
- **Dental Referral**, 800-336-8422, www.1800dentist.com
- **Lead Poisoning Prevention Program**, www.aclppp.org
- **Marin County Department of Health and Human Services**, 415-499-3696
- **Medical Board of California**, 800-633-2322
- **Medi-Cal Information**, 800-541-5555
- **Poison Control**, 800-876-4766
- **Public Health Department**, San Jose, 408-792-5050
- **San Francisco General Hospital**, 415-206-8000
- **San Francisco Department of Public Health**, 415-554-2500, www.dph.sf.ca.us
- **Sexually Transmitted Disease**, 415-487-5500
- **Suicide Prevention**, 415-781-0500

HIV TESTING
- **AIDS/HIV and Hep C Nightline**, 415-434-2437
- **AIDS Testing Hotline**, San Jose, 408-885-7000

- **California AIDS Hotline**, 800-367-2437, TTY 888-225-2437
- **HIV/AIDS and Hep C Testing Hotline**, Marin, 415-257-5687
- **UCSF HIV/AIDS Testing and Referral Hotline**, 888-448-8765

HOUSING

- **Bay Area Legal Aid, San Jose,** 408-283-3700; call for a pre-screening.
- **Bay Area Legal Aid, San Francisco,** 415-982-1300
- **Berkeley Rent Stabilization Program**, 510-981-7368, TTY 510-981-6903, www.ci.berkeley.ca.us/rent
- **California State Fair Employment and Housing Department**, San Francisco, 800-884-1684, TTY 800-700-2320, www.dfeh.ca.gov
- **California Tenant Law**, www.caltenantlaw.com
- **Contractors State License Board**, 800-321-2752
- **Franchise Tax Board**, 800-852-5711, www.ftb.ca.gov
- **East Palo Alto Rent Stabilization Program**, 650-853-3109
- **Eviction Defense Center**, 510-452-4541
- **Housing Rights, Inc., Berkeley,** 510-548-8776, 800-261-2298, www.housingrights.org
- **Legal Aid Society Housing Counseling Program**, 408-283-1540
- **Project Sentinel**, specializes in landlord/tenant disputes in Sunnyvale, 408-720-9888, www.housing.org
- **St. Peter's Housing Committee**, 415-487-9203
- **San Francisco Rent Board**, 415-252-4600
- **San Francisco Tenants Union**, 415-282-6622, www.sftu.org
- **San Jose Rental Rights and Referrals**, 408-975-4480

LEGAL MEDIATION OR REFERRAL

- **AIDS Legal Referral Panel**, 415-701-1100 or 510-451-5353 www.alrp.org
- **Alameda County Bar Association**, 510-302-2222
- **American Civil Liberties Union of Northern California**, 415-621-2488, www.aclunc.org
- **California Courts**, www.courtinfo.ca.gov
- **California Community Dispute Service**, 415-865-2520
- **East Bay Community Mediation**, 510-548-2377, www.seedscrc.org
- **Legal Aid Society of Santa Clara County**, 408-998-5200
- **Legal Aid of the North Bay Area**, 800-498-7666
- **San Francisco Bar Association Lawyer Referral Service**, 415-989-1616
- **San Mateo County Bar Association**, 650-298-4030
- **Santa Clara County Bar Association**, 408-287-2557
- **State Bar of California**, 415-538-2000

SMALL CLAIMS COURTS
See **Consumer Protection** section in the **Helpful Services** chapter.

PUBLIC LIBRARIES

- **Berkeley Central Branch**, 510-981-6100, www,berkeleypubliclibrary.org
- **Marin County Library**, 415-499-6051, www.marinlibrary.org
- **New Main**, San Francisco, 415-557-4400, www.sfpl.org
- **Oakland Public Library**, Main Branch, 510-238-3134, www.oaklandlibrary.org
- **Peninsula Library System**, 650-780-7018, www.plsinfo.org
- **San Jose Public Library**, 408-808-2000, www.sjlibrary.org
- **Santa Clara County Library System**, 408-293-2326, 800-286-1991, www.santaclaracountylib.org

See also the information listings following the description of each neighborhood.

MARRIAGE LICENSES

- **Alameda County**, 510-272-6363
- **Contra Costa County**, 925-646-2956
- **Marin County**, 415-499-3003
- **San Francisco City and County**, 415-554-4950
- **San Mateo County**, 650-363-4712
- **Santa Clara County**, 408-299-7310

PARKS AND RECREATION DEPARTMENTS

- **East Bay Regional Park District**, 888-327-2757, TTY 510-633-0460, www.ebparks.org
- **Golden Gate National Recreation Area**, 415-561-4700, www.nps.gov/goga
- **Golden Gate Park**, 415-831-2700
- **Marin County Department of Parks and Recreation**, 415-499-6387, www.marincountyparks.org
- **San Francisco Recreation and Parks Department**, 415-831-2700, www.parks.sfgov.org
- **San Mateo County Parks and Recreation Department**, 650-363-4020, www.co.sanmateo.ca.us
- **Santa Clara Department of Parks and Recreation**, 408-355-2200, www.parkhere.org

POLICE

- **BART Police**, 877-679-7000
- **California Highway Patrol**, Emergency, 911, Non-emergency, 800-835-5247, TTY 707-648-5363,

- **Domestic Violence Response Unit**, 415-553-9225
- **Emergency**, 911
- **Road Conditions**, 511
- **San Francisco Police Chief**, 415-553-1551
- **San Francisco Police**, Non-emergency, 415-553-0123; TTY 415-626-4357

POST OFFICE, 800-275-8777, www.usps.com

SANITATION—GARBAGE & RECYCLING

CALIFORNIA
- **California Department of Conservation**, 800-732-9253.
- **Earth 911**, 800-253-2687, www.earth911.org

SAN FRANCISCO
- **Golden Gate Disposal & Recycling Company**, 415-626-4000, www.goldengatedisposal.com
- **Norcal Waste Systems: Sunset Scavenger**, 415-330-1300, www.sunsetscavenger.com
- **Recycling Hotline**, 415-355-3700, www.sfenvironment.com
- **Recycle Central (Norcal)**, 415-330-1400
- **San Francisco League of Urban Gardeners (SLUG)**, 415-519-2006

NORTH BAY
- **Marin Recycling Center**, 415-453-1404
- **Marin Sanitary Services**, 415-456-2601, www.marinsanitary.com

EAST BAY
- **Allied Waste/BFI**, 510-657-3500
- **East Bay ROT-line**, 510-444-7645
- **Pleasanthill Bayshore Disposal**, serves most of Contra Costa County, 925-685-4711, www.pleasanthillbayshoredisposal.com
- **StopWaste.org** (Alameda County Waste Management Authority), 510-891-6500, www.stopwaste.org
- **Tri-Cities Waste Management**, East Bay, 510-624-5900

PENINSULA/SOUTH BAY
- **Allied Waste Daly City** (serving Daly City, Colma), 650-756-1130, www.alliedwastedalycity.com
- **Allied Waste San Mateo County**, 650-592-2411, http://bfisanmateocounty.com
- **Recycle Palo Alto Program**, 650-496-5910
- **RecycleWorks**, San Mateo County, 888-442-2666, www.recycleworks.org

- **Santa Clara County Recycling Hotline**, 408-924-5453 or 800-533-8414, www.recyclestuff.org
- **Santa Clara County**, Allied Waste, 408-432-1234
- **South San Francisco Scavenger** (northern San Mateo County), 650-589-4020, www.ssfscavenger.com

SENIORS

- **AARP California**, 888-687-2277, www.aarp.org
- **Elder Care Locator**, 800-677-1116, www.eldercare.gov
- **Legal Assistance for Seniors and HiCap**, Oakland, 510-832-3040
- **Institute on Aging**, 415-750-4180, www.ioaging.org
- **Legal Assistance to the Elderly**, 415-538-3333
- **Marin Adult Protection Services**, 415-499-7118
- **Meals on Wheels**, 415-920-1111, www.mowsf.org
- **Mission Hospice of San Mateo County**, 650-554-1000, www.missionhospice.org
- **Richmond Resource Center**, 415-752-2815
- **United Way of the Bay Area**, 415-808-4300, www.uwba.org

SHIPPING SERVICES

- **DHL Worldwide Express**, 800-225-5345, www.dhl-usa.com
- **FedEx**, 800-463-3339, www.fedex.com
- **United Parcel Service (UPS)**, 800-742-5877, TTY 833-0056, www.ups.com
- **US Postal Service**, 800-275-8777, www.usps.com

SPORTS

- **www.sfgate.com**
- **Golden State Warriors**, 510-986-2222, www.nba.com/warriors
- **Oakland Athletics**, 510-638-0500, http://oakland.athletics.mlb.com
- **Oakland Raiders**, 888-44-RAIDERS, www.raiders.com
- **San Francisco 49ers**, 415-656-4900, www.49ers.com
- **San Francisco Giants**, 415-972-2000, http://sanfrancisco.giants.mlb.com
- **San Jose Earthquakes**, 877-782-5301, http://sjearthquakes.mlsnet.com
- **San Jose Sharks**, 408-999-5757, http://sharks.nhl.com

STREET MAINTENANCE

- **Report an Overflowing Litter Receptacle**, 415-282-5326
- **Report Illegal Dumping**, 415-282-5326
- **San Francisco Department of Public Works**, 415-554-6920, TTY 415-554-6900
- **Sign Posting Guidelines**, www.amlegal.com

- **Street Cleaning**, 415-554-6920
- **Street Construction Coordination Center**, 415-554-5810
- **Street Use Permits**, 415-554-5810
- **Tree Planting, San Francisco Friends of the Urban Forest (FUF)**, 415-561-6890, www.fuf.net
- **Tree Removal and Pruning**, 415-282-5326

TAXES

- **Internal Revenue Service**, 800-829-1040, www.irs.ustreas.gov
- **San Francisco Tax Collector**, 415-554-4400
- **State Franchise Tax Board**, 800-852-5711, www.ftb.ca.gov
- **State of California Department of Finance**, 916-445-3878, www.dof.ca.gov

TELEPHONE

- **Astound**, 800-427-8686, www.astound.net
- **AT&T**, 800-222-0300, www.att.com
- **Credo Mobile**, 800-555-7774, www.credomobile.com, this company donates a portion of monthly fees to nonprofits
- **Sprint**, 866-866-7509, www.sprint.com
- **Verizon**, 800-837-4966, www.verizon.com

TICKETS

- **Ticketmaster**, 415-512-7770, www.ticketmaster.com
- **Theatre Bay Area**, 415-430-1140, www.theatrebayarea.org
- **Tickets.com**, 800-352-0212, www.tickets.com

TRAVEL AND TOURISM

- **International Association for Medical Assistance to Travelers**, 716-754-4883, www.iamat.org
- **National Park Service**, www.nps.gov
- **National Passport Information Center**, 877-4USA-PPT (877-487-2778), TTY 888-874-7793, www.travel.state.gov
- **San Francisco Convention and Visitors Bureau**, 415-391-2000, www.only-insanfrancisco.com
- **US Department of State, Bureau of Consular Affairs,** http://travel.state.gov

TRANSPORTATION

- **Bay Area Public Transportation**, go to www.511.org or dial 511 (no area code needed when dialed from anywhere in the Bay Area)
- **Carpool and Vanpool Services**, www.rideshare.511.org, 511, www.511.org

- **Real Time Traffic Updates**, http://cad.chp.ca.gov

TRAINS AND BUSES
- **AC Transit**, 510-891-4700; TTY 800-448-9790, www.actransit.org
- **Altamont Commuter Express**, 800-411-7245, www.acerail.com
- **Amtrak**, 800-872-7245, www. amtrak.com, www.amtrakcalifornia.com
- **BART (Bay Area Rapid Transit)**, 510-465-2278, 415-989-2278, 650-992-2278; TTY 510-839-2278, www.bart.gov.
- **CalTrain**, www.caltrain.com; 800-660-4287; TDD/TTY 415-508-6448
- **Contra Costa County Connection**, 925-676-7500; TDD/TTY 800-735-2929, www. cccta.org
- **Golden Gate Transit**, 415-455-2000, TTY 711, www.goldengatetransit.org.
- **Greyhound**, 800-231-2222, www.greyhound.com
- **MUNI (San Francisco Municipal Rail)** 415-701-2311, TTY 415-701-2323, www. sfmta.com
- **SamTrans**, 800-660-4287; TTY 650-508-6448, www.samtrans.com.
- **Santa Clara County Transit** (Valley Transit Authority) offers bus and light rail service to the South Bay, call 800-894-9908; TTY 408-321-2330, www.vta.org
- **Sonoma County Transit**, 707-576-7433, TTY 707-585-9817, www.sctransit. com
- **SuperShuttle**, 415-558-8500, www.supershuttle.com

AIRPORTS
- **Oakland International Airport**, 510-563-3300; parking, 510-563-3200, www.flyoakland.com
- **San Francisco International Airport**, 800-435-9736, www.flysfo.com
- **San Jose International Airport**, 408-277-4759, www.sjc.org

FERRIES
- **Alameda-Oakland Ferry**, 510-705-8204, www.eastbayferry.com.
- **Angel Island–Tiburon Ferry**, 415-435-2131
- **Baylink** (Vallejo-SF) 707-643-3779 or 877-643-3779, www.baylinkferry.com.
- **Blue and Gold Fleet**, 415-705-8200
- **Golden Gate Ferry Service**, (Marin-San Francisco) 415-455-2000 or http:// goldengateferry.org
- **Harbor Bay Ferry** (Alameda-SF), 510-769-5172, www.alamedaharbor bay-ferry.com

TAXIS, see **Transportation** chapter

UTILITIES

- **City of Palo Alto Utilities (CPAU)**, 650-329-2161

- **PG&E (Pacific Gas and Electric)**, 800-743-5000; TTY, 800-652-4712, www.pge. com
- **Santa Clara Green Power**, 408-244-SAVE
- **Silicon Valley Power**, 408-615-2300, www.siliconvalleypower.com

See **Water** in the **Getting Settled** chapter for water district numbers and web sites.

UTILITY EMERGENCIES
- **Pacific Gas & Electric**, 800-743-5002

WEATHER, Regional Weather Reports, www.wrh.noaa.gov/mtr/

ZIP CODE REQUEST, 800-275-8777, www.usps.com

SCOTT VAN VELSOR is a Bay Area native who is constantly on the prowl for outdoor diversion and a satisfying political argument. A Navy vet with a journalism degree and a flair for photography, Scott has written for many of the local news outlets like *SF Weekly*, *Oakland Tribune*, KALW, the *Contra Costa Times*, and for *Best Places Northern California*, a tourist guidebook. He is most at home while swimming in the chilly Pacific, backpacking the Sierra Nevada, or standing in one of San Francisco's numerous live-music venues.

READER RESPONSE

We would appreciate your comments regarding this fourth edition of the *Newcomer's Handbook® for Moving to and Living in the San Francisco Bay Area.* If you've found any mistakes or omissions or if you would just like to express your opinion about the guide, please let us know. We will consider any suggestions for possible inclusion in our next edition, and if we use your comments, we'll send you a free copy of our next edition. Please e-mail us at readerresponse@firstbooks.com, or mail or fax this response form to:

Reader Response Department
First Books
6750 SW Franklin, Suite A
Portland, OR 97223-2542
Fax: 503.968.6779

Comments: _____

_____

_____

_____

_____

_____

_____

_____

_____

Name: _____

Address: _____

_____

_____

Telephone: ( ) _____

Email: _____

6750 SW Franklin, Suite A
Portland, OR 97223-2542
USA
P: 503.968.6777
www.firstbooks.com

FIRST BOOKS

RELOCATION RESOURCES

Utilizing an innovative grid and "static" reusable adhesive sticker format, *Furniture Placement and Room Planning Guide...Moving Made Easy* provides a functional and practical solution to all your space planning and furniture placement needs.

MOVING WITH KIDS?

Look into *The Moving Book: A Kids' Survival Guide.*

Divided into three sections (before, during, and after the move), it's a handbook, a journal, and a scrapbook all in one. Includes address book, colorful change-of-address cards, and a useful section for parents.

Children's Book of the Month Club "Featured Selection"; American Bookseller's "Pick of the List"; Winner of the Family Channel's "Seal of Quality" Award

And for your younger children, ease their transition with our brand-new title just for them, *Max's Moving Adventure: A Coloring Book for Kids on the Move.* A complete story book featuring activities as well as pictures that children can color; designed to help children cope with the stresses of small or large moves.

NEWCOMERSWEB.COM

Based on the award-winning *Newcomer's Handbooks,* **NewcomersWeb.com** offers the highest quality neighborhood and community information in a one-of-a-kind searchable online database. The following areas are covered: Atlanta, Austin, Boston, Chicago, Dallas–Fort Worth, Houston, Los Angeles, Ninneapolis–St. Paul, New York City, Portland (Oregon), San Francisco, Seattle, Washington DC, and the USA.

NEWCOMER'S HANDBOOKS®

Regularly revised and updated, these popular guides are now available for Atlanta, Boston, Chicago, China, London, Los Angeles, Minneapolis–St. Paul, New York City, Portland, San Francisco Bay Area, Seattle, Texas and Washington DC.

"Invaluable ...highly recommended" – Library Journal

If you're coming from another country, don't miss the *Newcomer's Handbook® for Moving to and Living in the USA* by Mike Livingston, termed "a fascinating book for newcomers and residents alike" by the *Chicago Tribune.*

6750 SW Franklin Street
Portland, Oregon 97223-2542
Phone 503.968.6777 • Fax 503.968.6779
FIRST BOOKS **www.firstbooks.com**

BART AREA RAPID TRANSIT SYSTEM MAP

Visit our web site at

www.firstbooks.com

for information on all our books.